RAV CHESED:
ESSAYS IN HONOR OF
RABBI DR. HASKEL LOOKSTEIN

RAV CHESED

essays in honor of

Rabbi Dr. Haskel Lookstein

VOLUME II

EDITED BY

RAFAEL MEDOFF

KTAV Publishing House, Inc.
Jersey City, New Jersey

Copyright © 2009 by Rafael Medoff

Library of Congress Cataloging-in-Publication Data

Rav chesed : essays in honor of Rabbi Dr. Haskel Lookstein
edited by Rafael Medoff.
v. cm.
A two-volume collection of original essays by prominent rabbis, historians,
and other scholars, composed in honor of Rabbi Dr. Haskel Lookstein on the
occasion of his fiftieth year in the pulpit of Congregation Kehilath Jeshurun,
in New York City.

ISBN 978-1-60280-115-8

1. Orthodox Judaism. 2. Jewish women – Religious life. 3. Orthodox
Judaism – Relations – Nontraditional Jews. I. Lookstein, Haskel. II. Medoff,
Rafael, 1959-BM42.R375 2009 296.8'32 – dc22 2009010615

Published by
KTAV Publishing House, Inc.
930 Newark Avenue
Jersey City, NJ 07306

Email: bernie@ktav.com
www.ktav.com
Office: 201 963 9524
Fax: 201 963 0102

Dedicated to the memory of
Rabbi Joseph H. and Gertrude Lookstein

Contents

Talmud and Ma'asseh in *Pirkei Avot*

Aharon Lichtenstein

The relation between *talmud* and *ma'asseh*, study and implementation, can hardly be deemed a specifically modern concern. Nor does it constitute a uniquely Jewish issue. Endemic to the understanding of the spiritual life and its priorities, it recurs in varied civilizations and multiple contexts. Within the Western world, it constitutes a major crux of Greek – and, particularly, Athenian – philosophic speculation. During the Middle Ages, it engendered much debate among the Scholastics; and the claims of the *vita activa* and the *vita contemplativa* were subsequently perceived as central to the chasm dividing Christendom after the Protestant Reformation. Finally, in the modern period, echoes of the contretemps continue to reverberate – be it, often, in secular tones – at the planes of both theory and practice.

In our own Torah world, concern with the subject has been no less persistent, the discourse no less animated, and the attempt to attain a seemingly elusive resolution a major challenge. In Tanakh we do not encounter full-blown and directly explicit exposition of the issue, but many have sought to draw conclusions from their perspective upon the narrative portraying the lives and preoccupations of central figures within *Humash* or *Nevi'im*, or to identify prooftexts in *Ketubim* as sources supporting their

position. Hazal, however, report evidently charged debate, both
extensive and intensive, on the question of priority and stature of
talmud and *ma'asseh,* respectively:

וכבר היה רבי טרפון וזקנים מסובין בעלית בית נתזה בלוד, נשאלה שאלה
זו בפניהם תלמוד גדול או מעשה גדול נענה רבי טרפון ואמר מעשה
גדול נענה רבי עקיבא ואמר תלמוד גדול נענו כולם ואמרו תלמוד גדול
שהתלמוד מביא לידי מעשה.[1]

And Rabbi Tarfon and some [elders] were once convened
in the upper story of the house of Natza in Lod, and this
question was posed before them: Which is greater, *talmud*
or *ma'asseh?* Rabbi Tarfon responded and said, "*Ma'asseh* is
greater." Rabbi Akiva responded and said, "*Talmud* is greater."
The group responded and said, "*Talmud* is greater inasmuch
as *talmud* leads to *ma'asseh.*"

In light of the presumably sound Aristotelian dictum that the end
should be regarded as axiologically superior to a means that serves
as its instrument, the conclusion cited, its formulation notwithstanding, apparently predicates the primacy of implementation.
This was indeed assumed by Rashi in *Baba Kama.*[2] Elsewhere,
however, he appears to take a more literal approach and assigns
priority – or, at the very least, parity – to study, through which
both aims are achieved.[3] The Rambam, however, aligns himself
with the *Gemara* more fully and espouses its judgment consistently,
as is reflected in his comment, appended, pursuant to citation of
the *Gemara:*[4] לפיכך התלמוד קודם למעשה בכל מקום – "Therefore, everywhere, *talmud* precedes *ma'asseh.*" Subsequently, debate continued unabated, with *ba'alei halakha, ba'alei mahshavah,* and *ba'alei
mussar* – halakhists, philosophers, and ethico-pietists – deeply engaged, down to the present. If a contemporary exemplar needs to
be singled out, Rav Soloveitchik's first major essay, *Ish Hahalakha,*
may serve as an apt specimen;[5] but it hardly stands alone.

Despite the universal component, the issue does bear a
characteristically Jewish cast, for while both aspects are deeply

ingrained within general religious sensibility and experience, as has been noted, each is especially prominent within *yahadut* and hence the discourse is particularly relevant to Jewish tradition. On the one hand, Torah study, conceived as both normative duty and spiritual value, is posited as a central pillar of existence – personal, national, and even cosmic:

עַל שְׁלֹשָׁה דְבָרִים הָעוֹלָם עוֹמֵד, עַל הַתּוֹרָה, עַל הָעֲבוֹדָה, וְעַל גְּמִילוּת חֲסָדִים.[6]

The world is grounded upon three matters: *Torah, avoda,* and *gemilut hasadim.*

Moreover, this conception is not confined to a narrow coterie of *majores ecclesiae* but is defined in broad social and communal terms:

וְכָל בָּנַיִךְ לִמּוּדֵי ה' וְרַב שְׁלוֹם בָּנָיִךְ.[7]

And all your sons are instructed by Hashem, and great is the peace of your sons.

To a degree unparalleled in comparable cultures, the ordinary Jew is traditionally encouraged and expected to serve the *Ribbono Shel Olam* with intellectual faculties and cognitive tools no less than with physical organs and material goods, as he comes to grips with the niceties of often arcane legal minutiae.

On the other hand, the Jew's responsibility to the realm of *ma'asseh* is also more comprehensive than that of his Gentile counterpart. Whereas for the latter, *vita activa* largely denotes participation and initiative in the rough and tumble arena of public life, to the Jew it suggests primarily fulfillment of the divine will as expressed in the pervasive *halakhic* regimen which penetrates every facet of the mundane order, its venue coexistent with the scope of life itself. In light of the greater range and intensity of both factors, study and practice, the incremental Jewish component of our problem may indeed be significant.

This brief essay is obviously not intended to provide either an exhaustive analysis of the problem or a comprehensive survey of its history. Its focus will be far more modest. I shall attempt to delineate a bird's eye view of the issues, as reflected in relevant passages excerpted from one of the most familiar of Rabbinic texts, *Pirke Avot*. Familiarity is not the basis of its selection, however. Rather, I have chosen this tractate for three unrelated reasons. The first concerns its character. Perhaps best regarded as the Talmudic equivalent of Scriptural *Mishlei*, this amalgam of fully normative *halakhot*, moral wisdom, hortatory challenge, and outright prudential counsel is, in one sense, the least demanding of *massekhtot*, and in another, precisely because of its relatively amorphous nature, the most demanding.

Second, *Avot* confronts cardinal issues, at once fundamental and comprehensive, regarding the character and content of human life and the optimal mode of molding ideal personality. In a casual comment upon a *mishna* which, prima facie, is unrelated to these concerns, the Rambam nonetheless diverts its substance to this channel, noting that it stimulates תקון נפשו במעלות המדות ובמעלות השכליות, שזו היא כונת המסכתא, "For this, that is, perfection of the soul, morally and intellectually, is the aim of this tractate."[8] And indeed the bedrock question of the determination of priority regarding the spiritual quality of the good life is explicitly posed at several points. Rabbi Yehudah Hanassi, often simply denominated "Rabbi" – presumably, the *massekhet*'s editor and compiler – raises it as the opening wedge of the second chapter:

רבי אומר אי זו היא דרך ישרה שיבר לו האדם, כל שהיא תפארת לעושה ותפארת לו מן האדם.[9]

Rabbi [Yehudah Hanassi] said: Which is the right path which a person should select? That which reflects the luster of its pursuer, and redounds to him luster from others.

Several *mishnayot* later we learn that Rabbi Yohanan Ben Zakkai had five premier disciples, whom he confronted with a dual challenge:

צאו וראו אי זו היא דרך טובה שידבק בה האדם;

Go out and perceive which is a good path to which a person should adhere.

And, obversely:

צאו וראו אי זו היא דרך רעה שיתרחק ממנה האדם.[10]

Go out and perceive which is a bad path, from which a person should distance himself.

The responses vary widely. Rabbi's own formulation, "that which glorifies its agent, and confers upon him glory from others," is ambiguous insofar as it posits an ultimate goal but presents neither details regarding in what this *tif'eret* consists, nor any guideline concerning how the desideratum may be attained. In the latter *mishna*, the variety is of another sort. The factors cited range from designation of an overarching factor, "a good heart," be it *telos* or means, to selection of elements which can, tactically and instrumentally, lead to the promised land: companionship and/or community, or the capacity to anticipate the future. For our purposes, however, most important is the attention riveted upon the question and some of the premises implicit within it, since it is this focus that leads naturally to weighing the merits of *talmud* and *ma'asseh*, respectively, and limning the contours of their interaction.

The third reason for choosing this tractate is grounded in the *massekhet's* elements. *Pirke Avot* constitutes an anthology, within whose parameters are cited epigrams ascribed to a broad range of *tannaim*, some central and others relatively marginal. Obviously, the respective authors expressed themselves with regard to numerous issues, touching upon the entire corpus of *halakha* and/

or *mahshava*. Is it conceivable that Hillel's or Rabbi Akiva's dicta could be counted on the fingers of one hand? That the ethical legacy of giants in the forefront of our tradition consists of scattered morsels ascribed to each, and the composite compressed within five brief chapters? Evidently, in the process of selection and editing, attention was focused upon statements categorized as מרגלא בפומיה דרבי פלוני, recurrently repeated by a given *tanna*, as singled out by him for special awareness and dissemination, and, hence, characteristically identified with him. Given all three factors, we approach this treasure trove with an anticipatory eye for encountering distinctive insights.

To begin with the status of *talmud Torah*, independently considered, in *Avot*, there is no paucity of assertions trumpeting its prominence. Its designation as one of the pillars sustaining universal existence has already been noted,[11] but it is only the opening salvo. That is followed in short order by the admonition that one not credit himself as he contemplates his own virtue, expressed through learning much Torah, as לכך נוצרת, "it is to that end that you have been created"[12]; by the exhortation to persist diligently – הוה שקוד ללמוד תורה – in Torah study; by declaration that the absence of "Torah words" at a social gathering or a meal renders them מושב לצים, a "rogues' session," or זבחי מתים, "mortuary sacrifices," respectively, whereas, by contrast, Torah-centered gatherings ensure the presence of immanent *shekhina* in their midst.[13] This, in turn, is succeeded by the frightening asseveration that if, because of negligence and/or apathy rather than as a natural result of oblivion, one forgets any segment of the Torah he has learned, he is, figuratively, deemed as having endangered his soul.[14] Subsequently, Rabbi Meir urges minimizing commercial activity so as to enable concentrated Torah study[15]; while in the tractate's penultimate counsel Ben Bag Bag exhorts, evidently as classical *mefarshim* consensually assumed, with reference to the pursuit of Torah, הפך בה והפך בה דכולא בה, "Delve into it, and delve into it, for all is within it."[16] Much ink has been spilled in attempt to expound this much-debated charge, but whatever the details, the scope ascribed to *talmud Torah* and the status correspondingly accorded to it is beyond question.

The focus upon the value of Torah study is matched, however, by acknowledgment, both implicit and explicit, of the worth of *ma'asseh*. In Hazal's usage, the term denotes at least four distinct yet related referents. At its broadest, it signifies the full gamut of activity, including intellectual labor, as opposed to perception, observation, or total passivity. Somewhat more narrowly conceived, the term still encompasses the full range of physical action, to the exclusion of verbal or cerebral initiative. In a related and yet still more limited sense, it refers to a very specific act, often regarded as more significant than a comparable passive state. Thus a לאו שיש בו מעשה, a transgression of a negative prohibition, such as purchasing or leavening *hametz* on *Pesach*, is more seriously regarded – and is concurrently more subject to sanction – than failure to destroy *hamtez* that had already been owned prior to *Pesach*,[17] or than the neglect to eat *matzoh* on the first night. Finally, *ma'asseh* may simply be synonymous with an incident or its narrative.

All four senses appear in the text of *Avot*. However, for our purposes we shall focus primarily upon the first and shall discuss the last least. That first aspect alone, however, is abundantly reflected in numerous dicta strewn throughout the *massekhet*. And while it seems patently clear that not every *mishna* is equally and directly relevant to every reader, at either the personal or the collective plane, the composite image is one which certainly bespeaks and even exudes range and vibrancy in confronting the human condition. Thus we note from the outset that, in the *mishna* previously cited as defining the metaphysical legs of a universal tripod, both ritual and beneficence[18] stand firmly alongside Torah. As we read on, we sense consistently that engagement of the recipient of proffered guidance within the realm of the temporal and even the carnal order, whether out of choice or from necessity, is taken for granted as the point of departure for dialogue. He may be a judge or a plaintiff, a scholar or a tradesman, a host or a guest, a neighbor, good or ill, a teacher or a disciple, a friend or an adversary, indolent or energetic, humble or condescending, *homo economicus* and *homo religiosus*. With respect to all of these capacities and relations, the Jew is confronted, addressed, and advised, as concerns both scope and modality, as to how best to organize and lead a life of ethical rectitude, religious obligation, and practical accomplishment, which will enhance the prospect for entry into the order of felicity of the eternal abode. The citations vary considerably as to theme and range of their message. Some are pinpointed:

הוי מתפלל בשלומה של מלכות שאלמלי מוראה איש את רעהו חיים
בלעו;[19]

Pray for the welfare of government, as, were it not for fear of it, each would swallow his fellow alive;

others are mostly general and sweeping, as they postulate the element whose constant contemplation can instill the spirit and modality which will maximize, if not assure, virtue:

הסתכל בשלשה דברים ואין אתה בא לידי עברה – דע מאין באת ולאן
אתה הולך ולפני מי אתה עתיד ליתן דין וחשבון[20]

Regard three matters and you avoid lapsing into sin: from whence you have come, whither you are headed, and before whom you are destined to present judgment and accounting.

Some are descriptive, many prescriptive, while in others the description, given the values presumably energizing the reader, implicitly infers the mandated resolution. Throughout, however, the emphasis upon both *talmud* and *ma'asseh* is crucial.

The prominence of *talmud* and *ma'asseh*, each absolutely and independently considered and evaluated, is not, however, our sole – or even our primary – topic. We need to examine more fully their interaction and possible conflict. In this respect, it is important that the traditional parameters of discourse be borne in mind, especially as they include an asymmetrical component.

Yahadut optimally espouses and assumes the conjunction of *talmud* and *ma'asseh*, but the import of their severance is unevenly perceived. While enactment of the *halakhic* regimen, unaccompanied by learning and not buttressed by understanding, is regarded as inadequate but worthy, the obverse – *talmud Torah* bereft of faith and commitment to implement – is viewed as sacrilege, bordering upon blasphemy. In its milder form, this dissonance finds expression in two statements ascribed to the most frequently cited of *amoraim*, Rava. Commenting upon the *pasuk*,

ראשית חכמה יראת ה' שכל טוב לכל עושיהם (תהלים קיא:י)
Fear of Hashem is the origin of wisdom, [a source] of right thought for those who implement it.

he comments,[21] ללומדיהם לא נאמר אלא לעושיהם, "The verse does not say, 'For those who study them,' but rather, 'For those who implement them.'" Or, in a somewhat sharper vein, we note his admonitory plea to his students, במטותא מינייכו לא תירתון תרתי גיהנם, "I implore you, do not inherit a double Hell"[22] – to wit, as Rashi expounds, don't lead a life of self-sacrifice in the pursuit of Torah in this world, only to lapse postmortem into the inferno of the nether, if you have flagged in observance here. Elsewhere, however, we encounter far more extreme formulations, well beyond the pale of lassitude and retribution. Hazal saw the message writ large in a divine reproach to the wicked – variously identified in midrashim with Do'eg and Elisha ben Avuya – in verses of *Tehillim*:

ולרשע אמר א-לקים מה לך לספר חקי ותשא בריתי עלי פיך. ואתה שנאת מוסר ותשלך דברי אחריך.[23]
But to the wicked, God says, "What have you to do with pronouncing My statutes, and that you bear My covenant upon your mouth? And you have reviled guidance, and have thrust My words behind you."

And in a more general vein, the point is driven home graphically in a declaration cited as a challenge to the practice of Rabbi Shimon bar Yohai, who occasionally, and perhaps even habitually, abstained from reciting *Shema*, if it interfered with his learning:

ולית ליה לרשב״י הלמד על מנת לעשות ולא הלמד שלא לעשות שהלמד
שלא לעשות נוח לו שלא נברא.[24]

And does not Rabbi Shimon bar Yohai acknowledge that he who studies with intent to perform [is to be valued], but not he who studies without intent to perform, as, if one studies without intent to perform, it were preferable for him not to have been born.

Genuine severance is clearly no option. No matter how well motivated, it undermines the most fundamental premises of normative *halakhic* existence; and in addition to defiling commitment, interferes with the process of its realization, thus eviscerating both personal and communal spiritual well-being.

Prima facie, this assertion seems to be contravened by an inference possibly suggested by Rabbi Ishmael's statement in the fourth *perek*:

הלומד על מנת ללמד מספיקין בידו ללמוד וללמד והלומד על מנת
לעשות מספיקין בידו ללמוד וללמד לשמור ולעשות[25]

He who studies [only] with intent to teach is afforded the opportunity to study as well as to teach; but he who studies with intent to perform is afforded the opportunity to study, to teach, to preserve, and to perform.

The impression conveyed by the opening comment is that, while inferior in comparison with the personage described later, he who pursues knowledge with an eye to teaching, but not, evidently, to implementing, will be rewarded with support in realizing his aim, inasmuch as what he is doing, while partial, is nonetheless meritorious. But Rabbenu Yonah, *ad locum*, noted the implication and was consequently horrified:

פי' חס ושלום שאין זה מדבר בלומד על מנת ללמד ולא לעשות שזה אין
מספיקין בידו לא ללמוד ולא ללמד.

To wit: The *mishna* does not speak, Heaven forbid, of one
who studies with the intent to teach but with no intent to
perform, for such is denied the opportunity even to study
or to teach.

Hence he goes on to explain that at issue is the quality and level
of commitment, but not its bare existence. This view may strike
some as a bit forced and apologetic. In this respect the interpretation of the *Mahzor Vitry, ad locum*, may be more palatable. Its
author suggests that we are dealing either with a person who is
fully committed to observe but may be prevented from doing so
or who plans to fulfill but is motivated to teach by extraneous
factors:

שאין דעתו לקיים לפי שאינו יכול או אפילו יכול אינו עושה אלא לעשות
לו שם על מנת שיקראהו ר' ללמוד וללמד ולא יותר.

[The *mishna* refers to] one who does not expect to perform
[only] because he lacks the wherewithal; or, alternatively, of
one who is able [and does expect] to perform but shall do
so solely in order to establish his reputation as a master of
learning and teaching, but for no other reason.

As to why he then is assured of support, he explains:

שהמעשה עיקר כמו שמצינו בפ"א לא המדרש הוא עיקר אלא
המעשה.[26]

For *ma'asseh* is the main thing as we have encountered earlier (1:17), "The main thing is not exposition but implementation."

This reference introduces another issue, that of objective formal
observance versus inwardness, with a long history of its own, but
not to our present purpose. In any event, one is hardly inclined to

discard so deeply rooted and widely held an attitude on the basis of a single problematic inference.

The nature of the desired interaction is in one sense almost self-evident. The twin elements relate to varied aspects of human personality and diverse areas of personal and collective existence. Either is ignored at peril, and it is only their joint scope that enables us, like Arnold's Sophocles, to see life steadily and to see it whole – or rather, to live it as such. And yet, several strands may be discerned. In *Avot*, as elsewhere, we ought not perceive *talmud* and *ma'asseh* as merely twinned in shared and spiritual coexistence. Rather, within the *halakhic* tradition, they are regarded as entwined and fructifying; and reciprocally so. Thus on the one hand the *mishna* postulates, almost stridently, that לא עם הארץ חסיד, the unschooled cannot attain the higher levels of piety. On the other hand, with reference to the selfsame category of *hasid*, Rava asserts, in a somewhat complementary vein, that he who would attain it should *inter alia* enact the precepts of *Avot*.[27] Beyond that, the *mishna* proper states that the priority, presumably both chronological and axiological, of reverence to wisdom and the quest for it is a condition for the long-term viability of that wisdom-not of the reverence solely, but of the wisdom:

ר׳ חנניה בן דוסא אומר כל שיראת חטאו קודמת לחכמתו חכמתו מתקיימת, וכל שחכמתו קודמת ליראת חטאו אין חכמתו מתקיימת.[28]

Rabbi Hananyah bar Dossa stated, "If one prioritizes fear of sin to wisdom, his wisdom survives, but if his wisdom is prioritized to his fear of sin, it does not survive."

And we note that the assertion is presented as a fact and not just as a concern. The statement resembles attitudes encountered in a variety of parallel traditions but it is, for us, particularly noteworthy, precisely because the low-key and practically oriented tone of most of *Avot* is poles removed from the mystical mode.

Moreover, in this vein we might proceed a step further. The reciprocal dependency of *talmud* and *ma'asseh* is clearly stated. As, on the one hand, their conjunction, even at the vocational plane, constitutes a befitting mode of personal life:

יפה תלמוד תורה עם דרך ארץ שיגיעת שניהם משכחת עון;[29]

Talmud Torah goes handsomely with civility, as their joint pursuit obliterates sin.

so, on the other hand, the absence of one derails the other:

ר' אלעזר בן עזריה אומר אם אין תורה אין דרך ארץ, אם אין דרך ארץ אין תורה.[30]

Rabbi Elazar ben Azaryah said: "If Torah is absent, there shall be no *derekh ertez*; if *derekh eretz* is absent, there shall be no Torah."

The implicit message of the *mishnayot* in *Avot* is that *talmud* and *ma'asseh* are not just a sine qua non of each other. Each is, beyond that, a manifest realization of the other. *Talmud Torah* bears a dual aspect. It is both an independent value as a central aspect of *avodat Hashem*, fusing cognition and religiosity, and as a specific normative performance, a *mitzvah* in its own right – indeed, if properly motivated and faith-grounded, among the weightiest and noblest. Conversely, a life of submissive religious commitment provides the infrastructure for insight and perception and serves as an invaluable instrument of Torah learning and education.

While harmonious interaction can be idealized, the prospect of potential conflict cannot be averted. The possibility of internal contradiction must of course be anticipated by any legal system, and prescription for resolution is clearly requisite. In this regard, *halakha* is no exception. For the purpose of our discourse, however, it is essential that the substantive nature of the conflict under consideration be properly understood.

Primarily, the *halakhist* copes with two categories of conflict. In the first, itself divided into multiple subsections, the specific normative demands of diverse codicils stand in direct opposition.

The *mitzvah* of eating *matzah* on *Pesach* might, for instance, mandate eating a particular specimen if no other is available, while, if the specimen in question was baked with untithed flour, the prohibition against eating *tevel* proscribes its consumption. Similarly, the *mitzvah* of *tztizit* prescribes adorning a four-cornered garment with woolen strings even if its fabric is linen, whereas the injunction against wearing *shatnes* precludes it. Such conflicts abound and make their mark as a significant *halakhic* topic, and, depending upon variables such as the source and grade of commandment and restriction, respectively, are differentially resolved.

Very little of this rigorous discussion, however, finds its locus in the relatively flexible and less technical context of *Avot*. The conflict encountered in its *mishnayot* is focused upon the broader concerns of policy, attitude, values, and context. Inherently accidental head-on clashes are not so much at issue. Attention is riveted rather upon immanent questions – ideological, axiological, and practical – regarding the fabric and composition, the content and the direction, of human life as perceived from a Torah perspective. Hence conflict relates to the budgeting of energy, time, resources, and commitment, to the realization, both tragic and challenging, that *ars longa, vita brevis*, or, in the language of Rabbi Tarfon in *Avot*, that היום קצר והמלאכה מרובה והפועלים עצלים – "The day is short, the task is extensive, and the laborers lazy."[31] Hence our implicit charge with respect to ourselves is to ensure that the workers not be indolent.

At stake, however, is more than a laudable work ethic and pervasive dedication. The human agent qua agent, even if we momentarily omit fulfillment of David's charge to Shlomo, ודע את א־ לקי אביך ועבדהו (דברי הימים א' כח:ט), "And know the God of your father and serve Him," is mandated to be not only conscientious but wise, both passionately committed and intelligently perceptive, insightful as well as efficient – all of this presumably part of the labor which has been thrust upon his shoulders. And over all this effort the need to prioritize and the shadow of possible clash looms large.

If direct *halakhic* conflict is barely cited in *Avot*, diverse emphases and, at times, contradictory *hashkafic* formulations are nevertheless in evidence. The radical tinge of לא המדרש עקר אלא המעשה, as filtered through Rabbenu Bahyye's interpretation, serves to exemplify:

כלומר אין תכלית הידיעה ועמלו של אדם שילמוד תורה הרבה, אין התכלית אלא שיביא הלימוד לידי מעשה, הוא שכתוב ולמדתם אותם ושמרתם לעשותם בא להורות כי תכלית הלימוד אינו אלא כדי שיעשה.[32]

To wit: The *telos* of knowledge and one's related labor is not the study of much Torah [per se]. The purpose is but translating the study into implementation. Hence, it is written, "And you shall learn them and preserve them," in order to instruct us that the end of study is but that one should act, [*halakhically*].

To Volozhiner purists, this exposition of narrowness is sheer anathema. But even the less sensitive can readily agree that the message is hardly identical with that of הפך בה והפך בה דכלא בה; and neither *mishna* merely replicates the reciprocity of אם אין תורה אין דרך ארץ, אם אין דרך ארץ אין תורה. Or again, the gut response to דרך ארץ of Rabban Gamaliel's assertion that יפה תלמוד תורה עם דרך ארץ differs markedly from that of Rabbi Nehunyah's declaration that כל המקבל עליו עול תורה מעבירין ממנו עול מלכות ועול דרך ארץ, "Whoever accepts the yoke of Torah is released from the yoke of government and from that of *derekh eretz*."[33] The cognitive content of the two can unquestionably be reconciled. The feeling – tone is palpably different, however – a matter of no small moment.

Over all looms the magisterial sweep of the demand that וכל מעשיך יהיו לשם שמים, "And all your actions should be for the sake of Heaven."[34] This directive, justly singled out by the Rambam as the linchpin of religious living,[35] unquestionably encompasses *talmud* as well as *ma'asseh*, particularly insofar as intellection too is included in the realm of activity. And yet, as is amply attested in the details cited in the Rambam's presentation, whether in *Shemonah Perakim* or in *Hilkhot De'ot*, the focus is upon *ma'asseh*, more narrowly defined:

נמצא המהלך בדרך זו עובד את ה' תמיד אפילו בשעה שנושא ונותן
ואפילו בשעה שבועל מפני שמחשבתו בכל כדי שימצא צרכיו עד שיהיה
גופו שלם לעבוד את ה'...ועל ענין זה אמרו חכמים וכל מעשיך יהיו
לשם שמים.[36]

He who pursues this path thus finds himself serving Hashem constantly, even while engaged in trade or even in the midst of sexual relations, inasmuch as with respect to all he does he thinks how can he best meet his needs so that his body will be sound in order to serve Hashem…. And it is with respect to this that the Sages asserted, "And all your actions should be for the sake of Heaven."

Hence, the overarching formulation serves to secure the position of the *vita activa*, while yet promoting the conjunction of our two topics.

And there is, of course, subtler diversity. Commenting upon a series of *mishnayot* in the fourth *perek*, Rav Yitzchak Abravanel suggests that the core issue is the relation of our twin topics:

ואומר שהכוונה הכוללת בפרק הזה היא לבאר במה יקנה האדם שלימותו
בתורה כי אחר שהתבאר בפרקים הקודמים ששלימות האדם ותכליתו
הוא בקנין התורה וקיומה נשאר לבאר אם הוא העיקר בה הוא העיון והחכמה
התוריית או המעשה וקיום המצות ולכן באו דעות השלמים האלה כל
אחד כפי שטתו וסברתו.[37]

And let me say that the overall thrust of this chapter is to determine how one best attains his perfection with regard to Torah. For after it has been explained, in prior chapters, that the perfection of man and his ultimate purpose consists in the acquisition of Torah and its realization, we still need to determine whether the most essential is the probing and knowledge of Torah or its realization and the performance of *mitzvot*. Hence we encounter here the views of these noble persons, each in accordance with his theory and perception.

This perception should neither surprise nor alarm us. While some *bnei Torah*, fully acculturated to the welter of *mahloket* at all level of *halakhic* discourse, prefer to imagine that in the area of *emunot v'deot* – or even of *mahshava* generally – comity and unanimity are de rigueur, the distinction belies both theory and fact. Surely there is no reason to entertain it with respect to our particular topic. Even the advocacy of seemingly diverse values can be readily and variously understood. Given the prevalence of controversy as a staple of rabbinic discourse, it can be obviously contended that the variety confronted in *Avot* ought best be perceived as an exemplar of this characteristic, which at times constitutes a dispute over a relatively local issue, and at other times may emanate from conflict over fundamental Weltanschauung. In its more extreme formulation, this interpretation would hold that conflicting *mishnayot* argue over the adoption of one value and the concomitant negation of another, and vice versa. A milder version could be content with controversy over priority and emphasis. In either case, however, the reader or the student is encouraged to regard his endeavors in sifting the texts as a selective quest for a single and overriding phalanx of constricted guidelines.

Such a reading is grounded, generally, upon certain premises, both methodological and ideological, regarding the respective merits of dialectical, monistic, and harmonistic canons of exposition; and specifically upon one's grasp of particular texts and issues confronted in *Avot*. Allowing for some analogy between the realms of *halakha* and *mahshava* as regards *mahloket*, the possibility of unanimity or clear-cut recognition of advocacy of one contested value to the relative neglect of a rival can still not be ruled out. Nevertheless, in this case, given my own perspectives and proclivities regarding both *halakhic* training and *hashkafic* orientation, I freely admit to an inclination to multifaceted resolution and to the challenge of complexity. Even in the absence of such bias, I cannot fathom how the ethical life in its entirety could be encapsulated within the sphere of normative *talmud Torah* alone. Surely we, as advocates of Hazal's tradition, have nothing to gain and much to lose by any attempt to abandon, mute, or diminish the claims of both contemplation and action upon our consciences and upon our lives. In learning the *massekhet*, we err grievously in positing emphasis upon the two as diametrically opposed rather than conjoined. Surely, whatever the thrust of a particular text, the overall message in *Avot* is one of bonded values, and we shall lead purer and richer lives if we heed its call.

The linkage manifest in citations strewn through our *massekhet* foreshadows, in certain respects, its more explicit formulation in an early exposition penned by the first truly systematic master within our philosophic tradition. I refer, of course, to the Rambam and to the first of his major introductory prefaces. As the preface to his commentary upon the *mishna* draws to its conclusion, the Rambam feels impelled to raise the crucial issue, both ethical and teleological, of the purpose and nature of human existence. Tersely stated, in response, he states, "The end of our world and of that which is within it is 'a wise and good person.'"[38] After the contention that this conclusion is equally grounded in prophetic revelation and philosophic thought, the discussion moves, not surprisingly, toward judiciously balanced resolution of the relations of *talmud* and *ma'asseh*. First, in the spirit of Hazal, the Rambam emphasizes that, if it is to be genuine and meaningful, the quest for wisdom must be grounded in existential commitment and its concomitant lifestyle. Despite its enormous intrinsic value, learning that is bereft of religiously and ethically mandated discipline is fraught with arrogance and invites Yirmiyahu's critique[39]: איכה תאמרו חכמים אנחנו ותורת ה' אתנו וכו' "How can you say, 'We are wise and Hashem's Torah is with us'?' etc. However, in the reverse case, inasmuch as the relation is asymmetrical, while this option is imperfect because it may not be wholly bound to "the path of truth and certitude," the course has merit. Nevertheless, given the imperfection, as to the question of chronological priority, learning takes precedence: "Throughout the Torah, the למדתם comes before לעשותם, wisdom before practice, since through wisdom one attains practice, but practice does not induce wisdom. Hence Hazal's formulation, שהתלמוד מביא לידי מעשה, 'For *talmud* leads to *ma'asseh*.'"[40] On this balanced note – *ma'asseh* being acknowledged as the more essential, but *talmud* assigned sequential priority – the discussion ends, having made a number of salient points, but, like *Pirkei Avot*, having left a number of others open.

This brief synopsis of the Rambam's exposition strikes several familiar chords, the gist of the argument paralleling points that have been noted with respect to the treatment of *Avot*. At this point, however, the analogy is in large measure arrested. The themes are similar, but the contexts as well as the respective audiences are quite different. As to the latter, the *hakdama* is presumably oriented to readers who, while not all professional scholars, are apparently highly literate and sophisticated. With regard to *Avot*, the identity of the predominant projected audience is evidently in dispute. The Rambam envisioned it as aimed primarily at *dayyanim*;[41] and unquestionably a number of *mishnayot* relate directly to the formal judicial process. In all likelihood, however, the more prevalent view is that of the *Mahzor Vitry*, whose twelfth-century author prefaces his commentary upon *Avot* with the conjecture that the custom of reciting a *perek* on Shabbat afternoon derives from the limitations of the *hoi polloi*, for whom more difficult texts might be too challenging and who therefore imbibe requisite spiritual guidance from the milder fare of *Avot*.

לפי שעמי הארץ נאספים לקרית התורה, ומשמיעים אותם מידות תרומות
השנויות במסכת זו פרק ליום.[42]

For the ignorant are gathered in order to hear *keri'at hatorah*, and ideal virtues which are discussed in this tractate are expounded to them, one chapter at a time.

At a more significant level, however, we take note of distinctions concerning tone and content. With respect to the latter, note must of course be taken of the fact that the *hokhma* or *talmud* as well as the *ma'asseh* of *Avot* all refer primarily to the world of Torah and *halakha*, while the Rambam's discussion includes this dimension but is certainly not confined to it. And as to the aura, the systematic mode, characteristic of much of the Rambam's writing, is of course largely absent in *Avot*, as is the relatively more imperious tone of the Rambam's *hakdama*. In *Avot*, the prevalent human touch – reflected in direct personal guidance, much of it advisory, addressed by a *tanna* to a receptive listener in a fairly relaxed atmosphere, and, equally, in the absence of rigorous philosophic discourse or sharply honed argument – is in meaningful evidence. These observations do not obtain with respect to all of *Avot*, but I believe they are valid concerning a large segment, and assuredly with regard to this particular topic.

In a sense, the character of the interaction between author and reader – or shall we say between speaker and listener – contains the secret of *Avot*'s appeal and power. As in other respects, the collection's normative level is marked by diversity, the statements ranging from pragmatic advice:

הוו זהירים ברשות שאין מקרבין לו לאדם אלא לצרך עצמן, נראין
כאוהבין בשעת הנאתן ואין עומדין לו לאדם בשעת דחקו[43]

Be wary of governing authorities, as they only befriend a person in their own interests, and feign empathy when it is to their advantage, but do not stand by a person in his moments of stress.

which could have earned the assent of Lord Chesterfield or Machiavelli; through ethico-religious homily:

יהי כבוד חברך חביב עליך כשלך, ואל תהי נח לכעוס, ושוב יום אחד
לפני מיתתך[44]

May your peer's honor be as dear to you as your own, do not anger easily, and repent, [even] on the eve of death;

to outright *halakhic* imperative:

הוי זהיר בקרית שמע ובתפלה, וכשאתה מתפלל אל תעש תפלתך קבע
אלא תחנונים לפני המקום ברוך הוא.[45]

Be careful with respect to *keri'at Shema* and *tefilla*; and when you pray, do not render your prayer as a matter of rote, but, rather, as pleas addressed to Hashem, *Barukh Hu.*

The dominant chord, however, is relatively muted, in both tone and volume. We encounter little Sturm-und-drang. Voices are barely raised, threats hardly issued, fists largely impounded. The demands made upon us are far from minimal, in regard to both *talmud* and *ma'asseh*, and the standards to which we are held accountable are frequently imposing; and yet, even in *mishnayot* that present a panoramic view of the course of human life, inviting us to infer the consequences, we sense that by and large they provide knowledge, focus attention, and emphasize priorities but stop short of rubbing our noses in funerary earth. We are indeed reminded that

ולאך אתה הולך למקום עפר רמה ותולעה;[46]

And whither are you headed? To a locus of earth, decay, and worms.

but there is no danse macabre or Yorick to flesh out a *memento mori*.

The ability of *Pirkei Avot* to inculcate fundamental religious values within its relaxed atmosphere is in many respects quite remarkable, particularly with regard to values as central to Torah life as *talmud* and *ma'asseh*. However, I intuit that this fusion is, in no small measure, enabled by the broader context. The quietism of *Avot*, is in part very real but in part rather illusory, for the committed Jew indeed learns and absorbs the *massekhet* in its listener-friendly mode, but concurrently he captures its cadences as an aspect of his total religious experience. His ear is attuned to the קול דממה דקה, "the sound of evanescent silence," heard in the course of apparition to Eliyahu,[47] because that resonates with the קולות וברקים, the voices and flashes heard and seen at Sinai. Likewise, that ear is sensitive to the sotto voce tones of *Avot*, inasmuch as it experiences them against the background of the stern and imperative declaration emanating from Mount Horeb:

אמר רבי יהושע בן לוי בכל יום ויום בת קול יוצאת מהר חורב ומכרזת
ואומרת אוי להם לבריות מעלבונה של תורה שכל מי שאינו עוסק בתורה
נקרא נזוף.[48]

> Rabbi Yehoshua ben Levi stated: Daily, a celestial voice emerges from Mount Horeb and declares and pronounces, "Woe to persons over the affront to Torah, as anyone who does not engage in Torah is chastised."

Those to whom the din of the *bet* midrash is foreign may content themselves with the comment of Lionel Trilling – an interpreter, admittedly, drawn from outside the *halakhic* orbit, but surely an astute observer – that *Avot* "is not a system of ethics at all but simply a collection of maxims and pensees, some quite fine, some quite dull, which praise the life of study and give advice on how to live it."[49] And as to the quietism, they could readily accept his assertion that "we find in the tractate no implication of spiritual struggle. We find the energy of assiduity but not the energy of resistance.... Man in *Aboth* guards against sin but he does not struggle against it, and of evil we hear nothing at all."[50] Denizens of those *batei* midrash, to whom the challenging voices of tradition are an intrinsic facet of their perennial soundtrack, would rather apprehend and appreciate this quietism through the prism of the penultimate *mishna* of the first chapter in *Avot*:

כל ימי גדלתי בין החכמים ולא מצאתי לגוף טוב אלא שתיקה ולא המדרש
הוא העקר אלא המעשה וכל מרבה דברים מביא חטא.[51]

> Throughout, I was raised among sages, and found nothing better than silence for a person. And it is not exposition

but implementation which is most important. And he who speaks profusely invites sin.

The quiet I have touched upon is more ethical than auditory, and by no means literal *shetika*. But good for one's constitution and good for the soul, its tenor reverberates through *Avot* nonetheless; and therein lies, paradoxically, the source of much of its impact, its power, and its fascination.

⚜ NOTES

1. *Kiddushin* 40b and Sifri, *Eikev*, sec. 5 (in the edition of the Netziv). The two texts differ significantly in the details of the discourse described – as to location, individual ascription, etc. – but the basic thrust of the two narratives is largely identical. Of greater import is an impression possibly conveyed by an earlier statement in the Sifri: ולמדתם אותם ושמרתם לעשותם מגיד הכתוב שהמעשה תלוי בתלמוד ואין תלמוד תלוי במעשה וכן מצינו שענש הכתוב על התלמוד יותר מן המעשה (שם) – "'And you shall study them and take heed to perform them'. The *pasuk* hereby declares that *ma'asseh* is dependent upon *talmud*, but *talmud* is not dependent upon *ma'asseh*. Likewise, we find that Scripture reports greater punishment over *talmud* than over *ma'asseh*." This formulation raises the possibility that the priority of *talmud* derives from its superior worth and need not be grounded in its impact upon *ma'asseh*.
2. 17a, s.v. mevi.
3. See *Kiddushin* 40b, s.v. *shehatalmud*, where Rashi explains the superiority of *talmud* as grounded on the fact that it enables the attainment of both goals.
4. *Talmud Torah*, 3:3; c.f. ibid., 1:3. Two other suggestions for reconciling the implication and the statement of the Gemara might be briefly mentioned. One explains that the question raised in the gemara in *Baba Kama* relates to the sequence to be pursued, on a specific occasion, if one is confronted with both, rather than to overall policy. See *Tosafot, Baba Kama* 17a, s.v. *v'ha'omar*. This solution seems problematic, since sequence does not necessarily rest upon importance or reflect it, but may be due to other considerations. We eat a fruit cup before the main course but don't regard it as central. The second suggestion, cited in *Tosafot, Kiddushin* 40b, s.v. *Talmud* and *Shittah Mekubezet, Baba Kama* 17a, in the names of Rabbenu Peretz and Rabbenu Yeshayah, introduces another variable, that is, the stage in life with regard to which the question arises. This view found echoes in later centuries and is particularly relevant for the modern period, marked by lengthy schooling and training.
5. The Rav, was pulled in conflicting directions on this issue. He was, on the one hand, a scion of Volozhin and Brisk, with their focus on *Torah lishmah*, as well as under the impact of a highly abstract neo-Kantian orientation. On the other hand, the family tradition included a strong social conscience and activist streak, to which the Rav was both personally attracted and philosophically committed. The resultant tension is palpable in *Ish Hahalakha* and elsewhere.
6. *Avot* 1:2. It is noteworthy that Rav Haym Volozhiner severely circumscribed the scope of this dictum; see his qualifications in his commentary, *Rua'h Haym*, ad loc. The last two terms cited are not easily translated, since each has a broader and a narrower compass. The former could refer to some specific aspects of the ritual of *mikdash*, to the regimen of *mikdash* in its totality, or to part or all of the full range of service of God. The latter could be confined to specific assistance extended to one's fellow, material or spiritual, or to all actions, performed directly or indirectly, on his behalf. Commentators have differed as to the scope intended in this *mishna*.

7. *Isaiah* 54:15.

8. *Avot*, 5:2.

9. 2:1. In part, the thrust of the *mishna* consists in the fact that the opportunity and onus of conscious choice are assumed altogether.

10. 2:8–9. The question posed by Rabbi Yohanan resembles Rabbi's but is clearly narrower in scope. It is noteworthy that both texts speak of man universally, and not of the Jew alone.

11. I am assuming that the term *Torah* refers here to its study, as an activity parallel to the other elements, and not to the supportive existence of the Torah proper. This was apparently the understanding of the Rambam and Rabbenu Bahyye, but clearly not of Rabbenu Yonah.

12. 2:8. This formulation need not imply that future learning constitutes the sole raison d'être for personal creation, but it is a strong statement, on any reading. It should also be noted that Rabbenu Yonah adds that the caveat against self-satisfaction is not confined to *talmud* but applies equally to *ma'asseh*. וזאת המדה גם כן היא על המצות שאם עשית מצות הרבה אל תחזיק טובה לעצמך כי לכך נוצרת – "And this mode applies equally to *mitzvot*, that if you have performed many *mitzvot* do not credit yourself, for it is to this end that you were created."

13. 3:2–4, 6. These are not, strictly speaking, *halakhic* rulings, and they are not cited in the Rambam's *Mishneh Torah*. The axiological statement is, however, clear and forceful.

14. 5:28. This statement, too, was not codified by the Rambam, as defining a specific *halakhic* violation. However, the Ramban, in commenting upon the *pasuk* cited (*Deuteronomy* 4:9), did categorize it as such and included such forgetting as one of the 613 *mitzvot*. This, however, is only with respect to forgetting the events of *ma'amad har Sinai*, not regarding anything else that one has learned.

15. 4:10. Cf. the narrative implicitly criticizing some of Hazal who did not adopt this course – e.g., *Ta'anit* 21a, and *Avot d'Rabbi Nathan* 1:1.

16. 4:22. See, e.g., Rambam (in the common printed editions; in Rav Y. Shilat's edition of פירוש הרמב"ם לאבות, this *mishna* does not appear altogether), Rabbenu Bahyye, and Meiri.

17. See Rambam, *Hamez u-Matzah* 1:3.

18. As was previously noted, both terms are difficult to translate in this context, since they have multiple meanings. I have here used roughly accurate but not particularly elegant translations.

19. The resemblance to Hobbes is striking, but while the underlying base rests upon premises regarding unfettered human nature, I feel impelled to assume some difference. Hazal have no Rousseauistic illusions but also did not subscribe to extreme pessimism on this issue.

20. 3:1. See 2:1, where similar counsel is offered, but with regard to a different trio.

21. *Brakhot* 17a.

22. *Yoma* 72b. For a list of other primary sources in this spirit, see the references cited in Rav E. R. Zeeny's edition of *Magen Avot*, the commentary of the author of the Tashbez on *Avot* 1:17, pp. 74–76. To this we might add a remarkable interpretation of Rabbenu Bahyye in his *perush* upon *Deuteronomy* 30:15.

23. See *Tehillim* 50:16–17. For the identification, see *Sanhedrin* 106b and *Hagigah* 15b, respectively.

24. Yerushalmi, *Brakhot* 1:2. In reply, the rejoinder given is that R.S.b.Y. regarded the *mitzvah* of reciting *shema* as being of a piece with Torah study, and hence all *talmud Torah* could be a vehicle of its fulfillment. זה שינון וזה שינון זה. The Bavli, however, has a contrary factual tradition, according to which R.S.b.Y. abstained only from fulfilling Rabbinic *mtizvot*. See *Shabbat* 11a, and *Mo'ed Katan* 9a-b and *Tosafot* s.v. *kan* thereon.

25. 4:5. The opportunity cited as being afforded or denied refers, of course, not to a decision within the context of a formal proceeding but to providential intervention.

26. 2:522, commenting on *Avot* 4:5.

27. See 2:8 and *Baba Kama* 30a, respectively.

28. 3:9. The latter statement obviously invites the question of how the quantity is to be measured. But this is not my immediate concern.

29. 2:2. It should be noted, however, that the reason cited focuses upon avoiding evil rather than

upon creating good. The term *derekh eretz* has, in Hazal, a wide scope of meanings, ranging from social conduct – what Coventry Patmore denominated "the Traditions of civility" – to productive labor, conceived in both economic and quasi-metaphysical terms. Here, it probably refers to integration within the work force, which provides both economic sustenance and virtuous engagement in fulfilling God's primordial mandate to humanity, to place its stamp upon the natural order.

30. 3:17. The difference between the last two formulations is significant, but they obviously share a pietistic bent.

31. 2:15. Cf. 3:16 and 4:22.

32. 1:17.

33. 3:5. Here too, the referent is providential intervention.

34. 2:12.

35. See chs. 4–5 and *De'ot*, 3:3, respectively. It may be noted that much of the ideological controversy currently sundering the Torah world turns on the interpretation of to what extent does this dictum define what to do or how and why.

36. *De'ot* 3:3.

37. *Nahalat Avot* (New York, 1953), p. 212; on 4:1.

38. My own English rendering of Rav Yitzchak Shilat's Hebrew translation of the original Arabic. See his edition of הקדמות הרמב"ם למשנה (ירושלים, תשנ"ז), p. 57.

39. 8:8. The following *pasuk* continues: הבשו חכמים חתו וילכדו הנה בדבר ה' מאסו וחכמת מה להם – Lo, the wise are shamed, disheartened, and captured. Lo, they have contemned Hashem's word and what have they of wisdom?

40. *Hakdamot* p. 58.

41. This assumption serves as much of the basis for the Rambam's explanation of the position of *Avot* in *Seder Nezikin*, just after *Sanhedrin*. See *Hakdamot*, pp. 47–49. Of particular relevance to our discussion, we might note the Rambam's perception of *Avot*: בזו המסכתא מוסרי כל חכם מן החכמים עליהם השלום.

42. 2:461.

43. 2:3. This counsel may, to some extent, have been stimulated and sharpened by the catalyst of current historical events, but it hardly seems confined to a specific political constellation.

44. 2:9. The triad differs widely with respect to content and focus, but the overall direction is common to all three counsels.

45. 2:12. With respect to the motive force and character of *tefilla* as plea, cf. *Berakhot* 28b–29b.

46. 3:1.

47. See *Melakhim* I, 19:11–12.

48. 6:2. The citation is drawn from a chapter known as *kinyan Torah*, as it catalogs a list of 48 elements helpful to the acquisition of Torah. While not originally part of *Avot*, in the course of time it was linked to it as an appendage and is frequently printed with it.

   It is not clear from the text who is being addressed: universal humanity, collective Jewry, or those who lapse in *talmud Torah*.

49. "Wordsworth and the Iron Time," in *Wordsworth: Centenary Studies* (Princeton, N.J., 1951), p. 136.

50. Ibid, p. 140.

51. 1:17.

Standing Up Against Holocaust Deniers: *A Memoir from David Irving v. Penguin Books and Deborah Lipstadt*

Deborah E. Lipstadt

One of my teachers used to say, "Look at your week through *Parshat HaShavua* eyes." I always thought this a sweet but rather innocuous aphorism; something to rely upon to give contemporary relevance to one's *d'var Torah* but not much more. Shortly before my departure for London to fight a libel suit brought against me by Holocaust denier David Irving, I was given a new perspective on that teaching. It was New Year's weekend, 2000, and I was in my office packing up my books and papers to ship off to London. I was nervous and concerned. Though I knew that the truth was unequivocally on our side, I did not know how things would play out in the courtroom. Could Irving, as a result of some legal fluke or vagary, emerge triumphant and, as a result, give Holocaust denial a newfound legitimacy? Not surprisingly, the campus was largely deserted except for my colleague Michael Berger, professor of rabbinics and, prior to coming to Emory, a beloved teacher at Ramaz. Michael stopped by my office to ask when I was leaving for London. When I told him I would be going on the next Saturday night, he happily declared: "Oh, that's perfect because Shabbat afternoon

we begin reading *Bo*, the portion in Exodus." Puzzled, I tried to remember what in *Bo* might make it relevant. Unable to bring up a
textual reference, I asked a bit perplexed: "Why perfect?" Michael,
who has both a Columbia PhD and rabbinic ordination from one
of Israel's most elite Modern Orthodox yeshivot, supported himself
in college by serving as the Torah reader, chanting from the Torah
for a local congregation. Consequently he knows entire sections of
the text by heart. To him it was crystal clear: "*Bo* begins with God's
instruction to Moses: "*Bo el Pharaoh*," "Go to Pharaoh." He paused
and then added with great seriousness, "You are going to challenge a contemporary Pharaoh." I caught my breath, not because
of the connection, but because someone such as Michael, whose
life marches to the beat of Jewish learning, was using the Torah to
contextualize what loomed ahead of me.

✳ ✳ ✳

Despite the power of this moment, in the weeks that followed I
was barely aware of which Torah portion was being read. Grueling
days in court left me utterly spent. Most Shabbat mornings found
me fast asleep or luxuriating in the quiet and solitude of the day.

The months passed, and the evidentiary stage of the trial
ended one Thursday in March the right before *Shabbat Zakhor*,
the Shabbat of Remembrance. It occurs right before the holiday
of Purim and takes its name from the final section of that week's
Torah reading (Deuteronomy 25:17–19), which begins with the
word *Zakhor*, Remember. That section reminds the Israelites of
the brutal and unprovoked rear guard assault by the Amalekites
on them as they left Egypt. They were in fact the first group ever
to attack the Israelites. The Torah declares: "Remember, *Zakhor*,
what Amalek did to you" and instructs the Israelites to "wipe out
the memory of Amalek. Remember. Don't forget." Jewish lore
considers Haman, the antagonist of the Purim story, to be descended from Amalek, hence the choice of this particular reading right before Purim. Many people are discomforted by these
verses. Wiping out Amalek smacks to them of what Torah critics

call "Old Testament Vengeance." Holocaust survivors have taught me by example to see these verses in a somewhat different light. One would expect them to be driven by the desire to "wipe out," that is, to demonize the perpetrators and to be motivated by anger, hostility, and even vindictiveness toward those who attempted to destroy them. Instead I have found that most survivors expend little energy on these emotions. They are energized not by retribution, but by *not* forgetting. Their lives have been marked, not by the injunction to wipe out, but by *zakhor*, remember. Once, when I taught a course on "Judaism: Its Beliefs and Traditions" at Emory's Divinity School, my students were future Methodist and A.M.E. ministers. Many of them expressed their firm belief in the need to reflexively forgive one's enemies, irrespective of whether they have expressed remorse. A few years ago Bishop Desmond Tutu spent some time at Emory as a Visiting Professor. I was always tempted to ask him how, as head of South Africa's Truth and Reconciliation Commission, he could reconcile letting off those who had committed horrendous and unspeakable crimes with no punishment with the notion of individual responsibility for one's actions. It was an approach that seemed to run counter to Judaism, which posits that individual repentance does not obviate the mandate for justice. I have told some of my Christian acquaintances of my difficulty with accepting the notion of forgiving one's oppressors even if they have not repented of their ways. I suspect that they see me as a bit of a troglodyte or, to put it more bluntly, very "un-Christian" for harboring these sentiments. Ironically, Christianity, while preaching "forgiveness," has been responsible for the murder of millions of Jews while rarely, if ever, have Jews risen up to destroy those who have oppressed them. There are, of course, many contemporary Jews who are convinced that had Jews done a bit more "retaliating" their subsequent history might have been less tragic.

Before the trial there had been those who had wanted me to settle. (I was never sure precisely what it was they wanted me to settle for: four million victims? A few gas chambers? No gas chambers?) I eschewed their suggestions because I believed that this case, brought against me by someone who unashamedly lied about history and spread hatred and prejudice, left no room for compromise. Maybe, I mused, that was how these verses from Deuteronomy should be understood. Amalek represents an evil so extreme that one can simply not compromise with it.

The Saturday morning when *Parshat Zakhor* was to be read, I awoke and knew that I *needed* to be at services in order to hear this portion read. I momentarily toyed with the option of opening a *Tanakh*, a Hebrew Scriptures, and simply reading those verses, but that did not feel adequate. I felt a need to hear this portion in a communal setting. The drive to hear it in synagogue – *b'tzibur*, in a community – was unmistakable. When the Torah scroll was unrolled and the reader began to chant, I rose quietly in my place. I had not planned to do so, but did so instinctively. It is a brief reading so my standing was not an obtrusive act. I was sure no one noticed.

* * *

Two days later, on Purim, I returned to the synagogue for the reading of *Megillat Esther*, the Book of Esther. I had heard it read more times than I could count and was certainly not expecting a "*Parshat HaShavua*"[1] moment. Yet midway through the *megilla* one verse jumped out at me. Though I was familiar with the verse, that night I "heard" it in a different way. The verse comes at the moment when Mordecai tells Esther she must go to the king and inform him that Haman plans to destroy the Jewish people. Esther refuses because the king has not summoned her. To go before him without being summoned could result in her death.

Mordecai has little patience for her personal anxieties when the fate of an entire people – her people – hangs in the balance. Annoyed, he tells her three things. He warns her that she should not delude herself into thinking that, because she is queen, her fate will be any different from that of her fellow Jews. During the Holocaust this was a lesson learned by some of the secularized, assimilated Jews, those who had shed their traditional ways, any form of dress or practice that marked them as Jews, and any connection to their fellow Jews. Many of them assumed that, because they had Westernized themselves, they would not be the objects of antisemitism. Ironically, the Holocaust began in that country with the most acculturated Jewish community. In fact, the Nazis claimed that Westernized Jews posed a greater threat than traditional Jews. The latter, because of their clothing or practices, could be readily identified as Jews. The lesson to be learned is that ultimately, how a Jew dresses or behaves is irrelevant to the anti-Semite. Jew hatred is a form of prejudice. [Note the entomology of the word: pre-judge, i.e., don't confuse me with the facts.] As such, it is irrational and not a reaction to the actions of the Jews.

Mordechai then rather dismissively tells Esther that if she keeps silent and fails to act, *revach v'hatzalah ya'amode la'Yehudim mi'makom acher*, salvation will come to the Jews from some other place. If she does not act, someone else will. I reflected on the fact, that if I had not exposed Irving's claims, someone else would have had to do and certainly *would* have done so. But Mordechai is not yet finished with his admonition. Challenging Esther to use the blessings that have been bestowed upon her, he adds: "*Mee yodea im l'ate kazot higa'at la'malkhut?* Who knows, if not for this *very* reason, you became the queen?" Once again I fell back on my teacher's aphorism. I certainly do not equate, in any manner, shape, or form, being sued for libel by an anti-Semite and a racist with being anointed queen. But who knows if it were not for the need to defeat this man that I was given the education and the other opportunities that had brought me to this day? I might have been tempted to turn away in fear, as Esther was initially inclined to do. I did not do so, because I knew how many people – survivors in particular – were counting on me. I also knew – and had been reminded of such in a synagogue a few days earlier – that with evil there is no option to turn away. Esther responds by asking Mordecai to have the people fast and pray for her. She needs to know that, though she will stand alone before the king, she will *not be* alone. It was then that I understood my drive to get to synagogue to hear the verses from Deuteronomy and the Scroll of Esther in a congregational setting. While my reputation and work were on the line, this was a far larger struggle. I could not have done what I did without my magnificent legal team and without the material, emotional, and intellectual support of a host of people. When I stood up – whether it was in court, when the court usher would cry out each morning "All Rise," or in synagogue for the reading of *Zakhor* – many other people were standing with me.

*　*　*

The judge's overwhelming decision in my favor was handed down exactly one week before Passover. When my family and friends gathered for the Passover seder at my home, it was as if, one of my colleagues who was there observed, we were celebrating two liberations: one from Egypt and one from a legal morass. The seder moved along with great spirit and good cheer. After we ate, we reached the point when the door is opened for Elijah the prophet. That is accompanied by the recitation of *Sh'fokh Hamatkha* (*Psalm 79:6*), a short paragraph which makes many Jews profoundly uncomfortable because it calls upon God to pour out his wrath on those who have persecuted Jews. Let them be punished, the seder participants ask, because these enemies have "devoured" Jews and "laid waste" to their "dwelling place." It was apparently added to the Haggada during the medieval period at the time of the "blood libels," when Jews were falsely accused of using the blood of Gentile children for the preparation of *matzot*. Vile accusations, which even the Vatican condemned as without a basis in fact, and blood libels have persisted for centuries. Many modern Passover Haggadot, finding this paragraph too vindictive, have eliminated it. I, on the other hand, love it. Why my infatuation with *Sh'fokh Hamatkha*? I picture beleaguered Jews, particularly, but not only, in Europe, for whom Passover, with its proximity to Easter, was a dangerous time. Priests would preach about what the Jews supposedly did to Jesus. Christian children would be warned to avoid going near Jews. Many a Jew who grew up in Eastern Europe remembers the attacks perpetrated on them by Christians during these days. I imagine Jews who lived their lives, not just at Passover, but during much of the year, in fear of the violence the non-Jew could and often did direct their way. They knew from experience that when this happened they were on their own and that few – if any – non-Jews would come to their defense. On seder night, for one short paragraph, they opened the doors of their homes and unashamedly gave voice to their desire for justice. Of course, this act of bravery had a *faux* quality to it, because by that late hour most of their non-Jewish neighbors had already retired for the night. The danger of anybody actually hearing what they were saying was negligible. Those thirty-two words constituted a moment of uncharacteristic Jewish "machismo." And yet even then they did not ask God to let *them* pour out their own wrath. Instead, they asked God to render judgment. Moreover, they were quite specific about who should be the object of this wrath – not the entire non-Jewish world – but only those specific people who oppressed Jews and "did not call out in God's name," who failed to adhere to even a modicum of ethical standards. For one brief moment the Jew stood on an equal playing field. And yet even then this Jew turned to the Judge of all the world, the same Judge Abraham had challenged in the book of Genesis to do justice, and called upon that Judge to once again do justice. And then, as suddenly as it began, the door was shut, the Jew sat down, the Seder continued, and all returned to as it had been and as it would remain for too many years.

The hour was quite late as our Seder drew to an end with the singing of a number of wonderfully spirited songs. Then someone spontaneously began a refrain of *Dayenu*, the song enumerating all the good things that God has done for the Jewish people. After each verse the refrain proclaims, *Dayenu*, that alone would have sufficed. I was not sure if the person who began singing wanted to prolong the Seder a bit or was saying: "I've had enough." A s those assembled joined in song, I remembered a letter I had received a few days earlier from Rabbi Haskel Lookstein congratulating me on my victory. He closed with the line which introduces the song. *Kama ma'a lot tovot aleynu*, How many good things have come our way. Indeed, how many good things had come my way: I had been given the chance to stand up to a man who epitomized antisemitism, racism, and hatred. I had fought hard and I had won. I had been showered with thanks and praise – far more than I deserved – for doing that. I had given survivors a measure of satisfaction that this time Jew haters could not escape with no consequences. For all this *Dayenu* seemed like an insufficient refrain. Instead I thought back to one of the final verses of the 23rd Psalm, *Kosi revaya, my cup runneth over.*

And so it was. And so it is.

NOTES

1. Technically, *Megilat Esther*, since it is not part of the Five Books of Moses, is not in the category of *Parshat HaShavua*.

Dayeinu

Haskel Lookstein

(Adapted from a sermon given on June 14, 2008 on the occasion of Rabbi Lookstein's 50th anniversary as leader of Kehilath Jeshurun.)

I am deeply grateful to all of you who came this morning. I had thought that on a summer *Shabbat* the *shul* would certainly not be full; so many people would be away. I cannot tell you how moved I am by the packed synagogue with so many standees who gave up quite a bit on a beautiful weekend in order to be with me and my family on this once-in-fifty-years milestone.

Your presence, however, accentuates the fact that so many who would have *shepped nachas* from this occasion are no longer with us. Of course I miss my parents, but, in the nature of things, I could not have expected them to be here. I miss my uncle, Bernard Fischman, without whom I probably would not be standing here today. I miss my Aunt Nathalie Herman, whom I can visualize peeking out at me from the corner of the balcony to my right. I, of course, miss my sister, Nathalie Friedman, who was so vital a part of my life and my development. I am sad that my brother-in-law, Israel Friedman, the son of the sainted Boyaner Rebbe, is incapacitated and could not come across the park.

35

But, I also deeply miss my first brother-in-law, Dan Schacter, of blessed memory, who was taken from us at such a young age and who had a great impact on my life. I am deeply saddened by the absence of my nephew, Dr. Allen Gribetz, who would have loved this occasion and whose smile I can feel radiating from the section on my left.

I miss Mr. Joseph E. Adler who taught me how to *lain* and *daven* before the *amud* and set such a high standard for all of us in ritual matters. I, of course, miss my colleague Dr. Noam Shudofsky, who partnered with me in the development of Ramaz and KJ. Much of what we have today is a tribute to him. I miss Bob Leifert, whose creative mind and commitment to KJ was responsible for so many new initiatives over the course of his 25 years of service to the congregation, and I miss Florence Cohen, who for 35 years made it possible for me to do everything that I did.

I miss three past presidents of the congregation. The late Max J. Etra, Harry W. Baumgarten, and Nathan Salzman, who were so supportive of me, and two past chairmen of the Ramaz Board of Trustees, A. Philip Goldsmith and Joseph Lorch, who were similarly committed to my efforts in behalf of Ramaz.

☙ A RELEVANT STORY

My father, of blessed memory, loved to tell the story of a colleague of his, the late Rabbi Israel Goldstein, who was delivering a 40th anniversary sermon in Congregation B'nai Jeshurun (now known as BJ). Rabbi Goldstein, who was known for his somewhat long-winded sermons, was already in full homiletical stride when a woman entered the sanctuary and sat down quietly in the back. As the rabbi talked on and on and on, she asked a gentleman alongside her: "How long has he been speaking?" "Forty years," was the reply. "Oh well," she responded, "then I guess he can't go on much longer."

I thought about that anecdote as I reflected on my first sermon from this pulpit, 50 years ago today, June 14, 1958. It lasted 35 minutes, between my thank yous and what I thought at the time was a very important message on *Parshat Shelach* to the congregation into which I was born. I remember that, as I concluded the sermon, Max J. Etra and A. Philip Goldsmith, of blessed memory, left their presidential and vice presidential seats alongside the *Aron Kodesh* and presented me with a watch – a watch which I still wear every *Shabbat* and *Yom Tov*.

Some worshippers in this *shul* probably think it took me 50 years to get the hint – and some, no doubt, think I still don't get it - but, in fact, I am mindful of the change in attention span between 1958 and 2008. Those who sat through my first sermon will recall that back in 1958 when we went to the movies, we saw a double feature – two movies - plus the news of the day – five hours. If we went to the Polo Grounds, or, God forbid, Yankee Stadium or, worse still, Ebbets Field, on a Sunday, it was for a double header from 1:00 o'clock 'till 6:00 or 7:00. By the way, by a show of hands, who among you were here in *shul* for that inaugural address? I know that Larry Kobrin, Alice Smokler, and Steven Gross were present. Lillian Jacobs, who could not possibly make it here today but who called me yesterday, was present as was Sara Mandelbaum who also could not make the walk this morning. I see that Lionel Etra and Ray Ward were also there.

In any event, I assure you that I am mindful of *tircha d'tzibura* and I will limit my remarks accordingly. Of course, nothing I have said thus far counts towards my quota; it was just an introduction. So, those of you who regularly time my sermons, start the count now!

"Dayeinu!"

What were *B'nai Yisrael krechtzing* about in the wilderness? The *Torah* cites several specifics.

1. מי יאכילנו בשר? We want meat!
2. זכרנו את הדגה אשר נאכל במצרים חינם
   We miss the Egyptian caviar!

3. ‏ואת הקשואים‎ cucumbers;

‏ואת האבטיחים‎ melons;

‏ואת הבצלים‎ onions;

‏ואת השומים‎ garlic!

4. ‏ועתה נפשנו יבשה בלתי אל המן עינינו‎

All we have is boring *manna*; morning and night – *manna*!

Can you believe this scene! Could this *krechtzing* be real? Barely months after the Exodus, the Ten Plagues, the Crossing of the Sea, the Standing at Sinai and the Giving of the Torah?

Moreover, the fish they miss; the flagellating they forgot? Cucumbers they miss; the bricks they had to make by hand, they forgot? Onions and melons they miss; slave labor to build *Pithom* and *Ramses*, they forgot?

And why the disgust with *manna*? According to our sages, it tasted like whatever they wanted it to taste like. If they wished, it could taste like a Prime Grill steak with fries and onions or, if they preferred, a Häagen-Dazs Pralines and Cream Sundae topped with whipped cream and a cherry. Or, alternatively, a Starbucks latte or a glass of Macallans 18 year old single malt scotch! What did they have to *krechtz* about?

There is, of course, a simple answer to the whys of their dyspeptic exclamations. They forgot to be grateful for what they had and so they concentrated on what they didn't have. They did not have *hakarat ha-tov* for their liberation, for their freedom, for the revelation at Sinai; for *matan Torah*, for their myriad of blessings, and so their focus was on what was missing; what they lacked; what they thought they needed. They never felt *Dayeinu* for what they had, and therefore, they could never be grateful for what God had given them.

This was not just the character of the *Dor Ha-midbar* – the generation of the wilderness - this is a tendency of every human being in every generation.

The first human beings, Adam and Eve, lived in Paradise, but they desperately needed the apple from the tree of knowledge. They had everything, but they were not satisfied. They never felt *Dayeinu*.

Our children have relatively everything, but instead of saying thank you to parents and to God, they keep thinking of what they don't have. *Dayeinu* is not a fundamental word in their lexicon.

And we, as adults, are no different. We live in a virtual *Gan Eden* and yet, often, our focus is on what is missing in our lives, in our work, in our community and, sometimes even in our marriages. We, too forget to say *Dayeinu*.

I remember Roman Rutman, the leader of Moscow's refusniks, with whom Audrey and I spent many hours on our first visit to Moscow in 1972. The holder of two doctorates in cybernetics, he was hounded by the KGB because he applied for a visa to go to Israel. He was unemployed. He carried a briefcase with him on the street because he had to appear as if he had a job or risk arrest as a parasite, living off the dole. He was granted a visa in November of 1972, two months after we met. It was a miracle! His dream was fulfilled! He made *aliya*!

Did he say *Dayeinu*? Not quite! In December, he came to America to speak for the Soviet Jewry movement. He stayed in our home. It was clear to us that he was depressed, after only six weeks in Israel. "Why?" we asked him. He answered: "There isn't enough culture in Israel; and besides I miss the skiing!"

Skiing?! Culture?! What about the KGB outside your door? What about not being able to teach cybernetics? What about living off charity from visiting American Jews? What about the fulfillment of your dream of going from slavery to freedom?

I recall coming to my father in despair and consternation. He calmed me down and said, "Hack, it's no different from the response of *B'nai Yisrael* in the wilderness: 'We remember the caviar!'" No *Dayeinu* and, therefore, no gratitude.

So today, my feelings are crystallized in two words: *Dayeinu* and gratitude: for blessings that are above and beyond anything that I could have expected. *Dayeinu*!

If I had been blessed just with my parents and grandparents, *Dayeinu*. If I had had only my grandfather, Isadore Schlang, who gave me my love of *davening* and singing; or my father who modeled for me what a rabbi is supposed to be: an עבד לעבדי ה׳ – a servant to the servants of the Lord - and a lover of all Jews. If I could just talk to him for five minutes, there are so many questions I would want to ask him. He wasn't always the easiest person for me to get along with; he could be very critical, but how I miss the criticism. I recall that after every sermon that I delivered in *shul* we would come back together to his office and while removing our *tallesim* he would invariably say: "Hack, that was a beautiful sermon; of course, I would have…" I guess I bristled more than a few times at that "I would have" but, oh how I miss the honest and constructive criticism!

If I had been blessed only with my mother, who believed in me, *shepped nachas* from me, and whose wisdom helped me many times, especially after my father's passing. She would often call me on a Thursday or Friday and say, "Haskel, you're going to talk about such and such or so and so, aren't you?" In fact, I usually wasn't, but after hearing her suggestion, I did.

If I had been blessed only with Audrey, *Dayeinu*! Thank God for her father, of blessed memory, who convinced her to go out with me and who taught her his life principle שמח בחלקו – to be happy with one's lot. That's the way she lives her life and the way she brought up our children. She is absolutely selfless, always thinking of others first. I believe that the most important ingredient in a happy marriage is two people who look out for each other's interest. She is absolutely gifted in this and she sets the standard for me. Recently she had to choose a password for something on the computer. I was sitting alongside her so I happened to see it. You know what she chose? "Children!" That's what came first to her mind. (It never occurred to me to ask her why she didn't choose "husband"!) Her choice speaks volumes about who she is, why our family is so blessed, and how she has been so supportive of me and you for the last 49 years – actually 50; she began teaching second grade in Ramaz in 1958.

If I had been blessed only with our children, our children-in-law, and our grandchildren. *Dayeinu!* Thank God for them all. How blessed we are with their values and the way they live their lives: solidly, Modern Orthodox, Zionist, deeply involved in their synagogues, schools and communities, incredibly hospitable with an open door to all. Always putting others first – you see what Audrey has accomplished and what we have been blessed with! *Dayeinu!*

My teachers: What an incredible blessing to have had the opportunity to learn for four years with the *Rav* in his *shiur*; to have listened to years of lectures; and, yes, to have felt close to him personally. I recall at the *Rav's shiva*, his late son-in-law, Professor Twersky, telling me: "You know, the *Rav* really loved you; he used to tell me that he answered questions of yours that he wouldn't answer for others." His influence on me? Well, I recall studying *Ish Ha-halakha* in preparation for a lecture and I was so astonished that the *Rav* was articulating ideas and principles that I believed in so fervently. It was only upon reflection that I realized it was the other way around. After many years of listening to him I had internalized so much of his philosophy and outlook that I actually thought those ideas were mine – and, in a way, I guess that's the way he wanted it to be.

If I had had that privilege only – *Dayeinu!*

Finally, if I had been blessed only to have been able to be a rabbi in KJ and Ramaz, *Dayeinu.* What a privilege to work with lay leaders who served as president: Sandy Eisenstat, Benji Brown, Stanley Gurewitch, Fred Distenfeld, Chaim Edelstein, and now Eric Feldstein. What a blessing to have been able to work with chairmen of the Ramaz board of trustees, all of them Ramaz alumni: Larry Kobrin, Mel Newman, Arthur Silverman (an honorary alumnus because of his two sons who are alumni and because he is really a product of the KJ/Ramaz community), Steve

Gross, David Kahn, Steve Schacter, and, now, Pamela Rohr. What a gift to have had as my colleagues, and co-workers, such committed and capable professionals as Rabbi Bakst, Kenny Rochlin (another product of this total community), and now Judy Fagin who has given me an opportunity to step back from the day-to-day responsibilities in Ramaz and leave them in her wise and effective hands. And in KJ, to have had close association with *Hazan* Davis the first, and *Hazan* Davis the second, and, most recently, Leonard Silverman (another homegrown talent), Rabbi Weinstock, Rabbi Soloveichik, and, now, Riva Alper. And how can I not rave about Rudy for whom KJ and Ramaz are a religious commitment! If only for these lay leaders and co-workers, *Dayeinu*!

This community is really the *Gan Eden* of communities. There is such an appreciation here for what a rabbi is and does. It is unlike any other place. There is respect and love, a sense that we are all striving for the same thing; a modern, centrist, open, tolerant, nonjudgmental Orthodox life; a love of *Medinat Yisrael*; a respect for women and their needs and role in religious observance and education; a commitment to *Ahavat Yisrael*, especially toward those with whom we disagree; a concern for the total community and, particularly, for Jews who are in pain or distress; a loyalty to, and love for, America, and a belief in democracy and justice and fairness and freedom for all Americans and for all mankind.

It is amazing – and something which I do not take for granted – that this set of core values has remained constant and firm in KJ and Ramaz during these past 50 years. But they pre-date me. These were my father's values which he planted firmly in our community, beginning in 1923. These, I believe, were the values of my great grandfather, the RAMAZ who came here in 1906. The words may have been different; the methods and styles may have been different; but, fundamentally, *we have not changed*. We have grown. We have become a little less formal – we even allow men to wear brown shoes on Shabbat! We have loosened up some. But I believe that if my father and great grandfather were to walk into this *shul* today, while they might have some constructive criticism

(I know my father would), they would be very gratified that a vibrant Modern Orthodox Judaism is flourishing in the community they built. For that community and for that continuity, I am profoundly grateful – *Dayeinu*.

על אחת כמה וכמה טובה כפולה ומכפלת למקום עלינו

How much more so am I grateful to God for *all* of these blessings *together*.

Not many people are blessed this way. I pray for KJ and Ramaz, for all of you, for my family and for me that the blessings continue.

יהי ה' א-להינו עמנו כאשר היה עם אבותינו, אל יעזבנו ואל יטשנו

May the Lord, our God, continue to be with us as He was with our forebears; may He never forsake us; may He never abandon us.

There is a special blessing that one makes when one is grateful and happy and when that gratitude and happiness is not only personal, but shared with others. It is not the blessing of *shehechiyanu* – that one is for personal happiness only – but rather *ha-tov v'ha-meitiv*. I recite it now for myself and for all of us.

ברוך אתה ה' א-להינו מלך העולם הטוב והמטיב

Blessed art Thou, O Lord our God, King of the universe who is good and who makes things good!

Thank you!

Sephardi Traditionalism in Ceremonial Art and Visual Culture

Vivian B. Mann

Those groups that have successfully recreated themselves in a new environment appear to have done so by bringing a "cultural blueprint" of their former worlds and replicating their former lifestyle in their new surroundings. – James Deetz[1]

Some years ago, a collector of Jewish ceremonial art showed me a new piece he had acquired. It was a *ketuba*, a marriage contract, from Rhodes and had rather crude decoration. What was most interesting was the name of the bride, Malkah the daughter of Eliezer from Castile. In 1923, the year of the marriage, it was still a matter of pride to the bride's family that they had lived in Castile more than 400 years earlier. This is not an isolated example among the inscriptions that grace the ceremonial art of the Sephardi diaspora. The centuries of Jewish life on the Iberian Peninsula were remembered as a creative period in Jewish philosophy, Jewish thought, Hebrew literature, and science, and as a time when Jews could reach high levels of power.

It is widely recognized that distinctive aspects of Sephardi liturgy and particular customs still tie the descendants of émigrés from Spain and Portugal to their medieval homelands. But it is less well recognized that traditional forms of ceremonial art and the ways they are used echo medieval Iberian types. The decorated *ketuba* mentioned above is one example. Another is a *ketuba* from Spain dated 1479 on which the text of the *tenaim* and the *kiddushin* (the marriage and betrothal agreements) are written side by side, each in a horseshoe-shaped arch.[2] The same composition marks the earliest contracts written in Venice after the settlement of the Sephardim in 1589.[3] They are the beginning of a long tradition of decorated *ketubot* in the lands of the Sephardi diaspora (whereas Ashkenazim did not adopt this form of ceremonial art until the mid-twentieth century).[4]

Our knowledge of the ceremonial art and related material culture of Sepharad was for many years dependent on a small corpus of extant works that were preserved in public archives or museums, and even in church treasuries.[5] At the time of the Expulsion from Spain, the ban on exporting silver and gold ceremonial art extended to the ceremonial art of synagogues (even their textiles were burned to extract the bullion in the embroidery),[6] in addition to personal objects. This meant the loss of nearly all the Judaica of medieval Spain. Hebrew manuscripts and printed books were excluded from the ban and constitute the largest group of extant medieval Spanish Judaica. Among them are illuminated *haggadot* whose genre scenes, scenes of preparations for Passover and its celebration in the home and the synagogue, are an important source for the lost Judaica of Sepharad. By comparing works depicted in these genre scenes with forms of ceremonial art characteristic of the Sephardi diaspora, I suggested in a 1992 essay that other types of ceremonial art were used in Spain in addition to the known corpus.[7] These included the split-skirt type of Torah mantle (mantles that flair outward and have a slit to facilitate their placement over the scroll), the use of a set of Torah ornaments consisting of a crown and two finials on the Torah scroll, and the use of fruit-shaped finials as ornaments for the reader's desk. All of these examples are depicted in the synagogue scenes of *haggadot* from fourteenth-century Spain and appear later in the ceremonial art of Italy and the Ottoman Empire, and some even in Amsterdam and England.

Since the presentation of that research, the governments of the regions of Aragón and Murcia have undertaken numerous excavations in the juderías, or Jewish quarters, of various cities and towns that have enlarged the corpus of Judaica from Sepharad with the discovery of synagogues, cemeteries, ceramics, and metalwork. Noteworthy are the ceramic Hanukka lamps found in several cities such as Saragossa Lorca, and Burgos[8]; the silver plates inlaid with gold found in the synagogue level of a site later used for the church of Santa Maria in Burgos[9]; and the jewelry buried with the dead in Jewish cemeteries.[10] This paper will explore an additional source of knowledge for the Judaica and dress of the Sephardim prior to the Expulsion, representations of Jews and Jewish life on the large paintings placed behind church altars in the fourteenth and fifteenth centuries.

Concomitantly with the excavations, researchers began to mine the archives of the Crown of Aragón, as the medieval state was known, for documents pertaining to Jews. One result has been an expanded understanding of the role of Jews as artists, as both silversmiths and painters.[11] In the Middle Ages the silversmith or goldsmith was as significant an artist as the sculptor or painter who worked in churches, and the illuminator who decorated manuscripts with elaborate miniatures was on a par with the artist of panel paintings or frescoes. Occasionally the same artist worked in more than one genre. For example, an atelier or workshop active in fourteenth-century Barcelona known as the Workshop of St. Mark produced manuscripts in both Hebrew and Latin, as well as *retablos* or altarpieces.[12] One of the Hebrew manuscripts from the St. Mark Workshop, Maimonides' *Guide to the Perplexed* of 1324 (Copenhagen, Det Kongelige Bibliothek, Cod. Heb. xxx-vii), shows the impact of its production in a mixed workshop of Christians and Jews. In addition to having stylistic and compositional similarities to Latin manuscripts, one miniature (fol.

202r) is a composition developed initially in Byzantium and later found in the Christian West: the four "living creatures" of Ezekiel's vision, one placed in each corner of a square or rectangular frame. In Christian manuscripts, the figures are symbols of the Evangelists[13]; in the *Guide to the Perplexed* the same symbols are used to represent their original literary source, the four beasts of the heavenly chariot.

But manuscript illumination was not the only type of painting in which Jewish artists engaged in medieval Spain. Notarial documents dated 1316 to 1416 published by the Spanish historian Asunción Blasco Martínez reveal the existence of several Jewish painters who worked on a larger scale, such as Abraham de Salinas, who signed a contract with the See of Saragossa in 1393 to produce a *retablo*, a painting behind the altar table, on the theme of the life of the Virgin.[14] From the notarial texts, we know that Abraham painted at least four altarpieces for churches in the See of Saragossa, but he may also have produced others whose records are lost.

Another contract records the employment of Bernart de Alfarajín a Jewish silversmith, to create a frame for Abraham's *retablo* that was to include six cartouches on the theme of the Annunciaton to Mary. Many Jews were gold and silversmiths in Christian Spain, a calling that may have been a legacy of their role under Islamic rule.[15] Visual representations of Jews as silversmiths appear in the *Vidal Mayor*, the law code of James I of Aragon dated to the second half of the thirteenth century. Four recorded cases involve Jews; each is accompanied by a historiated initial.[16] Jews are shown as silversmiths, as merchants of metalwork, as pawnbrokers accepting metalwork as surety for a loan, and as litigants before the king in a case involving metalwork. Among the works made by Jewish silversmiths were objects for the church, to the extent that Pope Benedict XIII, at the beginning of the fifteenth century, prohibited Jews from fashioning chalices, crucifixes, or the bindings of holy books. Knowledge of the art of silversmithing was passed from father to son, resulting in generations of artists whose names are documented in archival records. One example is the Amalfi Family of Saragossa, who flourished during the fourteenth century.[17] The Jewish silversmiths of Spanish cities formed their own guilds and sometimes had their own synagogues; there was one in Saragossa known as the *sinoga de los argenteros* (the synagogue of the silversmiths).

Disputation between Moses and St. Peter, Cathedral of Tarragona, fourteenth century

Abraham de Salinas's altarpieces have not been identified, but it is possible to infer that other existing paintings are the work of Jewish artists. On a fourteenth-century *retablo* in the Cathedral of Tarragona, Moses and St. Peter dispute one another surrounded by a group of Christians and Jews (fig. 1). Moses holds the Tablets of the Law inscribed with correctly formed Hebrew letters, although the order of the Commandments is jumbled, while the scroll held by St. Peter is empty, which suggests that the artist was Jewish and knew Hebrew but did not know Latin. The combination of these two personalities in an anachronistic disputation is probably based on the *Dialoghi* of Petrus Alfonsi, whose text records a debate on the relative merits of Judaism and Christianity. Alfonsi was born Moses ha-Sephardi in Huesca in 1062; after his conversion to Christianity, he was called Peter. He used his strong knowledge of Jewish lore, including his own translations of biblical texts, as part of the argument with Moses.[18] The impact and popularity of the *Dialoghi* may be seen in the 75 manuscripts copied before the invention of printing.[19]

Large, multipaneled *retablos* became popular in the early fourteenth century. They are significant for the history of Sephardi visual culture because Jews appear in many of the scenes that accompany the large central figure of a saint or saints. They appear in scenes from the Hebrew Bible, in episodes from early Christian history at which Jews were present, and sometimes singly as representative worthies, such as kings and prophets. The *retablos* are particularly important for their recording of Jewish dress, known also from both written sources and Passover *haggadot*, and for the portrait-like faces of individual Jews. Occasionally there are glimpses of Jewish ceremonial objects that are otherwise unknown. In a "Presentation of Jesus in the Temple," now in the Hispanic Society in New York, the nature of the event, a circumcision, is indicated by the silver goblet and the semicircular knife and case on the altar (fig. 2).[20] This is the single representation we have of the knife from medieval Spain, and it is a type found in cities populated by Sephardi refugees in the sixteenth and seventeenth centuries.[21] Joseph carries a basket with two small birds, the required sacrificial offering of a postpartum woman in the time of the Temple.

Pere Espalargucs, "Presentation of Jesus in the Temple," Retablo from Enviny, 1490 (New York, Hispanic Society, A5)

On other *retablos*, in scenes that occurred in the Jerusalem Temple, the interior of the building is free of Christian decorations and appurtenances and is sometimes furnished with a Jewish ceremonial object, the *tik* or cylindrical case for the Torah scroll. That *tikim* were used in Spain was previously known from two synagogue scenes, one in the Sassoon Haggadah (Israel Museum, Ms. 181/41) and the other in the Barcelona Haggadah (London, British Library, Add. 14761, fol. 65v), in which the sexton holds a *tik* before the congregation.[22]

The altarpieces, like the *haggadot*, contain many depictions of Jews marked by signs of alterity. In 1215 Pope Innocent III convened the Fourth Lateran Council, which stipulated, among other edicts, that Jews must dress differently so that they were visually identifiable, thereby preventing sexual relations between Christians and Jews.[23] Exactly how this differentiation would be accomplished was left to local authorities.[24] The Law Code of Alfonso X of Castile (who reigned 1252–1284), which was adopted in all of Spain by 1348, stated:

> Many crimes and outrageous things occur between Christians and Jews because they live together in cities, and dress alike; and in order to avoid the offenses and evils which take place for this reason, we deem it proper and we order that all Jews, male and female, living in our dominions shall bear some distinguishing mark…so that people may plainly recognize a Jew, or a Jewess.[25]

In 1228 Jaime I of Aragon (1213–1276) required Jews to wear the circular sign, a decree that was later rescinded, but the wearing of a cloak outside the home by both men and women residing in the Crown of Aragon remained in force.[26] Legislation enacted in 1412 forbade Jews from shaving their beards or cutting their hair.[27] Their long and sometimes crooked noses or other flawed physical forms were identified with defects of character and moral failings. In sum, a Jew's appearance was a sign that he or she followed the wrong religion and was different from the majority. That these royal and ecclesiastical regulations were required implies the visual homogeneity of the Spanish population, a homogeneity that called for artificial means of differentiation in a context of identity confusion.[28] On the Iberian Peninsula, sartorial differentiation had first been instituted by the Muslim rulers of Al-Andalus, to signify the subordinate status of *dhimmi* or protected minorities.[29] Some articles of dress required by the Muslims, such as the *zunnar*, a rope belt, appear in the later altarpieces of Aragon that are discussed in this paper.[30]

The designation of clothing as a symbol of minority status was part of a general medieval view of dress as denoting class or occupation. Ann Rosalind Jones and Peter Stallybrass describe medieval and Renaissance clothing as material mnemonics.[31] Clothes signified an individual's place in society and were not "fashion" in the contemporary use of the term. Livery, for example, marked an individual as being in the service of another, more powerful person.

The Jewish view of the clothing regulations imposed by Christian authorities was eloquently expressed by Solomon Alami, who was born in Spain in 1370 and died in Portugal in 1420. He wrote in *Iggeret haMusar*, his 1415 treatise on moral behavior:

> We have suffered measure for measure. Because we adopted their dress, they required of us different vestments so that we would seem to be strangers among them, and because we shortened the corners of our hair and beards, they forced us to let our hair grow as if we were plunged into deep mourning.[32]

In the Jewish art of Spain, representations of women appear in biblical scenes and in scenes connected to the celebration of Passover in the *haggadot*. Most of them are generalized figures rendered according to the conventions of Gothic art, but in specifically Jewish genre scenes, those of the synagogue service and of the seder, the women wear individualized dress. Men and women in the synagogue wear the long, hooded cloaks that were required dress out of doors in the Crown of Aragon, as in the Sarajevo Haggadah of the second quarter of the fourteenth century and in the Barcelona Haggadah dated to mid-century.[33] In the seder scenes of some manuscripts, the mistresses of the house wear elaborate head coverings of pleated cloth (fig. 3).[34] According to the Spanish art historian María del Carmen Lacarra Ducay, these headdresses were generally worn by brides in medieval Aragon.[35] In other respects, the Jewish women's indoor dress is nondistinctive; the garments are basically flowing robes that hide the body in typical Gothic fashion.

The genre scenes discussed above provide evidence of the clothing worn by Jewish women on festive holidays. A responsum of Rabbi Yomtob ben Abraham Ishbili (ca. 1250–1330) suggests that the black robes worn by women mourning at Jacob's bier in *haggadot* miniatures represent another mode of female clothing in late medieval Aragon.[36] Rabbi Ishbili discussed the case of a woman whose husband went on a trip to a distant land and did not return.[37] After years passed, two men came and swore they had heard that her husband had died. She then donned widow's clothes. After some time, she removed her widow's weeds, covered herself with a veil, and was subsequently married to another man. Female mourners in black clothes may

Seder Scene, Sarajevo Haggadah, environs of Barcelona, ca. 1350, ink, gold and gouache on parchment (Sarajevo, National Museum)

illustrate the widow's weeds mentioned in Rabbi Ishbili's responsum.

Other representations of Jewish women appear in Christian altarpieces alongside the more numerous depictions of Jewish men. Since women lacked the beards required of Jewish men, the identification of female figures as Jews depends on their clothing and the narrative context in which they are seen. An example is an Exodus from Egypt included in the *Retablo de San Bernardi* from Banyoles (now in the Museo de la Catedral in Barcelona)

Jaime Huguet, The Exodus from Egypt from Banyoles, 1462–1470 (Barcelona, Museo de la Catedral)

that was painted by Jaime Huguet in 1462–1470 (fig. 4). The painter took great care to individualize the faces of the Israelites and to vary their dress. The foremost Jewish figures, representing Moses and Aaron, are thought to be portraits of the leading Jewish residents of Banyoles. The figure guided by Saint Bernard is tentatively identified as Bonjuà Cabrit, who became doctor-surgeon to the Royal House of Barcelona. He wears a striped garment over his head, probably a tallit or prayer shawl and a gold-bordered cloak, and he carries a codex with gilt edges. Although most of the women leaving Egypt wear simple scarves over their heads, one near the end of the procession wears an elaborate headdress that forms a roll around her head, with a protruding element at top dotted with pearls. A very similar headdress, but without the jewels, is worn by the mistress of the household in the seder scene of the Sarajevo Haggadah (fig. 3) and by Jewish women on a fourteenth-century relief in Barcelona Cathedral.[38] In the retablo, attention is drawn to this woman by her bright red cloak, which visually links her to Bonjua Cabrit, the man at the head of the procession.

The altarpieces also suggest that the source for the Sephardi use of gold embroidery on ceremonial costumes, well known from North Africa and the Ottoman Empire, was Spain. None of the archaeological finds mentioned above has included actual textiles. But there is important testimony to Jewish dress in Spain in a chapter of the *takkanot* of Valladolid, promulgated at a meeting of the Jewish communities of Castile in 1432.[39] The fifth chapter discusses sumptuary laws "because Jewish women wear costly clothes and jewels that cause offense to gentiles." Therefore, the communities ruled that no woman who is not about to be married or is not a bride in the first of her marriage shall wear:[40]

> garments with more than one panel of gold cloth, or of silk or silk taffeta…. Neither shall they wear trimmings of gold cloth or of silk on their gowns, nor a gold or pearl broach, nor a string of pearls on the lower part of the forehead, nor dresses with trains more than three meters in length…nor a dress of bright red color, nor cloaks embroidered in polychrome silks, nor Moorish garments with sleeves more than two palms in width. But they may wear crude silks and thin textiles, and silver and enamel jewelry or silver belts provided that there is not more than four ounces of silver in any of them.

"Offering of Isaac," Bible, Spain and Portugal, fourteenth century and 1471–1472 (New York, Hispanic Society, B241)

A hint of the appearance of this type of dress is a small miniature in the Lisbon Bible of 1471–1472, now in the Hispanic Society, New York (fig. 5). Its text was written in Spain during the fourteenth century; the manuscript was then brought to Lisbon, where it was decorated. The miniature of the Binding of Isaac shows the ram entangled in a bush and the arm of the angel descending from heaven holding a knife in the form of a *shofar*, a ram's horn. The angel's arm is clothed in deep pink silk embroidered in gold, a type of embroidery later found on Jewish wedding dresses of the Sephardi diaspora, specifically in the Ottoman Empire and Morocco. Other depictions of the dress cited in the Valladolid By-Laws appear in Aragonese altarpieces such as the *Retablo de la Santa Cruz* painted between 1481 and 1487 and now in the Museo de Zaragoza (fig. 6). In this scene, Saint Helena, the mother of the Emperor Constantine, is depicted as if she had just entered the arcuated gate of the *judería* in a Spanish town. She is engaged in questioning a Jew on the location of the true cross. Helena wears a cape of gilt metallic cloth over a deep red dress, while the lady behind her sports a string of pearls on her head. This visual evidence suggests that the *takkanot* of Valladolid were, in effect, forbidding "court dress" to be worn by Jewish women. But the *takkanot*, in specifying that this type of dress could be worn only by brides, also suggest that Spanish clothes served as the model for the *keswa el kbira*, the elaborate embroidered silk dress worn by brides of Sephardi families in Morocco, which is characterized by

Miguel Jiménez and Martín Bernat y Taller, *Interrogation of Judas, the Jew*, Retablo de la Virgin con el Níño, 1485–1487, temple on panel (Saragossa, Museo de Zaragoza)

fine silk, often of a deep red color, and wide sleeves (fig. 7). This traditional wedding dress is worn together with a Fez belt, a luxurious silk belt that to this day incorporates textile designs first used in medieval Spain. Another link to Spain is the ceremony of dressing the Moroccan bride, during which the women chant traditional poems and songs in Spanish. Despite a lack of medieval examples, these texts and works of art suggest that the women's costumes of Morocco and the Ottoman Empire continue types worn on the Peninsula.[41] Rabbi Shlomo ben Simeon (ca. 1400–1467), who was born in Algiers, gave testimony to sartorial continuity when he wrote that the Sephardim who immigrated to North Africa continued to wear their distinctive Spanish clothing.[42] Instead of the turbans worn by native Jews, the Sephardim wore the baretta.

Ceremonial Marriage Dress, Keswa el Kbira, Marrakech, twentieth century (New York, The Jewish Museum, 1993–1995)

That the Jews of Sepharad clung to their historic identity long after the Expulsion from Spain has been well known from writings and from the perpetuation of Sephardi customs in houses of worship with names such as the Seville Synagogue that once existed in Istanbul,[43] or the Spanish and Portuguese Synagogue in New York. What is less commonly realized is that the continuation of Sephardi identity is evident in forms of ceremonial objects and in their inscriptions. One example is the language of marriage contracts in northern Moroccan cities in which refugees from Spain settled. In the *ketubot* of Tangiers, Tetouan, Cuento, and Chefchouan, local families to this day, are described as *migorshei kastiliah* (among the refugees of Castile). As this paper has shown, another way Sephardi Jews expressed their identity in the diaspora was by perpetuating the forms of ceremonial dress they wore in Spain. From the depictions of Jewish women in Christian altarpieces and in *haggadot* miniatures showing preparations for Passover and the enactment of the seder, the modern viewer can now glimpse the appearance and dress of medieval Spanish Jewry described in the communal legislation of Valladolid in 1412. In all these ways, not only in the sphere of intellectual pursuits, but also in the spheres of art and visual culture, the Sephardim of the diaspora gave expression to their identity as heirs to a noble cultural and religious heritage.

❧ NOTES

1. James Deetz, *In Small Things Forgotten: An Archaeology of Early American Life* (New York, 1977), p. 58. I want to thank Susan Lockwood for bringing this quote to my attention.
2. Isidro G. Bango Torviso, ed., *Memoria de Sefarad* (Toledo, 2002), cat. no. 31.
3. For example, Vivian B. Mann, ed., *Gardens and Ghettoes: The Art of Jewish Life in Italy* (Berkeley and New York, 1989), cat. no. 103.
4. An exceptional illuminated contract was written in Kremsmunster in the fourteenth century (Vienna, Österreischische Bibliothek). For an illustration, see Cecil Roth, *A History of Jewish Art*, rev. ed. (Greenwich, CT, 1971), pl. 31 (opp. p. 149).
5. Vivian B. Mann, "Sephardi Ceremonial Art – Continuity in the Diaspora," *Crisis and Creativity in the Sephardic World, 1391–1648*, ed. B. Gampel (New York, 1997), pp. 282–395.
6. On the ban of exporting gold and silver, see F. Fita, "Edicto de los Reyes Católicos (31 Marzo 1492) desterrando de sus estados a todos los judíos, *Boletín de la Real Academia de la Historia* 2 (1887), p. 528. On the burning of textiles see Henry Kamen, "The Expulsion: Purpose and Consequence," in Elie Kedourie, ed., *Spain and the Jews* (London, 1992), p. 89.
7. See note 5 above.
8. On the Hanukka lamps, see P. Atrian Jordan, "Lámparas de Hanukkah en cerámica popular turolense, *Revista de Teruel* 65 (1981), pp. 175–184; Bango Torviso, ed., *Memoria de Sefarad*, cat. nos. 139–142; Angel Iniesta Sanmartin et al, Lorca. Luces de Sefaraa (Murcia, 2009), pp. 362-385.
9. Bango Torviso, ed., *Memoria de Sefarad*, pp. 181–185.
10. Bango Torviso, ed., *Memoria de Sefarad*, pp. 108–129.
11. See, for example, See, for example, Asunción Blasco Martínez, "Pintores y Orfebres Judíos en Zaragoza (Siglo XIV)," *Aragón en la Edad Media* 8(1989), pp. 113–31.
12. Millard Meiss, "Italian Style in Catalonia and a Fourteenth-Century Catalan Workshop," *Journal of the Walters Art Gallery* 4 (1941), pp. 45–87; Francis Wormald, "Afterthoughts on the Stockholm Exhibition," *Konsthistorisk Tidskrift* 22 (1953), pp. 74–78; Gabrielle Sed-Rajna, "Hebrew Manuscripts of Fourteenth-Century Catalonia and the Workshop of the Master of St. Mark," *Jewish Art* 18 (1992), pp. 117–128.
13. Ezekiel, ch. 1. An early example in the Latin West appears in the English *Bury Bible* of the twelfth century. For a reproduction of fol. 202r in the Maimonides, see Rosa Alcoy y Pedros, "The Artists of the Marginal Decorations of the Copenhagen Maimonides," *Jewish Art* 18 (1992), p. 131, fig. 4.
14. Blasco Martínez, "Pintores y Orfebres Judíos en Zaragoza (Siglo XIV)," pp. 116–118.

15. Vivian B. Mann, "The Unknown Jewish Artists of the Middle Ages," *Art & Ceremony in Jewish Life: Essays in the History of Jewish Art* (London, 2005), pp. 122–128.
16. *Vidal Mayor* (Los Angeles, The Getty Museum, Ms. Ludwig xiv 6, 83. Mq.165, fols. 114r, 175v, 180r, and 243v.
17. Blasco Martínez, "Pintores y Orfebres Judiós en Zaragoza (Siglo xiv)," pp. 120–124.
18. José González Luis, "Der 'Dialogus' des Petrus Alfonsi, ein polemisch-apologetischer Traktat," in *Jewish Studies in a New Europe*, ed. Ulf Haxen, Hannah Trautner Kronmann, Karen Lisa Goldschmidt Salamon (Copenhagen, 1998), pp. 308–311.
19. Ibid., p. 302.
20. *The Hispanic Society of America Handbook. Museum and Library Collections* (New York, 1928), pp. 6–7.
21. See, for example, Silvio G. Cusin and Pier Cesare Ioly Zorattini, *Friuli Venezia Giulia. Jewish Itineraries. Places, History and Art*, Venezia, Marsilio, [Udine], ca. 1998, p. 119.
22. The identification of the cases as *tikim* rests on their size and resemblance to an Italian *tik* now in Venice. Further, on an altarpiece dedicated to St. John now in the Cloisters, Metropolitan Museum in New York, the apparent Torah case in a scene of the High Priest in the Holy of Holies contrasts with the much smaller, but similar, ciborium in the church scene below it. For the Barcelona Haggadah scene, see Narkiss, *Hebrew Illuminated Manuscripts in the British Isles*, Vol. I, fig. 241.
23. For the relevant portion of proceedings, see Guido Kisch, *The Jews in Medieval Germany* (Chicago, 1949), p. 295.
24. Solomon Grayzel, *The Church and the Jews in the xiiith Century. Volume ii 1254–1314*, ed. Kenneth R. Stow (New York and Detroit, 1989), p. 110.
25. Jacob Rader Marcus, *The Jew in the Medieval World. A Source Book* (Detroit, 1999), p. 43.
26. Yom Tov Assis, *The Golden Age of Aragonese Jewry. Community and Society in the Crown of Aragon, 1213–1327* (London and Portland, OR, 1997), p. 283.
27. Elliott Horowitz, "Visages du Judaism. De la barbe en monde juif et de l'élaboration de ses significations," *Annales. Histoire, Sciences, Sociales* 49, 5 (1994), p. 1083.
28. Janina M. Safran, "Identity and Differentiation in Ninth-Century al-Andalus," *Speculum* 76, 3 (2001), p. 582.
29. Mark R. Cohen, *Under Crescent & Cross. The Jews in the Middle Ages* (Princeton, N.J., 1994), pp. 62–64; Safran, "Identity and Differentiation in Ninth-Century al-Andalus," pp. 582–583.
30. For example: Joachim and Anna, *Altarpiece of St. Mark of the Shoemakers*, ca. 1435–1445, tempera on wood (Manresa, Catedral).
31. Ann Rosalind Jones and Peter Stallybrass, *Renaissance Clothing and the Materials of Memory* (Cambridge, 2002), pp. 4–5.
32. Horowitz, "Visages du Judaism," p. 1084.
33. Roth, *The Sarajevo Haggadah*, final miniature preceding text of Haggadah (Cecil Roth, ed., Facsimile of the Sarajevo Haggadah [Belgrade, 1975]; also Bezalel Narkiss, *Hebrew Illuminated Manuscripts in the British Isles. A Catalogue Raisonné*, Vol. 1 (Oxford, 1982), figs. 187 and 241.
34. Roth, *The Sarajevo Haggadah*, Seder scene.
35. María del Carmen Lacarra Ducay, "Representacions de judíos en la pintura gótica aragonesa: siglos xiii al xv," *Boletín Museo e Instituto "Camón Aznar"* 99 (2007), p. 237.
36. For example in the Sister of the Golden Haggadah (London, British Library, Or. 2884; Bango Troviso, *Memoria de Sefarad*, p. 208); and in the Golden Haggadah (London, British Library, BL. Add. 27210); Narkiss, *Hebrew Illuminated Manuscripts in the British Isles*, fig. 175a.
37. Yom Tov ben Abraham al-Ishbili (haRitba), *Responsa*, ed. Joseph Kach (Jerusalem, 1959), no. 61.
38. For the Barcelona relief, see Elena Romero, ed., *La Vida Judia en Sefarad* (Toledo, 1991), p. 60.
39. A reproduction of the original accompanied by a translation into Spanish was published by Yolanda Moreno Koch, *De iure hispano-hebraico. Las Taqqanot de Valladolid de 1432. Un estatuto comunal renovador. Fontes Iudaeorum Regni Castellae* (Salamanca, 1987), pp. 92–95.

40. The following is a paraphrase of the text.
41. For examples of Ottoman wedding dresses with gold embroidery, see Esther Juhasz, ed., *The Sephardi Jews of the Ottoman Empire* (Jerusalem, 1989), pp. 120–171.
42. Isidore Epstein, *The "Responsa" of Rabbi Solomon ben Adreth of Barcelona (1235–1310) as a Source of the History of Spain and the Responsa of Rabbi Simon b. Zemah Duran as a Source of the History of the Jews in North Africa* (repr. New York, 1968), p. 14 and fn. 20.
43. Vivian B. Mann, *A Tale of Two Cities: Jewish Life in Frankfurt and Istanbul 1750–1870* (New York, 1982), cat. no. 197, a Torah Curtain dedicated to the Seville Congregation of Istanbul.

Meeting Again (and Again): Reading Pinkhos Churgin's Essay Seventy-Five Years Later

by Peter N. Miller

We *do not quite know when Pinkhos Churgin, my grandfather, first met Joseph H. Lookstein. But we do know that they became friends, and then intellectual collaborators – first on the Ramaz School, which Rabbi Lookstein founded and for which Dr. Churgin (as he preferred to be known, though he had rabbinical ordination from the Volozhin yeshiva) helped shape the Judaic Studies curriculum, and then on the making of Bar-Ilan University in Israel. Here Churgin was the founder and first president and Lookstein the consultant, fund raiser, ally, and then, after Churgin's early death, continuator. We are on a little more secure footing as to when Joseph Lookstein met my parents – because we at least know the date on which he married them. Similarly, I cannot remember when I first met Rabbi Haskel Lookstein – I must have been 9 years old – but I do know exactly when he married me and my wife.*

Meeting, meeting and meeting again. For the historian, the past lives still in the present, sometimes more in view, sometimes more hidden. One of Pinkhos Churgin's most intriguing publications is also one of his shortest and, on the surface, least consequential.

Churgin studied the history and literature of the Second Temple period, with focus on the targumic literature.[1] *On top of this he published regularly in the Hebrew and Yiddish press.*[2] *In 1932, as Associate Professor of Hebrew Literature and Dean of the Teachers Institute of Yeshiva College, and still towards the beginning of his career, Churgin agreed to contribute a brief essay to the College's yearbook,* The Masmid, *entitled "Meeting Again."*

The six paragraph-long essay, with each reflecting on an entire epoch of Jewish history (ancient, medieval, early modern, modern) is stunning. But its vision has been sharpened, not dulled, by time's passage. Seventy years' hindsight has only deepened its argument. In what follows, I reprint and comment on this remarkable document in the hope that others will take up its challenge in the years to come.

* * * * *

In its historical perspective. *Churgin took the long view, understanding that what was happening in New York City in the early twentieth century needed to be viewed against the deepest of context. Precisely this perspective is what the essay as a whole is designed to bring to bear.* The Yeshiva College. *Churgin had high hopes for this institution. Like a whole generation of European-born scholars, the institution's position mirrored his own. Even the very name, fusing two distinct horizons of learning, the Western and the Jewish, seemed to open possibilities that neither Jüdisches Theologisches Seminar (Breslau) nor Jewish Theological Seminar (New York) conveyed.* Rapprochement. *The first of a series of key words describing the possible convergence of Jewish and general culture. Churgin, who went from Volozhin to Yale, represented exactly this; in his circle of friends this kind of profile was not uncommon. Belkin, Mirsky, Ginzburg, Lieberman and others brought a depth of traditional learning together with real passion and enthusiasm for Western culture.* Jewish Hellenism. *We need here to understand not the "Channukah" narrative of Good Jews v. Bad Jews, nor the reading of Antiochus IV Epiphanes as an incipient anti-Semite, but the whole broader period to which the*

⊷ℬ MEETING AGAIN

In its historical perspective this college, the Yeshiva College, is attempting a new rapprochement between Jewish and general culture. Jewish Hellenism was the product of the first definite, friendly encounter of Jewish culture with foreign culture. It resulted in a union, delightful, curious, baffling, but intense with new thought—and no thought is devoid of a gleaming of truth. Judaism found in Hellenism a new form of expression for its basic ideas and conceptions; and philosophy, always eager to rediscover itself, could not remain unenticed by the charms of the new wisdom. It left its indelible stamp on human thought through the channels of religion. It influenced Jewish thought in a lesser degree because its era of bloom coincided with the most tragic experience of the Jewish people at the hands of the Romans.

unimpeachably orthodox Saul Lieberman would devote two still un-surpassed books, Greek in Jewish Palestine (1942) and Hellenism in Jewish Palestine (1950). **The first definite, friendly encounter.** *If we were yet uncertain of Churgin's position, it is now clear: Hellenism is viewed as a positive encounter, from which Judaism itself benefited.* **A union, delightful, curious, baffling.** *Union is an unambiguously powerful word, denoting complete interpenetration of two entities to create a third. This then refers to no mere dabbling or cultural tourism. There is no escaping the implications of union and certainly no fear from the unforeseeable consequences of a genuine "union." It bears noting that when Churgin came to the United States and Yale from Volozhin (via Jerusalem and then Alexandria) his doctorate in Semitics was, of all possible subjects, on* Targum – *the single Jewish mode which aspires precisely to this ideal of "union." The* targumim *were produced to bring the sacred text to an Aramaic-reading audience, and retained a sacred value even though clearly a human adjustment to a secular reality.* **No thought is devoid of a gleaming of truth.** *Another spectacular piece of open-mindedness. With this we are in fact taken back directly to ancient attitudes towards "Alien Wisdom" – whether amongst Jews, Greeks, Romans or Christians. Churgin's attitude keeps company with precisely that strain which we can identify in the worlds of Philo's Alexandria or Hasdai Crescas's Barcelona – not surprisingly, key figures in Harry Wolfson's parallel, contemporary project.* **Judaism found in Hellenism.** *The punchline: that Judaism was actually shaped by its encounter with Greek learning. Churgin leaves us with the thought that our Judaism, and that of the intervening centuries, still bears the impress of this embrace.* **It left its indelible stamp on human thought.** *This is glossing the position of Droysen in his classic biography of Alexander the Great which, as the great Italian-Jewish historian Arnaldo Momigliano has so beautifully written, was turned by Droysen into a reflection on the way in which Hellenism prepared the way for Christianity. Momigliano speculated that Droysen's inability to deal with the Jewish side of Hellenism, and its formative impact on Christianity and thus modernity, reflected Droysen's inability to come to* *terms with the place of Jews in nineteenth-century Germany. Some of his best friends, and even his wife, were Jewish converts to Christianity, but Droysen was unable to incorporate any of this experience into his scholarly vision. Churgin goes where Droysen himself could not.* **Tragic experience.** *The tragedy is two-fold: the Destruction, most obviously alluded to, and the permanent marking of Hellenism with the sign of the enemy.*

Arabic. *Not Christian. The point here is the unreceptivity of early medieval Christianity to Hellenism and thus its unavailability to Jews surrounded by Christian culture. Not until the Arab conquest and the recuperation of Greek learning was there a new possibility of Jewish contact with Hellenism.* **Fusion.** *An even more active way of describing union.* **Not a mere agent.**

Judaism met philosophy again in its Arabic overhaulings. The new fusion let off a stream of ideas which fertilized human thought, reaching its most desolate territories. It shook the European mind of its dormancy. But the Jewish philosopher was not a mere agent in planting philosophy among the European nations. Judaism was reasserted in this so-called Jewish Arabic philosophy. Maimonides was no copyist. He was no mere interpreter. He was one of the moulders of thought. It was this new Jewish thought which burst upon Europe in the Middle Ages. Western civilization was again vitalized by Judaism.

A succession of persecutions, of expulsions and butcheries called for a halt in the march of Jewish philosophy. Plunged in sorrow and repeatedly forced into exile, the Jew was groping to retrace the broken

Churgin here makes a strong argument: he is not merely saying that Jews were involved in the process by which Greek learning came via the Arabs to Europe. This would position the Jews as vectors for texts, whether, say, as merchants who carried them, or as translators working in multi-lingual teams in places like Toledo. But what Churgin is saying is that Judaism found another way of expressing its truths in the Hellenistically-inspired Arabic philosophical language of figures like al-Farabi (870-950). Again, the confident position is that the essential truth of a revealed religion can be manifested through all the very different means that human beings use to act on their divine nature. **Maimonides.** *The first of the few key figures who appear by name in the essay.* **Copyist. Interpreter.** *The Jewish philosopher does not transmit or even translate but creates something new. A union or a fusion makes something where nothing had been before. This is Churgin's view of Maimonides as a "Hellenizer," with no concession to those who burned his books.* **Vitalized.** *Another powerful word. Just as ancient Hellenism was enriched by its Jewish content, and then fed into the Christian mainstream, the synthesis of Greek philosophy with revelation modelled what could be done, and which then was done by Aquinas. Again, this is the kind of argument that was made by Wolfson in his 1929 masterwork on Crescas.*

Succession. *For the Jewish historian of ancient syntheses, modernity comes late. The period which for the West could be described as a breaking down of the ghetto walls of the mind was in fact, for Jews, the period in which those walls, both real and mental, were thrown up and then locked. From the Jewish perspective, the battle over where to draw the line between the Middle Ages and the Renaissance is moot: the same unhappy reality is more or less true everywhere.* **Retrace.** *And yet even in this period of uprooting, violence and confrontation, Churgin discerns a drive to recapture that possibility of union, as if there were always those confident enough to try and bring Judaism into a dialogue with its cultural surround.* **Broken path.** *The implication, then, is that the search for union is in some sense natural and that the condition of separation is the"brokenness" that needs mending.* **New attacks.** *The Spanish Inquisition; Counter-Reformation anti-Jewish edicts.* **Italian Jewish Scholar.** *Likely Azariah de' Rossi, or perhaps Judah Messer Leon, who read one culture off against the other.* **Marrano thinker.** *Possibly Spinoza, but more likely a composite, as in the preceding ideal type, suggesting a second possible path to symbiosis, through a clandestine union.*

Re-establish contacts. *There was no Renaissance for Jews if what we mean by Renaissance is, fundamentally, the recuperation of the symbols and structures of pagan antiquity by European monotheists. These centuries from 1500 to 1700 saw Christian scholars develop the competence to study rabbinic literature.3 This enabled them to produce four "Polyglot Bibles" – multi-volume folio books, with learned apparatus, which printed first the Hebrew, Greek, Aramaic and Latin versions of the Hebrew Bible and New Testament (Alacala, 1517), adding to these the Syriac to the Hebrew Bible (Antwerp, 1572), Samaritan Pentateuch, Arabic and Syriac to the New Testament (Paris, 1628-45) and, finally, Ethiopic to Song of Songs and Persian to the Pentateuch (London, 1653-57). Now, interestingly, the Persian Pentateuch had in fact first been printed a century earlier at Constantinople, in a Soncino-produced Polyglot Bible, containing the Hebrew text, Onkelos's targum, Sadia Gaon's Arabic commentary and then Jacob Taves's Persian translation – all in Hebrew characters. The sole monograph on this*

path of his spirit, groping for new contacts, but he was only to be thrown back by new attacks of religious fanaticism. Neither the Italian Jewish scholar nor the Marano thinker was able to re-establish the contacts between Jewish and general culture.

The modern period witnessed the remarkable dash of the Jew toward the freed domains of Western culture. He easily appropriated the new essences. Jews became masters in many fields of human thought. Some succeeded in ascending to its higher regions. But they all contributed as individuals. They exercised an excellence to which the nationality of its owner was a mere accident. Some Jewish landmark may be running through the work of the Jewish author, but, whatever its force, it is a note of an original endowment. The great bulk of Jewish men of letters and scientists of all description are singularly unaffected by Jewish culture. They have scarcely any knowledge of it. Some of the greatest lights in present-

*fascinating project is over a century old and there are only a smat-
tering of articles, focused on the printing history – in other words,
this rare early modern Jewish comparative project, albeit still shel-
tered within the Hebrew alphabetical world, has been completely
ignored. Why?*

Dash. *Again, the remarkable vigor of language used to signify Jews'
quest for contact with the wider civilization. But it is hard not to
sense also a psychological intimacy that was autobiographical. For
Churgin and his friends, the chance to drink in the learning of the
West was a heady experience. When he was at Yale, so the story goes,
he was frequently left with the key to the Divinity School Library
on Saturday afternoons while the librarians went to the football
game. That image of the Volozhin-educated "Yerushalmi" (so-called
in Lithuania because he had come there from Jerusalem) left free
to roam the stacks is a powerful visual metaphor.* **Freed domains**.
Locates us chronologically in the post-Emancipation period. **Appropriated. But all as individuals**. *This is important: for in the
modern condition, Churgin is arguing, even as Jews succeeded in
penetrating formerly closed domains and taking their content for
themselves, they did so not as Jews, but as individuals. As opposed
to the earlier moments when "union" and "fusion" were the goals,
here it is "appropriating" – a very different kind of chemical reaction.* **Nationality**. *In the post-emancipation dream of cosmopoli-
tanism, identity could be treated as accident. With this, the ground
has itself shifted, rendering the very notion of union unintelligible.*
Landmark. *Another fascinating word choice: landmark implies a
physical or spatial distinction, but is here applied to a spiritual or intellectual attainment.* **Original Endowment**. *We might be tempted
to view this as an unambiguously positive characterization, but for
Churgin it is contrasted with tradition, itself the much richer re-
pository of a long-running dialectic between the inertia of identity
and the drama of historical necessity.* **Unaffected**. *In nineteenth
and twentieth-century Europe, it was possible for the first time for
individuals to be individuals, unmoored from land or family or*

faith. Thus, Churgin concludes, it was now possible for there to be un-Jewish Jews. Achievements in the sciences and arts were achievements by the individual and did not – could not – redound to a new synthesis of Jewish and general culture. And so we have the spectacle, in both Europe and America, of intellectual heroes who were Jewish by birth but who brought no Jewish content to their work – and thus could not serve as conduits for the revitalization of Jewish culture by that general culture. **Bad taste.** *Here we are introduced to a concomittant phenomenon, the non-Jewish Jew who has seen but not understood rituals from his youth and who then makes fun of them, both because not understanding them, and – more insidiously – because by making fun of them he can make common cause with the wider culture. The Jew who aligns himself with "Them" in order to detach himself from "Us" echoes the injunction to the wicked son on Passover.* **Nearer. Contact.** *Neither the one nor the other.* **Actual.** *Thus it is the goal is for Judaism and the surrounding culture to meet. Its absence here comes across as a lament, as an indication of the modern impoverishment of Judaism.* **Correlate.** *Another of Churgin's interesting word choices. Correlate suggests bringing into a "a mutual or reciprocal relation."* **Mendelssohn. Cohen.** *Celebrated here for seeking to effect a reciprocal impact of Judaism on Western culture and Western culture on*

day European literature are Jews who have completely detached themselves from Jewish life and Jewish thought. The Jewish authors in American literature, with a few exceptions, have the bad taste to parade their ignorance also of Jewish habits. Jewish culture has not been brought nearer to Western culture through all of them than before – not to speak of an actual contact between these cultures. Two great thinkers of modern times have made a forceful attempt to correlate the distinct ideas of the cultures – Mendelssohn and Hermann Cohen. But in the absence of forces propitious to a real union between Jewish and Western culture, their attempt was doomed to isolation. They had no successors.

Judaism. Mendelssohn, who bested Immanuel Kant to win the essay prize of the Prussian Royal Academy of Sciences in 1763, also pro-duced the first Masoretic Bible. It could be said that Mendelssohn's Bible commentary in fact marked the arrival in the Jewish world of those late humanist Christian antiquarianized approaches to bibli-cal study that did not occur amongst Jews a century or more before. Herman Cohen's Religion of Reason out of the Sources of Judaism (1919) was his attempt to bring Kant and Judaism together, but he also, crucially, wrote books on Maimonides' "ethics" and the possible synthesis of Judaism and German philo-hellenism. Cohen was very important to many Jewish modernists in the 1920s, such as Gershom Scholem and Walter Benjamin (though they did not like him) and Joseph Soloveitchik (who did). It is interesting that Churgin preferred to celebrate Cohen's synthesis rather than Franz Rosenzweig's which, though based on Hegel rather than Kant, aimed at just this kind of "correlation." (Nor did Soloveitchik mention Rosenzweig in his Hala-chic Mind; perhaps existentialism and Judaism was not something that clicked in those decades). **Absence of Forces.** *The implication here is that within Judaism there was an inherent openness, but that it was the external circumstances – the realm of history – which ei-ther facilitated or, more often, blocked this drive.* **Real union.** *This was something that neither Mendelssohn nor Cohen could achieve – thus "correlation" is lesser achievement than "union." This, as in the Hellenistic, or Arab, model required a societal or cultural openness. Without it, those "external forces" would leave all such attempts isolated.* **Successors.** *The ending is nothing short of spec-tacular. To say that Mendelssohn and Cohen had no successors is to say that the modern period of Jewish history, despite – or, perhaps, even more interesting, because of – the civil emancipation of Jews did not account for a new Jewish creativity. Jews lived their Juda-ism, and Jews fled their Judaism for the easier world of the majority culture. But Judaism, as a way of thinking and living life – religion and philosophy both – was unaffected, did not grow, experienced nothing of that fruitful transformation that Churgin saw in ancient Hellenism. From Churgin's optimistic perspective, the perspective* *of a confident, grounded person, the wealth of the Jewish heritage could never be undermined or weakened through contact with the world's other great traditions. Indeed, the more substantial – and true – those traditions, the more they offered Jews, whether in Greek or Arabic or Italian or German dress.*

Radiating. *This is where Churgin's "Copernican Revolution" is fully revealed. Rather than seeing Judaism as the dependent body, the satellite subject to the gravitational pull of the larger general culture, Churgin confidently places Jewish culture in the center, a sun whose light and energy illuminates the space around it.* **College...Yeshiva.** *Again, instead of accepting the received – still today! – dichotomy between the Jewish late antique educational model, and the European medieval-modern one, Churgin views them as contiguous. In his mind, the foundation of a Yeshiva-College marked the culmination of this transformed vision of culture.* **Violence...**

The Yeshiva College represents an organized and concentrated effort to bring general culture within the radiating reach of Jewish culture. Here general culture is in intimate touch with Jewish culture. The College, the base of secular learning, rests on the fringes of the home of Jewish learning, the Yeshiva. Both mark their impression on the mind of the student. His will be a knowledge which fosters understanding. Spared the violence which accompanies passage into the fold of general culture, his creative faculties will be accessible to a natural interplay of contrasting ideas. He will seek to examine one in the light of the other. The creative mind will then respond to the flashes of a new Jewish philosophy.

Jewish culture is as resourceful as ever before. Its vigor is undiminished. It has the will to expand, to create. The Yeshiva College is creating the potentialities for its expansion. This is, as I can see it, the historical significance of the Yeshiva College. It has more comforts in store for the Jew. Yet in the realization of the fruit of the new union of cultures lies its strength and great promise

creative....creative. *Thus the connection between the Yeshiva and the University meant that passage from Jewish to general culture was never by force, never compelling the shedding of one identity, one body of learning, in order to participate in the other. Under conditions of "violence," and "Either/or," Churgin implies, no real creativity was possible. Recalling the opening of the essay, we can see that what Churgin invokes here in the context of an educational "Copernican Revolution" is the renewed possibility of a modern "hellenistic" age, in which Jewish creativity was sparked by its friendly and confident contact with the world of Greek learning.* **Jewish philosophy.** *And, tellingly, Churgin posits as the mark of this creative achivement nothing less than "a new Jewish philosophy" – not rabbinics, halacha, or even poetry, but philosophy, the archetypally Greek genre which had always been relegated with some suspicion to the margins of the Jewish canon, pace Maimonides, Cohen, etc.* **As ever before.** *Churgin the historian faced the future with tremendous optimism.* **To expand, to create…the new union of cultures.** *Churgin's concluding peroration confidently welcomes the future, certain in the intellectual resources of a Judaism rich with three thousand years of endeavor and experience.*

* * * * *

But now let us remember when Churgin wrote this, and where. In 1932 he was Professor of Hebrew Literature and Dean of Yeshiva's Teachers' Institute, to which he had come in 1920. He was soon to work with Joseph Lookstein on establishing the Judaic curriculum of a new experiment in Jewish education, the Ramaz School. Ahead of him lay long years of involvement with the Mizrachi Organization of America, including its presidency after 1949, and then, culminating his career, the establishment of Bar-Ilan University in Israel. Its symbol, a Torah scroll torqued into a microscope, makes concrete the notion of "union" that emerges in this essay as the highest vision of Judaism-in-the-world. (Even more, I would argue, than Yeshiva University's own "Torah u-mada" – in Churgin's terms this might only stand for "correlation" rather than the "fusion" of horizons captured in the Bar-Ilan symbol.) So Churgin lived his historical vision.

But what about the "absence of forces propitious to a real union"? Has the time since 1932 been more favorable, as Churgin would have hoped? Did the Yeshiva College do the work that Churgin so confidently envisioned? The emergence of modern Orthodoxy in America, the flourishing of Judaism in the new State of Israel, the many New Age fusings of Judaism with other traditions could all in some sense be booked on the positive side of the ledger. But among learned and observant Jews, those to whom Churgin was writing, and for whom he dedicated his life, it is surely still the case that "Hellenism," as both historical reality and metaphor for a self-confident Jewish openness to the cultural richness of the majority culture, is the enemy. It may even be the case that American-Jewish history of the past three-quarters of a century has added to Churgin's two categories of Jews, those who fled from their Judaism into the world, and those who fled from the world into their Judaism, a third type: Jews who have integrated into Western social life educationally, professionally, and financially, but who have managed to insulate themselves and their Judaism from the Western cultural tradition. Though we live in the greatest period of Jewish history since the end of Hasmonean sovereignty in 64 CE, we also live in the shadow of the Shoah. For too many of us, it seems, it is fear that dominates. And an age of fear will never be an age of "union," "fusion," "correlation," "friendly encounter" or one that could boldly proclaim that "No thought is devoid of a gleaming of truth."

❧ NOTES

1. Churgin's 1922 Yale Ph.D was published in 1927 as *Targum Jonathan to the Prophets* and remains in print; he later published *Targum Ketuvim* in 1945 and a collection of essays on the historical outlook of Jews of that period, *Studies in the Times of the Second Temple* [Hebrew], 1949.
2. A sampling of his scholarly and popular writing, along with a full bibliography, can be found in Pinkhos Churgin, *Vision and Legacy: Selected Papers with Essays on His Life and Work*, eds. Louis Bernstein and Raphael Yankelevitch (Bar-Ilan University Press, 1987).
3. The whole question of the meaning of the late humanist "miss" referred to by Churgin is one that I discuss further in "Lost and Found," *Jewish Quarterly Review*, 97 (2007), 502–7.

Is Coca-Cola Kosher? Rabbi Tobias Geffen and the History of American Orthodoxy

Adam Mintz

The ability of the American Orthodox rabbinate to enhance Jewish life through its involvement with the broader American community is taken for granted today. Yet for the immigrant Jewish community of the early twentieth century, such rabbinic influence was for the most part a distant dream. The American rabbi, whether educated in Europe or in the United States, rarely possessed the connections or credibility necessary to influence the outside community. One important exception was the successful effort in the 1920s and 1930s by Rabbi Tobias Geffen to convince the executives of Coca-Cola to make the necessary changes in the formulation of its famous beverage so it would meet the standards of *kashrut*. The story of Rabbi Geffen and the beginnings of his rabbinic supervision of Coca-Cola offers an early model of the ways in which the Orthodox rabbinate adjusted to changing circumstances in order to serve the Jewish community of America.[1]

Born in Kovno in 1870, Tobias Geffen was raised in a traditional Lithuanian Jewish home with its emphasis on the study of Torah.[2] As a teen, he studied under the renowned scholar Rabbi Eliakim Shapiro, and later he received rabbinical ordination from

Rabbi Zvi Hirsch Rabinowitz and Rabbi Moshe Danishevsky of Slobodka. In 1898 Geffen married Sara Hene Rabinowitz, the daughter of a prominent Jewish businessman in Kovno. In the wake of the Kishinev pogrom of 1903 and other eruptions of antisemitism in Eastern Europe, the Geffens decided to emigrate to the United States, ignoring criticism from friends and rabbis who felt that Rabbi Geffen should have taken a local rabbinic position.[3]

During their first months in the United States, Rabbi Geffen worked in a Lower East Side sweatshop owned by relatives of his wife. A brief stint as the rabbi of a neighborhood synagogue proved inadequate to support their family, but a subsequent position as a traveling fundraiser for Kovno's *Kollel Perushim* proved fortuitous. During a fundraising trip he was making to Canton, Ohio, leaders of a synagogue there were so impressed by his remarks that they hired him on the spot to serve as their spiritual leader. Among Rabbi Geffen's most notable achievements during his five years in Canton was the mending of a deep rift within the local Orthodox community, which he accomplished by serving simultaneously as the rabbi of two rival synagogues. In 1910, unable to adjust to Canton's difficult winters, Rabbi Geffen accepted the pulpit of Atlanta's Shearith Israel Synagogue. He would remain there for the next sixty years.[4]

When the Geffens arrived in Atlanta, the city had a Jewish population of about 4,000 out of a general population of 150,000. A majority of these Jews were, like the Geffens, of Lithuanian origin. At the turn of the century the only Orthodox synagogue in Atlanta was Congregation Ahavath Achim. However, its policy of permitting men who worked on Shabbat to be called to the Torah provoked the departure of its more devout members. In 1902 this group that broke away established Shearith Israel Synagogue.[5]

Rabbi Geffen quickly made his presence felt. He improved and streamlined *kashrut* supervision, initiated the community's first organized effort to raise funds for needy European Jewish families, and founded the city's first Hebrew school. A staunch Zionist,

Rabbi Geffen was a leader of the Atlanta branch of Mizrachi, the religious Zionist movement, as well as the Keren Hayesod and the Jewish National Fund. He also assisted Jewish prisoners in Atlanta's federal penitentiary and ministered to Jewish soldiers stationed in local military camps.[6]

Contrary to the insular image of East European rabbis, Geffen maintained friendly relations with a local Reform rabbi, David Marx, and even delivered the benediction at the dedication of Marx's synagogue. Many years later, in June 1965, he gave the benediction at the graduation exercises of the Jewish Theological Seminary of America when two of his grandsons were among the graduates.[7] For all the interesting and noteworthy items on Rabbi Geffen's impressive resume, it was his Coca-Cola *Teshuva* for which he would become best known.[8]

Coca-Cola was founded in 1885 in Columbus, Georgia, by John Pemberton as a coca wine. Later that year, when Fulton County, Georgia, passed Prohibition legislation, Pemberton responded by developing a carbonated, nonalcoholic version of his coca wine. The beverage was named Coca-Cola because the stimulus mixed in the drink was coca leaves from South America, the source of cocaine. Initially, each glass of Coca-Cola contained nine milligrams of cocaine. However, the cocaine stimulus was removed in 1903. As a marketing technique, the secret formula of Coca-Cola is reputed to be known by only a few Coca-Cola executives; the original recipe resides in the vault of the Sun Trust Bank in Atlanta.[9]

In his Coca-Cola *Teshuva*, Rabbi Geffen wrote that in 1935, "an inquiry was addressed to me concerning the well-known soft drink Coca-Cola, which is manufactured in the city of Atlanta, Georgia. Is it kosher for drinking during the entire year and on Passover?"[10]

The surviving correspondence from this episode, while unfortunately consisting only of letters that Rabbi Geffen received and not the ones he wrote, nonetheless indicates that Rabbi Geffen had in fact become involved in the Coca-Cola issue considerably earlier than 1935.[11] His earliest correspondence on the subject dates to 1925, when Rabbi Elihu Kochin, rabbi of the Orthodox Jewish Community of Pittsburgh,[12] wrote him: "I inquire of you to inform me concerning the kosher status of Coca-Cola.... For at this point, many of the people are drinking Coca-Cola without proper rabbinic certification and claiming that it is kosher. Please clarify this matter."[13] No reply to that inquiry is extant. A letter dated May 5, 1932, from an entity referred to simply as "Congregation Mischne" of Memphis, Tennessee, asked: "It has been a very long time since we have written to you but as we wish to get a little information from you as to let us know whether you have got the information concerning Coca-Cola which you stated that the company was not willing to give you the exact contents which goes into the manufacturing of this Coca-Cola. Lately we notice there are a few cities in the United States as well as Memphis that several Rabbi's [*sic*] O.K. the Coca-Cola as Kosher for Passover."[14] Rabbi Geffen evidently responded promptly to this letter, since we have another correspondence from Congregation Mischne to Rabbi Geffen dated May 20, 1932. In this letter Congregation Mischne made reference to the fact that Rabbi Geffen had written that he had inspected the Coca-Cola plants and that Coca-Cola contained glycerin, which was not kosher. They concluded the letter as follows: "The reason why Rabbi Taxon[15] is interested in same is that he happened to give a [*heksher*] on this drink through the Rabbi Pardes of Chicago."[16]

From this correspondence, it is evident that by 1932 Jews were drinking Coca-Cola and considered it kosher. Furthermore, there were some rabbis who were actually certifying Coca-Cola as kosher. At the same time, Rabbi Geffen had already investigated the Coca-Cola plant and determined that in fact Coca-Cola contained glycerin, a nonkosher ingredient. In line with the history of kosher supervision one would imagine that Rabbi Geffen's view would prevail and that Coca-Cola would be declared nonkosher by the rabbis. In this case, however, this is not what happened. It is possible that Rabbi Geffen's view was not known to the general public.

However, there seems to be another factor in the continuation of the rabbinic allowance of Coca-Cola, namely, the involvement of Rabbi Shmuel Pardes. Rabbi Pardes was a respected Orthodox rabbi in Chicago and the editor of the well-known rabbinic journal *Hapardes*. In the previously mentioned letter, Rabbi Pardes, together with Rabbi Taxon, was referred to as authorizing the kosher status of Coca-Cola in Memphis.[17]

As we learn from the following correspondence, Rabbi Pardes himself had already been in touch with Rabbi Geffen. In a 1931 letter, Rabbi Pardes wrote that he had heard that Rabbi Geffen believed Coca-Cola was not kosher. Rabbi Pardes explained that there were several cities in North America where Coca-Cola had received rabbinic supervision both for year-round use and for Passover, and that therefore the burden of proof fell upon Rabbi Geffen to prove that Coca-Cola was not kosher.[18] Rabbi Geffen's reply evidently arrived quickly, because Rabbi Pardes responded just ten days later stating that although he read Rabbi Geffen's response several times, he still did not understand what bothered him about the kosher status of Coca-Cola. He reported that in his own investigation of the Coca-Cola plant in Chicago, he found no nonkosher ingredients. He wrote that he could not imagine that the Coca-Cola plant in Chicago included different ingredients than the plant in Atlanta but would nonetheless travel to Atlanta to investigate the plant himself. He concluded the letter with the following comment: "I wrote last week to all the rabbis who give kosher supervision to Coca-Cola advising them of this problem."[19]

There is no further communication between Rabbi Pardes and Rabbi Geffen concerning Rabbi Pardes's visit to Atlanta to investigate the kosher status of Coca-Cola. There is, however, important information included in the contemporaneous rabbinic journal *Hapardes*. In his initial letter to Rabbi Geffen, the journal's editor, Rabbi Pardes, wrote that in 1930 several rabbis asked him to include advertisements in *Hapardes* for Coca-Cola announcing that it was kosher for Passover. Initially he refused, but after clarifying that Coca-Cola was indeed kosher, he included a notice in the December 1930 issue. The same issue included an article by Rabbi Pardes entitled, "Coca Cola: The American National Drink." After surveying the product's history and popularity, he concluded with a description of the ingredients and declared unequivocally, "Coca Cola is kosher with the ultimate standards of *kashrut*." He reported that the beverage had been inspected by chemists, who determined that there were no nonkosher ingredients.[20] In the next issue (January 1931), Rabbi Pardes published a Yiddish advertisement for Coca-Cola, which included this statement: "I have investigated and checked all the beverages in the Coca-Cola factory and I found that there is no problem of the inclusion of a nonkosher ingredient. This drink is made of all natural ingredients and it is worthy of being served at the table of rabbis."[21] Finally, in the March 1931 issue of *Hapardes*, Rabbi Pardes included another advertisement for Coca-Cola, with a slightly different statement signed at the bottom: "In the recent past I visited the main factory of Coca-Cola in Atlanta, Georgia. The workers in the factory revealed to me all the secrets and even the secret formula. I investigated and found that Coca-Cola is kosher and may be consumed."[22]

How did Rabbi Geffen respond to the imprimatur that Rabbi Pardes gave to the kosher status of Coca-Cola both during the year and on Passover? Did he continue to express his view that Coca-Cola was not kosher or did he take a different approach? In 1935, in an introduction to his *teshuva* concerning the kosher status of Coca-Cola, Rabbi Geffen wrote:

> A few months ago I sent a letter to the Orthodox rabbis of America in regard to the *kashrus* of the well-known drink known by the name Coca-Cola which is manufactured in Atlanta, Georgia. Since that date I have received many inquiries and requests for more information and positive proof according to the laws of the Shas in regard to this matter. It is a very difficult matter for me to answer each of these inquiries and

for this reason I have determined to give a reply [*teshuva*] in regard to this matter in my book "*Karnei Hahod*," which is now in press and will soon appear. Every person who is interested to know the real sources and reasons for this "*Heter*" of Coca-Cola will be able to find them in this book under the heading "The *T'shuvah* in Regard to Coca-Cola."[23]

In the *teshuva* that followed, Rabbi Geffen described in detail the process that led him to determine that Coca-Cola was kosher for all year and for Passover. Rabbi Geffen began by explaining what he found in his investigation of the ingredients of Coca-Cola. "The 'M' is a liquid product made from meat and fat tallow of nonkosher animals: it is an item which Jews are forbidden to eat and drink."[24]

The first curious aspect of this *teshuva* is the fact that Rabbi Geffen identified this liquid as "M." In the published Hebrew version of the *teshuva*, however, the word *muris* is used to describe this liquid.[25]

The letter "M" is an abbreviation of the Hebrew word *muris*, a Talmudic term defined as pickle brine. In a version of the Hebrew *teshuva* located in Rabbi Geffen's papers (and reprinted in 1963 in his collected essays, *Nazar Yosef*), Rabbi Geffen identified this liquid as glycerin oil.[26] This identification of glycerin is also found in a typewritten copy of the English translation found in the collection of Rabbi Geffen's papers.[27] As will be shown below, Rabbi Geffen was instructed to remove the name of the problematic ingredient by the attorney for Coca-Cola in order to maintain the secrecy of the formula.

Rabbi Geffen explained that glycerin was found in Coca-Cola only in very minute proportions – in a ratio of 1 to 1000. Generally such a small percentage would not make a product nonkosher; however, because this ingredient was a planned part of the recipe rather than an accidental ingredient that fell into the mixture by chance, it could not be consumed by Jews. There, was, however, a solution:

With the help of God, I have been able to uncover a pragmatic solution according to which there would be no question nor any doubt concerning the ingredients of Coca-Cola. This solution came to my mind when it was revealed to me by some of the expert chemists that the 'M' could also be prepared from plant oil such as that made from coconut, cottonseed oil and other plants.[28]

According to Rabbi Geffen, however, even after solving the glycerin problem, there remained an issue with the use of Coca-Cola on Passover: "in its processing the employees insert and mix the ingredient 'A,' which is made from *chametz*. Since any amount of *chametz* prohibits its use on Passover, it is expressly prohibited to drink Coca-Cola on this holiday."[29]

In the Hebrew *teshuva*, this "A" ingredient is identified as *anigron*, a Talmudic term defined as a sauce of oil and garum.[30] But in the version in Rabbi Geffen's papers, the ingredient is described as alcohol and it is so translated in the typewritten English translation.[31] Yet here too Rabbi Geffen found a solution:

Now, in regard to the prohibition of its use on Passover because of the question of *chametz*, I discovered that it is possible to prepare 'A' not from grain kernels but instead from sugar beets or sugar cane.[32]

Rabbi Geffen concluded his *teshuva* with the following reflection:

"I thank God for the opportunity that He has given me, making it possible to protect the general Jewish public from eating a mixture composed of tallow, a sin punishable by excommunication, and from eating *chametz* on Pesach. This matter is firmly established, and it has become possible for those who have been eating that which is forbidden to eat that which is permitted."[33]

Rabbi Geffen's *teshuva* is a fascinating statement of his view of the role of the rabbinate in America at the time. He had initially stated that he believed that Coca-Cola contained a nonkosher ingredient and that he deemed it unacceptable. He was opposed by Rabbi Pardes and the other rabbis who had followed Rabbi Pardes' lead. Rabbi Geffen could easily have stood his ground and continued to insist that Coca-Cola was not kosher. After all, he lived right there in Atlanta and had personally inspected the plant. While there was no guarantee that his decision would be generally accepted, his position was certainly legitimate and required no apology. Nevertheless, he chose to involve himself in a process that ultimately led the Coca-Cola Company to alter its secret formula regarding two ingredients, a process whose outcome Rabbi Geffen might have doubted until the very end.

Rabbi Geffen's attempt to find a means by which he could satisfy the regulations of Jewish law while not challenging common practice reflects an attitude that was critical to the development of Orthodoxy in America in the first half of the twentieth century. Rabbi Geffen was sufficiently astute to recognize that a position declaring Coca-Cola nonkosher, while *halakhically* valid, would have been ignored by most of the Jewish community. He would have defended a *halakhic* position but he would have made himself irrelevant to the Jewish community that was drinking Coca-Cola under what they considered to be acceptable rabbinic supervision. Instead, Rabbi Geffen took an alternative approach, as he wrote toward the end of his *teshuva*:

> Because Coca-Cola has already been accepted by the general public in this country and in Canada, and because it has become an insurmountable problem to induce the great majority of Jews to refrain from partaking of this drink, I have tried earnestly to find a method of permitting its usage.[34]

Rabbi Geffen's decision to lobby for changes in the ingredients of Coca-Cola in order to satisfy the needs of the Jewish community indicates his perception of American Jewry. Struggling to find their place in a land that was often hostile to their religion, American Jews respected and appreciated rabbis who sought to include them within the Orthodox camp rather than simply condemn them as sinners. Of course his approach would not have been possible had he not felt confident in his powers of persuasion, despite the fact that he was never comfortable speaking English since it was not his native tongue.[35]

Rabbi Geffen's decision to find a solution that would make Coca-Cola kosher would never have been possible without his ability to work with the decision makers at Coca-Cola. How was a Lithuanian rabbi whose preferred language was Yiddish able to accomplish this feat? According to Nathan Kaganoff, it was Harold Hirsch, the attorney for Coca-Cola and influential member of the Atlanta Jewish community, who introduced Rabbi Geffen to the company's executives.[36] Hirsch (1881–1939) was a native of Atlanta and a Columbia Law School graduate. In 1904 he joined the Atlanta law firm of John Candler, whose brother was one of the original owners of Coca-Cola. In 1909 Hirsch assumed responsibility for all of Coca-Cola's legal affairs, and in 1923 he was appointed vice president of the company. Among his many achievements, he fought for the trademark "Coca-Cola," which was finally granted in a decision by the United States Supreme Court. He was also influential in protecting Coca-Cola from its many imitators.[37] Hirsch was affiliated with the Hebrew Benevolent Congregation, an influential Reform synagogue founded in Atlanta in 1867, where he served as trustee, secretary, vice president, and president. He was also active in the American Jewish Joint Distribution Committee.[38]

According to Geffen family lore, Rabbi Geffen's daughter, Helen Geffen (1914–2003) attended public high school with one of Hirsch's children. Helen was chosen as the class valedictorian and delivered the valedictory address at the graduation. Harold Hirsch was so impressed with her address that he paid for Helen's college education at the University of Georgia, his beloved alma mater.[39]

Rabbi Geffen remained indebted to Hirsch, and a friendship developed between them. His volume of essays, which included the Coca-Cola *Teshuva*, was dedicated, "For his kind assistance and interest in the publication of this volume, the writer extends grateful thanks to Mr. Harold Hirsch of Atlanta, Georgia."[40] After Hirsch's death in 1939, Rabbi Geffen's eulogy was published as a pamphlet in Hebrew, Yiddish, and English.[41]

According to this family tradition, when Rabbi Geffen was initially approached by other rabbis concerning the *kashrut* of Coca-Cola, he asked Hirsch for permission to see the secret formula of Coca-Cola. Otherwise, he explained to Hirsch, he would have no choice but to declare Coca-Cola not kosher. Six months passed and finally Hirsch replied that he had gained access to the secret formula for Rabbi Geffen but that the rabbi would not be allowed to share this formula with anyone. Supposedly Rabbi Geffen's daughter Helen, who was studying chemistry at the University of Georgia, analyzed the ingredients for her father and found the two that were not kosher.[42]

The earliest extant communication between Rabbi Geffen and Coca-Cola is found in a letter dated April 6, 1934, from Roy Gentry, assistant to Coca-Cola Vice President Harrison Jones. Gentry apologized for the fact that there had not been enough time to prepare the Atlanta Bottling Company for the Passover season of 1934. He alluded to the fact that the rabbi had already been in contact with Coca-Cola and that a solution had been found for the *kashrut* problem. It seems the only obstacle had been the lack of sufficient time before the holiday. The letter also mentioned a visit that Gentry paid to the Geffen home.[43]

In a letter dated July 17, 1934, from Gentry to L. F. Montgomery, general manager of the Atlanta Coca-Cola Bottling Company, Gentry addressed Rabbi Geffen's bona fides:

I have found Dr. Geffen to be very conscientious and fair.... This is a matter of principle and not money with Dr. Geffen and he has signified that he will be more than pleased to cooperate with you next year when you get ready to kosher Coca-Cola in the bottling plant for the Passover season.[44]

A later letter from Gentry to Rabbi Geffen, dated February 25, 1936, reported that the vegetable glycerin which would substitute for the animal glycerin was going to be produced by Proctor and Gamble in Cincinnati. Gentry supplied affidavits from Proctor and Gamble verifying that the glycerin was completely derived from vegetable sources. In keeping with Coca-Cola's insistence on guarding the secrecy of its formula, Gentry instructed the rabbi to keep the glycerin information "most confidential."[45] In addition, in a letter to Rabbi Geffen dated February 7, 1935, Hirsch described how Rabbi Geffen had shown him a draft copy of the English translation of his *teshuva* on Coca-Cola. Hirsch made the following suggestion, which he asked Rabbi Geffen to accept: "We are most grateful for what you have done in this connection, but at the same time the information we have given to you in regard to 'Coca-Cola' is confidential and we should not like to have published to the world anything in regard the contents of 'Coca-Cola,' I ask, therefore, that you eliminate from your proposed article any reference to glycerine or alcohol as such."[46]

The Gentry-Geffen correspondence does not explicitly delineate the reasons for Coca-Cola's decision to accede to the rabbi's request. On the one hand, it appears that Rabbi Geffen, despite his accent and other traces of his foreign background, succeeded in making a strongly favorable impression on the executives at Coca-Cola. On the other hand, one would assume that Coca-Cola would have agreed to the changes only if it were in its business interests to do so. However, in Gentry's letter to General Manager Montgomery dated July 17, 1934, he wrote, "While I know that your volume of sales through this channel is going to be very small, I feel sure that Dr. Geffen's distinguished position in the orthodox church in this part of the country will cause those orthodox Jews who do feel inclined to buy Coca-Cola koshered for the Passover season to appreciate all the trouble and inconvenience that this may entail."[47] While engendering goodwill is always a good business practice, it seems unlikely, given the small number of Jews who kept kosher at that time, that this would have been enough reason to alter the special Coca-Cola formula.

In fact, while Coca-Cola's amenable position on the *kashrut* issue engendered goodwill among Jews, it also provoked some controversy that could have been bad for business. Nazi sympathizer Karl Flach, manufacturer of a German imitation drink called Afri-Cola, returned from a goodwill visit to the United States in 1936 with a handful of Coca-Cola bottle caps stamped "Kosher for Passover," which he had obtained while touring Coca-Cola's New York bottling plant. A photograph of the bottle caps soon appeared in Nazi literature to illustrate the extent of Jewish influence in the United States. Hirsch's role in the company was cited as evidence that Coca-Cola was secretly controlled by Jews, and the director of Coca-Cola's operations in Germany, Max Keith, urged the company to remove Hirsch from the board. To their credit, the executives of Cola-Cola stood by Hirsch and ignored both the Nazi attacks and Keith's pressure.[48]

The kosher status of Coca-Cola that Rabbi Geffen worked so hard to achieve came under attack several decades later from Rabbi Eliezer Silver, one of the leading Orthodox rabbis of the time and the head of the Agudath Harabbonim[49] Rabbi Silver issued a proclamation in 1957 stating that Coca-Cola had not been kosher up to that point and claiming that Proctor and Gamble, the source of the glycerin for Coca-Cola, did not adequately separate the meat and vegetable glycerin from one another. He reported that on a visit to the Proctor and Gamble plant in Cincinnati, he observed the use of glycerin from both animal and plant products running through the same pipes. He wrote that Proctor and Gamble had agreed to change its production methods but that until this change was achieved, Coca-Cola was not kosher.[50] Over the years, Coca-Cola has had a number of rabbinic supervisors, and ultimately, in 1991, the supervision was assumed by the Union of Orthodox Jewish Congregations of America.[51]

Tobias Geffen lived through several generations of American Jewry. He came to America as part of a wave of immigrants who struggled to find their place in this country while maintaining their religious commitment. He witnessed the steady erosion of traditional practices among much of the Jewish community, including in his own synagogue, where mixed seating was introduced in the main sanctuary in 1958. Willing to search for flexibility within *halakha* but unwilling to go beyond its parameters, Rabbi Geffen insisted on maintaining an additional *minyan* with separate seating in the synagogue's chapel, where he personally officiated until shortly before his death.[52] At the same time, he worked hard to ensure that American Jews would have an easier time maintaining their commitment to Judaism in the United States. His successful efforts to guarantee that Coca-Cola was kosher provide an instructive example of the creativity and adaptability of the early twentieth-century American Orthodox rabbinate.

ᛰ NOTES

To Rabbi Haskel Lookstein, my mentor in the rabbinate and in the appreciation of the history of American Judaism.

1. For a review of American Judaism at the beginning of the twentieth century, see Jonathan D. Sarna, *American Judaism* (New Haven, 2004), 135–207.
2. A biographical sketch of Rabbi Geffen's life was written by his son, Louis Geffen, in *Lev Tuviah: On the Life and Work of Rabbi Tobias Geffen*, ed. Joel Ziff (Newton, Mass., 1988), 19–40. While it contains much useful information, it is written from a son's perspective. There is an excellent biographical article on Rabbi Geffen by Nathan N. Kaganoff, "An Orthodox Rabbinate in the South: Tobias Geffen, 1870–1970," in *American Jewish History* 73:1 (September 1983), 56–70. This article is based on material from the Tobias Geffen Papers in the archives of the American Jewish Historical Society, including a typescript of an autobiography written in Yiddish in 1951 entitled *Fifty Years in the Rabbinate: Chapters of My Life*. For a complete list of Rabbi Geffen's writings and biographical material, see Moshe D. Sherman, *Orthodox Judaism in America: A Biographical Dictionary and Sourcebook* (Westport, Conn., 1996), 73–4.
3. Kaganoff, 57–58.
4. *Lev Tuviah*, 23, and Kaganoff, 59–61.
5. Steven Hertzberg, *Strangers Within the Gate City: The Jews of Atlanta 1845–1915* (Philadelphia, 1978), 232.
6. Kaganoff, 66–67, and *Lev Tuviah*, 33.
7. Kaganoff, 68, and *Lev Tuviah*, 39. The Hebrew text of Rabbi Geffen's benediction is found in *Lev Tuviah*, 57–58 (Hebrew section).
8. The Hebrew original of this *teshuva* can be found in Tuviah Geffen, *Karnei Ha-Hod* (Atlanta, 1935), 244–247. The English translation, prepared by his son Louis Geffen and his

grandson, David Geffen, is found in *Lev Tuviah*, 117–121. All references will be to the English translation.

9. The history of Coca-Cola has been documented in both popular and academic sources. The most recent and most complete history of Coca-Cola is Mark Pendergrast, *For God, Country and Coca-Cola* (New York, 1993). See esp. pp. 456–460 for a discussion of the legend of the "sacred formula." For an article on the "sacred formula" and the problems that *kashrut* presented, see Laurie M. Grossman, "The Big Problem Is: If They Tell, That Wouldn't Be Kosher, Either," *The Wall Street Journal* (April 29, 1992), B1.

10. *Lev Tuviah*, 117.

11. Rabbi Geffen's efforts to examine the ingredients of Coca-Cola and to determine its kosher status can be pieced together through an examination of some of the documents found in his collection of letters now housed at the American Jewish Historical Society. Rabbi Geffen was meticulous in preserving all communications that were sent to him. Unfortunately, we lack most of his responses to these letters.

12. For a short biography of Rabbi Kochin, see Yosef Goldman, *Hebrew Printing in America 1735–1926: A History and Annotated Bibliography* (Brooklyn, 2006), II:688.

13. Letter from Rabbi Kochin dated the third day of the portion *Matot/Massei* (July 14, 1925), Geffen Papers, Box 15, Folder 1.

14. Geffen Papers, Box 15, Folder 1.

15. Rabbi Morris Taxon was the rabbi of Baron Hirsch Synagogue in Memphis, originally called Congregation Mischne. For a short biography, see *Who's Who in American Jewry* 1926 (New York, 1927), 616, and *American Jewish Year Book* 44 (1942–1943), 345.

16. Letter dated May 20, 1932, in Geffen Papers, Box 15, Folder 1.

17. For a short biography of Rabbi Pardes, see Sherman, 161–162.

18. Letter from Rabbi Pardes, Tuesday *Parshat Terumah* (February 17, 1931), in Geffen Papers, Box 15, Folder 1.

19. Letter from Rabbi Pardes, Saturday night, *Parshat Tetzaveh* (February 28, 1931), in Geffen Papers, Box 15, Folder 1.

20. *Hapardes* 4:9 (December 1930), 3.

21. *Hapardes* 4:10 (January 1931) n.p. (back of cover).

22. *Hapardes* 4:12 (March 1931), 20.

23. This paragraph appeared as an introduction to the typewritten English translation of the Coca-Cola *Teshuva* and as the closing paragraph to the original Hebrew *teshuva* in Geffen Papers, Box 15, Folder 1. Interestingly, it is absent both from the printed edition of *Karnei Ha-Hod* and from the English translation published in *Lev Tuviah*. I am perplexed by the reason for this omission. The letter to the rabbis is dated July 2, 1934, and appeared in both Hebrew and English. This letter is found in the collection of Stanley Raskas, Rabbi Geffen's grandson.

24. *Lev Tuviah*, 117.

25. *Karnei Ha-Hod*, 244.

26. Tuviah Geffen, *Nazar Yosef* (Atlanta, 1963), II:157–61.

27. Geffen Papers, Box 15, Folder 1. In the English translation it is identified simply as glycerin without the word "oil."

28. *Lev Tuviah*, 120–121.

29. Ibid., 121

30. *Karnei Ha-Hod*, 246.

31. *Nazar Yosef*, II:161, and Geffen Papers, Box 15, Folder 1.

32. *Lev Tuviah*, 121.

33. Ibid.

34. Ibid., 120.

35. For an analysis of this rabbinic approach in America, see *Jewish Commitment in a Modern World: Rabbi Hayyim Hirschenson and His Attitude to Modernity* by David Tamar, reviewed by Marc Shapiro, *Edah Journal* (Tammuz 5765) 5:1 http://www.edah.org/backend/JournalArticle/5_1_Shapiro.pdf.

36. Kaganoff, 64.
37. For a biography of Harold Hirsch, see Mark Bauman, "Role Theory and History: The Illustration of Ethnic Brokerage in the Atlanta Jewish Community in the Era of Transition and Conflict," in *American Jewish History* 73:1 (September 1983), 79–85, and a wonderful, though brief, biography of Hirsch in *American Jewish Year Book* 42 (1940–1941), 165–172.
38. See *American Jewish Year Book*, 170–172.
39. Based on a conversation with Stanley Raskas, Rabbi Geffen's grandson, on February 26, 2008, and an email correspondence with Rabbi David Geffen, also a grandson, on February 23, 2008.
40. *Karnei Ha-Hod* (Atlanta, 1935).
41. Rabbi Tobias Geffen, *Memory in Script: Eulogy on That Noble Personage Mr. Harold Hirsch* (Atlanta, 1940).
42. Based on a conversation with Stanley Raskas, Rabbi Geffen's grandson, on February 26, 2008, and an email correspondence with Rabbi David Geffen, also a grandson, on February 23, 2008.
43. Geffen Papers, Box 15, Folder 1.
44. Geffen Papers, Box 15, Folder 1.
45. Geffen Papers, Box 15, Folder 1.
46. Geffen Papers, Box 15, Folder 1. As is mentioned above (f.n. 23), on July 2, 1934, Rabbi Geffen wrote a Hebrew document addressed to "Honored Rabbi" stating that he had visited the Coca-Cola plant and replaced the nonkosher ingredient. This letter is translated into English and typed with Rabbi Geffen's signature and stamp. This letter used the word "glycerine" in Hebrew and English. This was most likely the letter that Hirsch had in his possession, and he insisted that the word "glycerine" be removed. I have not been able to locate a corrected copy of the letter. It is also possible that there was another letter pertaining to Passover containing the word "alcohol," since Hirsch referred also to "alcohol." I have not been able to locate this letter either.
47. Geffen Papers, Box 15, Folder 1.
48. See Pendergrast, 219–220, and an excellent internet post at http://ajhistory.blogspot.com/2006/07/rabbi-tobias-geffen-harold-hirsch-and.html.
49. For a short biography of Silver, see Sherman, 199–200.
50. *National Jewish Post* (October 18, 1957) n.p. Located in Geffen Papers, Box 15, Folder 1.
51. In 2003 Rabbi Shmuel Gruber quoted Rabbi Geffen's *teshuva* and agreed with his argument that the glycerin could not be considered nonexistent since it was a necessary ingredient. However, Rabbi Gruber ignored the remainder of the *teshuva*, where Rabbi Geffen explained that Coca-Cola no longer used animal glycerin and Gruber argued that Coca-Cola is not kosher. See Rabbi Shmuel Gruber, "*Be-Din Bittul Davar She-Derekh Tikkun Asiato Be-Khakh*," in *Ohr Yisrael* 8:2 (Tevet 5763), 124.
52. Kaganoff, 69.

Middle Eastern Antisemitism: Indigenous Affliction or Imported Plague?

Michael Oren

*D*uring the siege of Beirut in the 1982 Lebanon War, when I was serving as a paratrooper in the Israeli Army, my unit stumbled upon the abandoned headquarters of the Popular Front for the Liberation Palestine. There, in addition to stacks of Kalashnikov rifles and Claymore mines, we found numerous Arabic translations of the *Protocols of the Elders of Zion* and *Mein Kampf.* Most poignantly, plastered to the wall was a large swastika flag and next to it a colored portrait of Adolf Hitler. The meaning of these items for the PFLP was, at the time, a mystery to me. What interest did these avowedly Marxist, secular Palestinians have in rank antisemitic paraphernalia?

A few weeks later I returned to the United States and began my doctoral studies in Middle Eastern history at Princeton University. My arrival at Princeton coincided with the beginning of a debate, which continues to this day, over whether Jews fared better under Islamic rule than under Christendom, particularly during the Middle Ages. One school of thought argued that there was basically no difference – Jews in Islamic lands were as subject to pogroms, discrimination, and sumptuary laws as were their counterparts in Europe. A second school held that Islam was far more tolerant of Jews than Christianity. I approached this question with an open mind, undecided which was right, until I read the work by another one of my Princeton professors, the great S.D. Goitein. In five immortal volumes based on the Cairo Geniza documents and collectively entitled *A Mediterranean Society*, Goitein reconstructed Jewish life in the neighborhood in Cairo between the eighth and eleventh centuries, the so-called Golden Age of Jewish – Muslim coexistence. What emerges is the portrait of a Jewish community living side-by-side with Muslims – there was no ghetto in Egypt – but also suffering. Much of their affliction arose from the poll tax, known as the *jizya*. The Jews of Cairo, just like their co-religionists throughout the Muslim world, had to pay a tax, which enabled them to live as Jews under Muslim rule. The sum involved was immense, and each year Cairo's Jews went into a profound malaise and panic over whether they could raise the money. So much for the Golden Age, I thought, and chose my side in the debate.

The debate over which was crueler to Jews, Islam or Christianity, became entwined with the question of whether anti-Jewish attitudes and actions in the Arab world were the by-product of Zionism and the creation of Israel. During the course of my research on the history of American involvement in the Middle East, I was surprised to encounter nineteenth-century diplomatic documents detailing blood libels and pogroms against Jews in Syria and North Africa – decades before the advent of Zionism. The documents also showed how, during World War II, American GI's had to physically intercede to save the Jews of Morocco and Algeria from massacre at the hands of their Muslim neighbors. In one infamous case, American soldiers entering Casablanca were attacked by Arab Muslims because a rumor circulated that the stars on the American jeeps were in fact the Stars of David.

Clearly, when we talk about Arab or Muslim antisemitism, we are not referring to a new phenomenon. But neither are we dealing with a static or singular phenomena. Rather, we are talking about a form of prejudice that has deep historical and theological roots in the Arab and Muslim world, but which also reflects foreign influence on the Middle East.

To gain any true appreciation of the nature and scope of Arab and Muslim antisemitism, we first have to start with the basics, with Islam. What does Islam tell us about Jews and the relationship of Jews to the Muslim community or *Umma*? The relationship between Islam and the Jews began poorly during the life of the Prophet Muhammad. Early in his career, in Mecca, Muhammad urged his followers to observe the Yom Kippur fast and to pray in the direction of Jerusalem. But forced to flee Mecca in 622, Muhammad arrived at the neighboring city of Medina, which was largely under the control of affluent Jewish tribes. Muhammad assumed that Medina's Jews would welcome him as the new and last prophet, but he was wrong. The Jews rejected him and made war against him, and in response, Muhammad eradicated them. He subsequently changed the direction of prayer to Mecca and Medina and replaced the Yom Kippur fast with Ramadan. He also set out what early Islamic sources describe as the Covenant of Medina.

The Covenant sets out the legal relationship between Jews and Muslims. The Jews are recognized as *ahl al-kitab*, People of the Book, that is, the Bible, and therefore cannot be forcibly converted. On the contrary, Jews are designated as *dhimmi*, protected individuals whose persons and property cannot be harmed. But the Jews are also subjected to the *jizya* tax and relegated to what we would describe today as second-class status.

The Covenant of Medina was significantly expanded after the conquest of Jerusalem in 717 by the second caliph, Umar. Prior to this time, the Jews had been excluded from the city by the Byzantines, but Umar allowed the Jews to return. At the same time, however, he also established a series of sumptuary laws detailing the legal status of *dhimmis* and the People of the Book, Christians as well as Jews. Accordingly, *dhimmis* were prohibited from riding on animals that would make them physically higher than

Muslims. They were not allowed to build new synagogues – or churches – and certainly not ones that were higher than mosques, and not allowed to bear witness against Muslims in court. Proselytizing Muslims was deemed a capital offense for Jews and Christians, and so too was a marriage between a Muslim woman and a *dhimmi* man in which the Muslim becomes an apostate. Jews and Christians were also required to dress in a distinct way: the yellow star, widely associated with Nazism, was in fact an early Islamic invention.

The Covenant of Umar, as it is broadly known, codified the legal relationship between Islam and the Jews. Though at certain times and in some places – in eighth-century Andalusia, for example – it was observed more in the breach, the covenant was widely applied. Moreover, it rested on substantial theological foundations. The Qur'an relates to the Jews as being untrustworthy, and it exhorts Muslims not to take them as friends. The Qur'an also advances the case that the Jews falsified the Bible and that the Talmud is a fraud. Some of the Islamic legends of the Prophet, or *hadith*, depict Jews as descendants of monkeys and pigs. One *hadith* asserts that when Jews take shelter from Muslims, the very trees and rocks will call out, "Listen, believing Muslim, there is a Jew hiding behind me; come and kill him." These notions have gained immense currency in the Arab and Muslim world today.

On the other hand, Islam did not regard Judaism as posing a theological threat of the same magnitude as Christianity posed. Islam absolves the Jews of the charge of deicide, for the elementary reason that God is not a human being and God cannot be killed. The Jews are not saddled with the responsibility for plagues and natural disasters, since they routinely were in medieval Europe, nor were expulsions and massacres the norm in the Islamic world. Tellingly, perhaps, the great Christian settlements of North Africa were completely obliterated by Islam, but the Jewish communities remained.

Racial antisemitism entered the Muslim Middle East relatively late in Islamic history, with the fifteenth-century conquest

of Byzantine lands by the Ottomans. Over the next 300 years antisemitic outbreaks were often triggered by Christian clergy and
European diplomats. The most nefarious of these, the Damascus
blood libel of 1840, was mounted by Capuchin monks with the
aid of a French consul general. Arabs also took their rising fear
of Europe out on the Jews, especially those Jewish communities
that enjoyed close connections with European imperialist powers. That was certainly the factor in the 1880 pogroms in Morocco
and the backlash against the Jews in North Africa in World War
II. In both cases, the Jews were perceived as being the natural allies of colonialism.

European-style racial antisemitism was thus well established
in the Middle East by the 1930s and the advent of Nazism. Wor-
shipful of military power and extending hope to the weak, the
Nazis put forth ideas that gained numerous adherents in the region. Fascist parties such as the Young Egypt Society and the Par-
tie Populaire Syrienne proliferated, and pro-Nazi revolts erupted
in Egypt and Iraq. Arabs and Iranians not only embraced Nazi
militarism and empowerment, but also Nazi antisemitism. Nazi
antisemitism was disseminated throughout the Middle East by
Hajj Amin al-Husseini, the Grand Mufti of Jerusalem, who had
been exiled by the British to Berlin. His publications and broadcasts, rife with the most pernicious images of the Jews, reached
an immense Arab audience. Later, after the war, many Nazi com-
manders and ideologues found refuge in Egypt and Syria and
some were employed in their propaganda ministries.

Though antisemitism had become a fact of Middle Eastern
life well before the establishment of Israel in 1948, that event undoubtedly fueled anti-Jewish sentiment throughout the area. The
Jews who caused the Arabs to fail in their first great postcolonial
test were not the representatives of a major European power, but
the remnants of a degraded people who had scarcely survived the
crematoria. Israel's victory therefore served as a source of unfath-
omable humiliation for Arab Muslims, and antisemitism provided
a convenient means for mitigating that humiliation.

By the 1950s we see the emergence of more readily recognizable European forms of antisemitism within the Arab world. First
translated into Arabic in 1925, *The Protocols of the Elders of Zion*,
the notorious Russian forgery that purports to be the minutes of
a meeting of a Jewish cabal that is planning to take over the world,
was reprinted and distributed by the Egyptian and Saudi governments in the 1950s, as was *Mein Kampf*. Both books, in fact, became best sellers. The image of the Jews as money-grubbers and
as weak and morally decrepit manipulators, on the one hand, and
as domineering and dominating the world, on the other, was unquestionably embraced by Arabs.

I wrote my doctoral dissertation on Egyptian policy in the
1950s, and I was very curious to follow the story of a young Egyptian reporter named Ibrahim Izzat, a correspondent for the then
prestigious weekly, *Ruz el-Yusuf*. In the spring of 1956 Izzat appeared at the Israeli Embassy in London and expressed interest in
writing a story about Israel. The Israelis were thrilled and extended
him VIP treatment. Izzat was able to interview Golda Meir and
Teddy Kollek, to visit kibbutzim and army bases. He returned to
Egypt and duly published his articles in *Ruz el-Yusuf*. What appeared, however, was not an insightful portrait of the Jewish state
but a compendium of every antisemitic canard. Israel, according
to Izzat, was created by an international Jewish cabal dedicated
to money laundering and world domination. Kibbutzim were
houses of prostitution for young Arab women kidnapped by ra-
pacious Jews.

The 1960s saw the wholesale adoption of Nazi antisemitic
motifs by the Arab press. Arab cartoons of the period almost invariably depicted Israelis as hook-nosed, ultra-Orthodox Jews
plotting to take over the world. And yet, Arab regimes claimed
that the frail and unmanly Jews could not have prevailed in the
Six-Day War; that was certainly the work of the British and the
Americans. The myth proved irrepressible. Many years later, while
I was researching my book on the 1967 war, almost none of the

Arab veterans I encountered believed that Israel had fought on its own.

Over the course of the next forty years, antisemitism in the Arab world became a standard, state-funded activity – what my former professor Bernard Lewis called "antisemitism from the top down." It found expression in an almost constant flow of antisemitic articles and cartoons, and in the official presses of Egypt, Syria, Saudi Arabia, and Libya. A long list of historical calamities were ascribed to the Jews, including the outbreak of the Russo-Japanese War and World Wars I and ii, the dropping of the atomic bomb on Japan, the collapse of the Ottoman Czarist Empires, and the triggering of the Great Depression.

Beginning in the 1990s, however, Arab and Muslim antisemitism underwent not one, but several profound transformations. The first of these was a process of "Islamization," in which Jews and Judaism were recast as the principal threats to Muhammad (eclipsing the medieval Christians) and as the embodiment of satanic evil. The charge that Jews were descended from monkeys and pigs and slated for mass slaughter became standard themes in Friday mosque sermons and Islamist propaganda. They became staples in school textbooks and even children's broadcasts from Gaza to Teheran.

The Islamization of Arab antisemitism spread from the Arab world into the world Islamic community, into Pakistan and Malaysia. It was exemplified by Malaysian Prime Minister Mahathir Mohammad, who, in a speech to an Islamic summit meeting in 2003, called on the 1.3 billion Muslims to unite against the mere 12 million Jews who currently controlled the world. The premier received a standing ovation.

The Islamization of antisemitism also meant popularization – no longer primarily from the top down, but also from the bottom up. Among the beliefs that have gained widespread credence in Arab and Iranian public opinion are that the Jews invented and spread the AIDS virus; they poisoned wells; and they distributed aphrodisiacs among Arab women and sexual suppressants among Muslim men. Jew-hatred, now thoroughly indistinct from anti-Zionism, became an obsession that was increasingly reflected in Holocaust denial. Numerous tracts were published and conferences held asserting that the murder of six million Jews never happened, that it is merely a myth devised by the Jews to manipulate the world's conscience. The Holocaust never happened but, in keeping with the popular Muslim image of Jews as at once weak and all-powerful, the Nazis were heroes for perpetrating it. Reports occasionally appear in the Israeli press of Palestinians whose parents blessed them with the name Hitler or Eichmann in the hope that they too would grow up to crush the Jews.

Another fixation – and another example of this paradox – are the events surrounding 9/11. Israel launched attacks on the World Trade Center in order to make Arabs and Muslims look bad, so the rumor holds. Four thousand Jewish employees were forewarned to leave the Twin Towers before the Mossad struck. But, at the same time, Bin Laden is revered as a hero for having struck a mortal blow at Zionist imperialism. Similarly, the war in Iraq is perceived in much of the Muslim Middle East as the first of many Jewish-orchestrated steps to conquer the region and appropriate its oil, and simultaneously as a pathetic attempt to save the Jews from their destruction by Saddam Hussein.

The Islamization and popularization of antisemitism has, in turn, spurred Middle Eastern regimes to escalate their antisemitic output. Recent years have witnessed anti-Jewish blood libels on the part of the Syrian and Saudi governments; Damascus even published a book on the subject. Dramatizations of *The Protocols* have appeared on Egyptian and Iranian state television and another appeared on Jordanian TV before being removed under American and Israeli pressure.

Confronted with this onslaught of hatred, it is essential to ask ourselves, "Why – why has antisemitism permeated much of the Muslim world?" Many Muslims would respond that antisemitism is a reaction to abhorrent Israeli policies, the suppression of the Palestinians, and the Israeli-promoted war in Iraq. But even allowing for a legitimate Islamic grievance, how can that sense of injustice serve to justify the almost unchallenged denial of the Holocaust, the blood libels, and the popularity of *The Protocols* and *Mein Kampf*?

The only plausible explanation, I believe, lies in Arab and Iranian frustration with the challenges of modernity. The failure to meet that challenge, to reconcile the Islamic promise of Muslim primacy with the reality of Western military and technological superiority, generates tremendous pain and anger. Antisemitism helps to salve that angst. The fact that the region's only successful Islamic regime, in Iran, has adopted Holocaust denial and other antisemitic tropes as its official policy serves as another compelling reason for Muslim hatred of the Jews.

Another important reason, however, is the near-absence of any serious international reaction to Arab and Iranian antisemitism. There was no American reaction, for example, when Yasir Arafat repeatedly claimed that Israel was dropping depleted uranium pellets into the West Bank water system to sterilize Arab men; no American reaction when King Abdallah of Saudi Arabia lectured the U.S. government on Jewish ritual slaughter. Indeed, in virtually every Arab country in which antisemitism has become commonplace, the West in general, and the United States in particular, have ignored it.

The failure to address this antisemitism poses a palpable threat, and not only to Israel and the Jewish people. The same defamation that is aimed at Jews is also launched at the United States. As the author and journalist Yossi Klein Halevi has pointed out, America has become the new Jew in Arab antisemitism – weak and immoral, all-powerful and voracious. Today, in the wake of Hamas's ascendancy in Palestinian politics and in the shadow of Iran's quest for nuclear weapons, it is essential that Jew-hatred in the Middle East not be dismissed as a mere nuisance or unpleasantness. It is, rather, a symptom of the madness that threatens Israel's existence and the security of

America and the West. The world should have learned its lesson from sixty years ago; ignoring antisemitism is the first step toward global cataclysm.

Compulsion or Choice?
The Jewish War and the Problem of
"Necessity" according to Josephus

Jonathan J. Price

The Jewish historian Flavius Josephus was a conflicted man. Born into an aristocratic family of priests in Jerusalem in 37 C.E., he was not yet 30 when the great rebellion broke out against Rome in 66 C.E. and he was appointed governor-general of the Galilee and Gamla, charged with organizing the first line of defense against the inevitable Roman attack from the north. After a self-described energetic and talented defense of the region, he chose to surrender to the overwhelmingly superior Roman forces, after which, using his wiles, he survived in the Roman camp by serving as translator, advisor, and spokesman, pleading with the militant rebels holding Jerusalem to surrender and accept Roman rule before they themselves caused the destruction of the holy city and Temple. After the Temple was destroyed in flames in 70 C.E., Josephus was taken back to Rome by the victorious general Titus, whose father, the Roman emperor Vespasian, rewarded the former Jewish general with Roman citizenship (changing his name from Yosef ben Matitiyahu to Titus Flavius Josephus), and with an apartment and pension in the capital. In these comfortable but compromising circumstances,

Josephus wrote five works: a history of the Jewish rebellion in Aramaic; a seven-volume history of the Jewish rebellion in Greek; a 20-volume history of the Jews and Judaism in Greek, from the biblical moment of Creation to the outbreak of the Jewish rebellion in 66 C.E.; a one-volume account in Greek of his own life; and a brilliant and learned two-volume defense of the Jews, in Greek, against the pernicious Judaeophobic slanders of the day. While Josephus' first literary venture, in Aramaic, has not survived, the other works, written in Greek, were lovingly preserved by Christian scholars and scribes and have come down to us in their entirety (highly rare for any ancient author), so that it is possible to read his entire Greek *oeuvre* and trace his development as an author.

Josephus' huge literary output is marked by the same contradictions and conflicting demands that marked his life. Although he was not forced by his Roman patrons to write anything at all, he took up his pen with energy and conviction for many reasons, first to defend his own part in the Jewish rebellion against Rome and explain his apparent change in policy and philosophy: how he started as a committed rebel and ended up counseling peace and accommodation with the Roman empire, and justifying both as expressions of God's will. He had a great deal of explaining to do, both to the Romans, who needed a sure sign of his loyalty, and to his fellow Jews, who accused him of the worst kind of betrayal of his own people. Josephus developed the theory that the destruction of the Temple, and ultimately the entire rebellion, was really the work of relatively small factions of militant extremists, who made the holy city and the entire Jewish people victims of their uncompromising and mistaken worldview. In his post-revolutionary phase as a writer – fully the second half of his life – he argued that acceptance of the yoke of Rome, with its attendant difficulties and bitterness, was part of God's plan for the Jewish people; he fit the destruction of the first and second temples into a theological and historical framework which made sense of the present in terms of the past and the anticipated future. And finally, disturbed by the incessant attacks on Jews and Judaism by Greek writers of different stripes, Josephus constructed a positive account of Jewish history against the backdrop of world history, in order to instruct an uninformed and often hostile Gentile world about the virtues of Judaism, its teachings and laws, historical vicissitudes, and political and religious culture.

Given the burden of these contradictory thematic demands, it is surprising that Josephus succeeded in writing a single word, for every time he wrote about one theme he was in danger of undermining another. His views were not static, but in a very human way changed in conjunction with the events of his momentous century. By reading through his works in chronological order, one can glimpse how he developed and refined his views on some of the most crucial issues impinging on his own life, in fact on his entire generation. The present paper focuses on one aspect of his intellectual development, namely, his presentation of the causes of the Jewish war against Rome and the involvement of the Jewish aristocratic class in that traumatic conflict.

Josephus published his first book in Greek, *The Jewish War* (BJ), within ten years after the destruction of the Second Temple.[1] Despite his main claim in that work that extremist revolutionary factions, such as the Zealots and Sicarii, were responsible for the war and its awful result, it is clear from Josephus' own evidence that he and much of his own class were active and even enthusiastic leaders of the rebellion in its initial stages. The first revolutionary government, formed in Jerusalem in the fall of 66 C.E., was led almost exclusively by members of the traditional Jewish aristocracy. Josephus' list of the original office-holders in that government includes the names of two former high priests and the son of another high priest, three other priests from noble families, and two members of the lay nobility[2]; other members of the Jewish elite are seen in posts of responsibility during the first year of the war.[3] Between the lines of Josephus' text, it is clear that these aristocratic leaders of the first revolutionary government were devoted to the rebellion.[4] Everything Josephus describes these leaders doing shows them to be so. The leader of the whole government, the former high priest Hanan ben Hanan, worked indefatigably to prepare Jerusalem for the siege, draw up a strategy, fortify defensible cities, build an army, and send the extremist units out on missions. Josephus says explicitly that every one of the new government's leaders "executed his commission to the best of his zeal or ability."[5] This includes the author himself: in books 2 and 3 of *The Jewish War*, Josephus portrays himself as a highly skilled general and adept politician who invested great energy and talent in defending the Galilee but perforce succumbed to the Roman military machine. According to his own account, he set up an administrative system for all Galilee, fortified towns, built and trained a large army, devised a military strategy, was everywhere at once worrying about the defense of the region under his responsibility – hardly a reluctant general. While Josephus had to worry about Jewish rivals and enemies in the region, his main theme in books 2 and 3 of *The Jewish War* is his own superior qualities as military and political commander – before, that is, he surrendered at Jotapata and changed his views about the wisdom of fighting the Romans. Unlike Josephus, many of the aristocratic leaders of the first government, that is, those who survived the violent *coup d'état* in the winter of 66/67 C.E., stayed in Jerusalem to the bitter end three years later, even when their lives were constantly endangered by the violent second government: these aristocrats would not have braved the purges and other dangers in the besieged city (such as famine) if not for their utter commitment to the revolution and belief that ultimately, with God's help, the Jews would prevail.

Throughout *The Jewish War* and his later works, Josephus portrays the Jewish ruling class as composed of sober, well-educated, worldly, and realistic men – the kind of men Rome could trust to help administer the province. Why, then, would they risk their own position and their nation in a hopeless uprising? Josephus' answer to this question developed and changed during his 30-year career as a writer in Rome. In *The Jewish War*, it is left unanswered, or answered only partially, and unsatisfactorily.

Josephus seems to waver between emphasizing the competence and true conviction of his rebellious colleagues and himself, on the one hand, and their sensible opposition to rebellion, on the other. For example, in the eulogy for the slain leader Hanan ben Hanan, Josephus wrote:

> A man on every ground revered and of the highest integrity, Ananus [= Hanan], with all the distinction of his birth, his rank and the honors to which he had attained, yet delighted to treat the very humblest as his equals. Unique in his love of liberty and an enthusiast for democracy, he on all occasions put the public welfare above his private interests. To maintain peace was his supreme object. He knew that the Roman power was irresistible, but, when driven to provide for a state of war, he endeavored to secure that, if the Jews would not come to terms, the struggle should at least be skillfully conducted. In a word, had Ananus lived, they would undoubtedly either have arranged terms – for he was an effective speaker, whose words carried weight with the people, and was already gaining control even over those who thwarted him – or else, had hostilities continued, they would have greatly retarded the victory of the Romans under such a general.[6]

Hanan is described as the Pericles of Jerusalem: the supreme orator, statesman, general, lover of democracy. Aside from the utter improbability that a high priest loved democracy and the practical impossibility that he was an experienced general, the phrasing of this encomium obscures the most important question: what was Hanan's real intention? Did he make every effort to achieve peace, was peace his "supreme object," and would it have in all likelihood been achieved had he remained? Or, in his alleged competence as general, did Hanan fight vigorously and unflinchingly against the Romans so that "undoubtedly," had he remained, their victory would have been greatly delayed? He cannot have done both.

106 | Jonathan J. Price

In truth, aside from this ambivalent eulogy, there is no sign in *The Jewish War* of Hanan's trying to bring about peace; in cold historical terms, he was a faction leader who devoted himself to revolution but was defeated in an internal struggle, by a stronger faction. In his conflicted praise of Hanan, Josephus reveals his own ambivalence and uncertainty about the war.

During the 15 years after he published *The Jewish War,* Josephus wrote his encyclopedic *Jewish Antiquities* (AJ). We know very little about what he was doing during that time in Rome, aside from extensive research and writing, which must have occupied much of his time. One thing that is known, from Josephus himself, is that he was forced repeatedly to respond to accusers from various quarters. He was not only under perpetual attack by Jews who suspected that he had betrayed them, but – contrarily, and more difficult for his status in Rome – he also had to answer constant charges by both Jewish and non-Jewish accusers that he helped foment rebellion in 66 C.E. and was still secretly aiding continued rebellion. At least two of his accusers are known by name: Justus, a Jew from Tiberias who himself wrote an account of the war and accused Josephus of fomenting the rebellion of Tiberias, and a certain Jonathan, a Jewish weaver from Cyrene, who also accused Josephus of rebellion (*neoterismos*) against Rome.[7] In each case, Josephus says, he defended himself successfully and was able to preserve the emperor's confidence in him.

Those same postwar years were momentous for the province of Judaea and the Jews in general. After the war the Romans reorganized the province of Judaea and administered it with their typical efficiency; the Jews there, in addition to suffering a steep population decline because of the devastating war, saw much of their property confiscated. The Romans established a special "Jewish tax," the *Fiscus Judaicus*, essentially a continuation of the former voluntary half-shekel tax to the Temple, now compulsory and redirected to Rome. The third and last Flavian emperor, the notoriously paranoid and volatile Domitian (81–96 C.E.), was especially thorough and cruel in his collection of this tax, and moreover executed certain Roman converts to Judaism on a charge of "atheism."[8] Many accounts of the Jewish War, praising the Romans and slandering the Jews, as well as simply anti-Jewish polemics, circulated throughout the Greek literary world in Josephus' time and afterwards. Very little of this literature has survived, and we know about it principally through Josephus' responses, especially his last work, *Against Apion*. The task of apology and explanation was made more burdensome by the widespread Flavian propaganda ostentatiously celebrating the Jewish defeat on triumphal arches (of which the Arch of Titus in the Roman Forum is one) and a massive series of coins issued from Rome bearing the legend *Iudaea Capta*, "Judaea Defeated/Captured," showing typically a spear-holding Roman soldier standing over a crouching, humiliated woman representing Judaea, often with her hands tied behind her back. It was not an easy period for Jews in the Empire.

At the same time, the revolutionary spirit and ideology remained alive among the Jews, perhaps even encouraged by the sting of defeat. Expectations of imminent apocalypse, or אחרית ימים, lived on in Eretz Israel and elsewhere, as represented in such visionary works known as Fourth Ezra, Second Baruch, and the Fifth Sibylline Oracle.[9] Remarkably, Jewish rebellious activities did not die out with the destruction of the Temple. On the contrary, the Sicarii remained defiant at Masada for three or four years after the Temple was destroyed, and others of that group not trapped on the mountain fortress fomented rebellion in Egypt until they were suppressed.[10] In 115–117 C.E. the Jews of Cyrene and Egypt launched a huge rebellion against Rome, resulting in near destruction of the once-thriving Egyptian Jewish community.[11] And in 132–135 Shimon Bar Kochba led another revolt with clear messianic aspirations, which were once again crushed by the Romans, with massive loss of life and property. Thus when Josephus wrote urgently of the need to accept Roman rule in order to preserve life, and when he wrote in a more veiled way against a theology that sanctioned armed uprising to initiate the End of Days, he was writing against people, ideas, and movements very much alive in his day, who he believed posed an immediate existential threat to the Jewish people.

In these circumstances Josephus had to improve his explanation not only of why the Jews rebelled against Rome, but especially why the Jewish rulers in 66 C.E. joined and led the uprising. This was important for all his multiple audiences: for general Greek readers, to show that neither the Jews nor their leaders were, contrary to the malicious propaganda, a perverse and lustful people despising the rest of humanity[12]; for Jewish audiences, to show that the aristocratic Jewish leaders of the rebellion in 66 C.E. had no true revolutionary convictions and thus provided no inspiration or encouragement for further revolt; and for the Roman authorities, who had to be persuaded that they could trust the surviving Jewish aristocrats as partners in administration (in this last purpose Josephus was singularly unsuccessful).

The idea that Josephus developed to explain the actions of the Jewish leaders to these three audiences was that the war was initially an act not of choice but of compulsion. Josephus opened his *Jewish Antiquities* with the declaration that he had written his previous book, *The Jewish War*, to correct the accounts "of those who in their writings were doing outrage to the truth," and that the Jews entered their latest war "involuntarily."[13] At the end of the *Antiquities* Josephus developed the idea that the rebellion was compulsory, in his account of the last procurator of Judaea in 66 C.E., Gessius Florus. He wrote that Florus, who had been sent by Nero because of a connection between his wife and that of the emperor, "filled the cup of the Jews with many misfortunes," was "wicked and lawless":

> Gessius Florus, as if he had been sent to give an exhibition of wickedness, ostentatiously paraded his lawless treatment of our nation and omitted no form of pillage or unjust punishment.... The ill-fated Jews, unable to endure the devastation

by brigands that went on were one and all forced to abandon their country and flee, for they thought that it would be better to settle among Gentiles, no matter where. What more need be said? *It was Florus who constrained us to take up war with the Romans*, for we preferred to perish together rather than by degrees.[14]

The corrupt, villainous Roman procurator Florus left the Jews no choice but to take up arms: thus Josephus' claim, in the late stages of his life. It should be noted that he does not here – or anywhere in his writings – indict the entire Roman administration as insupportably oppressive, or intimate that the Roman empire was inherently cruel and evil. He goes to great lengths to pin the blame on one or two ill-chosen Roman officials, but nonetheless the idea of necessity – "it was Florus who constrained us to take up war with the Romans" – is new to his interpretation of the war.

In his first account of the war, *The Jewish War*, Josephus had depicted Florus as a villain in stark terms similar to those used in the *Antiquities*,[15] and Florus is even said to have wished for a Jewish revolt as a cover for his own crimes,[16] but he is not assigned full responsibility for the rebellion by the historian; rather, in his first version of the rebellion, Josephus insists that it was not Florus's provocations but the reactions to them by the hot-headed, armed extremists which brought on the war. These "factious elements," in Josephus' language, adamantly refused to listen to the desperate repeated appeals for restraint from the high priests and other Jewish leaders[17] and took actions which committed the nation irrevocably to war.[18]

Florus therefore is depicted in *The Jewish War* as a contributory factor to the war, but his crimes were not in themselves sufficient to justify hostilities. On the contrary, in the great speech which Josephus puts in the mouth of Agrippa II, trying to dissuade the Jews in Jerusalem from starting a war against Rome, the Jewish king says:

Granted that the Roman ministers are intolerably harsh. It does not follow that all the Romans are unjust to you.... How absurd it were, because of one man to make war on a whole people, for trifling grievances to take arms against so mighty a power, which does not even know the nature of our complaints! The wrongs which we lay to their charge may be speedily rectified; for the same procurator will not remain for ever, and it is probable that the successors of this one will show greater moderation on taking office.[19]

Florus's crimes amount to "trifling grievances"; it was the extreme reaction to them that led to war. So said Josephus in *The Jewish War*. In the approximately 15 years between penning these words and writing the last sentences of the *Antiquities*, Josephus modified his view and made Florus's offenses a sufficient cause for war against Rome. Thus the *Antiquities* is framed by the idea of compulsion (Greek *anagke*), and it should be noted that Florus's greatest offense, his attack on the Temple Mount, was his last one; the Jewish reaction to this act required him to leave the province: all Jews at all social levels felt undying devotion to their Temple.

The problem of compulsion is developed even further in Josephus' autobiography, written as an appendix to the *Antiquities*. Here Josephus not only gives another reason, in a famous statement, why the Jews' uprising was a "necessity," but he combines that reason with an explanation of the questionable actions by aristocratic Jews such as himself. Josephus says that in the year 66 C.E. revolutionary movements were widespread in Judaea and there was "widespread elation at the prospect of revolt from Rome."[20] He claims that he tried to prevail upon the "promoters of sedition" to abandon their reckless course, for already at this stage – before he himself joined the rebellion! – he foresaw that "the end of the war would be most disastrous for us." In this state of confusion and danger, Josephus said, he and the other Jewish leaders of the time ("the chief priests and the leading Pharisees") employed a ruse:

In such obvious and imminent peril we professed to concur in their views, but suggested that they should make no move and leave the enemy alone if he advanced, in order to gain the credit of resorting to arms only in just self-defence.

Josephus finally solved the conundrum (whether or not satisfactorily is another question) of the Jewish leaders' true intentions – a conundrum, it will be remembered, which appeared in quite stark terms in Josephus' encomium on the high priestly leader Hanan ben Hanan in *The Jewish War*. It is true, he says here, that he and members of his class ("the chief priests and the leading Pharisees") joined the rebellion and professed enthusiastic support of it, but they were only pretending in order to gain control of it and bring it to a quick end. In his eulogy on Hanan, Josephus left open the question of whether that respected leader had planned to fight vigorously to the end or bring the war to a quick close. Now it is decided: the Jewish leaders were struggling to apply the brakes as quickly as they could. Their *apparent* support of the rebellion was only a sophisticated technique to end it as swiftly as possible.

There is another important shift: it is not only the cruel and oppressive Roman procurator Florus who gave the Jews no choice, but also the widespread attacks on Jews by their Gentile neighbors in cities throughout the East.

The inhabitants of the surrounding cities of Syria proceeded to lay hands on and kill, with their wives and children, the Jewish residents among them, without the slightest ground of complaint; for they had neither entertained any idea of revolt from Rome nor harbored any enmity or designs against the Syrians.

Similar outrages occurred in Scythopolis (Beth She'an), Damascus, and elsewhere. Josephus then pronounces his crucial conclusion:

I have given a more detailed account of these incidents in my volumes on the Jewish War [i.e., his first work]; and I merely allude to them here from a desire to convince my readers that the war with the Romans was due not so much to the deliberate choice of the Jews as to necessity (*anagke*).

Josephus says the whole nation was forced to war, without distinguishing levels of responsibility. While the same attacks were related in detail in *The Jewish War* in much greater detail,[21] as Josephus himself mentions, there is no mention there of these attacks compelling the Jews to war; rather they are presented as merely *accompanying* the outbreak of the rebellion. For at "the same day and the same hour" as Jewish extremists in Jerusalem treacherously massacred a Roman garrison, "as if by the hand of Providence," there were outbreaks of violence in Caesarea and elsewhere. One might even see an invidious equation between Jewish and Gentile violence in *The Jewish War*, but if so, Josephus abandoned it when he returned to the topic of the responsibility for the war. For by the end of his life these Gentile attacks on Jews had transformed in Josephus' thinking from a theological wonder to a concrete cause for action. Thus two elements which were contributing, secondary causes of the rebellion in *The Jewish War* – Roman abuses and pogroms by Gentiles – had become, in Josephus' changed view of history, primary and ineluctable causes of the tragic war against Rome.

A significant intellectual development is reflected in the apologetic statements of the *Antiquities* and the autobiography.[22] In fact, by this single shift in his thinking, Josephus was able to re-address the three audiences mentioned above. To Greek readers who questioned the practical wisdom of rebelling against Rome, or even saw in the rebellion an expression of Jewish misanthropy and separatism, Josephus asserted that Roman offenses and all-out violence had strained the Jews' endurance, including that of the elite leaders, beyond all human limits, and forced them to defend with their lives their dignity and freedom; Greek intellectuals, who with their proud past and humiliating present circumstances never entirely accepted the fact of Roman rule,[23] could have implicitly understood the predicament. To Jewish readers

Josephus was saying that although the nation was forced to war, it was by the actions of a single villainous Roman official and by many non-Romans whom the Romans usually restrained: one should not conclude that Rome should always be resisted at any cost. Many good Roman governors appear in Josephus' pages, as a counterbalance to the bad officials like Florus, such as the Roman governor of Syria, Petronius, who risked his life when he defied the order by the mad emperor Caligula, who wanted to put his statue in the Jerusalem Temple.[24]

For the Romans, Josephus' statement of "necessity" was a declaration of peaceful intentions: the Jewish leaders did not want the rebellion, he says, but, being men of high political and social status, they were offended by Florus' outrageous offenses and did what any men of dignity would do. Even Tacitus, no friend of the Jews, acknowledged: "The patience of the Jews lasted until Gessius Florus became procurator."[25] For this purpose, Josephus emphasizes Florus' mean background and his connection with the corrupt emperor Nero, whom Josephus' Flavian patrons used as a foil to enhance their own position and stature; Josephus was in tune with the official program. In any case, Josephus was telling his Roman patrons that the Jewish leaders made an effort to bring the war to a quick close but were thwarted in that attempt by the Jewish extremists, who are portrayed as more criminal than the Jews' Roman and Gentile oppressors.

In this respect, Josephus' assertion of the "necessity" of the war could also be read as a veiled warning: the Jews, who are spread throughout the Roman empire (especially the East), do not have unlimited patience for maladministration. When provoked and given good cause, the Jews are capable of unleashing violent rebellion, and even upper-class, peace-loving Jews like Josephus, who are accepting of Rome, have limits set by their Jewish identity and sensibilities.

✥ NOTES

This article deals with existential questions which vexed Jews at a critical juncture in history and still, in different forms, require answers today. I offer it in honor of Rabbi Haskel Lookstein, who throughout his distinguished career has unblinkingly faced similar questions of moral urgency.

1. Or 81 C.E. at the latest; see C.P. Jones, "Towards a Chronology of Josephus," *Scripta Classica Israelica* 21 (2002), 113–121.
2. BJ 2.562–568.
3. E.g., BJ 2.628, 4.160; Vita 29; etc.
4. See e.g. my book, *Jerusalem Under Siege: The Collapse of the Jewish State, 66–70 C.E.* (Leiden 1992), chapter 2; M. Goodman, *The Ruling Class of Judaea. The Origins of the Jewish Revolt against Rome A.D. 66–70* (Cambridge 1987). On the causes of the war, P. Bilde, "The Causes of the Jewish War according to Josephus," *JSJ* 10 (1979), 179–202.
5. BJ 2.569, trans. H. St. J. Thackeray for the Loeb Classical Library. This edition is the source of all translations of Josephus in this paper: H. St. J. Thackeray, R. Marcus, A. Wikgren, and L. Feldman, *Josephus* I–X (London, 1926–1965, Loeb Classical Library).
6. BJ 4.319–321.
7. Josephus' response to Justus (and our only source of knowledge about him) is contained in Vita (*passim*, see esp. pp. 357–360 on Justus's book); the story of Jonathan the weaver is told in BJ 7.437–450.
8. The imperial biographer Suetonius wrote: "I recall being present in my youth when the person of a man ninety years old was examined before the procurator and a very crowded court, to see whether he was circumcised." Suet. *Dom.* 12.2; apparently there were some Jews who tried to disguise their identity in order to avoid the tax; for text and commentary on Suetonius see M. Stern, *Greek and Latin Authors on Jews and Judaism* II (Jerusalem, 1980), pp. 128–131. The third-century historian Cassius Dio reports that the emperor Domitian condemned on charges of "atheism" many people, including a distinguished relative of his, who were Jewish converts (or perhaps "God-fearers"), Dio 67.14.1–2 see Stern, *ibid.*, 379–384; and in general see E.M. Smallwood, "Domitian's Attitude Toward the Jews and Judaism," *Classical Philology* 51 (1956), 1–13.
9. Translations in J.H. Charlesworth, *The Old Testament Pseudepigrapha* (Garden City, N.Y., 1983).
10. BJ 7.410–419, 437, 440.
11. On this lesser-known but very serious incident, see now M. Pucci Ben Zeev, *Diaspora Jews in Turmoil, 116/117 C.E.: Ancient Sources and Modern Insights* (Leuven, 2005); still good is G. Alon, *The Jews in Their Land in the Talmudic Age*, trans. G. Levi (Cambridge, Mass., 1989), pp. 382–405.
12. While the Greek anti-Jewish screeds of Josephus' time have mostly disappeared, it is instructive to read Tacitus' description of the Jews (Tac., *Hist.* 5.5), reflecting common opinion and knowledge of his day (and it is to be remembered that Tacitus was writing history, not a personal or polemical pamphlet against the Jews): he calls Jewish customs "perverse and disgusting," deems the Jews "the most degraded of other races," regarding the rest of mankind "with all the hatred of enemies; they sit apart at meals, they sleep apart, and though, as a nation, they are singularly prone to lust, they abstain from intercourse with foreign women; among themselves nothing is unlawful"; for the translated text of this entire passage and commentary, see Stern, *ibid.*, 39–43; and on anti-Judaism in antiquity, see P. Schäfer, *Judeophobia: Attitudes Towards Jews in the Ancient World* (Cambridge, Mass., 1997).
13. AJ 1.4, 6.
14. AJ 20.252–257.
15. "Gessius [Florus] ostentatiously paraded his outrages upon the nation, and, as though he had been sent as hangman of condemned criminals, abstained from no form of robbery or violence. Was there a call for compassion, he was the most cruel of men, for shame, none more shameless than he. No man ever poured greater contempt on truth; none invented more crafty methods of crime. To make gain of individuals seemed beneath him: he stripped whole cities, ruined entire populations, and almost went the length of proclaiming throughout the country that all were at liberty to practice brigandage, on condition that he received his share

of the spoils. Certainly his avarice brought desolation upon all the cities, and caused many to desert their ancestral haunts and seek refuge in foreign provinces." (BJ 2.77–79).

16. BJ 2.283.

17. E.g., BJ 2.320, 325.

18. BJ 2.330, 406–410, 425–456.

19. BJ 2.352–354.

20. The following quotations are from Vita 17–27. On this passage see two new detailed commentaries: S. Mason, *Flavius Josephus: Translation and Commentary IX: Life of Josephus: Translation and Commentary* (Leiden, 2001), *ad loc.*; and D.R. Schwartz, *Hayei Yosef* (Jerusalem, 2008), *ad loc.*

21. BJ 2.457–498.

22. This is not to revive the good, old, and wrong theory of R. Laqueur that Josephus' autobiography represents in fact an earlier work than *The Jewish War*, with much later additions such as the introduction from which I have just quoted, and that those later additions together with the entire *Jewish Antiquities* signify a more nationalistic position which Josephus had realized by the 90s C.E.: R. Laqueur, *Der jüdischer Historiker Flavius Josephus* (Giessen, 1920).

23. Among the massive bibliography on this topic see S. Swain, *Hellenism and Empire: Language, Classicism, and Power in the Greek World, A.D. 50–250* (Oxford, 1996); T. Whitmarsh, *Greek Literature and the Roman Empire: The Politics of Imitation* (Oxford, 2001); and the essays in S. Goldhill, ed., *Being Greek under Rome: Cultural Identity, the Second Sophistic and the Development of Empire* (Cambridge and New York, 2001).

24. BJ 2.184–203, AJ 18.261–309.

25. *Duravit tamen patientia Iudaeis usque ad Gessium Florum procuratorem.* (Tac., Hist. 5.10.1.).

A *Man of Egypt* Becomes *A Man of God*: Examining the Relationship Between Moses and Yitro

Sandra E. Rapoport

$\mathcal{A}$fter the enormous drama of the plagues, the exodus, and the splitting of the Red Sea, after God has brought the mighty kingdom of Egypt to its knees and freed the Children of Israel, Yitro surprisingly returns to the biblical stage in chapter 18 of the Book of Exodus.[1] Moses had taken leave of him back in 4:18, after spending years with him in the desert of Midian. Why does Yitro leave Midian and travel to Moses in the shadow of Mt. Sinai? Aside from the obvious fact that Yitro performed a vital service to Moses and the fledgling nation by structuring their nascent judicial system, this simple question masks a deeper inquiry: What is the nature of the bond that existed between Moses and Yitro that compelled Yitro to seek him out again?

I suggest that because both Moses and Yitro possessed a questing and spiritual nature, as well as a preoccupation with social justice, when they met in Midian those many years ago each instantly became the other man's "vital other." Yitro became Moses' mentor, the man who enabled Moses to explore, in desert solitude, his questions of morality, faith, and communal responsibility.

Moses, in turn, was the embodiment for Yitro of the moral man of action, who was highly cultured and educated yet who empathized with – and championed – the weak.

First, through text and commentary, we will explore Moses' character and his three early heroic acts, all for the purpose of understanding Moses' state of crisis when he arrives in Midian. Then we will explore the circumstances that led Yitro to *his* spiritual crisis, and we will arrive at an understanding of the need that Moses and Yitro filled in one another. We will then see that God personally takes over Moses' "education," girds him, and sends him on the mission for which he was readying him all these years, leaving Yitro bereft in Midian. Finally, we will return where we started, to the foot of Mt. Sinai, and we will witness Moses' penultimate encounter with Yitro.

Let us focus, first, on Yitro's name. According to Rashi, Yitro had seven names.[2] The meaning of "Yitro," the name by which he is best known – and the title of his eponymous Torah portion – is his most significant name for our purposes. The root of this name is the Hebrew word *yeter*, meaning extra, superfluous, or unnecessary. I ask you to keep this definition in mind as we approach the encounter between Yitro and Moses at Mt. Sinai.

Other than the cryptic words *a man of the House of Levi* in Exodus 2:1, the Torah text has not yet named or described a father figure for Moses (it mentions Amram, Moses' biological father, for the first time four chapters later, in Exodus 6:20). It is *Midrash Rabba*[3] that identifies Amram early on. Nor does the text even hint at any fatherly or grandfatherly influence on Moses by the Pharaoh. It is again the midrash[4] that depicts a king who indulges his daughter's adopted son but who nevertheless harbors strong suspicions about Moses. The implication, then, is that from Moses' own standpoint, he is in essence fatherless, an orphan. The same midrashic source[5] places Moses' age at twenty years, so we must appreciate that these first twenty years of his life have passed in a psychological neverland, where Moses is neither openly Hebrew nor wholly Egyptian.

In sketching the figure of the adult Moses, the Torah tells us (in Exodus 2:11) only that *When Moses was grown, he went out to his brothers and he saw into their burdens.* For clues about Moses' character and the people or events that mark him, we must look to that phrase in the text. Rashi tells us[6] that Moses did not merely *see* the burdens of the Hebrew slaves, he directed his eyes *and his heart* and he *shared* their distress. Here, then, are the first indications of the adult Moses' extraordinary nature. The words *he went out* signal to us, according to Ibn Ezra[7], that Moses felt compelled to leave the opulent comforts of the palace by a moral imperative. When he came of age in Pharaoh's palace, Moses already was a young man with a conscience. In Ramban's words[8], Moses was an *ish da-at*, a man of intelligence and insight. As an adopted Hebrew, he could have shunned his abject origins and remained in the royal court, physically as well as spiritually. He did not choose this course. He *went out* among the slaves, not as a voyeur, but in order to *absorb* their experience. We also learn from the Hebrew phrase, *he saw into their burdens*, that Moses was highly empathic. He did not merely look *at* the slaves' burdens: he peered *into* them. The implication of the oddly constructed Hebrew word meaning "into their burdens" (Exodus 2:11) is that paradoxically, Moses truly felt the Hebrew slaves' pain, despite his royal upbringing.

This interpretation allows us to infer another of Moses' signature qualities. Counterintuitively, Moses' superior, princely education at court, and his cultivated, aristocratic bearing, rendered him supremely fit for his future role as leader of the Hebrews. His brethren were pitiable slaves of body and of mind. Perversely, they would have had no reverence for Moses had he been raised as one of them. His "royalty," his "otherness," lent him a measure of credibility.

Moses' character is further elucidated in three heroic acts, in which he came to the aid of helpless people in hopeless situations, where otherwise no aid would have been forthcoming. First, Moses saved a Hebrew from a mortal beating at the hands of an

Egyptian. The Torah text says, *He saw an Egyptian man striking a Hebrew man, one of his brethren* (Exodus 2:11). Note the Hebrew verb *he saw – vayar –* once again preceding Moses' action. As we learned from Rashi, this verb, as it is applied here to Moses, indicates that Moses is seeing and absorbing the predicament of these oppressed people. In the process of interceding, however, Moses himself slew the Egyptian aggressor and buried the body. The Torah says, *And he looked this way and that, and he saw there was no one about, and he struck the Egyptian, and he secreted his body in the sand* (Exodus 2:12). He looked all about him before taking action. Again the text uses the verb *vayar*. An inquiring student of the text might ask: what was Moses looking for? Rather than interpreting his behavior as simply furtive, Ramban[9] takes a psychological approach and explains that since Moses had already been informed that he was really himself a Hebrew, he felt a compulsion to be among them, and *viewing* their suffering firsthand, he became overwrought and could not abide the Egyptians' cruelty. In this state of mind he killed the Egyptian aggressor.

The Netziv, in his *Ha-amek Davar,*[10] suggests that Moses looked this way and that and, seeing that in the slave camp there was certainly no Egyptian to whom he could appeal for justice against the abusive taskmaster, he took the law into his own hands. Nehama Leibowitz offers the interpretation that Moses had thought that surely one of the Hebrew bystanders would come to the aid of his brother as he was being beaten. But when Moses saw "there was no real man among them and that no one took an interest in his brother's misfortune",[11] he himself took action. The Netziv suggests that Moses' act here may well have been the model upon which Hillel the Sage based his precept, *In a place where there are no leaders, strive to be a leader – an ish.*[12] The Torah's phrase is that Moses looked about him and he could find no *ish.* He therefore stepped out of his detached, princely persona and *himself* behaved in the manner of an *ish.*

The next day Moses performed his second heroic act, this time interceding between two Hebrews. This time, however, Moses *speaks* to the aggressor, inquiring, *Why do you strike your brother?* (Exodus 2:13). The Torah is allowing us to see *the process* of Moses' moral inquiry. His first act was to save a Hebrew from an Egyptian; his second act is to save a Hebrew from another Hebrew. His first reaction was to use deadly physical force; the second time he speaks to the aggressor. Still, the Hebrew aggressor's response is chilling in its arrogant villainy. He turns on Moses saying, *Who appointed you as ruler and judge over us?* (Exodus 2:14) Although this angry comment is dramatically ironic for us as students of the text – for we know that Moses *is* destined to become the "ruler and judge" in years to come – the Hebrew aggressor was telling Moses that as Moses himself had just the day before committed a murder, he could not now preach from a moral high ground.

This retort causes Moses to stop in his tracks. He is terrified now, correctly deducing that his heroic action of the previous day had been carried as a tale not only among the Hebrews, whom he had regarded as his brothers and potential allies, but also, doubtless, to the palace. Moses instantly appreciated that he had become an anomie, an alien, a person who belonged in neither camp. He was rejected and betrayed by the Hebrews who bore him, and now he would be hunted down as a traitor by the Egyptians who raised him. This combination of mortal fear, deep agony over having witnessed acts of barbaric subjugation of an enslaved people, feelings of paralyzed helplessness to ease their burdens in any meaningful way, and an awareness of his own alien state precipitates Moses' existential crisis and causes his headlong flight into the desert.

A *midrashic heshbon*, or calculation, proposed in the Sifre,[13] divides Moses' life into thirds. The first third was spent in Egypt, the second third in Midian, the third segment in the *Midbar*, the wilderness. The Hebrew initial *mem* that begins the words *Mizrayim*, Midian, and *Midbar* has a numerical value of forty, and so we are taught that Moses lived approximately forty years in each locale, or at least that the man that Moses became was significantly influenced by his years in each place. The commentaries differ about precisely how old Moses was when he fled Egypt. Was he a teenager, was he twenty years old, or was he forty?[14] Yet if one accepts the intellectual thrust of the Sifre, we begin to appreciate that a prolonged period of time elapsed between Moses' flight from Egypt and his arrival in Midian. It could well have been twenty years or more, if we assume that Moses was even younger than twenty years old when he slew the Egyptian, and that he spent forty years with Yitro in Midian, returning to Egypt when he was eighty, as the Torah expressly states in Exodus 7:7.

The Torah goes on to narrate, all in the single verse 2:15 of Exodus: *The Pharaoh heard of this thing, and he sought to kill Moses; so Moses fled from before Pharaoh, and he settled in the Land of Midian, and he sat by the well.* Years have gone by, but the Torah ignores the passage of time and places us, in a balletic leap, alongside Moses at the well in Midian. We are poised to witness a "well scene," and in the vernacular of biblical analysis, we recognize "the well" as a typology. Important, life-changing events happen to the Bible's main characters at the well. Not only that, but we are about to witness a repetition of a special subset of the well scene: the fugitive-in-exile-at-the-well motif.

One canon of biblical exegesis holds that whenever the Torah repeats a familiar scene, it is fitting for us to analyze the *dissimi-larities* between the scenes in order to best understand its import. The most resonant biblical well scene took place in Genesis 29:1–13, at the well in Padan Aram, after Jacob has fled his father's house following his brother's enraged death threat. There, we recall, two dramas unfolded. First, Jacob heroically and single-handedly rolled the heavy wellstone from the mouth of the well and watered Lavan's flocks in full view of the neighborhood shepherds. Simultaneously, he gave up his heart to Rachel, who had come to the well to water her father's sheep.

Here, in Exodus 2:17, Moses' third heroic act is wholly in character with the preceding two. He again acts as a savior, this time to the seven daughters of the Priest of Midian, who are harassed and chased away from the well by the local shepherds. After rescuing them, Moses waters their flocks. Searching for the *dis-similarity* between Moses' well scene and Jacob's, we discern that here there is no mention of a love interest for Moses. The Torah does not single out one of the daughters as an object of Moses' gaze. We, and he, encounter them as a group of seven. The only person singled out for mention in 2:16 is their father, the priest of Midian.

In fact, the Torah goes on to describe that their father is amazed that his daughters have returned home from the well so quickly, and without their savior. In Exodus 2:18–19 they tell their father that an Egyptian man – *ish Mizri* – has saved them. Their father's immediate response is, *So, where is he? He* desperately wants to meet this man who champions the helpless, even if his daughters seem indifferent to him. So disinterested were *the daughters* in Moses that they forgot the surely basic tenet of nomadic life, and, as Sforno tells us,[15] they neglected to offer the wandering stranger refreshment or hospitality before they left for home.

Understanding why Yitro, their father, is avidly interested in meeting Moses will frame our understanding of the two men's affinity for one another. Let us briefly explore who Yitro is. A legitimate point of departure is to inquire why a Priest of Midian's daughters are in fear of daily harassment at the hands of thuggish local shepherds. We noted that *all seven* daughters must go to the well to water their father's flocks. Are Yitro's daughters following the principle of safety in numbers? It would seem so. *Midrash Rabba*[16] tells us that their father is a very unpopular man, since he has lately renounced idolatry and the cause of his priesthood. As a result, the Midianite priestly class issued a ban against associating with Yitro, so that he and his family were fair game for the bullies. According to Ramban,[17] Yitro's daughters hurried to the well that morning to complete the watering task, in hope of avoiding the dreaded daily encounter with the hostile shepherds. In fact, relates Ramban, as Moses had been sitting by the well, he witnessed that the women had arrived first, drawn the water for their flock, and were thereafter chased away by the shepherds.

This injustice is what roused Moses to intercede on the women's behalf; the water rightly belonged *to them*.

Midrash Rabba[18] is explicit in describing Yitro's spiritual provenance. We learn from the midrash and from the Talmud[19] that Yitro had been a respected high priest *in Egypt* years before and had actually been one of Pharaoh's court advisors. Yitro fled the Egyptian court when his own serious doubts about the idolatry he preached rose to crisis pitch and overwhelmed him. It was when the Pharaoh decreed that all the Jewish male babies should be killed that Yitro rebelled against the edict, refused to sanction it, and then fled Egypt for his life. The Talmud teaches us that Yitro's moral behavior of distancing himself from the immoral edict of a despot, especially in the face of certain and violent recrimination, merited that Yitro's descendants would sit in moral judgment on the high court, the Sanhedrin.

Whether or not Yitro actually sat as an advisor in Pharaoh's court before he became Priest of Midian, we can appreciate what the Talmud is trying to do. The rabbis are drawing an explicit temporal and moral link between Yitro and Moses. Both men had been in trusted positions close to Egypt's center of power; each had rebelled at the Pharaoh's inhumanity; both took the courageous step of rebelling, and thereafter of fleeing the evil. The Talmud wants us to understand that there is already more than a kernel of connection between the two men. It needs only proximity to sprout and flourish into a deeper relationship.

After Yitro's flight from Egypt, he spent years systematically investigating the various known religions, and by the time Moses appears at the well and rescues his daughters, Yitro already has also rejected the Midianites' cult and, as we have seen, is now considered a pariah. Furthermore, Yitro's excommunication by the Midianites extended to his family. Not only would no one agree to work for him as a shepherd, but no man would agree to court or marry his daughters. Thus unprotected, according to the midrash,[20] Yitro's daughters were considered fair game for sexual predators.

So we can understand Yitro's fascination with his daughters' savior, especially if the man is *ish Mitzri*, an Egyptian. Yitro must have thought to himself that this must be an entirely different breed of Egyptian if he aided seven defenseless women. The Egypt that Yitro fled would never have nurtured such a champion. Yitro is likely burning with curiosity to speak with him, and hence his invitation to Moses to visit in Yitro's tent and share a meal.

The midrash[21] fills in one miraculous detail that helps explain Yitro's avid desire to meet Moses. Apparently, when Moses watered Yitro's sheep that day, the daughters observed that the water *rose up* to greet Moses' vessel. Nomadic lore surely would have allowed the long-ago event of Rebecca at the well to reach mythic proportions. There, in Genesis 24:16, the midrash recounted how Eliezer, Abraham's faithful servant, saw the water in the deep well rise up to greet Rebecca, easing her task of watering his caravan of camels. Here, Yitro's daughters, in their recounting to their father all that befell them at the well that morning, included this amazing similar occurrence with the *ish Mitzri*, the "Egyptian." This event reinforced for Yitro, a man of questing spirituality and perception, that the *ish Mitzri* could not be an ordinary wayfarer. Miracles did not occur unless their object was worthy. According to Rashi,[22] Yitro was by now half-convinced that the *ish Mitzri* was a descendant of this same Hebrew line, and he desired to meet this living paradox.

The stage is now set on both sides. We already know that the fugitive Moses is on the verge of a personal moral and theological breakthrough. He fled Pharaoh's palace in an emotional torment, and God's hand has led him to the tent of the Priest of Midian, who *also* has recently experienced a crisis of faith, sufficient to have him break with his past, as Moses has done.

We see that it is not *the daughters'* desire for a husband that lures Moses to Yitro's tent; it is the fallen priest's fascination with the Egyptian stranger who would champion his outcast daughters. Appalled at his daughters' social gaffe, Yitro instructs them to belatedly summon Moses to his tent. In Exodus 2:20, Yitro admonishes them: *How is it that you have left the man? Summon him, so that he will eat bread!* The Torah next tells us that Moses desired to dwell with Yitro: *And Moses consented to dwell with the man.* The text is unambiguous. *Yitro* was the attraction for Moses here. The fact that Yitro gave his daughter Zipporah to Moses as his wife appears almost beside the point. If anything, Yitro sought to cement Moses' stay in his tent in Midian by giving his daughter to him in marriage. Also, the text's reference to both Moses and Yitro interchangeably as *ha-ish – the man –* in verses 20 and 21 reinforces our understanding of the mutual affinity between the two men: the effectively fatherless Moses who is spiritually bereft, and the former idol-worshipper who is fascinated by the *ish Mitzri –* the Egyptian man – who champions the weak.

Further textual proof of Moses' emotional comfort in Yitro's tent is offered in the next verse, Exodus 2:22, when Moses names his newborn son *Gershom.* The Torah presents Moses' own rationale for selecting the baby's name. He tells us it is *because I was a stranger in a foreign land.* The Torah uses the past tense. Perhaps this statement also implies that Moses no longer felt like a stranger; that Moses named his firstborn son after the period in his life that was now over; that by stark contrast, in Yitro's presence Moses felt *at home.* This idea is certainly borne out by the fact that Moses stays in Yitro's Midianite wilderness for the next forty years.

Verse 23 presents us with our only qualitative description of Moses' and Yitro's intervening years together in Midian. We are told cryptically that *much time passes.* Rabbi Moshe Lichtenstein is fascinated by this undifferentiated time gap in the text, calling it a "disappearance of the main character – Moses – mid-narrative."[23] Yet he supports the notion that the textual *silence* is itself an eloquent part of the story. In a kind of reverse onomatopoeia, where the sound of the word suggests its sense, the Torah's silence here is meant to convey to us, and to reflect, Moses' withdrawal, his concealment, and *his* silence. We are meant to infer that Moses secluded himself in the desert around Midian. Silent reflection became the essence of his life there.

As readers and students of the Torah text, we respond to the Torah's technique and envision a spiritually starved Moses, at first perhaps engaged in daily discussion with his friend and father-in-law, Yitro. Later, no doubt sensing Moses' solipsistic leanings – his need to examine his soul in hermetic solitude – Yitro sends Moses out to shepherd his flocks. In Exodus 3:1 we are told that Moses leads Yitro's sheep *far into the wilderness.* Yitro discerned that Moses' three heroic rescues had demonstrated to Moses that he could *not* find God in the corrupt and aggressive human society – whether in the enormity of Egypt or in the microcosm of Midian. Yitro thus provided Moses with the venue within which to seek out God: in the solitude of the distant wilderness beyond Midian. We should not assume that the Torah is *missing* a chapter in Moses' life by its silence about that time period. Rather, perhaps the Torah is telling it to us *in full,* if we would but heed the text. According to Sforno[24], Moses arrived alone at God's Mountain in the wilderness beyond Midian in order to meditate and to pray. The textual silence here reflects its main character's intentional solitude.

In Exodus 3 we see that after years in the desolation of the wilderness, Moses is moved to investigate the curious phenomenon of the burning bush on God's Mountain. Let us examine verse 2, which tells us, *And Moses saw, and behold the bush was burning fire, but the bush was not consumed.* We recognize the verb *he saw – vayar –* from its repeated use in the Torah text previously, when it signaled to us Moses' qualities of character. Perhaps it is doing so again. In the last verse in chapter 2 (v. 25) The Torah just told us, *And God saw the children of Israel, and God knew.* The verb *vayar* is echoing through the text, first with Moses, and now with God, so-to-speak, doing the "seeing." And once again, in verse 4, *God saw that Moses turned aside to see; and God called out to him from within the bush saying Moses! Moses! And he replied, Here I am!* Avivah Gottlieb Zornberg terms this important ability "to see," a "vulnerable empathy."[25] This unique quality of "seeing" others' suffering, of deep empathy, coupled with a firm belief in moral behavior, is precious to God.

Now it is evident to us that as Moses and God have converged here on *Har Ha-Elokim*, on God's Mountain, Moses and God have *the same vision.* The Torah is telling us, by its double use of the Hebrew verb "to see" in verse 4, that after all these years both God and Moses are "seeing" at the same time, in the same place! *God saw that Moses turned away to see....* This is no accident. It was God who aided Moses' flight to safety after his vigilante behavior plunged him into crisis; God who led Moses to Yitro's tent because Yitro was the perfect *"chavruta"* – study partner – for Moses at that time; God who prepared Moses for this very moment at the burning bush by granting him all those years of solitary introspection in Yitro's wilderness. Finally, Moses is ready, in God's view, to pronounce the word *Hineni! Here I am!* Moses had not been ready forty years earlier.

After Moses receives God's miraculous prophecy on God's Mountain – unbeknownst to Yitro – Moses is now propelled ahead of his friend, father-in-law, father-surrogate, and mentor. The Torah tells us in Exodus 4:18 that Moses returns from the wilderness to Yitro's tent and begs leave of him. He tells Yitro that he must return to Egypt in order to attend to his brethren's welfare; Yitro responds, *Lech l'shalom. Go to peace.* The Talmud[26] cites Yitro's parting words to Moses as a paradigm of the perfect way to take leave of a person. Yitro was, in effect, bestowing his blessing upon Moses when he said, *Lech l'shalom.* In a laconic, but nonetheless extremely touching farewell, Yitro is charging his friend and beloved son-in-law to "Go toward completeness." For the word *shalom,* meaning "peace," shares a root-word with *shlemut,* meaning "completeness;" and "completeness" is precisely what Moses has been seeking all these years. We learn from the Torah's terse eloquence that Yitro understood this fact. Though it is doubtless wrenching for Yitro to say it, he sends Moses off with the implicit blessing. Moses then goes, and he becomes great, and he succeeds in his mission.

We take special note of the Torah's use of the name *Yeter* in 4:18, when Moses begs his leave of Yitro. *And [Moses] returned to Yeter, his father-in-law.* Recall that the meaning of this name for Yitro means "extra," or "superfluous." The Torah may well be hinting to us that at the time Moses took his leave of his beloved father-in-law, Moses had moved beyond the lessons he could learn in Yitro's Midianite desert. His time with God on *Har Ha-Elokim*, God's Mountain, has transformed him from Yitro's protégé into God's servant; from an intriguing *ish Mitzri*, a man of Egypt, into *ish Ha-Elokim*, a man of God. Yitro is no longer vital to Moses' character development. He has been rendered extra, superfluous, *yeter*. It is time for Moses to go on God's mission and to leave Yitro behind.

We now jump forward in time, to Exodus 18, when Moses and the Children of Israel are standing at the base of Mt. Sinai. The first half of the chapter describes Yitro's surprise arrival at the Israelite camp. The text tells us in verses 1 and 2 that Yitro has heard all that God has done for Moses and *b'nai Yisrael*, presumably as an explanation for his arrival, unbidden, on Moses doorstep. Perhaps Yitro simply wanted to reunite his daughter and grandsons with their absent husband and father, or he wished to become part of *am Yisrael*. The commentaries suggest all these reasons.[27]

Could an additional reason be that Yitro desperately missed his son-in-law, his friend and protégé? Let us pay close attention to the text in Exodus 18:7: *And Moses went out to greet his father-in-law, and he prostrated himself before him, and he kissed him, and they each asked about the other's welfare, and they came into the tent.* Never dismissing Zipporah's place in Moses' present life, or that of his sons, we see what the Torah means us to see: that Moses' demonstrations of affection, honor, and fealty are paid only to Yitro. The commentaries note this fact. lbn Ezra[28] attributes Moses' behavior to his overt acknowledgement of Yitro's guiding wisdom. And Sforno[29] teaches us that despite Moses' high position as head of the Hebrew nation, nevertheless he publicly prostrated himself before Yitro as repayment of the great debt he owed Yitro for giving him refuge in his hour of extreme vulnerability, for mentoring him, and for affording him the time and solitude to seek God.

This desert meeting between Moses and Yitro can be seen, literarily, as a matching "bookend" to their first meeting in Exodus 3. The primary actors in both scenes are Moses and Yitro, with Zipporah an onlooker. The singular prop, so-to-speak, is the tent. At their first meeting, Yitro invited Moses into his tent; here, Moses invites Yitro into his. In the first scene, Yitro invited Moses to eat bread with him; here, Moses, Aaron, and the elders of Israel eat bread with Yitro. Both settings are, fittingly, in the vicinity of *Har Ha-Elokim*, God's Mountain. And both scenes are backdrops to Yitro's rendering vital assistance to Moses.

Here, Yitro's advice to Moses for configuring a system of judging the nation is offered for the express purpose of conserving Moses' energies. A primary piece of advice that Yitro gives to Moses in verse 22 is that every *large* matter should be referred to Moses to decide, and every *small* matter should be delegated to the chosen judges. Yet in verse 26, when Moses implements Yitro's advice, he alters it. The Torah says that Moses interpreted the advice so that he would adjudicate the *difficult* matters, not necessarily the *large* matters. We see from this change that Moses already is building upon Yitro's template. Intellectually, he has stepped beyond his mentor. Moses recognizes, in this one example given in the Torah text, that he should deal with matters that will be likely to have profound social implications, regardless of the size of the monetary amount at issue. Moses discerns that a matter could conceivably appear to be "small" while the principle at stake or its ramifications could be "difficult." Hence the Torah's word switch from *davar gadol*, a *large* matter, to *davar ka-sheh*, a *difficult* matter.

The Torah gives us one more clue to indicate that Moses has moved beyond his mentor. Note that the mention of Moses' second son's name in the text here, at the foot of Mt. Sinai (at Exodus

18:4), seems a bit out of place. The Torah says that *The name of the one [son] is Eliezer, because "the God of my father came to my aid, and saved me from the sword of Pharaoh."* The name "Eliezer" – meaning my God is my *ezer*, or helper – is stressed here, at this meeting of Moses and Yitro, perhaps as a hint to Yitro and to us that God has emerged as Moses' primary influence, replacing Yitro, Moses' surrogate father.

In verse 27, after Moses has implemented Yitro's judicial system, he sends his father-in-law back to his own land. Ibn Ezra says that Moses accorded Yitro much honor, even escorting him part of the way.[30] The crux of the matter for our inquiry is that Yitro has served his quite considerable function, and both he and Moses recognize that Yitro has no place beyond God's Mountain as Moses' mentor. Moses has outgrown Yitro. Yitro has rendered himself superfluous, unnecessary, *yeter*. Sforno suggests[31] that Yitro was feeling his age. He had performed his two gargantuan tasks on Moses' behalf and was not physically able to embark on a new adventure. Moreover, Moses did not need him anymore.

But while Yitro's name means "superfluous," it certainly does not mean "forgotten." We remember that the Torah has named one of its *parshiyot*, or weekly Torah readings, in Yitro's honor. Nor does *Yeter* mean "irrelevant." Actually, as a mentor Yitro remained critically important to Moses by saving him twice – first in Midian and again at the base of Mt. Sinai. But Moses had been transformed, during the forty years he spent in Yitro's tent and in the desert beyond Midian, from an *ish Mitzri*, a man of Egypt, into an *ish Ha-Elokim*, a man of God. Yitro's job was accomplished, and he knew this. Thus he heeded Moses' urging and returned home to Midian.

The implication, perhaps, is that we are, all of us, mentors – whether to our children, our students, our co-workers, or our friends. If we perform our functions well, we must sense when it is time for us to teach and when it is time for us to step away. Moses had found the God who champions the weak, and he now served Him by leading His people, teaching and judging them.

When Moses became *Ish Ha-Elokim*, a man of God, it was time for Yitro to go in peace, *Lech l'shalom*, which he did.

✥ NOTES

1. To be sure, we know that Yitro reappears briefly in Moses' life later on in the Bible, in Numbers (10:29–32). There, Moses pleads with his beloved father-in-law to stay with the Children of Israel as they travel to the land God has designated for them. Yitro declines to travel with the Israelites and elects to return to his own land. This article focuses on Moses' earlier, formative relationship with Yitro as it is discussed at length in the book of Exodus.

2. In his commentary on Exodus 18:1 Rashi lists the seven names to which Yitro ("Jethro") is referred in the Bible: Reuel, Jether, Jethro, Hobab, Heber, Keini, and Putiel.

3. *Midrash Rabba* 1.19 identifies Moses' father from the Torah's phrase *And there went a man of the house of Levi* (in Exodus 2:1): "It was taught: *Amram* was the leading man of his generation."

4. *Midrash Rabba* 1.26 describes Moses' early years in the palace of the Pharaoh:
   "Pharaoh's daughter used to kiss and hug him, loved him as if he were her own son, and would not allow him out of the royal palace. Because he was so handsome, everyone was eager to see him, and whoever saw him could not tear himself away from him. Pharaoh also used to kiss and hug him, and he [Moses] used to take the crown of Pharaoh and place it upon his own head, as he was destined to do when he became great…. The magicians of Egypt sat there and said: 'We are afraid of him who is taking off thy crown and placing it upon his own head, lest he be the one of whom we prophesy that he will take away the kingdom from thee.' Some of them counseled to slay him and others to burn him."

5. *Midrash Rabba* 1.27 defines the Torah's phrase *When Moses was grown up* (Exodus 2:11) to mean "Moses was twenty years old at the time; some say forty."

6. In his commentary on Exodus 2:11 Rashi explains the Torah's phrase *and he saw (into) their burdens* to mean Moses focused his eyes and his heart upon the Hebrews' burdens, and he was distressed over them.

7. R. Abraham Ibn Ezra, in his commentary on the Torah's phrase *He went out* (Exodus 2:11), explains that Moses had been dwelling in the palace of the king.

8. According to Ramban, the Torah's implication in the phrase *When Moses was grown up* (in Exodus 2:11) is that Moses grew to manhood not only physically, but also, perhaps more important – considering that he was to stand in the presence of kings – in maturity of mind.

9. Ramban, *loc.cit.*, explains that Moses went out to his brethren at this time because he had been told he was a Jew and he desired to see for himself their burdens, toils, and oppressions.

10. In the Netziv's commentary on the Torah's phrase *he looked this way and that* (Exodus 2:12), he explains that Moses was literally looking for someone to advise him about how to handle the situation he had just witnessed, where the Egyptian taskmaster had beaten the Hebrew slave for no reason.

11. Nehama Leibowitz, *New Studies in Shemot* (Jerusalem, 1981), Vol. I, p. 43.

12. *Avot (Ethics of the Fathers)* 2:6.

13. The commentary of the Sifre for Deuteronomy, at *Parshat Vezot Ha-Bracha* 34:7, explains the Torah's phrase *And Moses was a hundred and twenty years old (when he died)*: "He was one of four who died at the age of one hundred and twenty, and these were: Moses, Hillel the Elder, Rabban Johanan ben Zakkai, and R. Akiva. Moses was in Egypt for forty years and in Midian for forty years, and led Israel for forty years."

14. Ramban, *loc. cit.*, explains that while in his own opinion Moses was but a youth when he fled the murderous Pharaoh, meaning perhaps twelve years old, some even say he was eight, some say twenty, some say forty.

15. In his commentary to Exodus 2:20 R. Ovadia Sforno tells us that Yitro explained to his

returning daughters that because the stranger extended himself to perform an act of kindness to them at the well, they were remiss in not treating the man as one would treat a guest, that is, extending their kindly hospitality to him in return.

16. *Midrash Rabba* 1.32 describes Yitro's situation: "The fact is, say the Sages, that Jethro was at first a priest to idolatrous worship, but when he saw that there was no truth in it, he despised it and thought of repenting even before Moses came. He summoned his townsmen and said: 'Hitherto I ministered unto you, but now I have become old, choose another priest.' And he returned unto them all the insignia of his priesthood. Whereupon they excommunicated him, that no man be in his company or work for him or tend his flock; he asked the shepherds to look after his flock, but they refused, and he had to employ his daughters."

17. Ramban, *loc. cit.*, Exodus 2:16–1 9.

18. *Midrash Rabba, loc. cit.*

19. Babylonian Talmud, *Sotah* 11a. In describing the circumstances surrounding Pharaoh's infamous decree against the Jews (to drown all Jewish male babies at birth), the Talmud states that "As for Yitro, who fled to Midian in protest, his descendants merited to sit in the Chamber of Hewn Stone" as members of the Sanhedrin, the high court. The commentary explains that Yitro's future reward was measure-for-measure as recompense to him for having abdicated his position as an advisor to Pharaoh. In future years his own descendants, as members of the Sanhedrin, would function as advisors and counselors to Israel.

20. *Midrash Rabba, loc. cit.*, in explicating the Torah's phrase *But Moses stood up and saved them* (Exodus 2:17), tells us that "It does not say 'he delivered them' but 'he saved them.' Said R. Johanan in the name of R. Eleazar the son of R. Jose the Galilean: The shepherds came with the intention of violating them, therefore Moses saved them."

21. *Midrash Rabba* 1.32–33.

22. In his commentary on Exodus 2:20 Rashi states that Yitro recognized, from his daughters' recounting of the miracle of the water rising to greet Moses, that he was from the seed of Jacob.

23. R. Moshe Lichtenstein. *Yeshiva Har Etzion, Parshat Shemot.* [html//www.vbmHarEtzion]. Accessed 4/26/02.

24. Sforno states in his commentary to Exodus 3:1 that Moses "came alone [to the Mountain of God] to seclude himself and to pray."

25. Avivah Gottlieb Zornberg, *The Particulars of Rapture, Reflections on Exodus* (New York, 2001), p. 25.

26. Babylonian Talmud, *Moed Katan* 29a. In explaining the proper words to use when taking leave of a living person, the Talmud highlights Yitro's words to Moses in Exodus 4:18: "And R' Levi bar Chayata said: One who parts from a living person should not say to him Go *in* peace, but Go *to* peace…[as] when Yitro said to Moses, 'Go to peace,' [Moses] went and was successful."

27. See, e.g., *Midrash Rabba* 27.2, 27.6, 27.9; Sforno on Exodus 18:1; Ohr Ha-Chayim on Exodus 18:2, 18:6.

28. Ibn Ezra, in his commentary to the Torah's phrase *And Moses went out to greet his father-in-law* (Exodus 18:7), explicitly states that Moses was honoring not his wife and sons, but Yitro and his sage advice.

29. Sforno states in his commentary to Exodus 18:7 that although Moses was the leader of the Hebrew nation, nevertheless he publicly prostrated himself before Yitro in full view of the assemblage, to pay particular homage to the one who showed him kindness and understanding in his time of extreme trouble.

30. Ibn Ezra states that Moses escorted Yitro along part of his homeward journey in the same manner as Abraham, who walked alongside angels who visited him after his circumcision, when they took their leave of him.

31. Sforno, in his commentary to the phrase *And he returned to his own land* (Exodus 18:27).

Correcting the *Ba'al Koreh*: Punctilious Performance vs. Public Embarrassment

Moshe Rosenberg

⇢ INTRODUCTION

In 1947, Rishon LeTzion, Rabbi Ben Zion Meir Chai Uziel, the Sephardic Chief Rabbi of Israel, was approached with a sensitive query:

יורנו רבנו בענין העולה לתורה בשבת ברביעי ולא קרא את הטעמים בדקדוק, דהיינו ג' או ד' פעמים לא הבדיל בין פשטא לאזלא או בין זרקא לפשטא והנה זה שעלה אחריו בחמישי התחיל לחזור את רביעי מתחלתו באמרו שיש בזה דין נשתתק. ורק אחרי שהפצירו בו מחשובי הקהל חזר בו וקרא מתחילת חמישי, אבל בעגמת נפש ממש.

ולכן האם אין בזה ע"י החזרה משם בושה וכלימה לזה שקרא את רביעי, וייהרא לזה שעלה לחמישי ורצה לקרוא את רביעי מתחילתו? האם אין בזה הוראת הלכה שלא במקומה? אנו מחכים למעכ"ת שיפקח עינינו בהוראתו ויתן לנו לשתות לרויה מזרם מימיו הכבירים הטהורים.

Please teach us, our Master: Regarding a Torah reader who read the fourth aliya *on Shabbat, but did not read the trope accurately, that is, three or four times failing to distinguish*

135

between pashta *and* azla *or between* zarka *and* pashta. *Then the reader who followed him for the fifth* aliya, *began to reread the fourth* aliya, *saying that the previous reading was (unacceptable and) tantamount to the reader's having lost his voice. Only after important members of the congregation repeatedly insisted on it, did he relent and read from the beginning of the fifth* aliya, *but the incident involved tremendous anguish.*

Doesn't the second reader's attempt to repeat the fourth aliya *involve embarrassment and shame to the reader who read that* aliya, *as well as arrogance on the part of the second reader? Does it not involve passing judgment on a matter of law in an inappropriate context? We await His Torah Eminence to open our eyes with his decision, and allow us to drink our fill of the flow of his pure and powerful waters (of Torah).*[1]

No mitzvah of the Torah requires greater attention to detail and accuracy than the public reading of the Torah. Correct Hebrew pronunciation, memorization of vowels, placement of emphases and chanting of trope are all hurdles a *Ba'al Koreh* must overcome on the way to a competent Torah reading through which his listeners will discharge their obligation. If he is successful, his listeners will be uplifted and inspired, finding themselves back once more at Sinai receiving the Torah.

And yet no mitzvah of the Torah is so fraught with opportunities to publicly embarrass a fellow Jew. Every *shul* has its own horror stories of *ba'alei keriah* who finished their task with the bitter taste of public degradation in their mouths because of numerous corrections, necessary and unnecessary, whispered and shouted, by *gabbai* or *mitpallel*, which punctuated the *keriat haTorah*. Epithets, like "Captain Milra" or "The Gotcha Gang," have been lavished upon those irrepressible shul-goers who feel the need to call out corrections, not wanting to rely on the *rav* or *gabbaim*. An entire subgenre of humor has developed of how *ba'alei keriah*, infuriated by such corrections, have schemed to make the correctors look as foolish as those they purport to correct. Conversely, every *shul*-goer can recall when poor, even painful, readings were tolerated, and corrections not made, with the justification that the reader needed to be encouraged, not intimidated.

And the tension remains. Surely a congregation is entitled to expect an accurate and *halakhically* acceptable reading, but what of those times when the price to pay is the discomfiture of the reader? Surely a reader is entitled to dignity and respect, but what if the price is a flawed Torah reading; is that not a diminution of the dignity due to the congregation? Must a *ba'al koreh* be corrected at all? What errors warrant correction? Are there circumstances in which extra leniency can be applied, such as a bar mitzvah or easily bruised reader? This article will attempt to trace the development of the rules governing the correction of the *ba'al koreh* from Talmudic times to authorities of our own generation. It will focus on the view of the *Rama*, most prevalent in Ashkenazic circles, that only errors that change the meaning of the reading require correction. It will establish which errors must be corrected for those who follow the *Rama*, as well as which non-correctable errors, commonly unremarked upon, may be tightened up by those congregations with the ability to do so.

✥ RAMBAM VS. MANHIG

The primary dispute regarding the correcting of a *ba'al koreh* appears in the *Tur*.[2]

> כתב בעל המנהיג אם טעה הקורא או החזן המקרא אותו טוב שלא להגיה
> עליו על שגגותיו ברבים שלא להלבין פניו דאף על פי שטעה בה יצא ידי
> קריאה דאיתא במדרש שאם קרא לאהרן הרן יצא והרמב״ם ז״ל כתב קרא
> וטעה אפי׳ בדקדוק אות אחת מחזירין אותו עד שיקראנה בדקדוק:

The author of the Sefer HaManhig[3] *wrote: If the reader or the* hazan *erred, it is good not to correct him in public for his errors, in order not to embarrass him, for even though he erred, he has fulfilled the obligation of reading, for the Midrash says that one who reads "Aharon" as "Haron" has fulfilled his obligation. But Maimonides wrote: One who read and erred, even in a minor point (dikduk) of one letter, is sent back to repeat until he reads it with precision.*

What emerges appears[4] to be a dispute from one extreme to the other, with the *Rambam* requiring every minor error to be corrected, and the *Manhig* allowing them to be disregarded, at least when there is a possibility of embarrassment.[5] Let's take a closer look at both of these opinions.

ᨠ RAMBAM

The *Beit Yosef* suggests that the source of the *Rambam's* stringent view is a passage in the Jerusalem Talmud:[6]

טעה בין תיבה לתיבה מחזירין אותו אפילו טעה בין אם לואם

One who errs between words sent back, even between "im" and "v'im."

He suggests proofs for this position, including another passage in the *Yerushalmi*[7] which states that minor errors may be overlooked in the reading of the *Megilla*, implying that such a dispensation would not apply to Torah reading. This proof is considered conclusive by the *Gaon of Vilna*,[8] who rules in accordance with the *Rambam*. R. Yosef Karo records this as normative, first in his *Beit Yosef* commentary on the *Tur*, and then in the *Shulhan Arukh*.[9] A noted dissenting viewpoint, whose opinion continued to reverberate for centuries, is R. Yoel Sirkes, known as the *Bakh*, who writes[10] that, although the *Tur* seems to rule in favor of the *Rambam* by listing him last, nevertheless the common practice was in accordance with the *Manhig's* approach. R. Ovadia Yosef,[11] recording the practice among Sephardim who follow the rulings of R. Yosef Karo, prescribes the correction of all mistakes in words, though not those involving melody.

Even after a more moderate position was codified for

Ashkenazim by the *Rama*, as will be discussed below, there were still authorities who insisted on hewing to the *Rambam's* path. In a story related by his grandson, Rabbi Chaim Soloveitchik of Brisk is said to have ruled in accordance with the position of the *Rambam*.[12] Rav Yosef Dov HaLevi Soloveitchik related how once, as a youth, he was called to read a *Haftarah*. Flanking the sides of the *shulhan* were his grandfather and R. Simcha Zelig, the Dayan of Brisk. R. Chaim Soloveitchik warned his grandson not to make a mistake even in the trope-because they would correct him! In retelling the story, Rabbi Hershel Schachter provided his teacher's explanation: The *Yerushalmi* that formed the basis of the *Rambam's* position excuses minor errors in the reading of *Megillat Esther*, because the *Megilla* refers to itself as *iggeret*,[13] implying a less formal document. This leniency applies neither to the reading of Torah nor that of *Neviim*. Hence the most minor error, even in a *Haftarah*,[14] must be corrected.

❧ THE *MANHIG*

Before discussing the content of the *Manhig's* view, it must be noted that the citation to which the *Tur* refers does not appear in most of the editions of the *Sefer HaManhig* that are commonly available. The passage in question was restored to the text in the scholarly edition published by Mossad HaRav Kook, based upon a single ("New York") manuscript. This would seem to be the authentic reading, inasmuch as the view of the *Manhig* is referred to, in various ways, by the *Tur*, the *Terumat Hadeshen*, and the *Mahari Bruna*.[15] Moreover, similar views proliferate among *hokhmei Ashkenaz*, such as *Ra'aviah*, the *Agur*, the *Orhot Hayyim*, and the *Sefer Hasidim*, as we shall see.

In its simplest reading, the *Manhig's* position is that one need not correct errors even when they change the meaning of a word, because this might entail humiliation of the *ba'al koreh*. Rabbi Yehiel Mikhel Epstein, author of *Arukh Ha-Shulhan*, could not envision such far-ranging license, which flies in the face of the Jerusalem

Talmud cited above. Furthermore, he contested the *Manhig's* use of the midrash regarding the changing of *"aharon"* to *"haron,"* claiming that the language of the midrash refers only to a child or unlettered person in their private conduct, not a representative of the congregation.[16] These considerations led the *Arukh Ha-Shulhan* to argue that the *Manhig* only formulated his leniency with respect to mistakes in trope, but not those in words. The obvious difficulty with this resolution is that the Midrash is clearly referring to a mistake in a word – Aharon.[17] Likewise, neighboring midrashim in *Shir Hashirim Rabbah* deal with mistakes in words that change meaning, such as saying "v'ayavta," instead of "v'ahavta." Nevertheless, an examination of the complete citation from the Manhig supports the *Arukh Ha-Shulhan's* conclusion:

אם טעה הקורא בתורה או החזן המקרא אותו טוב לו שלא להגיה לו
על שגגותיו מלהלבין את פניו ברבים כי אע"פ שטעה יצא ידי קריאה,
דאמרי' במדרש מנין שאם קרא לאהרן הרן ולאברהם אברם שיצא ידי
חובתו שנא' ודגלו עלי אהבה פי' ושקר שלו במשלי קסם על שפתי מלך
במשפט לא ימעל פיו, בדינא לא לידגול פומיה, תלמ' חכמים המדגילין
זה לזה בהלכה, וכן פרש רבנו יעקב מ"כ פ' אין מעמידין בע"ז דיגלא
בחבריה ידע ואלו הן ראיותיו אך אם טעו ביתרון אות אחת או בחסרון או
שקרא לדלת ריש או לריש דלת בדבר שהוא כלפי מעלה שהוא כמחריב
את העולם אין עצה ואין תבונה לנגד יי', ויש עלינו להגיה לו בקול רם
עד שיחזור בו לקרות כהוגן וכדת.

*If the Torah reader or the hazan erred, it is good not to correct his mistakes (so as) not to embarrass him in public, for even though he erred, he has discharged his obligation to read. For we say in the Midrash, "From where (can we derive) that if he read 'Aharon' as 'Haran,' or 'Avraham' as 'Avram,' that he has discharged his obligation? As it says, 'And his banner ('diglo') is over me with love.'" This ('diglo') means 'his lie.' The verse in Proverbs (says) "A divine sentence is in the lips of the king; his mouth lies not in judgment," (and the targum renders the latter phrase:) "b'dina lo **lidgol** pumei." (And this is* *the same sense as the Talmudic phrase)* "scholars who lie (ha-**madgilim**) *to each other in* Halakha." *So Rabbi Jacob, may his rest be in honor, explained in the chapter* Ein Ma'amidin *of Tractate* Avoda Zara, *on the phrase* "digla b'havrei yada," *and these were his proofs.*

But if they erred with an extra or deficient letter, or read a (letter) dalet **as a (letter)** resh **or vice versa, in a matter which refers to the One above** (klapei ma'ala), **which is tantamount to destroying the world, then "There is no counsel or understanding before Hashem..." and we must upbraid him loudly, until he returns and reads it properly and according to law.**

In the latter part of his words, the *Manhig* makes clear that a mistake which is serious enough must be corrected. One could cavil over whether that means only those that are particularly blasphemous,[18] or any error that changes the meaning of a word, but the initial, all-encompassing license one would have expected based on the citation in the *Tur* undergoes limitation.

Even if the view of the *Manhig* is thus curtailed in scope, it must be observed that other authors of early *Ashkenaz* most certainly adopted the broader form of the leniency. The clearest such example is R. Yehuda Ha-Hasid in *Sefer Hasidim*:[19]

אם יפלא בעיניך על אותן המגמגמין בלשון וקורין לחי"ת ה"א ולשי"ן סמ"ך ולקו"ף טי"ת ולרי"ש דל"ית איך מתפללים או איך קוראים בתורה ואומרים דבר שבקדושה כשמגיעים לנפשנו חכתה לא נמצאו מחרפים ומגדפים אל תתמה על החפץ כי בוראינו אשר הוא בוחן לבות אינו שואל כי אם לב האדם אשר יהיה תמים עמו ואחרי שאינו יודע לדבר כענין מעלה עליו כאילו אומר יפה. וכן אותם הקוראים פסוקי דזמרה בקול רם ונעים זמר ואינם יודעים הפסוקים ואומרים בטעות תפילתם וזמירותם מתקבל כריח ניחוח. וגם הקב"ה שמח עליו שמחה גדולה ואומר כמה הוא מזמר לפני דעתו לפי זה נאמר (שה"ש ב' ד') ודגלו עלי אהבה מעילתו עלי אהבה. במשפט לא ימעל על פיו (משלי ט"ז י') מתרגמינן לא

ידגל פומיה. מעשה בכהן אחד שהיה פורש כפיו ואומר ישמדך והיה שם
חכם אחד והעבירו מלפני התיבה לפי שאינו יודע לחתוך האותיות אשר
בברכת כהנים והראוהו מן השמים לאותו חכם כי אם לא יחזרנו יענש
בדבר ע"כ.

*If you are surprised at how those who stutter in their speech,
and pronounce a het as a hey, a* shin *as a* samekh, *a kof as
a* tet *and a resh as a* dalet, *can pray (in public) or chant the
Torah and say* devarim she-bikedushah-*when they reach the
words* nafshenu hikta *(with a beginning* het, *meaning "our soul
awaits God," and say instead* nafshenu hikta, *with a beginning
hey, meaning "our soul strikes…") are they not blaspheming?
Do not be astonished at the matter. Our Creator, who sees
into every heart, requires only that ones heart be perfect with
Him, and when one cannot speak properly, considers it as if he
had. Likewise, those who recite the* pesukei de-zimrah *aloud,
with a melodic voice, but are unfamiliar with the verses and
err, have their prayers and melodies accepted like a offering
of pleasant aroma. Moreover, God rejoices greatly over such a
person, saying, "See how much he sings before me, according
to his understanding!" Concerning such a case the verse says
(Song of Songs 2:4)* Ve-diglo alay ahava - *(homiletically understood as:) his sin (*me'ilato*) against me is beloved, (as we find
the phrase in Prov. 16:10) "In judgment he sins not" translated
by the* Targum *as "lo* **yidgal** *pumei."*

*An incident occurred concerning a certain Kohen who used
to spread his hands in blessing, and say ("May God bless you
and) destroy you," (*yishmidekha, *rather than* yishmirekha-
"keep you.") A certain hakham *was there, and removed the
Kohen from the prayer stand because he did not know how
to pronounce the letters in the priestly blessing. From heaven
this* hakham *was told that if he did not restore the Kohen, he
would be punished.*

While not as emphatic as the *Sefer Hasidim*, other writers of the same period assume that the *Manhig's* position encompasses even errors which change the meaning of a word.

The *Ra'avia*,[20] after quoting the prohibition of appointing a *shaliah tzibur* who reverses letters, writes:

ובמדרש אגדה אמרינן מנין לקורא אהרן הרן שיצא תלמוד לומר ודגלו
עלי אהבה אפילו דגלים שבך עלי אהבה.

> The Midrash Aggada *states: From where do we derive that one who reads "Aharon" as "Haron" has discharged his obligation? Therefore the verse says: Ve-diglo alay ahava-even your degalim (lies? sins?) are beloved to me.*

The lack of qualification leaves open the possibility that the Midrash is to be applied even to gross errors.

The *Sefer Ha-Agur*[21] records:

איתא במדרש אע"פ שטעה הקורא בתורה בקריאתו יצא כמו קורא לאהרן
הרן.

> The Midrash records: Even if the Torah reader erred in his reading, he has discharged his obligation, such as one who reads "Aharon" as "Haron."

He balances this citation with the view of the *Rambam*, but leaves the permissive view in the most general terms, and clearly understands it to refer to a public discharging of ones obligation of *keriat ha-Torah*.

Interestingly, this view appears to have survived as far as the eighteenth century, in the writings of R. Jacob Lorberbaum of *Lissa*, author of the commentary *Derekh Ha-hayyi*m on the Siddur:

אמנם מי שאין חוזר אפי' במקום שהענין משתנה אין למחות בידו

However, if a reader does not repeat, even in a situation where the meaning is changed (by an error) one need not protest.[22]

The *Mishna Berura* cites the *Derekh Ha-Hayyim*, but disagrees with his position:

ובדה"ח הפריז על המדה ופסק דאפילו במקום שהענין משתנה מי שנוהג
להקל שלא להחזיר אין למחות בידו והביא זה מא"ר ולא מסתברא להקל
כ"כ בדבר שמעיקר הדין חוזר בכל גווני כמו שהוכיח הגר"א ודי לנו
להקל במה שהקיל הרמ"א:

The author of Derekh Ha-Hayyim *went too far and ruled that even in a situation where the meaning is changed, one need not protest the behavior of a reader who does not repeat, quoting this view from the* Eliyahu Rabba. *But it is not logical to be so lenient in a matter which one must, according to the letter of the law repeat in all cases, as the* Gaon *of Vilna has proven, and we must suffice in being lenient only as far as the* Rama *permits.*[23]

The Mishna Berura traces the Derekh Ha-Hayyim's view to the *Sefer Eliyahu Rabba*. The Eliyahu Rabba, in turn, attributed his stance to the Bach, who disagreed with the Beit Yosef-Rambam approach, and identified the prevailing practice as following the *Manhig*.[24] In dismissing this position, the *Mishna Berura* cites the *Gaon of Vilna*, who, as we have seen, supported the view of the *Rambam*. The *Mishna Berura* recommends following the ruling of the *Rama*, which represents the final step in the circumscribing of the permissive view of the *Manhig*, the *Sefer Hasidim*, the *Agur* and the *Ra'aviah*. Here are stages in that trend:

1. The *Orhot Hayyim*[25] limited the permissive approach to the

reading of the *Hazan beit ha-knesset*, since he did not make
a blessing, whereas the actual *oleh* would be corrected.

2. The *Terumat Ha-Deshen*,[26] in a responsum repeated verbatim by his student *Mahari Bruna*,[27] reported having seen
the leniency applied by his teachers only in cases of melody
and vocalization.

ואע"פ שכתב הרמב"ם שאם טעה הקורא בדקדוק אחד מחזירין אותו,
משמע קצת דאפילו בדיעבד לא יצא. הא כתב בטור א"ח דראבי"ה פליג
אהא, וכתב דאין להכלימו ולהחזירו על כך, מייתי ראייה ממדרש דאם
קרא לאהרן חרן יצא. ואותו מדרש מייתי נמי בהגה"ה באשירי בשם
מהרי"ח פרק במה אשה. משמע בפשיטות דבשעת הדחק קורין לכתחילה
בדרך זה, וכן ראיתי כמה פעמים לפני רבותי ושאר גדולים שטעו הקוראים
בדקדוקי טעמים, וגם בפת"ח וקמ"ץ סגו"ל וציר"י, אע"פ שגערו בו קצת,
מ"מ לא החזיר מהן.

*And although Maimonides wrote that we send back a reader
who errs even in a small detail, which might imply that even after the fact one has not fulfilled his obligation, nevertheless the
Tur in* Orah Hayyim *wrote that the Ra'aviya (sic[28]) disagrees
with that ruling, and wrote that one should not embarrass him
and send him back for this. He brings a proof from the Midrash
that if one called Aharon "Haron," he fulfills his obligation,
and the same Midrash is cited in the* Hagahot Asheiri *in the
name of* Mahariah, *in the chapter* Bameh Isha. *This implies
straightforwardly that in exigent circumstances we may read
this way in the first place. And I have seen a number of times
before my teachers and other great authorities that the readers erred in details of the trup, also (interchanging)* **patah** *and*
kamatz, *or* **segol** *and* **tzeireh**, *and even though they scolded
them a little, they did not send them back.*

The difference between *kamatz* and *patah*, *segol* and *tzereh*, would
likely imply minor errors, in which there is no change in the

meaning of a word. It is this nuance that is picked up by the *Rama*, who codifies the *Ashkenazic* position for future generations:[29]

ודוקא בשינוי שמשתנה ע"י זה הענין, אבל אם טעה בנגינת הטעם או
בניקוד, אין מחזירין אותו, אבל גוערין בו

...specifically a change through which the meaning is altered.
But if he erred in the melody or vocalization, we do not make
him repeat, but rather scold[30] him.

This, then, is the source of the oft-cited ruling that one only corrects the *ba'al koreh* for mistakes that change the meaning of the words. But reaching this point only raises new questions: What constitutes "a mistake that changes the meaning?" Does the *Rama* mean to say that no mistake involving melody or vowel need be corrected, even if it changes the meaning? What exactly is the difference between *machazirin oto* and *go'arin bo*? Answering these questions will occupy the next section of this paper.

❧ MISTAKEN CORRECTIONS

אֵת\אֶת

Certain corrections are commonly, but unnecessarily made, as the mispronunciations do not change the meaning of the word. For example, if a *ba'al koreh* reads *eit* instead of *et* (*tzeireh*, rather than *segol,*) or vice versa, he need not be corrected. The *tzeireh* form is used when the word has its own trope sign; the *segol* form is used when the word is connected through a *makaf* to one or more other words, under the same trope sign.

❧ PAUSAL FORM

Similarly, in the following cases, no correction is necessary when a *segol* and *kamatz* are interchanged:

דֶּלֶת   דָּלֶת

קֶבֶר   קָבֶר

יֶלֶד   יָלֶד

In these and similar cases, the *kamatz* replaces the *segol* at a pause in the verse, but the meaning is not changed.

❧ NON-SHABBAT READINGS

Before defining the paramaters of error, we must limit the expanse of readings in which correction plays a crucial role. Of course, when there is no consideration of *kavod ha-beriyot* or fear of confusing the *ba'al koreh*, one would correct everything, all the time, but in deciding what to correct in typical circumstances, it is important to know when the failure to correct would disqualify the reading. Here it is important to note that during the readings of Monday, Thursday and Shabbat *mincha*, unlike that of Shabbat morning, the failure to correct would not automatically disqualify the *keriya*. The basis for this exception is the difference between the obligation to read on Shabbat, as opposed to the other readings. Whereas on Shabbat, there is an obligation on the *tzibur* to have the entire *parsha* read, on Monday, Thursday and Shabbat *mincha*, the obligation is to call three *olim*, each to read a minimum of three *pesukim*, and to read, with rare exceptions, a minimum total of ten *pesukim*. If the minimum numbers are met, even if mistakes are subsequently made, the *halakha* is satisfied, and the whole *parsha* will be read correctly on Shabbat. This leads to the following leniencies:

1. If a *ba'al koreh* omits a word or a verse, but his omission is only discovered after three *olim* have read ten *pesukim*, as well as the concluding blessing, he need not repeat.
2. If a *ba'al koreh* makes a mistake that changes the meaning of a word (and certainly if the error is in the vowels or melody),

once three *olim* have read ten *pesukim*, he may not need to repeat.[31]

⌘ DETERMINING ERRORS

On a Shabbat morning, in accordance with the ruling of the *Rama*, errors which change the meaning of a word must be corrected. At first glance, it might appear that determining which errors fall into the correctable category would be a simple matter, able to be performed by any reasonably intelligent and literate listener. On closer examination, it becomes clear that at least three factors have to be taken into account in the split seconds one has to make the decision whether or not to correct a ba'al koreh:

(1) Objective considerations of language, grammar, trope, etc.
(2) The assumptions of the listeners.
(3) The reading style of this particular *ba'al koreh.*

In the course of analyzing particular types of errors, the interplay between these factors will become clear. In general, the first factor serves to identify an ostensible error, while the latter two sometimes mitigate the identification, and eliminate the need to correct.

⌘ OMITTING/ADDING WORDS OR LETTERS

A *ba'al koreh* who omits a word or a letter, even if the meaning is not thereby affected, must return and read the verse correctly.[32] The addition of a letter that doesn't change the meaning need not be corrected.[33] The addition of a word that doesn't change the meaning is discussed on a case by case basis by *poskim.*[34]

⌘ VOCALIZATION

From the language of the *Rama*, cited above ("…but if he erred in the vocalization or melody we do not send him back"), one might have concluded that errors in *nikkud* or *ta'amei ha-mikra* are not correctable. This, however, is not the understanding of the *Mishna*

Berura and other *poskim* within the *Rama*; rather, the *Rama* meant that usually such mistakes do not change the meaning, and, if so, would not have to be corrected. If they do change the meaning, correction is required. Here are some examples, ranging from the obvious to the subtle and often overlooked. When relevant, the stressed syllable is in bold font – sometimes both *nikkud* and accent are at issue in a given example.

Meaning	Should have read	Meaning	Word read
he went out	וַיֵּצֵא	he shall go out	וְיֵצֵא
milk of	חֲלֵב	fat (of)	חֵלֶב
I have sinned	חָטָאתִי	my sin	חַטָּאתִי
they feared	וַיִּירְאוּ	they saw	וַיִּרְאוּ
it shall be done (binyan nifal)	יֵעָשֶׂה	he shall do (binyan pa'al)	יַעֲשֶׂה

The first example in the table above demonstrates a most common error: When the letter *vav* with the vowel *patah* is the prefix for a verb, it is called the *vav ha-hipukh*, and serves to reverse the tense from future to past. *Vayetzeh* – he went out; *v'yatza* – he will/should go out. Sometimes the *vav* with a *sheva* can reverse the tense from past to future – e.g. *asa* (he did) becoming *v'asa* (he will do). This example shows one way the nikkud of the vav can change the tense.

The third example shows how easy it is for incorrect vocalization to convert a word from a verb into a noun or vice versa. It should be noted that for a *ba'al koreh* reading with *havara sefaradit*, the only difference between the two forms would be in the placement of the accent.

❧ MAPIK HEH

One common error in vocalization which can change the meaning of a word is the omission or addition of a *mapik heh*. The *dagesh* in the concluding *heh* of a word can demonstrate possession, and thus

her husband	אישה	woman	אשה

Rabbi Avraham David Wahrman rules that the failure to pronounce the *mapik* is not cause for repeating. His reasoning is that there is at least one verse in which the Torah itself does not insist on the *mapik* – in Bamidbar 32:22, the word *"la"* appears without a *mapik*, even though the rules of grammar would dictate the need for one. If the Torah is not insistent on the *mapik*, the *ba'al koreh* who omits it elsewhere cannot be held fully accountable.[35]

However, R. Mordechai Carlebach[36] suggests three categories of *mapik heh*: 1) Where it is clear that there is no change in meaning, because no alternative word exists with a different meaning. *"La"* would be an example of this type – it is never found meaning anything else without a *mapik*, and so no correction is called for. 2) Where it is clear that the meaning is changed by the addition or deletion of a *mapik*. *"v'hishka(h)"* (*Bamidbar* 5:24, 27) would be an example – the meaning changes, and it bears correcting, and finally, 3) Where it is unclear whether the change implies a different meaning. His example is *"ba,"* ending with a *mapik* – perhaps the absence of the *mapik* would make it possible to be confused for *"ba"* ending with *alef*, meaning "come" or "came." He leaves this as a doubt.

A final consideration which may be relevant is the particular style of the *ba'al koreh*. Below we will cite the view of Rabbi Mordechai Willig, that a *ba'al koreh* who never distinguishes between *sheva na/nah* or *kamatz gadol/katan* would not be corrected on those errors. It may well be that a *ba'al koreh* who is sadly oblivious to the existence of *mapik hehs* would be in the same category. Thus one would be advised to correct a mistake in the placement or omission of a *mapik heh* in cases where the meaning is changed, provided the *ba'al koreh* generally does correctly pronounce such words.

❧ ACCENTS

There are many cases in which misplacing the stress from one syllable to another can change the meaning. Some such examples are documented in *poskim*. Probably the most famous is the difference between

בראשית כט, ו	וְהִנֵּה רָחֵל בִּתּוֹ בָּאָה עִם־הַצֹּאן	And behold his daughter Rachel **is coming** with the sheep

and

בראשית כט, ט	וְרָחֵל ׀ בָּאָה עִם־הַצֹּאן	And Rachel had come

In this case, the difference between the *mil'el* (first syllable) and *milra* (later syllable) accentuation is a change in tense. The need to correct such an error is documented by the Arukh HaShulhan,[37] among others.

A similar potential error is found in *Megillat Esther* (2:14):

אסתר ב, יד	בָּעֶרֶב ׀ הִיא בָאָה	In the evening, she would come

Here, too, shifting the accent to the first syllable would yield "she came." The *Arukh HaShulhan* rules that such an error be corrected.[38]

There are occasions when the misplacing of an accent not only changes the tense of a verb, but actually substitutes one totally different verb for another. Joshua R. Jacobson[39] points to one verse which incorporates two unrelated verbs that are identical, but for the stress.

מלכים א ח, מח	וְשָׁבוּ אֵלֶיךָ בְּכָל־לְבָבָם וּבְכָל־נַפְשָׁם בְּאֶרֶץ אֹיְבֵיהֶם אֲשֶׁר־שָׁבוּ אֹתָם	(But if, in the land of their captivity, they repent of their sinful ways) and **re-turn** to you with all their heart and with all their soul, in the land of their enemies who **led them away cap-tive...**

The first instance in the verse derives from the root *shin-vav-vet*=return, while the second comes from *shin-vet-heh*=take captive.

✎ v'*aHAvta* – v'*ahavTA*

Based on the principles developed in the last two sections, namely that either a vav misvowelized or a stress misplaced can change the meaning, it should follow that the combination of the two would certainly bear correction. Hence the following common error:

Meaning	Should have read	Meaning	Word Read
You should love	וְאָהַבְתָּ	And you loved	וְאָהַבְתָּ
You should draw	וּמָשַׁחְתָּ	And you drew	וּמָשַׁחְתָּ
You should be happy	וְשָׂמַחְתָּ	And you were happy	וְשָׂמַחְתָּ

In each of the above cases, the *vav ha-hipukh* is replaced by the *vav ha-hibur* (the conjunction *and*), the accent shifts from the last syllable to the penultimate one, and the result is a shift in tense and meaning. Surely, one should have to correct the *ba'al koreh* on the spot, and even send him back after the fact. Indeed, many grammar-focused writers have singled out this error.[40] It is certainly an error that one should correct if possible, and a standard towards which one should steer the the Torah reading in any *minyan*.

However, modern decisors have ruled that in a typical con-temporary minyan, *in which embarrassment of the* ba'al koreh *is a consideration, and sensitivity to the nuances of Biblical Hebrew is only average, it would not be necessary to correct this error.*

A clear statement of this counter-intuitive position is found in a letter of Rav Shlomo Zalman Auerbach.[41] Rabbi Menacham Jacobowitz had asked, "In words like '*ve-amarta*' or '*ve-yashavta*,' if they do not coincide with a *sof-passuk* or *etnahta*, and are not followed by a word that begins with an accented syllable, if they refer to the future, they must be pronounce *milra*, (otherwise they would refer to the past). However, most *ba'alei keriya* are not familiar with the grammatical rules, and do not distinguish. In these matters, should one not be insistent, since most people do not distinguish (just as Ashkenazim do not not distinguish between *ata*, with an *ayin* and *ata* with an *aleph*), or perhaps one should follow the grammatical experts and correct this imprecise reading?"

Rav Shlomo Zalman responded, "In *keriat Shema*, as well, people say '*ve-ahavta*,' and the like, and are not so punctilious, and yet they discharge their obligation even though this is the first verse of the *Shema*."

Among contemporary American *poskim* queried, this position is also taken today by Rabbi Hershel Schachter, Rabbi Mordechai Willig and Rabbi Dovid Cohen.[42]

The popular rationale for this position is predicated on the fact that how languages are pronounced and understood changes over time, and that an error is measured based on how the language is pronounced and understood at that time by its audience. Just as Ashkenazic Jews no longer insist on a distinction between the pronunciation of *aleph* and *ayin*, despite the Mishna's clear requirement of such a distinction, so, in an era when many, if not most listeners to *keriat ha-Torah* are not sensitive to the difference between *ve-aHAVta* and *ve-ahavTA*, we need not correct for the wrong pronunciation.[43]

Factoring audience expectation into the calculation for determining errors can be found explicitly in the commentary *Eshel*

Avraham to the *Shulhan Arukh*.[44] In considering whether it would be necessary to correct a *baʾal koreh* who read *le-ohvdam* (with a *holam*) rather than *le-ovdam* (with a *kamatz katan*), the *Eshel Avraham* writes, among other factors, that since the public does not generally distinguish between the two sounds, it is not necessary to correct.

✺ ADDITIONAL CHANGES IN MEANING

Having reached this stage, it should be clear that even finer distinctions exist which can change the meaning of a word, but would generally not bear correction. If *ve-ahavTA* need not be corrected, many of these gradations of error should follow a fortiori. We will list them nonetheless, because a few instances still would bear correction, and because it is important, as we shall soon discuss, to constantly perfect the level of *keriat ha-Torah* in our synagogues, and strive to reach the level at which we polish even the slightest imperfections without creating ill will.

✺ SHEVA NA VS. SHEVA NAH

A slight stress in pronunciation is placed on letters that bear a *sheva na*. On occasion, omitting that stress, or stressing a *sheva nah* can result in a change of meaning undetectable to most listeners. For example, in the phrase

וַיִּיקַץ יַעֲקֹב מִשְּׁנָתוֹ

the *shin* is to be pronounced with a *sheva na* – *mishenato*, and translated *from his sleep*.

Substituting a *sheva nah*, and pronouncing *mishnato*, would yield the translation *his learning*. Nevertheless, as we have said, this mistake would not bear correction in the typical *minyan*.[45]

✺ MISTAKES IN TROPE

Even misgrouping words by applying incorrect trope signs can change the meaning of a word or phrase. One clear example is the phrase *Arami oved avi*, found in *Devarim*. The trope signs on these words read *pashta*, (pause) *munah, zakef-katon*, and naturally lend themselves to the translation **An Aramean tried to destroy my father**. Such is the translation of *Rashi*, which is also adopted in the Pesah Hagaddah. Change the trope to *mahpah, pashta, zakef-katon*, however, and you have linked the first two words, and made possible the translation of the Ibn Ezra: *My father was a wandering Aramean*. See the chart below for a graphical rendition of this example.

אֲרַמִּי֙	An *Aramean* tried to destroy	אֲרַמִּ֤י אֹבֵד֙	A wandering Aramean
אֹבֵ֣ד אָבִ֔י	my father	אָבִ֔י	was my father

This is but the tip of the iceberg, when it comes to possible meanings changed by the misapplication of trope,[46] but again, most *minyanim* would not be required to correct such errors.

Rabbi Mordechai Willig suggested that trope errors which misplace pauses in such a way as to convey a different or opposite meaning should be corrected. If the Biblical brother-in-law of *Devarim* 25:8 is represented as saying, *lo! hafatzti l'kahta*, ("No, I do want to marry her,") rather than *lo hafatzti l'kahta* ("I do not want to marry her), then correction is in order. This may be the intent of the *Shulhan Atzei Shitim* quoted in the *Mishna Berura* (142:5), who refers to reversing a *mesharet* (connecting) and *mafsik* (separating) trope sign. Clearly most trope errors do not fall into this category.

⌘ MISAPPORTIONING THE PAUSES GENERATED BY TROPE

Prof. Aharon Dotan[47] goes even further, asserting that it is possible to change the meaning of a verse, by assigning too long a pause to one trope sign, relative to another. His example:

פְּקֻדֵיהֶם לְמַטֵּה רְאוּבֵן || שִׁשָּׁה וְאַרְבָּעִים אֶלֶף וַחֲמֵשׁ מֵאוֹת:
פְּקֻדֵיהֶם לְמַטֵּה רְאוּבֵן שִׁשָּׁה וְאַרְבָּעִים || אֶלֶף וַחֲמֵשׁ מֵאוֹת:

The first version correctly inserts the main pause after the *etnahta* trope, and therefore the number yielded is 46,500. The second version, on the other hand, incorrectly prolongs the pause on the *tevir* trope, and forces one to translate 46+1500=1546.

Dotan notes, "It is important to remember that there is not always a correspondence between the length of a trope sign and the degree to which it serves as a pause. The trope signs employing the highest notes and most intricate melodies – like *pazer, telisha-gedola, gershayim* – are among the briefest pauses, and *telisha ketana* is even a connective sign. One must pause the reading after the major pausive trope signs, even if the melody doesn't seem to require it."

Dotan himself admits that he has never seen a *ba'al koreh* sent back for such an error, and indeed, according to what we have said, it would not be necessary to send him back, but this, too, is an area to bear in mind when striving for the perfect *keriat ha-Torah*.

☙ ERRORS THAT CONTRADICT A *HALAKHIC* MIDRASHIC INTERPRETATION

There are times that an error, even in trope, can change meaning, not of the literal translation of a word, but of a rabbinic gloss or midrash based on it. An example takes us back to the dawn of the era of American *tikkunei keriya*. The Scharfstein *tikkun*, from which many *ba'alei keriya* trained in the mid twentieth century, was a valiant pioneering effort, but left some accuracy to be desired. For our purposes note its rendition of Bereishit 7:14, listing the winged creatures that were taken aboard the ark by Noah –

כָּל־צִפּוֹר כָּל־כָּנָף:

whereas the correct rendition, as found in more accurate texts, is

כֹּל צִפּוֹר כָּל־כָּנָף:

The seeming trifling difference is highlighted by Rashi, who maintains that the second version, which emphasizes and isolates the word *kol*, by giving it the entire *tipha*, implies that any winged creatures at all were included in the command, even insects. Of course, this would not require the correction of the *ba'al koreh*.

❧ SUMMARY

Thus far we have traced the question of when to correct Torah reading errors to a dispute between the *Rambam* and the *Sefer Ha-Manhig*, who base themselves on sources in the *Talmud Yerushalmi* and Midrash. We traced both views through history down to their most recent proponents, and examined the differing opinions of R. Yosef Karo (the *Mehaber*) and R. Moshe Isserles (*Rama*) in the *Shulhan Arukh*, the former adopting the strict approach, and the latter espousing a circumscribed version of the lenient approach. Finally, we expanded upon the view of the *Rama* that only errors which change a word's meaning bear correction. We showed how such errors can be caused not only by the omission or substitution of words, but also by incorrect vocalization or misplaced accents. We also showed that contemporay *poskim* do not, in the final analysis, require correction of the *v'aHAVta/v'ahavTA* error, nor of numerous other finer errors, although grammatically they do change the meaning, and should be discouraged.

❧ RAV UZIEL'S CONCLUSION

Armed with this information, we can now understand the answer Rav Ben Zion Hai Uziel gave to the question with which we opened this article. When asked if the *ba'al koreh* of the next *aliya* had acted properly when he re-read the previous *aliya* to correct the errors of his predecessor, who had "three or four times fail(ed) to distinguish between *pashta* and *azla* or *between zarka* and *pashta*," he replied that, inasmuch as these errors do not change the meaning of the text, they certainly did not need to be corrected, especially in light of the public discomfiture of the *ba'al koreh*. This ruling, it should be noted, would satisfy both the *Mehaber* and the *Rama*, since we are dealing only with trope errors. At the same time, Rav Uziel's implication is clear: If the meaning of the verse had been changed, one would have been obligated to correct the *baʾal koreh*, regardless of any embarrassment the correction would cause. The factor of *kavod ha-beriyot*, while sufficient to obviate the need for correction of minor errors, does not trump the actual fulfillment of the commandment. Thus the oft-heard claim that "*keriat ha-Torah* is only a rabbinic commandment, but public embarrassment is a Biblical prohibition," is not accepted in this context – apparently because the accurate rendition of the reading, through which listeners can discharge their obligation, should be the paramount concern of the *baʾal koreh*, as well, who should welcome necessary corrections toward that end.

This last point leads us to a final necessary element. If a *rav* of a *shul* is at the stage of deciding whether to opt for a kosher reading or the avoidance of public embarrassment, then the battle is already lost in that *shul*. The only effective way to regulate this very sensitive area of synagogue life is by making sure that it never becomes necessary to make that stark choice. By creating the proper culture of *keriat ha-Torah* in his synagogue, and adopting certain procedures to insure that both accuracy and dignity can co-exist, the *rav* can keep his congregation far from the precipice of such no-win scenarios. In another venue, I hope, God willing, to outline the parameters and implementation of such a culture.[48]

Maintaining a quality standard to *keriat ha-Torah* is a never-ending, often thankless, behind the scenes task. Like housework, its value is only realized in its absence. Unlike housework, it can never be allowed to lapse, because a case of public embarrassment may be only one *parsha* away, and one such situation in a congregation is one too many.

A well read *parsha* is a delight to hear and a pleasure to read. It pleases the mind and uplifts the soul. It is not incompatible with the ideal of training new readers, and need not lead to any compromise of *kavod ha-beriyot*. With the necessary education of all parties involved, and the proper system in place, the re-experience of the spectacle of Sinai is not a pipe dream, but a goal within reach of every *kehilla*.

דרכיה דרכי נעם וכל נתיבותיה שלום

✢ NOTES

For over a quarter century, my father, Rabbi Israel D. Rosenberg, z"l, was connected to Rabbi Haskel Lookstein, as he had been to Rabbi Joseph Lookstein, z"l, before him, through two of the most inseparable bonds known to Jewish life – those of ba'al tokeia *and* makri, *as well as* ba'al koreh *and* rav. *It is impossible to communicate to the outsider the ineffable unity that forms between the bearers of these responsibilities to G-d and congregation. Beyond becoming attuned to each other's habits and nuances, the partners form a mystical oneness whose unselfish substance is the perfect fulfillment of a mitzvah. These collaborations were perhaps the most sublime expression of the decades-long partnership of these two men in the service of the Jewish people.*

When I was privileged to read the Torah at kj, *I never fully appreciated the rarity of serving under a rav who himself was an accomplished* ba'al koreh, *knowledgeable not only in* halakha *and homiletics, but in* dikduk *and trope, as well. Rabbi Haskel seemed wistful that rabbinic duties kept him from the joy of laytning more frequently. He reveled in the first aliyot of Beshalah, my bar mitzvah parasha, which, he said, almost read themselves. He introduced me to the joke of the hapless* ba'al koreh *who was left with too much melody at the end of the words conluding the rishon of Mishpatim. Years later, when I encountered mistake-riddled readings presided over by oblivious rabbis, I came to better value the culture in which I was raised.*

And I came to realize that a major reason that I chose the rabbinate as a calling was because of the rabbis I was privileged to watch, listen to and learn from as a child. The same rabbi who drove me to the old 82nd Street Primary school building, spoke to me under my huppah, and has always been there in the years since, for support, advice, and example. This article is a small way of saying "Thank you."

I wish to express gratitude to Rabbi Hershel Schachter, Rabbi Mordechai Willig, Rabbi Dovid Cohen and Rabbi Zvi Harari for giving of their time and wisdom in discussing issues related to this paper, and to Dr. David Berger and Mr. Eric Freudenstein, z"l, for graciously reading an earlier version of it, and offering illuminating comments.

An expanded version of this article will appear in the Fall 2009 issue of The Journal of Halakha and Contemporary Society. *I am grateful to that publication for the permission to use the material in this forum, as well.*

This article is dedicated to the memory of my father, Rabbi Israel D. Rosenberg, הרב ישראל דוד צבי בה"ר יצחק מרדכי *who served as Ritual Director of Congregation Kehilath Jeshurun from 1954–1990, and taught* keriat ha-Torah *at Ramaz. He made the love of accurate Torah reading a part of my soul, even as he inspired generations of bar mitzvah boys, one at a time.*

1. Responsa Mishpetei Uziel Vol. 3, addenda, no. 8
2. Orah Hayyim 142.
3. R. Avraham b. Natan (ha-Yarchi) of Lunel (1155–1215).
4. But see below for what is more likely the precise view of the *Manhig*.
5. Here is a good place to note the obvious: Barring the potential for embarrassment, every *posek* would advocate correcting all errors, whether or not they change the meaning, be they in words, vowels or melody. It is only because such a practice is often impossible, and leads to embarrassment and strife, that leniency is suggested by some. Were a *ba'al koreh* to explicitly request to be corrected, officially forgiving any potential embarrassment in advance, the door would be open to correcting everything, in accordance with the view of the *Rambam*. More about this later.

6. *Megilla* 5:5.

7. Ibid 2:2.

8. *Biur HaGra*, O. C. 142.

9. O.H. 142:1.

10. *Tur* O.H. 141:2.

11. *Yalkut Yosef*, Laws of *Keriyat HaTorah*

12. See R. *Tzvi* (Hershel) Schachter, *Nefesh HaRav*, p139; *Masorah* (periodical of Orthodox Union), Vol. 6, p.25.

13. Esther 9:29.

14. This is not the prevalent attitude towards corrections in *Haftarot*.

15. A student of the Terumat ha-deshen, who reproduces his teacher's responsum verbatim, with a brief addendum, in his teshuvot, no. 90. This duplication was explained by Prof. Ephraim Kanarfogel, in a private communication, as follows: "The phenomenon that you describe is not uncommon, if not fully explained. There are number of such 'reproductions', both by R. Yisrael Bruna who was a student of Terumat ha-Deshen and by others of this period. (A number of *teshuvot* Maharil, for example, are also reproduced by various of his students or their students). Whether this was for preservation, for sharing the material with others or mostly in order to respond is not always clear. Indeed, as you may have noticed, #180 in Terumat ha-Deshen is reproduced verbatim in Mahari Bruna #89 with no addendum, the one (181/90) that you are working with ratifies the Terumat ha-Deshen and adds what Mahari Bruna did (without his mentioning his name), and the next set has two from the Terumat ha-Deshen (182-83) with a long discussion by Mahari Bruna (#91), in which he includes and 'signs' his name. And these are not the only cases, as I mentioned. Yedidya Dinari has a brief discussion of this phenomenon in his *Hakhmei Ashkenaz be-Shilhei Yemei ha-Benayim* but doesn't offer a full explanation, other than the possibilities that I mentioned above."

16. The *Arukh Ha-Shulhan's* objection might be sustained against the language of the Midrash in *Shir Hashirim Rabba*, but it is clear from the *Manhig's* language and his application, that he was working from a version of the Midrash more akin to the formulation found in *Tosafot* to *Avoda Zara* 22b s.v. *digla*, where the language clearly refers to the discharging of an obligation, and not the mistaken act of a child or boor: מנין לקורא בתורה שקרא לאהרן הרן שיוצא

17. See his way of solving this difficulty in 142:3.

18. I believe a case could be made that the reference to "destroying the world" and the example of interchanging the dalet and resh letters may be a reference to the error mentioned in the *Sefer Hasidim* below, in which a kohen said "*ve-yishmidekha*," rather than "*ve-yishmirekha*." This would leave the *Manhig's* position basically intact regarding all but the most egregious errors.

19. Cp. 18; p. 81 in *Margaliyot Ed.*

20. R. Eliezer ben R. Yoel Halevi, (1140–1220), Germany Cp. 53; Aptowitzer Ed. p. 31.

21. R. Yaakov Barukh b. Yehuda Landau, 15th Century, Germany; Cp. 191; p. 44 in Hirshler Ed.

22. Laws of *Keriyat Ha-Torah.*

23. *Biur Halakha* 142 s.v. *aval im ta'ah.*

24. Though it appears that this most permissive view faded into obscurity with the acceptance of the ruling of the *Rama*, I have come across two recent sources that make practical use of it.

    The *Steipler Gaon* (*Karyana D'Igrita* no. 139, cited above), rules that in a case of doubt as to whether an error changed the meaning of a word, if the *ba'al koreh* has read on several verses, one can depend upon the opinion of the Bach not to send him back.

    In a discussion in the listserv MailJewish, (http://www.importersparadise.com/mj_ht_arch/v22/mj_v22i72.html#cwz), the question was raised whether to complete a verse which had contained the name of God, once an error was made, or whether one should leave the verse incomplete, and immediately go back to reread. One contributor cited Rabbi Hillel David as saying that once an error was made, the verse is no longer a valid verse, and therefore no purpose would be served by "completing" an invalid verse. Mordechai Pearlman countered with the opinion of his Rav (unnamed) that the view of the Bach that the correction need not be made is enough to render the verse a valid verse despite the error, and make it worthwhile to complete it before going back to reread.

25. R. Aharon ben R. Jacob ha-Cohen of Narbonne, (13th-14th century), France; laws of *keriyat ha-Torah* sec. 18.

26. Rabbi Israel ben Petachyah Isserlein, (1390–1460), Germany; *Pesakim u'khtavim*, no. 181

27. R. Yisrael ben R. Chaim, (ca. 1400–1480), Germany; no.90.

28. This is, of course, the *Manhig's* opinion, as cited in the *Tur*. The misattribution is seen by Aptowitzer in his glosses to the *Ra'aviya* (p. 31) as the source for the mistaken assumption of the Peri Megadim that the *Ra'aviyah* authored the *Sefer Ha-Manhig*.

29. *Orah Hayyim* 142:1

30. My friend and colleague Rabbi Jeremy Wieder, in a *shiur* to *gabbaim* sponsored by the Orthodox Union, and available at OU.org, maintained that the term *"go'arin,"* (scold), actually means that one must correct the reader. *"Ein mahazirin"* simply means that, if the *ba'al koreh* went on, we need not send him back, if the meaning was not changed. According to this much stricter approach, any mistake, even if it does not change the meaning of the word, must be corrected, or one does not discharge one's obligation. This is not the approach that I am presenting in this paper. I understand *"go'arin"* to mean that, after the reading, the rav or other figure of authority must chastise the reader, and ensure that the error will not recur. *"Mahazirin"* means that a correction must be made on the spot, and, if necessary, the reader who has read on must be sent back. I have not found another authority who adopts R. Wieder's stricter reading, and have found my understanding confirmed explicitly in the *Eshel Avraham* and the *Teshuvah Afarkasta D'anya* II, *Orah Hayyim* no. 23. Furthermore, it is hard to explain the phrase *"go'arin bo ketzat,"* used by the *Terumat Ha-deshen* and others, if *go'arin* means to correct. How would one correct "a little"?

31. The *Biur Halakha* to *Orah Hayyim* 142, end of s.v. *mahazirin oto* expresses a doubt whether an error has the same status as an omitted verse, or is more severe.

32. *Biur Halakha* to *Orah Hayyim* 142:1 s.v. *aval im ta'ah*.

33. *Mishna Berura* 142:4

34. See Lerner, Yosef Yitzhak, *Shegiot Mi Yavin* (Otzar Ha-Poskim, Jerusalem, 5760), I:18 f.n.101. Rabbi Simcha Rabinowitz, in *Piskei Teshuvot* II (Jerusalem, 5762), 142:3 writes that in a case where an added letter or word does not change the meaning, it is not necessary to repeat. Both of the above works are treasure troves of information, and recommended for issues not covered in this article.

35. *Eshel Avraham to Orah Hayyim* 142 in discussing Vayikra 21:3. (The *Eshel Avraham* is the commentary on *Shulhan Arukh* by R. Avraham David b. Asher Anshel Wahrman, (1770–1840), Rav of Boczacz in Galicia, to be distinguished from the commentary of the same name penned by the *Peri Megadim*.)

36. *Havatzelet Ha-Sharon Al Ha-Torah* (Jerusalem, 5767 p.1022), to be distinguished from the Responsa of the same name. I am indebted to Rabbi Tzvi Harari of Yeshiva University for drawing my attention to this source.

37. *Orah Hayyim* 690:20 regarding Esther 2:14. Note that if the correction was not made, the *Arukh Ha-Shulhan* rules that one nevertheless fulfills one's obligation.

38. Unlike the first example, here the shift in tense would not be between present and past, but between the usage of the past to indicate a habitual activity ("She was wont to come"), and the simple past tense.

39. *Chanting of the Hebrew Bible*, Jewish Publication Society, 2002, p.21.

40. In an erudite article in the journal *Ohr Torah* (5748, p. 608), Nisan Sharoni collects an impressive group of sources to argue for the need to correct. Some of those sources deal with *tefilla*, as opposed to *keriyat ha-Torah*, and stress the need to pronounce our supplications properly if we hope for a positive Divine response. Some are general exhortations for careful pronunciation, without specifying whether or not correction would be required. Others, like Rav Yosef Shalom Eliashiv and Rav Yisrael Yaakov Fisher, work off of the example of *"ba'ah,"* a specific case already enshrined in *halakhic* literature, and which all authorities would

apparently correct. They are quoted as saying that an error like "*ba-ah*," which changes the meaning would require correction, but no examples nor written source is given. Sharoni cites a letter of the Steipler Gaon, R. Yaakov Yisroel Kanievsky (*Karyana De-igrita* no. 139, p. 155) as ruling strictly, but fails to quote the very telling context:

ובדבר ושמעתי כי חנון אני שקרא הנגינה מלעיל וכותב מעכ"ת שזהו שינוי המשמעות דכשהנגינה
מלרע משמעותו על העתיד וכשהנגינה מלעיל משמעותו לשעבר, בעניותי איני בקי בחכמת הדקדוק ולא
ידוע לי מי הוא הקדמון שאמר כלל זה. ואם כלל זה הוא מגדולי הפוסקים לכאו' הוא שינוי בהענין וכתב
במ"ב שם סק"ג דה"ה בשינוי בנגינת הטעמים כשהענין משתנה מחזירין אותו. אבל מ"מ צ"ע דמתוך
דברי הפרשה מוכח דקai על העתיד וצ"ע.

The Steipler both professed his lack of familiarity with the grammar involved, and entertained the possiblity that no correction would be needed because of clarity through the context of the verse. (The factor of clarity through context, also raised by the Eshel Avraham (with reference to *Devarim* 10:2 – *ve-ekhtov/va-ekhtov*), is clearly assumed by some *poskim*, but I have not found clear guidance as to the extent of its efficacy.) Once more it is important to stress, that of course, ideally all of these errors need to be extirpated, but the point of this article is to provide *Halakhic* guidance in typical situations, where one must curtail corrections to the minimum required.

41. Stepansky, Nahum, v'alehu Lo Yibol, Jerusalem, 5759, Vol. 1 p. 268.

42. A second possible explanation, offered by Rabbi Tzvi Harari, involves an extension of the reasoning mentioned above regarding the *mapik heh*. We find at least one verse in which the Torah itself seems to disregard the difference in vav and stress which we have been discussing. In *Devarim* 6:18, the word *u-VAta* is used, when we would have deemed *u-vaTA* to be more appropriate. Attempting to say "You shall come," which would normally require a *vav ha-hipukh* and the *milra* stress, the Torah uses a form which seems to incorporate the *vav ha-hibur* ("and") and the *mil'el* stress, which would normally mean "and you came." Therefore, the argument goes, if a *ba'al koreh* blurs the distinction elsewhere in the Torah, he need not repeat.

43. This explanation is alluded to in the question of Rabbi Jacobowitz, and was given, in similar ways by Rabbis Schachter, Willig, and Cohen. Rav Dovid Cohen actually used the *aleph - ayin* analogy. Rabbi Willig added one additonal factor to the mix – the style of the *ba'al koreh* himself. Even if we were normally to correct for a certain error beyond the vocalization, but the style of the *ba'al koreh* is such that it is clear that he never distinguishes in such cases, one would not correct. If, for example, a *ba'al koreh* switches a *sheva na* with a *sheva nah*, in such a way that would change the meaning, but this particular *ba'al koreh* is not at the level of proficiency where he usually distinguishes between the two types of *sheva*, we would not correct his error. The specific example adduced by Rabbi Willig is the word *shafta/shofta*, depending on whether the first *shin* has a *kamatz gadol* and means she judged, or a *kamatz katan*, and means judge! If a *ba'al koreh* never distinguishes between *kamatz gadol* and *kamatz katan*, it does not make sense to correct him.

As to why *poskim* insist on correcting *ba'ah*, but not *ve'ahavta*, Rabbi Mordechai Willig suggested that the former is found in both *mil'el* and *milra* forms in the Torah (see *Bereishit* 29:6 and 29:9 and *Rashi*), and one could be confused for the other, whereas it is exceedingly rare to find a *vav ha-hipukh* word which is pronounced *mil'el*.

44. R. Avraham David b. Asher Anshel Wahrman, (1770–1840), Rav of Boczacz in Galicia. *Orah Hayyim* 142. The extensive comments of the *Eshel Avraham* deserve a treatment of their own. Later sources draw heavily from his examples, which span the entire Torah reading cycle. Moreover, many of his entries read like a rabbi's log, inviting the reader to share the thought processes of a skilled rav and posek, as he struggles to make split second decisions, and revisits them later. In additon to his opinion scattered through these footnotes, it is worthwhile pointing out three of his more startling ideas: 1) If a rav corrects the *ba'al koreh*, and the congregation hears the correction, but the *ba'al koreh* reread with the same mistake, there is no need to send him back again, because the correct reading was made clear to the *tzibbur*. 2) A *ba'al koreh* may look in a *humash*, and then immediately read from the Torah,

even saying the words before he sees them, because of the rule of *tokh k'dei dibbur.* 3) A shift from future to past in a command of God may not require correction, because the will of God is considered as if it were already done.

45. An eyewitness reported to me seeing this exact error corrected twice in one week at morning *minyanim* at Yeshiva University. The correction is not normatively mandated. Rabbi Mordechai Willig suggested that this type of correction might depend upon the level of the *ba'al koreh,* and whether he normally distinguishes between *sheva na* and *sheva nah.*

46. For some contemporary literature that deals with the trope in its interpretive capacity see Breuer, R. Mordechai, *Ta'amei Ha-miqra be-khaf alef sefarim u-v'sifrei emet,* Mikhlala Publishing, 1982, pp. 368–90; Ahrend, Moshe, *Aleph Bet Be-ta'amei ha-miqra u-v'mashma'utam ha-parshanit* in his *Yesodot be-hora'at ha-miqra,* Bar Ilan University Press, 1987; Kogut, Simha, *Bein Te'amim le-parshanut,* Magnes Press, 5756.

47. *Inyanei hagiya be-tefilla u-ve-keriat ha-Torah,* Sefer Shavtiel, 5752, pp. 68-76.

48. See my forthcoming article in fall issue of *The Journal of Halacha and Contemporary Society.*

The *Halakha* According to B'nai B'rith

Jonathan D. Sarna

$\mathcal{A}$ccording to an oft-repeated tale, the Jewish fraternal organization B'nai B'rith, founded in New York City on October 13, 1843, was
established by recent German immigrants in response to antisemitism.[1] Hasia Diner's account reflects this dominant view:

> Twelve young Jewish men, all from Germany, got together
> informally on a regular basis on Sundays at Sinsheimer's
> saloon on New York's Essex Street. These young merchants
> with a few artisans among them had all been in the United
> States less than a decade and at Sinsheimer's found a place to
> relax and interact with their fellows. Four of them belonged
> either to the Masons or the Odd Fellows. In the 1840s, when
> those organizations began to systematically reject Jewish ap-
> plicants for membership, these young Jews decided to create
> a Jewish equivalent.[2]

Thanks to Cornelia Wilhelm's careful research, we now know
that this is a complete myth. First of all, the founders were *not* all
immigrants; Isaac Dittenhoefer, for example, was born in America. Second, they were not just starting off in life; instead, they
were "already successful, middle class self-employed men with

a bourgeois consciousness and standing."[3] Finally, and most important, antisemitism had almost nothing to do with the organization's founding. Most of the founders, in fact, were members in good standing of Masonic or Odd Fellows lodges, and those lodges did not change their policies toward Jews in the 1840s. Instead, individual Jews were turned down on other grounds, such as lack of personal morality and a dearth of genuine religious motivation. Some of them blamed religious prejudice for their misfortune, but those charges, at the time, were considered baseless.[4]

The complaints of the rejected fraternity members served, nevertheless, as the catalyst for establishing what was originally conceived to be "a society for the purpose of supporting its members in the event of illness and other untoward events."[5] Even Jewish members of the Masons and Odd Fellows sought the company of their fellow Jews during times of severe illness or when a death occurred. Those rejected by non-Jewish fraternities required Jewish companionship at such times all the more. Two decades earlier their needs would have been met by what was then New York's only synagogue, Shearith Israel, which assumed responsibility for the entire New York Jewish community. In the interim, however, the "synagogue-community" of early America had collapsed into a community of eight competing synagogues.[6] While many of the founders of B'nai B'rith belonged to Congregation Anshe Chesed, growing numbers of New York Jews were "indifferent"; they belonged to no synagogue whatsoever.[7] Already in 1841 a group of New York Jews who were unconnected with synagogues formed what they called the "New Israelite Sick-Benefit and Burial Society," supposedly the first "overtly secular Jewish philanthropy in the United States."[8] The new society, one suspects, looked to follow in its footsteps, forging links among Jews that reached beyond the synagogue's now delimited sphere.

Within weeks, however, the plan had broadened from the creation of a "society" – the equivalent, perhaps, of a traditional "hevra" with provisions for branches in other cities – into a full-fledged fraternal order. That idea had actually been percolating for several years, influenced by the example of the Masons and Odd Fellows, and in response to the growing fragmentation and factionalism in American Jewish life. Since synagogue disputes and an array of other religious differences now divided Jews from one another, the new goal, according to B'nai B'rith's longtime president and first historian, was to create a fresh basis for unity based on the fraternal and covenantal ties among Jews:

> A society which, based on the teachings of Judaism, should banish from its deliberations all doctrinal and dogmatic discussions and by the practice of moral and benevolent precepts bring about union and harmony, where before had existed strife and dissension. Such a society, eliminating geographical lines and bringing together upon a common platform German and Pole, Hungarian and Hollander, Englishman and Alsatian; extirpating the narrow prejudices and superstitions of sections and provinces; inculcating lessons of discipline and toleration; of mutual forbearance and respect, of brotherly love and harmony, could not fail, it was thought, of producing a complete and radical change in the manners, habits, thoughts and actions of its adherents.[9]

The new organization bore the German name Bundes Brüder and the euphonious Hebrew name B'nē B'rīth (as it was originally spelled). The German name stressed fraternity ("league of brothers") without a Jewish component, while the Hebrew name denoted connection to the covenant (*brith*) that linked Jews across time and space. Revealingly, it was the Jewish name that quickly became the dominant one. By 1851, when B'nai B'rith published a revised constitution, its German name had been discarded.[10]

Nevertheless, the secular universalism that underlay the original German name remained influential within some lodges of B'nai B'rith. Emanu-El Lodge in Baltimore, for example, defiantly admitted a non-Jew to membership in 1850, warning against "exclusivity." The Grand Lodge, however, firmly rejected the Baltimore lodge's decision. Acknowledging the universalistic hope that someday the "mission of Israel" would be fulfilled and all the nations of the earth would worship one God, the Grand Lodge ruled that, for now, "we must...abide [sic] our time." B'nai B'rith, it decreed, was open only to Jews. Emanu-El lodge, dissatisfied with that decision, disbanded just as B'nai B'rith's new constitution came into effect.[11]

By the time its 1851 constitution appeared, B'nai B'rith was benefiting from surging Jewish emigration, principally from Central Europe. The size of the American Jewish community had more than tripled over the previous decade, ballooning, according to some estimates, from 15,000 in 1840 to 50,000 in 1850. The Jewish population of New York City, at the same time, grew from about 7,000 to over 16,000. These numbers would increase at the same rate during the 1850s.[12]

"Many land on this shore, ignorant of the vernacular, without direction how to proceed, without home to settle down," the new constitution observed. "Thus they wander about, longing for the brotherhood, which is willing to help, to render assistance, and to counsel them how to make a living."[13] This was essentially the mission that B'nai B'rith took upon itself at that time. Its goal was not so much to create a "secular synagogue," as Deborah Dash Moore argued,[14] as to establish a secular *kehilla*, an organized lay-led Jewish community that would bind together religiously divided and geographically dispersed Jews into a single covenanted community:

Therefore this new covenant of peace; that its children should not only extend to each other the friendly brotherhand in all changes of life, where aid and assistance becomes necessary, when misfortune here and sufferings there make their appearance but where their strength may unite also to higher and usefull [sic] objects, to call into existence benevolent institutions, to found associations for instruction, art and knowledge, but more especially to cultivate and guard faithfully the common inheritance of Israel, the precepts of its covenant and to insure to it that public dignity and respect, which its possessors cherish for it....[15]

Communities operate under laws. This was true of the early synagogue communities in the United States, which all produced constitutions with extensive laws and bylaws as well as stipulated punishments for those who violated them.[16] It was even more true of the organized *kehillot* or *gemeinde* of the lands from which most nineteenth-century B'nai B'rith members emigrated. The American Freemasons, of course, also had an internal judicial system of their own.[17] So it comes as no surprise that B'nai Brith's constitution likewise set forth rules for "fines and trials." Indeed, this topic formed the longest single article in the whole entire constitution – 21 paragraphs long (see Appendix). According to the constitution, those who violated the order's rules, insulted fellow members, or engaged in "unbrotherly and immoral conduct" were liable to punishment and "entitled to a proper trial." Those found guilty at the local level could appeal to the District Grand Lodge and beyond that to the Constitution Grand Lodge, B'nai B'rith's highest tribunal.

Nobody, to my knowledge, has analyzed the cases brought before B'nai B'rith's tribunal. Thanks to a weighty tome entitled *Jurisprudence of the Independent Order of B'nai B'rith: A Compilation of Appeals and Questions Officially Submitted To, And Decided Upon, By The Constitution Grand Lodge, Court of Appeals, and the Respective District Grand Lodges of the Independent Order of B'nai B'rith Since the Institution of the Order. With Digest of Decisions and Manual...*(1879), edited by M[ayer] Ulman,[18] the secretary of B'nai B'rith's Seventh District Grand Lodge and a trained jurist, such analysis is possible – at least for the first two decades of cases that confronted the organization. Several of these cases, as we shall see, cast interesting light not just on issues internal to B'nai B'rith, but on the organization's attitude toward Jewish law, Jewish tradition, and questions of Jewish identity. They reveal that traditional *halakha* and the *halakha* according to B'nai B'rith did not easily mesh.

In 1871, for example, Joseph Lodge No. 73, in St. Louis, asked "whether a member who is a *Cohen* is compelled to sit up with the corpse of a deceased brother, or if he is exempt from such duty as a Cohen." The Grand Secretary replied that "If his Lodge requires him to sit up with a deceased brother, and he has conscientious scruples which makes it objectionable to him, he must in such case provide an acceptable substitute." Ulman's legal note on the case makes clear that Jewish laws governing descendants of priests (*kohanim*) – the biblical ban on their coming into contact with the dead – had no impact on the fraternity: "Laws are indiscriminate on all members; and no one can claim exemption upon the claim of religious scruples or usages."[19]

The same approach decided a more tragic case in 1875. According to B'nai B'rith's endowment law, a man without a living wife or child needed to make a sworn statement to his lodge concerning who should receive his $1,000 death benefit following his demise; otherwise, the money was retained by the lodge itself. In this case, the wife and sole heir of P.L. Bachman of New York City died childless. Bachman "being of an orthodox tendency… did not, while holding his week of mourning, consider it right to go to the Lodge room to make a formal declaration [of his new intended heir], but intended to do so immediately thereafter, but died while in the week of mourning, without having made such a declaration." The majority of the lodge members sought to pay the benefit to his heirs anyway, on the grounds that his failure to comply with the Endowment Law was an unavoidable consequence of *shiva*: "[B]eing an orthodox Israelite, he observed the week of mourning with punctiliousness in all its forms, did no work or writing of any description, and by a singular coincident his week of mourning and his life expired at the same moment." But the Court of Appeals by a vote of 4–2 disagreed, insisting that the rules of the Order must be carried out to the letter. "Laws cannot discriminate between orthodox and reformed," Ulman explained in his note on the case. "One law must be for all."[20]

In at least one case, however, a lodge that attempted to apply this principle in a manner favorable to Jewish tradition found itself reversed. District Grand Lodge #3 passed a regulation compelling all of its members to cover their heads during one portion of the lodge's ceremony. A visitor from another B'nai B'rith lodge refused to comply. Rather than insisting on "one law for all," the court permitted the visitor, acting presumably on the basis of his Reform Jewish principles, to keep his head bare. "A Lodge," it ruled, "cannot compel a brother to cover his head during any portion of the ceremonies." At the same time, it discouraged such separatist behavior. "A visiting brother," it warned, "exhibits a great want of courtesy and respect to the others by refusing to comply with a rule of the Lodge in which all the members unite."[21]

Where the "one law must be for all" principle was strictly enforced by B'nai B'rith, the "one law" generally meant the law of the land; it was loathe to impose any Jewish law on its members. In 1873, for example, Haggai Lodge dealt with the case of a member who had been divorced through a rabbinical *get* [bill of religious divorce] but had not gone to court to obtain a civil divorce. This was a not an infrequent occurrence among immigrant Jews of that time, since the countries from which they emigrated generally did not require civil divorce and they failed to understand why any was needed. When the member remarried and wanted to declare his new wife and children his heirs, however, the lodge demurred. "Can the Lodge accept this declaration and not come in controversy," it wondered, "since the brother is not divorced legally from his former wife?" The District Grand Lodge's decision left no room for compromise: "The Lodge has to recognize that wife who can prove herself the *legal wife*." The complexities of the case – the fact that Jewish law and American law recognized different "legal wives" – went unmentioned.[22]

The most wrenching cases that confronted B'nai B'rith during its first decades of existence entailed boundary controversies:

vexing questions concerning who could and could not be a member of the order, and what kinds of actions warranted a member's expulsion. Not surprisingly, moral turpitude always resulted in separation from the order. Such cases also remind us that the nineteenth-century Jewish family was hardly as strong and as wholesome as hagiographers would have us believe.[23] Jacob Solomon, for example, was charged in 1875 with "living in adultery," "immoral conduct," and "desertion of his family." The lodge suspended him indefinitely, and his appeal was turned down. "Adultery and desertion of family, if proven, is just cause for punishment," Ulman piously opined in his remarks on the case.[24]

For "ill-treating and whipping his brother's wife," Moritz Wolf was expelled from the order altogether. On appeal in 1869, he was granted a new trial, based on a flaw in the original proceedings, but the punishment was not questioned.[25] Nor did the order find itself sympathetic to A.S. Honnett of Pine Bluff, Arkansas, who was tried in 1876 for "seducing a maiden of our race," "employing medical skill to procure abortion," and after "being compelled to undergo marriage ceremony," deserting his new wife during her pregnancy, "leaving her destitute, and reviling and slandering her." Indeed, so shocked were some when the lodge declared Honnett "not guilty," despite overwhelming evidence to the contrary, that the "Grand Saar" (President) of B'nai B'rith "was instructed to prepare articles of impeachment" against the whole lodge.[26]

In one case, even nonpayment of a debt to a synagogue provided grounds for a member's expulsion:

> Myers, a member of Congregation Anshe Ameth, resigned without paying his dues. The resignation was accepted on condition that he was clear in the books. He refused to pay up and was sued. Meyers participated in all the deliberations of the Congregation, attended meetings, and paid up his dues whenever called, exept [sic] in the last instance, when he resigned *and* refused to pay.

The Congregation sued him, and on the trial before the circuit court of the county he pleaded that he was not a *member*, never having signed the Constitution. To this he made oath, and there is the evidence of three parties to the fact. On this technicality the judge ruled that although morally bound to pay the same, he was not so legally, not having signed the Constitution.

We hold that a man who is guilty of such a conduct in the manner charged before the Lodge, and proved by disinterested witnesses, is not a proper person to be a member of the Order and a Lodge. The Lodge on these facts suspended him indefinitely, and we therefore recommend that the action of the Lodge be sustained.[27]

The District Grand Lodge approved the lodge's actions. Its argument, Ulman explained, was that "fraudulent means employed to forego the payment of an honest debt makes a person unfit to be a member of a Lodge in the Order."[28] What makes the case particularly significant is that B'nai B'rith, in this instance, held to a higher standard than the American court. Even though under U.S. law the congregation proved unable to collect its debt, B'nai B'rith, perhaps influenced by ethical proscriptions requiring Jews to conduct business fairly and amicably with their fellow Jews, suspended the member indefinitely.

If Jewish religious laws and traditional values lurked in the background of that case, they failed to do so in the case of intermarriage. Here the rulings of the grand lodge were unambiguous: "The fact of an Israelite being married to a Gentile is no disqualification."[29] In one case, in 1872, Dan Lodge, having elected an individual to membership, did subsequently conclude that he was "unworthy of being a member or receiving the degrees of the Lodge, he having married a non-Jewess." Upon appeal, though, that decision was unanimously reversed. The District Grand Lodge insisted that "the fact of having married a non-Jewess does not disqualify an applicant in the Order of B'Nai B'Rith, and certainly does not constitute a man *unworthy* in a legal sense."[30] When four years later another lodge sought clarification of B'nai B'rith's policy, observing that in the past it had "refused admittance on this ground," it was informed that "the Court of Appeals...has decided that such a law [proscribing the intermarried] would be unconstitutional."[31]

Intermarriage between Jews and Christians became more common in the 1870s. By then, immigrants' American-born children had grown up, liberal Jews and Christians looked hopefully toward a "new era" of universal brotherhood, and ardent proffers of love were proving more powerful, in a romantic age, than the pious proscriptions of religion. Rabbinic leaders, including most Reform rabbis, decried the rising tide of intermarriages, but B'nai B'rith came to terms with them. It insisted that whom a man took for his wife was a private affair and not the business of the order.[32]

One might have imagined that the same policy would govern the Order's policy concerning circumcision, but that proved not to be the case. While intermarriage did not disqualify a man from being Jewish, lack of circumcision, in the view of many B'nai B'rith members, did. In their eyes, male circumcision marked the very covenant that the Order pledged to uphold. District Grand Lodge No. 3, as a result, announced a firm policy against admitting the uncircumcised. The language it employed in setting forth this standard makes clear that it understood its position to be unpopular in more universalistic B'nai B'rith circles:

A person who is not circumcised cannot become a member of the Order in this District. Our name implies that a member must be "a son of the Covenant" of Abraham. Our Order is still a Jewish Order, for the benefit of the Jewish people, and for the advancement of Jewish interests.[33]

Indeed, the decision aroused substantial debate. B'nai B'rith leader

Simon Wolf insisted that "any one declaring himself to be a Jew in faith, a believer in one God and all the accessories incident to Jewish religion, whether circumcised or not, is a fit and proper Candidate, and no lodge for that reason solely can exclude him." He also pointed to the awkwardness "of a personal physical examination" of potential members. Rabbi Bernhard Felsenthal, likewise a B'nai B'rith leader, noted that some influential rabbis were prepared to accept proselytes without circumcision and that, in any case, it was "not the province of B'nai B'rith as such to decide theological questions." In the end, though, the Order's Court of Appeals reached no decision on the matter and the District Grand Lodge's original action stood.[34]

In 1879 the question came up again in what was described as the most widely-discussed case ever to be decided by the Order's highest court. Genero Henrickson of Lincoln, Illinois, the uncircumcised son of a non-Jewish mother and a Jewish father who was a member of B'nai B'rith, applied to be initiated into the Order. The young man, according to the documents presented to the court, had "not been raised up in any faith, and until now has not made any profession to religion of any sort." Could he be admitted into an Order that defined its mission as "uniting Israelites in the work of promoting their highest interests and those of humanity"?[35]

Some sought to ban Henrickson unilaterally, since he had neither a Jewish mother nor evidence of conversion and circumcision. Others insisted that his application to join the order was itself "equivalent to a confession" of commitment to the Jewish people. The District Grand Lodge proposed a compromise, a two-step profession of faith:

> [I]f a candidate applies for membership in a Lodge, of whom it is doubtful or disputed whether he is a Jew or not, such candidate shall declare in writing:
>
> 1. That he confesses his belief in Judaism.

2. That he does not belong to any non-Jewish church or other non-Jewish religious organization.[36]

The resulting controversy, anticipating twentieth-century controversies concerning "who is a Jew" and patrilineal descent, divided leaders of B'nai B'rith, pitting conservatives against liberals, those who insisted that Judaism was a "race" against those who considered it a system of beliefs, and reopening questions concerning the order's attitude toward non-Jews. Documents in the case eventually occupied 72 closely printed pages of text. In addition to arguments based on B'nai B'rith's own precedents, the District Grand Lodge at one point solicited opinions from five different Reform rabbis connected with B'nai B'rith: Isaac M. Wise, Samuel Hirsch, Max Lilienthal, Bernhard Felsenthal, and Solomon Sonneschein. Revealingly, no Orthodox rabbis, such as Sabato Morais or Henry Pereira Mendes, were queried. Even so, the two questions – (1) "Is a candidate applying for admission into a lodge, whose one parent is an Israelite and whose other parent a Gentile, to be considered an Israelite?" and (2) "If not, should such a candidate undergo some initiatory rites, and which, in order to become an Israelite?"[37] – elicited a wide range of opinions. Then, as later, Reform rabbis varied in regard to their definition of who is a Jew (Isaac Mayer Wise asserted that, in his view, "any man declaring to be a Jew by conviction and faith is a Jew"[38]) and in regard to what rituals of conversion they deemed essential.[39]

B'nai B'rith leaders who weighed in on the question disagreed even more emphatically. Some feared too "exclusive" a definition of membership in the Order while others, more sympathetic to tradition, insisted that "either the Order is a Jewish organization or none at all."[40] Many warned the Order to avoid trespassing into theological territory. A few, hoping that the whole issue might just go away, argued that the Court of Appeals lacked jurisdiction in the case.

In the end, the Court threw out the District Grand Lodge's compromise and held unequivocally that "The Independent Order of B'nai B'rith is exclusively a Jewish Order and only Jews are

eligible as members." While it granted lodges the right "to determine that an applicant is an Israelite," it warned them of their
"duty to see that no stranger enters into our covenant." Implicitly, it
found "belief in Judaism" – the standard proposed in Henrickson's
case – to be insufficient. B'nai B'rith members, it ruled, had fully to
be Jews: "[N]either this Court nor any existing body in the Order
can declare that those are Jews who are doubted so to be."[41]

This decision carried far-reaching consequences for B'nai
B'rith, preserving its Jewish character. The case demonstrated that
any Jewish community, even one that was determined to be secular and all-embracing, needed to establish boundaries. However
dismissive B'nai B'rith may have been of *halakhic* practices concerning *kohanim*, *shiva*, head coverings, *gittin*, and even intermarriage, when it came to membership in the Jewish people it took a
much firmer line, identifying the order as a "Jewish Order" and
limiting its membership to "Jews."[42] As a result, B'nai B'rith retained its Jewish character. Even as a "secular *kehilla*," it remained
a covenanted community defined by mutual obligations, ethnic
ties, and its own distinctive "*halakha*."

❧ APPENDIX
Rules Concerning Fines and Trials[43]

Article VIII
Fines and Trials

§1. Any member acting contrary to the Constitution, Bylaws and
Regulations of a Lodge, violates the usages of the order, or uses
improper or insulting language against the officers of the Lodge,
District, or Constitution Grand Lodge, or towards any member
of the order, or is guilty of unbrotherly and immoral conduct,
shall be fined, reprimanded, suspended or expelled, according
to the established laws and usages of the order or as the Lodge
may decide.

§2. The Lodge shall suspend all members who owe their dues
over twelve months, and who refuse or neglect to pay the same.

§3. Every member is entitled to a proper trial, in all cases where the charge is of such a nature, as to be unprovided for by the By-laws, and which involve a fine, suspension or expulsion (those for non payment of dues excepted).

§4. The charge must contain a detailed account, submitted to the Lodge in writing, and such being accepted without debate, shall be entered on the minutes by the Secr[etary] and a copy thereof handed to the accused.

§5. A trial can be instituted only on the merits of the specifications contained in the complaint.

§6. The P. then has to select an investigating committee consisting of five members, having as many degrees as the accused; to the latter however the right shall be reserved to object to the one or [t]he other, yet he must select five out of ten brothers thus appointed.

§7. When the accused is not present, the names of the committee shall be sent to him in writing and he has the same right to object, until the next following meeting, to all those he is dissatisfied with.

§8. The accused has the right to select a brother of his own, or of a sister Lodge, as his counsel.

§9. The committee shall proceed to examine into the merits of the complaint, and make all proper efforts in order to arrive at a clear view of the case. For this purpose the plaintiff and the defendant shall appear with their resp[ective] witnesses before the committee for examination, written notice as to the definite time and place shall be served upon them.

§10. The committee has to keep correct minutes of the evidence elicited and to transmit the same to the lodge, accompanying it with a report, in which it has to transmit also the result of its own carefull examinations, as to the guilt or innocence of the accused.

§11. The committee report shall then be read to the Lodge and an opportunity given first to the plaintiff and then to the defendant or to his counsel to speak on the case once, whereupon the accuser and the accused and his counsel have to leave the room.

§12. The Lodge shall then proceed to take the case into consideration and decide in the same meeting as to the guild or innocense of the accused.

§13. The decision is effected by written tickets, of which every member receives two, one written with *guilty*, the other with *not guilty*; Of these two, each member may deposit one in the ballot box. The votes are then counted by a committee of three, appointed for this purpose by the P. and if he found guilty by a majority of votes, the accused shall be subject to such punishment as the By-laws provide or the Lodge imposes.

§14. If the defendant is dissatisfied with the decision of the Lodge, he has a right to appeal to the District Grand Lodge.

§15. When the accused neglects to appear to trial after having been duly notified, a new trial shall be ordered and definite notice given to him to that effect. If he should then again refuse to appear, and should neglect to give sufficient excuse for it, he shall be found guilty, and dealt with as prescribed in § 13 of this article.

§16. After a member is suspended or expelled, all Lodges of the district shall forthwith be informed thereof, and no expelled member shall be reinstated again in the order, without the express consent of the District Grand Lodge.

§17. When a member wishes to forward charges against a brother of a sister Lodge, such complaint must be presented through his Lodge to the Lodge to which the brother belongs, which shall then proceed to the provisions made in this article; and when the committee submits its report in agreement with the §10 of this article, the plaintiff shall have the privilege to speak once in the case before the Lodge.

§18. In order to secure brotherly love against all infringements, it shall be the duty of every Lodge to elect a committee of reference, whose duty it shall be, to seek in all instances, to bring about a peaceable adjustment of all controversies between brethren; and it is therefore recommended to all brothers, not to resort to a public tribunal, before submitting their controversies to this committee, and until all efforts to bring about a friendly settlement have failed.

§19. No member shall be allowed to fill an office whilst a charge is pending against him.

§20. Whenever charges are preferred against a member of a Lodge, who is at the same time a member of the District Grand Lodge, notice of said charge shall be send forthwith to the District Grand Lodge.

§21. Members found guilty of any criminal offence before any public tribunal shall be expelled without delay from the Lodge.

☙ NOTES

This essay is dedicated with admiration and deep gratitude to my former principal and longtime Sarna family friend, Rabbi Haskel Lookstein, on the fiftieth anniversary of his pulpit at Kehilath Jeshurun in New York.

1. Standard histories in English are Edward Grusd, *B'nai B'rith: The Story of a Covenant* (New York: 1966), and Deborah Dash Moore, *B'nai B'rith and the Challenge of Ethnic Leadership* (Albany, N.Y.: 1981), but by far the best researched and most accurate history has now appeared in German: Cornelia Wilhelm, *Deutsche Juden in Amerika: Bürgerliches Selbstbewusstsein und jüdische Identität in den Orden B'nai B'rith und Treue Schwestern, 1843–1914* (Stuttgart, 2007). Most histories rely on the account of the early years of B'nai B'rith published in English by Julius Bien in the *Menorah*, beginning in 1886. Wilhelm cites a wide range of other sources, many of them in German. These sources disagree concerning many details of the fraternity's founding. I rely on the date in Grusd, *B'nai B'rith* 18, since it is based on the original B'nai B'rith minute book and echoes Julius Bien's recollections in the *Menorah* 1 (1886), 121.
2. Hasia Diner, *A Time for Gathering: The Second Migration 1820–1880* (Baltimore, 1992), 109; cf. Hasia Diner, *The Jews of the United States* (Berkeley, 2004), 140.
3. Wilhelm, *Deutsche Juden in Amerika*, 60–61.
4. Ibid., 59–63; see Julius Bien, "History of the Independent Order B'ne B'rith," *The Menorah* 1 (1886), 65–68: "It has been asserted that the origin of this society was owing to the action of some Odd Fellow lodges, in rejecting, on account of their religion, Israelites who had applied for admission. This statement, however, seems hardly probable, considering that some of the founders of the new society were members and officers in high standing and position in that organization (p. 65)."
5. Quoted in Grusd, *B'nai B'rith* 18.
6. Hyman B. Grinstein, *The Rise of the Jewish Community of New York 1654–1860* (Philadelphia, 1945), 472–473. On the collapse of the "synagogue-community," see Jonathan D. Sarna, *American Judaism: A History* (New Haven, CT, 2004), 52–61.
7. Wilhelm, *Deutsche Juden in Amerika,* 60; on the rate of unaffiliated Jews at this time, see Sarna, *American Judaism*, 73.
8. Jacob R. Marcus, *United States Jewry 1776–1985* (Detroit, 1989), I, 335–336.
9. Bien, "History of the Independent Order B'ne B'rith," 64; William Renau, one of the founders, recalled that it was he who "proposed to establish a new Order with the principal aim of

uniting and elevating the Sons of Abraham, who had come to this country, from all parts of Europe, with all their provincial prejudices towards each other" (p.67), but other founders made similar claims; see also Wilhelm, *Deutsche Juden in Amerika*, pp. 62–64.

10. See the bilingual German-English constitution published that year: *Constitution of the Independent Order of B'nai B'rith as Revised and Adopted in the General Meeting of the Constitution Grand Lodge in the Year 1851 (5611)* (New York, 1851); Bien, "History of the Independent Order B'ne B'rith," pp. 121–122.

11. Grusd, *B'nai B'rith*, pp. 30–31; Wilhelm, *Deutsche Juden in Amerika*, p. 80.

12. Jacob R. Marcus, *To Count a People: American Jewish Population Data, 1585–1984* (Lanham, MD, 1990), pp. 149, 238–239.

13. *Constitution of the Independent Order of B'nai B'rith*, p.3.

14. Moore, *B'nai B'rith and the Challenge of Ethnic Leadership*, esp. ch. 1, "A Secular Synagogue," 1–34. Moore seems to me much closer to the mark when she explains that "B'nai B'rith…helped transform American Jews into an associational community, and, to the extent that American social realities corresponded with the American ethos, into a voluntary community" (p.33). While Moore stresses the American context, Wilhelm underscores the important German influences upon the order.

15. *Constitution of the Independent Order of B'nai B'rith*, p.3.

16. See Daniel J. Elazar, Jonathan D. Sarna, and Rela G. Monson, *A Double Bond: The Constitutional Documents of American Jewry* (Lanham, MD, 1992) for examples and analysis.

17. See James E. Morrison, ed., *The Code, Index and Digest of the Laws of Freemasonry* (New York, 1877), pp. 46–90, for the "Masonic Code of Procedure."

18. None of the usual biographical sources identify "M. Ulman," who is listed as the author of this book. His identity as secretary of the lodge is listed on the title page and his death was memorialized by the lodge in 1884; see Mendel Silber, *B'nai B'rith in the Southland: Seventy Years of Service* (New Orleans: 1943), p. 23. The same Memphis publisher (Rogers & Co.) who issued *Jurisprudence* also published a volume entitled *Co-operative Insurance: A Review of the System and Practice of Mutual Benefit Societies* (1882) by Mayer Ulman, and I am assuming that these are the same person. Whether this is a relation of the tavern keeper, Mayer Ulman of Philadelphia, I do not know; on the latter, see Henry S. Morais, *The Jews of Philadelphia* (Philadelphia: 1894), pp. 72, 447.

19. M. Ulman, *Jurisprudence of the Independent Order of B'nai B'rith…*(Memphis: Rogers & Co, 1879), p. 273 (case 284). For the laws governing priests and dead bodies, see Leviticus 21:1–2; and Maurice Lamm, *The Jewish Way in Death and Mourning* (New York, 1969), pp. 211–215.

20. Ulman, *Jurisprudence of the Independent Order of B'nai B'rith*, pp. 52–55 (case 34).

21. Ibid., p. 36 (case 21).

22. Ibid., p. 117 (case 109); for various cases involving the *get* in American law, see J. David Bleich, "Jewish Divorce: Judicial Misconceptions and Possible Means of Civil Enforcement," *Connecticut Law Review* 16 (Winter 1984), pp. 201–289. On the rabbinic principle that "the law of the land is the law" (*dina de-malkhuta dina*), see *Encyclopaedia Judaica* (2nd ed, Jerusalem, 2007), vol. 5, pp. 663–669 and bibliography cited therein.

23. For parallel cases in Russia, see ChaeRan Y. Freeze, *Jewish Marriage and Divorce in Imperial Russia* (Waltham, MA, 2002).

24. Ulman, *Jurisprudence of the Independent Order of B'nai B'rith*, 414 (case 426).

25. Ibid., pp. 241–242 (case 257).

26. Ibid., pp. 488–489 (case 489).

27. Ibid., p. 421 (case 435).

28. Ibid., p. 422.

29. Ibid., p. 612.

30. Ibid., pp. 356–357 (case 366).

31. Ibid., p. 155 (case 150); see also pp. 519 (#70), 555 (#437), 612 (#14).

32. Sarna, *American Judaism*, pp. 124, 132; on Reform Judaism and intermarriage during this era, see William Rosenblatt, "The Jews: What Are They Coming To," *Galaxy* 13 (June 1872),

pp. 47–60. Michael A. Meyer, *Response to Modernity: A History of the Reform Movement in Judaism* (New York: Oxford, 1988), pp. 257, 280, summarizes Reform attitudes.

33. Ulman, *Jurisprudence of the Independent Order of B'nai B'rith*, p. 345 (#36); see also p. 36 (case 21) and p. 613.

34. The case of *D. Goldman and Others* vs. *District Grand Lodge No. 3* is briefly summarized in Ibid., p. 36 (case 21). Extensive quotations from the arguments on different sides of the case may be found in I.O.B.B., *Appeal XLVI* (New York: 1880), pp. 30–31 (This item is listed as #2894 in Robert Singerman, *Judaica Americana* [New York, 1990], and I have used the copy found at HUC-JIR, Cincinnati.) In another case, *Emek Beracha Lodge No. 61* vs. *D.G.L. No.2*, a lodge passed a bylaw declaring that "Any brother who marries a non-Jewess or who does not circumcise his children [sic] according to Jewish Ritual shall be expelled from the Lodge." The Court of Appeal declared the bylaw unconstitutional since "no individual Lodge could impose restrictions, such as the one in question, which affect the membership of the whole Order (Ulman, *Jurisprudence of the Independent Order of B'nai B'rith*, 33 [case 18])." Ulman generalized that "an Israelite not having his male children circumcised is thereby not disqualified for admission (p. 612, #14). For the German background of the circumcision question, see Robin Judd, *Contested Rituals: Circumcision, Kosher Butchering and Jewish Political Life in Germany 1843–1933* (Ithaca, NY, 2007), pp. 21–57.

35. I.O.B.B., *Appeal XLVI*, 5–8.

36. Ibid., p. 5.

37. Ibid., p. 21.

38. Ibid., p. 34.

39. Ibid., pp. 34–48.

40. Ulman, *Jurisprudence of the Independent Order of B'nai B'rith*, p. 613.

41. I.O.B.B., *Appeal XLVI*, pp. 63, 68.

42. Ibid., p. 68.

43. *Constitution of the Independent Order of B'nai B'rith...1851*, pp. 52–58. Misspellings in the original have been retained.

Tikkun Olam: Defining the Jewish Obligation

Jacob J. Schacter

The issue is clear and straightforward: What is *tikkun olam* and are Jews obligated to engage in it?

This phrase is variously translated as repairing, fixing, mending, or improving the world. Insofar as it relates to the theme of this article, it connotes four basic assertions:

- The world as it is known to be is not what the world is ultimately meant to be; there is a fundamental disconnect between the real and the ideal.
- Human beings are empowered with the capacity to transform the real into the ideal. Not only is this within the purview of God, but human beings are granted by God the capacity do something about it. Human beings can make a difference.
- Not only do human beings have the capacity to make a difference, but it is part of the religious obligation of Jews to make a difference. Jewish religious tradition expects and requires Jews to be engaged in the effort to bring about this transformation.
- This obligation includes bettering the welfare of all peoples who populate the earth, not only Jews. Of course, the primary responsibility of all Jews is for one another (*hayekha*

kodmim; see *Bava Mezi'a* 62a and Rama, *Yoreh De'ah* 251:3), for family members and then for other Jews, both in terms of the time as well as the money spent. But these universalistic obligations make demands upon Jews as well. Jews also bear a fundamental religious responsibility not only to ensure Jewish moral, spiritual, and material welfare but, albeit secondarily, also to ensure the moral, spiritual, and material welfare of the world as a whole. And this comes with the awareness that every minute or every dollar spent on those activities is a minute or dollar taken away from Jewish causes and Jewish needs.[1]

The fact is that such an obligation is absent from the vast majority of Jewish primary sources from the post-biblical to the pre-modern period. The authoritative texts of the Jewish tradition – the Talmud and its commentators, responsa literature and codes – are almost silent on the obligation, and even the desirability of Jewish involvement in what is known as social justice, activity aimed at universal social or communal betterment.

Furthermore, even when such statements do appear, one gets the impression that the sentiment they reflect is very far from the notion of *tikkun olam* just described. Very often the justification is primarily, if not exclusively, a pragmatic or self-serving one, for the sake of advancing parochial Jewish interests. For example, note the injunction of Jeremiah (29:7), "Seek (*ve-dirshu*) the welfare of the city to which I have exiled you and pray (*ve-hitpalelu*) to the Lord on its behalf, for in its peacefulness you will enjoy peace." Rabbi Samson Raphael Hirsch notes the significance of both verbs in this verse, suggesting that while *hitpalelu* clearly refers to prayer, *dirshu* obligates the Jew "to do everything to promote the welfare of the countries in which we live."[2] But the end of the verse is most significant. The rationale offered is not that such behavior is intrinsically worthwhile but that it will bring benefit to the Jew, "for in its peacefulness you will enjoy peace."

The text of the Mishna in *Avot* (3:2), which serves as the locus for this comment of Rabbi Hirsch, is another case in point.

Rabbi Hanina is quoted there as having made a wonderful universalistic statement: "Pray for the welfare of the government." But the reason that immediately follows negates its relevance for us. "Because if people did not fear it, a person would swallow his fellow alive" is about as self-serving an explanation as one can find. One gets the impression that the Mishna is really stating, "Pray for the welfare of the government, because if people did not fear it, Gentiles would swallow Jews alive." Jewish self-interest, then, is what animates the desire expressed here for Jewish engagement in ensuring a just and moral society.

This point becomes even more clear in the parallel text in *Avoda Zara* (4a): "As it is with the fish of the sea, the one that is bigger swallows the other up, so it is with man. Were it not for fear of the government, everyone who is greater than his fellow would swallow him up. As it is taught, Rabbi Hanina the Deputy Priest said…." There is no doubt as to who was considered "bigger" or "greater" in this Talmudic perception of the world.[3]

Another possible example. A well-known passage in the Talmud (*Gittin* 61a) states that a Jew supports the Gentile poor, visits the Gentile sick, and buries the Gentile dead "*mipnei darkei shalom*," because it will lead to peace and harmony between us and them. Once again, the ruling appears to be self-serving. Support them, visit their sick, and bury their dead, not because such behavior is necessarily intrinsically worthwhile and laudatory but because of the Jew's desire to foster "ways of peace" [read, perhaps: Jews do not want Gentiles to beat them up].

Furthermore, there are those who suggest that the Jewish people best fulfills whatever responsibility it may have for the welfare of mankind not by busying itself directly in the moral, spiritual, and material welfare of the world but by acting appropriately before God as pious and observant Jews. In other words, to the extent to which the impact of the Jew on the world at large is considered something of value, it is an indirect impact. For example, Rabbi Samson Raphael Hirsch wrote that "Abraham's descendants should follow with love and justice in the ways of

God and by this silent example become a blessed monument to God and humanity among the peoples of the earth."[4] Note also the following quote from Theodor Herzl: "The world will be liberated by our freedom, enriched by our wealth, magnified by our greatness. And whatever we attempt there [in the Jewish state] for our own benefit will redound mightily and beneficially to the good of all mankind."[5] Jews are to affect the world by serving as an example; their actions within the confines of their homeland will bring benefit to the world as a whole.

A famous Talmudic passage at the end of *Yoma* (86a) comes to mind in this context:

> "You shall love the Lord your God" (Deut. 6:5), [meaning] that the name of Heaven should become beloved through you. One should read [Scripture], learn [Mishna] and serve Torah scholars, and his dealings with people should be conducted in a pleasant manner. What do people (*beriyot*) say about him? "Fortunate is his father who taught him Torah. Fortunate is his teacher who taught him Torah. Woe unto people who do not learn Torah. This person who studied Torah, see how pleasant are his ways, how refined are his deeds." Regarding him Scripture states, "He [God] said to me, 'You are my servant Israel through whom I am glorified'" (Isa. 49:3).[6]

The Jew should behave as a Jew should, and the rest of the world (*beriyot*) will become inspired and ennobled; the world will become more just and more peaceful when the non-Jew will watch and emulate the moral, ethical, and spiritual behavior of the Jew. This is also how some explain the biblical verses, "And all the families of the earth will be blessed through you (*ve-nivrikhu vekha kol mishpihot ha-adamah*)" (Gen. 12:3) or "And all the nations of the earth will be blessed through him (*ve-nivrikhu vo kol goyei ha-arez*)" (Gen. 18:18). "All the families of the earth" and "all the nations of the earth" will be blessed by observing the behavior of the Jew and by being inspired to emulate it.[7] In fact, it is in this sense, perhaps, that the well-known biblical mandate for Jews to be *le-or goyim* (Isa. 42:6) is to be understood.[8]

Indeed, to put it mildly, the classical authoritative texts of our tradition do not abound with statements requiring Jewish involvement in activity designed solely for the purpose of advancing the general good.[9] What does one make of this apparently striking lacuna? Does it reflect a reasoned ideological position that, in fact, such activity was deemed unimportant in principle, or is it a reflection perhaps of something else? In other words, is this position prescriptive, the way it should be, *lekhathila*, or is it descriptive, reflecting a specific set of historical realities, *bi-dieved*?

It seems clear that this silence in the Talmud and subsequent rabbinic literature does not reflect any principled objection to the values here being discussed but is rather the product of historically grounded mitigating circumstances. To extrapolate a negative Jewish attitude toward this kind of universalism from the absence of a significant universalistic emphasis in post-biblical pre-modern classical Jewish texts is to misunderstand a fundamental value of Judaism.

First of all, one may wonder to what extent the notion of a moral imperative for the universal good which transcends religious boundaries is present at all in any religious tradition prior to the eighteenth century. Perhaps this value is also not articulated outside the Jewish community in pre-modern times, in which case the significance of its absence in Jewish sources is significantly minimized. Nevertheless, there are special considerations that are relevant specifically to Jews. The fact is that the big world out there has not been good to the Jews. Throughout the ages, from ancient through modern times, the Jewish people was repeatedly forced to confront demographic dispersion, political disintegration, economic dislocation, social alienation, psychological oppression, subtle as well as crude discrimination, and, at worst, of course, brute physical annihilation.[10] Can there be any wonder, then, that a genuine sense of obligation to the welfare of society at large was not high on the list of the national, communal, or personal priorities of previous Jewish generations?

In a collection of poems published just five years after the end of the Holocaust, the Israeli poet Uri Zvi Greenberg voiced the deep disillusionment widely shared by many members of his shattered generation:

בינינו לבין אמות העולם מנחים טבוחי משפחתנו

"Between us and the nations of the world lie the slaughtered of our family…"[11]

Under such circumstances, can one blame Jews for not feeling a burning responsibility for the welfare of mankind, for not placing this responsibility high on their scheme of obligations? As a vulnerable and beleaguered community shouldering the difficult burden of a long and arduous exile, other internal priorities were much more pressing. Jews needed to expend whatever precious little resources they had on keeping their own house in order, on caring for their own, on simply ensuring their own survival. Simply put, they had enough trouble just taking care of themselves. The struggle for survival in the dispersion of the Diaspora sapped all their strength. Nothing was more important than self-preservation.

True, in the nineteenth century the situation somewhat changed. Emancipation and Enlightenment joined to create a much more favorable external situation for Jews. But even then one does not find forthcoming any real support for the kind of obligation being described here. In analyzing the thinking of some of the major Jewish thinkers of the nineteenth century on this subject – Solomon Maimon, Saul Ascher, Samuel Kirsch, Nachman Krochmal, Samson Raphael Hirsch, Zechariah Frankel, Heinrich Graetz, and Solomon Ludwig Steinheim – Eliezer Schweid came to the striking but not unexpected conclusion that not a single one of these thinkers, writers, or communal leaders promoted political

Jewish engagement with society at large. With all the improvements modernity had brought to the Jews, and there were many, those living even at the end of the nineteenth century could not even imagine being in a position of having significant political influence in the countries in which they lived.[12]

A major shift occurred in America shortly after the turn of the twentieth century. In 1919 Mordecai M. Kaplan was using his pulpit at the Jewish Center on the Upper West Side of Manhattan to "fulminate" in favor of unions, workers' rights, a five-day work week – positions that evoked significant opposition among his wealthy congregants.[13] And the value of social justice became very important in the Reform movement. At its annual meeting in 1918 the Committee on Synagogue and Industrial Relations of the Central Conference of American Rabbis (CCAR) adopted the first social justice resolution of Reform Judaism: "[In] the next few decades...the world will busy itself not only with the establishment of political, but also with the achievement of industrial democracy through social justice. The ideal of social justice has always been an integral part of Judaism." The CCAR submitted a "declaration of principles" calling for a more equitable distribution of profits, a minimum wage, a compulsory day of rest for workers, a safe and sanitary working environment, the abolition of child labor, universal workmen's health insurance, and more.[14] Michael Meyer ascribed this emphasis to two influences, both of which came from outside Judaism: the American Progressive movement and the Christian Social Gospel movement. Nevertheless, as Meyer points out, and as was made clear in the platform cited above, the Reform rabbis adopting it did not consider themselves as importing from Christianity but as drawing from the heritage of prophetic Judaism common to both Jewish and Christian religious traditions.[15]

However, this emphasis and interest were not widely shared across the American Jewish denominational spectrum. In the larger American Jewish community, social justice was simply not a priority. On one end, Jews were still not interested in becoming involved in the broader society and, at the other end, no one was interested in asking them to do so.

But in the second half of the century the situation changed, and in both directions. Jews became significantly more involved in *tikkun olam*, and the "world out there" welcomed and became much more supportive of that involvement. In midcentury, Abraham Joshua Heschel wrote: "Religion becomes a mockery if we remain callous to the irony of sending satellites to the sky and failing to find employment for our fellow citizens, of a highly publicized World's Fair and insufficient funds for the extermination of vermin in the slums. Is religion to be a mockery?"[16] More recently Ruth Wisse wrote about how in the Montreal Jewish school she attended in her youth, "Jewish values were transmitted as a passion for justice."[17] In the 1960s, Jews played a prominent role in the civil rights movement disproportionate to their numbers.[18] In his 1986 acceptance speech for the Nobel Prize for Peace, Elie Wiesel said:

> Of course, since I am a Jew profoundly rooted in my people's memory and tradition, my first response is to Jewish fears, Jewish needs, Jewish crises. For I belong to a traumatized generation, one that experienced the abandonment and solitude of our people. It would be unnatural for me not to make Jewish priorities my own: Israel, Soviet Jewry, Jews in Arab lands…. But others are important to me. Apartheid is, in my view, as abhorrent as antisemitism. To me, Andrei Sakharov's isolation is as much a disgrace as Joseph Begun's imprisonment and Ida Nudel's exile.[19]

A series of national polls of American Jews conducted in the last twenty years shows that "commitment to social equality" tops "religious observance" or "support for Israel" as the most important factor in American Jewish identity by a factor of more than two to one.[20] In reflecting upon his campaign for the vice-presidency in 2000, Joseph Lieberman wrote: "Today, Jewish Americans are broadly represented in all aspects of American civic life.... We all have a stake in the health of this unique, free, pluralistic country. And America needs the commitment to justice, spirituality, and the communitarian ethic of Jewish tradition."²¹ In December 2007 the Melton Centre for Jewish Education of the Hebrew University in Jerusalem sponsored a conference on the occasion of the hundredth anniversary of the birth of Heschel which focused specifically on linking Jewish religious thought to the value of social justice that was so central to his life. The conference theme was described in the Centre's newsletter as follows: "Heschel's uniqueness as an educator was in his understanding that being Jewish was not simply about a set of particularistic practices, but also about giving voice to God's vision of social justice, often in opposition to the status quo."²² Also a special supplement to New York's *Jewish Week* in June 2008 was devoted to highlighting the many efforts being made in this area across the American Jewish communal and religious spectrum.²³

In fact, *tikkun olam* has become a widely bandied about code word within the Jewish community as well as in American culture at large. *The New Republic* reported on a speech former New York governor Mario Cuomo delivered in 2000 to a group of lawyers. In response to a question about what his advice would be to law students, he said: "*Tikkun olam*. That's Hebrew for 'repair the world.' Complete the task of creation."²⁴ In 2001 *The New Yorker* published a story about African American Studies professor Cornel West which included the following: "He fingered his cufflinks, which were gold and molded in the shape of the Lion of Judah. ('*Tikkun olam* all the way,' he said. 'Hebrew scripture, uh-huh.')."²⁵ An April 2008 article in the *New York Times Magazine* about the Kabbalah Center in Los Angeles noted how "Madonna brings the Kabbalah center's message of egoless dedication to *tikkun olam* (repairing the world) home to her fans both in her music and in personal appearances."²⁶ In a speech delivered before an audience at the AIPAC National Policy Conference in Washington, D.C. on June 4, 2008, then–Senator Barack Obama said:

As any Israeli will tell you, Israel is not a perfect place but like the United States it sets an example for all when it seeks a more perfect future. These same qualities can be found among American Jews. It is why so many Jewish Americans have stood by Israel while advancing the American story, because there is a commitment embedded in the Jewish faith and tradition to freedom and fairness, to social justice and equal opportunity – *Tikkun Olam* – the obligation to repair this world.[27]

And, finally, the first major exhibition at San Francisco's new Contemporary Jewish Museum, entitled "In the Beginning: Artists Respond to Genesis" and on display from June 2008 to January 2009, included an installation by Mierle Laderman Ukeles named, "*Tsimtsum/Shevirat Ha-Kelim*: Contraction/The Shattering of the Perfect Vessels: Birthing *Tikkun Olam*."[28]

What then are sources from Jewish tradition that we can draw upon to serve as the foundation for a commitment to *tikkun olam* or social justice as we now understand it? What follows is surely not an exhaustive presentation but merely some sources that should be considered as particularly relevant.

First, the Bible, of course. The Bible is replete with references to the broader social responsibility of the Jew, both via explicit verses as well as implicit lessons to be drawn from various biblical narratives. Abraham's interest in caring for his noontime visitors, whom he took to be traveling nomads, as well as his efforts on behalf of the sinners of Sodom are instructive, as are Rivka's concern for Eliezer and his flock (Gen. 24:46) and Moshe's assertive defense of seven Midianite daughters (Ex. 2:17). And there are many other examples as well. Various prophecies in Jeremiah, Ezekiel, Zekhariah, and other biblical books also underscore this value.

The second source brings us back to the Talmudic passage (*Gittin* 61a) cited earlier regarding the Jewish responsibility to support Gentile poor, visit their sick, and bury their dead. Some would question its relevance to the topic being considered here, for a number of reasons, even without taking into consideration the possible self-serving nature of its attendant rationale of *mipnei darkei shalom* as suggested above. There are those who point to the fact that in each case the Talmud couples helping Gentiles with simultaneously helping Jews: "One provides support to the Gentile poor *along with the Jewish poor* (*im aniyei Yisrael*). One visits the Gentile sick *along with the Jewish sick* (*im holei Yisrael*). One buries the Gentile dead *along with the Jewish dead* (*im metei Yisrael*)." This juxtaposition leads them to limit the obligation to help Gentiles only to circumstances where Jews are also being helped as well,[29] a position that would clearly minimize the usefulness of this text as a broad expression of *tikkun olam*. Furthermore, some do not read the phrase "one provides support to the Gentile poor" as constituting an obligation to do so, as in "one is obligated to provide support to the Gentile poor" but rather understand it as optional, as in "it is permitted (*mutar*) to provide support to the Gentile poor."[30] Clearly these scholars assume that some would consider such behavior as actually being prohibited and therefore feel the need for Jewish law to allow it as optional. Once again, the relevance of this text to the more overarching principle of *tikkun olam* is clearly minimized.

However, with regard to the suggestion that Jews must also benefit when Gentiles are being helped, the majority of commentators and decisors disagree with this limiting reading and, on the basis of the formulations in the *Yerushalmi* and *Tosefta*, do understand this Talmudic passage as requiring assistance to Gentiles independent of any concurrent help for Jews.[31] With regard to the question of whether this passage is to be understood as merely providing permission to assist Gentiles or requiring it as an obligation, most instructive – and most relevant – is a Maimonidean formulation codifying this Talmudic passage. In some places in his *Mishneh Torah* (*Hil. Avoda Zara* 10:5; *Hil. Matnot Aniyim* 7:7; *Hil. Avel* 14:12) Maimonides simply cites the Talmudic ruling that one supports the Gentile poor "*mipnei darkei shalom*" without any further comment or elaboration. Elsewhere, however, his language is more expansive and significant. In *Hil. Melakhim u-Milhamot* (10:12) he writes:

> Even with respect to Gentiles (*ha-Goyim*), *our Sages admonish us* (*zivu Hakhamim*) to visit their sick, bury their dead along with the dead of Israel, and maintain their poor as well as the Jewish poor in the interests of peace (*mipnei darkei shalom*). Behold it is written, "The Lord is good to all, and His mercies are over all His works" (Ps. 145:9). It is also written, "Its ways are ways of pleasantness and all its paths are peace (*ve-khol netivoteha shalom*)" (Prov. 3:17).[32]

Unlike the other places in his *Mishneh Torah* where Maimonides cites this ruling, here he introduces it with the important phrase *zivu Hakhamim*. For him, supporting Gentile poor is clearly not simply optional; it is required. Second, and even more significant, Maimonides concludes his ruling by adducing two different verses to support it. Two points are relevant here. First, by citing the second verse, "Its ways are ways of pleasantness and all its paths are peace," Maimonides is drawing the reader's attention to a Talmudic passage (*Gittin* 59b) that associates that verse with the totality of Jewish law. "The entire Torah is also for the sake of [fostering] the interests of peace (*mipnei darkei shalom*), as it is written, 'Its ways are ways of pleasantness and all its paths are peace (*ve-khol netivoteha shalom*).'" And note Maimonides' concluding statement of *Sefer Zemanim*, the third of his fourteen books of the *Mishneh Torah*: "Peace is great, for the entire Torah was given to make peace in the world as it is written, 'Its ways are ways of pleasantness and all its paths are peace'" (*Hil. Hanuka* 4:14). "In the interests of peace (*mipnei darkei shalom*)" must be seen within the broader overarching context of "and all its paths are peace (*ve-khol netivoteha shalom*)." And this latter phrase is a blanket statement about the ethical sensitivity of Torah in general, clearly with no reference to anything that might be construed as reflecting any level of personal or communal self-interest. Hence *mipnei darkei shalom* in this Maimonidean passage must be understood as a rationale for supporting Gentiles, which is not to be circumscribed by any ulterior or self-serving motives. One must act this way because it is the right thing to do; such behavior is in keeping with the overall goal or purpose of "the entire Torah."

In addition, Maimonides went out of his way to cite another verse first, one that is unrelated to the value of peace but that stresses God's indiscriminate and universal goodness, a trait that is incumbent upon His people to follow. Clearly, for Maimonides there is another factor central to this ruling: the religious obligation to imitate the ethical behavior of God. Indeed this same verse is cited by Maimonides in a similar context elsewhere in his *Mishneh Torah* (*Hil. Avadim* 9:8):

> Cruelty and effrontery are not frequent except with heathen who worship idols. The children of our father Abraham, however, i.e., the Israelites, upon whom the Holy One, blessed be He, bestowed the favor of the Law and laid upon them statutes and judgments, are merciful people who have mercy upon all. Thus also it is declared by the attributes of the Holy One, blessed be He, which we are enjoined to imitate: "And His mercies are over all His works." (Ps. 145:9).

Once again, emulating God's attributes is in itself an independent religious obligation, absent any considerations of self-interest or ulterior motive.[33]

That this is Maimonides' understanding of the phrase *mipnei darkei shalom* can also be inferred from one of his responsa dealing with the religious status of the Karaites, an issue to which he, as well as many others, devoted significant attention.[34] He ruled that as long as the Karaites act respectfully to "us," they should be treated in a similar fashion. In support of his position, he cited the Talmudic passage in *Gittin* that one is obligated to inquire as to the welfare of Gentiles *mipnei darkei shalom*. And, he continues, "If this is the case for idol worshippers, then certainly (*kal va-homer*)" it should apply to Karaites.[35] If acting favorably to Gentiles *mipnei darkei shalom* was only permitted (*mutar*) and not required, or if it was only self-serving, it would be irrelevant here. Applying this ruling to the Karaites via a *kal va-homer* makes sense only if it is understood as an independent, objectively morally appropriate act.

Later rabbinic authorities also seemed to follow this approach. It would appear that Rabbi Jacob Emden, writing in the eighteenth century, applied the obligation to bury Gentile dead, comfort their mourners, and support their poor *mipnei darkei shalom* even during a time and in a place when and where Jews had authority over them and did not need to fear retaliation from them.[36] One century later Rabbi Samson Raphael Hirsch referred to Maimonides' *Hil. Melakhim* 10:12, among other sources, while waxing eloquently about how positively Jews must treat a *ger toshav*, a Gentile who accepts the Seven Noahide Laws as a part of divine revelation, thereby considering them to be binding.[37] In the twentieth century Rabbi Eliyahu Eliezer Dessler understood that these obligations of Jews toward Gentiles, predicated upon this rationale of *mipnei darkei shalom*, represented a fundamental general requirement for Jews to treat all human beings with *derekh eretz*, no strings attached. He made the point that Abraham's greatest test was having to negotiate with the Bnei Het for a burial place for his wife while her dead body still lay before him and while his grief over her passing was still fresh and intense. Yet, despite his deep distress, he made sure to treat them properly and respectfully in keeping with "a fundamental principle with regard to *derekh eretz*. The other need not suffer because I am in pain." In this context he quoted the rabbinic and Maimonidean ruling that one must seek the welfare of Gentiles *mipnei darkei shalom*. For Rabbi Dessler, a human being is deserving of respectful behavior simply and only by virtue of their being human (*Avot* [3:14]: "Beloved is the human being [read: including a non-Jew] who was created in the image [of God]"). There are no alternative considerations, no ulterior motives.[38] And in 1966, addressing the scandal that erupted regarding the alleged refusal of some to desecrate the Shabbat in order to save the life of a non-Jew, Ashkenazi Chief Rabbi of Israel, Rabbi Isser Yehudah Unterman, wrote that the concept of *darkei shalom* "does not have the status of a *middat hasidut* and is not a means to defend ourselves, but it emerges out of the core ethical values of the Torah."[39]

A third source. In commenting on the last verse in the book of Jonah, R. Menahem Azaryah of Fano (d. 1620) noted that God has greater compassion for a large group of Gentiles in danger than for a smaller one. The verse (Jonah 4:11) highlights that "more than a hundred and twenty thousand people" could have been destroyed because numbers matter. The potential danger to such a large number of Gentiles aroused a special, greater, degree of mercy from the Almighty.[40]

A fourth source remains an important one even though it has often been cited in this context. Toward the end of his well-known essay outlining his position on interfaith dialogue, Rabbi Joseph B. Soloveitchik characterized the nature of the obligation of the Jew to the world at large. "We are human beings, committed to the general welfare and progress of mankind...interested in combating disease, in alleviating human suffering, in protecting man's rights, in helping the needy, *et cetera*." A few pages later he formulated the Jew's relationship to the world by reference to the apparently mutually exclusive categories of stranger (*ger*) and sojourner (*toshav*):

> Our approach to and relationship with the outside world has always been of an ambivalent character, intrinsically antithetic, bordering at times on the paradoxical. We relate ourselves to and at the same time withdraw ourselves from, we come close to and simultaneously retreat from the world of Esau.... Yes, we are determined to participate in every civic, scientific, and political enterprise. We feel obligated to enrich

society with our creative talents and to be constructive and useful citizens.[41]

On another occasion Rabbi Soloveitchik addressed the question of why the book of Jonah, surely the biblical book most reflective of Judaism's universalistic concerns, is read on the afternoon of Yom Kippur, the holiest day of the year. After all, are there not other biblical passages that one may have considered more appropriate on that most solemn and awe-filled occasion?

Said Rabbi Soloveitchik:

> During the Yom Kippur services, our prayerful concerns are almost exclusively with our own people…. We are often accused of being parochially clannish. This may be true, for otherwise we would have succumbed long ago, considering our historical vulnerability. But this self-involvement is not hermetically exclusionary. The universal emphasis is prominent in all our prayers, in Scripture, the Talmud and the Midrash; and when opportunities were benign and conditions propitious, we have contributed far more than our proportionate share to the welfare of humanity….
>
> It is, therefore, characteristic of the universal embrace of our faith that as the shadows of dusk descend on Yom Kippur day, after almost twenty-four hours of prayer for Israel, the Jew is alerted through the book of Jonah, prior to the closing of "the heavenly gates" (*Ne'ilah*) that all humanity is God's children. We need to restate the universal dimension of our faith.[42]

As the holiest day of the Jewish calendar begins to come to an end, the focus of the Jew turns outward to a sense of responsibility for the larger world in which he or she lives.

The fifth source is a strong letter of endorsement written by Rabbi Aaron Soloveichik in the late 1980s or early 1990s on behalf of the Jewish Fund for Justice, an organization committed to social and economic justice in America, particularly for non-Jews. The undated letter included the following:

> It is obvious that, from the Judaic perspective, righteousness is to be practiced equally towards Jews and non-Jews. Rabeinu Bahya ben Asher in his comment on the verse in Deuteronomy chapter 16 v. 20: "Righteousness righteousness thou shalt pursue" says that the reason as to why the Torah reiterates the term righteousness twice is to impress upon us the notion that righteousness is to be practiced equally to Jews and non-Jews alike. Rabeinu Menachem Hameiri – one of the outstanding Torah giants in the thirteenth century – writes that decent Christians and decent Moslems are to be treated like proselytes of the gate (*ger toshav*). And in respect to a *ger toshav* (a Gentile who observes the fundamental obligations of humanity as represented by the seven Noachide Laws) Maimonides in the *Yad Hachazaka Hilchot Melochim* chapter 10 writes: "It is my view that we are obligated in our relationship with a *ger toshav* to deport ourselves with the same degree of consideration and generosity as we display towards our Jewish brethren. Even in respect to pagans our Sages commanded us to support their poor, to visit their sick, to comfort their mourners in the same way as we do it towards our Jewish brethren. For it is written: 'G-d is kind to all and His compassion extends to all His creatures.' And it is written: 'Its ways are pleasant and all its paths are conducive to peace.'"[43]

Finally, Rabbi Aharon Lichtenstein also affirmed the importance of demonstrating concern for and acting to ensure the welfare of non-Jews. He wrote:

> There is no gainsaying the fact…that Judaism has espoused a double ethic. The *Halakha* indeed has championed a double standard grounded in recognition of *kedushat* Israel and the

perception…that intensive ethnocentric *hesed* is preferred to bland universalism. Yet the tendency, prevalent in much of the contemporary Torah world in Israel as well as in the Diaspora, of almost total obliviousness to non-Jewish suffering is shamefully deplorable. Surely Avraham Avinu and Moshe Rabbenu felt and acted otherwise, and intervening *mattan* Torah has not changed our obligation in this respect. Priorities certainly need to be maintained, as regards both practical and emotional engagement; but between that and complacent apathy there lies an enormous moral gap…. but the notion that only Jewish affliction is worthy of Jewish response needs to be excoriated and eradicated. In this respect, the Hafez Hayyim's remark – that if the Gentiles knew how much we pray for them on Rosh Hashana, they would publish *Mahzorim* – serves as an instructive guide.[44]

It is thus clear that there is a Jewish obligation to engage in *tikkun olam* as it has been defined here. It should also be noted that this entire enterprise of seeking *halakhic* sources for the obligation to engage in *tikkun olam* raises the larger question of whether Jewish tradition recognizes the legitimacy and binding nature of ethical imperatives outside the structure and parameters of *halakha*. If, in fact, it does, would it not be possible to argue that the search for specific source texts supportive of engagement in *tikkun olam* might be unnecessary? But this discussion raises large and complicated questions that are beyond the scope of this paper.

In any case, rabbinic authorities have ruled that supporting Gentile poor is required, and is the case even when doing so will inevitably result in the diminution of money available to support the Jewish indigent.[45] A place has been set at the table of Jewish obligation for needy non-Jews as well. But, as Rabbi Lichtenstein noted, the matter of priorities is important, and it needs further attention.[46] What about percentages? *Halakha* has determined that one should donate one tenth (*ma'aser*) of one's income to charity with a maximum of 20 percent.[47] *Halakha* has also determined that certain categories of needy individuals have priority in laying claim to one's charity dollar: for example, one's relatives, righteous Jews and Torah scholars, the poor of one's own city and the land of Israel, those in greatest need, and a poor bride.[48] In addition, certain causes also have priority, such as ransoming captives, facilitating Torah study, and supporting a synagogue.[49] Clearly not all these causes can be supported in full; giving more to one will inevitably result in less to another. If *tikkun olam* then, as defined in this essay, is a religious obligation and therefore also has a claim to the Jewish charity dollar, how much of a priority should it have? How much of one's *ma'aser* money should go to help victims of the hunger crisis in Darfur (since 2003), the tsunami in the Indian Ocean (2004), Hurricane Katrina in New Orleans (2005), the Sichuan earthquake in China (2008), and Cyclone Nargis in Myanmar (2008)?[50] While this is an issue that still requires further clarification, the question is an important one and needs to be asked. For, indeed, "all humanity is God's children."

✥ NOTES

In honor of Rabbi Haskel Lookstein, who has spent a lifetime teaching an expanded vision of the parameters of Jewish obligation.

My thanks to Rabbi Dr. Gil Perl and Rabbi Kenneth Hain for their thoughtful suggestions.

1. For some of my thoughts on this subject, I am indebted to David Shatz, Chaim I. Waxman, and Nathan J. Diament, eds., *Tikkun Olam: Social Responsibility in Jewish Law and Thought* (Northvale, N.J. and London, 1997). For a more recent treatment of the full range of meanings of this term, see Gilbert S. Rosenthal, "*Tikkun ha-Olam*: The Metamorphosis of a Concept," *The Journal of Religion* 85:2 (April 2005):214–240. See also "Israel Among the Nations: A Symposium," *Jewish Action* 50:4 (Fall 1990); Jonathan Sacks, "Tikkun Olam: Orthodoxy's Responsibility to Perfect G-d's World," at *www.ou.org/public/Publib/tikkun.htm*; Jill Jacobs, "The History of 'Tikkun Olam,'" at *www.zeek.net/print/706tohu*; idem, "From Pumbedita to Washington: Rabbinic Text, Urban Policy and Social Reality," *Shofar* 26:3 (2008):105–126; Or N. Rose, Jo Ellen Green Kaiser, and Margie Klein, eds., *Righteous Indignation: A Jewish Call for Justice* (Woodstock, N.Y., 2008) and the critical review of this book by Hillel Halkin, "How Not to Repair the World," *Commentary* 126:1 (July–August, 2008): 21–27.

   In one of his earliest articles, my late teacher Dr. Isadore Twersky addressed the *halakhic* nature of the responsibility of Jews for others and asked three questions, the third being: "Is charity a particularistic performance of the Jew – like Sabbath observance – or is it a universal expression of the basic dignity of man and the concomitant sense of reciprocal helpfulness? On the practical level, this question revolves around the historic position of Judaism vis-à-vis non-Jewish philanthropic enterprises." It is regretful that, because of "limitations of time and endurance" Dr. Twersky decided to "eliminate the third question for the time being," and I am not aware of his coming back to it again. See Isadore Twersky, "Some Aspects of the Jewish Attitude Toward the Welfare State," *Tradition* 5:2 (Summer 1963):138–139.

2. See *Chapters of the Fathers: Translation and Commentary by Rabbi Samson Raphael Hirsch* (Jerusalem and New York, 1967), p. 40.

3. On the implication of these statements, see Martin Sicker, "A Political Metaphor in Biblical and Rabbinic Literature," *Judaism* 40:2 (Spring 1991):208–214. Parenthetically note also that even the first part of Rabbi Hanina's statement mandates only prayer; the text does not read, "*Act* for the welfare of the government...."

4. R. Samson Raphael Hirsch, *Horeb* 2 (London, 1962), p. 465, #613. For this theme in the writings of Rabbi Hirsch and other nineteenth-century figures like his teacher, Rabbi Yaakov Ettlinger, and Rabbi Naphtali Zevi Yehudah Berlin, see J. David Bleich, "*Tikkun Olam:* Jewish Obligations to Non-Jewish Society," in David Shatz, Chaim I. Waxman, and Nathan J. Diament, eds., *Tikkun Olam: Social Responsibility in Jewish Law and Thought*, pp. 87–96.

5. Theodor Herzl, *The Jewish State: An Attempt at a Modern Solution of the Jewish Question* (London, 1872), p. 79.

6. See too Rambam's formulation of this concept in his *Sefer ha-Mizvot, Mizvat Aseh* #3.

7. For the uniqueness of this interpretation of these verses, see Gerald J. Blidstein, "*Tikkun Olam,*" in David Shatz, Chaim I. Waxman, and Nathan J. Diament, eds., *Tikkun Olam: Social Responsibility in Jewish Law and Thought*, p. 54. This article first appeared in *Tradition* 29:2 (1995): pp. 5–43.

8. For a very different perspective on the meaning of this very important phrase, see Harry M. Orlinsky, "'A Light of the Nations:' A Problem in Biblical Theology," in Abraham A. Neuman and Solomon Zeitlin, eds., *The Seventy-Fifth Anniversary Volume of the Jewish Quarterly Review* (Philadelphia, 1967), pp. 409–428.

9. This point is sharpened by reading Elliot N. Dorff, *The Way Into* Tikkun Olam (*Repairing the World*) (Woodstock, N.Y., 2005, 2007). Despite its title, this book deals virtually exclusively with Jewish obligations and responsibilities to other Jews, not Gentiles. One searches the entire volume almost in vain for any sources that specifically address the Jewish obligation toward non-Jews, which is how the phrase *tikkun olam* is generally understood.

10. This felicitous formulation comes from Isadore Twersky, "Survival, Normalcy, Modernity," in Moshe Davis, ed., *Zionism in Transition* (New York, 1980), p. 349.

11. Uri Zvi Greenberg, *Rehovot ha-Nahar* (Jerusalem and Tel Aviv, 1950), p. 172, cited in J. David Bleich, "*Tikkun Olam:* Jewish Obligations to Non-Jewish Society," p. 98.

12. Eliezer Schweid, "The Attitude Toward the State in Modern Jewish Thought Before Zionism," in Daniel J. Elazar, ed., *Kinship and Consent: The Jewish Political Tradition and Its Contemporary Uses* (Ramat Gan and Philadelphia, 1981), pp. 127–147.

13. Jeffrey S. Gurock and Jacob J. Schacter, *A Modern Heretic and a Traditional Community: Mordecai M. Kaplan, Orthodoxy, and American Judaism* (New York, 1997), pp. 102–103.

14. Leonard J. Mervis, "The Social Justice Movement and the American Reform Rabbi," *American Jewish Archives* 7:2 (June 1955):178–179.

15. Michael A. Meyer, *Response to Modernity: A History of the Reform Movement in Judaism* (New York and Oxford, 1988), pp. 286–289. See too Albert Vorspan and Eugene J. Lipman, *Justice and Judaism: The Work of Social Action* (New York, 1956), highlighting the centrality of social justice in the Reform Jewish community over a half-century ago.

16. Abraham Joshua Heschel, *The Insecurity of Freedom* (Philadelphia, 1966), p. 111.

17. Ruth R. Wisse, *Jews and Power* (New York, 2007), pp. x–xi.

18. See, for example, Sidney Schwarz, *Judaism and Justice: The Jewish Passion to Repair the World* (Woodstock, N.Y., 2006), pp. 108–112.

19. *www.eliewieselfoundation.org/nobelprizespeech.aspx*, cited in Sidney Schwarz, *Judaism and Justice*, p. 134.

20. Elliot N. Dorff, *The Way Into* Tikkun Olam (*Repairing the World*), p. 1; Sidney Schwarz, *Judaism and Justice*, p. xxi.

21. Joseph I. Lieberman, "Introduction" to L. Sandy Maisel and Ira N. Forman, eds., *Jews in American Politics* (Lanham and Boulder, Col., 2001), p. xxii.

22. Eilon Schwartz, "Social Responsibility and Educational Audacity: Heschel's Challenge to 21st-Century Jewish Education," *Kol Hamercaz* 10 (Nisan 5768/April 2008):1.

23. "The New Activism: Repairing the World – With a Vengeance," *The Jewish Week* (June 20, 2008):25–39.

24. See Dahlia Lithwick, "Devil's Advocate," *The New Republic* (July 31, 2000):20.

25. Eric Konigsberg, "Cornel West Busts a Rhyme," *The New Yorker* (August 20 and 27, 2001):56.

26. Daphne Merkin, "In Search of the Skeptical, Hopeful, Mystical Jew That Could Be Me," *The New York Times Magazine* (April 13, 2008):52.

27. *www.aipac.org/Publications/SpeechesByPolicymakers/PC_08_Obama.pdf*, p. 9.

28. *www.thecjm.org*.

29. Mordekhai, *Gittin* #464.

30. See, for example, *Sefer ha-Hinukh* #426; *Tur, Yoreh De'ah* 151, end; *Shulhan Arukh, Yoreh De'ah* 151:12. See *Taz, Yoreh De'ah* 151:9, who strongly argues that supporting Jewish poor is a *mizvah* while supporting Gentile poor is not.

31. *Ran, Gittin (dapei ha-Rif* 28a), *s.v. kovrin*; *Hiddushei ha-Rashba, s.v. ha de-tanya* and *Hiddushei ha-Ritva, s.v. ve-ha de-amrinan, Gittin, ad. loc.* In addition, see, for example, *Bah, Tur Yoreh De'ah* 151, *s.v. asur*; *Shakh, Yoreh De'ah* 151:19, 251:2, 335:8; *Taz, Yoreh De'ah* 151:9; *Perishah, Yoreh De'ah* 151:21, 335:16; *Bi'ur ha-Gra, Yoreh De'ah* 151:20, 251:2, 335:12; 367:1; *Be'er Hetev, Yoreh De'ah* 251:1. See *Enzyklopediah Talmudit* 7 (Jerusalem, 1993), p. 723.

32. I translate from the Shabsai Frankel edition of the *Mishneh Torah* (Jerusalem and Bnei Berak, 1999), vol. 12, p. 288.

33. For this point, see Walter S. Wurzburger, "Darkei Shalom," *Gesher* 6 (1977–1978):84; idem, *Ethics of Responsibility: Pluralistic Approaches to Covenantal Ethics* (Philadelphia, 1994), pp. 50–51.

34. Maimonides' attitude to the Karaites has also been the subject of much scholarly interest. See, for example, Isadore Twersky, *Introduction to the Code of Maimonides* (*Mishneh Torah*) (New Haven and London, 1980), pp. 84–86.

35. Joshua Blau, ed., *Teshuvot ha-Rambam* 2 (Jerusalem, 1986), pp. 729–730, #449.

36. R. Jacob Emden, *Sheilat Yaavez* 1 (Lemberg, 1884), #41, *s.v. u-lefima'sh*, p. 36b.

37. R. Samson Raphael Hirsch, *Horeb* 2 (London, 1962), pp. 379–380, #503.

38. R. Eliyahu Eliezer Dessler, *Mikhtav me-Eliyahu* 4 (Jerusalem, 1983), pp. 245–246. See also the editor's note on p. 246.

39. For a discussion of this position as well as a bibliography of sources where this statement by Rabbi Unterman appeared, see Binyamin Lau, "'Bivoah shel Emet': Rabbanut ve-Akademiah be-Kitvei ha-Rosh Rosenthal al Hazalat Goy be-Shabbat," *Akdamot* 13 (April 2003):11–12. Some considered this position to be "apologetics." See Yosef Salmon, "Nozrim ve-Nazrut be-Sifrut ha-Pesikah mi-Shilhei ha-Me'ah ha-Shemonah Esreh ve-ad ha-Mahzit ha-Sheniyah shel ha-Me'ah ha-Tesha Esreh," in Uri Erlich, Hayyim Kreisel. and Daniel Y. Lasker, eds., *Al Pi ha-Be'er: Mehkarim be-Hagut Yehudit u-be-Mahshavat ha-Halakhah Mugashim le-Yaakov Blidstein* (Beer Sheva, 2008), p. 645, n. 56.

40. R. Menahem Azaryah of Fano, *Sefer Asarah Ma'amarot* (Jerusalem, 2005), p. 110. My thanks to Rabbi Yehuda Kelemer for this reference. Rabbi Kelemer also informed me that when asked if someone could donate part of his *ma'aser* money to the American Cancer Society, Rabbi Shlomo Zalman Auerbach responded in the affirmative and explained that his reason was not that Jews would also benefit from a cure for cancer but that there is an obligation to help rid the world at large from this terrible disease.

41. R. Joseph B. Soloveitchik, "Confrontation," *Tradition* 6:2 (1964):20–21, 26–28. See also p. 17.
    For a sense of how central this text is for this discussion, note that it is cited and discussed no less than nine times in David Shatz, Chaim I. Waxman, and Nathan J. Diament, eds., *Tikkun Olam: Social Responsibility in Jewish Law and Thought*. See pp. 4, 6, 9 n. 23, 10, 19–20, 145–146, 161–162, 179, and 220.

42. Abraham R. Besdin, *Man of Faith in the Modern World: Reflections of the Rav* 2 (Hoboken, N.J., 1989), pp. 142–143.

43. My thanks to Rabbi Kenneth Brander for bringing this letter to my attention. Dr. David Luchins, who solicited the letter from Rabbi Soloveichik on behalf of the Jewish Fund for Justice, told me that parts of it had already been publicized by that organization and had appeared in print in the Jewish press, and he encouraged me to publish this excerpt here.

See also Rabbi Soloveichik's comments on this subject in his "Civil Rights and the Dignity of Man" and "Jew and Jew, Jew and Non-Jew," *Logic of the Heart, Logic of the Mind* (Jerusalem, 1991), pp. 61–91.

44. Aharon Lichtenstein, "The Duties of the Heart and Response to Suffering," in Shalom Carmy, ed., *Jewish Perspectives on the Experience of Suffering* (Northvale, N.J., 1999), p. 59.

45. See the passages in Maimonides cited earlier; *Perishah* on *Tur, Hoshen Mishpat* 249:2, "Even if there are Jewish poor, a person should not say, "If I support Gentile poor I will have less for the Jewish poor." Cf. *Taz, Yoreh De'ah* 251:9.

46. Rabbi Lichtenstein revisited this issue in his paper "Jewish Philanthropy – Whither," prepared for the Twentieth Orthodox Forum Conference held in New York City in March 2008. There he also offers further rationales for the obligation of Jews to be engaged in "outward looking" philanthropy, among them an *a fortiori* argument from the *mizvah* of *za'ar ba'alei hayyim* and an explanation of the implication of the requirement for Jews to be engaged in *yishuvo shel olam*.

47. See *Ketubot* 50a; Rambam, *Hil. Matnot Aniyim* 7:5; *Hil. Eirikhen ve-Haramin* 8:13; *Shulhan Arukh, Yoreh De'ah* 249:1. See also Cyril Domb, *Ma'aser Kesafim* (New York, 1980).

48. Rambam, *Hil. Matnot Aniyim*, Chapter 8; *Shulhan Arukh, Yoreh De'ah* 251.

49. *Shulhan Arukh, Yoreh De'ah* 252.

50. See n. 40 above.

בגדר קדושת ישראל

הרב צבי שכטר

א. איתא בגמ' ברכות (ו.) וראו כל עמי הארץ כי שם ד' נקרא עליך ויראו
ממך, ותניא ר' אליעזר הגדול אומר אלו תפילין שבראש. ודבר ברור הוא שאין
זה פשוטו של מקרא אלא דרשה נוספת בבחינת אחת דבר אלוקים שתים זו
שמעתי וגו' (תהילים סב:י"ב), שמקרא אחד יוצא לכמה טעמים (סנהדרין ל"ד
ע"א).[1] אכן להבין פשוטו של מקרא עי' אדרת אליהו להגר"א (שמה לפ' כי
תבוא), כי פסוק זה הוא המשך לסוף הפסוק הקודם – והלכת בדרכיו. והיא
מ"ע ח' במנין המצוות של הרמב"ם – להדמות בדרכיו. כלומר, שכל אדם
נברא בצלם אלוקים, כלומר, עם מדות אלקיות, ואפשר לנו לשמור על הצלם
ההוא וליזהר שלא לאבדו.[2] ואח"כ ממשיך הפסוק שלאחריו – וראו כל עמי
הארץ כי שם ד' נקרא עליך – כשיראו אומות העולם שהצלחנו לשמור על
הצלם האלקי אשר בתוכנו (דהיינו – שם ד' נקרא עליך) ואף הם נבראו בצלם
א', וזה גם באפשרותם לעשות, ליזהר שלא לאבד את צלם הא' שלהם, ויראו
ממך – ילמדו ממנו ענין זה של יראת שמים, ואף ענין זה של להדמות אליו ית'.
ופסוק זה שבפ' כי תבא הוא המקור בחומש למושג המפורש ע"י ישעיה הנביא
(מ"ט:ו) ונתתיך לאור גויים, שלכלל ישראל יש חובת שליחות בעוה"ז – לשמש
כאור לגויים, להראות לאוה"ע את הדרך ילכו בה. ואין הכוונה בזה לדיני שבת,
כשרות, וטהרת המשפחה, כי מה אלו ענין לאוה"ע, אלא הכוונה על הזהירות
בצלם הא' שלא לאבדו.

ונראה דהיינו נמי פשוטו של מקרא דר"פ קדושים, קדושים תהיו כי
קדוש אני ד' אלוקיכם. כלומר, שכולנו חביבים שנבראנו בבחינת בנים למקום,
וכמו שהקב"ה הקדוש, כמו"כ נולדנו כלנו בניצוץ של קדושה בתוך נשמותינו,

ושפיר אפשר לכולנו לשמור על הקדושה שבנו, וליזהר בה שלא לאבדה, וזאת היא משמעות מצוה זו של קדושים תהיו – לשמור וליזהר שלא לאבד בחינת הקדושה שישנה כבר בתוכנו מבטן ומלידה.

ב) ובהקדמת הג"ר שמעון שקאפ ז"ל לספרו שערי יושר הביא מדברי המדרש עה"פ ההוא, קדושים תהיו, יכול כמוני, (כלומר, באותה הדרגה והרמה של קדושה), ת"ל, כי קדוש אני, קדושתי למעלה מקדושתכם, ויתבאר בהמשך דברינו. ובפשוטו אין הדרשה הזאת מובנת, דפשטיה דקרא ר"ל שנשמור על אותה הקדושה שכבר יש בנו, ודומיא דהפסוק שהבאנו מקודם והלכת בדרכיו. ומ"ל לתנאים לדרוש מכאן שקדושתי למעלה מקדושתכם. ונכון שמצד הסברא העניין מאוד מסתבר להניח כן שקדושתו ית' בודאי למעלה מקדושתנו, אך צריכים להבין היאך הבין זה מתוך לשון הפסוק.

ומצאתי בס' הנפלא מלא וחסר בתנ"ך (מאת הרב אברהם בן מאיר יאקבס, ז"ל) שדרשת הספרא שבכאן מיוסדת על כך שתיבת קדשים כתובה חסר וא"ו, ואילו תיבת כי קדוש אני, כתובה מלא וא"ו, להורות שקדושתו ית' היא מלאה, ואילו הקדושה שהוא מחייב אותנו לנהוג בה-קדושה בלתי-שלמה ובלתי-מלאה היא.[3]

ובמס' יומא (מג:) הובאה דרשת החכמים [כנגד דעת הצדוקים שהיו טוֹעֲנים שטבו"י פסול לעסוק בפרה], דילפינן מקרא דכתיב והזה הטהור על הטמא, טהור מכלל שהוא טמא, לימד על טבו"י שכשר בפרה. ובפשוטו, דברי הגמ' תמוהים, מהיכן דייקו לומר כן, שהטהור המזה את מי הפרה אינו צריך להיות טהור לגמרי. ובספר הנ"ל ביאר שאף דרשה זו יסודה במה שתיבת "הטהור" כתובה בתורה חסר וא"ו, לומר שיש לו רק טהרה בלתי-גמורה ובלתי שלמה. ואף שלא נזכרה מדה זו (לדרוש את ההבדל שבין מלא לחסר) בברייתא דר' ישמעאל בין יתר המדות שהתורה נדרשת בהם, מכ"מ דבר זה מפורש הוא בגמ' כתובות (מ:) שלרבנן דר"מ, שיש קנס לקטנה, הדין הזה נדרש ממאי דכתיב נערה חסר ה"א (להורות שהכונה אף על נערה בלתי-שלמה, דהיינו – קטנה) חוץ ממוציא שם רע, ששמה כתיב נערה מלא ה"א, (שהכונה על נערה שלמה), דנערה מלא דבר הכתוב, שהמוצש"ר על הקטנה פטור, דנערה מלא דבר הכתוב.

ג) והנה הרמב"ם במשנה תורה כתב (רפ"י מהל' ס"ת) שס"ת שהוא פסול אין קורין בו ברבים. ועיי"ש בכס"מ, שבתשובתו כתב הרמב"ם להיפך, ושכבר העיר בזה הרשב"א על הסתירה שבדבריו, וסבור הוא לומר שבילדותו כתב כן (להקל), וחזר בו בזקנותו. ולכתחילה הכי קיי"ל, שלא לקרות בציבור מס"ת שאינו כשר, אכן במקרה שכבר קראו חצי הפרשה ונמצאת טעות בס"ת, בכה"ג מיקרי בדיעבד, וסמכינן אתשובת הרמב"ם. כן כתב הכס"מ שם בשם רבו הגדול מהר"י בי רב זלה"ה.

ויש מן האחרונים שיעצו, שאם אפשר לחלק את יתר הפרשה (שקורא בס"ת השני הכשר) לז' עליות, מן הנכון לעשות כן, כי לגבי זה, זהו כבר לכתחילה, וכן הביא המשנ"ב (סי' קמ"ג ס"ק ט"ז).

ד) וזכורני היאך שפ"א התפללתי בבהכ"נ אחד ונמצאת טעות בס"ת באמצע קריאת פ' האזינו, והורה הרב של אותו המנין להחמיר כן ולעשות ז' עליות בספר השני. וכשהתאספו כל המתפללים שוב באותו היום לתפילת מנחה, הכריז הרב, שדברים שאמרתי בפניכם בבקר טעות הן בידי, שהרי מבואר בגמ' ר"ה (לא.) שפרשת האזינו צריכים לחלק באופן מיוחד (הזי"ו ל"ך), ושאינו נכון לעשות בה הוספות, ומה שהחמיר (לעשות ז' עליות בספר החדש) היתה חומרא שהביאה לידי קולא וקלקול, שלא נזהרנו בדין הגמ' דהזי"ו ל"ך. (ועי' מש"כ בספר נפש הרב (עמ' ק"מ) בשם רבינו הגרי"ד סאלאווייטשיק ז"ל, שקיימת אפשרות שזה דין דאורייתא, ושהמפסיק במקום אחר בפ' האזינו נחשב כקורא שלא ככתבו.)

וכשלמדנו או"ח הל' קרה"ת אצל רבינו ז"ל הביע את דעתו בזה, שאם המתפללים בני תורה הם, ואפשר לשכנע אותם בלי מלחמות ומחלוקת שכדאי לשמוע קריאת כל הפרשה כולה עוה"פ מתחילה מן הס"ת השני (הכשר), מן הנכון להתחיל מתחילת הסדרה, כי אף זה בבחינת לכתחילה הוא בציור שכזה, ולכתחילה קיי"ל כפסק הרמב"ם שבמשנה תורה.

ה) ודבר ידוע הוא שיש ספק (בפ' כי תצא) היאך לכתוב תיבת פצוע דכא, אם באל"ף או בה"א. וכבר עמדו על כך האחרונים, דהלא לפי מאי דקיי"ל כדעת הרמב"ם, שס"ת שחסר אות א' או שיש בו יתור של אות אחת פסולה, היאך קוראים קרה"ת בשום מקום בברכה, הלא כולנו מסופקים לגבי האות הנכונה של תיבת דכא. והמקובל לדינא בזה הוא מש"כ בזה הרב מנח"ח (במצוה תרי"ג) שמה שאנו פוסלים ספר תורה שחסר אות אחת, היינו דוקא כשיש טעות בכתיבה, כגון שכתבו בראשית חסר א', או שכתבו תיבת נח עם שבע טעויות (כפתגם הידוע ביידיש). אבל במקום שכתבו תיבה שלא לפי המסורה אבל לא נכתבה בטעות (מכפי המופיע במלון), ואין השינוי שבכתוב משנה את ענין התיבה, אז אף שמן הנכון לתקנו בהקדם האפשרי, מכ"מ אין זה פוסל את הספר, חוץ ממקרה של קרי וכתיב, שאם נכתב כפי מה שצ"ל הקרי, אז יש לפסול אותו הספר, אפילו בדעבד, דקרי וכתיב הללמ"ס היא שכן צריך שיהיה (כדאיתא בגמ' נדרים ל"ז ע"ב). וכתיבת תיבת דכה (בה"א או באל"ף) בשני האופנים כתיבה נכונה היא, אלא שרק האחת נכונה ע"פ המסורה, אך מפאת זה אין לפסול את הספר בדעבד.

והגדולים שבאו לאחר המנ"ח נסתפקו מה יהיה הדין בכתב תיבת היא ביו"ד, והיתה צריכה להכתב בוא"ו (הוא, וקריאתה – כאילו הי' הוא"ו יו"ד)

אם יש לפסול בכה"ג, שדינה כקרי וכתיב, או דנימא דב' אופנים נכונים יש
לאיות תיבה זו (עי' ס' אורחות חיים (ספינקא) לסי' קמ"א אות ח', ובהערות
שערי רחמים שעל הס' שערי אפרים, שער וא"ו, לפ' אמור.) וכה"ג נמי יש
להסתפק בכותב נערה (מלא) במקום נער (חסר), האם דינו כקרי וכתיב, שיש
לפסול הספר אפילו בדעבד, או שנאמר שבלשון התנ"ך יש שני אופנים נכונים
לכתיבת התיבה נערה, או מלא או חסר, ושאין לפסול הספר מפני טעות זו.

ו) והנה, מנהגנו לקרוא מגילת רות בחג השבועות. וכמה טעמים נאמרו
בזה. ושמעתי מרבנו ז"ל בשם הגר"א, שכמה פרטים בהל' גרות נלמדו (ביבמות
פרק החולץ) מתוך הפסוקים באשר תלכי אלך וגו' עמך עמי וגו' ותרא כי
מתאמצת היא ללכת וגו'. והיות שבקשר לחג השבועות נתגיירו אבותינו, שהרי
בכריתות (ט.) קבעו, שמה אבותיכם נכנסו לברית ע"י מילה, טבילה, והרצאת
דמים (כלומר, קרבן הגר), שאף לדורות הדין כן, הרי שהבינו שבקשר למעה"ס
הי' שמה גירות לכלל ישראל, לפיכך הוא שנהגו לקרוא מגילת רות בחג
השבועות, שתוכנה ועניינה – גרות, והוא היו"ט של גרות של כלל ישראל.[4]

ז) ודברי הילקו"ש (סי' תר"א) ידועים (עה"פ יעש ד' עמכם חסד כאשר
עשיתם עם המתים) שהמגילה הזאת אין בה לא טומאה ולא טהרה, לא היתר
ולא איסור, ולמה נכתבה, ללמדך שכר של גומלי חסדים. ולפי הנ"ל, שעיקר
תוכנה של מגילת רות הוא ענין הגרות, אולי י"ל דהכל אחד, דעיקר תוכנה של
קדושת ישראל (החלה מכח הגרות) היא באמת ענין זה של גמילות חסדים.

ועיי"ש בתחילת ההקדמה להס' שערי יושר שביאר, שענין הקדושה
היינו – שיהיו כל עבודתנו ועמלנו תמיד מוקדשים לטובת הכלל, שלא נשתמש
בשום מעשה ותנועה, הנאה ותענוג שלא יהיה בזה איזה ענין לטובת זולתנו,
וכמובן בכל הקדושות שהוא התיחדות למטרה נכבדה. והנה כשאדם מיישר
הליכותיו ושואף שתמיד יהיו דרכי חייו מוקדשים להכלל, אז כל מה שעושה,
גם לעצמו להבראת גופו ונפשו, הוא מתיחס ג'"כ אל מצות קדושה, שעי"ז
יטיב גם לרבים, שבטובתו לעצמו הוא מטיב עם הרבים הצריכים לו...וביחס זה
מתדמה ענין קדושה זו לקדושת הבורא ית' באיזה דמיון קצת, שכמו שבמעשה
של הקב"ה בהבריאה כולה...כל מעשיו הם מוקדשים לטובת זולתו, כן רצונו
ית' שיהיו מעשינו תמיד מוקדשים לטובת הכלל, ולא להנאת עצמו. [וזהו
ביאור ההו"א של המדרש הנ"ל, יכול כמוני, כלומר,...אם יאמר האדם להכניע
את טבעו, להגיע למדה יתירה עד שלא יהיה בנפשו שום מחשבה ושאיפה
להיטיב לעצמו, וכל שאיפותיו יהיו רק להיטיב לאחרים, (מה שנקרא אצלנו
"אלטרואיזם"), ובאופן כזה תהיה שאיפתו להגיע לקדושת הבורא ית', שרצונו
ית' בכל הבריאה...רק להיטיב להנבראים,[5] ולא לעצמו ית' כלל וכלל...ולכן

הורו לנו חז"ל במדרש זה שלא כן הוא, שאין לנו להשתדל להדמות לקדושת
הבורא ית' בצד זה, שקדושת הבורא למעלה מקדושתנו וכו'.

הרי שהבין הגרש"ש שעיקר תוכן קדושת ישראל זהו ענין ההטבה
לאחרים, והיינו – גמילות חסדים. והשוה גמ' שבת (לא.) שוב מעשה בנכרי אחד
שבא לפני שמאי, א"ל גייריני ע"מ שתלמדני כל התורה כולה כשאני עומד על
רגל אחת. (וביאר שמה בח"א מהרש"א שכונתו לומר, שילמדו היסוד העיקרי
שעליו בנויים כל המצוות.) דחפו באמת הבנין שבידו (כלומר, שכמו שבנין א"א
לעמוד על יסוד אחד, כן התורה רחבה במצוותיה, וא"א ליתן לה יסוד אחד,
מהרש"א שמה). בא לפני הלל, גייריה, א"ל דעלך סני לחברך לא תעביד, זו היא
כל התורה כולה, ואידך פירושה הוא, זיל גמור. ופשטות משמעות הגמ' כדברי
הג"ר שמעון ז"ל הנ"ל. וכן עי' גמ' יבמות (עט.) שלשה סימנים יש באומה זו,
רחמנים ביישנים וגומלי חסדים...כל שיש בו שלשה סימנים הללו ראוי להדבק
באומה זו. והובאו דברי הגמ' הללו בשו"ע אה"ע (סי' ב' סוף ס"ב), וכן מי
שיש בו עזות פנים ואכזריות...ואינו גומל להם חסד, חוששים לו ביותר שמא
גבעוני הוא. ובב"ש שמה (סק"ג) הבין שאין צריכים לחוש אא"כ חסרים אצלו
כל ג' הסימנים. והאחרונים דנו שם בדבריו, שבאמת יש מקום לומר אחרת,
ועי' באור הלכה (שבס' דרך אמונה) פ"י מהל' מתנות עניים ה"ב, שפשטות
לשון הרמב"ם (שמה) משמע דאפילו אם אחד מהסימנים יש לחוש, דענין
גמ"ח הוא כ"כ עקרוני לקדושת ישראל, מי שאין בו מדה זו צריכים לחוש שמא
באמת חסרה לו קדו"י.

הערות

1. ועי' עוד מש"כ בזה בס' גנת אגוז (עמ' קפ"ו).
2. והשוה דברי רבינו (שהובאו בס' מפניני הרב ד"ה נאמנות): מה שיש לכל אדם מישראל נאמנות (באיסורים ובממונות וכו') היינו מפני שכל אדם נברא בצלם אלקים, וחותמו של הקב"ה – אמת (יומא סט:), וממילא, אף מדה זו (של אמת) ג"כ נטועה היא באדם מתחילת לידתו, כשאר מדות האלקיות, אך הבזויים המקלקלים את צלם האלקים שלהם, ומאבדים בידים את אלו המדות האלקיות, אף מדת האמת ג"כ בכלל, וממילא נפסלים הם מלהעיד...ומה"ט נמי פסולים הרשעים לעדות, כדכתיב ומוראכם וחתכם יהיה על כל חית הארץ, דאין חיה שולטת באדם עד שנדמה לו כבהמה, שנאמר, אדם ביקר בל ילין נמשל כבהמות נדמו, כשהאדם משתקע בעוונות, צלם האלקים מסתלק מעל פניו.
3. וכעת מצאתו כדברים האלה ממש בספר עקיבא סופר (ד"ה סופר דקדושים").
4. ועי' בית יצחק (תשנ"ב, עמ' ע"ח).
5. כנראה, כונת הגאון בזה למש"כ המקובלים, שמה הניעו הקב"ה לברוא את עולמו הוא, כי טבע הטוב להטיב, וקודם שנברא העולם לא הי' ביכולתו ית' להטיב לאחרים, ועמש"כ בזה בס' מפניני הרב (ד"ה טעמי המצוות) בשם הגר"ח.

To be German and Jewish: Hermann Cohen and Rabbi Samson Raphael Hirsch

Meir Soloveichik

✿ MODERNITY AND ORTHODOXY

In his book *After Emancipation*, David Ellenson notes that academics studying the encounter between German Jews and modernity all too often ignore the Orthodox community in Germany. It is frequently assumed, he notes, that German Orthodoxy lived a life unimpacted by modernity.[1] This view of German Orthodoxy, Ellenson admits, is understandable, because the German Orthodox often portrayed themselves in this way. Yet scholarship, Ellenson notes, has produced a new appreciation of the fact that German Orthodoxy in general, and Rabbi Hirsch in particular, was quite modern in certain respects. Similarly, Rabbi Aaron Lichtenstein has noted that while R. Hirsch's "humanism is genuine and genuinely Jewish," the fact that it contains a modern "element that has been engrafted is inescapable."[2] Ellenson therefore argues that an understanding of how German Orthodoxy responded to modernity is necessary "if a full portrait of modern Judaism and its struggle with the reformulation of tradition is to be complete."[3]

It is with this concept in mind that a fierce traditionalist such as Rabbi Samson Raphael Hirsch and a modern German Jewish intellectual such as Hermann Cohen can be compared. It may seem at first that no commonalities between the two should exist. Rabbi Hirsch was the zealous proponent of German Orthodoxy, who insisted that any authentic philosophy of Judaism must be founded on the premise that, in his own words, "the Law, both Written and Oral, was closed with Moses at Sinai."[4] Cohen, on the other hand, studied with, and was impacted by, the Positive-Historical school of Zacharias Frankel. In his *Religion of Reason out of the Sources of Judaism*, Cohen argues that though Judaism at its outset clung to ancient superstitions, mythology, and an ethical system that excluded many members of society, the rabbis discarded all of these flaws in developing a religion that, once properly understood, could be admired by as brilliant and modern a man as Immanuel Kant.

Ellenson notes, however, that one would be wrong to assume that no similarities exist between the approach to Judaism of Hermann Cohen and that of Rabbi Hirsch. Like Cohen, Rabbi Hirsch was eager to illustrate that there was nothing superstitious about Judaism, and Rabbi Hirsch, like Cohen, utilized modern philosophy "as the medium to explain and defend Judaism to Jew and Gentile alike." Interestingly, it was precisely in Rabbi Hirsch's assuming, like Cohen, that no tension existed between the Talmud on the one hand and modern philosophy on the other that allowed him to argue against the Positive-Historical school in the first place. Insisting that Judaism embodied eternal truths, Rabbi Hirsch argued that Judaism did not develop these notions over time; rather they are the philosophical essence at the heart of the Bible. Thus, Ellenson concludes, "philosophy, not history, became a weapon to wield on behalf of Orthodoxy in a world hostile to tradition."[5]

In defending the eternal relevance of all 613 commandments to German Jewry, Rabbi Hirsch insisted that every *mitzvah* symbolically conveyed a philosophical concept – and that this concept was one fully reconcilable with modern philosophy. As an example, Ellenson cites Rabbi Hirsch's explanation of perhaps the most cultic ritual in the Torah: the rite of the Azazel goat, the Temple scapegoat whose death ensured the forgiveness of the Jewish people on Yom Kippur. The reader of the Bible might well understand the importance of the ritual for Temple-era Israelites to be mystical in nature. Rabbi Hirsch, however, insists that the rites are symbolic of philosophical truths. In his commentary on the Bible, Rabbi Hirsch argues that the Azazel goat, thrown off the cliff, is "the embodiment of that mistaken way of life which misuses the divine gift of free decision by giving oneself up to be mastered by one's senses and which turns that which was given to us to devote to moral freedom, to devotion, into moral lack of freedom." Any hint of the cultic is thus removed; as Ellenson put it, "Through his emphasis on the human ability to decide between good and evil, obedience and rebellion, Rabbi Hirsch supplies a Kantian understanding of these passages in keeping with nineteenth-century German moral sensibilities." Thus Rabbi Hirsch propounds a philosophy of Judaism which "would not offend a Kantian notion of ethics."[6]

Cohen and Rabbi Hirsch therefore differ greatly in their attitude toward the cultic rites of biblical Judaism and in their respective beliefs regarding the history of the *halakha*; but in their search for synthesis between Jewish ethics and Enlightenment they are actually somewhat similar. Both present philosophical justifications of Judaism, and both draw on the vast corpus of Jewish legal literature – Bible, Talmud, Midrash, Maimonides – in order to do so. Further, both take for granted that the philosophical worldview derived from these sources will in no way stand in tension with the Kantian values of their age. Ellenson cites Rabbi Isaac Breuer, Rabbi Hirsch rabbinic and intellectual heir, who articulated the following as a summation of German Orthodoxy's worldview: "In Judaism, law and ethics are absolutely identical." This statement by a leader of German Orthodoxy, Ellenson notes, is "reminiscent of Hermann Cohen."[7]

A closer study of Rabbi Hirsch's writings confirms Ellenson's thesis, and indicates that the some of the philosophical similarities

between Rabbi Hirsch's writings and Cohen's are even more striking than Ellenson suggests. While Rabbi Hirsch was a fierce de-
fender of tradition, the fact is that some forty years before the
publication of Cohen's *Religion of Reason*, Rabbi Hirsch argued
for an ethical philosophy whose universalism was, in certain respects, quite modern. In justifying the divine origins of the Torah
and *halakha*, Rabbi Hirsch built a philosophical system of ethics
different from that of some earlier traditional *halakhic* exegetes.
In defending the chosenness of Israel and the eternal relevance
of the Torah, Rabbi Hirsch insisted that Judaism required no
preferential ethical treatment for, or love of, Jews by other Jews.
Furthermore, Israel's being chosen by God does not indicate any
divine favor bestowed upon the Jewish people. On the contrary,
Israel, chosen in order to educate all mankind of the ways of God,
is in no way especially beloved by God. All men, created in the image of God, are brothers; all are blessed with moral intuition and
therefore ought to relate to each other equally, with no thought
to kinship or covenantal affiliation. Hatred of evildoers, Rabbi
Hirsch insisted, is forbidden by Jewish law; and evildoers will
ultimately be defeated not by violence but by ethical inspiration.
In other words, in defending the importance of tradition, Rabbi
Hirsch argues for a universalism that was quite reconcilable with
the ethos of nineteenth-century Germany.

In this respect Rabbi Hirsch's writings are, at times, strikingly similar to those Hermann Cohen, who, a few decades later,
argued in like fashion that a universal ethic of love lay at the heart
of Jewish law and observance. And though neither Cohen nor
Rabbi Hirsch gives any indication that their universalism is at
times almost complete contradiction with Jewish legal literature,
both were all too aware of the problems presented by specific Talmudic sources, and they took pains to address them. We cannot
be sure of the exact influence that Rabbi Hirsch may have had on
Hermann Cohen. Yet whether or not Rabbi Hirsch's commentary
on the Bible, and his other writings on Judaism, impacted Cohen's

philosophy of Judaism in a direct fashion, a thorough examination of Rabbi Hirsch's universalism allows us to put Cohen's own writings in proper perspective. While Cohen's belief in the evolution of Judaism was certainly very different from that of Rabbi Hirsch, Cohen's placing of universal ethics at the heart of Judaism was quite consistent with the approach of German Jewish Orthodoxy. In presenting a philosophical defense of Judaism, Cohen saw himself as following in the tradition of Moses Maimonides. But Cohen's enlightenment-influenced universalism and his rejection of any notion of Jewish political power and military might are foreign to the Maimonidean perspective, and indeed to much of the medieval Jewish tradition. It is all the more striking, then, that the traditional Jew with whom Cohen's ethical philosophy has the most in common was the man who led German Jewish Orthodoxy when Cohen was himself coming of age.

This essay will attempt to place Hermann Cohen's philosophy in perspective by comparing his writings with those of Rabbi Samson Raphael Hirsch. When possible, both Cohen and Rabbi Hirsch's writings will be contrasted with legal statements made by Maimonides. This contrast will indicate how different Cohen and Rabbi Hirsch are in their philosophy of Jewish ethics from that of certain earlier traditional Jewish writings, while at the same time exhibiting how much they themselves have in common with each other. Since Rabbi Hirsch's writings are vast, this essay will limit itself to singling out some of the essential concepts in Cohen's Jewish thought and illustrating the striking similarities between them and ideas propounded by Rabbi Hirsch in his commentary on the Pentatauch. Rabbi Hirsch's and Cohen's beliefs regarding the history of *halakha* were quite different from one another, and I certainly do not mean to minimize the enormous theological gap between them. But this essay will illustrate that in their interpretations of certain Jewish texts about ethics, they are strikingly similar in their reconciliation of Judaism and Kantian universalism.

ᛰ COHEN, RABBI HIRSCH, AND NEIGHBOR-LOVE

We begin by examining the foundation of much of Jewish ethics: "Thou shalt love thy neighbor as thyself; I am the Lord."[8] The verse was singled out by Rabbi Akiba as an embodiment of the entire Torah. In his *Mishneh Torah*, Maimonides clearly limits the obligation of neighbor-love to Jews: "It is an obligation upon every person to love every single member of Israel like his own self, as it is written, 'and thou shalt love thy neighbor as thyself.'"[9] Maimonides indicates likewise in his Book of the Commandments that the verse obligates "a member of our minority to love a member of our minority (*le-ehov ketzateinu et ketzateinu*) as we will love ourselves, and that our love and mercy to our brother should be like our love and mercy for ourselves." David Novak, in his analysis of Hermann Cohen's philosophy, notes that prior to Cohen most Jewish commentators had limited the obligation of neighbor-love to Jews, while at the same time insisting that the Jewish approach to the Gentile world be one of "justice for all." The most obvious argument for the traditional reading, notes Novak, is the verse's concluding "I am the Lord." Jews, Novak suggests, have long understood the obligation of neighbor-love as commanding Jews to bestow upon fellow Jews the preferential, covenantal love that all of them enjoy from the God of Abraham, Isaac, and Jacob. God therefore concludes the commandment, Novak writes, by identifying Himself as "the God of the covenant."[10]

It is the notion that Judaism limits covenantal love to members of the Jewish people that Cohen sets out to refute. In his *Religion of Reason*, Cohen insists that Judaism obligates every individual to "discover man as fellowman." The foundation of love, according to Cohen, is determined not by kinship or faith, but rather by the fact that all human beings are created in the image of God and are therefore brothers. He notes that Genesis warns that "at the hand of every man's brother, will I require the soul of man," with the Bible subsequently explaining its statement by stating that "in the image of God He made man." Man, made in the image of God, is called the brother of all other human beings created in His image. "Consequently," Cohen concludes, "according to the covenant with Noah, every man is already the brother of every other."[11] The notion that neighbor-love is an obligation extending only to one's countryman is, Cohen argues, "a biased misinterpretation."[12]

Interestingly, Rabbi Hirsch's commentary on the verse obligating neighbor-love is even more enthusiastically universal in approach; he makes no mention of the possibility that the commandment is limited to Jews. For Rabbi Hirsch, just as for Cohen, it is not the Jew that is the exclusive object of religious love, but rather the "fellowman." In contrast to the traditional Jewish approach, which, as Novak noted, sees in the statement "I am the Lord" an implication of the exclusivity of the commandment, Rabbi Hirsch singles out the phrase as indicating the contrary: that all human beings are obligated to love each other. "For the demand of this love is something which lies quite outside the sphere of the personality of our neighbour, is not based on any of his qualities. *I am the Lord* is given as the motive for this demand. It is something that is expected from us towards all our fellow-men in the Name of God, who has given all men the mutual calling of *rei'im*."[13] That the embodiment of German Orthodox resistance to modernity accepted, without question, the universality of religious love, in stark contrast to the traditional interpretation, is strking.

Having insisted that in obligating us to love the neighbor, the Bible referred not to Jew but to "fellowman," both Rabbi Hirsch and Cohen must now grapple with a passage whose implication is to the contrary.

> Akiba says: "Thou shalt love the neighbour as yourself." This is a great principle in the Torah." Ben Azai says: "This is the book of the generations of man." This is a greater principle than the other.[14]

The clear implication in the passage is that the second verse is all-encompassing to an extent that the first verse is not. Indeed, the simplest reading, and the one taken by most traditional commentators, is the following: while Rabbi Akiba chooses the commandment of neighbor-love as a central principle of the Torah, which is a verse limited to commanding love of fellow-Jews, Ben Azai stresses that there exists a verse more universal in essence, since it speaks of a common ancestor of all mankind. For Rabbi Hirsch and Cohen, however, the passage is problematic. In their view, Rabbi Akiba has already understood neighbor-love to be a universal principle. In what way, then, is Ben Azai's verse a greater principle of the Torah? Rabbi Hirsch and Cohen both respond by noting the second part of Ben Azai's verse, though Ben Azai himself does not stress that clause in the Talmudic text: "On the day on which God created Adam, he formed them in the likeness of God." It is true, they both argue, that Rabbi Akiba cites as the embodiment of Judaism a verse obligating universal love. But the verse does not cite the *grounds* of that love, the ultimate bond between individuals, which must be only the fact that all men are created in God's image. "Which foundation," queries Cohen, "is the superior? Perhaps the first, which stresses the equality between man and man, which makes man into the 'the other,' and therefore into the fellowman? Or the one that makes man, as God's creature, the image of God? Evidently Ben Azai is right."[15] Ben Azai's verse, Cohen insists, implies that the unity of man is founded not on the Torah, nor on the Noahide code, but rather on the fact that man is created in God's image: "The Israelite is a son of Noah before he is a son of Abraham.... But before he is a son of Abraham and a son of Noah, the Israelite is, just as every man is, God's creature and is created in his image." Similarly, Rabbi Hirsch, in his commentary on the Torah, *does not* explain that Rabbi Akiva's verse is limited to less people than Ben Azai; rather, he argues that Ben Azai stresses that all human beings, moral and immoral, are alike, and that Ben Azai believes this to be an even more important, though no more universal verse, than Rabbi Akiva's. While Rabbi Akiba, in establishing the universal principle of neighbor-love, indicated that "at the bottom there is, after all, only one sin, selfishness, egoism," Ben Azai's verse indicates that "the greatest criminal, the greatest degeneration, the greatest bestiality, all as developing out of the one Adam, the one creation in the likeness of God."[16]

Both Rabbi Hirsch and Cohen, then, confront and deftly deal with a problematic passage in a similar way: by insisting that neighbor-love was always understood by the Talmud to be universal, and by explaining that Ben Azai was stressing that this universal neighbor-love is founded solely on the concept of *imagio dei*.

✠ GOD, MAN, AND HATE

Just as Rabbi Hirsch and Cohen take the universalization of religious love for granted, so do they take a similar approach to its corollary: "Thou shalt not hate thy brother in thy heart." Jews long understood that this prohibition does not apply to the wicked, as Jews are permitted to hate the egregiously evil, Jew or non-Jew. The *Sefer ha-Hinnukh*, an anonymously composed compilation on the commandments modeled on Maimonides' code, notes that the Bible itself has instances of expressed hate. When it comes to hating the wicked, he notes, "there is no prohibition, but rather an obligation to hate them after we have reproved them many times for their sins and they have not repented, as it is written, 'Will I not hate them, or Lord, who hate thee?'"[17] (Psalms 139:11).

Rabbi Hirsch argues that the prohibition against hatred is a corollary of the obligation of the neighbor-love; the universality of one demands the universality of the other.

> These principles of social life lived under the dictates of that which God considers social life should be, are not complemented by indicating what our relations are to be towards those of our fellowmen who, forgetting these principles, have misbehaved towards us, and who thereby might be considered to have forfeited their right to demand our consideration and love. Against that idea comes the holy and

sanctifying Word of God: *Thou shalt not hate thy brother in thy heart.* The Torah assumes that, left to ourselves, the behaviour of our fellowmen towards us might have allowed the feeling and the conception of hatred to arise in our heart… Such a feeling, which may be quite a natural one to a human heart not ennobled by the control of God's Torah, we are not allowed to arise within us. However badly our fellowman may have behaved towards us, however much, by his forgetting his duty towards our welfare…one name he can never lose, our brother he remains. This he remains by the common thread of Divine descent, joined in brotherhood to us in God, and through God. We remain brothers, children of the same Paternal House.[18]

Similarly, Cohen, in his chapter on the virtues, also assumes that one cannot hate the wicked. Even one's enemy is a proper object only of love, and not of hate. Cohen argues that when the Bible instructs us not to hate one's brother, the implication is that "hatred is determined as opposition to the brother and to the heart, hence as opposition to the fellowman and to man's own foundation, which lies in his heart."[19]

Cohen and Rabbi Hirsch both proceed to grapple with the following possible problem with their point of view, though neither of them openly acknowledges that a problem presents itself. One sin cited by the Talmud as responsible for the destruction of the Temple is *sinat hinam*, or "baseless hatred." The fact that the rabbis singled out some types of hatred as being baseless indicates that some types of hatred do have a legitimate foundation. Here Rabbi Hirsch's and Cohen's answers differ. Rabbi Hirsch counters the problem by arguing that while all forms of hatred are forbidden, some are more baseless than others. Even hatred of an enemy is forbidden by the Torah, "however badly he may have behaved toward us;" but the prohibition is "all the more necessary, as human feelings, left to their own natural, unnobled trend, know even *sinat hinam*, an unjustified and unprovoked hatred." This hatred,

Rabbi Hirsch explains, involves resenting one's "brother-man" who, in his struggle for daily sustenance, competes and thereby "threatens to overtake" the other, an action leading to a feeling of resentment of hate. Specifically this form of *sin'ah*, Rabbi Hirsch argues, is *hinam*, baseless, because worldly competition is inevitable, and we must look "on every other human being working alongside us as a 'brother' in our Father's house."[20]

Cohen's answer is even more creative. The Talmud's reference to "baseless hatred" is not in any way an indication that some forms of hatred are properly founded. On the contrary, the phrase is itself proof positive that hatred is always forbidden. If one of the worst sins in the Talmudic worldview is "baseless hatred," that, Cohen argues, is so because *all hatred is baseless*. Hatred, in his words, "is always wanton hatred." It is not enough, he argues, that we are obligated to love our enemy; "I can remove hatred from the human heart only insofar as I do not know any enemy at all."[21] All *sin'ah* is *hinam*; all "hatred is vain." Cohen admits that the Bible does have verses authorizing hatred of the enemy, but argues that rabbinic Judaism, in the course of its development, progressed beyond such vengeful sentiments. It is true, Cohen acknowledges, that there are psalms "which in this line of thought seem to breathe vehement hatred and insatiable vengeance." But the "wisdom of the Talmud has progressed beyond the Bible."[22] In developing the philosophical notion of baseless hatred, the rabbis declared that "people persuade themselves that they hate one another, but this is their delusion, the fateful outcome of their ignorance about their own soul and their consciousness." Cohen and Rabbi Hirsch, then, both argue for an ethics fully consonant with the Kantian worldview, but Cohen combines his philosophical defense of Judaism with his belief in the development of Judaism in order to avoid scriptural objections to his ethical worldview.

☙ RABBI HIRSCH AND BIBLICAL HATRED

Rabbi Hirsch, of course, will not argue that the rabbis developed an ethical philosophy more perfect than that found in scripture.

But Rabbi Hirsch, apparently, cannot countenance the notion of hating a human being. He therefore has a difficult time dealing with biblical passages that clearly endorse the hatred of wicked individuals. Let us examine, for example, an excerpt which is quite well known, since it is one of the prophetic portions read in synagogues on the Sabbath. In the beginning of the book of Malachi, Israel is depicted as concerned that it lacks any self-worth, that the Israelites are loved only because of their ancestors. As an answer, the Almighty responds that Jacob and Esau shared the same righteous ancestors but God loved Jacob specifically because he lived up to his ancestors' legacy, and that is why Israel is loved. In contrast, Esau betrayed his heritage and therefore God does *not* love him; on the contrary:

> The fate of the Word of God sent to Israel, by Malachi. I have loved you saith God! But you retort: Wherein hast Thou loved us? Saith God: Was not Esau Jacob's brother? And yet I loved Jacob. But I hated Esau, and laid his mountains waste, and made his inheritance into a lamentation for a wilderness.[23]

The classical Jewish exegetes all accept the plain meaning of the prophet's words: God hates Esau because of his wickedness. For the modern Jew, however, any anthropomorphic description of God is difficult; a depiction of the Almighty as a passionate hater is excruciating. As an example, we need only examine the biblical commentary of the British Chief Rabbi Isaac Hertz. In composing his commentary, Rabbi Hertz attempted to accomplish in England exactly what Rabbi Hirsch did in Germany: to present to the public an interpretation palatable to a modern audience while at the same time going on the offensive against proponents of the documentary hypothesis. Therefore Rabbi Hertz insists that God, in this passage, in is no way actually expressing that He hates Esau. At times, he notes, the Bible refers to someone as "hated" when they are loved less than others. For example, Genesis describes

Leah as "hated" (*senuah*) because Jacob loved Rachel first and foremost. This, Rabbi Hertz insists, is what is intended in Malachi. In this prophetic passage, Rabbi Hertz argues:

> loved and hated…are relative terms only, denoting that one has been preferred to another; cf. the similar phraseology applied to Leah and Rachel, and also used in Deut. 21:15.[24]

As apologetics this is acceptable, but as exegesis it is not. According to Rabbi Hertz, Esau is not hated; he is only not loved as much. But this interpretation renders the passage unreadable. If Esau is not hated, if Esau is actually loved by God, it is not quite clear why God "laid his mountains waste, and made his inheritance into a lamentation for a wilderness." Rabbi Hirsch does not take this approach. Instead, in his commentary on the *haftarot*, Rabbi Hirsch is cited as arguing that God is referring not to Esau personally, but rather symbolically:

> The principle of Esau-Edom is: the worship of force, the laurel of blood is its highest ornament…conquest of the world form the dream of the greatest of its world-historic great ones. With them the care and development of all the material, spiritual and moral forces and wealth of men stand in the service of this ideal. We know that our sages saw in the Roman Empire the strongest embodiment of this Edomite principle. But this Esau-principle is in complete contrast to the Divine order of the world…. It is on this contrast that the mighty kingdoms of Edom founder, however "mountain-like" they reach to the skies, and, to the contemporary outlook, seem established for ever. "Esau-principle is what God hates, the Jacob- principle what he loves," this is what the downfall, the ruins of the empire of Edom teaches, that is what the survival of Israel teaches.[25]

What emerges from this interpretation? Esau himself is not hated;

it is only what he stands for that is hated. Nor, according to this interpretation, is God saying that he loves Jacob preferentially; it is the principles to which he adhered that the Almighty admired. The anthropomorphic elements of this passage have been dealt with; God is no longer the passionate lover of Israel and the hater of Esau. Instead, the Almighty *hates the sin but not the sinner.* This very untraditional interpretation will emerge throughout several important passages in Rabbi Hirsch's exegesis: when God singles out an evildoer with His hatred, the hatred is directed not against person but against principle, against the ethos expressed by one who is engaging in evil acts. God hates not Esau, but the "Esau-principle": the worship of force and military power.

✣ RABBI HIRSCH, MAIMONIDES, AND THE PROBLEM OF POWER

Let us sum up what we have discovered thus far. For Rabbi Hirsch, the doctrine of universal love is part and parcel of Jewish ethics. Further, hatred has no part to play in the Jewish ethical tradition, and God's statement that He hates Esau is actually to be interpreted as saying that God hates any valuing of power and military might. All of these aspects of Rabbi Hirsch's thought come together in a stunning departure from traditional Pentateuchal interpretation found in Rabbi Hirsch's interpretation of the Jewish commandment to wage war against Amalek, which has always embodied the Jewish obligation to defend itself against its enemies. We begin with the relevant biblical passage:

> Remember what Amalek did unto thee by the way, when ye were come forth out of Egypt; How he met thee by the way, and smote the hindmost of thee, even all that were feeble behind thee, when thou wast faint and weary; and he feared not God. Therefore it shall be, when the LORD thy God hath given thee rest from all thine enemies round about, in the land which the LORD thy God giveth thee for an inheritance

to possess it, that thou shalt *blot* out the remembrance of *Amalek* from under *heaven*; thou shalt not forget it.[26]

For the *halakha*, three commandments are listed in this passage. First, Jews are forbidden from forgetting what Amalek did to the Jewish people immediately after the Exodus. Second, they are called upon to repeatedly remind themselves that they are to return Amalek's hatred of Israel with hatred of their own. Finally, these reminders are meant to motivate Israel to actively wage war against its enemies. As Maimonides writes in his *Book of the Commandments*:

> This commandment…is that we are commanded to remember what Amalek did to us when he made haste to do us harm, and that we are to repeat this at every moment, and to urge people by spoken word to fight against him, and that we must encourage the people to hate him, until we do not forget this *mitzvah*, and that the hatred of him not weaken and become missing from people over the length of time.[27]
> …That we are warned not to forget what the descendants of Amalek did to us, and made haste to attack us. And we have already explained…the obligation to remember what Amalek did to us and to thereby renew hatred of him.[28]

Similarly, the author of the *Sefer HaHinnukh* states that "we are obligated to remember what Amalek did to Israel," and, by way of explanation, writes that "the root of the *mitzvah* is to place to our hearts that anyone who attacks Israel is hated before God, and the degree of his evil and damage done will be the extent of his downfall, as we find with Amalek, that because he performed this great evil to Israel…God commanded us to destroy his memory and to keep after him until the end." Here, traditional commentaries agree: the point of the commandment is that Israel is called to hate those who hate her, and to wage war against them. The *mitzvah*, then, stresses the importance of everything that, as we have seen, Rabbi Hirsch decried: not only hatred of evildoers but also the manifestation of Jewish military might.

In contrast, in Rabbi Hirsch's commentary on the passage in Deuteronomy, what emerges is an interpretation of the obligation to remember and wipe out Amalek, and an approach to the Jewish messianic era, that is very different from that quoted from Maimonides above. Recall that Rabbi Hirsch interpreted God's hatred of Esau as a philosophical rejection of the "Esau-principle," which Rabbi Hirsch defined as "the worship of force" and an ambition to achieve the "conquest of the world." In a similar sense, the war against Amalek is, for Rabbi Hirsch, a battle against the worldview embodied by Amalek, who, like Esau, "only finds its strength in the might of its sword." Rabbi Hirsch cleverly notes that God instructs Moses to wipe out the *"memory* of Amalek." Thus, he argues, the war against Amalek is not a military battle against evil; on the contrary. In the command to wipe out Amalek, God summons Israel to wage a war of ideas by eschewing any glorification of war against people: "It is not Amalek who is so pernicious for the moral future of mankind, but *zekher Amalek*, the glorifying of the memory of Amalek which is the Danger."[29] Rather than waging war against evil, the Torah reminds us that "as long as the annals of humanity cover the memory of the heroes of the sword with glory," Amalek wins. It is only "when the divine laws of morals have become the sole criterion as to the worth of the greatest and smallest of men," then and only then "will the reign of Amalek cease for ever in this world."[30] For Rabbi Hirsch, then, the battle against Amalek is to be understood not as a physical or military battle; on the contrary, we fight Amalek by rejecting the value of force and cleaving solely to the will of God. In reading Rabbi Hirsch's writings, it is difficult not to conclude that he believes that it is precisely by practicing pacifism that the war against Amalek is waged: for "only with the doing away with the remembrance of devastations and conquests will the perpetrators of these deeds disappear."[31] We are called to remember Amalek not in order to incite our revenge, but rather to remind us not to harm anyone. The ultimate Jewish defense against evil can only be achieved by Israel, wandering throughout the diaspora, acting ethically earning the admiration of others:

> Zachor (Remember): Keeping afar from every *avel*, from the misuse of every position of power over others – even if only momentarily – to their disadvantage, from the misuse of the confidence which one person must place in the other if people living together is to be at all possible, being penetrated with the conviction that we can only call God our God as long as we anxiously avoid doing the slightest wrong to any of His human beings on earth…. The people in whose national character the traits of sympathy, consideration, kindness and doing good to every living creature are to shine forth…the people to whom "doing harm" should be an impossibility, who are to wander over the earth in the most complete ideal condition of *Yeshurun*, in their intercourse with other people are to show themselves as *yashar*, as the straightest, most honest, most upright nation amongst the nations; and *She-eirit Yisrael* (the remnant of Israel), those who last through the ages and all the trials to the ultimate stage of the Jewish perfection are seen, in the words of the Prophet, to be those "who do no wrong, speak no deceit, and in whose mouths no word of fraud is to be found; they alone find their pasturage and repose on earth, they alone have not to tremble before anything or anybody."[32]

Rabbi Hirsch further argues that the end of evil, and the end of Amalek, will occur not by the sword, but by the turning of mankind to the word of God: "The last page of this war will not be closed until the sword of Amalek shatters against a mightier sword, when the Power of the Sword collapses before the Power of the Word, before a force which will blossom out in the world depending solely on faithful obedience to god's Law of Morality."[33]

For Rabbi Hirsch, the Torah's insistence that Amalek be wiped out when "God has given thee rest from thine enemies," is not a reference to the Jewish waging of war. Rather, this state of being will be achieved only by the *rejection* of force. God, Rabbi Hirsch writes, will give the Jewish people rest from its enemies "if you, in just the opposite of all these traits of Amalek, order all your doings in accordance with His Will, and thereby – not by your sword and your might – by His protection which you have won by your faithful adherence to duty." The Holy Land, writes Rabbi Hirsch, is "nothing that you have obtained possession of by your own plenitude of power."[34] What emerges, then, is a stunningly untraditional and pacifist messianic vision, one utterly unlike most eschatologies of Rabbi Hirsch's predecessors.

✌ RABBI HIRSCH, COHEN, AND THE MESSIAH

For Maimonides, the Messiah is primarily a military leader; he wields influence not merely by moral authority, but also, and primarily, through power and the conquering of the land of Israel. Moreover, it is important to note that for Maimonides, the Messiah becomes an unparalleled Jewish leader not only through religious inspiration, but through waging war. Maimonides' messiah is depicted at the very end of his *Mishneh Torah*:

> Do not imagine that the anointed King must perform miracles and signs and create new things in the world or resurrect the dead and so on. The matter is not so...if a king shall stand up from among the House of David, studying Torah and indulging in commandments like his father David, according to the written and oral Torah, *and he will coerce all Israel to follow it, and to strengthen its weak points, and will fight God's wars*, this one is to be treated as if he were the anointed one. *If he succeeded and defeated all nations surrounding him* and built a Holy Temple in its proper place and gathered the strayed ones of Israel together, this is indeed the anointed one for certain, and he will mend the entire

world to worship the Lord together, as it is stated: "For then I shall turn for the nations a clear tongue, to call all in the Name of the Lord and to worship Him with one shoulder."[35] (emphasis added)

In insisting that violence is an essential aspect of Jewish eschatology, Maimonides draws on the Bible. While it is true that the messianic era is meant to usher in a time when the lion will lie with the lamb and when swords will be reforged into plowshares, scripture, in the book of Joel, also insists that this era will be preceded by war:

> Prepare for war, awaken warriors, come forth and arise men of war! Beat your plowshares into swords and your pruning-hooks into spears! Let the weak say "I am a hero!" Let the nations come round and assemble, for there the Lord has placed your warriors. Let the nations awaken and come up to the valley of Yehoshafat, for there I shall sit to judge all the nations around...for great is their iniquity.... The sun and moon have darkened, and the stars have withdrawn their splendor. And the Lord will roar from Zion, and from Jerusalem will send his call, and the heavens and earth will shudder – yet the Lord will be merciful to his people, a strength to the children of Israel. And you will know that I am the Lord your God, who dwells in Zion on my holy mountain; and Jerusalem will be holy, and foreigners will no longer pass through it.[36]

A very different depiction of the messianic era than that of Maimonides can be found in the writings of Rabbi Hirsch and Cohen. Cohen describes the Messiah not as a historical figure but as a moral ideal, a suffering servant who is the embodiment of the ethical; he is an archetype to which all mankind must be attracted. Whereas Maimonides spoke of a messiah who wielded power in order to restore Israel to its original national grandeur, Cohen visualized a messianic ideal that in its essence embodied the *rejection of power*. The Messiah, then, exists as an idea, an archetype of peacefulness toward which all mankind is attracted.

> Only through the Messiah's taking the earthly suffering of man upon his shoulders does he become the ideal image of the man of the future, the image of mankind, as the unity of all peoples. He becomes through this not a Tantalus of Sysyphus but the Atlas who supports the moral world of the future. Only through this concept of the representation of human suffering could the messianic concept of history be fulfilled. For the concept of power in history is only naturalistic, anthropological, ethnological, or nationalistic. The ethical concept of world history must be basically free of all eudaemonism. Therefore power cannot be the standard of ethical history.[37]

Of course, Rabbi Hirsch, like Maimonides, affirms the traditional Jewish notion of a personal Messiah. Yet in Rabbi Hirsch's approach no mention of Maimonides' military messianism is made. In fact, not only does power play no role in Rabbi Hirsch's messianism, but the Messiah is depicted as the ideal human being who eschews both power and wealth. In his commentary on Genesis, Rabbi Hirsch notes that Jacob speaks of the Messiah as one who binds "his ass's colt to the choice vine branch." In other words, the redeemer chooses a humble animal as his steed. In this Rabbi Hirsch sees symbolism of enormous significance. "So Jacob visualizes the Messiah," write Rabbi Hirsch, "and how does he see him? He sees the saviour of mankind, the conqueror of nations, not on a steed, but on a young ass's foal." The reason for this, he insists, is that "the ass is always used to represent *peaceful* well-being, *peaceful* national greatness, whereas 'steed' is used to represent military might."

How, then, will the Messiah redeem the world, if not by means of military might? Rabbi Hirsch depicts the Messiah as the moral ideal, who through his righteousness and peacefulness attracts the nations to him. In a clever act of exegesis, and an implicit criticism of Chritianity, Rabbi Hirsch cites the prophet Zechariah's description of the Messiah: "For see, thy King cometh unto thee, he is righteous and saved" (9:9). Rabbi Hirsch notes that the Messiah is not called a savior (*moshia*) by the prophets, but rather a *tsaddik ve-nosha*, one who is righteous and saved. "He is no savior," Rabbi Hirsch writes, "the Messiah does not come to help us, but to teach us by his example how we would be helped. He is a righteous man, and therefore that is why he has been helped. He is no God, Who helps, but a man, whose greatness lies in his being so eminently righteous that, because of his righteousness, God has helped him."[38] For Rabbi Hirsch, the Messiah is a righteous man whose relationship with God will inspire all mankind. He is not a conqueror, but rather an awe-inspiring moral ideal. He rejects any notion of coercion and will draw the world to Judaism only by acting as an extraordinary example of religious righteousness.

⅋ GOD'S LOVE FOR MAN

Let us conclude by examining how Rabbi Hirsch and Cohen approach the concept that seems most at odds with modern universalism. If man must love all men equally – if the foundation of religious love is not kinship or chosenness but rather the fact that all men are created in God's image – then it stands to reason that God must love all human beings equally as well. That notion, of course, stands in tension with the notion of the election of Israel, the concept that God chose the Jewish people, in Deuteronomy's words, "because the Lord loved you, and because he would keep the oath which he had sworn unto your fathers." The implication is that God, while a benevolent Creator, maintains a preferential love for the Jewish people. As Rabbi Akiba states in the Mishna, man is beloved, "for he is created in the image of God," while "beloved are the Israelites, for they are called the children of God."[39] Israel is termed God's "nation of kingly priests," whom God singles out as a *segulah*, or treasure, "from among the nations."[40]

While many traditional exegetes may interpret the appellation *segulah* as implying a unique love for God on behalf of the Jewish people, Rabbi Hirsch argues that the verse implies exactly the opposite. "The use of the word for the fundamental condition which is demanded of us in our relationship to God indicates that we must become completely and exclusively His possession in every phase of our being, that our whole existence and all our desires be dependent on Him." But dedication to God is divinely desired of all mankind. Therefore, Rabbi Hirsch argues, in deeming Israel His possession, God is essentially saying to them that "this relationship you are to bear towards Me is really nothing exceptional, is nothing but the beginning of the return to the normal condition which the whole world should bear towards Me. The whole of humanity, every nation in the world really is destined to belong to Me and will be ultimately educated by Me up to Me."[41] God's informing Israel that it will be his "special treasure" is, for Rabbi Hirsch, actually a statement that they are not really special at all. Rather, God is choosing the Jewish people as an indication of what mankind ought to, and ultimately will, become. Israel is chosen solely for the sake of mankind, and no preferential love for the Jewish people is implied.

In his chapter on "Religious Love," Cohen likewise argues that God in no way favors the Jewish people. It is necessary, he maintains, "to clear God's love for Israel of the suspicion that it is an anomaly in regard to God's universal love for mankind." God has no special love for the Jewish people; He "does not love Israel more or differently from His love for men in general, nor, needless to say, could God's love for Israel limit and impair His love for the human race." In His love for the Jewish people, Cohen maintains, "God loves nothing other than the human race."[42] Cohen explains the word *segulah* in the same manner as does Rabbi Hirsch: "Israel is His property; or however one may translate this Hebrew word, God loves Israel only as a model, a symbol of mankind, a mark of distinction within it, for only monotheism is able to establish the unity of the human race." Cohen asserts what would appear to be an enormous Jewish concession to Kantian universalism; but he is only asserting what a leader of German Orthodoxy has taken for granted.

✥ CONCLUSION

In their approach to the ethical issues discussed above, Rabbi Hirsch and Cohen, in my view, concede too much to universalism, and I have elsewhere defended what I believe to be the traditional approach to subjects such as chosenness, war and hate.[43] This essay, however, is meant as intellectual history rather than theology. One cannot minimize the significance of the divide between Rabbi Hirsch and Hermann Cohen – they are debates over the history of Jewish law, indeed over the very foundations of Judaism itself. But what is evident is that both Orthodox and non-Orthodox German Jews took certain modern ideas and ideals for granted, maintaining an approach to modernity that continues to reverberate through modern Judaism to this day.

✥ NOTES

1. David Ellenson, *After Emancipation Jewish Religious Responses to Modernity* (Cincinnati, 2004), p. 237.
2. Rabbi Aharon Lichtenstein, "Legitimization of Modernity," published in Moshe Z. Sokol (ed.), *Engaging Modernity: Rabbinic Leaders and Challenge of the Twentieth Century* (Northvale, NJ 1997), p. 30.
3. Ibid., p. 238.
4. Cited in Ellenson, p. 248.
5. Ibid., p. 249.
6. Ibid.
7. Ellenson, p. 254.
8. Leviticus 19:18.
9. *Mishneh Torah, Dei'ot* Chapter 6.
10. David Novak, *The Election of Israel: The Idea of the Chosen People* (New York, 1995).
11. Hermann Cohen, *Religion of Reason*, p. 118.
12. Cohen, *Religion of Reason*, p. 119.
13. Rabbi Hirsch, *Leviticus*, p. 527. I will be using, for all my citations from R. Hirsch's commentary on the Pentateuch and the *haftara*, the translation by Isaac Levy published by the Judaica Press (London, England, 1966).
14. Jerusalem Talmud, Nedarim Ch. 1.
15. Hermann Cohen, *Religion of Reason out of the Sources of Judaism* (New York, 1972), p. 119.
16. Rabbi Hirsch, *Genesis*, p. 118.
17. *Sefer ha-Hinukh*.
18. Rabbi Hirsch, *Leviticus*, p. 522.
19. Cohen, *Religion of Reason*, p. 458.

20. Ibid.
21. Cohen, *Religion of Reason*, pp. 452–453.
22. Ibid.
23. Malachi 1:1–3.
24. Hertz, *The Pentateuch and Haftorahs.*
25. Rabbi Hirsch, *Haftarot*, p. 48.
26. Deuteronomy 25:17–23.
27. *Sefer Ha-Mitzvot*, Positive Commandment 189.
28. *SeferHa-Mitzvot*, Prohibition 59.
29. Rabbi Hirsch, *Exodus*, p. 234.
30. Rabbi Hirsch, *Deuteronomy*, p. 525.
31. Rabbi Hirsch, *Exodus*, p. 234–235.
32. Rabbi Hirsch, *Deuteronomy*, p. 523.
33. Ibid., p. 535.
34. Ibid.
35. *Mishneh Torah*, Melakhim 11:4.
36. Joel 3:9-17. On this, see David Hazony's "Plowshares Into Swords: The Lost Biblical Ideal of Peace," *Azure* 3, (Winter 1998).
37. Cohen, *Religion of Reason.*
38. Rabbi Hirsch, *Genesis*, p. 666.
39. *Pirkei Avot*, 3:18.
40. Exodus 19:5–6.
41. Rabbi Hirsch, *Exodus*, p. 250.
42. Cohen, *Religion of Reason*, p. 149.
43. See, for example, my essays "God's Beloved: A Defense of Chosenness," *Azure* 19 (Winter 2005), and "The Virtue of Hate," First Things (February 2003).

The Right of Others to Think Differently from Us

Joseph Telushkin

1. Tolerance is among the most difficult of virtues. The Hebrew word for it, *sovlanut*, derives from *sevel*, "to suffer.[1] In other words, we have to endure a certain amount of discomfort and sometimes even suffering in order to tolerate views with which we disagree."[2]

   Savlanut, a related Hebrew word, means "patience," suggesting that one aspect of tolerance is patience with those who hold views we believe to be wrong.

2. Practicing tolerance also is difficult because its benefits are not necessarily obvious (as is the case with such virtues as justice and fairness). In fact, one might well question why tolerance should be regarded as a virtue at all. For if we feel certain that a view is wrong, and perhaps even harmful, should we not strive to suppress it? What is good about permitting people to spread misguided or harmful ideas or advocate behavior we believe to be wrong?

✣ THREE REASONS TOLERANCE IS NECESSARY

(1) People Have the Right to Think Differently

3. The basis of tolerance is the acknowledgment that other people have the right to think about the world differently from the way we do. Rather than regarding such differences as irritating and unfortunate, a Talmudic passage suggests that they are natural: "Rabbi Meir used to say, 'In three things people are different one from the other: in voice, appearance, and opinions.'" (*Sanhedrin* 38a) Thus, just as it does not bother us if our neighbor's voice or appearance differs from ours (indeed, it would be extremely boring if everybody looked and sounded exactly alike), so it should not bother us if our neighbor's views differ from ours as well (Rabbi Menachem Mendel of Kotzk).[3]

   One upshot of Rabbi Meir's teaching is that parents should not try to make all their children alike or copies of themselves. Rather, as Proverbs teaches, "Raise a child according to his way" (22:6; emphasis added). Observe your child carefully, and support her interests and enthusiasms in order to develop her potential. If your daughter is artistic, don't impose upon her your long-cherished dream that she become a doctor, or make her feel that she is disappointing you by pursuing a path that differs from what you want. Children, too, are entitled to their own "opinions" about the kind of life they wish to lead.

4. While the sight of a large crowd causes many people to have dismissive thoughts (e.g., "a mindless mob"), the Talmud commands us to recite a blessing, "Blessed is the Wise One who knows secrets" (that is, everyone's innermost thoughts; *Brakhot* 58a). This implies that we should remember that each person in the crowd has a different way of understanding the world, and "we bless God for having created such diverse minds" (Reuven Kimelman).[4]

A Midrash expresses a similar thought: "Just as the faces of people [in a large crowd] are not like each other, so their minds are not the same; rather, each has his own way of thinking" (Bamidbar Rabba 21:2).

(2) Different People Have Different Needs

5. When it comes to ethical behavior, such as laws against harming others, we need a uniformly binding code of conduct. But in many other areas of life, uniformity is unnecessary and can cause pointless, and sometimes great, misery. For example, some people's longings for spirituality are satisfied through a lengthy prayer service with a great deal of singing; others prefer a shorter service, with a focus on study. There is no reason to believe that one approach is better than the other, although many people look down upon those whose spiritual longings differ from their own.

Similarly, because we are all different, it is wise to offer a variety of approaches to people in need: *When it comes to human emotions, one size definitely does not fit all.* Psychologist David Pelcovitz relates how Israel's educators have learned to take into account people's diverse styles of coping with tragedy: "I was in Jerusalem shortly after a suicide bombing and was asked to join an Israeli psychologist in meeting with a group of adolescents who had just lost a beloved teacher in the bombing. The school set up five rooms for the adolescents. One room was set aside for writing condolence letters to the family of their teacher, other rooms were designated for a discussion group (led by the psychologist), music, art, and saying *Tehillim* (Psalms). The teens chose the room that best matched their style and seemed to find solace in finding an opportunity to deal with their grief in a manner that uniquely suited their styles." Pelcovitz concludes: "There is no one correct way to deal with upsetting situations."[5]

Thus, tolerance emanates in part from the realization that people have different needs and that, as long as meeting their needs does not cause suffering to others, they should be free to act as they wish rather than being made to feel inferior.

(3) Truth Is Multifaceted

6. While Jewish law generally tries to reach uniformity on basic legal and ritual issues (for example, all followers of Jewish law agree that pig and shellfish are not kosher), the Talmud supports the validity of divergent views in nonlegal areas. For example, in a dispute between Rabbis Evyatar and Yonatan concerning each one's understanding of a biblical passage about an incident with a "concubine" (described in Judges 19), the rabbis conclude that "These and these are the words of the living God" (*Gittin* 6b). In other words, not only does each of the rabbis have the right to understand the passage differently, but each one's view may well be legitimate. Thus, tolerance is rooted not simply in acting amicably toward those whom we believe to be wrong, but also in recognizing that there might be some truth in positions with which we disagree; indeed, they may well be "the words of the living God."

7. Elsewhere the Talmud teaches that intellectual growth depends on exposing oneself to a variety of viewpoints: "One who studies Torah from only one teacher will never achieve great success" (*Avoda Zara* 19a).[6] We therefore need to expose ourselves even to views with which we disagree. Otherwise we will end up with a one-sided and incomplete understanding of a subject, or of the world.

8. As these texts suggest, on many of life's most important issues, there is no one truth. Rabbi Aryeh Kaplan has suggested that perhaps that is why God gave humankind the Torah, which can be interpreted in so many different ways ("maybe [God] wanted a certain amount of variety and interchange"), as opposed to the *Shulhan Arukh*, the sixteenth-century code

of Jewish law, which lends itself to less interpretation.[7] The rabbis taught that there are seventy faces (*shivim panim*) to the Torah, an expression meant to convey that there are dozens of *legitimate* ways to interpret it.

9. The Talmud frequently records views that the majority of the rabbis rejected. The Mishna explains that this was done so that later generations or different courts could rely on these views if changed conditions led them to reach a different conclusion than that of earlier sages: "Why do they record the opinion of a single person among the many, when the law [*halakha*] must be according to the opinion of the many? So that if a court prefers the opinion of the single person, it may rely on him" (Mishna *Eduyot* 1:5).[8] The rabbis understood that the best decision for one generation might turn out not to be the best for a later one and thus wanted all students of the law to be aware of the views that were rejected.

To cite a well-known example of this principle drawn from American law: In 1896, in Plessy versus Ferguson, the Supreme Court ruled 7–1 that "separate but equal" facilities (in this case, referring to separate railroad cars for whites and blacks) were constitutional. At the time of this ruling, the one dissenting justice, John Marshall Harlan, recorded his view that the constitution was intended to be "color-blind" and that it recognized "no superior, dominant, ruling class of citizens. In respect of civil rights, all citizens are equal before the law." Following this decision, legislation based on the doctrine of "separate but equal" and promoting racial segregation expanded steadily throughout the American south. Then, almost sixty years later, in 1954, in Brown versus Board of Education, Plessy versus Ferguson was overturned, and the justices (this time ruling in a case involving segregated public schools) concluded that "separate educational facilities [were inherently] unequal." Justice Harlan's insistence that the constitution was

*color blind, though rejected in his own day, was embraced by
a 9–0 verdict of the court.*

*While members of the Sanhedrin were obligated to abide
by the court's rulings, a member who was in disagreement was
permitted to teach his dissenting views, both in private and in
public, and to criticize the court's decisions, as long as he continued to obey the court's ruling and counseled others to do the
same (see Mishna Sanhedrin 11:2).*

ॐ THE INTELLECTUAL ADVANTAGES GAINED BY BEING TOLERANT

10. The one other instance in which the Talmud uses the expression "These and these are the words of the living God" (*Eruvin* 13b) is in its description of the *Bat Kol* (heavenly voice)
that applied these words to the more than 300 legal disputes
between the Schools of Hillel (*Beit Hillel*) and of Shammai
(*Beit Shammai*). In this case, however, the *Bat Kol* goes on
to declare that Jews should follow the rulings of Hillel and
his disciples.[9]

The Talmud explains why: "Because they [the School of
Hillel] were kindly and humble, and because they studied
their own rulings and those of the School of Shammai, and
even mentioned the teachings of the School of Shammai
before their own" (*Eruvin* 13b). Apparently, Hillel's and his
disciples' greater humility and tolerance made them not
only ethically worthy of being chosen over their opponents,
but also more likely than the School of Shammai to reach
accurate conclusions than did their opponents.[10]

Why? Shammai and his followers apparently were so
certain that they possessed the *whole* truth that, the above
text suggests, they did not bother to study their opponents'
views in depth. In contrast, the School of Hillel's tolerance
led it to study Shammai's views as alternatives to be carefully
considered. Consequently, the members of the House of Hillel
were repeatedly forced to defend, refine, and deepen their

own views. The Talmud records instances in which Hillel's disciples, after studying the opposing positions, reconsidered and changed their views (see, for example, Mishna *Eduyot* 1:12–13).[11]

In short, tolerant people are not only more likely to be "kind and humble," but also are more likely to reach accurate conclusions.

Two differing traditions exist in the Talmud concerning the personal relations between the Schools of Hillel and Shammai. One teaches that members of the two groups married one other and "treated each other with affection and kinship" (Yevamot 14b). But another describes an incident in which disciples of Shammai ambushed and killed many of Hillel's disciples so that they could outvote them and institute the law according to their interpretation. The Talmud refers to this "triumph" of the School of Shammai (a ruling that was later overturned) as being "as grievous for Israel as the day on which the Golden Calf was made" (Jerusalem Talmud, Shabbat 1:4; Shabbat 17a).

Obviously, these accounts do not necessarily negate each other; they might simply be describing events that happened at different times. However, the disturbing account from the Jerusalem Talmud reminds us of intolerant individuals' unhealthy potential to turn violent.

Another Talmudic passage reinforces the view that challenges to authority can lead to more, not less, truth. After the death of his study partner Reish Lakish, Rabbi Yochanan lamented: "With Reish Lakish, whenever I would say something, he would pose twenty-four difficulties [i.e., challenges] to me, and I would give him twenty-four solutions and as a result the subject became clear." (Bava Metzia 84a)

Serious challenges, as long as they are not offered just to be provocative, should be treated with respect, since they deepen understanding and lead to a fuller appreciation of the truth.

❧ UNIFORM THINKING CAN PRODUCE ERRORS

11. The Talmud rules that if the 71 members of the *Sanhedrin* (Jewish High Court) unanimously believe a defendant in a capital case is guilty, not only is the death sentence not carried out, but the defendant, it would seem, is released: "Rabbi Kahana said: A Sanhedrin, all of whose members felt that he was guilty, [must] acquit him. What is the reason? We have learned that [where the vote is to convict], the judgment [in capital cases] must be delayed overnight [to give the judges the opportunity] to search for a defense [for the accused], but these judges [having voted unanimously to convict] will no longer consider any basis for acquittal" (*Sanhedrin* 17a).[12] In other words, the rabbis feared that in so one-sided an environment, one in which no member of the court seemed to be seeking out alternative evidence or exonerating circumstances, the truth may become distorted. In modern times, only authoritarian and totalitarian governments seek uniformity and unanimity. Thus, leaders in communist, fascist, and other dictatorships often claim election majorities of 99 percent and higher.

❧ TOLERANCE TOWARD OTHER RELIGIONS

12. The author and radio talk show host Dennis Prager suggests that one of the most important days in the life of a religious person is when he meets a member of a different religion, or of a different denomination within his own religion, who is both a good and intelligent person. After such an encounter, one can no longer dismiss the other group's followers as being of low intelligence or character, the way intolerant people often do.

Those who spend time only with those who are of like mind often regard other groups with contempt. But to dismiss out of hand views that differ from, or challenge, our own is wrong. In a remarkable statement of tolerance dating from 1598, Rabbi

Judah Lowe, the Maharal of Prague (c. 1520–1609), taught that it is worthwhile to listen and respond even to alternative religious viewpoints, as long as the person expressing them is not malicious or coercive:[13] *"If a person does not intend to goad, only to convey his faith, even if his words are opposed to your own faith and your own religion, you should not say to him: 'Do not speak and keep your words to yourself....' On the contrary, let him speak as much as he wants.... Reason requires that nothing be hindered, that no mouth be closed, and that religious dispute be open for everybody.... This is the only way by which men can reach ultimate truth. Any proponent who wants to overcome his opponent and demonstrate his own correctness would very much want his opponent to confront him to his utmost."*[14] *(Be'er Ha-Golah, Vol. 2, pp. 424–426)*

Yet I believe that it is unwise, in general, for Jewish groups to engage in interfaith dialogue on issues of theology; for example, to take part in a formal, public discussion in which Christian participants explain why they believe Jesus to have been God's son and the messiah, and then Jews explain why they do not. When done on a group level, there is little to be gained by such a discussion, and a good chance that bad feelings will ensue. However, if I understand the Maharal correctly, he does think it both acceptable and worthwhile for individuals to speak of their deepest beliefs one-on-one. Conversations between individuals are less likely to harden into annoyance and antagonism than are group discussions. Indeed, personal conversations on issues of faith (and sometimes struggles with faith) can sometimes lead to mutual respect and affection. I once came across a story that Rabbi Walter Wurzberger told of visiting Rabbi Soloveitchik in the hospital. As he walked in, a doctor was thanking the Rav over and over. When Wurzberger asked Rabbi Soloveitchik what had happened (normally one hears patients thanking the doctor, not the reverse), the Rav answered that the doctor was a Catholic man who was having issues of religious doubt, and the Rav was able to supply him with thoughts about faith and God that the doctor found help-ful and reassuring. That is why he was thanking him.[15]

As opposed to formal forums on theological issues, inter-faith cooperation and dialogue on matters of social justice are definitely worthwhile. It is beneficial for each side to consider the other's perspective on what their religious tradition be-lieves are the best ways to address problems of racial injustice, confronting oppressive foreign governments, and helping poor people to improve their lot.

13. Many religious Jews believe that Judaism's monotheistic faith, which is based upon God's revelations to the Patriarchs and to Moses, is the only true expression of God's will, and that other religions are therefore wrong. In recent years the United Kingdom's Chief Rabbi, Sir Jonathan Sacks, has ar-gued forcefully against this view: "Judaism is a particularist monotheism. It believes in one God but not in one religion, one culture, one truth. The God of Abraham is the God of all mankind, but the faith of Abraham is not the faith of all mankind.[16]

In Rabbi Sacks's striking formulation: "God is God of all humanity, but no single faith should be the faith of all humanity.... God no more wants all faiths and cultures to be the same than a loving parent wants his or her children to be the same.[17]

The dangers and evils that ensue when people are convinced that they possess the whole truth was noted by Isaiah Berlin (1909–1997), the political scientist and philosopher: "Few things have done more harm than the belief on the part of individuals and groups (or tribes or states or nations or churches) that he or she or they are in sole possession of the truth.... It is a terrible and dangerous arrogance to believe that you alone are right... and that others cannot be right if they disagree. This makes one certain that there is one goal and only one for one's nation or church or the whole of humanity, and that it is worth any amount of suffering (particularly on the part of other people) if only the goal is attained."[18]

In similar manner, Jacob Bronowski, author of The Ascent of Man, *declared in the television series based on his book: "We have to cure ourselves of the itch for absolute knowledge and power…In the end, the words [we all need to hear] were said by Oliver Cromwell: 'I beseech you…. Think it possible you may be mistaken.'"*

14. The same tolerant approach should apply in the political realm. Ideologues on the left and right often demonize each other, seeing their opponents not only as wrong and foolish, but also as possessing evil intentions – an ugly aspect of American political life.

In an effort to defuse this sort of intolerance, during election campaigns I like to ask partisans of each candidate: "Can you think of at least one reason someone would vote for the candidate you oppose that does not reflect badly on either the person's character or intelligence?" I am constantly amazed and saddened at how rarely people can think of a single intelligent and/or nonselfish reason someone would vote for the other side. Their inability to do so means that many politically passionate people end up regarding about half of the populace as either unintelligent or of poor character.

⚖ TOLERANCE AND INTOLERANCE WITHIN THE JEWISH WORLD

15. While antisemitic writers have long claimed that Jews are united in an international conspiracy to control the world's economies and governments,[19] anyone familiar with Jewish life from within knows that Jews are hardly united. As is the case with many groups, Jewish communal life has its share of tension, intolerance, and often mutual contempt.

Unfortunately, this has often been the case between Orthodox and non-Orthodox religious denominations. Rabbi
Irving (Yitz) Greenberg has cautioned: "I don't care what
denomination in Judaism you belong to, as long as you're
ashamed of it." Since each denomination is committed to
tikkun olam, repairing the world, each movement can hardly
claim that this perfection has not been achieved only because
of the other movements' misguided teachings or behavior.
Intolerant people have a tendency to look for, and exaggerate,
their opponents' faults while minimizing their own.

Rabbi Abraham Twerski, a psychiatrist and a Chassid, recalls:
"I was once traveling on a bus, dressed in my customary garb,
wearing a broad black hat and a [long] black coat. A man ap-
proached me and said, 'I think it's shameful that your appear-
ance is so different. There is no need for Jews in America to be
so conspicuous, with long beards and black hats.'

"'I'm sorry, mister,' I said to the man. 'I'm not Jewish. I'm
Amish, and this is how we dress.'

"The man became apologetic. 'Oh, I'm terribly sorry, sir,'
he said. 'I did not mean to offend you. I think you should be
proud of preserving your traditions.'

"'Well, well,' I said. 'If I am Amish, then my beard and
black hat don't bother you, and I should be proud of my tradi-
tions. But if I am Jewish, then I must be ashamed of my Jew-
ishness? What is wrong with you that you can respect others
but have no self-respect?'" [20]

In 1938, in the days following the Nazi nationwide pogrom
known as Kristallnacht, the Reform congregation in Provi-
dence, Rhode Island, conducted a special service to which it
invited recently arrived Jewish refugees from Europe. Many of
the refugee Jews came to the synagogue wearing hats or kip-
pot, which violated the Reform congregation's practice of men
remaining bare-headed in temple. [21] *A prominent member of*

the congregation insisted that the refugees remove their head-coverings, and he kept pressing the rabbi, William Braude, who was also a renowned rabbinical scholar, "Did you give permission to these people to wear hats?" Rabbi Braude was so upset by the man's mean-spirited intolerance that he felt too intimidated to tell him to let these poor refugees from Nazism alon, and to permit them to keep their heads covered.[22]

Some years ago an Orthodox rabbinic organization put out advertisements before the High Holy Days urging Jews to remain at home rather than attend a Reform or Conservative service. Ironically, when a prominent American Baptist leader said that God does not hear the prayers of Jews because they are not offered through Jesus, Jews of all denominations were understandably outraged.[23] But should not all Jews be equally upset by advertisements such as those of the rabbinic organization? And if we should not be (some would argue that those who took out the ad honestly felt they had to warn people away from what they regard as sinful behavior), then what right do we have to be annoyed at men like the Baptist leader who obviously felt that he was also trying to warn people away from wrongful behavior?

A friend, a Reform rabbi in Jerusalem, attended an Orthodox synagogue to recite kaddish for his recently deceased father (his Reform congregation does not have daily services). He was recognized by members of the Orthodox congregation, one of whom stood up and announced that it was forbidden to answer "Amen" to his kaddish since, as a Reform rabbi, my friend was a heretic and responsible for other people acting sinfully.[24] Obviously, refusing to answer "Amen" – an act that can be compared to refusing to return a handshake after another has extended his hand – when a Reform rabbi offers a prayer to God only further alienates non-Orthodox Jews from Orthodox ones.[25]

✣ SOURCES OF INTOLERANCE WITHIN JUDAISM

16. The Torah regarded idolatry with abhorrence: Idolatry led people to sacrifice their children and to deny not only the universal God but also His universally binding morality. Furthermore, given that within the context of ancient idolatrous societies it would have been difficult if not impossible to establish monotheism,[26] the Torah's absolute prohibition of, and contempt for, idolatry becomes understandable.

However, even aside from its unbending opposition to idolatry, there is a strong streak of intolerance in Judaism. Oddly, it is epitomized in the thinking and writing of Moses Maimonides, medieval Judaism's premier rabbinic scholar, philosopher, and intellectual. Relying in part on certain Talmudic precedents, Maimonides outlined societal norms that he thought should be instituted in a state that is run according to Jewish law. For example, he ruled that Jews who deny a tenet of Judaism, such as that the entire Torah is the revealed will of God, or who eat unkosher food to show their contempt for God and Judaism (and not simply because they like it), deserve to die (even though eating unkosher food was never a capital offense in Jewish law). "If it is within one's power to kill them with a sword in public view, then kill them. If doing that is not possible, one should devise schemes that can bring about their deaths." He then offered the following guidance as an example of how to act toward a heretic: If you see such a person fall into a well, and there is a ladder in the well, you should remove the ladder, and even lie to the would-be victim, "I must hurry to take my son down from the roof. I shall return the ladder to you soon." (*Laws of Murder* 4:10) Maimonides' rationale for killing such people, or for indirectly causing their deaths, is that they alienate Jews from God. (*Laws of Idolatry* 10:1)[27]

Maimonides intended his code to serve as the legal code of a future Jewish state, but had the modern state of Israel chosen a political and legal system based on his directives, Israel would today be a highly repressive society. Hence, while Maimonides has been among the greatest influences on my own understanding of Jewish law, it seems to me that his code *alone* cannot function as a fully sufficient ethical and legal code for contemporary Jews.

> *In the twentieth century, sages such as Rabbi Abraham Isaac Kook, and the Chazon Ish, one of the preeminent figures of right-wing Orthodoxy, ruled that we no longer apply the laws concerning heresy to any Jews, even those who deny Judaism's most basic beliefs; not only should we not harm such people, but if the situation presents itself, we should save them. The Chazon Ish wrote that we live today in "a time of God's conceal-ment," that is, when divine providence is more obscured than it was in the ancient past, "when miracles were commonplace" and God's existence was apparent to all. Therefore, he ruled that it is wrong to regard nonbelievers today as acting with the same "maliciousness and lawlessness" as the heretics of old (see his book* Chazon Ish, Yoreh Deah, *chapter 2).*

ᛒ THE MORAL DANGER OF INTOLERANCE

The belief that we possess the whole truth can cause us to act in-appropriately and sometimes cruelly. Intolerance emanates from the belief that one's position is so right, and one's opponent's so wrong, that it would be catastrophic to respect the opposing view-point and those who hold it. This attitude can be likened to the *deserved* contempt with which mainstream doctors regard faith-healing sects that will not, for example, permit diabetic members to take insulin injections but insist that they try to heal themselves through prayer alone. In some cases, when members of certain religious sects have done this, the diabetics have drifted into ir-reversible comas and died.

17. While this behavior is abhorrent, such instances are rare, although those involved in disputes often claim that they are fighting for a matter of life and death, or of absolute right and wrong. Thus throughout Jewish history leaders have often

argued that the positions advocated by their adversaries are so dangerous that they must be suppressed; and yet later assessments by both Jewish scholars and the general community have rarely supported these claims. Rabbi Elijah, the Gaon of Vilna (1720–1797), was probably the greatest Jewish religious scholar since Moses Maimonides (twelfth century), and the recognized spiritual leader of his age.[28] During the Gaon's lifetime the Chasidic movement was begun by Rabbi Israel Baal Shem Tov (1700–1760). The Gaon believed that the Chasidic leadership was composed of ignoramuses who were not committed to the proper observance of Jewish law. So certain was he of this fact that when the Chasidic leaders Rabbis Menachem Mendel of Vitebsk and Shneur Zalman of Liady tried to meet with him to demonstrate that the new movement did not conflict with traditional Judaism, the Gaon refused to see them. Furthermore, he issued bans of excommunication, ruling that it was forbidden for other Jews to do business with, marry, maintain social relations with, or even assist at the burial of Chasidim. At one point, the Gaon declared: "If it were within my power, I would do to the Chasidim what Elijah the Prophet did to the priests of Ba'al." In other words, he would kill the Chasidim, just as Elijah led the Jews to kill 450 idolatrous priests of Baal (see I Kings 18:40).[29]

Because of the Gaon's preeminence, his words deeply influenced his followers, who persecuted the Chasidim. Shortly after the Gaon's death, an anti-Chasidic rabbi made a false accusation of treason to the Russian government against Rabbi Shneur Zalman of Liady, the founder of the Lubavitch movement, and it almost led to the rabbi's execution.

Yet two hundred years later, how do Jews view the Vilna Gaon and the Chasidim? Almost all knowledgeable Jews regard the Gaon as a great intellectual and spiritual figure and simultaneously view the rise of Chasidism, and its rabbinic figures such as the Ba'al Shem Tov, as a very important spiritual development in Jewish life. Of course, the Vilna Gaon would have been horrified by this attitude. Ironically, had this great but intolerant man been granted the power to deal with the situation, he would today be regarded as a brilliant man who nevertheless brought about the deaths of innocent people. Sometimes the greatest blessing for intolerant people is to be denied the power that they desire.

✷ WHEN INTOLERANCE IS A VIRTUE: A RARE BUT IMPORTANT EXCEPTION

18. On both moral and rational grounds, it makes little sense to tolerate those who, if they gain power, will deny freedom to those with whom they disagree. Thus it seems morally wrong to grant democratic rights to those whose intention is to utilize democracy's tolerance to overthrow it.[30] That was Hitler's tactic: to come to power through democratic elections and then to destroy democracy. Nor did he and his followers make any effort to deny that this was their goal. As Joseph Goebbels, the future Nazi minister of propaganda, wrote in 1928: "We become members of the Reichstag [the German parliament] in order to paralyze the Weimar...with its own assistance. If democracy is so stupid as to give us free tickets and per diem [daily expenses] for this blockade, that is its own affair.... We do not come as friends nor even as neutrals, we come as enemies. As the wolf bursts into the flock, so we come." Seven years later, after the Nazis had come to power and ended democracy, Goebbels acknowledged yet again that doing this had always been their intention: "We National Socialists never asserted that we represented a democratic point of view, but we declared openly that we used democratic methods only in order to gain power and that, after assuming power, we would deny to adversaries without any consideration the means which were granted to us in the times of opposition." Similar tactics – using free elections in an attempt to destroy the democratic process – have been

tried by Communist parties as well as by certain Islamist groups today.

Granting democratic rights to those who intend to use these rights to destroy democracy makes as little sense as allowing someone who announces that he intends to commit a crime to acquire a weapon.

The Talmud records that in the first century C.E., *a man named Bar Kamtza slandered the Jews of Israel to officials in the Roman government, telling them that the Jews were fomenting rebellion. Upon hearing of Bar Kamtza's behavior, the rabbinical leadership wished to execute him before his accusations could cause any further harm, but Rabbi Zechariah ben Avkulas ruled that Bar Kamtza had as yet committed no capital offense and that it would therefore be wrong to kill him. Bar Kamtza continued his slanders, and the results were catastrophic. Rabbi Yochanan later commented: "The tolerance displayed by Rabbi Zechariah ben Avkulas [in refusing to allow the traitorous Bar Kamtza to be put to death] destroyed our Temple, burned down our Sanctuary, and [caused us to be] exiled from our land." (Gittin 56a)*

✣ FINAL THOUGHTS: TWO ANTIDOTES TO INTOLERANCE

19. *Disagree with people but do not impugn their motives.* The contemporary Talmud scholar Prof. Reuven Kimelman summarizes the authoritarian and potentially violent mindset of the religiously (and politically) intolerant: "Two opposing sides cannot both be in possession of the truth. If I have the truth, then what you have is false. If I am right, then you are wrong. And since falsehood has no rights, I, in service of the truth, am duty-bound to work for your conversion or, failing that, your destruction."

The hatred such thinking promotes can be prevented only "as long as both parties entertain the possibility of the other acting for the sake of Heaven."[31] Therefore, even when you disagree with someone, unless you know for a fact that the other person's motives are malicious and/or self-serving, do not impugn your opponent's motives.

This mode of thinking is also helpful in cases involving forgiveness of someone who has hurt us but has not sought our forgiveness. My friend Rabbi Leonid Feldman suggests that we try to focus on the other person's intentions, which are usually more benign than their actions. For example, I know a man who felt misunderstood and cruelly mistreated by his father. Prior to his father's death, the two men had a perfunctory reconciliation, but the son's anger at his father remained fierce. When he conducted this exercise, he was able to realize that although his father had hurt him, his father had never thought, "What can I do to really hurt my son and destroy his emotional well-being?" True, he had been a bad father, but not out of a desire to be a bad father. This realization finally enabled the man's anger at, and demonization of, his father to subside.

20. *Judge people by their behavior far more than by their beliefs.* Rabbi Harold Kushner has noted that "There are people whose theologies I do not share, but I consider their religions to be 'true' when I see the way they live their faith."[32] In other words, while not accepting as true basic tenets of another belief system, Kushner nonetheless recognizes that these faiths have the capacity to inspire their adherents to live lives of kindness, integrity, and holiness. For example, Jews obviously do not believe the claims that Christianity makes for Jesus (e.g., that he was the son of God and perfect). But they can still appreciate that such beliefs, among others, motivate many Christians to lead righteous lives. Similarly, Orthodox Jews find Reform Judaism's willingness to overturn, suspend, or regard as optional many biblical and Talmudic laws as profoundly wrong, while Reform Jews regard Orthodox

insistence that Torah laws cannot be abrogated and that Talmudic legislation is still obligatory as wrong as well. But once one meets those who hold these beliefs and who are leading day-to-day lives of goodness, can one dismiss such people as lacking in value because one dislikes their theology? There is, it would seem, more than one way to lead a moral life, and this can sometimes be done even by those who possess theological beliefs we regard as wrong. We can feel passionately about our own religious tradition without regarding with contempt and disdain those who live by another set of beliefs but who lead lives of goodness.[33]

✌ NOTES

1. In English the word "tolerance" is related to "tolerate."
2. Rabbi Aharon Lichtenstein relates tolerance to the possession of power. Thus, "to tolerate is to suffer the pressure of what is…by my lights, thoroughly erroneous, and to refrain, nonetheless, from the exercise of power to coerce its devotees to cease and desist" ("The Parameters of Tolerance," in Moshe Sokol, ed., *Tolerance, Dissent, and Democracy*, p. 140).
3. *Emet ve-Emunah*. The Talmudic passage itself narrowly restricts the meaning of Rabbi Meir's aphorism, saying that if people all thought alike, they would hide their valuables in the same place, and this would be a great boon to thieves.
4. See Reuven Kimelman, "Judaism and Pluralism," *Modern Judaism*, May 1987, p. 147.
5. David Pelcovitz, *Keeping Faith in the Face of Terror*, 2.
6. Literally, "will never see a sign of blessing [in his studies]."
7. See Rabbi Aryeh Kaplan's discussion of this point in Cope-Yossef, "Reflections on a Living Torah: Rabbi Aryeh Kaplan," in Ora Wiskind Elper and Susan Handelman, eds., *Torah of the Mothers: Contemporary Jewish Women Read Classical Jewish Texts*, pp. 44–45.
8. Another reason to list minority positions is so that people in later generations who would argue on behalf of such views would realize that the earlier Rabbis had already considered and rejected them; see Mishna *Eduyot* 1:6.
9. If the rulings of both sides were valid expressions of God's will, why did Jewish law find it necessary to choose one set of rulings over another? Because when it comes to law, anarchy results when there is no uniformity on basic legal requirements. For example, a century after the incident of the heavenly voice, two leading rabbis, Gamliel and Joshua, had a dispute over the day on which Yom Kippur would fall that year. As president of the Sanhedrin, Rabbi Gamliel had supreme authority, and he compelled Rabbi Joshua *not to* observe Yom Kippur on the day on which Joshua thought it fell (Mishna *Rosh Hashana* 2:8–9). Gamliel feared that, otherwise, followers of each rabbi would start to observe two different calendars, and the Jewish community would split apart.
10. This is despite the fact that one Talmudic passage (*Yevamot* 14a) claims that Shammai's followers had greater analytic abilities than did Hillel's disciples.
11. There is only one instance (in the context of a highly technical legal dispute) in which Shammai's disciples acknowledged the validity of the position offered by Hillel's followers (see Mishna *Terumot* 5:4).
12. Regarding the logic of disregarding a unanimous verdict, Aaron Schreiber, a professor of law and a Jewish legal scholar, writes: "[P]art of the 'due process' accorded to a criminal

defendant in Jewish law was that after the deliberations of the court and before any judgment was reached, the judges were required to spend the night together in pairs, searching for a possible defense for the criminal defendant (see Mishna *Sanhedrin* 5:5). Here, since the judges of the Sanhedrin unanimously felt that the defendant was guilty, they would no longer search for a possible defense in his behalf. Accordingly, he was deprived of the 'due process' requirement. He could not therefore be convicted and had to be acquitted. This rule would reflect the extreme lengths to which Jewish law would go to accord a criminal defendant 'due process.'" Schreiber compares the release of a criminal who is undoubtedly guilty to "the 'Miranda' and 'Poisoned Fruit' doctrines in the United States, which prevent the imposition of sanctions upon defendants who clearly appear to be guilty of crimes, where the police have engaged in acts that violate the defendants' constitutional rights" (*Jewish Law and Decision-Making*, pp. 270–271).

13. Coercion occurred when Jewish communities in premodern Europe were forced to come to the synagogue and listen to Christian clergy's proselytizing speeches. For example, Pope Gregory XIII (1572–1585) ordered missionizing sermons to be delivered in synagogues every Sabbath and on Jewish holidays. Lest Rome's Jews stay away from services to avoid these sermons, he further decreed that a minimum of 100 Jewish men and 50 Jewish women, all over the age of twelve, be in attendance when sermons were delivered. The Church even established a special school to train preachers for this work. A half-century later, in 1630, Austrian Emperor Ferdinand II similarly ordered the Jews of Vienna to attend such sermons, and he mandated that any Jew who was observed talking or sleeping during the sermon be punished (Ben Zion Bokser, *Jews, Judaism, and the State of Israel*, pp. 125–126).

14. The medieval Christian-Jewish debates in which Jews were forced to participate were pointless, in addition to being cruel, because the Jews generally feared to present their most powerful arguments since these provoked wrath, and sometimes attacks, against them. Also, only when we overcome our opponent's best arguments do we feel confidence in our own position. One strongly suspects that the most important reason authoritarian rulers do not allow their opponents freedom of speech is fear that they won't be able to respond to their critics in a convincing manner. Indeed, one feature Communist, Fascist, and all other totalitarian regimes share is that they jail and otherwise muzzle those who express opposing viewpoints.

15. This incident is particularly interesting because of Rabbi Soloveitchik's well-known opposition to interfaith dialogue on matters of faith; this story would seem consistent with the Maharal's view, allowing for one-on-one discussions of spiritual matters between people of different faiths. I am thankful to Dr. Joel Wolowelsky and Dr. David Berger, who helped me track down this story.

16. Jonathan Sacks, *The Dignity of Difference*, 53.

17. Ibid., pp. 55, 56.

18. Cited in ibid., p. 63. This 1981 text is found not in Berlin's essays but in notes he had prepared for a friend who had solicited his help in preparing a lecture. Berlin was to go abroad the following day, and these hurried notes, Sacks explains, "convey as well as anything he wrote, his lifelong opposition to intolerance and what he believed to be its source."

19. According to anti-Semites, the document proving this conspiracy is *The Protocols of the Elders of Zion*, a late nineteenth-century forgery by the Russian secret police. *The Protocols* were translated by Henry Ford's *Dearborn Independent* in the early 1920s (additional, false material was added), and the Nazis distributed millions of copies during the 1930s. As of the early 2000s, the *Protocols* remain a perennial best-seller in the Arab world.

20. Abraham Twerski, *Generation to Generation*, 92.

21. Today in most Reform congregations men cover their heads, but in the past, particularly in temples that followed the tradition known as Classical Reform, they were bare-headed.

22. Jonathan Magonet, *Returning*, 28.

23. It is infrequently noted that the Reverend Bailey Smith, the Baptist leader who made this statement, went on to say that he would defend with his life the right of Jews to offer such prayers.

24. The man who made this announcement might have been relying in part on a decision of Rabbi Moshe Feinstein, who ruled that non-Orthodox rabbis attending a service at an Orthodox synagogue should not be given *aliyot*, called to the Torah. In Rabbi Feinstein's view, since these rabbis do not accept the traditional understanding of divine revelation (precisely that which is asserted in the blessing recited when one is called to the Torah), the blessing for them is a mere verbal formula and it is forbidden to answer "Amen" (*Igrot Moshe, Orach Chayyim*, Vol. 3, # 21).

25. My friend found another Orthodox synagogue in which the members did answer his *Kaddish*. While he was grateful to them for doing so, he noted that nobody there spoke to him during the eleven months he was reciting *kaddish*.

26. Once monotheism was established as a widespread belief, however, rabbinic intolerance for idolaters declined. Thus, in a famous Talmudic ruling, the Rabbis declared that contemporary idolaters outside the land of Israel should not be viewed as evil; rather, "they are only carrying out *customs* learned from their ancestors" (*Chullin* 13b; emphasis added).

27. Maimonides himself, or rather his writings, subsequently became the victims of terrible intolerance from fellow Jews. Less than three decades after his death, three leading rabbis in France, arguing that there were heretical teachings in Maimonides' books, denounced his writings to the Dominicans, who headed the French Inquisition. The Inquisitors were happy to intervene and burn some of Maimonides' writings. They also used this incident as an excuse to start looking into other Jews' books. Eight years later, when the Dominicans started burning the Talmud, one of the rabbis involved, Jonah Gerondi (author of the classic work *Gates of Repentance*) concluded that God was punishing him and French Jewry for their unjust condemnation of Maimonides. He resolved to travel to Maimonides' grave in Tiberias, Israel, to beg forgiveness.

28. In popular Hebrew parlance, the term *gaon* means "genius." Thus he was called "the genius of Vilna."

29. See the discussion of the Gaon's animus to the Hasidim in Elijah Judah Schochet, *The Hasidic Movement and the Gaon of Vilna*, pp. 8–10.

30. On pragmatic, as opposed to moral, grounds, it might make sense not to outlaw Communist or Nazi groups in countries such as the United States, where they pose no threat of achieving political power. Withholding rights from such groups might prompt some people to regard them as martyrs and, therefore, extend them support. On the other hand, in a country such as Germany, in which the people did vote the Nazis into power, it would make sense to outlaw even small groups – and even if they are currently nonviolent – that intend to destroy democracy.

31. Kimelman notes that the intellectual flaw in concluding that your view is absolutely right is that it "seeks to absolutize a particular configuration of the tradition into universal validity" ("Judaism and Pluralism," in *Modern Judaism*, May 1987, p. 32; also 35).

32. Harold Kushner, *The Lord Is My Shepherd*, 83.

33. Kushner's notion of assessing others on the basis of their behavior, not theology, corresponds in some respects to the Meiri's (thirteenth-century) willingness to suspend all anti-Gentile legislation in the Talmud on the grounds that such legislation was directed against idolaters, and he judged idolatry primarily on the basis of the immoral behavior it sanctioned: "It has already been stated that these things [anti-Gentile legislation] were said concerning periods when there existed nations of idolaters, and they were contaminated in their deeds and tainted in their dispositions…but other, 'nations that are restricted by the ways of religion,' which are free from such blemishes of character…are without doubt exempt from this prohibition [that is, from anti-Gentile legislation]." (Meiri commentary on *Avoda Zara*, p. 53.)

Becoming Human: What's in a Name?

Shera Aranoff Tuchman

The first book of the Hebrew Bible, Genesis or *Bereishit*, begins with a narrative of God's creation of the world, describing the six days of creation which culminate in the appearance of man. According to the *p'shat* or plain understanding of the text, the world is created in a sequence of increasing complexity, from nothingness to the inanimate world, to the plants, fish, birds, and animals, and finally to God's ultimate creation, the human being.

What I would like to suggest is that the *Bereishit* story of creation of man in the first chapter describes only the *physical* creation of the human being, and in fact a very naïve being. And just as in the creation of the *world* there is a progression from simple to the complex, so in the creation of the human there is a progression from a naïve state to that of a complex human being. The Torah gives us a synopsis not only of the creation of the *external* world but of the development of the human's *inner* world as well. Whereas the progression of God's creation of the physical world is marked clearly by changing of *days*, changes in human development are not mentioned outright but, I would suggest, are alluded to and revealed by changes in the human's *name*.

This maturation of the human being takes place over the first several chapters in *Bereishit*. In the beginning of *Bereishit* it is clear that there are two narratives describing the creation of the human being. The first is narrated in *Bereishit* 1:26–29, the second, which we will discuss later, in *Bereishit* 2:21–25.

> *And God said let us make Adam in our image after our likeness and let them have dominion over the fish etc. And He created Adam in His image, in the image of God He created him, male and female He created them.*[1]

Noting the variations in the text as the newly created human is described both in singular and in plural, Chizkuni suggests that in this story of creation God created a male-female human *duo*, given the same one name, Adam. "*Let us make Adam* – this means human, male and female."[2] Chizkuni instructs us to look forward to *Bereishit* 5:2, where it explicitly states "*and He called their name Adam on the day they were created.*"

Rashi further explains that this human duo was a composite, a fused male and female. He realizes that one may initially see an apparent contradiction between this narrative and the narrative in chapter 2 which describes the creation of Eve, but he does not perceive it as a difficulty. Rashi states that in the first chapter, man was created as a duo, and the Torah is giving us the bare facts. In the second chapter, Rashi continues, this duo is separated, and we are given the fleshed-out details of the creation of the human being: *And God created man in His image, male and female He created them. Yet further on it states (2:21) and He took one of his ribs. So how was woman created? The first human was created with two faces, as one conjoined being. This is described in the first narrative. Later, in the second narrative, it states how this entity was divided.*[3]

This human creature of two faces described by Rashi is mentioned in the Babylonian Talmud in the tractate *Eruvin*. Here, the Talmud explains that the first human was created as a joined entity, male on one side and female on the other. As for the differing story in the second chapter, which describes the creation of woman from the side of man, the tractate *Eruvin* states that the creation of woman was the separation of the male-female entity, either into equal parts or into unequal parts, from which God later builds Woman:

> God created the first human as a combined duo, or two-faced, du partzufim, *male on one side and female on the other. But it is written in the second chapter that the female was created separately, that God built her from the original human's side, the* tzelah! *Some say that the second creation story was an equal separation of the original Adam and others say only a small part, an insignificant part, was separated from the* tzelah, *and that God completely rebuilt the female entity.*[4]

Bereishit Rabba adds a second possibility to the creation of this original human, stating that at first man was created not as a duo as Siamese twins, but rather as a hermaphrodite, a single being who had both male and female organs. According to this description, it was only in the *second* narrative of creation that this primitive creation was divided into two distinct beings: *He initially created the Adam as a hermaphrodite, bisexual, with the capacity to be both male and female. In the second creation story He separated them.*[5]

According to the commentaries, this first created *human* was a dual entity of absolute equality, of complementary halves, with no tension between them on either a physical or emotional level. Perhaps this *human* could rightly be called humanoid, since it can hardly be called a complete human being. Amazingly, this primitive human being does not interact with its Creator. It does not respond at all to being created. It says nothing. It does nothing. It breathes. *It is.* This existence is described in *Bereishit*: *And God formed the Adam, from dust from the ground, and breathed into him the soul of life, and so the Adam became a living being.*[6]

Surprisingly, it is to this newly created mute creature that God gives two commandments, the first positive commandment and the first negative commandment in the Bible. First, God instructs this human creature to *be fruitful and multiply and fill the earth, and conquer it.*[7] Again, as after creation, there is no response from this human. This creation is alive, *God breathed into him the breath of life*, but has no consciousness of self.

We can now picture the Adam creature living in the newly created magnificence of paradise, obeying the *only* given commandment, that of being fruitful and multiplying, but with no thoughts of which we are aware, no speech, no human emotions. But, in fact, if this Adam is a conjoined entity, then one would not expect a reaction to procreating. Reproducing becomes a bodily function only, like eating or digesting.

Then God issues to the Adam the first *negative* commandment. This human is commanded to eat and enjoy of all the fruits in the Garden of Eden save one, the fruit of the tree of knowledge of good and evil. This is a very strong prohibition, with very serious consequences. The disobeying of this commandment will result in the punishment of death, an undoing of the ultimate creation of man:

> *And out of the ground made the Lord God to grow every tree that is pleasant to the sight, and good for food; the tree of life also in the midst of the garden, and the tree of the knowledge of* tov *and* rah: *good and evil. And the Lord God commanded the man saying, "Of every tree of the garden thou may freely eat. But of the tree of the knowledge of good and evil, thou shall not eat of it; for in the day that thou eat thereof thou shall surely die.*[8]

Amazingly, there is still no response from the human: no response, no questioning, no agreeing, and no disagreeing.

The reader must by now wonder about the nature of the human who is commanded to procreate, who is prohibited from eating of the tree of knowledge of good and evil, and who does not respond to either edict. Can the human think? Can the human feel? In fact, one may wonder if this creation is really human! Furthermore, is it God's desire that, with this prohibition, knowledge is to be kept from the human? In the twelfth century Rabbi Moses ben Maimon, known as Maimonides or the Rambam, explains this at length and definitively in his *Guide of the Perplexed*:

> It does appear at first sight from scripture that man was originally intended by this commandment not to eat from the tree of knowledge, and thus to be perfectly equal to the rest of the animal creation, which is not endowed with intellect, reason, or power of distinguishing between good and evil, and that it would be only Adam's *disobedience* to the command of God that would procure that great perfection which is the peculiarity of man, the power of distinguishing between good and evil, the noblest of all the faculties of our nature, the essential characteristic of the human race. It appears strange that rebelliousness would be the means of *elevating* man to a pinnacle of perfection by giving him knowledge! Examine the matter more deeply; for it is not to be understood as we may understand it at first glance. *Man was created in the form and likeness of God* (*Bereishit* 1:26), and thus the gift of intellect was granted to man as the highest endowment and was bestowed on him *before* his disobedience. It is on account of this gift of intellect that man *could* be addressed and commanded by God, for no commandments are given to a brute creation or those devoid of understanding. After disobeying the commandment and eating from the tree of knowledge of good and evil, the human became aware of desires that had their source in fantasy, imagination, and gratification of bodily appetites. By sinning, he obtained knowledge of relative, personal, subjective desires, but at what price? He lost absolute clarity of truth and falsity, as right and wrong became muddled in his imagination and desires.[9]

Rambam here makes a sharp distinction between objective

facts – true and false – and subjective desires – good and bad. He states clearly that the tree was not simply the tree of knowledge, but in fact the tree of a *special kind* of knowledge – knowledge of good and bad.

According to the Rambam, the human had intelligence, an objective knowledge of *facts*. Through his intellect, the Adam knew scientific truth. When the human was in a state of innocence, Adam was guided only by objective, intellectual perception, by reason. So the human was in fact given commandments that he could understand with his *intellectual* faculty. The human possessed this knowledge perfectly and completely. But Adam was not able to understand personal *subjective* desires, *tov* and *rah*. So the newly created human could understand commandments, though the human could not understand subjectivity and had no human emotions.

The twelfth-century scholar Ibn Ezra confirms and brings a prooftext to Rambam's explanation to describe how intelligent this primitive human, in fact was. Ibn Ezra reasons that "this human had to have knowledge *before* he ate from the tree of knowledge of good and evil, for God wouldn't demand one to obey a commandment if he were like an animal, incompetent, and without knowledge."[10] Also, Ibn Ezra continues, "before eating from the forbidden tree, God paraded all the animals before the human, who then named every animal."

And God brought all the animals and all the birds to Adam to see what he would call them, and whatever Adam named them that would be their name forever.[11] The human was actually very knowledgeable in absolute knowledge, in facts. In Adam's naming the animals, that name became their essence, their nature, forever.

Strangely, nestled between the prohibition regarding eating of the tree of knowledge of good and evil and the parading of the animals in front of Adam, the text states, *It is not good for Adam to be alone. I will make him a helpmate opposite him.*[12] But it is only after God parades all the animals before the human and Adam names them that he realizes that he is alone, that there is no animal who is a match for him. *The human gave names to all the cattle, and to the fowl of the air, and to every beast of the field, but for Adam there was not found a helpmate for himself.*[13]

Ramban, the thirteenth-century scholar Moshe ben Nachman, or Nachmanides, not only invests our Adam with intellectual knowledge, as described by Rambam and Ibn Ezra, but adds another dimension to this primitive being. He explains that Adam did have a passionate animal nature even before he ate from the prohibited tree. Ramban states that Adam acted according to an innate biological imperative, with animalistic hormonal drives. He explains that before he ate from the prohibited fruit, there was no human attraction or desire between male and female, but mating was done like animals in heat, and the reproductive organs were to them like arms or faces. It was only after eating from the tree of knowledge that *human* passion was born. The forbidden fruit stimulated desire and passion, which could be a desire for good or for bad.

> *It was no longer a biological imperative, as with animals, but human passion that would drive man. The "tree of knowledge" is in effect, "tree of desire for good or bad." After eating from the tree of knowledge, humans now had desires, and with those desires, choice to do good or to do harm, and they could use that free will wisely or do evil to fulfill his desire and pleasure.*[14]

Sforno, biblical commentator of the fifteenth and sixteenth centuries, describes this knowledge of good and bad as knowledge of desire. "The knowledge imparted from the tree was knowledge of the senses, a twisted sort of knowledge which encouraged one to pick the enticing, even if it was harmful, and to reject the bitter, even if it would be beneficial."[15]

To summarize the characteristics of the original human according to the commentaries just discussed, we have learned that Adam was extremely intelligent with total clarity of vision (Rambam). This was proven by the fact that he named the genus and species of every living creation (Ibn Ezra). He did have a primitive sort of desire, but it was of the innate animal nature. After eating of the tree, that passion became complex and fraught with difficulties (Ramban). After eating from the tree of knowledge of good and evil, he was no longer able to see facts objectively. Adam's intelligence became distorted with imagination, fantasy, and desires (Sforno).

David Hume, one of the most important eighteenth-century British philosophers, clearly distinguishes between intellectual knowledge and knowledge born of desire:

> The rules of morality are not conclusions of our reason. Since reason has no influence on our passions, it is in vain to pretend that morality is discovered by a deduction of reason. Reason is the discovery of truth or falsehood. Truth or falsehood consists in an agreement or disagreement either to the real relation of ideas or to real existence and matter of fact. Now 'tis evident our passions and volitions are not susceptible of any such agreement. Reason cannot be the source of distinguishing between moral good and evil. Moral distinction, therefore, is not the offspring of reason.[16]

A troubling question now arises. When God forbade Adam from eating of the tree of knowledge of good and bad, did He really *not* want us to have passions and desires? Aren't these emotions precisely what make us truly human? Rabbi Adin Steinsaltz grapples with these questions:

> The problems are profound. If man's superiority rests on his mental capacity, why should God forbid him to eat of the tree? What is there about this type of knowledge that is so dangerous and terrible? "On the day you eat from it you shall surely die." Man's knowledge, which comes from the forbidden tree, is a mixture of good and evil, hopelessly jumbled in a medley of both. The good and evil keep influencing

each other and drawing upon each other. Good and evil is a Rorschach test, of smells, tastes, appearances, tactile feelings, memories, and anticipations. There is always a duality. It is man who is the decisive factor. Evil then is not necessarily ugly or repellent. It can be genuinely beautiful. For man then, knowledge of good and evil is an awareness of, and an involvement in, a complexity that he generally cannot hope to overcome in his lifetime. Only angels *know* properly, and keep good and evil separate and distinct, not by a mental effort, but naturally. We cannot distinguish twilight – *hamavdil ben kodesh lechol*. An angel can *know* good and evil, and remain an angel. When a man gets to *know* good and evil, he can only with difficulty remain a man. Knowledge in Hebrew is always linked to an emotional element, *Adam knew his wife*. A mature person can remain good, but not innocent. For man, knowledge of good and evil becomes his beginning.[17]

What emerges from this discussion is that the tree of knowledge is not the tree of absolute knowledge, but of relative knowledge – the tree of emotions – desires and passions, struggles and needs, of all that makes us truly human. And it is from this tree that Adam is prohibited from eating.

According to *Ohr Hachayim*, Adam's naming of the animals immediately after the prohibition to eat from the tree of knowledge is twofold. First, it reveals to *us* his computer-like intelligence, but the naming is also part of God's plan to have the intellectual *Adam realize* that, as intelligent and knowledgeable as he is, there is something he lacks. Immediately before he parades the animals God says that *it is not good for man to be alone*.[18] *Ohr Hachayim* relates that this whole scene of parading the animals before Adam was to make him aware that something was missing, what one might call *intellectual desire*, to bring forth the separation of the duo-Adam into two separate beings, not only to procreate but to be an appropriate complement for each other. According to the commentary, Adam in fact did search for a suitable helpmate among all the other creatures he was naming, but he did not find one acceptable to him. "Naming the animals, that is, identifying their essence, was part of that search for a suitable helpmate. Eve's existence as a separate body became mandatory from Adam's point of view."[19]

Chizkuni adds that this divine plan for man to have a mate was decided from the beginning of creation. "God *wanted* there to be a human pair, but He waited for the right moment, until the human saw that all the animals had mates, and there was no corresponding *other* for Adam. This was part of God's plan so that Adam would *desire her, and thus appreciate her more*."[20] It would seem that the parading of pairs of animals awakened within Adam an intellectual desire, though an emotionally childlike one, for a mate.

Ramban fleshes out this explanation, stating that the calling of names refers to the division into species so that the animals could beget offspring from one another. "Adam watched them mating and realized that he didn't find a mate for himself. It was God's will not to take Adam's rib from him until he himself would know that among the created beings there was none suitable for him and he would crave to have her.[21] In effect, God planted the seeds of desire. God wanted Adam to develop his potential for desire, although Adam's first desire was a rudimentary intellectual one!

Sha'arei Aharon, an encyclopedic commentary by Rabbi Aharon Yeshaya Rotter, adds that although God said it isn't good for man to be alone, "the mate doesn't appear until man prays for a mate," until man *feels* an existential aloneness.[22]

God wanted Adam to feel a void, a consciousness as a being alone, needing another for completion. And that could not be taught. It had to come from within oneself. God wanted Adam to feel that existential aloneness. Only then would the desire to transcend it take place. Adam is missing the *other*.

French philosopher Jean-Paul Sartre states that "man cannot

be anything unless others recognize it as such. In order to get any truth about myself, I must have contact with another person. The other is indispensable to my own existence as well as to my knowledge about myself. Inter-subjectivity, this is the world in which man decides what he is and what others are."[23]

The human is beginning to have a glimpse of self-awareness, stirrings of consciousness. Adam is aware of being alone. Until now, the only action of the human that the Bible has revealed to us is naming the animals. No other thoughts, words, or actions have been attributable to the first created person. Now, after his having named the animals, we are finally privy to his thoughts. The Bible clearly states that Adam did not find a helpmate. But now, for the first time, Rashi gives voice to these thoughts. "When God brought the animals before Adam, he said, 'They all have mates, and I don't have a mate.'"[24]

Recent Nobel Prize winner for physiology or medicine, Dr. Gerald M. Edelman, describes human consciousness. "As human beings we are conscious of being conscious. Dogs and other mammals, if they are aware, have primary consciousness…animals with primary consciousness are not conscious of being conscious and do not have a nameable self.[25]

Dr. M. Esther Harding, M.D., twentieth-century founding member of the Medical Society of Analytical Psychology of America, explores the stages in which consciousness develops in the human being:

From being merely an integer in the continuum, he gradually becomes a person in his own right, developing the part of the psyche we call "I." Until this differentiation takes place, we are merely the puppets of unknown forces, having hardly any power or choice of self-determination at all. We speak of a person's being conscious as opposed to his being asleep or comatose, yet a human being may be unconscious in the psychological meaning of the word. He may perform many acts, even quite complicated ones, without being aware that he is doing so. The biblical account that *God breathed his spirit into man (Bereishit 2:7)* and so made him different from the animals means that the creation was *capable* of consciousness.

A person who is unconscious of himself does not live life, life just happens to him. Such a condition is very infantile, very primitive. At first it is not even aware of its own body limits. There is no differentiation whatever between I and *not I*. It is not until this step is taken that it *can* dawn on an individual that others too may have a similar sense of being I. And indeed, *this* state of consciousness is by no means always achieved by the average man. Many people go through their lives still under the impression that they are the only *I*, blind, primitive, and amazingly unconscious.[26]

This analysis aptly describes our original Adam. The human was intelligent – Adam named all the animals – but had no sense of self-consciousness, no sense of I, let alone an awareness of an *other*. Consistent with Harding's analysis, one could say that Adam accomplished this naming while still in a state of *un* consciousness. It is only afterward, observing the animals pairing as male and female, that Adam begins to feel stirrings of aloneness, and a need for there to be an *other*. The human is developing a rudimentary consciousness by observing the animals relating to their *other* in the animal kingdom. The human is now aware of being existentially alone.

In the sentence immediately following Adam's awareness of his aloneness, God causes the human to fall into a deep slumber. It is precisely at this moment that a second human will be created. God creates an *other* for Adam. *God made a deep sleep to fall upon Adam, and he slept, and God took one of his ribs-sides, and closed the flesh under it. God built the side that was taken from man into a woman and He brought her to the man."*[27]

God finally creates an *other*. The commentaries offer their opinions regarding the nature of this creation. Sforno describes this creation as Adam's mirror-image equal. "She may have the form of man and his qualities, differing from him only in the physical vessels, the organs of reproduction, this being the difference between them. Otherwise, both have the possibility for the attainment of perfection, be the attainment abundant or meager."[28]

Ibn Ezra questions the statement that God *brought* her to Adam. How did God bring her to him, when she was right there already, having been created from Adam's side! He explains that God did not physically bring the newly created being to Adam, but psychologically. This was not a physical bringing, since she was created from the rib, right next to Adam; rather it was a conscious awareness of an "other," someone like himself but distinct from himself. "He brought her to him in his, Adam's *mind*."[29]

And now, for the first time in the biblical text itself, Adam speaks! Because these are the human's first spoken words, the commentaries pay close attention to them. *This time, bone of my bone, flesh of my flesh, this will be called woman* (eesha) *because this was taken from man* (eesh)."[30]

The Zohar, the foundational work of medieval Jewish mysticism, describes this verse as perhaps the world's first love poem. "This verse is spoken lovingly, so as to draw her to him and to win her affections. Observe how tender and coaxing Adam's language is: '*bone of my bone, flesh of my flesh*.' Adam begins to sing her praises, *this shall be called wo***man**, and this is the peerless and incomparable one, who merits the title of *wo***man**. Every word is inspired by love."[31]

The Malbim, nineteenth-century commentator Rabbi Meir Leibush, observes that when Adam was a dual entity, the female part and the male part had the same name, *ha'adam*, Adam. This was the name of the initial creation of the human. Now the two were separated and separate, man and woman, *eesh* and *eesha*. This time the female is defined by herself. What the Malbim astutely adds is that by her having her own essence, Adam gets his own essence as well. Thus it was an "additional name to Adam also, named here as *eesh*."[32]

This is a radical change in the development of man. When

Adam describes the woman as *flesh of my flesh, for from man she was taken*, he is appreciating a self-awareness which has eluded him until now. With the creation of woman, Adam is able to see himself subjectively. The human is now aware of an *other*.

In contrast to the Zohar, I would suggest that there is another way to read this text. Rather than see Adam's first words as a love poem, a close reading of the text reveals that the human is talking *about* the newest creation, not *to* her. Yes, the human is finally conscious, aware of himself and of *other*. Unfortunately, he sees this woman as an object. Martin Buber, a twentieth-century Jewish philosopher, expands upon this notion in his book *I and Thou*:

> There is no "I" as such, but only "I" as the basic word I-you, or I-it. Man becomes an *I* through a *you*. The man who has acquired an I and says *I-It* (*this will be called woman*) assumes a position before things but does not confront them in the current of reciprocity. He bends down to examine particulars under the objectifying magnifying glass of close scrutiny, or he uses the objective telescope of distant vision, to arrange them as mere scenery. In his contemplation, he isolates them without any feeling for the exclusive or joins them without any world feeling. But whoever lives only with that *is not human*. The real association of the real duality, *I* and *you*, is different from the *I* of *It*. The *I* of *It* appears as ego, the *I of I-you* appears as a person. Egos appear by setting themselves apart from other egos, Persons appear by entering into relations of other persons. Every feeling has its place in polar tension (*ezer kenegdo*). It derives its color and meaning not from itself alone, but also from its polar opposite. *I* require a *you* to become an *I*. It is in the encounter. Nothing reveals itself, except through the reciprocal force of confrontation.[33]

Our primitive Adam is at the earliest stage of human development.

He realizes he is a unique being, *eesh*, and is aware of an *other*. But clearly, Adam doesn't speak *with* her in an *I-You* confrontation. He speaks *about* her as *I-It*.

With deep psychological insight, the Netziv, nineteenth-century rabbi and scholar, develops ideas similar to Buber's. According to the Netziv, Adam felt that the woman was created for *his* purposes only, to fulfill his own needs, just as his needs were met with other body parts as his arm or his leg. For this reason, the Netziv explains, she is at first called *eesha* (woman, meaning from *eesh* (man). The Netziv continues that later on it will not be like that, for her nature changes. After she eats from the tree of knowledge, she will become a woman with her own desires as well. Then she will not just be Adam's object, but a subject in her own right.[34]

Radak, the twelfth-thirteenth century biblical scholar Rabbi David Kimchi, builds upon this idea by stating that the name he gives the woman, *eesha*, is not a specific, individual name for this newly created woman, but rather refers to the entire species. He is naming her as he named all the other animals. Adam is naming her objectively as his mate. Later we will learn that he does give her a specific name when he calls her Chava, which is unique and personal to her.[35]

Until now everything has been concrete from man's point of view. The animate world was created with living creatures, animals, mammals, *man*, and now, finally, *woman*. And Adam has named them all. His consciousness of self is embryonic. Human drives have certainly not been documented so far in the biblical text.

But the Torah is a timeless book, as relevant to us today as it was to the millions of people who studied it over thousands of years. The Torah knows that we are not only physical beings with objective, scientific thoughts. The Bible knows of human passions, of desire, and of wants that become needs, even beyond that which is acceptable. It is into this precarious world that we now enter. We are now on the brink of what makes us truly human, for better or for worse.

This is a most difficult concept. And the Bible presents this concept in the simplest terms, perhaps in a metaphor. The text describes a fable-like story of a fanciful garden with a talking snake and a magical, enticing fruit. The two human creations, man and woman, are placed by God Himself into this paradise of the Garden of Eden to enjoy the bounty of its blessings. There is but one restriction. They are instructed that they are forbidden to eat the fruit of one of the trees, mysteriously called the tree of knowledge of good and evil. They disobey this one prohibition, with cataclysmic consequences.

An understanding of this metaphor allows us a glimpse into the most intrinsic nature of a human being. This Garden of Eden story then becomes a psychological manual to aid us in understanding man's existential nature and all that makes us truly human – our drives, desires, and passions.

> Now the serpent was more subtle than any beast of the field which the Lord God had made. And he said to the woman, "Moreover even if God said it, should you not eat from all the trees of the garden?" And the woman said unto the serpent, "Of the fruit of the trees of the garden we may eat; but of the fruit of the tree which is in the midst of the garden, God has said, you may not eat from it, nor may you touch it, for you may die." And the serpent said to the woman, "You surely won't die, for God knows that on the day you eat from it, your eyes will be opened, and you will be as God, knowing good and evil." And when the woman saw that the tree was good for food, and that it was tempting to her sight, and that the tree was to be desired to make one wise, she plucked one of its fruit and ate, and she also gave to her man who was with her, and he ate. And the eyes of them both were opened, and they knew that they were naked, and they sewed fig leaves together, and made themselves coverings.[36]

Sforno understands the serpent and the fruit to be a metaphor, representing the power of "imagination, desire, and images of pleasure."[37] We can understand then that in the Garden of Eden, the woman's subconscious desire is *projected* onto the serpent and onto the forbidden fruit.

Esther Harding, in her book *Women's Mysteries*, describes this phenomenon of projection. She explains, "This occurs when subconscious factors are not sensed in *concepts*, but are instead projected onto the *outer world*."[38]

Radak takes a close look at the beginning of chapter 3. Radak notes that when the serpent first addresses the woman, the text begins with the peculiar use of the word *af*, which translates as "in addition to" or "moreover," so it would seem that there was more to the conversation than that to which we are privy. We apparently enter in the midst of an intimate dialogue between the woman and the serpent, though we cannot hear the beginning of the conversation.[39]

Amazingly, the Torah records several sentences of the dialogue between the woman and the serpent. His words, her words, volleying back and forth – he said, she said. What we must realize here is that, finally, someone is speaking *to* the woman. The snake and the woman are engaging each other in conversation. They are relating as *I-You*, as subjective individuals. And surprisingly, though the *snake* and the woman are having a long intimate conversation, there are still no recorded words in the Torah text between the *man* and the woman!

> *And when the woman saw that the tree was good for food, and that it was tempting to her sight, and that the tree was to be desired to make one wise, she plucked one of its fruits, and ate, and she also gave to her man who was with her, and he ate.*

One might ask, how could the woman *see* that the tree was good for food, that the fruit was desirable, and that it would give her a certain kind of knowledge? According to Ibn Ezra, this was *not* knowledge of the taste, texture, or sweetness of the fruit. Nor was it intellectual knowledge, but an understanding of the *heart*. What an amazing pronouncement! The woman is *seeing* her heart's desire. Woman is evolving. She is feeling desire for the first time since her creation.

And she also gave to her man who was with her, and he ate. Ibn Ezra discloses further that the woman told the man the secrets of the snake, and they ate the fruit together. According to his commentary, the man was not duped into eating the forbidden fruit but was an accomplice in disobeying God's commandment. He was *not* an innocent bystander. The man and woman together enjoyed the forbidden fruit and were therefore equally guilty. Ibn Ezra then states clearly that the kind of knowledge offered by the tree of knowledge of good and evil is the knowledge of desire, specifically of sexual desire. The commentary explains that it is only *after* the man eats from the tree of knowledge that the text uses the term *knew*. (4:1) *And the human knew Chava, his wife, and she became pregnant.* This knowledge, according to Ibn Ezra, implies knowledge of sexual desire. [40]

It is clear from the biblical story that the woman is the first to eat from the forbidden fruit. One wonders why. Was it a weakness in her nature that made her the first to disobey, and did she then influence the man to join her? I would like to suggest an alternative reading. I would suggest that both man and woman had innate inchoate awakenings of desire. Adam realized he was alone when he named the animals and realized that he did not have a mate. He then desired a mate, even if on an intellectual level. It was at this time that God created woman for him. One could say, therefore, that his embryonic desire was satisfied by the appearance of woman. He knew he was alone. He desired a mate. God made him one. But what of woman's desire? When did her desire have a chance to be awakened? She was created and set down before the man, given to him, as it were. She had no chance to *not* have him, no chance to feel a lack, no time to desire him. She was created, and he was there, waiting for her. It is only with the snake, and with the forbidden fruit, that she could appreciate the stirrings of desire, the *not having*. And so, to fulfill her nascent stirrings, she took that first step to reach toward her *own* desire.

The Zohar describes this newly born desire very clearly. "She gave it to her husband, because she was aroused with desire for him, aroused with will and love."[41] The Netziv adds that this birth of desire was mutual, that the man also developed an intense physical desire. "And the eyes of them *both* were opened. In that one second, they became human, as we now are!"[42]

It is immediately after sharing the passion fruit that the man and woman interact as fully developed human beings, knowledge of both intellect and passion. "*And the eyes of them both were opened, and they knew that they were naked, and they sewed fig leaves together and made themselves coverings.*"

Harding describes this type of moment as "the rise of instinct released from ancient taboos, the flood of emotions of ecstasy, rising from the unconscious depths of the psyche."[43]

Rabbi Adin Steinsaltz summarizes this change. He states that "after eating of the tree the man and woman knew that sexuality was not structured in the rhythm of biological necessity as were other natural functions. Man has to grapple with that, constantly. That knowledge had become part of man's being, and with it, a loss of innocence."[44]

And so, by eating from the forbidden tree, the primitive Adam has become a distinctly human man and woman, with not only intellectual knowledge but emotional knowledge as well. The Malbim expressly warns us, however, that this all too human quality of passion is a double-edged sword. "When intellect precedes passion, good will result. But when passion is unbridled and precedes intellect, it will harness the intellect and degrade it to be its servant. It will be preoccupied with evil designs with the invention of justifications and excuses for a man's actions."[45]

Following their eating of the fruit of the tree of knowledge of good and bad, with the concomitant discovery of desire and passion, the man and the woman, being aware of, and having clothed their nakedness, try to hide from God. God accosts them, asking them what had made them aware of their nakedness. Had they, in fact, eaten of the tree from which He had commanded them *not* to eat? The man responds, immediately blaming the woman.

> *And they heard the voice of God's presence in the garden during the breezy part of the day, and they hid, the man and his wife, among the trees in the garden. Then God called out to the man and said, where are you? And he answered, I heard your voice in the garden, and I was afraid, for I am naked, so I hid. And He said, who told you that you were naked? Did you eat from the tree of which I commanded you not to eat from? And the man said, the woman you gave to me at my side, she gave me from the tree, and I did eat. And the Lord God said to the woman, what is this you have done? And the woman said, the serpent beguiled me, and I did eat.*[46]

Bereishit Rabba gives us a twist on the man's response to God's query: *Did you eat from the tree of which I commanded you not to eat from?* It paraphrases the man's response to be interpreted as "Not only I *did* (va'ochayl) eat, but I will *continue* (va'ochal) to eat." In the Hebrew language, different vocalization of the vowels of same word changes the tense. According to *Bereishit Rabba*, not only does the man disobey God's commandment and deny God by thinking he can hide and not get caught, but he states resolutely, uncontritely, that he will do it again! [47]

Rashi gives us insight as to how her disobedience affected the woman as well. When asked by God as to why *she* ate from the tree, the woman answered, "The snake beguiled (*hisiani*) me." Rashi notes that the woman uses the word *hisiani*, which is similar to the word for marriage (*nisuin*); the double entendre of the word implies, according to Rashi, that the snake *married* her.[48] She too has now become a passionate being, forever changed as well.

The humans have become truly human. They are not willing to return to the intellectual, passionless creations that they had been before the moment of sharing the forbidden fruit.

From this moment on, passion will inform their actions. Their existential nature has been forever altered.

Later in the chapter Adam renames his wife, giving her the name Chava: *And Adam called his wife Chava, for she was the mother of all living.*[49]

According to the Netziv, Adam understands that not only has there been a radical change in his relationship with his wife, but she too has changed. She no longer exists to serve him; henceforth her desires will be based on what is good or bad *for herself.* Finally Woman has her own name and her own identity.

The Netziv discusses the new name Adam gives his wife – Chava. The simple meaning of the name, according to the Torah text, is that *Chava* is derived from *kol Chai,* meaning "all living things." The Netziv acknowledges that though indeed she is the forbearer of mankind, humans are not the only living creatures! She is certainly *not* the forbearer of insects and animals! The Netziv queries next, why does Adam name her only *after* they eat from the tree of knowledge of good and evil?

To answer these questions, the Netziv looks at alternate meanings for the word *Chai.* He equates *Chai* with *simcha umelui ratzon* – "joy and the fulfillment of desire" – based on a sentence in Brakhot 86, *Lahachayot bahem nefesh kol chai,* meaning fulfillment not of man's essential needs, but fulfillment of *desire.* "Until she ate from the apple, the woman had only inchoate desire. Once she attached to the serpent and ate the forbidden fruit, desire was created, and from that desire were created all desires. Therefore, Chava is the mother of all (living) *desires.*" And, the Netziv continues, "The reason she is called *Chava* and not *Chai* is to remind us that most desires can ultimately cause harm. The word *Chavya* ("ankle") reminds us of a snake that bites us, unawares, at the ankle."[50]

At first the female's name was part of the Adam-duo. Then Adam names her *Eesha,* as his objective counterpart to *Eesh.* Finally, now he gives her own name, *Chava.* We have seen how her names changes reflect not only Adam's perception of her, but their relationship and maturation as well.

> *And Adam knew Chava his wife and she became pregnant and gave birth to Cain and she said I have acquired a man, with God.*[51]

Finally, according to the Netziv, Adam now truly *knows* his wife. *And Adam knew.* "He knew *her.* He knew that the person with whom he was having intimate relations was Chava, his wife, not just a woman. He no longer acted like an animal that procreates for biological necessity with no cognizance of the female counterpart as a distinct being." The Netziv further teaches us that "this is how man and woman should relate, with an awareness of the *other* as a subjective human being."[52]

The second half of the sentence in the biblical text sentence is surprising. It is Chava, not Adam, who names her child! Chava, who had been named by Adam with an individual, personal name for herself, now names her own child. *And she names her son Cain, saying she has acquired a man with God.*[53] This is a confusing statement. To whom in fact is she referring? Which *man* has she acquired, her husband Adam or her son Cain?

Rashi explains that Chava is stating that she has a acquired a *son* with the help of God. According to Rashi, she is saying, "When He created me and my husband, He by Himself created us, but with Cain we are partners *with* Him."[54] *Bereishit Rabba* offers the alternative explanation, positing that Chava is speaking about Adam, her husband: "When a woman sees that she has children, she says 'My husband is now in my possession.'"[55] Rashi on this commentary explains, "Now that I have a child, I have a husband who will never leave me."[56] Maharaz, a commentary on *Bereishit Rabba*, explains that the text is speaking about Adam: "If the Torah text meant *son*, it would have said, I have in my possession my *son*, not my *man*. By giving him children, the husband feels closer to her."[57]

However one chooses to understand this sentence regarding the naming of Cain, we know now that Adam and his wife are intimately connected as thinking and feeling human beings, complete with human knowledge and desire. Their second child's birth is recorded in the next sentence: *And she again gave birth, to his brother Abel.*[58] With the birth of their third son, Seth, the text states: *And he knew, Adam, more (again) his wife, and she bore him a son and she called his name Seth, saying God has given me another offspring instead of Abel.*[59]

Bereishit Rabba makes astonishing comments on the evolution of the relationship between Adam and Chava which he derives from this sentence: "Desire was heaped upon desire. In the past, when he didn't see her, he didn't desire her. Now, whether he was seeing her or not, he desired her."[60] Maharaz explains this assumption on the basis of structure of the sentence when compared with the word sequence describing the first pregnancy. "With the first conception, it states *And Adam knew Chava his wife,* and now it states *And he knew, Adam, more (again), his wife.* What do we learn from the addition of the word "more"? We learn that he was now never free of desire, even when he was not with her! If it said, *And he knew, Adam, his wife more,* it would mean he had relations with her *again.* But as it says, *And he knew, Adam, more, his wife,*" it means that he *knew* her *more* – that he desired her always.[61] This is to be explained, not that Adam desires her at every moment, but that now, and for always, *desire* will be part of the human condition.

In summary, this paper follows the humanization of man from a primitive being at the first creation, an intelligent creation devoid of human feelings, to his progression to a fully human being with the full gamut of human emotions. I would suggest that name changes are markers for this evolution: At first the human is known as *the Adam.* When separated from the created duo, they become *eesh and eesha,* man and woman. Finally, as they become independent individuals, Adam retains the name of Adam, and the woman becomes Chava.

A serious reader must still have the same question in the forefront of her or his thoughts, a question that has yet to be answered. If God wanted us to be fully human, with intelligence and emotions, with knowledge and desires, why were the first created humans expressly forbidden from eating of the tree of knowledge of good and bad, more specifically, the tree of human desire?

According to the Chatam Sofer,[62] an eminent eighteenth-century Hungarian Torah scholar, God did in fact want us be fully human. He posits that God wouldn't have created the tree if humans would never have been able to eat from it! But, the Chatam Sofer continues, primitive man was not yet developed enough to be ready to eat from the tree. Had he waited until the Sabbath, he would have had the extra *neshama*, or spiritual strength, that the Sabbath brings. This added spirit would have given humans the strength to deal with the type of knowledge the tree offered. But they ate too early! In fact, it was absolutely necessary for the human to eat from the tree, he explains. The Chatam Sofer quotes Ramban's theory that, by eating from the tree, mankind developed desire and free choice. Before their eating from the tree. even man's worship of God was rote and without emotion. If there is no desire and no free choice, then there can be no reward or punishment. It is the human condition to make choices.

Sartre describes this human condition succinctly and eloquently with an emphatic statement of human freedom and individual responsibility. "Desire expresses all human reality. I am my choices. Choice is nothing other than the being of each human reality."[63]

And so, according to the Chatam Sofer, God didn't want the humans to eat from the tree that would transform them into complete human beings – creating in them desire, and with it the necessity of free choice – until the Sabbath. Then the extra Sabbath spirituality, the Sabbath *neshama*, would have guided their desires and subsequent choices so that these would have consistently been for the moral and ethical good. And that would have been humankind's foundation. But such was not to be. Adam and Chava ate from the tree of knowledge of good and bad before Shabbat, before they had internalized a foundation that would enable them always to desire and choose the good. Desires and individual free choice of how to act upon those desires – for better or for worse – became the human condition.

✣ NOTES

1. *Bereishit* 1:26–27.
2. Chizkuni for 1:26.
3. Rashi for 1:27.
4. *Eruvin* 18A.
5. *Bereishit Rabba* 8.1.
6. *Bereishit* 2:7.
7. *Bereishit* 1:28.
8. *Bereishit* 2:15–18.
9. Moses Maimonides, *Guide of the Perplexed* Section 1, Chapter 2, excerpts from pp. 33–39.
10. Ibn Ezra for 2:17.
11. *Bereishit* 2:19.
12. *Bereishit* 2:18.
13. *Bereishit* 2:20.
14. Ramban for 2:9.
15. Sforno for 2:17.
16. David Hume, *A Treatise of Human Nature, Book 3: Of Morals* (London: Penguin Classics 1985) excerpts from pages 456–459.
17. Adin Steinsaltz, *In the Beginning: Discourses on Chasidic Thought* (Northvale, N.J.: Jason Aronson, 1992), excerpts from pp. 53–62.
18. *Bereishit* 2:18.
19. *Ohr Hachayim* for 2:18.
20. Chizkuni for 2:18.
21. Ramban for 2:20.
22. *Sha'arei Aharon* for 2:20.
23. Jean-Paul Sartre, *Existential Psychoanalysis* (Washington, D.C.: Regnery-Gateway, 1988), excerpts from pp. 36–38.
24. Rashi for 2:20.
25. Gerald M. Edelman, M.D., PhD, *Second Nature: Brain Science and Human Knowledge* (New Haven, Conn.: Yale University Press, 2006), p. 15.
26. M. Esther Harding, *The I and the Not I: A Study in the Development of Consciousness* (Princeton, N.J.: Princeton University Press, 1973), excerpts from pp. 7–15.
27. *Bereishit* 2:21–22.
28. Sforno for 2:22.
29. Ibn Ezra for 2:22.
30. *Bereishit* 2:23.
31. *Zohar Bereishit* 49B Volume 3: 137–138.
32. Malbim for 2:23.
33. Martin Buber, *I and Thou* (New York: Charles Scribner's Sons, 1970) excerpts from pp. 78–111.
34. Netziv for 2:23.
35. Radak for 2:23.
36. *Bereishit* 3:1–7.
37. Sforno for 3:1.
38. M. Esther Harding, *Woman's Mysteries* (Boston: Shambhala, 1990) pp. 18–19.
39. Radak for 3:1.
40. Ibn Ezra for 3:6.
41. *Zohar Bereishit*, 49B Vol. 3:139.

42. Netziv for 3:7.
43. Harding, *Woman's Mysteries*, p. 207.
44. Steinsaltz, *In the Beginning,*excerpts from pp. 53–62.
45. Malbim for 3:6.
46. *Bereishit* 3: 8–13.
47. *Bereishit Rabba* 19:12.
48. T.B. Shabbat 146A.
49. *Bereishit* 3:20.
50. Netziv for 3:20.
51. *Bereishit* 4:1.
52. Netziv for 4:1.
53. *Bereishit* 4:1.
54. Rashi for 4:1.
55. *Bereishit Rabba* 22:2.
56. Rashi for *Bereishit Rabba* 22:1.
57. For *Bereishit Rabba* 22:2.
58. *Bereishit* 4:1.
59. *Bereishit* 4:25.
60. *Bereishit Rabba* 23:5.
61. *Bereishit Rabba* 23:5.
62. Chatam Sofer on *Bereishit*.
63. Jean-Paul Sartre, *Existential Psychoanalysis* (Washington, D.C.: Regnery-Gateway 1988), excerpts from pp. 5, 53, 60.

קבע בתפילה
הערות על מושג הקביעות בפרק ד' של מס' ברכות

הרלן ג׳יי ווכסלר

רבה של ק"ק אור זרוע
ניו-יורק

מס' ברכות, רובה ככולה, מבקשת קביעות בעניני עבודה שבלב. החל מן
המשנה הראשונה, "מאימתי קורין את שמע בערבית", עד למשנה האחרונה,
"חייב אדם לברך על הרעה כשם שהוא מברך על הטובה," קובעים חז"ל צורות
המגבשות יחס האדם למקום. ובכן המלה "קבע" היא מלה מלה בעלת משמעות
חשובה במסכת.

אבל דע לך שמילים הן לבושי מושגים, ובטיבה של מילה יש קסם, קסם
גם גלוי וגם כסוי – לשאול מנוסחתו של ביאליק.[1]

עוד יותר מזה, ברור הוא שתפילה שבלב כחוויה דתית יכולה להתנגד
לקביעות כל שהיא. ובכן יש לראות פרדוקסליות בחווית התפילה. למשל, מורי
הרב אברהם יהושע השל בספרו God in Search of Man דן בפרק אחד על
"בעיית הקטביות", באנגלית: "The Problem of Polarity". וכך הוא כותב:

> "Our great problem...is how not to let the principle of regular-
> ity (*keva*) impair the power of spontaneity (*kavana*)."[2]

השל רואה ניגוד קטבי בין קבע וההפך שלו כוונה. אבל כדרכו של השל הניגוד

283

הזה הכרחי. מטרתי להבין מתיחות כזאות ביתר דיוק. ובכן הבה ונדון בפרטי
המושג כפי שהוא מופיע בפרק ד' של מס' ברכות. שמה יש למילת "קבע"
שלשה מובנים:

א. קביעות זמן

ב. קביעות חובה

ג. קביעות נוסח מדויק.

מפני שיש מובנים רבים למלת "קבע" לפעמים הגמרא צריכה לברר מה פירוש
המלה בסוגיה מסוימת.

א. קבע פירושו זמן קבוע ‏‎&‎

כבר במשנה הראשונה של פרק ד' מופיעה הקביעות בולטת לעין. לומדים
במשנה פרקי הזמן מתי יש חיוב להתפלל תפילות היום: תפלת השחר, עד
חצות. רבי יהודה אומר: עד ארבע שעות. תפלת המנחה, עד הערב. רבי יהודה
אומר: עד פלג המנחה. ואז: תפלת הערב אין לה קבע.

ובכלל לא קשה להבין מה פירוש המילים "אין לה קבע." המשנה דנה
בשעות הקבועות לתפילות היום. השעות הקבועות לתפילת שחרית הן שעות
הבקר עד חצות. על זה חולק רבי יהודה באומרו: עד ארבע שעות, ז"א עד שעה
עשר בבקר לפי שיטת השעות הזמניות אשר לפיהן מחולקת היום. אז לומדים
על תפילת מנחה שיש להתפלל אותה עד הערב. ועוד פעם חולק רבי יהודה
עד שעה אחרת והיא עד פלג המנחה, ז"א עד שעה ורבע של השעות הזמניות
לפני סוף היום.

אז מספרת המשנה על תפילת ערבית ואומרת: תפלת הערב אין לה קבע.
פירוש המילים "אין לה קבע" ברור הוא שאין להטיל ספק. ברור הוא כאור היום
שתפילת הערב מותר להתפלל אותה כל הלילה ובכן אין לקבוע גבולות לתוך
הלילה עצמה. אלא כל הלילה זמן תפילת הערב. וכן גם אומר רש"י בפירושו:
כל הלילה זמנה.

הרי הגמרא עצמה מבינה את המילים "אין לה קבע" בזה האופן כשהיא
נותנת רקע על התפילות ולמה תקנום. בדעה של רבי יהושע בן לוי האומר
תפילות כנגד תמידים תקנום, מסבירה הגמרא בברייתא, בין היתר, "ומפני מה
אמרו תפילת המנחה עד הערב? שהרי תמיד של בין הערבים קרב והולך עד
הערב." ועל זה חולק רבי יהודה באומרו: "עד פלג המנחה שהרי תמיד של בין
הערבים קרב והולך עד פלג המנחה."[3] זמני התמידים קובעים זמני התפילה.
אז ממשיכה הגמרא ואומרת: "ומפני מה אמרו תפילת הערב אין לה קבע?"
עונה הגמרא: "שהרי אברים ופדרים שלא נתעכלו מבערב קרבים והולכים כל

הלילה."[4] ז"א זמן תפילת ערבית כל הלילה מפני שבלילה היו אברים ושומן מקרבנות היום (שנזרק דמן לפני שקיעת החמה) על המזבח כל הלילה.

גם לתוספתא יש דוגמא בולטת של שמוש המושג קבע במובנו הפשוט: שעות קבועות. אומרת התוספתא: "כשם שנתנה תורה קבע לקריאת שמע, כך נתנו חכמים לתפילה."[5] ליברמן פירש את הקטע הזה לפשוטו, לדעתי, באומרו שהתורה נתנה שעות לקריאת שמע כאשר אומרת התורה: ובשכבך ובקומך.[6] אע"פ שאין אנו לומדים מזה שעות מדוייקות, בכל זאת לומדים שעות פחות או יותר מדוייקות, שקוראים שמע בערב ובבקר. לעומת זה, אין התורה אומרת כלל מתי יש להתפלל. באו חז"ל וקבעו לנו שעות התפילה.[7] עד כאן פירוש המילים "אין לה קבע": זמנים קבועים.

ב. קבע פירושו חובה

אע"פ שלי ברור הוא כאור היום שפירוש המשנה האומרת "תפילת הערב אין לה קבע" היא אין לה שעות קבועות, לא ברור הוא לבבלי. ובכן שואלת הגמרא: "מאי אין לה קבע?" ז"א מה פירוש המלים של המשנה: אין לה קבע? ומגבשת הגמרא את השאלה עוד יותר כשאומרת הגמרא: אילימא דאי בעו מצלי כוליה ליליה – אם נאמר שפירושו: אם רצו יכולים להתפלל כל הלילה – היתה צריכה הגמרא לאמר: תפילת הערב כל הלילה! ואז הגמרא מציעה פירוש אחר: מאי "אין לה קבע"? תפילת ערבית רשות.[8]

הנה הגענו לפירוש השני של המושג "קבע." לא של זמן קבוע אלא של חובה קבועה. כנראה לא זה פשט הדברים, אע"פ שאולי אדם חושב שאין הבבלי בא אלא לפרש פשוטם של דברים. וגם אולי אפשר להביא רמז לדבר ואולי אפילו ראיה לדבר שכן פירוש "קבע" הוא חובה. שאפשר לפרש משנה אחרת בכיוון הזה – ואני מתכוון לדברי שמאי במשנה הידועה של מס' אבות[9] כשאומר שמאי: עשה תורתך קבע. עד עכשיו הפירוש היה תמיד ברור לי: יש לקבוע שעות קבועות ללימוד התורה. אבל אולי יש להציע פירוש אחר: עשה לימוד התורה חובה עליך.[10]

עכשיו השאלה חוזרת בעוד תוקף: למה הבבלי דוחה הפשט ומקבל את הדרש? ואל תהא דבר זה קל בעיניך. אריות העולם קיבלו פירוש זה כשדנו בנושא אם תפילת הערב חובה או רשות, והתקוטטו עליו וכתוצאה נפלה עטרה מראשו של רבן גמליאל,[11] לגבי תפילת ערבית היתה מחלוקת חמורה. רבן גמליאל אומר: חובה. רבי יהושע אומר: רשות. מעשה שהיה כך היה. תלמיד אחד בא לפני רבי יהושע, אמר לו: תפילת ערבית רשות או חובה? אמר לו רבי יהושע: רשות. בא לפני רבן גמליאל, ואמר לו: תפלת ערבית רשות או חובה? אמר לו: חובה. אמר לו: והלא רבי יהושע אמר לי רשות.

אמר לו: המתן עד שיכנסו בעלי תריסין (ז"א עד שיתאספו כל החכמים) לבית
המדרש. כשנכנסו, עמד השואל ושאל: תפלת ערבית רשות או חובה? אמר לו
רבן גמליאל: חובה. אמר להם רבן גמליאל לחכמים: כלום יש אדם שחולק בדבר
זה? אמר לו רבי יהושע: לא. אמר לו רבן גמליאל: והלא משמך אמרו לי רשות?
יהושע – המשיך רבן גמליאל – עמוד על רגליך ויעידו בך. עמד רבי יהושע
על רגליו ואמר: אלמלא אני חי והוא מת – יכול החי להכחיש את המת, ועכשיו
שאני חי והוא חי – היאך יכול החי להכחיש את החי? היה רבן גמליאל יושב
ודורש, ורבי יהושע עומד על רגליו, עד שכל העם התלוננו על רבן גמליאל.
ובסוף הורידוהו ממשרתו והמליכו רבי אלעזר בן עזריה במקומו.

כנראה היתה המחלוקת הזאת חשובה ומכריעה בעולמם של רבותינו.
וברור הוא שלפי דעתו של רבן גמליאל תפילת ערבית היתה חובה ולפי רבי
יהושע היתה רשות. ובכן למה לא קיבלו את הפשט?

כנראה שאלה כזאת היתה אש קודחת אז. מסכם אלבוגן,[12] למשל, שרבן
גמליאל קבע שכל יחיד בעדה חייב לאמר את התפילה בפני עצמו. לפני כן
העמידה היתה תפילת צבור ואמר שליח צבור את התפילה כנציג הקהל ולאחר
כל ברכה ענה הקהל אמן. בדור שראו התגבשות התפילה כסדר מקובל על
העם, ענין כזה עמד במקום חשוב. ובסופו של דבר מפורשת המשנה להטעים
טעם לדברי האומר: רשות.

גורם מעשי, תולדות התפתחות התפילה, גרם לגמרא להוציא את המלה
"קבע" מידי פשוטו ולתת לו פירוש אחר: חובה, ו"אין לה קבע," פירושו
רשות.

הדו־משמעות הזאת ניכר על ידי ראשונים. אומר הרשב"א, למשל,
בתשובה לאחד משואליו: ומה שהקשית בתפילת הערב אין לה קבע. במקום אחד
פירשו שאין לה זמן קבוע שהרי אברים ופדרים קרבים כל הלילה, ובמקום אחר
פירשו "אין לה קבע" שאינה חובה אלא רשות...זה אינו קשה בעיני כלל דמלשון
אין לה קבע תרתי שמעינן מינה (שני דברים אנחנו לומדים ממנה).[13]

‎❧ ג. קבע פירושו נוסח קבוע

בוא וראה עוד שמוש של המלה קבע בפרק ד' של ברכות, וזה יביא אותנו
ישר לבעיות של השל – המתיחות בין קבע וכוונה. הנה המשנה אומרת: רבי
אליעזר אומר: העושה תפלתו קבע, אין תפלתו תחנונים.[14] מה פירוש "קבע"?
א) המתפלל בשעות קבועות אין תפילתו תחנונים? ב) המתפלל תפילותיו מפני
שהן חובה עליו, אין תפילתו תחנונים? אבל לא זה ולא זה הנכון.

אלא, מן המשנה עצמה נראה שכאן המחלוקת על דבר אחר. לא אם יש
חיוב, אלא מה מחויב. ליברמן מציין שיש להבין דברי רבי אליעזר כפי שהם

מופיעים בירושלמי, בהקיש וברציפות לדברי רבנים אחרים שדנים בשאלת נוסח התפילה שיש להתפלל.[15] רבן גמליאל אומר בכל יום מתפלל אדם שמונה עשרה. רבי יהושע אומר מעין שמונה עשרה. רבי עקיבא אומר אם שגורה תפלתו בפיו, יתפלל שמונה עשרה ואם לאו, מעין שמונה עשרה.[16] אז המילים הבאות הן אלה של ר' אליעזר: העושה תפלתו קבע, אין תפילתו תחנונים. ובכן ר' אליעזר חולק על עצם הקבע של מילים קבועות לקיים חובת התפילה.

הנה יש לנו פירוש שלישי לקבע: לא קבע במובנו של זמנים, ולא קבע במובנו של חובה. אלא קבע במובנו של נוסח קבוע.

הנה אנחנו רואים שלב אחר בדיוני חז"ל ובתולדות התפתחות התפילה, גם מצד הסטורי וגם מצד החוויה הדתית. הצד ההסטורי הוא: גישות שונות בעיני חז"ל עצמם לערך נוסח מדויק וגם לבעיות העולות מנוסח מדויק. הצד החוויתי הוא חלק מן הפרדוקסליות של תפילה-הלב מבקש קירבה לאלהים שהוא מעל כל צורה. ונוסח התפילה קושר המתפלל לצורות מוגבלות ומוגדרות. יתר על כן יכול נוסח קבוע להביא לידי שעמום ולתפילה כמצות אנשים מלומדה.[17]

מעניין הוא לראות איך שהבבלי מבר מברר פירוש דברי ר' אליעזר: העושה תפילתו קבע אין תפילתו תחנונים.[18] וכדרכו הבבלי שואל: מאי קבע? תמיד יש צורך להגדיר פירוש המלה. ומציעה הגמרא ד' אפשרויות. מאי קבע? א. לפי דעתם של רבי יעקב בר אידי ורבי אושעיא: כל שתפלתו דומה עליו כמשוי. ב. הרבנן אמרו: כל מי שאינו אומרה בלשון תחנונים. ג. רבה ורב יוסף שניהם אומרים: כל שאינו יכול לחדש בה דבר.[19] ד. אביי בר אבין ורבי חנינא בר אבין שניהם אומרים: כל שאין מתפלל עם דמדומי חמה, דאמר רבי חייא בר אבא אמר רבי יוחנן: מצוה להתפלל עם דמדומי חמה.

מה המשותף בדעות האלה?

המשותף שכולם מתעסקים בחוויה הדרושה מן התפילה עצמה. במילים אחרות, הם מתעניינים בחיי הרוח ופנימיות החוויה הדתית. דברי רבי אושעיא – דומה עליו כמשוי – למשל, פונים אל בעיית החיוב. אם פעולה מחויבת, אז אפשר שהפעולה תתגנה עליו. דבריו מזכירים דברי פרא פרנז רוזנצווייג שביקש להפוך את ה-Gesetz ל-Gebot הלכה פסוקה ויבשה למצווה טריה ופורחת. הדעה השניה, של רבנן, פונה גם היא לעצם החוויה ומזהירה שעל המתפלל לשמור שתהיה תפילתו תחנונים – עם כוונה ואולי גם עם רגש. זה מזכיר כמובן דברי רבי שמעון במס' אבות:[20] וכשאתה מתפלל, אל תעש תפלתך קבע, אלא רחמים ותחנונים לפני המקום ברוך הוא.

הדעה השלישית – שצריך המתפלל לחדש דבר בתפילתו – מעניין הוא כתרופה לבעיית תפילה מסודרת של מילים קבועות. וממליץ הוא להוסיף מילים

כפתרון לבעייה. בדעה הרביעית מוסיף עוד דבר לתהליך הרוחני של התפילה: שיש לקשר אותה עם דמדומי חמה, עם סדר ויופי טבע העולם.[21]

מרחיב הירושלמי את המושג באומרו דברי ר׳ אבהו בשם ר׳ אלעזר: ובלבד שלא יהא כקורא באגרת.[22] והירושלמי עצמו מספר לנו על פתרונותיהם של ר׳ אלעזר ור׳ אבהו לבעית מי שיתפלל כמו שהוא קורא אגרת. רבי אלעזר היה מתפלל תפילה חדשה בכל יום. רבי אבהו היה מברך ברכה חדשה בכל יום.[23]

⅏ סכום

הדיון הזה לגבי דברי רבי אליעזר – העושה תפילתו קבע אין תפילתו תחנונים – מביא אותנו למטרה שלנו, והיא מטרה של שאלות פנומנולוגיות ולא רק הסטוריות. עצם החוויה של אלהים מביא גם לידי קבע וגם לידי מה שאי-אפשר לקבוע.[24] אבל אני רוצה להציע שיש לדייק ולראות שלשה תחומים שהם תחומי החוויה הדתית מבחינת עולמם של חז״ל בפרק ד׳ של ברכות. והם א. ענין הזמן, ב. ענין החובה ג. מילים קבועות – איך אדם מתיחס לצורות המוחשיות של הדת. בחויה דתית יש לרכז את הדעת על שלשה תחומים אלה ולראות איך הדת נוצרת ומתקדמת, בחיי הפרט ובחיי הכלל. המתיחות של השל בין קבע וכוונה חשובה היא, ומבקשת דיוק עדין כדי לברר איך פנימיות האדם חי בתחום הזמן, החובה, והמילים.

וכל זה ראינו בלבושיה של המילה ״קבע,״ הגלוי והכסוי בלשון.

⅏ NOTES

Each year, before Yom Kippur, I listen to Rabbi Haskel Lookstein's tape of the Neilah Service. I learn, again and again, the importance of paying attention to the words, of being accurate and of leading prayer with proper kavannah. How does one thank the teacher who conveys such lofty advice? This essay is token of gratitude.
– Harlan J. Wechsler

1 ח.נ. ביאליק, ״גילוי וכיסוי בלשון,״ אודסה, תרע״ז (1917), ועכשיו מתוך ח. נ. ביאליק, דברי ספרות, הוצאת דביר תשל״ח (עמ׳ כד-לא). ר׳ על ״גילוי וכיסוי בלשון״: עיונים במסתו של ביאליק, עריכה ומבוא צבי לוז וזיוה שמיר, הוצאת אוניברסיטת בר-אילן, 2001.

   Abraham Joshua Heschel, *God in Search of Man*, Ch. 33, "The Problem of Polarity." 2

3 בר׳ כו, ב.

4 השו׳ דברי התוספתא בר׳ ג,ב (ליברמן ע׳ 11): ״תפילת הערב אין לה קבע ר׳ יוסי אומר עם נעילת שערים. אמר ר׳ לעזר בר׳ יוסי אבה היה מתפלל אותה עם נעילת שערים.״ ברור הוא שפירוש ״אין לה קבע״ אין שעות קבועות לתפילת ערבית.

5 תוספתא מס׳ ברכות ג,א (ליברמן, ע׳ 11).

6 שם.

7 כמו שמזכיר ליברמן (תוספתא כפשוטה בר׳ ע׳ 27, הערה 1), זהו דעת הרמב״ם, ס׳ המצוות, מ״ע י׳. שם אומר הרמב״ם: ״...זמני התפילה אינם מן התורה. אמנם חיוב התפילה עצמה מן התורה... וחז״ל סדרו להם זמנים. וזהו ענין אמרם (בר׳ כו, ב) תפילות כנגד תמידים תקנו. רוצה לומר שתיקנו זמניהם כפי זמני הקרבן.״

8 בר' כז, ב.

9 מ' אבות א, טו.

10 ר' פירוש הרמב"ם: עשה לימוד התורה עיקר־שהוא קרוב. הש' אבות דרבי נתן (נוסחא א', פ' יג, ד"ה עשה תורתך ונוסחא ב', פ' כג, שהוא קרוב לדברי הרמב"ם. וכאשר כתוב בבבלי (שבת לא, א): אמר רבא: בשעה שמכניסין אדם לדין אומרים לו: נשאת ונתת באמונה, קבעת עתים לתורה וכו' – אולי כאן פירוש "קבע" הוא "קביעת זמן," ושם, בדברי שמאי, פירושו: קביעת חובה! פירוש זה, לדעתי, דחוק.

11 בר' כז, ב.

12 התפילה בישראל, ע' 21.

13 רשב"א, שו"ת חלק א' סימן רע"ט. ראה גם רבינו יונה על הרי"ף בר' פ' ד' במקום של הדיון בגמרא: אין לה קבע ר"ל לומר ב' דברים שהיא רשות ושזמנה כל הלילה.

14 מ' בר' ד, ד'.

15 ליברמן, תוספתא כפשוטה בר' ע' 31–32.

16 שם. ליברמן מצטט את המשנה בר' ד,ג.

17 ליברמן שם.

18 בר' כט, ב.

19 ורבי זירא מוסיף שהוא יכול לחדש בה דבר, אבל הוא מפחד שמא הוא יתבלבל.

20 מ' אבות ב', יג.

21 פירשתי לא כפירש רש"י: אינו מקפיד לחזר אחר שעת מצוה ועת רצון.

22 יר' בר' ד',דף ח', ע' א.

23 שם. שאלה: האם יש לדייק מדבריהם שר' אלעזר היה מחדש תפילה במובנו של שמונה עשרה בכל יום? ובכן הוא לא הסתפק בשמונה עשרה קבוע ואולי היתה דעתו כמו דעת ר' אליעזר, ז"א העושה תפילתו קבע, אין תפילתו תחנונים? ואולי היה ר' אבהו פחות קצוני, והוא היה מברך ברכה חדשה בכל יום, להדגיש "ברכה חדשה" ולא כל התפילה כולה.

24 ר' (Max Kadushin, *Worship and Ethics* (Northwestern, 1964 ע' 117-120.

Nation as Family: The Key to Redemption in Tanakh

Avraham Weiss

✤ TWO COVENANTS

Rabbi Abraham Isaac HaCohen Kook describes two different covenants between God and the Jewish people. The first is called *brit avot*, the covenant with the patriarchs. This covenant was established with Abraham in the *brit ben ha-betarim*, the covenant of the pieces. ביום ההוא כרת ה' את אברם ברית – "On that day the Lord made a covenant with Abram." (Genesis 15:18) Ultimately the covenant includes Sarah, as it continues through Isaac, Sarah's son, and not Ishmael, Hagar's son. (Genesis 17:19)

It is the individual or individuals, though, who make up a **family**. If you are born into that family, whether you are committed or not, deserving or not, worthy or not, you're part of the *brit* (covenant), you're part of the *mishpaha* (family). Rabbi Kook puts it this way:

שני דברים עקריים ישנם שהם יחד בונים קדושת ישראל וההתקשרות
האלהית עמהם. הא' הוא סגולה, כלומר טבע הקדושה שבנשמת ישראל
מירושת אבות.

There are two main elements that together unite and build the sanctity of the Jewish people along with their connection with God. The first is "treasure" (*segulah*), i.e., the holy nature that rests in the souls of Israel as an inheritance from their patriarchs.[2]

Rabbi Kook calls the second covenant *brit Sinai*, because it took place at Mount Sinai, where the Jewish people received the Torah from God. While *brit avot* is with family, *brit Sinai* is with **nation**, ויקח ספר הברית ויקרא באזני העם – "He took the Book of the Covenant and read it in earshot of **the people**." (Exodus 24:7) While Jews remain part of *brit avot* no matter what they do, *brit Sinai* is a function of choice, as a person may decide to keep or reject the commandments. This idea is based on the verse וַיֹּאמְרוּ כֹּל אֲשֶׁר דִּבֶּר יְקֹוָק נַעֲשֶׂה וְנִשְׁמָע – "And they said 'all that the Lord has spoken, we will do and we will listen.'" (Exodus 24:7) As Rabbi Kook explains:

> והב' הוא ענין בחירה, זה תלוי במעשה הטוב ובתלמוד תורה. – And the second element is the concept of selection (*behirah*), which depends upon good deeds and the study of Torah.[3]

Lest the second covenant be thought of as more valuable, he then boldly writes:

> החלק של הסגולה הוא הרבה, באין ערוך כלל, יותר גדול וקדוש מהחלק התלוי בבחירה. The share of the *segulah* [in this aspect of the Jewish people] is great, without any measurement, greater and holier than the aspect that depends upon *behirah*.[4]

Rabbi Kook was a deeply religious and observant Jew, whose commitment to mitzvot, the Sinaitic covenant, was central to his being. Still, what ultimately defines the Jew for Rabbi Kook is being part of the family. Family supersedes ideology; it weighs most heavily when evaluating one's connection with Judaism.

⚡ DISSOLUTION OF FAMILY

Rabbi Kook's analysis may explain why Genesis precedes Exodus. If the Torah is a book of law given to the Jewish people, it would be logical to begin with those laws as they are found in the Book of Exodus.[5] It can be suggested, though, that Genesis is the story of the dissolution and then reconstruction of the family.[6] Only when the family comes together can the nation be born and the Book of Exodus begin. This teaches that the best model of nation is family.

A cursory review of the Book of Genesis from the onset of the patriarchal and matriarchal period, reveals how fragmentation of families became more pronounced with each succeeding generation. Abraham's eldest two sons, Isaac and Ishmael, have a serious falling out. Ishmael, according to the Torah, is *mezahek*, prompting Sarah to demand he be expelled. (Genesis 21:9, 10) While the Midrash relates *mezahek* to the three cardinal sins of idolatry, immorality and murder,[7] a more literary interpretation is that Ishmael tried to be Isaac, he tried to supplant Isaac and become the covenantal heir.[8] They part, but never threaten each other. Truth be told, they themselves never argue, as it is their mothers who are at odds, and, at the end of their father Abraham's life, both Isaac and Ishmael join to bury him. (Genesis 25:9) In fact, the Torah records that Isaac returned to באר לחי ראי, the place where Hagar was first told that she would give birth to Ishmael. (Genesis 25:11; 16:14) By going to באר לחי ראי, Isaac reveals that his spiritual yearning interfaces with Ishmael.

Isaac and Rebecca's children, Jacob and Esau, have a more serious falling out. At the behest of Rebecca, Jacob takes the blessing from Esau, an act that results in Esau's threatening his life. וַיִּשְׂטֹם עֵשָׂו אֶת יַעֲקֹב עַל הַבְּרָכָה אֲשֶׁר בֵּרְכוֹ אָבִיו וַיֹּאמֶר עֵשָׂו בְּלִבּוֹ יִקְרְבוּ יְמֵי אֵבֶל אָבִי וְאַהַרְגָה אֶת יַעֲקֹב אָחִי – "Now Esau harbored a grudge against Jacob because of the blessing which his father had given him, and Esau said to himself, 'Let but the mourning period of my father come, and I will kill my brother Jacob.'" (Genesis 27:41) Whereas the end of Abraham's life brings his sons together, the end of Isaac's life is seen by Esau as the time to kill Jacob.

Jacob's children have an even more serious falling out. Joseph dreams of sheaves and stars. (Genesis 37:7, 9) Sheaves represent land, growing as they do from the ground. Stars are the metaphor for children, as God tells Abraham his seed will be like the stars in the heavens. (Genesis 15:5) Together, land and children are the foundation of the covenant.[9] Thus the brothers believe that Joseph, by the nature of his dreams, sees himself as the sole covenantal heir. As Sforno comments,

> The brothers were convinced that Joseph was beguiling and deceiving them with the interest of destroying them... hence they felt justified in slaying (or selling) him to prevent him from slaying them...as the Torah teaches us, "He who comes to kill you, arise to slay him."[10]

The brothers, therefore, take action, and try to kill Joseph. The Torah describes their throwing him into a pit, leaving him to die. (Genesis 37:24) When Jacob concludes that Joseph is gone, he cries out כי ארד אל בני אבל שאלה – "For I will go down to the grave mourning for my son." (Genesis 37:35) The death of Abraham brings his children together; the death of Isaac is seen by Esau as the time to kill Jacob; and Jacob talks about his death as the time when he will still be in mourning for the loss of his son Joseph.[11]

What emerges is a Genesis narrative in which sibling rivalry becomes increasingly irreconcilable from Isaac and Ishmael, who separate but live peacefully; to Esau, who threatens Jacob's life; to the sons of Jacob, who actually attempt to kill their brother Joseph.[12]

✠ TAMAR AND JUDAH

At this point, the Joseph narrative is seemingly interrupted by the story of Judah and Tamar. (Genesis 38) A closer look, however, shows that the chapter is key to understanding how the Joseph story reveals a central teaching of the Book of Genesis, and, for that matter, the Torah itself – the coming together of all of *Am Yisrael* through which all of humankind will be united.

It begins with Judah, the prime mover of the Joseph sale, going down. (Genesis 38:1) Judah lost standing with his siblings as he bears the primary responsibility for the loss of Joseph, having suggested that Joseph be thrown into the pit and left there to die.[13] The narrative continues with Judah marrying the daughter of Sh-uah and fathering three sons, Er, Onan, and Sha'lah. Er marries Tamar, but he dies. Onan weds Tamar, as prescribed by the laws of "levirate marriage [*yibum*]," but he also dies. Sha'lah – which some have suggested could be vocalized as "shelah," meaning hers, connoting that he belongs to her (Tamar) through the laws of levirate marriage – is blocked by Judah from marrying Tamar. Judah fears that since Tamar was married to his two eldest sons when they died, Sha'lah would also be in jeopardy.[14]

In time, Judah's wife dies. Tamar dresses as a harlot and has relations with Judah. While Judah's intentions were impure, Tamar's were pure, as she seeks to have a child from Judah's family.[15] Judah promises Tamar payment later,[16] but Tamar insists on a guarantee, an *ei'ravon*. Judah gives Tamar his seal, string, and staff. The items given may have deeper meaning. *Ei'ravon* relates to *areivut*, feeling a sense of responsibility for the other. Assuming responsibility is the foundation of leadership. Yet Judah gives this away. Not coincidentally, the objects he gives Tamar are all related to different forms of leadership. The seal was used by the high priest to indicate the purity of a ritual object.[17] The staff was carried by the prophet wherever he went.[18] The string is associated with a coat from which it flows.[19] The coat is the symbol of executive or royal leadership. If one wears the coat, one leads. Without it, his leadership is in jeopardy.[20] Judah gives it all away as he has abandoned his leadership role.[21]

In time, Judah seeks to recoup his guarantee by sending payment to Tamar. Thwarted in these attempts, Judah declares תקח לה פן נהיה לבוז – "Let her keep them, lest we be shamed." (Genesis

38:23) On its simplest level, Judah declares that in seeking the guarantee, he may be embarrassed, because his true identity may be revealed. On a deeper level, the Hebrew for "shamed" (*la'vuz*) is strikingly similar to the Torah's description of Esau's selling of the birthright to Jacob – ויבז עשו את הבכורה. (Genesis 25:34) Just as Esau abdicates leadership, Judah does the same as reflected in his refusal to pursue the retrieval of his leadership symbols.[22]

Tamar becomes pregnant. Judah self-righteously proclaims that she should be killed, since she violated her quasi-relationship with Sha'lah, whom she should have wed in a levirate union. Tamar reveals the seal, cord, and staff and declares, לאיש אשר אלה לו, אנכי הרה – "I am with child by the man to whom these belong." (Genesis 38:25) At that moment, Judah is faced with a choice. He could remain silent and save face. The consequences of that decision would be that Judah would have no progeny; the very future of the Jewish people would be in jeopardy – and Tamar would be killed. Instead, he proclaims, "צדקה ממני – She is right and I am wrong." (Genesis 38:26) In doing so, Judah signals his readiness to reclaim leadership, to assume responsibility (*areivut*). Twins are born – Peretz and Zerah. In reality, a double *yibum* takes place, as the seed of both Er and Onan continue through the birth of the twins. Here Judah commits himself to continue his deceased sons' progeny.[23] And, of course, Peretz is the ancestor of Boaz, husband of Ruth, from whom David comes and the Messiah will ultimately arrive. (Ruth 4:18–22)

❧ TWO SETS OF TWINS

Comparing the twins born to Judah and Tamar to the better known set, Jacob and Esau, born to Isaac and Rebecca, illustrates how the Book of Genesis takes a sudden turn – moving from dissolution of family to family becoming whole. At first glance the two sets of twins seem similar, with Zerah interfacing with Esau while Peretz interfaces with Jacob. Zerah has this red-like quality. The name "Zerah" literally means "to shine," like the red sun. Zerah also seems to emerge first as he stretches his hand from the womb. To prove he is the eldest, the midwife ties a string of scarlet (in Hebrew *shani*) around his hand. Scarlet is a reddish color. In the words of the Torah, ויהי בלדתה ויתן יד ותקח המילדת ותקשר על ידו שני לאמר זה יצא ראשנה – "And when she gave birth he stretched out his hand and the midwife tied scarlet on it, proclaiming 'this one has emerged first.'" (Genesis 38:28) Similarly, Esau is associated with redness. He emerges from the womb ruddy, ויצא הראשון אדמוני. (Genesis 25:25) Also, when Esau comes back from the field hungry, he says to Jacob, הלעיטני נא מן האדם האדם הזה – "Pour unto me from the red lentil soup." (Genesis 25:30) Moreover, Esau's descendants are referred to as Edom, עשיו הוא אדום, literally, "Esau is Red." (Genesis 36:8)[24]

There is also an intersection between Peretz and Jacob. As Jacob runs from Esau, God appears to him and says, והיה זרעך כעפר הארץ ופרצת ימה וקדמה צפנה ונגבה – "And your seed will be like the dust of the earth, **and you will burst** forth to the west and east, the north and south." (Genesis 28:14) The term *peretz*, an unusual word for the covenantal blessing of many children is used only vis-à-vis Jacob. Additionally, when describing what he's done for his father-in-law Laban, Jacob says, כי מעט אשר היה לך לפני ויפרץ לרב – "For the little you had before I came multiplied exceedingly." (Genesis 30:30) In the end, the Torah describes Jacob as having had fabulous success, using the verb *paratz*, ויפרץ האיש מאד מאד – "And the man swelled up mightily." (Genesis 30:43)[25]

Not only are the names of the two sets of twins linked, their storylines are parallel. Their mothers, Rebecca and Tamar, are the only women who bear twins in the Bible. (Genesis 25:24 and 38:27) In addition, both women veil themselves. When Rebecca sees Isaac for the first time, just prior to their marrying, she takes her veil and covers herself – ותקח הצעיף ותתכס. (Genesis 24:65) In the Bible, the covering of the face is the symbol of a woman's marrying.[26] Similarly, as Tamar prepares to win Judah over by seducing him, the Torah states ותכס בצעיף – "And she covered herself with her veil." (Genesis 38:14) While Judah intends an immoral act, Tamar's intentions are holy, as she prepares for a levirate marriage to bear a child from Judah. It is also very clear that both women were strong personalities playing major roles in preparing and building their respective families covenantally. They accomplish this task by deception. Rebecca plans the deception of her husband so Jacob can be blessed, and Tamar deceives Judah to have children with him.

The twins are linked through their fathers as well; both Isaac and Judah are fooled at critical moments. Thus the twins and their respective mothers and fathers have much in common.

The key in comparing narratives is to see not only similarity, but dissimilarity as well. And it is in the dissimilarity that an important idea emerges. When Jacob and Esau were struggling in Rebecca's womb, the oracle tells her, ולאם מלאם יאמץ – "one people shall be mightier than the other." (Genesis 25:23) In other words, they will remain in unresolved conflict. Through the ages Jacob, father of our people, and Esau, father of Edom, struggle.[27] In the words of Rashi לא ישוו בגדולה, כשזה קם זה נופל – "They will not be equal in greatness, when one rises the other will fall."[28] The text continues, ורב יעבד צעיר. (Genesis 25:23) While this is normatively translated "And the older will serve the younger," that is, Esau will serve Jacob, it could also mean the younger will serve greatly. In other words Jacob will serve Esau. It is purposely ambiguous because the conflict will forever continue.

Peretz and Zerah are different. There the ambiguity as to who is first and second is resolved. Consider the scene: Zerah puts his hand out; but that doesn't make him first. Life begins when the head, or majority of the body, emerges.[29] Not coincidentally, in wanting to designate Zerah first, the midwife ties a *shani* (red string) on his hand, which is a clear association with the word *sheini*, implying that this child would in the end be second.[30]

Herein lies the difference between the two sets of twins. Jacob and Esau are in constant conflict; only one is chosen to be the next patriarch. Peretz and Zerah have their conflict resolved; both are included. Whereas Jacob and not Esau inherits the covenant, both Peretz and Zerah are counted among the children of Judah, as the Torah states, ‏בני יהודה...לפרץ משפחת הפרצי לזרח משפחת הז־‏ ‏רחי‏ – "The children of Judah...of Peretz the family of Perezites, of Zerah the family of Zerahites." (Numbers 26:20) For this reason, the descriptive term for twins in the Peretz and Zerah case – unlike Esau and Jacob – includes an *aleph* and *yud*, ‏תאומים‏. This is so because, in contrast to Jacob and Esau, both Peretz and Zerah were righteous. In the words of Rashi, "The word for twins [in the case of Jacob and Esau] is written defective [without *aleph* and *yud*] while in the case of Tamar it is full [with an *aleph* and *yud*] because in the latter case both children proved righteous."[31] From this perspective, Peretz and Zerah represent a fixing of Jacob and Esau. Jacob and Esau struggle, and only one will be a covenantal heir. Peretz and Zerah are both embraced, each playing an important part in Judah's family.[32]

In the end, Judah becomes the worthy figure to father twins who would both be part of the Jewish covenantal community, since he had learned the message of *areivut*. Tamar had successfully reminded Judah to take leadership by recognizing his role in perpetuating his family.[33] The father who assumes such responsibility raises children who, in the spirit of *areivut*, make room for each other to play critical roles with respect to the Jewish people.

✥ JUDAH BRINGS ABOUT RECONCILIATION

Up to this point, Genesis is a book of selection. Adam and Eve have three children: Cain, Abel, and Seth. Abel is murdered; Cain's descendants die in the flood; only Seth, from whom Noah comes, remains. Noah had three sons, Shem, Ham, and Yafet. Abraham and Sarah come from Shem. From Abraham, Isaac and not Ishmael is chosen. From Isaac, Jacob and not Esau is chosen. Tamar teaches Judah to structure the family differently; for the first time there is no choosing. Both their children, Peretz and Zerah, are included. The entire family continues, each playing a significant role. Rabbi David Silber argues that the restructuring of Judah's family foreshadows the restructuring of Jacob's family, where all of

Jacob's children are blessed. And who inspires that restructuring? Judah, who understands the importance of unity, as he had united his personal family. Far from interrupting the Joseph narrative, the Tamar-Judah rendezvous is a crucial part of the story, since it explains why Judah was suitably qualified to be the uniter.[34]

The moment when Judah steps into the breach and starts to bring the larger family of Jacob together occurs soon after Joseph, as viceroy of Egypt, declares that if the brothers wish to come for more food and retrieve Simeon, they must bring Benjamin. Jacob is hesitant to allow Benjamin to go. Judah rises and declares אָנֹכִי אֶעֶרְבֶנּוּ – "I will be the **guarantor**." (Genesis 43:9) Most often, an *arev*, a guarantor, is a third party who guarantees the loan if the debtor is unable or refuses to repay. Here, the guarantor becomes the debtor. That is, Judah himself says, I obligate myself to bring Benjamin back, and if I do not, וחטאתי לך כל הימים – "I will forever be a sinner before you." (Genesis 43:9)[35] In this spirit, Rabbi Ahron Soloveichik writes:

> Why are the Reuveni and Shimoni, all Israelites of whatever of the tribes of Israel called "Yehudi"? And the answer is given: Because he, Yehudah, said "For your servant is surety for the boy." (Genesis 44:32) It is this principle of surety that constitutes the distinguishing feature of the Jew.[36]

The same Judah who had relinquished leadership when giving away his *ei'ravon* to Tamar assumes leadership by declaring his readiness to be the *arev*. This is precisely what Judah does. Standing before Joseph, who is disguised as the viceroy of Egypt, Judah declares, כי עבדך ערב את הנער – "Now your servant has pledged himself for the lad." (Genesis 44:32) Judah had first learned of this obligation when he admitted his mistake before Tamar, saving his inner family; this makes him more able to now save the larger family of Jacob.

Interestingly, on the brothers' return home, Joseph's cup is found in Benjamin's belongings, having been placed there at Joseph's behest. Judah states מה נאמר לאדני מה נדבר ומה נצטדק האלוקים מצא את עון עבדיך – "What shall we say to my Lord? What shall we speak? Or **how can we justify ourselves?** God has found the iniquity of your servants." (Genesis 44:16) These words are problematic because Judah knew he and his brother had not stolen the cup. But more deeply, writes Nehama Leibowitz, Judah was "confessing to the iniquity, not which the Egyptian had 'found' in him, but that 'God has found out the iniquity of your servants.'"[37] In other words, Judah was expressing remorse for past deeds, including his lead in the sale of Joseph.[38] Judah's declaration מה נצטדק also reminds the reader of his declaration to Tamar, צדקה ממני. (Genesis 38:26) The link illustrates the connection between Judah's bringing his inner family together by proclaiming צדקה ממני – "Tamar was right and I [Judah] was wrong," and Judah's bringing the larger family of Jacob together by proclaiming מה נצטדק – that is, Joseph was right, and I [Judah] was wrong.[39]

✢ REUNIFICATION

At the end of the Book of Genesis, three powerful images of reconciliation emerge. The first occurs when Judah defends Benjamin, who, in the absence of Joseph, is his key adversary.[40] Judah declares, כי עבדך ערב את הנער – "For your servant has pledged himself for the youth." (Genesis 44:32) The same Judah who sold Joseph, seeing him as a threat to becoming the covenantal heir, rises to defend Benjamin and becomes Benjamin's *arev* (guarantor).[41]

The second image of reconciliation is when Jacob inverts his hands while blessing his grandchildren and gives Ephraim the lead *brakha* over Menashe, שכל את ידיו – "He switched his hands." (Genesis 48:14) Unlike earlier, when Esau was upset when his younger brother Jacob received the *brakha*, Menashe is at peace when his younger brother Ephraim is favored.

The third image of reconciliation is when Jacob basically adopts his grandchildren, Ephraim and Menashe – כראובן ושמעון יהיו לי – "They will be mine like Reuben and Shimon." (Genesis 48:5) Perhaps Jacob adopts them knowing that there would never be real peace between Joseph and his brothers, because the rift was so great that they would always be wary of each other. The text makes this point when, after Jacob dies, the Torah states: וַיֹּאמְרוּ לוּ יִשְׂטְמֵנוּ יוֹסֵף וְהָשֵׁב יָשִׁיב לָנוּ אֵת כָּל הָרָעָה אֲשֶׁר גָּמַלְנוּ אֹתוֹ – "And [the brothers] said, perhaps Joseph will nurse hatred against us and he will surely repay us for all the evil that we did him." (Genesis 50:15) The Midrash emphasizes this idea when it relates that after burying Jacob, the brothers saw Joseph go to the pit from where he was sold, presumably, they thought, to plan an attack against them.[42]

Sometimes achieving the goal must wait for the next generation. Although Joseph could not make peace with his brothers, perhaps Joseph's children, Ephraim and Menashe, would be up to the task.[43] To paraphrase a popular Israeli peace song, Jacob tells Joseph:

בני יוסף, בני יוסף, בחייך לא יבא השלום, אבל בחיי בניך, אפרים ומנשה, יבא השלום – הנה בא השלום – My son Joseph, my son Joseph. Peace will not come in your lifetime, but it will come in your children's lifetime. Behold, the peace will come.

This situation explains why there is no tribe of Joseph, only the tribes of his children Ephraim and Menashe. To be a tribe, the tribe must have a possibility to live in peace. The tribe of Joseph could never live in peace with the rest of Israel. Perhaps the tribes of Ephraim and Menashe could.

It follows that Genesis ends with a powerful sense of family unity. Judah defends Benjamin, Ephraim and Menashe get along, and Joseph, through his sons Ephraim and Menashe, is in a position to make real peace with his brothers. Genesis, which is the story of fragmented families and sibling rivalries, ends on a high note. The family is reconstituted; it is reunited; there is reconciliation. Only when this happens can the book of Exodus, the story of *Am Yisrael*, begin. The best model for a nation is family. Just as a family that works must be together, so, too, must the Jewish people.[44]

This analysis gives us a deeper understanding of Rabbi Kook's concept of the two covenants. For Rabbi Kook, the foundation of *brit Sinai* is *brit avot*, the foundation of nation is family. If one wants to understand how to relate to the Jewish nation, one should ask how to relate to one's own inner family. Put simply, every time one sees the word "nation," he or she should insert the word "family."

✿ UNRAVELING

The period of the judges and prophets is an unraveling of Genesis. The unity of family is shattered. The nation is divided. It is interesting to note the conflict between Benjamin and Judah. In the story of *pilegesh be-Givah*, the concubine of Givah, the tribe of Benjamin is temporarily excised from the Jewish People, with the tribe of Judah taking the lead and going to war against Benjamin. (Judges 20:18) Not long after, King Saul from the tribe of Benjamin, and David from tribe of Judah, are locked in a bitter battle. In the words of the Navi: ויהי שאול עוין את דוד – "And Saul eyed David with suspicion from that day on." (Samuel 1, 18:9) Judah and Benjamin are no longer at peace.[45]

Ephraim and Menashe engage in civil war with 42,000 Ephramites killed by the tribe of Menashe in the Yiftach story. (Judges 12:6) Here, Ephraim and Menashe are also no longer at peace.[46]

After King Solomon, the kingdom of Israel splits. The protagonists of this split are Rehavam from the tribe of Judah and Yeravam from the tribe of Ephraim (1 Kings 11). The hope that the children of Joseph, led by Ephraim, would be at peace with the brothers, led by Judah, has gone awry.[47]

From a certain perspective, redemption depends on the unity of *Am Yisrael*, most important on how Ephraim, who is considered the spiritual heir of Joseph, gets along with Judah. Even in the spy story, which ends in tragedy – as God proclaims that the Jews who left Egypt would not enter Israel – has a positive side. This occurs when Ephraim and Judah get along as their descendants Joshua and Calev form an alliance to speak favorably about Israel (Numbers 13 and 14). Their alliance reaches its crescendo

at the conclusion of the Torah, when Joshua is appointed to succeed Moses. Joshua, of the tribe of Ephraim, is accepted by Judah
and all of the Jewish people, as he leads them into Israel. While
the Torah ends with the Jewish people united, the prophets end in
discord. The nation splits into two kingdoms of Judah and Israel,
beginning with Yeravam, who comes from Ephraim.[48] This division ultimately leads to the destruction of the Temple.

While the Tamar story in the Torah is the precursor for
bringing Jacob's family together, the Tamar story in the Prophets
precipitates an opposite result. The Book of Samuel records that
David had several sons. His eldest was Amnon, who rapes Tamar,
the full sibling of Absalom – David's third son.[49] The text records
Tamar begging Amnon not to rape her. כִּי תְּעַנֵּנִי אַל אָחִי אַל לוֹ וַתֹּאמֶר
הַזֹּאת הַנְּבָלָה אֶת תַּעֲשֵׂה אַל בְּיִשְׂרָאֵל כֵן יֵעָשֶׂה לֹא. – "And she said to him,
'No, my brother; do not violate me, for such things are not done
in Israel. Do not commit this despicable act.'" (II Samuel 13:12)
Amnon is from the tribe of Judah. Unlike his ancestor Judah, who
heard Tamar's teachings and admits his wrongs, Amnon refuses
to listen. אֹתָהּ וַיִּשְׁכַּב וַיְעַנֶּהָ מִמֶּנָּה וַיֶּחֱזַק בְּקוֹלָהּ לִשְׁמֹעַ אָבָה וְלֹא – "But he
refused to heed her voice; and being stronger than she, he violated
her, and lay with her." (II Samuel 13:14) Judah embraces Tamar's
teaching, and as a result the family is brought together. Amnon
rejects Tamar, and as a result the family is shattered. The result is
horrific. Amnon is killed by Absalom; Absalom rebels against David and is killed. David is never able to fully recover and reunite
his kingdom. (II Samuel 19) Soon after Absalom's defeat, Sheva
ben Bikhri, a Benjaminite, rebels against David (II Samuel 20:1),
and the Benjamin-Judah alliance is shattered. All this paves the
way for the ultimate break between the ten tribes (led by Ephraim)
and Judah. The Joseph-Judah alliance is in shambles.

The two Tamar stories are further joined by the only mentions of *ketonet pasim* (coat of many colors) in all of Tanakh. After
being raped by Amnon, Tamar is described as wearing a *ketonet
pasim*. She rents her garment, places dirt on her head, and cries
as she walks. In the words of the text:

וְעָלֶיהָ כְּתֹנֶת פַּסִּים, כִּי כֵן תִּלְבַּשְׁןָ בְנוֹת הַמֶּלֶךְ הַבְּתוּלֹת מְעִילִים; וַיֹּצֵא
אוֹתָהּ מְשָׁרְתוֹ הַחוּץ, וְנָעַל הַדֶּלֶת אַחֲרֶיהָ. וַתִּקַּח תָּמָר אֵפֶר עַל רֹאשָׁהּ, וּכְתֹנֶת
הַפַּסִּים אֲשֶׁר עָלֶיהָ קָרָעָה; וַתָּשֶׂם יָדָהּ עַל רֹאשָׁהּ, וַתֵּלֶךְ הָלוֹךְ וְזָעָקָה. "Now
she had a garment of many colors upon her; for such robes were
worn by the maidens among the king's daughters. And his servant brought her out and bolted the door after her. And Tamar
put ashes on her head and rent her garment of many colors that
was on her; and she laid her hand on her head and went her way,
crying aloud as she went." (II Samuel 13:18–19)

In the Genesis story Jacob is shown Joseph's *ketonet pasim*
dipped in blood, which casts him into interminable mourning.
(Genesis 37:31–34) The story, however, ends in euphoria as Judah
listens to Tamar, assumes responsibility, and unites his inner, and
ultimately his larger, family. In the Prophets, Tamar is also wearing a *ketonet pasim*, "crying aloud as she went." Here, however,
the story ends in tragedy. Amnon fails to listen to Tamar, his inner family is split, and this division becomes the precursor of the
larger family of Israel forever broken.

❧ THE CHALLENGE

Genesis ends with the family intact; the narrative of the Prophets
takes us in the opposite direction – the family is shattered. The
challenge in contemporary times is to repair the brokenness of
the Jewish people that ended the prophetic era and return to the
blueprint that ended Genesis, of family and nation together. In
the words of the prophet Ezekiel, וְאַתָּה בֶן אָדָם, קַח לְךָ עֵץ אֶחָד, וּכְתֹב
עָלָיו לִיהוּדָה, וְלִבְנֵי יִשְׂרָאֵל חֲבֵרָיו; וּלְקַח, עֵץ אֶחָד, וּכְתוֹב עָלָיו לְיוֹסֵף עֵץ אֶפְ-
רָיִם – "Son of man, take a wooden tablet, and write upon it for Ju-
dah and for the children of Israel his comrades; and another, and
write upon it Joseph, it is Ephraim's...." וְקָרַב אֹתָם אֶחָד אֶל אֶחָד...וְהָיוּ
לַאֲחָדִים, בְּיָדֶךָ – "and bring them close one to the other, and let them
become one in your hand." (Ezekiel 37:16, 17)[50]

Not coincidentally, the last words of the prophets forecast
that redemption will arrive when Elijah announces the coming of
the Messiah. And what will Elijah do to facilitate the redemptive

period? Here the prophet declares, הַנֵּה אָנֹכִי שֹׁלֵחַ לָכֶם אֵת אֵלִיָּה הַנָּ־ בִיא לִפְנֵי בּוֹא יוֹם יְקֹוָק הַגָּדוֹל וְהַנּוֹרָא: וְהֵשִׁיב לֵב אָבוֹת עַל בָּנִים וְלֵב בָּנִים עַל אֲבוֹתָם – "Behold, I will send you Elijah the prophet before the coming of the great and awesome day of the Lord. And he shall turn the heart of the fathers to the children, and the heart of the children to their fathers." (Malakhi 3:23–24) In the time of re-demption, families will be united. This event forms the segue to the redemption of the Jewish people through which the world will be redeemed. (Isaiah 2:1–4)

The goal is elusive, but an attempt must be made to reach it. The key is to understand what *ahdut Yisrael* means. Just as the test of family unity is not how its members love each other when agreeing, but how they love each other when disagreeing, so too the test of Jewish unity is not how Jews love each other when get-ting along, but how we love each other when we do not. *Ahdut Yisrael* means that a spirit of unity prevails. Unity does not mean eradication of differences. That is uniformity. Rather it means liv-ing together despite differences.

A story illustrating this idea of *ahdut Yisrael* occurred dur-ing the last days of the disengagement from Gaza in the summer of 2005. It took place in Nezer Hazani, one of the Gush Katif settlements. Some soldiers, led by Segan Aluf (Lieutenant Colo-nel) Lahat, came to the home of Benny and Rachel Yefet. A few years earlier their son, Itamar Yefet, was murdered by terrorists, and now the Yefets were being taken out of their home. After an hour-long discussion, Segan Aluf Lahat told the Yefets it was time to leave. Benny asked if he could take his two most prized pos-sessions. He proceeded to remove the mezuza from the door and the Israeli flag from his roof. As the family walked out with the soldiers, Benny turned to Lahat and said, I do not know where we are going. Could you please hold on to the mezuza and flag. Lahat nodded and said he would. Benny then said to the Segan Aluf, Promise me that when we move to our new home you will come and put the mezuza on the door and raise our *degel Yisrael* (flag of Israel) on our roof. Benny and Segan Aluf Lahat were on opposite sides of the political and religious divide, but they both broke down and tears flowed, as they fell into each other's arms. What a moment of Jewish unity and love.

This is an era of *humrah*, of being stringent in *halakha*. But the greatest *humrah*, whatever one's political, religious, or *halakhic* bent, should be to be *mahmir*, absolutely *mahmir* on *ahavat Yisrael* (loving one's fellow Jew). *Lu-yehi, lu-yehi*, let it be, let it be.[51]

☙ NOTES

1. This essay is dedicated to Rabbi Haskel Lookstein, one of the leading Modern Orthodox rabbis in America today. As senior rabbi of congregation Kehilath Jeshurun and leader of the Ramaz School, he has, during his fifty years of *avodat hakodesh*, touched the souls of tens of thousands of people.

   My association with Rabbi Lookstein was at times strained. We sometimes clashed as activists as he worked within the establishment and I worked outside of that framework. However, in recent years I have come to understand that Rabbi Lookstein's approach is nothing less than heroic. When working from within, one has to deal with systemic change. There are major personalities to be coddled and pushed so that the desired outcome can be attained. Rabbi Lookstein did just that. He went to the brink, cajoling, insisting, demanding that more be done. In the end, he was able to achieve extraordinary results.

   I have often wondered why Rabbi Lookstein always chose to work from within. My answer is simple. Bringing individuals together under a common cause is a natural extension of Rabbi Lookstein's love for and his embrace of all people.

   It is in this spirit that this essay has been written. Hopefully it will spark a greater consciousness concerning the meaning of *ahdut Yisrael* – the lifelong mission of the rebbe of uniting our people, Rabbi Haskel Lookstein.

2. Rabbi Abraham Isaac HaCohen Kook, *Iggrot ha-Ra'iyah*, vol. ii, letter 555.

3. Ibid.

4. Ibid.

5. See Rashi, Genesis 1:1, s.v. *be'reishit*

6. See Julian Morganstern, *The Book of Genesis* (New York, 1919), p. 305.

7. See *Bereshit Rabba* 53:11 and Rashi, Genesis 21:9 s.v. *mezahek*.

8. See *The Jewish Study Bible Commentary*, ed. Adele Berlin and Marc Zvi Brettler (Oxford, 2004), Genesis 21:9. "Playing (*mezahek*) is another pun on Isaac's name. Ishmael was 'Isaacing,' or 'taking Isaac's place.'"

9. I first heard the connection between Joseph's dreams and the covenant in the name of Rabbi Menachem Liebtag.

10. Sforno, Genesis 37:18, s.v. *va-yitnaklu ohto le-hamito* quoting Sanhedrin 72a. Sforno translation by Rabbi Raphael Pelcovitz, Mesorah Publications, p. 181.

11. Death is a time to take stock of the well-being of a family, as the bereaved often do during *shiva*. In Genesis, death serves as a barometer to measure the state of togetherness of the patriarchal and matriarchal families.

12. I first heard the idea of fragmentation increasing among the Genesis siblings from Rabbi David Silber. While the kernel of the idea is his, the formulation and embellishment of the idea presented here are my own.

   Some have suggested the reverse – with the passing of generations the rivalries become less strained. Isaac and Yishmael part forever, coming together only for a brief moment when their father dies. Jacob and Esau reunite after twenty-two years and actually embrace. True, they quickly go their own ways, but they seem at least on the surface to make peace. Joseph and his brothers are apart for twenty-two years but reconcile in Egypt, where they all remain. See B. S. Jacobson, *Meditations on the Torah*, (Tel Aviv, Israel, 1964), p. 54.

The Exodus story as it relates to sibling relationships takes us to an even higher level. When Aaron hears that his younger brother Moses has been appointed prophet, he reacts with absolute elation (Exodus 4:14, 27). Far from sibling rivalry, there is only joy in the other's success and appointment to becoming leader of the Jewish people.

13. See Rashi, Genesis 38:1, s.v. *va'yehi ba'et ha-hi*.

14. The Torah records that both Er and Onan had sinned, perhaps explaining why they died. Judah may have been unaware of their wrongdoings.

15. This also was a kind of "levirate marriage," as after Sha'lah, Judah was the closest relative. This situation parallels Ruth's marriage to Boaz, who is also the second relative in line (Ruth 3:12; 4:13).

16. Judah's promise to send Tamar *gedi ezim*, a kid of the goats, signals that a deception will soon take place. Wearing *gedi ezim*, Jacob had fooled his father Isaac and taken the blessings. Dipping Joseph's coat of many colors (*ketonet passim*) into goat's blood, the brothers, probably led by Judah, deceived Jacob. And now Judah himself is soon to be deceived. All these deceptions revolve around the theme of birthright and covenantal continuity. They teach that what goes around comes around, the deceiver becomes the deceived.

17. See, for example, *Shabbat* 21b.

18. Moses, for example, is instructed to carry a staff in his hand (Exodus 4:17).

19. Note the text in the Torah which deals with *tzitzit* (fringes) attached to a four-cornered garment (Numbers 15:37–41).

20. Note that when Samuel tells Saul that he no longer will be king, his coat is torn (Samuel I, 15:27). Note also that David rips Saul's coat, de facto taking the kingdom from him (Samuel I, 24:5). In the Joseph story itself, Joseph could not be sold until the brothers take off his coat of many colors (Genesis 37:23). See Robert Alter, *The David Story* (New York, 1999), pp. 92, 148.

21. The idea that these symbols represent leadership is found in the Midrash and is quoted by classical commentators. See, for example, *Bereshit Rabba* 85:9, where the seal symbolizes royalty, the cord alludes to the Sanhedrin, and the staff refers to the royal Messiah. See also Ramban, Genesis 38:18, s.v. *ho'tamkhah u'fe-tilekha*.

22. I heard the *va-yivez-la-vuz* comparison from Rabbi David Silber.

23. See Leon R. Kass, *The Beginning of Wisdom* (New York, 2003), p. 537.

The key letters of *yibum* are *bet* and *mem*, *bam*, which literally means, "in them." The *yud* may turn the word into the future tense. By performing this act, Judah unites with his children Er and Onan, seeing to it that their legacy lives on.

More generally, the term *yibum* speaks to the intermingling of the living brother with his deceased sibling. By performing *yibum*, the living brother is with them, with those left behind, childless. Conversely, the deceased brother "will be in them," as his name is kept alive through his wife and brother.

24 Robert Alter draws this parallel in his commentary *The Five Books of Moses* (New York, 2004), pp. 219–220. In his words:

"The twins of course recall Jacob and Esau…The name Zerah means 'shining,' as in the dawning of the sun, and so is linked with the scarlet thread on his hand. The scarlet in turn associates Zerah with Esau – the-Red – another twin displaced from his initial position as firstborn."

See also Leon R. Kass, *The Beginning of Wisdom*, p. 537.

25. See Ibn Ezra, Genesis 38:29, s.v. *mah parazta*, who mentions the *peretz* parallel. See also Alter, *The Five Books of Moses*, pp. 219–220, who sees Peretz as a Jacob figure since both struggle for the right of the firstborn, seemingly taking it away from their respective elder brothers.

26. This may be the source of *badekin*, the veiling ceremony performed at weddings.

27. See Nechama Leibowitz, *Studies in Genesis* (Jerusalem), pp. 283–284. She writes "In the

Aggada, Esau (like Pharaoh and Haman) is not an individual, a specific historical figure who appeared at a certain time, but a prototype, a symbol, a milestone of Jew hatred."

28. Rashi, Genesis 25:23, s.v. *mil'om yeh-eh-matz.*

29. See Mishna Ohaloth 7:6 and commentary of Rabbi Ovadiah M'Bartenura, s.v. *yatzah.* See also Mishna Niddah 3:5.

30. See Or Ha-Chaim, Genesis 38, s.v. *al yado shani lay-mor.*

31. Rashi, s.v. *ve-hinei tomim,.* Genesis 25:24.

32. Alter, *The Five Books of Moses,* pp. 219–220. He sees the struggle between Peretz and Zerah as corresponding to Jacob and Esau, since Peretz, like Jacob, struggles for the right of the firstborn. In Alter's words, "Zerah, sticking his hand out first, seems to be the firstborn, but he is overtaken by *Peretz,* who makes a 'breach' or 'bursts forth' (the meaning of the Hebrew *Peretz*)."

    Rabbi David Silber argues the reverse: Esau and Jacob is about constant struggle; Peretz and Zerah is about struggle resolved.

33. The name Tamar has as its key roots *mem reish,* short for *morah.* It can mean "she will teach," as Tamar was the teacher par excellence.

34. Some suggest that this chapter teaches that even in the most dire of circumstances, God is busy planting the seeds of redemption. This occurs in the Judah-Tamar story as one of the twins, Peretz, is the ancestor of David, from whom the Messiah will come. See B. S. Jacobson, *Meditations on the Torah,* p. 48.

35. This is a far cry from Reuben, who offers his two sons as guarantee, an offer rejected by Jacob. Alternatively, Ramban argues that Reuben's offer is rejected because food from Egypt was just brought into Jacob's home. Judah waits until the food is gone. With no food available, Jacob is left with no choice but to allow the brothers to return to Egypt with Benjamin.

36. Rabbi Ahron Soloveichik, "Jew and Jew, Jew and Non-Jew," reprinted from *Jewish Life* by the Orthodox Union, p. 9.

37. Leibowitz, *Studies in Genesis,* p. 467.

38. See *Bereshit Rabba* 92:9.

39. נצטדק is in the plural, as Judah's brothers participated in the sale.

    Umberto Cassuto notes that when Tamar confronts Judah, the Torah uses terms found in the sale of Joseph. In the Tamar story the words include *shalhah, leimor, haker na, va-yaker,* and *va-yomer* (Genesis 38:25,26). They remind the reader of the words found in the sale of Joseph story. These words are *va-ye-shalhu, va-yomru, haker na, va-ya-kirah,* and *va-yomer* (Genesis 37:32,33). It is extraordinary that these words in both narratives are in precisely the same order. The Torah may be teaching us that Tamar confronts Judah not only for impregnating her, but also for his role in the sale. Judah's response צדקה ממני is an admission that he has been wrong in both incidents – the sale, and the liaison with Tamar. See B.S. Jacobson, *Meditations on the Torah,* pp. 44-45.

40. Reuben, the eldest son of Leah, is not in the running for the birthright, since he had an inappropriate relationship with Bilhah, his father's concubine/wife (Genesis 35:22; 49:3,4). Simeon and Levi are also non-candidates, because they destroyed the city of Shekhem (Genesis 34; 49:5–7). Judah is therefore in line to inherit. His competition is Benjamin, who in the absence of Joseph is the primary son of Rachel.

41. This may explain why Joseph was not in touch with his father for twenty-two years. It was important that his brothers, especially Judah, express remorse for having sold him (Joseph) before Joseph revealed himself. Only then could they live in peace. What better way than for Joseph to orchestrate a similar situation wherein Judah is given the opportunity to defend Benjamin, who in effect is Joseph's surrogate. See Ramban to Genesis, 42:9; Rambam, Yad, Laws of Repentance 2:1; and Leibowitz, *Studies in the Book of Genesis,* p. 460.

42. Mishnat R. Eliezer, ch. 7 (this is Midrash Agur) according to Torah Shelemah *va-yehi* paragraph 50, quoted in *Studies in Genesis* by Nechama Leibowitz, p. 558. The Midrash goes on to say that Joseph meant no harm. He went to thank God for delivering him from the pit.

43. Rabbi David Silber on disc 7 of his lectures on *The Joseph Narrative: The Reconstruction of a*

Family argues that although the brothers may dislike Joseph that doesn't mean they dislike their nephews (Ephraim and Menashe). In his words, "There is no tribe of Joseph, there is a tribe of Menashe and a tribe of Ephraim. But through Ephraim and Menashe Joseph is brought back."

See also Rabbi E.J. Duschinsky, *B'Ikvei Parshiyot* (Tel Aviv, 1977), p. 108. He hints that in adopting Ephraim and Menashe, Yaakov expresses confidence in Joseph's Jewish commitment. It follows that through the adoption, Jacob reclaims Joseph.

44. The term עַם, "nation," is never found in the Book of Genesis. It first appears at the beginning of the Book of Exodus, which deals with the coming into being of the Jewish people (Exodus 1:9).

45. It has been suggested that Saul was chosen as the first king precisely because he came from the tribe of Benjamin (I Samuel 9). A fundamental role of the king is to unite Am Yisrael. Choosing Saul was an attempt to do just that by bringing in a leader from the tribe most alienated from the larger nation of Israel.

In the Mossad Harav Kook commentary on the Book of Samuel by Moshe Kil, (Jerusalem 5741), the demand of Nachash Ha-Amoni to have the residents of Yavesh Gilad, a close ally of the tribe of Benjamin (Judges 21:8) to cut out their right eye (*ein yamin* – I Samuel 11:2) was an attempt to sever Benjamin (*Binyamin*) from the Jewish people. Note the similarity between *yamin* in *ein yamin*, and *yamin* in *Binyamin*. Saul responds vigorously by rallying all of Am Yisrael to come to the aid of Yavesh Gilad. The narrative goes out of its way to communicate the number of soldiers who came from the tribe of Judah (I Samuel 11:8). Through this process Saul unites the kingdom and brings Benjamin and Judah together. See Rabbi David Silber in his essay "Anarchy and Monarchy" published in the Yeshivat Chovevei Torah Rabbinical School *Tanakh Companion the book of Samuel*, Ben Yehuda Press, Teaneck, NJ, 2006, pp. 51–54.

And of course the special relationship between Jonathan from the tribe of Benjamin and David from the tribe of Judah, reflects the unity between these two tribes (I Samuel 18:1).

Midrash Tanhuma 11:8 suggests that Judah fulfills his commitment to be a guardian for Benjamin when David of the tribe of Judah steps in for King Saul of the tribe of Benjamin to battle Goliath. Notice the phrase ויגש הפלישתי השכם והערב, literally, "the Philistine (Goliath) would approach [the Israelite camp] every morning and evening" (Samuel I 17:16). *Ha'arev* reminds the reader of the term *orev*.

Notwithstanding these noble attempts to bring Benjamin and Judah together, Saul and David become bitter enemies. Still, while David steps in for Saul, they become and remain bitter enemies.

46. In the narrative, the Ephraimites flee. The people of Menashe ask them to say *shibbolet*. Unable to pronounce the "sh" sound, the Ephraimites respond *sibbolet*. This pronunciation indicated to the Menashe'ites that they are Ephraimites, and they are killed (Judges 12:5,6).

The simple approach is that the Ephraimites had a speech impediment. The deeper meaning may be that *shibbolet* means "wheat," the symbol of strength. *Sibbolet* is related to *sahval* or *sabal*, the person who suffers, or a porter, the person who carries heavy loads and in a certain sense is compliant to others. The Menasheh'ites dare the Ephraimites to say *shibbolet*, i.e., we are in power; in fact they are forced to say *sibbolet*, we are under the rule of others. Here Menashe overlords Ephraim, a far cry from the Genesis story when Menashe is content when Jacob declares Ephraim will be greater.

This interpretation resonates when one considers that *shibbolet* in the text is spelled with a *shin* and *sibbolet* is spelled not with a *sin* but with a *samekh*, the letter used in the word *sahval* or *sabal*.

47. The split occurs when Rehavam (of the tribe of Judah) fails to heed the advice of the elders to tell Yeravam (descendant of Ephraim, the key son of Joseph) that he and his followers would be treated with kindness (1 Kings, 12:13,14). This is a far cry from the reverence Judah shows his elderly father (Jacob) who instructs him to return to Egypt in peace, a plan which ultimately leads to the rendezvous with Joseph (Genesis 43:11–14).

48. As it turns out, the kingdom of Israel is led by kings who come from other tribes as well. For example, the Yeravam dynasty is destroyed by Baasha of the tribe of Issakhar (1 Kings 15:27–29). Still, the split begins with Yeravam, who comes from the tribe of Ephraim.

49. Some suggest that sexual acts in the Tanakh are political. In raping Tamar, Amnon is declaring that he, and not Absalom, who was vying to succeed David, is the worthy successor to the throne.

50. There are other examples of the prophetic period ending in failure, leaving it up to us to do the repairing. Jeremiah, the prophet of the destruction of the First Temple, prophesized וְהִשְׁבַּתִּי מֵעָרֵי יְהוּדָה, וּמֵחֻצוֹת יְרוּשָׁלַיִם, קוֹל שָׂשׂוֹן וְקוֹל שִׂמְחָה, קוֹל חָתָן וְקוֹל כַּלָּה – "Then will I cause to cease from the cities of Judah, and from the streets of Jerusalem, the voice of mirth and the voice of gladness, the voice of the bridegroom and the voice of the bride" (Jeremiah 7:34). And yet under every *chuppah* we recite מהרה... ישמע בערי יְהוּדָה, וּבְחֻצוֹת יְרוּשָׁלַיִם, קוֹל שָׂשׂוֹן וְקוֹל שִׂמְחָה, קוֹל חָתָן וְקוֹל כַּלָּה – "Soon there will be heard in the cities of Judah and in the streets of Jerusalem, the voice of mirth and the voice of gladness, the voice of the bridegroom and the voice of the bride." Here, bride and groom are challenged to fix the words of the prophets by bringing joy and gladness to Jerusalem and the larger world. This may be a deeper meaning of breaking the glass under the *chuppah* as bride and groom recall the Temple's destruction and devastations in the world, and resolve to fix the broken pieces. This is, in fact, what Jeremiah envisions when he proclaims, עוֹד יִשָּׁמַע בַּמָּקוֹם הַזֶּה...בְּעָרֵי יְהוּדָה, וּבְחֻצוֹת יְרוּשָׁלָם... קוֹל שָׂשׂוֹן וְקוֹל שִׂמְחָה, קוֹל חָתָן וְקוֹל כַּלָּה... – "Yet again there will be heard in this place...in the cities of Judah, and in the streets of Jerusalem...the voice of mirth and the voice of gladness, the voice of the bridegroom and the voice of the bride..." (Jeremiah 33:10,11).

In a similar fashion, the experiment of kingship as recorded in the prophets ended in tragedy. With the establishment of the State of Israel, we are in a position to begin repairing that failure. This idea may be predicated on Rabbi Kook's notion that in the absence of the biblical king, the people vote. The leadership they elect then has the status of biblical king. See Rabbi Kook's *Mishpatei Cohen*, n. 144.

51. I am grateful to Rabbi David Silber, Founder and Dean of the Drisha Institute, whose classes have brought me much joy and reshaped my approach to the Genesis text. In particular, his insights on the Judah-Tamar story as found in his Jewish Holidays Audio-Cassette Series (Shavuot) were critical in the development of this paper. I am also indebted to Rabbi Nati Helfgot, Chair of the Bible and Jewish Thought Departments of Yeshivat Chovevei Torah Rabbinical School (YCT), whose teachings and persona have influenced my understanding of Tanakh. Many thanks also to my students at YCT and the Bayit (the Hebrew Institute of Riverdale), who have challenged me and offered insights that contributed to this essay.

Law and Narrative in the Book of Ruth

Avivah Zornberg

ॐ LAW AND LOVE

R. Ze'ira said: This scroll (of Ruth) tells us nothing of purity or impurity, of prohibition or permission. For what purpose was it written? To teach how great is the reward of those who do deeds of lovingkindness (*chasadim*).[1]

The central message of the *Book of Ruth*, declares R. Ze'ira, is embodied not in law but in narrative. The book tells a story about the good things that happen to good people. For modern readers, of course, whose assumptions have been shaped by empirical and cultural experience of the *bad* things that often happen to good people, this conventional moral theme is not a simple teaching. But R. Ze'ira is careful with his terms: he refers specifically to "those who do *chasadim* – deeds of lovingkindness": *chesed* is the elemental quality often translated as "love," in the expansive sense that opens out into kindness, loyalty, and courage. But the core meaning of the word resists translation. *Ruth* is the narrative that displays that core meaning in dynamic form.

Here *chesed* moves and breathes and generates; here, one can take the measure of its uncanny power. Here are Ruth and Orpah, in their devotion to their mother-in-law'[2] and Ruth in relation to Boaz (and perhaps to her dead husband, Machlon).[3] But here too

313

is Boaz, encouraging Ruth to glean in his field, and instructing his reapers not to shame her but to leave the "forgotten" stalks for her gleaning. He too is one of the *chesed* people who, the midrash affirms, will receive great reward. His goodness, however, is precisely an expression of the *legal* requirements of his situation, that is, of the "prohibitions and permissions" that the midrash maintains are *not* the subject of the book. The laws of the field, as they are sketched out in Leviticus (19:9–10) are given dramatic form in Boaz's words of *chesed*.

In this narrative, then, law and *chesed* are not schematically opposed to one another. Indeed, law and custom inform many aspects of the narrative of *chesed*.[4] It is precisely the licit and the illicit – prohibition and permission – that provide a structure of meaning within which human desire and fear may resonate. Nevertheless, the *main* purpose of the book is "to teach how great is the reward of those who do deeds of *chasadim*." In the end, the book tells a tale of a certain kind of human being. How does this way of being human relate to the concept of law that defines the world of *Ruth*?

The law that most significantly defines this world is an exclusionary law that is never articulated in the text. Throughout the whole course of her narrative, its shadow looms over Ruth: "No Ammonite or Moabite may enter into the community of God; none of their descendants, even in the tenth generation, shall ever enter into the community of God."[5]

This law, repressed in the text, bans Ruth from ever marrying into the community that she has so passionately insisted on claiming as her own. ("Your people are my people and your God my God" [1:16]). In the presence of this law, the unguarded desire with which she solicits Naomi resonates poignantly. When one looks more closely at this opening scene, Ruth's being described, repeatedly and redundantly, as Ruth *the Moabite* is a way of intimating the legal barriers that frame her world. Although no explicit mention is made of this law, its presence nevertheless informs all the interactions, in speech and silence, in the narrative. Repressed, it is everywhere operative.

✢ THE CONVERSATIONAL FABRIC AT RISK

However, perhaps the most radical claim that the midrash has to make about law in the world of this book is in its reading of the opening words: "And it was in the days when the Judges judged." As a historical framework for the narrative, the expression "when the Judges judged" (*b'shfot ha-shoftim*) has a tongue-twisting, ambiguous quality: "In the days of the Judges" would have served the purpose more simply. The mirroring noun/verb structure raises questions: does it mean "when the Judges judged" or "when the Judges were judged"?

It was a generation that judged its judges. If the judge said to a man, "Take the splinter from between your teeth," he would retort, "Take the beam from between your eyes." If the judge said, "Your silver is dross," he would retort, "Your liquor is mixed with water."[6]

If the judge is subject to harsher criticism than the defendant, this fact signifies a breakdown in the rule of law. If judges cannot rule on the improprieties of those they judge without provoking much more serious charges against themselves, this fact indicates how seriously disabled the legal system has become. The images – the splinter between the defendant's teeth, the beam that grotesquely emerges from between the judge's eyes – indicate the greater gravity of the judge's misdeeds. The splinter may be embarrassing, inappropriate, but the beam – massive, distorting the judge's vision – compromises the radar by which he evaluates the world.[7]

In another round of metaphors, the judge compares the defendant to alloyed silver: hidden acts have compromised his integrity. The latter responds with a counterimage: the judge is like watered-down liquor: at what point does diluted liquor stop being liquor? By imperceptible degrees, the judge has lost his claim to represent justice; or worse, in a world of such judges, the very concept of justice may lose all meaning.

From a sociological perspective, the corruption of judges signifies the collapse of a shared world of meaning. Peter Berger discusses the challenge posed by the sociology of knowledge to the maintenance of a particular worldview. Concerned with "studying the relationship between human thought and the social condition under which it occurs," this discipline proposes that "the plausibility...of views of reality depends upon the social support these receive." Individuals are subject to powerful pressures to conform to the views of others. "It is in conversation, in the broadest sense of the word, that we build up and keep going our view of the world."[8] Social networks or "conversational fabrics" produce practices and explanations to bolster conviction: controls, therapies, legitimations create the "plausibility structure of the conception in question."[9]

In this view, the mystery of faith disappears as the theologian's world becomes "one world among many," a community of faith constructed in a specific human history. Similarly, when judges lay themselves open to serious charges of personal corruption, a world of expectation and belief begins to crumble. "Woe to that generation," declares another midrash, that judges its judges – who require judgment!"[10] The woe of this condition is socially determined, but its effects endanger the survival of a world of meaning.

In a similar vein, the midrash indicates the reason for the catastrophe that befell the aristocratic house of Elimelech. The death of father and sons, which effectively sets in motion the narrative of Naomi and Ruth, demands moral explanation. What was the family's sin that brought down such calamity?

> It has been taught: In time of pestilence and in time of war, gather in your feet, but in time of famine, spread out your feet. Why then was Elimelech punished? Because he struck

despair into the hearts of Israel. He was like a prominent man who dwelt in a certain country, and the people of that country depended upon him and said that if a drought should come he could supply the whole country with food for ten years. When a drought came, however, his maidservant went out and stood in the marketplace with her basket in her hand. And the people of the country said, "This is the man upon whom we depended that if a drought should come he would supply our wants for ten years, and here his maidservant stands in the marketplace with her basket in her hand!" So with Elimelech! He was one of the notables of his place and one of the leaders of his generation. But when the famine came he said, "Now all Israel will come knocking at my door [for help], each one with his basket." He therefore arose and fled before them. This is the meaning of the verse, "And a certain man of Bethlehem in Judah went…"[11]

Even though it is legitimate to flee the country in famine, Elimelech bears responsibility for the social effect of abandoning his city. As a leader, a wealthy man, a *parnas* [lit. a feeder], he is the focus of economic expectations; when famine comes and his servant is found begging for bread in the market, this action deals a blow to morale in Bethlehem. An unwritten contract has been betrayed; his power in the community had been based on a implicit network of social expectations.

The midrash emphasizes the inner world of the community, the narrative it has created around its feeder-leader. Beyond any specific law that might have prevented him from fleeing the country, his place in the "conversational fabric" of Bethlehem makes its own moral demand. Indeed, he flees not at the prompting of hunger, but in a kind of nervous recoil: he speaks of being besieged at every aperture by hands grasping begging bowls – What will remain of him? He flees, that is, in apprehensive fantasy of depletion, of loss of selfhood. To be a feeder means power; but it also raises the specter of the self consumed by the needs of others. In face of this dilemma, Elimelech abandons his position in his social world.

Nurturing life, maintaining vital connections with others, fulfilling needs – this is the world of *gomlei chasadim*, of "those who do deeds of kindness." In fleeing, Elimelech removes not only his food resources but his role in the "plausibility structure" of his world. Essentially, he fails as a *father*: the death of his sons testifies to this larger failure.

☙ NOMOS AND NARRATIVE

In his important essay, "Nomos and Narrative," Robert Cover writes of the normative universe that is created and maintained by the interaction of law and narrative:

> We inhabit a *nomos* – a normative universe. We constantly create and maintain a world of right and wrong, of lawful and unlawful, of valid and void…. The rules and principles of justice, the formal institutions of the law, and the conventions of a social order are, indeed, important to that world; they are, however, but a small part of the normative universe that ought to claim our attention. No set of legal institutions or prescriptions exists apart from the narratives that locate it and give it meaning. For every constitution there is an epic, for each decalogue a scripture.[12]

The commitments of those who administer and live in this world determine what law means. Law may be viewed as a "bridge linking a conception of a reality to an imagined alternative – that is, as a connective between two states of affairs, both of which can be represented in their normative significance only through the devices of narrative."[13] This "alternity," is one element of a *nomos* which is a present world constituted by a system of tension between reality and vision…. Our visions hold our reality up to us as unredeemed…. But law gives a vision depth of field,

by placing one part of it in the highlight of insistent and immediate demand while casting another part in the shadow of the
millennium....[14]

Cover illustrates the tension between law and narrative by the
example of the biblical law of inheritance, by which the eldest
son receives a double portion of the family inheritance.[15] This
concept is formulated as case history: the rights of the son of the
less favored wife are pitted against those of the loved wife, already
suggesting the human complexity that law addresses. But accompanying these legal texts are many significant biblical narratives,
in which the first-born is passed over in favor of the younger son:
Cain and Abel, Ishmael and Isaac, Esau and Jacob, Joseph and his
brothers, Moses, Solomon.

Cover argues that the formal precept is not ignored; indeed,
these narratives owe their power to the fact that the rule was
normally obeyed. However, in each narrative where succession
is contested,

> there is a layer of meaning added to the event by virtue of the
> fact that the mythos of this people has associated the divine
> hand of destiny with the typology of reversal of this particu-
> lar rule.... Revelation and...prophecy are the revolutionary
> challenges to an order founded on revelation.... The bibli-
> cal narratives always retained their subversive force – the
> memory that divine destiny is not lawful.[16]

৪৪ NAOMI'S BITTERNESS

In terms of Cover's analysis, the normative world in which Ruth's
story plays out displays, from the start, symptoms of collapse. Law
no longer acts as the bridge linking reality and vision. The judge's
vision is skewed, yielding no depth of vision but mere fragmentation. Skeptical narratives are generated in this world, where the "is,"
the "ought," and the "what might be" are separated by impassable
gaps. Midrashic stories illustrate the failure to maintain a world of

meaning: stories of hypocrisy and resentment at norms that have lost their power to inspire.

One such midrashic theme describes the famine at the beginning of the narrative as a spiritual drought, a hunger for the word of God.[17] Law has been rendered problematic by the way it is embedded in narrative. The very idea of the world-builder, world-protector, the feeder, the parent, has become hollow, and with it the sense of a normative universe. An unacknowledged "hunger" pervades the world to which Naomi returns with her two Moabite daughters-in-law, Ruth and Orpah.

All three are widows, childless, the wreckage cast up after the storm. "She remained," we are twice told of Naomi – the debris of her husband's death, and then that of her sons.[18] Eviscerated of meaning, Naomi is compared in the midrash to the husk that is left over after the meal-offering goes up in smoke; after her sons die, she becomes "the husk of a husk" (*shiyarei shirayim*).[19] Inessential, connected to nothing, she returns with her daughters-in-law to Bethlehem – like the walking dead...

Naomi is absorbed in persuading the younger women to leave her, to return to their proper place – *isha beit ima*: "each woman to *her mother's house*" (1:8). "May God deal kindly with you, as you have with the dead and with me! May God grant that each of you finds security in the *house of a husband!*" Either within the mother's world or within the husband's, a woman finds her home. Even the Hebrew word-play, *isha beit isha* – lit. "each woman the house of her man" – conveys the mirroring of identity that is to be sought. In this way, the hunger that these Moabite women bring with them may be appeased.

For their sakes, Naomi works to detach them from her. Speaking with affectionate gratitude, she calls them *B'nottai* – "My daughters...." But in the same breath, tenderly, imperatively, she presses them: *Shovna b'nottai* – "Go back, my daughters!" Even as they link their destiny with hers: *ki ittach nashuv* – "No, we will return with you" – she insists on the empirical meaning of "return:"

for them, this refers to Moab; for her, to Bethlehem. Three times she urges them, *Shovna*, pathos mounting as she demonstrates the absurdity of their journey.

At this point Naomi's speech becomes charged with complex meaning: "It is very bitter to me because of you" (1:13). Her passion to send them back to Moab is, on one level, concern for their future, for their sterile prospects if they attach themselves to one so wounded by fate. At the same time, however, she tells of her bitterness, which is *because* of them: these Moabite marriages have undone her sons, and the presence of these forbidden wives in her future life in Bethlehem would be a constant irritant and reminder of her losses. Naomi thus is driven by a real desire to rid herself of these clinging foreigners. She refuses their love, kissing them goodbye even as they weep, until Orpah returns her kisses, yielding to Naomi's bitter desire.

Naomi's bitterness is the main burden of her response to the women of Bethlehem. She repudiates her own name; she has outlived its meaning. ("Don't call me Naomi [sweetness]. Call me Mara, for God has made my lot very bitter" [1:20].) Unrecognizable now as the wealthy patroness of an ordered world, she addresses those who had been abandoned by her family, telling them about her own inner world, grown rank and sterile. God is the agent of her bitterness. The taste in the mouth conveys an intimate experience, which comes from God. For if He is the God of justice, and the world is a world of law, her suffering must be a sign of guilt. "God has afflicted me" (*anah bi*), she declares (1:21); but also, "God has *testified* against me."[20] This alternative translation is offered by Rashi and Ibn Ezra: Naomi declares that her sufferings proclaim her failure; the bitterness of her fate becomes a source of humiliation.

Here Naomi speaks like Job, justifying God and reproaching Him. Ibn Ezra in fact refers to Job's use of a similar metaphor of suffering as testimony to guilt. "You renew Your witnesses against me" (10:17). But in Job's speech, we can clearly hear the complexity of his feeling:

If I am wicked, woe is me; and if I am righteous, yet I will not lift up my head, for I am filled with disgrace, and I see my affliction;

If my head is lifted up proudly, you hunt me like a lion; and again work wonders against me:

You renew Your witnesses against me, and increase Your indignation against me; You bring fresh armies against me. (10:15–17)

Job's state of mind, like Naomi's, is one of bitterness: "I will speak in the bitterness of my soul" (10:1). Baffled by God's vindictiveness, Job wishes both to justify it and to reaffirm his innocence. Desiring a meaningful world, he searches for the law he has transgressed, but he can never quite convince himself that this accounting is true. Naomi similarly brings God into her narrative, as both rationale and enigma. If she is implicated in her husband's guilt, her sin is that she betrayed the expectations of her world, and her punishment that she is left empty, isolated: "I went away full, and God has brought me back empty" (1:21). But if she is not to be held responsible for her husband's dereliction – if, that is, her status as a woman exonerates her from blame for his decisions – then she is wrecked indeed: of husband, children, and a meaningful world.

Throughout her Job-like speech, Naomi ignores Ruth's silent presence – as, indeed, do the townspeople, the women of Bethlehem. Ruth's attachment does not at all, it seems, mitigate Naomi's emptiness. Nothing in her resonates to Ruth's equally passionate speech of devotion ("Where you go, I will go…"). Fiercely dedicated to her rhetoric of bitterness, Naomi had responded to Ruth's passion with silence: "And when Naomi saw that she was determined to go with her, she ceased speaking to her" (1:18). Out of that silence came her testament of bitterness and utter loneliness. And now Ruth stands silent and unnoticed, her loving words fallen on deaf ears. At this point in the narrative, Naomi allows Ruth to accompany her, but her silence becomes an attack on Ruth's consoling presence.

In a well-known anecdote, Freud describes his infant grandson playing with a reel and string, throwing it into the crib and pulling it back, at the same time uttering sounds that Freud interpreted as *Fort! – Da!*: "Gone! – Here!" In play, the child is enacting his mother's absence, repeatedly staging her disappearance and return.[21] Jonathan Lear comments that "the game is prompted by a rip in the fabric of life…. The outcome of the game is to convert what would otherwise be a nameless trauma into a loss."[22]

"In being able to get to '*da*,' the child is able to bring his experience together." The game "creates a cultural space in which the child can play with loss: in this way he comes to be able to tolerate it and name it…it is only now that the mind can wander around the idea of mother's absence…. Inventing the game, the child thereby creates the capacity *to think* about mother's absence…. This is courage-in-the-making…."[23]

If, however, the child could never get to "*Da*," if he kept endlessly repeating "*Fort!*" he "would never be able to get a thought together…. Rather than face his own loss, the child might opt to attack his own ability to understand what had happened to him."[24]

Naomi, I suggest, is engaged in such an attack on her own capacity for making meaning. Imaginative activity might link loss with recovery. Instead, Naomi's rhetoric isolates her in bitterness. For her, hope can mean only a grotesque scenario of the aged body giving birth to infant husbands for aging wives (1:11–13).

৪৪ THE PARADOX OF RUTH

The ironic aspect of this situation is that her one resource, that might have motivated her to hope, is Ruth – who is invisible, inaudible, and banned by law from entering the community of God. Because she is a Moabite, Ruth is excluded from Naomi's world. This is the law, and its reason is clear: "because they did not come out to greet you with bread and water on your journey after you left Egypt…" (Deut. 23:5).

The Moabite stigma originates in a historical failure of *chesed*, of connectivity, of acknowledgment of the other's need.[25] The Moabites are not feeders, maintainers of the world. But in this narrative, as we have seen, it is precisely the Judean world that has failed to sustain the social networks, the conversational fabrics that keep faith alive. And it is Ruth the Moabite who has offered to be a link between past and future, a possible resource of meaning in Naomi's destitute condition.

Here, then, is the problem constituted by Ruth. Her situation is sharply defined by law: she can never find her place within the community of God. But, as every reader has always known, the *Book of Ruth* will conclude in the way legislated by history: Ruth will marry Boaz, and their child will be grandfather to King David. In a sense, then, all the delays in the narrative, the episodes drawn out over a summer, the outrageous move that sends Ruth, dressed and scented, to the granary floor and to Boaz's feet on a harvest night – all contain a hidden necessity: the ending is legislated in advance.

✣ NARRATIVE AND ITS DISCONTENTS

"*Une chose*," says Sartre, "*commence pour finir.*"[26] Since everyone – writer and readers – knows that Ruth must marry Boaz, what is holding the narrative back? What, in fact, allows there to be a narrative at all? What makes this piece of history narratable? The answer is related to Ruth's identity, to the problem that she poses to the *nomos*, the normative world of law and story that, even before she arrived, had already been in palpable crisis.

Problems, crisis, conflict, instability – these are the very substance of narrative. Ruth constitutes the possibility of narrative, as well as the necessity of closure. But narrative is often radically at odds with the utopian state of closure. This central tension in the traditional novel, for instance, is the subject of D. A. Miller's *Narrative and Its Discontents*. Miller argues that "closure" and "narratability" are essentially in conflict. If the *ending* of a Jane Austen novel, for instance, yields "a state of absolute propriety: proper understanding expressed in proper erotic objects and proper social arrangements," her *narratives* are "generated precisely by an underlying instability of desire, language, and society, and, as such, they are inevitably felt to threaten the very possibility of this definitive, 'finalizing' state of affairs."[27]

Such a fiction, then, is a "perverse" project, since it longs to eliminate the narratable: it "is a quest after that which will end questing; or a distortion of what will be made straight..." Since "only insufficiencies, defaults, deferrals, can be 'told,'" the very idea of a narrative of happiness is put in question.[28] For to bring the narrative to a state of fulfillment is virtually to end it. Miller argues, therefore, that narratives are never fully or finally governed by their endings.[29] There is an ongoing tension between the two states:

> [O]ne might say that the traditional novelist gives play to his discontent only to assuage it in the end, much as the child in Freud makes his toy temporarily disappear the better to enjoy its reinstated presence.... [It] would therefore work on the principle of vaccination; incorporating the narratable in safe doses to prevent it from breaking out.
>
> If the novel attempts to master the narratable, it rarely succeeds. Even in Freud, the "anxiety of disappearance is intrinsically stronger than the gratification of return, for the former is not merely a moment in the game, it is the underlying inspiration of the game itself."[30]

In the book of Ruth, the narratable dimension is generated by Ruth herself, by the problem, the instability that she constitutes for the normative world that she enters. The resulting turbulence in some sense survives even the fulfillment, legislated in advance, of the ending. Simply by being Ruth, she raises questions and disrupts norms. She represents the "quest after that which will end questing," the "distortion of what will be made straight."

The "distortion of what will be made straight" embedded in Miller's rhetoric refers to the verse from Ecclesiastes which inaugurates the following midrash:

It is said, "That which is crooked cannot be made straight; and that which is wanting cannot be counted" (Eccles. 1:15). In this world, he who is crooked can be made straight, and he who is straight can become crooked; but in the hereafter he who is crooked cannot be made straight, nor can he who is straight become crooked. "And that which is wanting cannot be numbered." Consider two wicked men who associated with one another in this world. One of them repented of his evil deeds before his death while the other did not, with the result that the former stands in the company of the righteous while his fellow stands in the company of the wicked. Seeing him there, he says, "Woe is me, is there favoritism here? We both of us committed robberies, we both of us committed murders together, yet he stands in the company of the righteous and I in the company of the wicked!" And they [the angels] reply to him and say, "You fool! You were despicable after your death and lay for three days, and did not they drag you to your grave with ropes? 'The maggot is spread under you, and the worms cover you' (Isa. 14:11). But your old acquaintance understood and repented of his evil ways, while you too had the opportunity to repent but you did not take it."

He immediately replied, "Let me go and repent!" And they answer him, "You fool! Do you not know that this world is like the Sabbath and the world from which you have come is like the eve of the Sabbath? If a man does not prepare his meal on the eve of the Sabbath, what shall he eat on the Sabbath? And do you not know also that this world is like the sea, and the world from which you have come is like the dry land? If a man does not prepare his food on the dry land, what shall he eat at sea? And do you not know also that this world is like the wilderness and the world from which you have come is like cultivated land? If a man does not prepare his food on cultivated land, what shall he eat in the wilderness?"[31]

The verse from Ecclesiastes becomes a description of *Olam HaBa*, of the world-to-come. There, the distorted can never be made straight. Herein lies a bittersweet paradox: our present world is the world for *teshuva*, for repentance, while, in the world-to-come, character and destiny are determined on arrival. The case of the two sinners, whose ways part so dramatically in the hereafter, stages the classic idea: repentance, transformation is possible in this world only. Our hero is slow to comprehend this radical difference between worlds: he can no longer transform himself and his fate. The world he came from was the place and time for making the crooked straight. Three classic images conclude the Midrash: the Sabbath, the sea, the wilderness – all must have food prepared in advance if one is to eat there. Or rather – from the perspective of the world-to-come, where the sinner now finds himself – if you want to eat *here*, you had to prepare *there*.

This Midrash draws its narrative power from its shifted perspective. A classic notion about the relation between worlds looks different from the viewpoint of the hereafter. The world-to-come represents to the human being in this world a consummation devoutly to be wished, a prospect of clarity and fulfillment after the turbulence of this world. But it turns out that there is a sting in the sweetness. A melancholy limitation invests the hereafter: nothing there can change.

In Miller's terms, this world is the world of narrative, while the hereafter represents closure. Once instability and error have been resolved, one may find oneself at sea, or in a wilderness, or in the quiescence which is the Sabbath, without access to the "food" which can be prepared only in the energy of narrative. Narrative and closure are incongruous worlds; but they yearn for each other. In the world of narrative, ultimate meanings are veiled; desires and fears, multiple possibilities, suspense, insufficiency keep the story going. But when the end comes, nothing further can develop; all is arrested in the condition to which its turbulent history has brought it.

✄ THE RIGORS OF NARRATIVE

From this midrashic perspective, Ruth and Orpah represent these two modalities. Ruth has the capacity to generate a story. Precisely because of her vulnerability, her "outsider" status, as well as her mysterious desire to find her way in, she sets episodes in motion. Lacking everything, she makes a decision to leave behind her the stability of family, nation, and religion and to embark on a *narrative*: on a course that offers no visible fulfillment. Orpah starts out with her but soon yields to the blandishments of closure: "Return," Naomi urges, "*isha beit isha* – each woman (*isha*) to the home of her man (*isha*)" (1:9). The play on words enacts closure, fulfillment. Orpah chooses the resolution that will liquidate a senseless journey.

But Ruth knowingly declares her commitment to a future that can bear no imaginable fruit. To Naomi's plea that she *go after* her sister-in-law, she responds, "Do not urge me to leave you, to turn back and not *go after* you. For wherever you go, I will go; wherever you lodge, I will lodge; your people shall be my people, and your God my God. Where you die, I will die, and there I will be buried. Thus and more may God do to me if anything but death parts me from you" (1:16–17).

Her famous speech holds no hint of fantasy, of utopian closure. Her desire is to go with Naomi – or rather, to *go after* her – and to be with her unto death and burial. The dynamic of the moment is stark: urged to follow Orpah's lucid journey to womanly fulfillment, she redescribes this choice as a movement away from the essential magnetic connection to Naomi. *Going after* Naomi evokes an entranced state, an attachment blind to rational interest. "I remember for you the devotion of your youth, your love as a bride – how you went after Me in the wilderness, in a land not sown" (Jer. 2:2). Like the children who follow the Pied Piper into the mountain, she knows only the life she senses in this connection. This is the future she chooses, soberly, undeluded; it leads to the only plausible consummation: death, burial. She has no argument with Naomi's grim realism about the possibility of a conventional happy ending. Marriage and children do not figure in her expectations. Instead she commits herself to the unmitigated rigors of her desire. Naomi is the essential clue in her labyrinth: for Ruth, she opens up a vista of movement and rest, of nation and God.

Orpah acts out the classic consummation of narrative: tearfully, she kisses her mother-in-law farewell, and goes toward her foreseeable ending. Ruth, on the other hand, *clings* to Naomi (*davka bah*). To cling is to affirm the passionate desire that constitutes its own gratification. It is to refuse to flee the rigors of narrative. The word *davak* is most resonantly used of erotic and of mystic connections: "Therefore, a man shall leave his father and mother and cling to his wife, so that they become one flesh" (Gen. 2:24). "And you who cling to God your God are all alive today" (Deut. 4:4). Implicitly, to cling is to move away from the given relationships of childhood, to desire a life beyond infantile fantasy.[32] At the same time, it evokes a risky persistence, a courage of desire that bears one through the drifts of the narratable. Ironically, this courage is subject to ambiguous judgments: it can be viewed as a clinging *to* infantile fantasy.

The tactile imagery of *devekut* (clinging, stickiness) accompanies Ruth throughout her narrative. She holds fast to Naomi, whose emptiness, as we have seen, is at first unappeased by her. Ignored by the women of Bethlehem, Ruth then proposes to find a field in which to glean – "following someone in whose eyes I may find favor." She is casting herself into the drift of chance and desire. In this world of narrative, the traveler has no guarantee of finding safe harbor. With unusual pungency, the narrative declares, *va-yiker mikreha* – "*as luck would have it* – it was the land belonging to Boaz, who was of Elimelech's family" (2:3). Unwittingly, she has fallen upon her destiny; her trajectory now holds out hope of a real "return" to Naomi's family. But, from Ruth's perspective, she is *taking her chances* (lit., "her chance chanced it").

The coincidence that brings her to Boaz's field is of the kind that, retrospectively, can be read as an accident that was meant to happen. But Ruth has no knowledge of the ending of her story. In the drift of contingency, she enters a field; unknown to her, Boaz asks his servant about her: "Whose is this young woman?" And the servant answers: "She is the Moabite woman, who returned with Naomi from the fields of Moab" (2:5–6).

The reader is caught in the subtle anguish of narrative. Ruth is being maligned: twice in one sentence, the servant has managed to refer to her Moabite origin – and this, after the narrator has reintroduced her at the beginning of the chapter as Ruth *the Moabite*. All the hopelessness of her situation is here, insult added to injury. What is the servant implying as he harps on her background?

> "Whose is this young woman?" Did he not then recognize her? But when he saw how attractive she was, and how modest her comportment, he began to inquire about her. All the other women bend down to gather the ears of corn, but she sits and gathers; all the other women hitch up their skirts, and she keeps hers down; all the other women jest with the reapers, while she is reserved; all the other women gather from between the sheaves, while she gathers from that which is already abandoned.
>
> In the same way one must understand the verse, "And when Saul saw David go forth against the Philistine, he said to Avner.... 'Whose son is this youth?'" (1 Sam. 17:55). Did he not then recognize him? But yesterday he sent to Jesse saying, "Let David, I pray you, stand before me: for he has found favor in my sight" (16:22); and now he inquires about him. But when Saul saw the head of the Philistine (Goliath),

he began to ask about David, "Is he a descendant of Perez, a king? Is he a descendant of Zerah, a judge?"

And Doeg the Edomite was present at that time, and he said to him, "Even if he is a descendant of Perez, is he not of impure descent? Is he not a descendant of Ruth the Moabitess?" Avner said to him, "But has the law not been revised: *Ammonite but not Ammonitess, Moabite but not Moabitess?*" He answered him: "But if so, we could also say *Edomite but not Edomitess, Egyptian men but not Egyptian women.* Why were the men repudiated? Was it not 'because they did not meet you with bread and water?' (Deut. 23:5). The women ought to have met the women!" And for the moment, Avner forgot the law.

Saul said to him, "Go and inquire about that law which you have forgotten from Samuel and his court." When he came to Samuel and his court, he said: "Where did this come from? Not from Doeg? Doeg is a heretic and will not leave this world in peace! And yet I cannot let you go without an answer: 'All glorious is the king's daughter within the palace' (Psalms 45:14). It is not for a woman to go out and bring food [to foreign armies], but only for a man. 'And because they hired Balaam against you' (Deut. 17:5) – A man hires, but not a woman.'"

And the servant who was in charge of the reapers answered and said, "'It is a Moabite woman' (2:6) – and yet you say that her conduct is praiseworthy and modest? Her mother-in-law has taught her well!"[33]

The midrash finely inflects the dialogue. Why did Boaz ask about Ruth? Surely he knew of her? Soon after, in fact, he will tell her of her admirable reputation for *chesed*, lovingkindness. His question, however, is "*Whose is she?*" meaning that he is impressed by her bearing, her modesty, and her intelligence, and implying: "Could she be mine? Could she belong to my world?" Generations later, the same question will be asked by Saul about David, implicitly about his potential for positions of power. Immediately David will be disparaged by Doeg, on the grounds of his impure descent from Ruth the Moabitess. A debate breaks out: on a closer look at the biblical text, it has become clear that only the male Moabite is banned from the community of God, not the female. The law has been revised, since this gender distinction makes room for Ruth to marry Boaz. But is this not a mere verbal quibble, which could be extended *ad absurdum* to all such marital bans? No, declares Samuel; here the issue of greeting and feeding strangers would exempt women on the ground of modesty; the cultural codes of the time would make that obvious.

On Samuel's view, the biblical text always contained this nuanced gender distinction which might have been interpreted at any time. The fact remains that this interpretation was never made until Ruth came on the scene; she is the first Moabite woman to benefit from the change in the law.[34] It is striking, too, that in the time of David the issue is still controversial, so that the malicious counselor, Doeg, can still cast aspersions on David's ancestry, while even the honest counselor, Avner, forgets the law. The question has to be taken to Samuel as the final court of appeal. He determines the gender functions in such a way as to make the new reading unassailable. But the midrash concludes by returning to Boaz and the servant in the field. His disparaging answer directly addresses Boaz's admiration of Ruth: she has merely benefited from good coaching [lit. healing] by Naomi. In other words, once a Moabite, always a Moabite.

The midrash dramatizes the hostility of the social world that Ruth is trying to penetrate. The premise, both now and in the future, in the story of David, is that the law has been changed: otherwise, how could Boaz marry her? But the change has just happened, and society retains its sense of a normative world that excludes Moabites. Such classifications of inside/outside are hard to shift. One hears in the tone of the servant in the field, as well as of Doeg, generations later, a malicious satisfaction in ruling the other out. In Doeg's case, he himself is then paradoxically *ruled out* from the world ("He is a heretic and will not leave this world in peace") precisely because of his rigidity. Revisions in the law constitute its organic life. But Ruth will nevertheless remain suspect; the taint of her ancestry will remain troubling in the narratives, if not in the law books, of her new people.

Moreover, the fact that the law is changed just as Ruth meets Boaz suggests that it is Ruth's presence that has made this change necessary. The servant's grudging answer defines her as merely *well coached*. But clearly it is her distinction that rouses Boaz's interest; in combination with her taboo status, it constitutes her as an irresoluble question. *Whose* is she? Her nation is under the stigma of lacking *chesed*, the instinct to nurture the vulnerable other. But this national character is not reflected in Ruth's bearing, which is charged with *chesed*. To what world, then, does she belong?

The law will make space for her inside the world of Judea. Boaz will beautifully describe her to her face in terms that evoke the epic heroes of his world.[35] Law and narrative both include her – and yet, poignantly, she remains an outsider, foreign in the eyes of others as well as in her own eyes.

৪৪ POWERS OF HORROR

One specific dimension of her reviled status is the sexual notoriety of Moabite women. *Zenut*, sexual seduction, sexual waywardness, has marked the Moabite story from its origins. We remember how, after the destruction of Sodom, Lot's daughters made their father drunk and had sexual relations with him.[36] But it was the daughter who inscribed the incest into her son's name (Moav = *Me'avi* [from my father]) who exposed the act of darkness to the light. Later it was the women of Moab who enticed Israel into the sin of Baal-peor (Num. 25:1).

This association of Moab, and particularly of its women, with lasciviousness accompanies Ruth throughout her dealings with the world of Bethlehem. She becomes the embodiment of what

Julia Kristeva calls *the abject*: that which is *cast out* of the self and considered loathsome:

> The abject confronts us, on the one hand, with those frag-ile states where man strays on the territory of *animal*. Thus by way of abjection, primitive societies have marked out a precise area of their culture in order to remove it from the threatening world of animals and animalism, which were imagined as representatives of sex and murder.
>
> The abject confronts us, on the other hand, and this time within our personal archeology, with our earliest attempts to release the hold of maternal entity even before existing out-side of her, thanks to the autonomy of language.[37]

Both being upheld by taboos and remaining a focus of fascination, the abject rouses fear of the loss of boundaries.

Ruth's transactions with Boaz can be read as marked by such an ambiguity. After the servant has answered Boaz's question and Boaz has kindly opened up the field for her gleaning, her first speech transforms her from an object discussed by others into a linguistic being, neither animal nor the mother of early, prever-bal life:

> And she fell upon her face and bowed down to the ground and she said to him, "Why have I found favor in your eyes to recognize me, though I am a stranger." (2:10)

In addressing him, she in a sense responds to his question: "Do you not hear me, my daughter?" (2:8). Something unresponsive in her moves him to ask, *Do you hear? Do you understand my lan-guage?* But strikingly her answer questions the very possibility of his *recognition* of her. The Gaon comments:

> Falling on her face expresses a certain dejection. Ruth sees that Boaz has spoken kindly to her, as though he means to

marry her, and yet he adds, "So shall you cling to my servant – girls," classing her with his servants and making no further move of courtship. Nevertheless, she bows down in gratitude for his kind words, and she says, "Why have I found favor in your eyes to recognize me, to single me out, as though you will know me as a wife?" But again, "I am a stranger" – it is clear from your last words that I am a foreigner. I don't understand your meaning!

On this reading, Ruth is acutely sensitive to the ambivalence that Boaz displays toward her. The law may have been changed, but Ruth is depressingly conscious of the residues of the old boundaries: Boaz is blowing hot and cold. What might have been a moment of closure remains tantalizingly ambiguous – and keeps the narrative going in all its danger and possibility.

And yet, even as closure eludes her, Ruth speaks with a certain lucid pleasure in the sheer paradox of the moment. She plays with language: "Why have you acted as though you *know* me [*l'hakireini*], as though I were recognizable to you, when I am a *stranger* [*nochriya*]?" To be known *as the other*, this too is recognition. Perhaps Ruth senses the hopefulness in being known in her very difference? Perhaps her foreignness can even become a gift that she can offer Boaz? As Edmond Jabes suggests, "The foreigner allows you to be yourself by making a foreigner of you."

At any rate, the Gaon indicates a certain confidence in Ruth's tone, as she responds again to Boaz's second, and even more kindly speech: "And she said, 'May I find favor in your eyes, my lord, for you have consoled me and you have spoken gently to your maidservant – *though I am not so much as one of your maidservants*" (2:13). Between this usual reading and the Gaon's ["*I shall not be like one of your maidservants*"], the complexity of Ruth appears: modest and assertive, dejected but hopeful.

This complexity is her response to the ambivalence of Boaz and his world toward her. At the same time, we can say that it is precisely this complexity that arouses hostility and suspicion in a solidly demarcated world. As one who *clings* – serially, to Naomi, to the servants in the field, to Boaz during the night on the granary floor – Ruth is perceived as disturbingly anomalous.

In a classic essay, Sartre writes of the *viscosity*, stickiness, neither solid nor liquid, which is among our primary experiences. Mary Douglas amplifies Sartre's notion to discuss cultural categories and their relation to anomalies. She engages with the threatening quality of the viscous as "aberrant fluid or…melting solid":

> Its stickiness is a trap, it clings like a leech; it attacks the boundary between myself and it. Long columns falling off my fingers suggest my own substance flowing into the pool of stickiness…. In this way the first contact with stickiness enriches a child's experience. He has learnt something about himself and the properties of matter and the interrelation between self and other things…. It makes the point that we can and do reflect with profit on our main classifications and on experiences which do not exactly fit them…. So from these earliest tactile adventures we have always known that life does not conform to our most simple categories.[38]

The public character of a culture makes its categories more rigid, so that the anomalies that inevitably occur must generate new interpretations to reduce the threat to its definitions of reality.

In her *stickiness* – her persistent desire, her bold modesty – Ruth poses a disconcerting challenge to the world of Bethlehem. On the one hand, she is obedient, malleable: according to the midrash, she is submissive to all the legal stringencies with which Naomi tries to deter her. Even her great speech of devotion is read in this way, as a point-by-point response to the difficult demands of the law: Naomi warns her, "It is forbidden for us to go beyond the Shabbat boundary," and Ruth answers, "*Where* you go, I will go."[39] She accepts the boundaries of law, in its 613 forms: she will not visit theaters and circuses; she will not sleep in a house without a *mezuza*; she acknowledges the sanctions for serious crimes – four types of executions and two types of ignominious burial. All these limitations she accepts.

On the other hand, her very existence challenges the imaginative boundaries that have defined the world she desires to penetrate. Moreover, in her poetic declaration of love for what she senses in and through Naomi, she has the courage to "play" with the imaginings of death, destruction, and loss. She not only *clings*: she *reflects* on *devekut* (the clinging posture), on the ways that language creates boundaries and dissolves them. Naomi acknowledges Ruth's capacity to play, but only, at first, by "ceasing to speak to her" – that is, she yields to Ruth's wish not to be separated from her, but she yields without any corresponding wish of her own.

Boaz acknowledges Ruth's spiritual parentage: like Abraham, she has left her father and mother in her quest for an unknown alternative.[40] She belongs to the world of Abraham, which for her is represented by Naomi. As a *mother*, however, Naomi is far from incarnating the soft mother of infancy. Her words create her as separate, distinct, not the loving mother of primal desire, but the mother whom Christopher Bollas describes as a *process of transformation*. From the mother who constantly alters the infant's environment to meet her needs, the child is born into her own emerging capacities to transform the world – to handle and differentiate objects, to speak their distinctness. This transformational impact of the mother in early life is carried over into adulthood, when there will appear "the object that is pursued in order to surrender to it as a medium that alters the self."[41] The Ruth who is able to articulate her experience, to play in the potential space between desire and reality, is also the Ruth who seeks *devekut*, the transformative moment of uncanny fusion.[42]

It is at the hands of a somewhat austere mother, then, that Ruth seeks out her own transformation. Confronting the image of her own abjectness, she persists in her desire for the *devekut*, the unthinkable intimacy that is its other face. Treading a fine line, she assumes the risks of narrative: clinging to Naomi, seeking out someone in whose eyes she will find favor, even twining herself round Boaz's feet on the granary floor. Haunted by racial stereotypes both of sexual license and of emotional stinginess, she neither acts them out nor violently repudiates them. If she is to find the transformation she so devoutly wishes, she must open herself to the vagaries of narrative, and to its dangerous language of becoming.

✛ THE WINGS OF THE DOVE

And her process has its palpable effect on Naomi and Boaz. Naomi at first responds to Ruth's initiative of gleaning with just two words: *L'chi bitti* – "Go, my daughter." But at the end of the day, she greets Ruth returned from the field as *her mother-in-law*, three times repeated (2:18,19). She speaks a language of blessing, that is, of wishfulness, previously unheard on her lips: "May the one who acknowledged you be blessed…. Blessed be he by God, who has not abandoned His love (*chesed*) to the living and the dead!" (2:19–20) She is now able to speak of God's love persisting through all, as falling on the living and the dead. That is, where previously she had spoken dismissively of Ruth's *chesed* "with the dead and with me" (1:8), she now defines herself and Ruth as *the living*. God's love is now a sensed reality, affecting even the traumatic past. Redundantly, she addresses Ruth as her daughter-in-law (2:20, 22), as well as her daughter (2:22). The increased vitality and warmth of Naomi's language is her tribute to Ruth's very being. Most strikingly, Ruth is once again named, both at the beginning of the chapter and at the end, as *Ruth the Moabite* (2:2, 21). Outsider still, evoking complex associations, Ruth has palpably brought Naomi to life and to a language of attachment.

The dynamic effect of Ruth's presence on Naomi is felt most clearly in Chapter 3. Here Naomi takes the initiative and plots for Ruth the nighttime encounter with Boaz that will bring her narrative to its consummation: "And Naomi her mother-in-law said to her, 'My daughter, shall I not seek for you *a resting place* that shall be good for you'" (3:1). Naomi declares the nature of her quest: an end to questing for Ruth, a full closure that will meet her desire.

The idea of *manoach*, a resting place, reminds us of Noah's dove, sent out to test the waters after the Flood: "And the dove did not find *a resting place* for the sole of its foot, so it returned to him to the ark, for there was water over all the earth" (8:8). Like the dove, Ruth seeks a place of stability in the volatile world. By now Naomi identifies sufficiently with Ruth's quest to wish it happily over.

But the dove's flight configures a question (Have the waters abated?); whether or not she returns to the ark will become the answer. Ruth's quest, too, raises an existential question, one about the possibility of fulfillment for such desires as she harbors. Naomi demonstrates how deeply she has been affected by Ruth's courage, by her stamina in the face of danger. To find consummation for Ruth – and for herself – she adopts Ruth's "narrative" mode, endangering her reputation in the most Moabite way imaginable.

She sends Ruth to the granary where Boaz lies during the night after the harvest, to uncover his feet and lie there. Ruth's preparations are to be those of a woman before a sexual encounter: washing, scenting, dressing, and secrecy. Boaz's acts are precisely foreseen: he will eat and drink and lie down–and he will tell her what to do. Ruth obediently replies, "Everything you tell me I will do"; her obedience includes obedience to Boaz's instructions. Naomi, it seems, has entered into Ruth's risk-taking mode, coaching her for a role that unnervingly resembles the role of the harlots, the *zonot*, who haunt granary floors and who are the target of prophetic anger[43] – the role for which Ruth's Moabite background has prepared her. Only by such ambiguous means, it seems, can the world of law, of normative order, be accessed.

Ruth, in fact, follows Naomi's instructions, but not their timing: first she goes down to the threshing floor and only then does she make her preparations. The Talmud notes the change: she prefers not to walk in public in her perfumed finery.[44] Another midrash adds that she fears being accosted by "one of the dogs."[45] Her own intelligence guides her to modify Naomi's instructions.[46]

Naomi thrusts Ruth into the eye of the storm, into all the turbulence of narrative. It is as though she now loves Ruth sufficiently to take risks with her. Indeed, she makes common cause with Ruth, referring to Boaz as *our kinsman*.[47] The Jerusalem Talmud indicates the depth of Naomi's identification with Ruth by noting her instructions: "Wash, perfume yourself, dress up, and go down to the granary...and lie down" (3:3): the Hebrew verbs are read in the second person but written, strangely, in the *first person*. "She told her: 'My merit shall go down there with you."[48] In other words, Ruth does not go alone: Naomi is with her as she moves into her moment of greatest narrative suspense.

In her relation with Boaz, too, Ruth displays a *chesed* quality that affects him profoundly. Here too the paradox is that the humble outsider, needy, suspect, abject, generates a movement of reciprocal recognition and gratitude in the other. The teacher is redeemed by the student, the older man is guided by the younger woman, Israel is regenerated by the woman from Moab.

Ruth is under Naomi's instructions to obey his wishes: "He will tell you what to do." But when he wakes at midnight, shuddering at the mysterious being who grips his feet, and asks, "*Who are you?*" she answers by identifying herself and, in the same breath, *giving him, too, an identity*: "I am Ruth your maidservant. Spread your robe over your maidservant, *for you are a redeemer*" (3:9). She is, in fact, proposing marriage to him.[49] In a sense, too, she is answering his question to the servant in the field: "*Whose is this woman?*" She is his, she tells him, soliciting his care, protection, warmth, sexual intimacy, his concrete representation of the "wings[50] of the Lord God of Israel." He himself had described her as seeking refuge beneath those wings (2:12). Bringing his rhetoric in the field into intimate focus, she makes him the very emissary of the Lord God of Israel.

In soliciting him in this way, however, she is also expressing her solicitude for him: she is giving him an opportunity to be a redeemer. By redeeming Naomi's estate, in the legal sense, and by becoming Ruth's metaphorical redeemer – by taking her under his wing – Boaz will find his own redemption.[51] She has given him a place in her narrative, which, it will transpire, is to become *the* narrative. Through his connection with her, he will endow Elimelech's family with a future. And as this connection takes form in her words, he is affected by the *chesed*, the beauty that her words create. He responds with strange gratitude: "Blessed are you of God, my daughter! Your latest deed of *chesed* is finer than the first, in that you have not gone after young men, whether poor or rich." (3:10)

He addresses her as a source of blessing, and of *chesed*, precisely in her relation with him. He had woken, shuddering at the mysterious pressure at his feet; at first he had not identified her as a woman – perhaps she was a demon embodied from his dream.[52] His initial terror modulates into acknowledgment of the loving energy that emanates from her. In soliciting his redemption, she has drawn out of him, with gentle force, a possibility of larger life. Demonic, uncanny, speaking with numinous authority, she regenerates both herself and him.

Chesed intimates, among other translations, love, kindness, devotion, courage, and *beauty*. The grace, the favor (*chen*) that she characteristically hopes to find in the eyes of others is the twin of *chesed*: a beauty of being and of language.[53]

In the potential space created by their words, they sleep until dawn. She rises before the light, "so that none may know that the woman came to the granary." And the next day Boaz brings the work of narrative to its conclusion. What has been acknowledged in the darkness is publicly ratified in the daylight, at the gate of the city. Here, it turns out, the other redeemer, Mr. X, is willing to undertake the legal redemption of Naomi's estate – but not the metaphorical redemption of Ruth. His reason is clear: "... lest I destroy my own estate." (4:6) Ruth would bring confusion, anomaly to his condition. In economic terms, he would be investing his own resources in a son who would legally be regarded as Machlon's. A banal and immediate "happy ending" to his narrative is endangered by Ruth's ambiguity, by her neediness, her viscosity.

So Boaz consummates the narrative: by legal transaction before witnesses, he claims both land and woman, assuming responsibility, allowing intimacy, freeing all three from limbo.

Ruth, meanwhile, returns unseen in the dark to her mother-in-law, who asks her, "*Who are you*, my daughter?" What quality in Ruth leads both Naomi and Boaz to ask this question? Boaz, of course, asked it in a midnight daze, between sleep and waking. Naomi knows her as "my daughter." And yet, for both, Ruth retains to the end an *unknown* quality. Something in her remains strange. In both cases, she has an answer. We have seen how deeply Boaz is affected by the authority of her words. For Naomi, Ruth produces the barley that Boaz has given her in token of promised plenitude. The dove has found a resting place in the midst of many waters. But both answers only partially eliminate the force of the question. There is a residue of inscrutable *chesed*, of sheer unknownness, in the woman whose impact they both know.

✥ IF BOAZ HAD KNOWN…

The end of the story is, of course, triumphant. It is also public knowledge, an ending legislated in advance. A baby is born of the marriage of Boaz and Ruth, whose genealogy is then doubly traced: he is grandfather to David, and descendant, generation by generation, of Perez, son of Judah. The roll call of generations from Perez leads to Boaz and continues onward to David. This is closure in its most utopic, definitive form: a list of male names, quasi-mythical, making for full and final meaning.

But what are we to make of the relation between this ending and the narrative that has come before? The midrash raises an uncanny question:

> "And he reached her parched corn, and she ate and was satisfied and had some left over." (Ruth 2:14) R. Isaac ben Marion said: This verse can teach that if a person is going to perform a good deed, he should do it with all his heart. For had Reuben known that Scripture would record of him, "And Reuben

heard it, and saved him from their hand" (Gen. 37:21), he would have borne Joseph on his shoulder to his father. And had Aaron known that Scripture would record of him, "And also, behold, he comes forth to you" (Exod. 4:14), he would have gone forth to meet him with timbrels and dances. And had Boaz known that Scripture would record of him, "And he reached her parched corn, and she ate and was satisfied and had some left over" (Ruth 2:14), he would have fed her fatted calves.

R. Cohen and R. Joshua of Siknin said in the name of R. Levi: In the past, when a person performed a good deed, the prophet placed it on record; but nowadays when a person performs a good deed, who records it? Elijah records it and the Messiah and the Holy One, blessed be He, add their seal to it. This is the meaning of the verse, "Then they who feared God spoke with one another; and God listened, and heard, and a book of remembrance was written before Him." (Malachi 3:16)[54]

If Boaz had known how his narrative would be written, he would have acted with greater panache – less equivocally, less hesitantly. Instead of a pinch of parched corn, he would have fed Ruth fatted calves! In the light of retrospective knowledge – that is, of full and final versions – how much better would we play our roles! If we knew the camera was focused on us, we would acknowledge one another with drums and dancing. The midrash seems to be advocating a kind of imaginative awareness that will intensify the good deed – *as if* we knew the final record.

However, in using the rhetoric of "If Boaz had known…," the midrash paradoxically stages the unbridgeable gap that must exist between act and record, between narrative and closure. In the conditions of this world, the world of narrative, human beings struggle, ignorant on many levels, to act well, to "perform good deeds." The deeds of *chesed* in this world are often hesitant, partial, expressing the instability, complexity, insufficiency of narrative.

Moreover, if Boaz had known how his story would be recorded, his act of kindness to Ruth might have been more fulsome, but it would have lost its human force, which was born precisely of the tensions of the situation that Ruth has precipitated. The fraught moment of his gift, the pinch of parched corn, if recorded on camera, would need an inspired director to communicate its mute expressiveness. The narrator of the Book of Ruth achieves just this in quietly observing, "And she ate and she was satisfied" – she was well satisfied by his gift. A pinch of corn has become an epiphany within this narrative world.

Narrative and closure constitute incompatible worlds. It is in the nature of narrative to be plagued by ignorance, oscillations, misunderstanding. Within these risky parameters, Ruth expresses, passionately but incompletely, her desire. Without knowing how the text will inscribe her, she clings, seeking that uncanny fusion, the *devekut* that her words can only intimate.

In fact, the midrash goes on to speak of the "nowadays" reality as one of pure narrative: when one does a good deed, who records it? In the past, the prophet was at hand to record such deeds; the gap between narrative and closure was narrowed, the prophet effecting almost simultaneous translation, so that full and final meanings were to some extent, even in this world, to be understood. But now such record is a matter of faith: Elijah, the Messiah, God Himself ensure that the significant moments of narrative are written, their meanings elucidated. But that writing happens in some other world. Here, now, Ruth must speak her desire without hearing its ultimate resonance.

The midrash ends with a verse from Malachi, the last prophet: "Then they that feared God spoke[55] with one another; and God listened, and heard, and a book of remembrance was written before Him." The conversation of the righteous is heard and recorded by God. In Radak's reading, the prophet is recording a contest of conversations: the disbelievers speak to one another, questioning God's appeals to them to consider their ways ("It is useless to serve God..." [3:14]); in response, "those who feared God and esteemed His name" maintain a conversation of faith. The constructive conversation is thus doubly recorded – by the prophet and, in his account, by God too.

After the prophetic period, however, the existence of such a divine record becomes a matter of faith. We remain essentially uncorroborated in this world, with our various social networks, normative worlds, conversational fabrics. Although the midrash maintains that all is ultimately on record – signed by God – in this world we have no access to the divine text. Those who belong to the society of believers sustain their world of belief in God's providence and in the larger repercussions of human action. They may discuss theology and interpret reality; but final meaning – the divine writing – is not available to them. Like Reuven, and Aaron, and Boaz, they live in this world, which is the world of narrative. Here, a pinch of parched corn may have to do in place of fatted calves; Boaz's heart will have to be whole enough to sustain the energy of Ruth's desire.

In *Ruth*, even if theirs is only one among many conversations, those who seek meaning generate a world of meaning. In the end, Ruth's narrative is written, and brought to triumphant closure. All the emptiness is filled, the distortion made straight. The child that is born to Ruth and Boaz is set in a line of names that lead to David and to the Messiah himself. A world of narrative desire is consummated.

✽ RUTH EFFACED

But there remains one disturbing dimension to this fulfillment: Ruth disappears from the text. Just as the whole community seems to welcome her among them, ratifying Boaz's redemption, blessing her with the destiny of Rachel and Leah, the matriarchs who built the House of Israel, her disappearance begins. She becomes "the woman who is entering your home" (4:11), "this young woman." (4:12) For the women who congratulate Naomi on the birth of the child, she is "your daughter-in-law who loved you." (4:15) It is they who name the child, after Naomi has taken him into her bosom and become his foster mother; deliberately, they displace Ruth: "A son is born to Naomi!" (4:17) Only for Boaz is she simply Ruth: "And Boaz took Ruth; she became his wife, and he came unto her." (4:13)

Ruth has faded out of this triumphant pageant. In uncanny fulfillment of her own absurd scenario of hope, Naomi has in old age given birth to this child and suckled him. Some translators evade this implication: in using the word *yulad* (born), the women may be referring simply to Naomi's rearing the child; so too the word *omenet* may refer to her nurturing role.[56] But these are metaphorical expansions; the literal meanings, with their strong physical base, shockingly displace Ruth and set Naomi at the center of the closing vignette, as mother and nurturer.

In a sense, Ruth's disappearance is inevitable. So powerfully is she associated with the turbulence and contingency of narrative that no place can be found for her in the world of full and final meaning. Perhaps her presence in the utopian pageant would be too disturbing; the ending might not fully govern the discomfort that Ruth arouses, the questions that her narrative has evoked. If there is to be a sense of total coherence at the close of her book, she must be effaced.

With the disclosure of the birth line that leads from Ruth to David, a hidden necessity comes to light; it has all been for this; *une chose commence pour finir*. But if all has been legislated in advance, how is it that this narrative remains readable, even strangely compelling? Perhaps we return to it again and again because its discontents, its drift of desire, are not totally assuaged. If the subversive questions that she evokes are not to get out of hand, Ruth must be effaced from the ending. Pressing against too many boundaries, she endangers the magnificent necessity of this closure.

❧ CHOOSING RUTH

Might there have been an ending that read Ruth back into the text? The midrash offers such an alternative ending, where narrative and closure, desire and law, find, in all their tension, a moment of meeting:

> "There they dwelt, occupied in the king's work." On the strength of this verse, they said that Ruth the Moabite did not die until she saw her descendant Solomon sitting and judging the case of the harlots. That is the meaning of the verse, "And set a throne for the king's mother," that is, Bathsheba. "And she sat at his right hand" (1 Kings 2:19), referring to Ruth the Moabite.[57]

It seems that there is more to tell after all: another story about a mother and child. The midrashic writer begins by speaking of Ruth's death – the true closure of narrative – as deferred, so that she may see a narrative unfold which is not, properly, her narrative. "Ruth the Moabite did not die until she saw her descendant Solomon sitting and judging the case of the harlots." Until she witnesses this scene, she *cannot die*. Effaced from the public record at the moment she gives birth, she can be laid to rest only after she sees how Solomon her grandson stages her life in his judgment.[58]

In this last scene, Solomon, her great-great grandson, is powerfully, and famously, maintaining a world of law: judging a case of disputed maternity, he sets a seat for his mother, Bathsheba. By midrashic license, the biblical description is complicated, its folds unfurled, to make room for Ruth. "She sat at his right hand – that is, Ruth the Moabite." A spectral presence, unable to die, she is read into the scene to witness the judicial narrative that now unfolds.

In what will become Solomon's flagship case, two harlots lay claim to the surviving baby. One woman narrates the circumstances of the case at great length: how both mothers gave birth, alone in the house, how the other woman lay upon her baby during the night and smothered him, how she switched the babies, how the speaker rose to nurse her baby in the morning and "behold it was not my son, whom I did bear." The other woman disputes the narrative, creating a deadlock of versions: "No, the dead child is yours, mine is the living one." (1 Kings 3:16–23) The king repeats the deadlocked stories, calls for a sword, and commands that the live baby be cut in two, half for each mother. The true mother responds: "Give her the living child – only don't kill him!" But the other woman insists, "He shall be neither yours nor mine – cut him in two!" The king's verdict follows: "Give her the living child – only don't kill him; she is his mother."

With this judgment, Solomon gains his extraordinary reputation: "divine wisdom was within him to do justice." (3:28) This is the case that Ruth the Moabite witnesses before she dies. Here, like nesting boxes, narrative within narrative, we have Ruth's closure, Solomon's initiation into divine wisdom, the two harlots' stories, each excluding the other. Solomon orders the babies to be cut in two, a brutal gesture of justice,[59] which the false mother accepts: *gezoru* – Cut! It is only fair, even-handed, in such a case of conflicting desires and versions, that neither woman shall have the baby. The true mother prefers to lose the baby to her rival. Solomon's true verdict now emerges, once the counterfeit has done its work. But his majestic words of law simply repeat the words of the true mother, adding simply *hi imo* – "*she is his mother.*"

It turns out, then, that the first verdict, Cut him in two! was simply a charade, an incitement to extend the narrative. Apparently an expression of pure legality, his verdict acts performatively to generate a yet unknown justice. It provokes both women to show their true colors. Essentially, it provokes the true mother, in all her blind despair, to *frame the verdict*. It is as though Solomon is quoting her in a self-evident decision.[60] The true mother identifies herself in the very words with which she yields her child to the lying mother, in her readiness, that is, to live the confusion and anguish of narrative, rather than cut through to the inhumanly incisive gesture of law: "Cut!" Solomon, in a sense, does no more than *listen* to the language of a woman struggling in and with her desire. Unwittingly, she speaks the words that he simply redirects to her.

Where did Solomon learn to listen so well? In the midrashic narrative, the two women who flank the king, Bathsheba and Ruth, become more than witnesses: both are associated with the issues that are brought into brutal focus in the case of the harlots. Solomon is in fact the child born of the illicit relationship between David and Bathsheba; he is also the great-great grandson of Ruth *the Moabite*, once liminal, abject, full of desire. Perhaps Solomon has learned from these women to inform law with narrative, to bring the incompatible universes into dynamic relation.

Perhaps Ruth in particular, who once chose for herself a new mother, has been chosen by him as his ancestor. When he is faced with the challenge of recuperating and sustaining a viable normative world, his version of law seeks to bridge the reality and the vision, what is and what may be. As Robert Cover says, "Choosing ancestry is always a serious business." Solomon chooses Ruth the Moabite, as a constant reminder of the narrative anguish out of which transformations emerge.[61] Perhaps her willingness to be effaced from the written text of her own narrative, to give up her child as an act of devotion, is what gives her the grace of the "true mother" in the moment of Solomon's choice.

THE UNKNOWN WOMAN

In making this choice, Solomon has in a sense undermined the totality of closure. He has placed Ruth in a position where he can see her while he comes to his verdict. But perhaps more important, he is *seen by her*: "She did not die before *seeing* Solomon rendering judgment in the case of the harlots." To arrive at a true judgment that will reverse the *anomie*, the normative collapse with which Ruth's story began – "In the days when the judges judged" – Solomon must know himself as seen by the woman, the ultimately unknown woman, whose gaze has been acknowledged with such difficulty.

In the closing moment of Max Ophul's film *Letter from an*

Unknown Woman, the man covers his eyes with both hands in horror and exhaustion, as images from earlier in the film assault him. Stanley Cavell suggests that this is

> an ambiguous gesture, between avoiding the horror of know-
> ing the existence of others and avoiding the horror of not
> knowing it…he is in that gesture both warding off his see-
> ing something and warding off at the same time his being
> seen by something, which is to say, his own existence being
> known, being seen, by the woman of the letter.[62]

As in the ending of Henry James's "The Beast in the Jungle," the "unknown woman" becomes a figure for the difficulty of seeing the other as other, of acknowledging her animate human existence and significance. To have missed her would mean to have missed everything.

The midrash responds to a similar concern with seeing and being seen in relation to Ruth. In the biblical story this question animates her connections with Naomi, with Boaz, with the people of Bethlehem. She is the invisible heroine whose impact of *chesed*, of beauty, flows from her words.[63] The midrashic ending to her narrative allows her to see and to be seen in a mode of full acknowledgment.

Ruth's paradoxical closure comes when she sees Solomon *dan dinan shel zonot*, "absorbing the voice of the harlot," the wayward voice of pure narrative; he regenerates a normative world that had lost plausibility. In some private sense she presides over this scene; she is Solomon's teacher. Seeing this, she can die. As her descendant, Solomon learns from her a transformative dimension of Torah.

> R. Joshua b. Levi said: One who teaches his grandson Torah
> is regarded by Scripture as though he had received it [direct]
> from Mount Sinai, for it is said, "And you shall make them
> [the things your eyes have seen] known to your sons and your

sons' sons," which is followed by, "the day you stood before God at Horeb." (Deut. 4:9–10)[64]

The Torah one teaches a grandchild is the Torah of "the things your eyes have seen." (Deut. 4:9) This is the Torah that flashes back to Sinai, to the subversive moment of pure narrative. That foundational experience, before the Law was given, aroused "dread, fear, shuddering and trembling."[65] Desire and fear sent the people plunging back and forth at the base of the mountain, in overwhelming attraction and recoil.[66] The grandparent teaches a Torah of *r'iyah* (seeing), of personal experience, of oscillation, reversals, suspense, insufficiency. Unlike the parent who transmits what has been handed down, generation to generation, the grandparent, across a gap, dares to tell a narrative of danger, of an unmediated vision of great love, of the impact of a passion that shook her being into movement, unfurling it into a new language.[67]

Ruth's story makes it possible to reimagine Sinai. Ruth becomes the source of a teaching that Solomon acknowledges and makes his own. She returns us, her grandchildren, across a gap, to that subversive force of narrative that is never lost. This is the Torah that, like its teacher, can never be fully known, that is always discontinuous, of which we ask, *Who are you?* And rejoice in the silence that animates its response.

✣ NOTES

1. *Ruth Rabba* 2:15.
2. See 1:8.
3. See 3:10.
4. Beyond the details of the agricultural laws that shape the charitable responses of Boaz and his reapers, the text intimates other areas of law that engage with the proselyte, with the issues of redeeming land, and with the levirate problem: the law concerning the childless widow who is to marry her brother-in-law. Technically, this is not the situation in this narrative, but its moral residue creates a diffuse sense of obligation. Since Ploni Almoni (Mr. X) will not fulfill this obligation, Boaz assumes it as his own. These indications become the subject of many midrashic amplifications.
5. Deuteronomy 23:4.
6. *B. Baba Batra* 15b.
7. See the refrain that expresses the resulting anarchy in *The Book of Judges:* "Each man did what was right *in his own eyes.*"
8. Peter L. Berger, *A Rumor of Angels* (New York, 1970), p. 34.

9. Berger, p. 36.

10. *Ruth Rabba*, Preface (*Petichta*).

11. *Ruth Rabba* 1:4.

12. Robert Cover, *Narrative, Violence, and the Law* (University of Michigan Press, 1993), pp. 95–96.

13. Cover, p. 101.

14. Cover, pp. 101–102.

15. See Deuteronomy 21:15–17.

16. Cover, pp. 117–120.

17. See *Amos*, 8:11: "I will send a famine upon the land: not a hunger for bread or a thirst for water, but for hearing the words of God."

18. *Ruth* 1:3,5.

19. See *Ruth Rabba* 2:8,10.

20. Ibn Ezra cites 20:13 for the root *anah*: to testify.

21. Freud, *Beyond the Pleasure Principle*, SE 18:23.

22. Jonathan Lear, *Happiness, Death, and the Remainder of Life* (Cambridge, MA, 2000), p. 92.

23. Lear, pp. 94–95.

24. Lear, p. 93.

25. Rashi comments: "*On your journey*: When you were exhausted" (*b'teruf*, in a state of madness, disarray). This emphasizes the need of the travelers for the symbols of an ordered world.

26. *La Nausee*. Quoted in Miller, *Narrative and Its Discontents*, (Princeton, 1981), p. xiii.

27. Miller, p. x.

28. Miller, p. 3.

29. Miller, p. xiv.

30. Miller, pp. 265–266.

31. *Ruth Rabba* 3:3.

32. See Targum Onkelos on Genesis 2:24: "...a man shall leave his parents' bedroom."

33. *Ruth Rabba* 4:8.

34. See J. Yevamot 8:3.

35. See 2:11. Boaz translates her narrative into the language of Abraham's election by God (Gen. 12:1).

36. According to the midrash the incest is justified in the context of the apparent destruction of the world. Lot's daughters are moved to lie with their father to perpetuate the doomed human species.

37. Julia Kristeva, *Powers of Horror* (Columbia University Press, 1982), pp. 12–13.

38. Mary Douglas, *Purity and Danger* (Routledge, 1994), p. 39.

39. *B. Yevamot* 47:2.

40. See 2:11.

41. Christopher Bollas, *The Shadow of the Object* (Free Association Books, 1991), p. 14.

42. See Bollas, pp. 15–17.

43. See Hosea 9:1.

44. *B.Shabbat* 113b.

45. *Ruth Rabba* 5:13.

46. "Everything you tell *me* I will do" is written with the word *li* (*me*) missing: the word is not written but it is read [the *kri u-ketiv* feature in the biblical text]. The midrash interprets this wording: "I will obey you – but it is *up to me* to make sense of your words." Ruth is deliberately reserving the right to her own interpretation.

47. Cf. 2:20, where Naomi uses a similar idiom.

48. J. Peah 8:7. This is again the *kri u'ketiv* feature: written *you shall go down* and read *I shall go down*. Some scholars note that this is an archaic form of the second person verb. Its arbitrary occurrence here still requires explanation.

49. Cf. Ezekiel 16:8.

50. The word for "wings" and for "robe" is the same: *kenafayim*.

51. Redemption of land and levirate marriage are distinct biblical categories.

52. See Rashi to 3:8.

53. I am grateful to Francis Landy for his eloquent discussion of Ruth as a "beautiful subject." See "Ruth and the Romance of Realism" in *Beauty and the Enigma* (Sheffield Academic Press, 2001), pp. 224–225 and *passim*.

54. *Ruth Rabba* 5:6.

55. *Nidbaru* indicates continuous discourse.

56. The same chorus of women does refer to Ruth as "having given birth" to the child (4:14). But even this is said in tribute to Naomi: Ruth is praised for loving her and producing the child as a token of that love – he is "born for Naomi." At best, Ruth's role has become instrumental.

57. *Ruth Rabba* 2:2.

58. My thanks to David Shulman for sharpening my reading of this point.

59. In rabbinic Hebrew, the word for "decree" is *gezera*, derived from the verb "to cut."

60. It is striking that Solomon's selection of the true mother at first appears ambiguous, since the last speaker before "She is his mother" was the *false* mother. However, his repetition of the true mother's speech leaves no doubt as to which woman he means. Judicial clarity is compromised to enact the performative point.

61. On a different level, of course, it is the Rabbis who have chosen Ruth by inserting her into a text that bears no indication of her. The effect is to admit her in a new way into their own world of law: as if to acknowledge that they see her and know themselves seen by her.

62. Stanley Cavell, "The Melodrama of the Unknown Woman," in *The Trial(s) of Psychoanalysis*, ed. Francoise Meltzer, (Chicago, 1987).

63. It is striking that the Hebrew word *ra'ah*, "to see," is absent from *Ruth*, as are all references to physical beauty.

64. *B. Kiddushin* 30a.

65. *B. Brachot* 22a.

66. See Rashi to Exodus 20:15.

67. My reading is based on *Pachad Yitzhak Shavuot*, 26.

On Sunday the Rabbi Stayed for *Bensching*

Joshua Lookstein

Adapted from remarks given at Kehilath Jeshurun on June 14, 2008, on the occasion of Rabbi Haskel Lookstein's 50th year in its pulpit.

✥ I. THEME I: HISTORICAL VS. USUAL

We begin with a verse from this week's portion, *Beha'alotcha*, that deals with the Passover Sacrifice:

> The Lord spoke to Moses in the wilderness of Sinai, on the first new moon of the second year following the exodus from the land of Egypt, saying: Let the Israelite people offer the Passover sacrifice at its set time (*bimoado*): you shall offer it on the fourteenth day of this month, at twilight, at its set time; you shall offer it in accordance with all its rules and rites. (Numbers 9:1–3)[1]

Rashi notices the extraneous word *bimoado* (at its set time): If it says explicitly that the sacrifice is brought on the fourteenth *at twilight* (*bein haarbayim*), then why add "at its set time"? Rashi answers:

355

> Even on the Sabbath; ["in its appointed time,"] even in a state
> of impurity (Numbers 9:2).²

He says that it adds that it is given at its set (or appropriate) time
regardless of other factors, other factors being the Sabbath or impurity. So *bimoado* means that the Passover sacrifice is sacrificed
even if the 14th falls on the Sabbath and even if most of the community or the priests who performed the sacrifice or the vessels
used for the sacrifice are impure.

From where does Rashi know this? From the Talmud in
Tractate *Pesachim*, which makes an analogy of common terms
(*gezeirah shavah*) from a verse in the portion of *Pinchas*:

> Command the Israelite People and say to them: Be punctili-
> ous in presenting to Me at its set time (*bimoado*) the offer-
> ings of food due Me, as offerings by fire of pleasing odor to
> Me. (Numbers 28:2)³

The verse in *Pinchas* talks about the daily sacrifice (*Korban Tamid*)
that was brought in the morning and toward the evening, and it
uses the same word, *bimoado* (at its set time).

The Talmud presents the analogy of common terms (*gezeirah shavah*):

> …Just as the phrase *its appointed time* that is stated with re-
> gard to the *tamid* offering refers to a sacrifice whose service
> overrides the Sabbath restrictions, so too does the phrase *its
> appointed time* that is stated with regard to the *pesach* offer-
> ing refer to a sacrifice whose service overrides the Sabbath
> restrictions.
>
> The Talmud asks: And the *tamid* offering itself, from
> where do we know that it overrides the Sabbath?…from the
> verse: *The olah of each Sabbath on its Sabbath, besides for the
> olah of the tamid offering*. This verse implies that the *olah* of
> the *tamid* offering is brought even on the Sabbath.

...from where do we know that they override the *tumah* restrictions as well?

...Just as the law of the *pesach* offering is derived from the law of the *tamid* offering [through the exposition of *in its appointed time*] with regard to overriding the Sabbath, so too is the law of the *tamid* offering derived from the law of the *pesach* offering [through that same exposition] with regard to overriding the *tumah* restrictions.

...And the *pesach* offering itself – from where do we know that its service overrides the *tumah* restrictions?

...the verse states: Any man who will be *tamei* from a corpse. The verse's use of the singular (any man) implies that only a *tamei* individual is deferred until *Pesach Sheni*, but a *tamei* congregation is not deferred until *Pesach Sheni*; rather, it (i.e., the congregation) makes the regular offering on *Pesach Rishon*, in a state of *tumah*.

The Talmud explains that we know the daily sacrifice (*tamid*) is brought even on the Sabbath, and that the Passover sacrifice is brought even in a state of impurity. Since the word *bimoado* (at its set time) is found in both cases, we cross-legislate and the resulting law is that both are brought on the Sabbath and both are brought in a state of impurity – two sacrificial peas in a pod, so to speak.

Rabbi Samson Raphael Hirsch takes this technical, legal connection and assigns it a philosophical implication as well:

A truth of no small importance lies in the inclusion of the "daily" occurrences of morn and even in the sphere of the "special" once-occurring events in the history of the world proving the existence of God and inviting us to Him...Just as the revelation of God in Egypt...at Sinai, the manna, etc... were appointed at every anniversary of their happening as a *moed*, a time appointed to refresh our minds with thoughts of God...so did He appoint every daily appearance of morn and even, occurring regularly without any special overcoming of His laws of nature, to be just such a *moed*. It makes every rising and falling ray of light a daily no less intense witness and messenger which shows us God's presence in the world. (Numbers 28:2)[4]

Hirsch seems to be answering an unasked question: How could the daily sacrifice (*Korban Tamid*) be called a *moed* (holiday)? Isn't that almost insulting to the real holidays? He says no. If *moed* is designed to be a Godly experience, then there are two types of such experiences: the historical and the usual, the one-time, powerful experience, and the everyday, consistent experience, or the extraordinary and the ordinary. And the ordinary is no less important than the extraordinary. In fact, the use of the same word transforms the ordinary into the extraordinary, each ray of light, appearing and disappearing, becomes a witness to God's presence.

So the cross-legislation between the Passover sacrifice and the Daily Sacrifice becomes the unifying theme of God's presence in the historical and the usual, between the extraordinary and the ordinary.

✿ II. THEME 2: COMMUNITY VS. INDIVIDUAL

At the end of the portion of *Pinchas*, after all of the holiday sacrifices are listed, the Torah recaps and adds information:

All these you shall offer to the Lord at the stated times, in addition to your votive and freewill offerings, be they burnt-offerings, meal offerings, libations, or offerings of well-being. (Numbers 29:39)[5]

The verse instructs that certain sacrifices are to be brought during the holiday, but certain others are not. And the Talmud in Tractate *Temurah* explains the verse:

...These shall you make for Hashem in your appointed times.
These are your obligatory offerings that are brought on the
festivals. The verse continues: *aside from your vowed offerings and your donated offerings.* This teaches that vowed and
donated offerings may be brought on Hol HaMoed. The next
term in this verse is: *for your* olah *offerings.* With respect to
which type of *olah* is the verse speaking?...[the verse] must
be speaking only of the *olah* of a woman who has given birth
and the *olah* of a *metzora.* (Temurah 14b)[6]

The obligatory offerings that the Talmud mentions as being
brought on the holiday (*yontif*) are the *Olat reiyah* (for being in
Jerusalem on the holiday) and the *chagiga* (in honor of a holiday). All the rest – *neder, nedava,* and for our purposes, *yoledet*
(a woman who has given birth) *and metzora* – are brought on the
intermediate days of the holiday (*Hol Hamoed*).

Again, Hirsch assigns a philosophical implication to this
seemingly straightforward and technical law:

The sanctification and getting near to God by dedications of
private life is in no way a cutting down of the spirit of national feeling, the intensified feeling of being a member of
the national brotherhood which the festivals are to engen-
der. But the fresh impetus which the moed is to give to the
national relationship to God and the sanctuary of His Torah
is rather to benefit private life and its relationships to God.
(Numbers 29:39)[7]

Again Hirsch answers an unasked question: If the holiday was supposed to be this grand, communal event, everyone coming from
everywhere to be together as a community in Jerusalem, then how
could bringing a personal sacrifice be allowed? Let the woman
who has given birth wait. We're dealing with public sacrifices! His
answer is basically that the purpose of holidays on our calendar is

misunderstood. While the holiday is a public event, the celebration is to benefit "private life and its relationship to God". Pretty amazing! Yes, holidays and major events are about community and coming together, but they are also about using the community to impact the individual; the major event is supposed to make a difference in each person's relationship to God.

So theme number 2, the personal sacrifice of a woman who has given birth that is brought during the holiday reminds us that the community is significant but the impact is to be felt on an individual level.

✢ III. THEME 3: *MOED* (HOLIDAY) = TIME

The portion *Emor* presents all of the holidays. The following is the verse that introduces *Shemini Atzeret* (the "eighth day" of *Sukkot*):

> Seven days you shall bring offerings by fire to the Lord. On the eighth day you shall observe a sacred occasion and bring an offering by fire to the Lord; it is a solemn gathering: you shall not work at your occupations. (Leviticus 23:36)[8]

We're all familiar with the midrash quoted by Rashi as to why the eighth day is called *Atzeret*. Nachmanides quotes Rashi and then continues:

> "I keep you back before Me." It is similar to the case of a prince who invited his children to a banquet for a certain number of days. When the time came for them to leave, he said, 'I beg of you stay with me for yet one more day, for your departure is so hard for me!'"...Now with respect to the Festival of Unleavened Bread He commanded that it be observed for seven days, with the first and seventh [days] being holy... From then on...we are to count forty-nine days...and then to sanctify the "eighth day" [i.e., the Festival of Weeks] just as the eighth day of Tabernacles [is holy]; and [the forty-

nine days] counted between them are in the "intermediate days" of the festival, in the interval separating the first day and "eighth day" of the festival, this being the day of the Giving of the Torah...Therefore our rabbis, of blessed memory, always called the Festival of Weeks by the name *atzeret*...for it is on the "eighth" day of the festival, which Scripture here so called by that name.[9]

Just as Shemini Atzeret is the extra day added on to Sukkot, the Ramban says that so too Shavuot is the extra day added on to Passover, which is also why the Talmud refers to Shavuot as *Atzeret*. So the holiday of Passover is really an amalgam of Passover, the counting of the *Omer* – playing the role of the intermediate days of the holiday (*Hol Hamoed*) – and Shavuot. Just as God wants the Jewish People to stick around longer after *Sukkot* – and presumably Rosh Hashana, *Aseret yimei teshuva*, and Yom Kippur (as Rav Goldvicht, of blessed memory, the former *Rosh Yeshiva* of Kerem B'Yavneh once said) – so too God wants them to stay longer after this period of the year as well.

Why, though? What's going on here? What is it about these periods that causes God to be more attached to the Jewish People?

I think the answer is simply: time. It's just a tremendous amount of time, intense time that we spend with God. Days and days of synagogue, *sukka*, commandments, repentance, matzoh, *seders*, counting, mourning, refining ourselves, learning all night, eating, eating, eating. It's time. The more quality time we spend with anyone, the deeper, stronger, more meaningful the relationship is. So God says, "Don't leave. Stay a little longer."

So theme 3 is holiday (*moed*) as time – quality, intense, long-lasting time spent with God.

I think these three themes are key ingredients of my father's relationship with this community.

Every rabbi will have in his rabbinate, both the one-time, historical events and the regular, daily life of building a community. My father certainly has had his share of historical moments: Soviet Jewry, Ethiopian Jewry, Israel, the Intifadas, Iranian Jews, even China! He is a major force on the international scene, someone who is looked to by other communities in times of international crisis. But I'm not sure if it will surprise you that my father once told me that years ago, members of the synagogue wanted him to be more international, like my grandfather was, but that he never saw himself that way. "I have a community right here to build," he said. "I can't be running around the world." For someone who so clearly has made an international impact, he always saw himself – and sees himself – first and foremost as a builder of this community, as a caretaker of the needs of this community, both the *shul* and the school as a necessary component of this community. His place is on the Upper East Side, in his office, doing the budgets, giving sermons, teaching his Wednesday morning *parsha* class.

It's interesting that this event could have been elsewhere. We could have organized a major trip to Israel! Or the former Soviet Union or somewhere exotic. It would have been an extravaganza! But it didn't happen and it shouldn't have happened. There is no better place to celebrate than right here, in the shul, in this community, because that's where my father most sees himself, as a builder and pastor to this community.

But even the word "community" is complex. As Hirsch says, it's a community of individuals, and communal events are designed to impact its individuals. Again we have both aspects of my father. On the one hand, is the image of him as leader of communal events: leading the community in *Neilah*, Purim, in the *sukka* for hundreds on *Sukkot*, leading a *seder* in Israel for 200 people, leading a conga line at midnight to "Who Knows One," at the head of the Ramaz contingent at the Salute to Israel Parade, and on the grandstand on Solidarity Sunday.

But when it comes down to it, as strong as his relationship to the community is, his personal relationship with its members is stronger. His involvement in everyone's life-cycle events, pre-marital meetings – he doesn't speak about marriage, he speaks about the bride and groom – pre-bar/bat mitzvah meetings, asking teachers to find out what makes each child unique, conversions – how he changes into a bathing suit to take a baby into the mikvah – funerals, *shiva* calls, hospital visits, even to new mothers, dealing with crises. His fundraising. Yes, he needs the money, but he also views each of the almost 500 calls he makes as opportunities to connect to each person, to make sure he is doing right by those people. He will sometimes get off the phone after a not-so-pleasant call and say, "He's right. I should be paying more attention to him and I'm not." Even leading the community on every holiday, it is like Rav Hirsch said, that it's "to benefit private life and its relationship to God."

I remember at the conclusion of Rosh Hashana after the September 11 attacks, I was in my office, desperately longing to go home. I, like every other rabbi in the country, had worked hard rewriting my sermon. It was physically, mentally, and emotionally draining. I had visions of getting into bed, pulling the covers up, and watching TV. My father comes into my office and says that a friend of one our members just passed away and they have no one to do the funeral, and the member asked if we could do it; my father couldn't do it himself because he had an appointment, and as I look at him in disbelief he hands me the family's address and says that they are waiting for me to come over. Words can't describe what I was feeling at that moment. I did do the funeral though. But there was no disbelief in my father, nothing out of the ordinary. The major communal event of Rosh Hashana in no way distracted him from the needs of an individual. I am positive that everyone in this room feels that he or she has a personal relationship with him.

The unasked question is: how does he do it? How could someone be an international force, a community leader, and yet be available to everyone?

The answer is "time." He devotes all the time that he has for everything and everyone. I know it because I've seen it first-hand. There isn't a time that I call him that he doesn't answer if I need him. I remember when I was a rabbi in Stamford, Connecticut. and three people unfortunately passed away in the first three days I was there, and I called him hundreds of time with probably ridiculous questions. And it still happens today. Every so often my phone will ring and I'll see that it's him calling and I'll hesitate because I'm busy (of course!), and then I'll catch myself. What? Busy? Who are you kidding? There's no one busier than he is, and *he* always answers *my* calls! And I'll answer it of course.

He has time for everyone. He is always in meetings with people or teaching a class or at the hundreds of annual life-cycle events that he and my mother go to, or doing mail – and now email – until all hours of the night, or at the graduation or play of one of my nieces and nephews, or traveling to and from all of these places. This past Sunday, amidst the chaos at my sister's house before my nephew Daniel's bar mitzvah, my cousin Jessica said that her daughter Kate was trying to reach him. He asked me for the number, he went outside, and he talked to her and they made a plan to learn together. He made the time to call her. He makes the time to spend with her.

But what I'm always most amazed at might seem normal to everyone, and that is how long he and my mother stay at the various life-cycle events that they attend. Inevitably, my father leads the *bensching*. I would venture to say that most people in the room, myself sometimes included, don't always stay at weddings or bar/bat mitzvahs until the end. I would also venture to say that most people in this room don't attend a fraction of the number of events my parents attend. I would also say that many, if not most, rabbis leave after their speaking parts are over – entirely understandable because of family and communal time constraints – and if my parents leave it's usually because they have another event to go to. That *bensching* that my father does at every wedding, when he fills the glass of the bride almost to the top and then the glass of the groom only an ounce and then says that whoever finishes the wine first runs the house and then swaps the glasses, people love it every time. I used to dread it! "Not again, Dad, they've all seen it a hundred times." The truth is, they haven't seen it a hundred times because most people are long gone by that time, but if you have seen it a hundred times, chances are you still laugh because, consciously or not, you realize that he's still there. To the end, not trying to find a convenient time to leave, but there because he wants to be there, for the duration.

Because that's how relationships are formed. Like eight or almost sixty days of a holiday. Quality time, intense time, dedicated time. My father knows that, and he'll quote Woody Allen about showing up, that eighty percent of success is showing up, but Woody Allen should be quoting him or watching him because no one shows up more or for longer than he.

Like the set times of the Passover and daily sacrifices, the sacrifices of the holidays and the mother who has given birth, and the duration of the holiday, so is the experience of my father for these past 50 years.

✢ CONCLUSION

It can't be a coincidence that my father's 50th year anniversary comes in such close proximity to Shavuot, the 50th day since the beginning of Passover. It is our *Atzeret* after forty-nine years. In reality, we don't leave God after Shavuot or after Sukkot. The experiences just intensify our relationship and infuse the rest of the year. So, Dad, may this 50th year celebration only intensify your relationship with the Jewish People, this community, and each of its members for many more years to come, only in health and happiness. *Mazal Tov.*

✢ NOTES

1. Nahum M. Sarna, Chaim Potok, and Jacob Milgrom, *JPS Torah Commentary* (Philadelphia, 1990), Numbers, p. 67.
2. Yisrael Isser Zvi Herczeg, *Rashi/Commentary on the Torah*, Artscroll Series/The Sapirstein Edition, Vol. 4, Bamidbar/Numbers (Brooklyn, 1997), p. 98.

3. Sarna, Potok, and Milgrom, *Torah Commentary*, p. 238.
4. Samson Raphael Hirsch, *The Pentateuch*, Vol. iv Numbers (London, 1960), pp. 469–470, 502 (see also pp. 138–139 commentary on 9:2).
5. Sarna, Potok, and Milgrom, *Torah Commentary*, pp. 249–250
6. Yehezkel Danziger, The Artscroll Series/Schottenstein Edition, Talmud Bavli/Tractate Temurah (Brooklyn, 2004), p. 14b3.
7. Hirsch, *Pentateuch*, p. 502.
8. Baruch A. Levine, Leviticus, jps *Torah Commentary* (Philadelphia, 1989), p. 162.
9. Charles B. Chavel, Ramban (Nachmanides), *Commentary on the Torah*, Leviticus (New York, 1974), pp. 392–393.

Rav Chesed: The Life and Times of Rabbi Haskel Lookstein

Rafael Medoff

❦ INTRODUCTION

BY THE HON. MICHAEL B. MUKASEY

Biography – the venture of trying to capture on paper the story of someone else's life – is often a risky enterprise, and all the more risky when the life in question is still being lived. To the usual hazards of not telling at least all that is significant must be added both the distinct possibility that some event will overtake what is already recorded, and the certainty that the subject will be present to offer his own view, which is bound to differ from his biographer's. However, when one looks at the title and the ten chapter headings in Rafael Medoff's fascinating account of Rabbi Haskel Lookstein's journey among us, what becomes clear is that whatever disadvantage may lurk in those mundane hazards is far outweighed by the importance of having this volume, and particularly of having it while Rabbi Lookstein continues to lead and to teach us.

The ten chapter headings – beginning with "The Student" and ending with "The Teacher" – describe aspects of Rabbi Lookstein's life that are ongoing. Although many people lead lives sequentially, with one chapter ending and another beginning, sometimes with indeterminate gaps between, none of the chapters in this book, even as they may describe particular events and activities that are in the past, has an end. Pick any at random – "The Scholar" or "The Activist" or "Women's Issues" or "The Zionist" – and you will call to mind events and concerns that are ongoing in Rabbi Lookstein's life. The key lies in the title: *Rav Chesed*. These chapters are facets of a person whose motivating and defining force is chesed. This is a volume that is important not only to help us to understand a person who is among us, but also thereby to improve the lives of those around us, k'lal yisrael, and ourselves. Its force is enhanced by the happy fact that if there is this or that point that we don't get, we have the subject to teach it to us, by explanation if necessary but in any event by example. This is a good read insofar as it tells us about some of Rabbi Lookstein's achievements; it is an important one insofar as it reminds us of our own unrealized potential.

Michael B. Mukasey*
May 2008

* Mr. Mukasey is a member of Congregation Kehilath Jeshurun and a former student of Rabbi Lookstein at Ramaz School. He served as the Attorney General of the United States from 2007–2009.

On a crisp Monday morning in early September 1937, Rabbi Joseph H. Lookstein led his five year old son, Haskel, into a classroom in the fledgling Ramaz elementary school on East 85th Street, next door to its sponsor, Congregation Kehilath Jeshurun. The inauguration of the school launched a major new attempt to combine Orthodoxy and modernity in a Manhattan neighborhood that few considered fertile ground for Jewish religious observance. The experiment would ultimately succeed far beyond its sponsors' expectations. Under the leadership of Rabbi Lookstein, and later of his son, Ramaz would come to be recognized as one of the most influential Jewish day schools in the United States, Kehilath Jeshurun would emerge as one of America's most important synagogues, and the Upper East Side would blossom into a thriving center of Jewish life. Nurturing a local community while at the same time influencing the entire American Jewish community, the Looksteins would make their mark with an innovative blend of traditional observance, respect for modernity, social activism, tolerance, and personal compassion.

*   *   *

Joseph H. Lookstein first came to Kehilath Jeshurun in 1923, as assistant rabbi under the renowned sage Rabbi Moses Margolies, better known by the acronym RaMaZ. Three years later he married Margolies's granddaughter, Gertrude Schlang, and when their daughter Nathalie reached the age of five, in 1932, he began exploring the possibility of establishing a day school on the Upper East Side. The 1930s were hardly an auspicious time to establish a new Jewish school, especially in an area with a small Jewish presence such as the Yorkville section of Upper Manhattan, where Kehilath Jeshurun was situated. The Great Depression drastically reduced the pool of potential donors, and the neighborhood was best known for pro-Nazi rallies by the German-American Bund. By 1937, when Rabbi Lookstein's son Haskel turned five and was ready to enter first grade, the rabbi was determined to launch a Jewish elementary school, regardless of these obstacles.[1]

The neighborhood and the national economy were not the only hindrances to his plan. It was also a period of intense turmoil for American Judaism. Many Jewish immigrants chose to leave behind their old-world religious observances and assimilate into American society. Only a small minority clung to the traditional lifestyle they had known in Europe. Rabbi Lookstein was among those who sought a middle ground between these two extremes, as he worked to build a community that would remain loyal to tradition while at the same time embracing the best of modern American life.

At a meeting of the KJ board of trustees in 1937, he presented his vision of an institution that would integrate Judaic learning with secular studies, embodying the spirit of the modern, Americanized Orthodoxy to which they subscribed. Such a school was "an imperative necessity for an entire generation of growing young people," he argued. Most of the approximately fifteen Orthodox day schools in New York City were widely perceived as "ghetto schools." They were situated "in underprivileged neighborhoods and were considered as suited for poor underprivileged children." The children of more successful American Orthodox Jews did not regard such schools as "congenial or acceptable." Judaic studies were taught in Yiddish, by teachers who did not understand "the modern American Jewish children," while secular studies were relegated to the end of the ten-hour school day, when "tired teachers were expected to teach tired children."[2]

The school Rabbi Lookstein proposed to build would be unique in two important respects. First, it would bring to the Upper East Side a type of day school unknown to that area and barely represented elsewhere in New York City: a modern Orthodox alternative to, on the one hand, a traditional *cheder* that would leave their children ill equipped to succeed in the outside world, and, on the other hand, a public school that would leave the youngsters bereft of Jewish knowledge. Ramaz would offer the best of both worlds. Second, it would consciously seek to recruit students from less religiously observant families. Doing this was a virtual necessity given the small size of the neighborhood's Orthodox community, but it also created an unusual opportunity to influence Jewish families to become more observant.

R. Joseph's proposal met with some skepticism among KJ board members. Some regarded day schools as "too parochial," preferring that Jewish children be sent to public schools and receive a limited supplementary Judaic education. Others doubted that the synagogue could shoulder the financial burden of a new school, which would inevitably run a deficit at least in its early years.

Rabbi Lookstein would not yield. He informed the board that if Kehilath Jeshurun were unwilling to take on the project, he would resign and find another synagogue that would implement his vision. The stalemate was resolved when Max J. Etra, a prominent attorney and lay leader in the congregation, pledged to cover the first year's deficit, which the rabbi estimated would be $5,000.[3]

Lookstein named the school after Rabbi Margolies, a renowned scholar from Vilna whose intellectual feats included studying the complete Talmud each year. Significantly, the RaMaZ was also known for his substantial involvement in community affairs. A famous photograph shows Rabbi Margolies participating in the founding meeting of the American Jewish Joint Distribution Committee, the overseas relief agency run primarily by non-Orthodox Jews. His willingness to work side by side with Jews of other backgrounds and differing levels of religious observance was emblematic of a spirit of tolerance for which his grandson and great-grandson would become well known.[4]

In 1932, shortly after his son was born, Rabbi Joseph Lookstein visited the RaMaZ to receive a blessing. As the story goes, Rabbi Margolies had just read about the passing of Rabbi Hatzkel [Yehezkel] Kalischer, a distinguished scholar with whom RaMaZ had been close. He suggested to Rabbi Lookstein that the baby be named Hatzkel, "so he will grow up to be like Reb Hatzkel." Lookstein was pleased with the idea, regarding it as a harbinger of success for his son, but he worried that his wife and mother would be less than thrilled "about naming him after some Polish rabbi" instead of a relative. They conspired to present the name as connected to RaMaZ's father and uncle, both of whom were named Yechezkel. Gertrude Lookstein accepted the proposal but planned to also give him Charles as his English name, to which Rabbi Lookstein objected on the grounds that the boy, named for a renowned rabbi, would undoubtedly be called "Chuck." Their compromise solution was to use the slightly Americanized "Haskel," although the future Rabbi Lookstein was immediately nicknamed "Hack" or "Hacky" by family and friends alike.

As a child, Haskel exhibited musical ability which he attributed to two influences. One was his maternal grandfather, Isidore Schlang, a devout "*shul yid*" who was always the first to come to morning *minyan* and the last to leave, reciting his prayers slowly and punctiliously. When Haskel led the service, his grandfather would remind him of the importance of pronouncing every word – "Hacky, say woids!" he would implore him. Schlang's passion for Shabbat *zmirot* made a strong impression on young Haskel, who subsequently adopted his grandfather's tune for *birkat ha-mazon* [grace after meals], as would his children and grandchildren.[5]

An equally profound influence on Haskel was Joseph E. Adler, who began working at Kehilath Jeshurun in 1933 as sexton, Torah reader, and second *hazan*. Adler, who would later gain renown in the kosher food industry for Mrs. Adler's Gefilte Fish (based on his wife's recipe), was deeply involved in community affairs and worked closely with Rabbi Joseph Lookstein in building the synagogue and the school. He was Haskel's model for Torah reading and as *shaliah tzibur* [leader of the communal prayer service], and Adler's *nusach* became Haskel's. "I just loved to listen to him," he recalled. "My *davening* is his *davening*."[6]

After Haskel turned thirteen, Adler would call on him to read *maftir*, without advance notice, if the scheduled person did not show up. "I was able to read the *haftorah* without preparation simply because I loved it," he noted. "When you enjoy something so much, you get good at it." The text commonly used in those days was a nineteenth-century edition by Isaac Leeser, which had the esoteric textual variations and corrections at the bottom of the page rather than in the text itself as in contemporary versions. Thus Haskel needed to check those variations at the bottom of the page during the *misheberakh*. When he concluded the reading, Adler, sitting at the back of the *bima*, instead of complimenting his protégé, would inevitably point out to Haskel some obscure error he had made. Haskel considered this the ultimate compliment, realizing that his consummate mentor expected from him nothing less than absolute perfection.[7]

Rabbi Lookstein has described Torah reading and leading the *davening* as "my biggest *yetzer hara*." A small part of him would have preferred to follow in the footsteps of Joseph Adler rather than of his father, Joseph Lookstein, although ultimately he would come to derive satisfaction from the realization that his *davening* in fact supplemented his rabbinical leadership. Making the prayers meaningful helped inspire congregants to feel more connected to the synagogue and the community, an ingredient crucial to the success of a rabbi's mission. Over the years, he had the opportunity to indulge himself on the few Shabbatot when the *hazan* was absent, and, most notably, during the High Holidays. From his father and maternal grandfather, Rabbi Haskel Lookstein learned the importance of "emphasizing every word, and putting feeling into every word." His style left a strong impression on his congregants. A Ramaz alumnus who attended only one Yom Kippur service at KJ, twenty-five years later still vividly remembered the rabbi leading *shaharit* and *ne'ila*, "with a powerful but musical voice, filled with emotion and concentration, leaving behind his day-to-day rabbinic persona and becoming a true *eved Hashem* [servant of God]."[8]

"Some day, I am sure, my voice will begin to crack and waver, and I will have to very reluctantly accept the fact that I can do only *ne'ila* but not *shaharit*," he conceded. "Somebody, perhaps my wife, will find a gentle way to alert me that the time has come. I won't be happy about it, but it's inevitable."[9] In the meantime, however, the KJ-Ramaz community made clear its appreciation for his singing. R. Haskel's solo rendition of the song "*hazak, hazak*," performed according to the tune and style of noted Jewish singer Avraham Fried, has been a highlight of the Ramaz Upper School's annual banquet since 1999. The congregation's celebration of R. Haskel's seventieth birthday, in 2002, with a gala dinner at the Marriott Hotel, included a video clip of him singing that song. It took little coaxing to convince the rabbi to do a live version on stage at the birthday event, where he was joined by a surprise guest – Avraham Fried himself.[10]

Haskel grew up in a family that was close-knit, with a full-time, stay-at-home mother and a father to whom he felt close despite the elder Rabbi Lookstein's hectic professional life as spiritual leader of KJ and principal of Ramaz. Gertrude Lookstein managed an equally busy life as mother, wife, and *rebbitzen*. She founded and led the KJ Sisterhood; instructed the *shul's* young women in caring for *shiva* houses, visiting the sick, and performing other social mitzvahs; and hosted a constant stream of Shabbat and Yom Tov guests. "We had open house in our home, visitors for dinner Friday night and Shabbos lunch and every holiday," she recalled. "Both my husband and I enjoyed it. And the people enjoyed it. We never sat down alone."[11]

Haskel looked up to his older sister, Nathalie, whom he regarded as "a wonderful role model but a tough act to follow – she rarely got less than an 'A' in anything." He remembered attending her graduation ceremony (from Hunter High School; Ramaz did not exist when she began school), at which Nathalie and another Jewish girl received seventeen of the eighteen scholastic awards, and wondering if he would earn even one award in his high school class. Nathalie would go on to earn a PhD in sociology and lead a distinguished academic career at Barnard College and Stern College.

Haskel's years at Ramaz were not always a smooth ride. When he reached eighth grade, he "hit a wall," as he later put it, engaging in frequent mischief that caused his teachers and parents considerable aggravation. R. Haskel would later attribute this difficult period to the pressure of fellow students targeting "the principal's son," together with his anxiety over his height. He was four foot five at the time of his bar mitzvah in March 1945 and needed to stand on a platform in order to read from the Torah. "But, thank God, I grew eleven inches in the next two years," he recalled.[12]

Some of the eighth-grade troublemaking was comical. If a student was caught talking while their Hebrew teacher that year, Morris Nieman, was writing on the board, "Nieman would suddenly pivot like a baseball pitcher throwing to second base to pick off a runner – only he would throw his eraser at the student. And he had good aim." R. Haskel recalled the day when Nieman wheeled and hurled the eraser at him, assuming that he was, as usual, the culprit. But with his fast reflexes, Haskel flipped up his desk in time to cause the eraser to ricochet and strike the guilty student, Peppy Friedberg (later chairman of Loews Entertainment Corporation). Other episodes were less amusing. One teacher, Samuel Goodside, would make a notation in his roll book next to a student's name each time that student engaged in unusually bad behavior. Aside from Haskel, the worst student in that eighth-grade class racked up six notations; Haskel had twenty-five. After the twenty-fifth, some horseplay in which a fellow student accidentally injured Haskel, R. Joseph gave his son "a tongue-lashing that I can remember clearly, even though it's sixty-two years later.... It was a very sobering event in my life."

For Haskel, the incident was a turning point. By the time he began ninth grade, he had become a serious and devoted student. Rabbi Nachum Bronznick, whose first full-time teaching position, at Ramaz, fortunately coincided with the year Haskel was in ninth grade and therefore took his class, later recalled his anxiety at the prospect of having the principal's son as one of his pupils. "To my great relief, however, I discovered soon enough that I had nothing to be uneasy about," he noted. "This student, happily, did not show any sign that he was expecting any special treatment. He acted and behaved as a true and sincere young *mensch* in every respect." Rabbi Bronznick noted that while it was common for students to approach him after an exam was returned and argue for additional points, Haskel came to him after a particular test, saying, "I am not coming to argue why I didn't get credit for this particular answer, but I want to understand what is wrong with it, and what is the correct answer." The incident convinced the teacher that this pupil "was destined to become a person with many great achievements to his credit, as he indeed became."[13]

Haskel excelled throughout his remaining high school years, finishing as the second highest student in his class. In retrospect, that rough patch in eighth grade offered him a valuable lesson:

> As a result of that experience, when I look at students whom the educational system is ready to give up on, I have an entirely different perspective. I know that students can change. Sometimes the kid who is most out of line can get back in line and straighten himself out. What happened to me gave me a lot of empathy for kids in junior high school, who can go through a difficult time before turning out very well. When I run into such students, I often tell them, and their parents, about my own experience, to help them realize that there's hope.[14]

Many of young Haskel's crucial formative experiences took place at Camp Massad, where he sepent ten consecutive summers beginning in 1945. The Hebrew-language camp, run by Shlomo and Rivka Shulsinger, was situated in Tannersville, Pennsylvania, in the Pocono Mountains. There Haskel exhibited a prowess at basketball, tennis, and softball that would last long after his camp years were over. With Lookstein as its star pitcher, the younger campers' softball team (13 year-olds) defeated not only their peers but the older division as well, and the year Haskel turned 15, his team beat the teams of counselors and waiters as well. His enthusiasm for basketball carried over into the school year, when as captain of the team in his senior year – "it was me, at five foot three, with four boys who were six feet or taller" – he averaged more than ten points per game. Those experiences, together with occasional teenage forays to the Polo Grounds with his father to watch the New York Giants, nurtured Haskel's lifelong passion for professional sports. Six decades later he would describe as one of the highlights of his life the day in 2006 that KJ members arranged for him to throw out the ceremonial first pitch at a New York Mets game. Surrounded by KJers with "Lookstein Puts the RBI in Rabbi" t-shirts, R. Haskel threw a strike. When the Mets fell behind in the first inning, a fan sitting near R. Haskel and his friends shouted, "Hey rabbi, maybe you should get back out there, we need you!"[15]

Haskel made a quick transition from ordinary camper to a leader-in-training in the summer of 1947, when the counselor in charge of *tefilla* for the older campers seven days a week asked 15-year-old Haskel if he would supervise the weekday *minyan*. Haskel felt a special affinity for *davening* and accepted the offer without hesitation. "I taught the boys how to *daven* correctly, practicing the *nusach* with everyone out loud," he recalled. "At the time, I didn't realize what a major turning point it was, but looking back now, I realize that was the point where I started becoming interested in Jewish education and the rabbinate as a possible career." For the rest of the summers while he was in high school, and all through his college years, Haskel continued to serve as the *rosh tefilla* for the campers at Massad.[16]

Michael Mukasey, who in 2007 became Attorney General of the United States, was a camper in Massad's "Degania" division of older campers, over which counselor Haskel presided one summer. "He had everyone's respect in part because he could do everything we thought was important – which is to say he could hit, pitch, field, take a jump shot, get his first serve in, and hit a backhand – and do it better than we could," and in part because of his "fine and gentle demeanor, the kind that makes people lean forward to listen when he speaks." Mukasey remembered Haskel "unobtrusively looking in on even the most spontaneous and unorganized of activities, just to make sure that everyone was included (and that we were all speaking Hebrew)." But most of all, he remembered Haskel as "the only person I have ever seen participate in a water fight and maintain his dignity."[17]

Haskel graduated from Ramaz in the spring of 1949, as valedictorian of his class and president of the student government. He entered Columbia University that fall. He was, his father later noted with considerable pride, "the first student of Ramaz to have gained admission to Columbia and, therefore, the one who blazed a trail which was followed at Columbia and Barnard by a generation of Ramaz graduates." The fact that a significant percentage of Ramaz graduates attend Ivy League colleges became more than a badge of pride for Ramaz. It demonstrated the school's educational quality and also made a broader statement about the ability of modern Orthodox Jews to reach the highest echelons of American society. In effect, it helped validate one of the major contentions of the Centrist Orthodoxy that the Looksteins so passionately advocated.

Uncertain as to his career direction, Haskel enrolled in a wide range of courses at Columbia. Friends and relatives, his father included, assumed that in view of his oratorical and intellectual skills, Haskel would become an attorney; in fact, however, Haskel had no interest in doing so. Finally, late in his junior year, he sought his father's counsel in choosing a career path.

"In one more year I will graduate from Columbia as an educated bum," he recalled. "My father was not much interested in self-pity. He pressed me to name the field that interested me most. I said Jewish education, recalling how, at Massad, I had developed an interest in other people's religious behavior and ways in which I could help them. 'Well', he said, 'do you want to be a teacher or do you want to someday be principal of the school?' In our conversations, my father often criticized me but he also had an insightful way of clarifying issues and choices."[18]

Interestingly, Rabbi Lookstein had never spoken to his son about becoming a rabbi, although in retrospect Haskel assumed that some people in the congregation did harbor expectations that he would follow in his father's footsteps. R. Joseph told his son that if his goal was "to be a Jewish educator," then he had to "become educated Jewishly." It would not suffice to take courses in education – "if that is all you do, you'll become a plumber in Jewish education." The way to do it, he advised, was "after finishing your BA at Columbia College, enroll at Yeshiva University, attain rabbinical ordination, and then go into Jewish education." Haskel later speculated that his father may have had an unstated agenda, urging his son to pursue s'micha ostensibly for a career in education but quietly hoping it would lead him down the path to the rabbinate.

Haskel decided to test the waters. Never having studied gemara for long periods of time, he wanted to be sure he was capable and enjoyed it sufficiently before making a multiyear commitment. For six weeks in the summer of 1952 [the end of his junior year at Columbia] he traveled each day to Crown Heights to study Gemara with Rabbi Norman Lamm, Joseph Lookstein's rabbinic assistant at KJ. "My pupil was alert, quick, and took to the material – which could be quite abstruse – very readily," Rabbi Lamm recalled. "His native intelligence helped him overcome the inertia and listlessness urged on us by the summer heat." From Haskel's perspective, too, the experiment was a success; he concluded that he was both able and interested, so much so that he opted to complete his final courses at Columbia in the fall of 1952 in order to begin his studies at Yeshiva University in the spring of 1953, forgoing his final semester at college.[19]

Haskel being accustomed to the quiet, dignified atmosphere of Columbia's Butler Library ("If you whispered, you would be expelled," he joked), the scene he encountered when he entered the Y.U. beis midrash for the first time was something of a culture shock. "When I heard the level of noise, I thought to myself, 'How can anyone study with such a cacophony of voices?' People were yelling, wrestling with each other over a *tosefos*, hurling arguments back and forth in a way that was completely new to me."

His years at the Rabbi Isaac Elchanan Theological Seminary [RIETS], Yeshiva University's rabbinical school, exposed Haskel to some of the leading lights of contemporary Orthodox scholarship. In his first year he learned in the highest-level *shiur* of Samuel Sar, dean of students, while also learning privately with Rabbi Joseph Weiss, a *rosh yeshiva*, whom Haskel soon came to regard as his first "rebbe." The following year he studied Tractate *Sanhedrin* with Rabbi Avigdor Cyperstein. That year he also began a limited but formal connection to Ramaz by tutoring eighth graders for their bar mitzvahs.[20]

From there he moved up to the Gemara *shiur* of Rabbi Joseph B. Soloveitchik, the Rav. "I was very fortunate," he recalled. "He admitted me to the *shiur* even though I had much less background in serious Talmud study than the boys who had gone to Yeshiva College as undergraduates. But he evidently felt I had enough ability and potential to succeed, and so his approach toward me became, as he put it, 'stuff him like an ox.'"

Haskel's participation in Rabbi Soloveitchik's shiur created an unexpected dilemma. He had already completed two and a half years of study at Y.U. at that point, meaning he could complete his remaining requirements with other instructors and graduate in two more years. But as fate would have it, the Rav was just then inaugurating a special three-year study plan for rabbinical students, which involved learning Talmud and *Shulhan Arukh* together, with him. Haskel was torn between continuing on his path to graduate in two years or switching to the Rav's multiyear program and considerably delaying his graduation. Dean Sar provided the advice that "completely changed and informed my life," as Rabbi Lookstein later put it: "Spending an extra year in Y.U. won't reduce your life expectancy – but being able to spend four years learning with the Rav could make all the difference in the world." Rabbi Lookstein recalled:

> No one has ever given me better advice than that. Intellectually, religiously, and philosophically, the Rav was the greatest influence on my life. He was so influential that when I read his book, *Ish Ha-Halacha*, I was astonished at how much he was in tune with my whole worldview. Then, of course, I realized that it was the other way around – that after so many years of exposure to him, I had so internalized his teachings, it looked to me like he was speaking my language – rather than me thinking some of his thoughts.[21]

✤ NOTES

1. Rafael Medoff interview with Rabbi Haskel Lookstein (hereafter cited as RHL interview), 10 July 2007.
2. Rabbi Joseph H. Lookstein, "Ramaz at Forty – A Sentimental History," undated (1977) (New York: Kehilath Jeshurun, 1977), pp. 3–4.
3. RHL interview, 10 July 2007.
4. Rabbi Margolies's willingness to work with non-Orthodox Jews is explored in Jeffrey S. Gurock, *American Jewish Orthodoxy in Historical Perspective* (Hoboken, N.J.: Ktav, 1996), pp. 19–23.
5. Ibid.
6. Ibid.
7. Ibid.
8. Ibid.; Francesca Lunzer Kritz interview with Rafael Medoff, 2 December 2007.
9. RHL interview, 10 July 2007.
10. RHL interview, 12 February 2008.
11. "Oral History," *Kehilath Jeshurun Bulletin* (hereafter KJB), December 1997, p. 12.
12. RHL interview, 10 July 2007.
13. Nachum Bronznick memoir in *Ner L'Echad Ner L'Meah: Rabbi Haskel Lookstein* (New York: Kehilath Jeshurun, 1998).
14. RHL interview, 10 July 2007.
15. RHL interview, 12 February 2008.
16. RHL interview, 10 July 2007; Dr. Shlomo Shulsinger-Shar Yashuv memoir in Adele Tauber, ed., *Haskel Lookstein: Teacher, Preacher and Leader* (New York: Kehilath Jeshurun, 1983) (hereafter *Teacher, Preacher*), p. 14.
17. Michael Mukasey memoir in *Teacher, Preacher*, p. 14.
18. RHL interview, 10 July 2007.
19. Ibid.; Dr. Norman Lamm, "Unintended Consequence," in *Teacher, Preacher*, p. 24.
20. RHL interview, 10 July 2007.
21. RHL interview, 25 July 2007.

✂ II. THE RABBI

In the spring of 1958, five and a half years after he began his studies at RIETS, Haskel Lookstein received his rabbinical ordination. He had been one of the top students in the Rav's *shiur*, focusing almost all his time on his studies there. The only exception had been for the limited time he devoted to teaching the bar mitzvah and cantillation classes at Ramaz, something he had taken on after Joseph Adler departed for the gefilte fish business. It was a job that had become a labor of love for Haskel; teaching the boys how to *layn* [read from the Torah] and *daven* was actually what he enjoyed most, and there was an important practical achievement as well: "For five and a half years I developed boys who were really proficient at reading the Torah – not just reading their bar mitzvah portion, but giving them the skills for a lifetime of *layning*."

R. Joseph, however, felt strongly that bar mitzvah tutoring was no longer an appropriate task now that Haskel had achieved ordination. In his view, that was a job better left to a rabbinical student. Haskel reluctantly agreed to give it up.

But there is an exception to every rule, and in the late spring of 1958, after Haskel's final year at RIETS, a prominent lay leader at KJ, Alexander Gross, asked him to tutor his son Steven for his bar mitzvah (to be held in June 1959). "I told him I knew that Steven was a good student," he recalled, "and I would love to teach him, but my father had instructed me not to do any more bar mitzvah tutoring, especially in view of the possibility that I would become assistant rabbi at KJ." Gross was insistent. "Of course your father is right," he said. "But my Stevenyu!" Haskel made an exception, and never regretted it. Gross grew up to become an important leader in the Jewish community, chairman of the board of Ramaz, and a major force behind the building of the Ramaz middle school and other projects. "And he can still read a flawless *haftorah*," Rabbi Haskel noted with pride.[1]

During his final year at RIETS, Haskel, like all *s'micha* students, met with Victor Geller, director of Y.U.'s Office of Rabbinic Placement. As is customary, he was offered two possible positions.

"One was in Detroit and I didn't want to go there, because I naively believed there were few single Jewish girls there," he recalled. "I was the most provincial person you ever saw – I had lived my whole life between 84th and 86th Streets, and Lexington and Madison Avenues. I could not imagine viable Jewish communal life existed as far away as Detroit." The second possible pulpit was for a Sephardic shul that was being developed in Cedarhurst, Long Island. "I was not ready to become a Sephardic rabbi either."[2]

Dissatisfied with those prospects, Haskel approached his father about the possibility of a position at KJ. "Both my son and I were excited about the idea but we entertained serious reservations as well," according to R. Joseph's account. "It is never easy for a father and son to work together in the same profession and under the same roof. In the rabbinate it is almost unheard of." Moreover, Haskel recognized that it would have been better if he had served his first pulpit in some other congregation, where he could gain some experience and establish a record of institutional success, before coming to KJ. But given the circumstances, he thought KJ might work. Victor Geller was less than encouraging: "Haskel, you could do it, but you have to understand what you're getting into," he said, and then offered a baseball analogy that the sports-loving young rabbi could readily appreciate: "It's like the seventh game of the World Series, the last of the ninth inning, the score is tied, the bases are loaded, there are no outs and the count is 3 and 0. And you are summoned from the bullpen. It's possible to get out without a run scoring. But you can't make a single mistake." Haskel's interpretation: it's difficult but feasible. Geller laughed when he recalled the story many years later; he was, in fact, trying to warn him against taking the job.[3]

Kehilath Jeshurun's lay leaders were not of one mind regarding the possibility of Haskel becoming assistant rabbi at that time. Max Etra, who had been president of the synagogue since 1940, felt strongly that Haskel should first obtain experience in a different community prior to working at KJ. But a group of supporters, led by Alexander Gross, Oscar Perlberger, and Yeshiva

University president Dr. Samuel Belkin, pressed ahead with a board of trustees meeting, in Rabbi Joseph Lookstein's home, to decide the matter.[4]

The episode highlights R. Joseph's unusually powerful position. In most synagogues the rabbi is an employee who does not typically attend board meetings, much less play a significant role in its decisions. Joseph Lookstein, by contrast, completely involved himself in the governance of the synagogue and the school. He took part in board meetings and, although they did not normally take place in the rabbi's home, none of the board members looked askance at the fact that the meeting concerning R. Haskel's status was held there, even though that very fact could be seen as influencing the board's decision. Whatever the private qualms of the board members about hiring R. Haskel at that time, it is hard to imagine them defying their revered rabbi in his own living room. Sure enough, whatever opposition might have existed had melted by the time Dr. Belkin made the nomination. "Then, it is reported, something most unusual occurred," according to the KJ newsletter. "Everyone among those present seconded the nomination." Two weeks later R. Haskel was formally installed as assistant rabbi and "accepted the mantle of his new post with dignity," the newsletter reported.[5]

R. Haskel's transition from rabbinical student to assistant rabbi was facilitated by two key relationships. One was with Dr. Belkin, who happened to sit in the front row at KJ, immediately adjacent to R. Haskel. "Whenever I delivered a sermon, as I returned to my seat, he would spring to his feet, his hand extended, and give me a big *"yasher koach"* – even if the sermon wasn't so great," R. Haskel remembered. "It was indicative of the fact that he was, beneath his reserved exterior, a warm, gracious, and extremely kind man."

The other important relationship was with the Rav, Rabbi Joseph Soloveitchik. Because of his stature as a scholar and leader, some of his students and admirers hesitated to approach him personally. R. Haskel, however, established a closer than usual *talmid-rebbe* rapport with him early on and always felt comfortable consulting with him about matters large and small. In an address in the main synagogue on the occasion of the 100th anniversary of Kehilath Jeshurun, Rabbi Soloveitchik, after strongly praising Rabbi Joseph Lookstein, turned to R. Haskel, sitting in the front row, and said, "Chatzkel, do you want me to say something about you too?" ("I would have liked to fall through a trap door at that moment," R. Haskel later mused.) He then remarked, "Your father, I respect. You, I love."[6]

On one occasion, during a *shiur* after the Rav had developed an extensive analytic argument about a certain subject in the Talmud, Haskel noticed what he perceived to be a contradiction between the Rav's argument and a point the Rav had made during a *shiur* some months earlier. "Rebbe," he asked, "how does this fit with the analysis that we developed some months ago?" The Rav, his eyes wide with surprise, thought for a moment and then said to the class: "You are right, I am wrong. Do you hear, students? Lookstein is correct, I am incorrect. I'll have to go home and relearn the entire subject and present it again tomorrow."[7]

The detailed memoranda of his conversations with the Rav in the early 1980s, which Rabbi Lookstein composed for his private reference, indicate that he routinely consulted the Rav on a range of issues, from the minutiae of traditional ritual observances to the unique concerns of the modern era. One session in early 1982 included discussions about women dancing with a sefer Torah on Simchat Torah, the use of prenuptial agreements to ameliorate the *aguna* problem, requirements for conversion, the permissibility of spelling out the word "God," and the reheating of foods on Shabbat. Another, in the autumn of 1984, addressed such issues as aborting a Tay Sachs pregnancy, calling a Reform rabbi to the Torah in an Orthodox synagogue, and what kind of public transgressions would disqualify someone from serving as a witness at a Jewish wedding.[8]

The topics raised in the conversations between R. Lookstein and R. Soloveitchik point to the difficulties facing rabbis in the modern era, the changing role of the rabbi in his synagogue and community, and the unique problems confronting modern Orthodoxy in navigating between old-world-style Judaism and the lures of American society. From the moment he assumed the position of assistant rabbi at Kehilath Jeshurun, Haskel Lookstein became acutely aware of these challenges.

The examples set by his great-grandfather, and especially, his father, offered R. Haskel additional guidance as he embarked on his new position. The historians Adam Ferziger and Jeffrey Gurock have pointed out that although the RaMaZ was in many respects a "rabbi from the old school," some of his actions belied that stereotype, including his support for Zionism, his willingness to work with non-Orthodox rabbis in Jewish organizational functions, and his invitation to Hebrew University chancellor Judah Magnes to speak at KJ on Yom Kippur eve despite Magnes's affiliation with Reform Judaism.[9] Rabbi Joseph Lookstein went considerably further, shaping and promoting Americanized Orthodoxy not as a grudging concession to modern pressures – as some of his colleagues in the Orthodox rabbinate regarded it – but as an approach that stood on its own as a comprehensive ideology.

When R. Joseph became assistant rabbi at KJ back in 1923, Orthodox synagogue life in Manhattan had not been at all to his liking. Contemporary critics described the typical Lower East Side synagogue of that era as small, overcrowded, unkempt, and even "un-American" – that is, out of step with modern, American houses of worship.[10] KJ was just beginning to attract "self-consciously, upwardly mobile immigrants [for whom] the indecorous and informal downtown synagogue served as an uncomfortable reminder of their immigrant origins and of their un-Americanized selves," the historian Jenna Joselit has pointed out. R. Joseph made it one of his priorities to improve KJ's physical appearance. He believed that with the right presentation, Orthodoxy could constitute a viable alternative to Reform and Conservative Judaism on the Upper East Side. He went so far as to "personally inspect the building from top to bottom, making sure that the bathrooms were clean, the brass finishings of the sanctuary polished, and its prayer books untattered and regularly dusted."[11]

Prayer services adhered to Orthodox liturgy but were conducted in as orderly and dignified a manner as possible. "Our intention," Rabbi Lookstein later recalled, "was to conduct the kind of public worship that would be as dignified as the most Reform and as pious as the worship in a *shteibbel*."[12] A small portion of the services were even conducted in English, a practice not forbidden by Jewish law but unusual in an Orthodox synagogue. "From personal experience, I have seen the welcome thrill on the faces of worshipers when, for example, during a *Yizkor* service an English psalm or prayer is read," he wrote. "I am convinced that a slight concession in this regard might keep within the folds of Orthodoxy a multitude who might otherwise desert us."[13]

Throughout his career, R. Joseph closely scrutinized his congregants' behavior to ensure appropriate comportment. As late as 1976, near the end of his tenure at KJ, he was admonishing the congregation for its "overindulgence in handshaking" after someone was called to the Torah. "The handshaking syndrome has become almost a compulsive act," he wrote in an appeal in the KJ newsletter. "People have been seen to walk from a far end of the synagogue in order to shake the hand and congratulate someone who had an *aliya* or any other honor. It is utterly unnecessary to do that and, moreover, it is a disturbing practice and interferes with the dignity and the order of public worship." He proposed that "a friendly and dignified nod of the head" would constitute a more appropriate gesture.[14]

In R. Joseph's view, personal attire too constituted an integral part of congregational dignity. The *KJ Bulletin* often featured his appeals for appropriate dress. A typical remonstrance, appearing in the newsletter in 1965, pointed out that when one observes "devotees of other faiths going to their respective places of worship," the men "wear dark clothes and black shoes" and "the women invariably are dressed becomingly but in modesty." KJ members should do no less, R. Joseph admonished: "A dark suit and black shoes – not tan, not loafers – should be the standard for men," and "as for the ladies, they will understand what modesty in dress is."[15]

For all his emphasis on order and decorum, R. Joseph seems to have harbored a certain limited fondness for the exuberance that characterizes Chassidic worship. While his idea of appropriate behavior during services was quite different from what would be found in a Chassidic shteibel, he proudly noted in the KJ newsletter in 1965 that "Chassidic spirit is a rare phenomenon in Yorkville but on Simchat Torah it is experienced in full in our synagogue."[16] Likewise, his description of a teenagers' Shabbaton at KJ that year expressed pleasure that the youths "sang Chassidic songs and danced with a fervor not usually associated with groups in our neighborhood."[17]

The years that Joseph Lookstein occupied the KJ pulpit were a period of struggle and change for Orthodox Judaism in America, and R. Joseph was often on the front lines. The pressures of integrating into American life had pushed many Jewish immigrants and children of immigrants to leave Orthodoxy for Conservative Judaism. In the late 1930s, when R. Joseph succeeded the RaMaZ as senior rabbi at KJ, Orthodoxy was numerically the largest of American Judaism's denominations. But many of its adherents practiced what Jeffrey Gurock has characterized as "inconsistent Orthodoxy"; that is, they were lax in their personal religious observance, although they chose to be members of an Orthodox synagogue.[18] On the infrequent occasions when they took part in synagogue life – typically on the High Holidays – they felt more comfortable doing so in an Orthodox setting. Rabbi Lookstein built KJ in the 1940s and 1950s by actively competing for the support of these inconsistent Orthodox. Making KJ physically attractive helped win the affections of aesthetic-minded, upwardly mobile, and religiously casual Upper East Siders.

In the 1950s and 1960s American Orthodoxy continued to lose some of its less observant members to Conservative Judaism. At the same time, however, the Orthodox community was strengthened by a postwar influx of East European Orthodox immigrants from Europe and the coming of age of more religiously strict children of modern Orthodox families. After decades of steady erosion in levels of religious observance, the pendulum began to swing in the other direction, at least for some segments of the Orthodox community.[19]

R. Joseph continued advocating a centrist religious path, amid what he regarded as alarming signs of a religious shift to the right among some of KJ's own rank and file during the 1960s and later. In a note to his son – he would often put his suggestions to Haskel in writing – the elder Rabbi Lookstein in 1968 warned against what he called the "chnokerization" of KJ, that is, a tendency on the part of some members to put exaggerated focus on observances that were customary rather than required by Jewish law. He urged Haskel to remain steadfast in resisting such trends. As for those at the other end of the KJ religious spectrum, R. Joseph never compromised on KJ's official fealty to basic Orthodox principles, but he refrained from pressuring less observant congregants to become more scrupulous in their personal practice. His sermons typically commented on news events or important Jewish principles rather than admonishing his listeners over their level of observance. He was convinced that by setting the proper example and creating an attractive environment, he could "make Conservatism or Reform unnecessary and undesirable to a substantial number of families in the neighborhood."[20]

Although he was competing with Conservatism and Reform, R. Joseph approached non-Orthodox Jews with utmost respect and civility, and he taught his son to do likewise. "My father loved every Jew, no matter what his state of religiosity, piety or observance," R. Haskel noted. "He used to say, 'The only Jew I don't love is one who doesn't love other Jews.'" Significantly, his father "was prepared to meet every Jew where he was, and, through warmth and genuine affection, he tried to bring him closer to tradition. Kehilath Jeshurun and Ramaz were built on this foundation of love and acceptance."[21] It is noteworthy that in 1959 a front-page report in the *KJ Bulletin* describing recent academic achievements by "young people of KJ" announced with evident pride that one young man "was ordained as Rabbi by the Jewish Theological Seminary," Conservative Judaism's rabbinical institution. On a similar note, the speaker chosen to deliver the sermon following Thanksgiving Day services in 1962 was a professor at Reform Judaism's rabbinical seminary, Hebrew Union College, and was involved in a Bible translation project, no less – and was identified as such in the KJ newsletter.[22] This open approach to intra-Jewish relations reflected both Joseph Lookstein's personality and his philosophy of Jewish communal life. His son would do likewise. For example, when Rabbi Dr. Mordecai Kaplan, founder of Reconstructionist Judaism, passed away in 1983, R. Haskel placed a paid obituary for him in the *New York Times*, acknowledging that Kaplan had once been an assistant rabbi at KJ and praising his intellectual contributions to American Jewish life.[23] In a similar spirit, R. Haskel in 1986 invited a Conservative rabbi, Reuven Kimmelman, to serve as Scholar in Residence for KJ's Annual Synagogue Shabbaton.[24]

Compassion was another trait that R. Haskel absorbed from his forebears. According to Lookstein family lore, a woman once came to the RaMaZ on a Friday afternoon with a chicken that had a hole in its stomach. She wanted to know if it was kosher. Rabbi Margolies and R. Joseph inspected the chicken together. The younger rabbi felt certain that the chicken had swallowed a sharp object which had punctured its stomach, one of the eighteen primary criteria for deciding that something is nonkosher. The RaMaZ took a *sefer* from his bookshelf and located a similar case in which an early *halakhic* authority had permitted eating the chicken. He then found a second rabbinical authority, in another *sefer*, who had likewise issued a lenient ruling in such a case. "This is a poor woman," Rabbi Margolies told R. Joseph. "If we declare her chicken to be *treif* she will have nothing to eat for Shabbos. Let's rely on these two [authorities] and you take a little responsibility on your shoulders and I'll take some on my shoulders and let this woman have a good Shabbos."

This, R. Haskel later wrote, was an example of the "*Torat chesed*" that his father learned from the RaMaZ and passed on to him. "It demonstrated [Rabbi Margolies's] care for people…. He embodied in his personality the Talmudic principle that *koach d'heteira adif*, the power to permit, is preferable to the power to prohibit." The RaMaZ "believed that it was the responsibility of a *posek* [religious authority] to make Judaism livable for people and not difficult for them," a principle R. Haskel deemed especially important "in an era like ours, where so many Orthodox Jews seem to belong to the '*Chumra* of the Month Club.'"(elevating the observance of nonobligatory customs almost to the level of religious requirements).[25]

While the new assistant rabbi was in some respects his father's son – "my father was, after all, larger than life and in many ways I idolized him" – R. Haskel also had ideas of his own that he hoped to implement at KJ.

> Yes, the services were very dignified, and that was appropriate, at least to a certain extent. But they were also somewhat stuffy. Men were expected to wear a black *kippa* in *shul*; if you showed up with a knitted *kippa*, an usher would ask you to take it off. Nor was the atmosphere child-friendly – since there was so much emphasis on the services being orderly, people were less likely to bring their children. I understood what my father was doing. He was trying to create an Orthodox synagogue in which people would feel just as comfortable as if they were in Temple Emanuel. And his approach was absolutely right for the first half of the twentieth century. But as we entered the 1960s, people's needs were starting to change. I thought it would be possible to loosen things up a little, not in terms of the content of the services, but in the overall atmosphere of the *shul*.[26]

One of R. Haskel's first initiatives was the creation of a Young Marrieds Club. Beginning in the autumn of 1958, the club met monthly at members' homes to discuss current social and political issues, sometimes with multiple speakers to explore issues from various angles. The inaugural meeting, for example, which focused on birth control, brought speakers to address the medical, legal, and socioeconomic aspects of the issue, with Rabbi Lookstein presenting "the Jewish view." The level of audience participation was "spotty at best," perhaps, according to R. Haskel's notes, "due to the delicate nature of the subject."[27] The next session, however, dealt with "The Parent-Child Relationship," and "everyone participated and aired his views on the subject…if success is measured by liveliness, it was quite successful," the rabbi noted.[28] The Young Marrieds Club continued to court controversy over the years. For example, one 1966 meeting focusing on the adoption of racially mixed Jewish babies generated "a heated discussion" that turned "explosive," according to the KJ newsletter.[29]

In 1958 Yeshiva University launched a Department of Adult Education to help modern Orthodox synagogues undertake their own adult learning programs. Under R. Haskel's direction, the KJ Adult Institute grew in its first two years from three courses and 25 part-time students to seven courses with 116 full-time students. Featuring classes in Talmud, Hebrew language, Jewish history, festival laws, and liturgy, the program was so popular that many of the classes in the first year were extended through the summer months. By the second year, R. Haskel reported to the Y.U. Department of Adult Education "a phenomenal rise" in the congregation's interest and participation in the program. The Jewish history class was particularly popular, with 90 registrants. Attendees in the various courses "ranged from the president of the congregation to the most recently elected member."[30] Course offerings expanded significantly in the years that followed. Hebrew calligraphy, Jewish music, and Holocaust literature joined the list, as well as a course on the New York Jewish community, taught by Malcolm Hoenlein, then executive director of the Jewish

Community Relations Council, and a session on the thought of Martin Buber, taught by Professor Michael Wyschogrod.

To judge by the topics selected for various synagogue programs in the early 1960s, KJ under the Rabbis Lookstein was a congregation that was somewhat ahead of its time. For example, although the Soviet Jewry protest movement in the United States did not become a significant part of the major Jewish organizations' agenda until 1970–1971, the KJ Men's Club as early as 1964 featured a film about the plight of Soviet Jewry. Likewise, although public discussion of the world's response to the Holocaust began in earnest only with the publication of Arthur Morse's 1968 book, *While Six Million Died*, KJ's Cultural Luncheons series in 1964 and again in 1965 featured mock trials of the international community for standing idly by during the Holocaust.[31] The KJ adult education offerings were also notable for their recognition of the growing interest among women in advanced Jewish studies. A Talmud *shiur* by the noted scholar Rabbi Hershel Schachter was open to women, and although only a small number of the attendees were women, they described it as a groundbreaking experience.[32]

Some of the programs R. Haskel initiated responded to specific problems in the congregation. For example, a proposal for a "Sabbath Seudah Seminar" that he drew up in the early 1960s sought to combat indications of religious laxity during the final hours of the Sabbath day. "As the day draws slowly to a close, the tendency to ignore [the restrictions of] Shabbat becomes more pronounced," he wrote. "The violations of Shabbat afternoon can vary from a television program to an early start for an evening appointment.... Now, we regularly have an attendance of 60 to 70 men, women, and children [at Shabbat *mincha* services] – no mean feat in a community such as ours. I don't know what the men and women do at home when they don't come to *mincha* on Shabbat. The chances are that they are not saying *Gott fun Avrohom*[33] with their children as they watch the evening shadows lengthen. When they are in *shul*, however, I can be certain that their Shabbat is ending on the right note."

As he envisioned it, the program would consist of the *mincha* prayer service, a communal meal with singing, and then a discussion period that would include questions for the rabbi and a ten-minute talk by a layman (which, he felt, would increase attendance because "laymen bring their own rooting section"). The topics to be discussed should be cleared with the rabbi first, "otherwise Jacob will be described as a cheat, Joseph a spoiled brat, and Miriam a gossiping virago, with the rabbi left to defend them." Speakers too needed to be chosen "with the utmost caution" since, as he put it, "not every layman is a Demosthenes although there will be no shortage of men and women who think they are." Not coincidentally, the κj *Bulletin*'s report on the success of the opening program (70 people attended) asserted that speakers Fred and Rosemiriam Zuckerman spoke "with the eloquence, lucidity, and cogency of a Demosthenes." The program was so successful that R. Haskel was invited to deliver a report on it at the following year's annual convention of the Yeshiva University Rabbinic Alumni.[34]

R. Haskel invested considerable energy in developing an array of youth groups, and as early as 1961 his father noted approvingly that the κj building was "humming with youth activity," so much so that "two doormen had to be engaged to provide adequate protection until late in the evening." A Junior Congregation program on Shabbat mornings, under the leadership of future Ramaz administrator Noam Shudofsky, grew quickly in the early 1960s, as did a group for κj teenagers called Shachar. "Our teenage group is the only one of its kind throughout the city that does not depend upon such activities as 'Jewish basketball' and 'Jewish bowling' for its main attractions," R. Haskel proudly reported to the board of trustees in 1964. "Our young people are deeply involved in other forms of creative expression." The Father and Son Minyan, a Sunday morning program combining prayer, breakfast, and basketball, more than doubled its attendance during the 1960s, from an average of 25 in its early days to more than 50 each week. Even a storm that left 17 inches of snow could not keep 38 men and boys from attending one Sunday in the winter of 1968.[35]

At R. Haskel's initiative, KJ also introduced a Men's Club Shabbat and a Young Couples Club Shabbat, in which congregants active in those clubs led the services in place of the regular *hazan*. "Of course not everyone was as talented as the regular *hazan*, but it was much more participatory," he noted. Later an annual "Sabbath of Welcome for New Members" was launched, with as many as 70 new members joining the Looksteins for a buffet lunch in their apartment on Shabbat.[36]

The cumulative impact of all these programs could be seen in the KJ membership's evolving demographic profile. One Shabbat morning in 1965, R. Joseph – prodded, he said, by a worshipper who "remarked about the bountiful representation of young people at the services" – decided to "take the liberty of making an educated estimate" and concluded that of the 300-plus congregants on hand, "better than one third of the worshippers were between the ages of 13 and 35." This "delightful trend," he wrote, extended to other aspects of congregational life: almost 50 children attended that day's Junior Congregation; the Young Marrieds Group "now numbers some 40 couples"; KJ's teen group, Shachar, "now numbers 68 members"; and on Shabbat afternoons "the synagogue house is filled with young children who are engaged in club activities." Not too long before, he noted, the number of worshippers and club attendees "was much smaller." A 93-year-old synagogue with such an "active, young constituency" is "a happy combination of tradition and progress.... We have every reason to hope that our greatest accomplishments are yet to come."[37]

These trends continued in the years that followed. At the 1971 annual meeting, KJ president Harry Baumgarten spoke of "a steady infusion of young and fresh blood into the veins and arteries of this old congregation." Noting that it was "a time when we hear much about young people abandoning their ancestral faith," and when "we hear sighs and groans about the rebellion of youth and about the 'new breed' which is drifting from us," he pointed with pride to the fact that "we at Kehilath Jeshurun can report that our young people are following in the footsteps of their forebears."[38]

Although R. Haskel's innovations arguably played a significant role in these advances, his father often responded cautiously to proposed changes. "This is not Kehilath Jeshurun" was the reaction R. Haskel sometimes received at first, but eventually, after further discussion and his son's prodding, the elder Rabbi Lookstein would reluctantly authorize his son to "go ahead and try it," often conceding afterwards that the change was worthwhile.

Sukkot 1971 provided a vivid example of this process. That year the first days of the holiday fell on a Monday and Tuesday. Catered meals were offered in the synagogue's *sukka* for $19 per meal, a substantial sum for those times. Ninety-two people attended the first meal, but only 45 came to lunch the next day. No meal was offered Monday night because, as R. Joseph put it, "Who wants to eat two big meals in one day?" By Tuesday lunch, attendance was down to 19. R. Haskel, who was focused on the importance of finding ways to bring the congregants together, was convinced that an important opportunity for communal celebration and bonding had been missed.

Sitting at the Tuesday lunch with his father and KJ president Harry Baumgarten, R. Haskel reported that Lincoln Square Synagogue had served TV dinners for $5 per person – and attracted 200 participants. He proposed doing likewise for Shabbat chol ha-moed and, in fact, had already discussed it with a caterer. R. Joseph was indignant at the suggestion: "Absolutely not. That's not the Kehilath Jeshurun style; we will attract every freeloader around." R. Haskel was insistent, but when he saw that he was not persuading his father, he said bluntly, "If you won't try it out, my family and I will go to a private *sukka* on Friday night and Shabbat lunch. I can't sit here with a group which is so small because we have made the meals too expensive for ordinary people to afford." Baumgarten weighed in on R. Haskel's side, urging Rabbi Lookstein to give the idea a chance. The rabbi reluctantly gave in, although he was still convinced that the experience would be terrible. In actuality, 200 people attended the Friday night dinner and also returned for lunch the next day. ĸj teenagers served the meals. "It was a tremendous, delightful community event," R. Haskel later recalled. "The teenagers from the *shul* served the meals and did a wonderful job. There was a spirit of togetherness, lots of *ruach*. My father agreed it had gone very well, but said we shouldn't do it again. I said, on the contrary, we have to do it, because that's the way to have Sukkot."

The following year the first days of Sukkot were due to fall on Shabbat and Sunday. Three months before the holiday, R. Haskel was invited to participate in a mission to the Soviet Union (see below). He asked his father to make the necessary arrangements for another ᴛᴠ dinner-Sukkot event. Agreeing only with the greatest reluctance, R. Joseph became increasingly anxious about the plan as his son's date of departure approached. The elder Rabbi Lookstein predicted that the experience would be "a disaster"and expressed regret that he had ever agreed to it. R. Haskel was incommunicado for nearly the entire two weeks of his trip behind the Iron Curtain. Stopping briefly in London on his way back to the United States, he found two letters from his father waiting for him at the hotel.

The first was postmarked the Friday before Sukkot. Sparks were flying off the page. "Hack, everything I feared is going to happen. All the cheapskates are making reservations, it's going to be a real mess. This is not ĸj style. We will never do this again!" The second letter was postmarked the Monday of *Hol ha-moed*. "Dear Hack, I have to apologize to you. I was wrong. It was fabulous. Mike Barany, a ĸj member who volunteered to organize the meals, did a great job, the kids served nicely, the spirit was wonderful, the *Sukka* was filled with singing. It was very very special." I give my father alot of credit for saying that. Doing it that way was not at all his style.[39]

Joseph Lookstein had built Kehilath Jeshurun according to a strategy that placed utmost emphasis on dignity and propriety. "That Sukkot, by contrast, was positively *heimish*," R. Haskel said. "It was orderly, but with a good deal of planned disorder. Teenagers instead of waiters? Paper plates and paper tablecloths instead of dishes and nice linen tablecloths? It was unheard of at kj." R. Joseph and others of his generation were accustomed to synagogue's events that reflected the station in life that most of the congregants had attained. By contrast, R. Haskel's approach sacrificed luxury for affordability in order to include members who were less well off.

The experience was indicative of a young assistant rabbi beginning to "loosen things up a bit," leaving his mark in ways that would ultimately facilitate the growth of the synagogue and the community around it. By 2007 kj was serving as many as 600 people in three separate *sukkas*, possibly the largest communal Sukkot celebrations in the United States at the time. The tv dinners are a thing of the past, and waiters have replaced the teenagers, but the synagogue still keeps the price low, often taking a loss in order to make the event accessible to congregants and their families of all economic levels, and even permitting participants to bring their own meals if they cannot afford the price.

In the same spirit of fostering what he called "a family feeling," R. Haskel sought to introduce the practice of singing briefly after a *misheberach* is recited at the Torah reading in celebration of a family *simcha*. After a *misheberach* for the birth of a girl, the song would be *Siman Tov U'Mazel Tov*; for the birth of a boy, *Ureh Vanim*; for an engagement, *Od Yishama*; for an *aufruf* [pre-wedding celebration], *Vayehi Biy'shurun Melech*. R. Haskel was not the first modern Orthodox rabbi to do this, but it represented such a sharp break from R. Joseph's regimented style that the elder rabbi Lookstein insisted his son bring the issue before the board of trustees. One trustee did, in fact, object, charging that such singing was "not in keeping with the dignity of our congregation" and warning that the assistant rabbi was "trying to turn this place into a Young Israel" by permitting a level of disorder comparable to that for which some Young Israel synagogues are known. But with R. Joseph's support, the proposal gained approval by consensus and became standard KJ practice, occasionally even branching out into a chorus of "Happy Birthday."[40]

R. Haskel's modest innovations at KJ and the father–son disagreements they occasionally engendered were all part of the apprenticeship experience. "Everything I do as a rabbi, I learned from my father," he said. "From watching him, I learned everything from preaching to running a funeral or a wedding to administration of the synagogue. He taught Practical Rabbinics and Homiletics at RIETS – but I was blessed to have the living role model." R. Joseph was also a helpful critic. "On a Shabbat when I gave the sermon, we went to his office after the services to take off our *taleism*, and he would invariably say, 'Hack, that was a very fine sermon, thoughtful and very well organized; of course, I would have said….' Sometimes, deep down, I might have bristled a bit because of the critique, but after his passing I came to miss that criticism very much. I miss having someone who will tell me straight when I am off base – the congregants are too respectful and my wife loves me too much. For a while, my daughter Debbie filled the role – walking home from shul, she would say, 'Daddy, I think that was a pretty good sermon; I would give it an A-minus,' and then she would explain why it wasn't an A."[41]

The transition from R. Joseph's leadership to R. Haskel's would have proceeded very gradually had health issues not intervened. In 1965 R. Joseph's doctor, alarmed by the rabbi's developing heart condition, ordered him to withdraw from at least one of his major areas of work. Until that time, he had served simultaneously as rabbi of KJ, principal of Ramaz, and, since 1954, acting president and then chancellor of Bar Ilan University. He chose to give up his role at Ramaz. R. Haskel replaced him.

✢ NOTES

1. Ibid.
2. Ibid.
3. Rabbi Joseph H. Lookstein, "Rabbi Haskel Lookstein: An Evaluation and a Tribute," undated (1978), File: Rabbi Joseph Lookstein, KJ, p. 3; RHL interview, 25 July 2007.
4. RHL interview, 10 July 2007.
5. "Haskel Lookstein Elected Assistant to Rabbi Lookstein," KJB XXV:36 (6 June 1958), p. 1; "Rabbi Haskel Lookstein Installed as Assistant Rabbi in Congregation," KJB XXV:38 (20 June 1958), p. 1.
6. RHL interview, 25 July 2007.
7. Rabbi Lookstein recounted this anecdote in a memorial article he wrote in the Spring 2003 issue of *Jewish Action*, after the Rav's passing. In that version, however, Rabbi Lookstein did not reveal that in fact he was the student who spotted the discrepancy.
8. Memoranda of Rabbi Haskel Lookstein's conversations with Rabbi Soloveitchik, 24 March 1982 and 1 November 1984, File: Rabbi Joseph Soloveitchik, Kehilath Jeshurun Archives, New York (hereafter KJ).
9. Adam S. Ferziger, "The Lookstein Legacy: An American Orthodox Rabbinical Dynasty?" *Jewish History* 12:1 (Spring 1999), pp. 128–129; Jeffrey S. Gurock, *American Jewish Orthodoxy in Historical Perspective* (Hoboken, N.J.: Ktav, 1996), p. 120.
10. Jenna Weissman Joselit, "Of Manners, Morals, and Orthodox Judaism: Decorum Within the Orthodox Synagogue," in Jeffrey S. Gurock, ed., *Ramaz: School, Community, Scholarship & Orthodoxy* (Hoboken, N.J.: Ktav, 1989), p. 24.
11. Joselit, op.cit., p. 27.
12. Ferziger, "Lookstein Legacy," p. 131.
13. Joselit, op.cit., pp. 40, 65.
14. Joseph H. Lookstein, "The Handshake," KJB XLIV:4 (12 November 1976), p. 3.
15. "Appropriate Attire for the House of God," KJB XXXIV:3 (17 September 1965), p. 1.
16. "Hakafoth at Kehilath Jeshurun," KJB XXXIV:5 (8 October 1965), p. 3.
17. "Ramaz and Shachar Weekend Attracts Exuberant Gathering of Teenagers," KJB XXXIII:34 (28 May 1965), p. 1.
18. Jeffrey S. Gurock, "The Winnowing of American Orthodoxy," *Approaches to Modern Judaism* II (1984), pp. 41–54.
19. Jeffrey S. Gurock, "From Fluidity to Rigidity: The Religious Worlds of Conservative and Orthodox Jews in Twentieth Century America," David W. Belin Lecture in American Jewish Affairs (Ann Arbor: University of Michigan, 1998), p. 14.
20. Ferziger, "Lookstein Legacy," pp. 130–131.
21. Rabbi Haskel Lookstein, "Words of Eulogy," undated (1979), File: Rabbi Joseph Lookstein, KJ, p. 5.
22. "Young People of K.J. Advance Academically," KJB XVII:37 (19 June 1959), p. 1; "Dr. Harry M. Orlinsky to Discuss New Bible Translation at Thanksgiving Service," KJB XXXI:9 (16 November 1962), p. 1.
23. R. Haskel credits his mother, Gertrude Lookstein, for the suggestion to place the obituary.
24. "Rabbi Reuven Kimmelman to Be Scholar in Residence at Annual Synagogue Shabbaton," KJB LIII:6 (21 March 1986), p. 3; "Face to Face with Pope John Paul," KJB LV:2 (12 October 1987), p. 3.
25. "The Ramaz on His 70th Yahrzeit – A Sermon of Tribute by His Great Grandson, Rabbi Haskel Lookstein, Shabbat Ki Tetze," September 2, 2006, File: Rabbi Moses Margolies, KJ, pp. 3–4.
26. RHL interview, 10 July 2007.
27. "Young Marrieds Meeting No. 2, November 15, 1958," File: Young Marrieds, KJ.
28. "Young Marrieds Meeting No. 3, January 10, 1959," File: Young Marrieds, KJ.

29. "Rabbi Isaac N. Trainin Addresses Young Marrieds on Matter of Great Concern," KJB XXXIV:30 (29 April 1966).
30. Martin Markson, "Adult Institute" (undated), File: Adult Institute, KJ.
31. "Another Capacity Audience Attends Men's Club Meeting," KJB XXXIII:11 (21 November 1964), 1; "Report on Activities of Congregation Kehilath Jeshurun 1964–1965" (New York: Kehilath Jeshurun, 1965), pp. 8, 21; "Cultural Luncheon Serves as Forum for Youth," KJB XXXII:27 (27 March 1964), p. 4.
32. Kritz interview.
33. A Yiddish-language prayer recited by some Orthodox Jewish women shortly before the conclusion of Shabbat.
34. Rabbi Haskel Lookstein "A Sabbath Afternoon Program" (undated), File: Sabbath Seudah Seminar, KJ; "Sabbath Seudah Seminar Opens Auspiciously," KJB XXVI:9 (7 November 1958), p. 3; "Rabbi Haskel Lookstein Reads Paper Before Rabbinic Alumni," KJB XXVIII:10 (13 November 1959), p. 2.
35. Rabbi Joseph Lookstein, "Father and Son Minyan Report," undated (apparently 1968), File: Father–Son Minyan, KJ; Minutes of the KJ Board of Trustees, 3 December 1961, p. 6; RHL, "Youth Activities Report, November 8, 1964," in Minutes of the KJ Board of Trustees, 8 November 1964, p. 2.
36. RHL; "Special Projects Committee – Minutes of First Meeting held in two parts on May 23 and 29, 1974," File: Special; Projects, KJ, p. 7; Audrey Lookstein interview with Rafael Medoff, 20 January 2008.
37. "Young People in a 93 Year Old Congregation," KJB XXXIII:1 (22 January 1965), p. 3.
38. Mr. Harry W. Baumgarten, "President's Address, Annual Meeting, Congregation Kehilath Jeshurun, May 4, 1971, " p. 3.
39. RHL interview, 25 July 2007.
40. Minutes of Meeting of the Board of Trustees, March 25, 1971, pp. 8–9.
41. Mindy, Debbie, and Shira Lookstein memoir in Teacher, Preacher, p. 94; Debbie Senders interview with Rafael Medoff, 5 February 2008.

✌ III. HUSBAND AND FATHER

While devoting himself to building the "KJ family," R. Haskel was also building a family of his own. In late 1958 he began dating Audrey Katz, a teacher at the Ramaz elementary school whom he had first met when they were both active in Mizrachi Hatzair, the youth wing of the Mizrachi religious Zionist movement. She was impressed from the start by his warmth, considerate nature, and strongly positive outlook on life. After a six-month courtship, Haskel and Audrey were married in the spring of 1959. Their first child, Mindy, was born in 1961. Debbie followed sixteen months later, then Shira in 1966 and Joshua in 1970. As assistant rabbi at KJ and assistant principal and instructor at Ramaz, R. Haskel juggled an array of professional responsibilities. The bulk of the child rearing naturally fell to Audrey – "which is why they turned out so well," he later quipped – although he tried to be home for dinner each evening and in general to play as active a role in their family life as his hectic schedule permitted.

To R. Haskel, Audrey was always his "anchor," the one who "keeps me balanced" and who always exhibited "an uncanny ability to instinctively know what's right, what to do in particular situations." Her caring nature, her generous approach to *tzedaka* both in terms of their financial contributions and the time she devoted to volunteering, and her selflessness – "of which I am the prime beneficiary," as he put it – are what he credited for making it possible for him to accomplish everything he has done in the world outside their home.[1]

The Lookstein children still have vivid and pleasant memories of how their father incorporated their needs into his crowded daily routine. When R. Haskel needed to inspect the *kashrut* of the Burry Best cookie factory each month, it became a fun outing (for whichever of the children could wake up at 4:30 A.M.). The teens were able to get driving lessons on the narrow roads of a cemetery after an unveiling concluded. Entertainment sometimes meant opera tickets that someone had given to the rabbi, "with special pre-opera appreciation lessons on the living room couch thrown in for good measure," as they put it. "So while we didn't always get the gifts that other kids got, we got the greatest gift of all – Daddy."[2]

Family vacation time offered a more substantial break from the daily routine. From 1963 until 1970, summers were spent in a rented house at Lake Mohegan. In a reverse of the typical New York Orthodox family's summer vacation routine, R. Haskel stayed with Audrey and the children during the week but returned to KJ for each Shabbat. In 1971, when Mindy and Debbie were old enough to attend Camp Massad, the rest of the family began going there too. R. Haskel assumed the position of camp rabbi and tennis instructor. Some children would regard the presence of their parents in their summer camp as an unnerving intrusion on their private space. The Lookstein children, however, recall feeling no such unease; in fact, Shira enjoyed seeing them there, feeling that her personal identity was intertwined with them and strengthened by their presence.[3]

There were vacations in the winter as well. These often consisted of a 23-hour drive, straight through the night, to south Florida. They would stay for a week or so with the elder Looksteins, who by then had taken to spending that time of year in the warmer climate. Even on vacation, R. Haskel felt a strong sense of responsibility to the KJ community, a perception of himself as a "servant of the people" who must "always be there" for their needs. This meant interrupting his vacation time to answer phone calls from congregants, help them resolve pressing problems, and console them in times of grief. Sometimes it meant cutting the family's vacation short and leaving Florida – or even Israel – earlier than planned so he could visit someone who had fallen gravely ill or could deliver the eulogy at a funeral. In one instance he was already at Kennedy Airport with his mother-in-law, wife, and three of their children, preparing to leave for Israel, when he received a call informing him that the wife of a former chair of the Ramaz board had suddenly become extremely ill. R. Haskel rushed to the hospital to visit her; two days later he officiated at her funeral. He then joined the family in Israel.

Through it all, the Looksteins strove to maintain as normal a home life as possible. Shabbat was still Shabbat, with its special atmosphere, homemade delicacies, and parents prodding children to join in singing *zmirot* (Shira's lack of cooperation earned her the nickname "*Lo Shira*," ['doesn't sing,' in Hebrew]). More than one prominent visiting rabbi found his shoelaces tied together by young mischief-makers. Almost every Shabbat table in the Lookstein home included guests, whether KJ members, cousins, or celebrities, some of whom became close personal friends, such as the families of Israeli diplomats Chaim Herzog and Yehuda Blum. The Lookstein children, weary of listening to their father share all-too-familiar anecdotes with the Shabbat guests, later fondly recalled their delight at discovering that the children of the famous violinist Yitzhak Perlman were likewise bored to the point of snickering and eye-rolling when their father shared timeworn anecdotes with R. Haskel and Audrey. The abundance of Shabbat guests left its mark; all four Lookstein children regard the plethora of guests at their own tables as the product of their childhood experiences. Especially true to form, a prominent Israeli diplomat in Atlanta is today a frequent guest at Mindy's Shabbat table.[4]

Daily life in the Lookstein home featured the same array of joys and conflicts that one finds anywhere, irrespective of R. Haskel's role in the school and synagogue. Report cards were still a source of tension between parents and children. Birthdays were still celebrated with parties or outings to Shea Stadium. Teenagers were still admonished to cut short their long-distance phone calls, unless they happened to be speaking with their married siblings. And children, even as adults, still turned to their parents for advice. Josh, as a young rabbi in his first pulpit (in Stamford, Connecticut), sometimes telephoned his father a dozen or more times in a single day for guidance on various synagogue issues. "He took my calls every single time – he never even said he would call me back in a few minutes, he spoke to me right then, whenever I needed him." From his family's point of view, that willingness to make himself available to anyone in need is one of R. Haskel's most admirable qualities. "He does not know the concept of turning down a request," according to Josh. "His sense of responsibility is really extraordinary." Although Josh later became a professional in the world of Jewish philanthropy rather than a pulpit rabbi, he continued to call on his father for guidance and found him always available.

Josh noted that from his earliest days in the rabbinate, R. Haskel chose to attend an inordinate number of his congregants' life cycle events, whether bar mitzvahs, consoling mourners, engagement parties, hospital visits, bar and bat mitzvahs, or weddings. "He attends probably more than three hundred such events each year," Josh estimated. "And when he and my mother go to a wedding, they don't necessarily leave after the *huppah*, as most rabbis would do. They frequently stay all the way until the very end of the evening."[5]

"Haskel's attitude in such situations is that while a particular *simcha* might be the second or third such event for us that weekend, it's the only *simcha* for that particular family," Audrey noted. "He tries hard to put himself in the other person's shoes so that he can be sensitive to their needs and concerns." This level of dedication requires an extraordinary amount of energy on R. Haskel's part, which KJ members find both admirable and remarkable. They note that when he leads a public Passover *seder*, as for example during a mission to Israel, R. Haskel is on his feet virtually the entire time, nearly four hours of speaking, reading, and going from table to table to encourage everyone's participation and discussion. Similarly, on Yom Kippur, between the portions of the service he leads in KJ's auxiliary *minyan* and those he leads in the main *minyan*, he is standing nearly the entire time.[6]

In addition to celebrations of congregants and Ramaz alumni, the Looksteins' calendar has always been crowded with *simchas* of cousins, nephews, and nieces.

R. Haskel maintained a close relationship with his sister Nathalie (d. 2004), her four children, and sixteen grandchildren. "Haskel was always very devoted to his nephews and nieces, and even more so since Nathalie's passing," Audrey pointed out. The families are scrupulous about participating in each other's *simchas*, to the point of refraining from choosing dates for the events until everyone's availability is confirmed.[7]

✿ NOTES

1. RHL Interview, 12 February 2008.
2. Shira Baruch interview with Rafael Medoff, 15 January 2008; Debbie Senders interview.
3. Debbie Senders interview; Shira Baruch interview; Audrey Lookstein interview; Mindy Cinnamon interview with Rafael Medoff, 17 January 2008; Joshua Lookstein interview with Rafael Medoff, 11 January 2008.
4. Ibid.
5. Joshua Lookstein interview.
6. Audrey Lookstein interview; Debbie Senders interview.
7. Audrey Lookstein interview.

✸ IV. THE SCHOLAR

R. Haskel's additional responsibilities at Ramaz compelled him to cut back in the area of his own education. As a rabbinical student at RIETS, he was required to simultaneously complete a master's degree at Y.U.'s Bernard Revel Graduate School. In 1963 he earned an MA in Medieval Jewish History and Philosophy, with a master's thesis on "The Organization of Maimonides' *Sefer Ha-Mitzvot*," under the supervision of Prof. Irving Agus. He described Agus as "a major intellectual influence on my life."

In the years that followed, R. Haskel inched his way toward a PhD in Jewish History, gradually completing the requisite coursework as time allowed, particularly during the summer. In late 1972 he presented his doctoral advisory committee with a proposed topic for his dissertation: a follow-up study of Ramaz alumni. The committee rejected the topic on the grounds that it was more sociology than history. Committee members also wondered whether the principal of Ramaz could be truly objective in studying his own former students. At a social occasion a few days after the committee's decision, Jerry Goodman, executive director of the National Conference on Soviet Jewry, suggested to the visibly downcast rabbi that he consider writing a dissertation comparing American Jewry's response to the persecution of Soviet Jews to its response to news of the Holocaust. "Bells went off in my head," he remembered. "I was incredibly excited. It was as if I had just been reborn as a doctoral student." R. Haskel had long exhibited a particular interest in the Holocaust. As early as 1963 the topic he had chosen for his remarks at a Youth Sabbath at KJ was "the relationship of the Warsaw Ghetto to the current crisis in Israel," as the KJ *Bulletin* put it. Now here was an opportunity to study a topic that combined his interest in the Holocaust and his own continuing experiences in the Soviet Jewry struggle.[1]

Two colleagues helped refine the topic. Prof. Hyman Grinstein urged him to focus on the Holocaust period alone, since the Soviet Jewry movement was too new to study as history. Elie Wiesel – a friend and, at the time, a member of KJ – suggested that instead of trying to cover the entire vast period of the Holocaust, he should take five or six specific episodes or narrow periods. In the spring of 1973 R. Haskel set to work on "The Public Response of American Jews to the Holocaust, 1938–1944." The months stretched into years as the dissertation research vied for his attention with his heavy load of work at the school and the synagogue.

Three factors ultimately provided the final push to complete the dissertation. The first was Audrey's insistence that instead of his teaching at Camp Massad in the summer, as he had been doing for years, they should stay home for one or more summers until he finished the work. He ended up spending the summers of 1976, 1977, and 1978 in New York City. The second factor was the position of Revel dean Dr. Haym Soloveitchik. In the autumn of 1977 the dean gave R. Haskel a deadline of December 1978 to complete the dissertation or face termination of his student status and loss of all his credits. The ultimatum compelled R. Haskel to drop a number of projects that were draining his time but were not necessary to his basic responsibilities at Ramaz and KJ. The third factor was the influence of his father. "He said to me, 'Hack, you have to finish your dissertation and you have to do it now – otherwise, something will happen to get in the way and then you'll never get it done.'" R. Joseph spoke from experience: after completing his own MA in sociology at City College, he had been studying for a doctorate and even had selected a topic for his dissertation, but the outbreak of World War II and its consequences made it impossible for him to complete it. He feared something similar would happen to his son.

Two prominent scholars of American Jewish history, one a veteran and the other a newcomer, participated in overseeing the dissertation process. Prof. Henry Feingold of CUNY initially served as his advisor for the dissertation, and Prof. Jeffrey Gurock, who, ironically, had once been a student in R. Haskel's American Jewish history class at Ramaz, was assigned to refine his writing style, "essentially to remove all traces of homiletics from his history."² The dissertation was finalized in March 1979, and father and son proudly strode together in cap and gown at the Yeshiva University graduation ceremony in May. "I remember my father's absolute delight at seeing me complete what he had never been privileged to finish in his career," R. Haskel recalled. "But my father also proved prescient. Two months after the Y.U. graduation he died from a stroke. My life changed radically. Had I not finished the dissertation then, it would never have been completed. Something had happened, as he predicted."³

The impetus to publish the dissertation as a book came from R. Haskel's uncle, Bernard Fishman, with whom the young rabbi was particularly close. Fishman felt strongly that it was important for American Jewry to face up to its record during the Holocaust, and that it would be helpful to his nephew's standing in the community for his scholarly achievement to be brought to public attention. Fishman, an attorney and activist with a wide range of contacts, shared copies of the dissertation with associates in the publishing world and found considerable interest.⁴

Published as *Were We Our Brothers' Keepers? The Public Response of American Jews to the Holocaust, 1938–1944*, the dissertation was released in hardcover by Hartmore House in 1985 and then in paperback in 1988 by Random House, with a foreword by Elie Wiesel. "Unbelievable but true: the American Jewish community had not responded to the heart-rending cries of their brothers and sisters in Nazified Europe," Wiesel wrote. "At the very least, not as they should have…. Too harsh a judgment? Rabbi Haskel Lookstein judges no one. No one has the right to judge. Lookstein can only relate his own pain. It overwhelms us. It reflects a broken heart. But a broken heart is an open heart, open to suffering and to prayer, to anger and to hope, to hope in spite of anger, to faith too, to faith in spite of despair."⁵

Rabbi Lookstein used the Jewish and general press to analyze the Jewish community's response to major events of the Holocaust period, such as the 1938 Kristallnacht pogrom, the confirmation in 1942 of the Nazi genocide, and the 1943 Anglo-

American conference in Bermuda which was supposed to devise ways to rescue Jewish refugees but failed to do so. The result was an incisive yet readable portrait of a community anxious to help its persecuted brethren but handicapped by intraorganizational rivalries, fears of stirring domestic antisemitism if they protested too loudly, and most of all, a business-as-usual mentality among Jewish leaders, who failed to recognize the urgency of the crisis.

Were We Our Brothers' Keepers? broke important new ground. Although several major scholarly studies of the American government's response to the Holocaust were published in the late 1970s and early 1980s, and those books had included some material on American Jews, Lookstein's was the first book-length scholarly study of the American Jewish community's response to the Holocaust. His final paragraph summed up both the book's findings and his personal philosophy: "The Final Solution may have been unstoppable by American Jewry, but it should have been unbearable for them. And it wasn't. This is important, not alone for our understanding of the past, but for our sense of responsibility in the future."[6]

The book nearly sold out its hardcover print run of 5,000, and the paperback did almost as well. The reviews were overwhelmingly positive. Prof. Deborah Lipstadt praised it as "most important," and the worst that Prof. Edward Shapiro, a critic, could charge was that R. Haskel had indulged in "moralism," but an undue emphasis on morality is not an accusation at which the rabbi necessarily took offense. Not surprisingly, readers took from the book a variety of lessons, depending on their particular perspective. U.S. Senator Howard Metzenbaum [D-OH], for example, wondered after reading the book, "Are we going through some of the same in our indifference to the effort to Christianize America now?" A letter writer in a Florida Jewish newspaper, citing *Were We Our Brothers' Keepers?*, charged that "too many Jewish leaders today spend their time fighting for other people's causes – a sad fact which suggests that they really have not learned the lessons from the silence of the Jewish leadership during the Holocaust."[7]

Significantly, a number of prominent figures in the Jewish establishment responded sympathetically to the book despite R. Haskel's criticism of the 1940s Jewish leadership. "Through Haskel Lookstein's volume, we must finally acknowledge our error," wrote Philadelphia Jewish leader Rabbi David Wortman. "We must commit ourselves to never again be silent in the face of the banality of evil and the stark reality of human suffering." Council of Jewish Federations vice president Donald Feldstein commended "Lookstein's honest examination…he writes in sorrow and not in anger, and has therefore produced a useful, true, and valuable document."[8]

The positive reception that greeted *Were We Our Brothers' Keepers?* may be attributed to a number of factors. First, the research was solid and the tone of the writing was measured. It was scholarship, not a polemic. Second, the author was a widely respected figure in the Jewish community, someone with a track record of credibility and integrity. Third, American Jewry had matured sufficiently to be able to take a sober look at the controversies of the 1940s. It might not have been possible for such a book to have gained a serious audience in the 1960s or early 1970s. The memories of the Holocaust and the intra-Jewish quarrels of that period were still too fresh. The publication of the first books critiquing the Roosevelt administration's response to the Holocaust, Arthur Morse's *While Six Million Died* and David Wyman's *Paper Walls*, both published in 1968, made it easier for American Jews to begin looking at their own record. The rise and fall of the Goldberg Commission, a group of Jewish leaders and scholars who during 1981–1983 examined the U.S. Jewish response to the Holocaust, stirred controversy but also helped pave the way for the community to consider the subject. Most of all, the passage of time since the Holocaust brought to the fore a new generation of American Jews for whom the partisan battles of the 1940s were irrelevant. *Were We Our Brothers' Keepers?* asked the right questions at a time when American Jews were finally ready to ask them too.

R. Haskel's research findings assumed a central role in his view of the American Jewish community, past and present. The Jewish leadership's response to news of the Holocaust became the quintessential model of how Jewish leaders should not behave. In his speeches, writings, and classes in the years that followed, he would often cite the failures of the 1940s in commenting on issues such as the plight of Soviet Jewry, the threats facing Israel, and the consequences of Jewish disunity.

One episode in particular vividly illustrated Rabbi Lookstein's application of the lessons of the Holocaust period to contemporary situations. Shortly before Purim in 1996 a wave of Arab terrorist attacks left 63 Israelis dead and more than 200 wounded. R. Haskel, who in his book had bemoaned the failure of American Jews in the 1940s to alter their daily behavior patterns in response to the news of the Nazi killings, decided to drastically alter KJ's Purim services and celebration. Upon entering the synagogue that evening for the reading of the *megilla*, worshippers found the ark draped with a black curtain, and some of the lights in the sanctuary extinguished. In his explanatory remarks, R. Haskel said that in view of the murders in Israel, "it would be impossible for us to conduct business as usual in our observance of Purim…. The fact that it happened six thousand miles away was irrelevant. In our minds, it happened in our own neighborhood." Thus, before the reading of Megillat Esther reading, special prayers were recited for the terror victims; KJ's post-*megilla* pizza party and Vice Presidents' Breakfast, and Ramaz's annual Purim *Chagiga*, were canceled; and the singing, dancing, and Purim *Spiel* which were the most prominent feature of KJ's communal Purim *Seuda* were eliminated. Just bfore the holiday began, Rabbi Lookstein and the dean of the Ramaz Upper School, Rabbi Joshua Bakst, addressed the student body on the importance of recognizing that "our family suffered a loss and, while Purim had to be observed in a proper *halakhic* manner, there was no room for joy and festivity."[9]

✣ NOTES

1. KJB XXXI:33 (17 May 1963), p. 2.
2. Jeffrey S. Gurock, "Called to the Principal's Office in Triumph," in *Teacher, Preacher*, p. 26.
3. RHL interview, 10 January 2008.
4. Ibid.
5. Elie Wiesel, "Foreword," in Haskel Lookstein, *Were We Our Brothers' Keepers? The Public Response of American Jews to the Holocaust, 1938–1944* (New York, 1988), pp. 9, 11.
6. Haskel Lookstein, *Were We Our Brothers' Keepers*, p. 216.
7. Deborah E. Lipstadt, "America and the Holocaust," *Modern Judaism* 10:3 (October 1990), p. 290; Edward S. Shapiro, "Historians and the Holocaust: The Role of American Jewry," *Congress Monthly*, May /June 1986, p. 7; Howard M. Metzenbaum to RHL, 20 March 1986, File: Book, KJ; Sarah Stein, "Have Jewish Leaders Learned Their Lessons?" (letter), *Miami Jewish Tribune*, 2 December 1988. Surprisingly, Henry L. Feingold, who had been R. Haskel's advisor for the first few chapters of the dissertation and at that time did not dispute its main contentions, wrote in *American Historical Review* (vol. 91, pp. 1015–1016) that R. Haskel's central argument was "unsubstantiated."
8. Rabbi David A. Wortman, "Book Review: *Were We Our Brothers' Keepers?*" *Jewish Exponent* of Philadelphia, 27 December 1985; Donald Feldstein, "Book Review: *Were We Our Brothers' Keepers?*" *Journal of Jewish Communal Service* 61:2–3 (Spring–Summer 1986), pp. 273–275.
9. RHL, "A Memorable Purim But One We Would Not Like to Repeat," KJB LXV:3 (22 March 1996), p. 2.

✝ V. ON HIS OWN

Six weeks after his son's graduation, Joseph Lookstein, then living part time in Florida, suffered a major stroke. R. Haskel recalled:

> My sister and I rushed to Miami to be with him. The first two days, Thursday and Friday, we couldn't get a smile out of him no matter how hard we tried. On Shabbat morning, I came back to the hospital after attending services at a shul nearby, one of the major synagogues in Miami Beach. Of course my father was very interested to hear my report. I said, "It was such a *balagan* [chaotic atmosphere] in there – it was so noisy before the Torah reading that the rabbi had to wait five minutes for everyone to quiet down, and the same thing happened before he began his sermon. I looked around and it seemed like the congregation was similar to ours – a mixture of some older people and some younger, some refugees and some American-born, some wealthier and some less so. If we're not careful, KJ could become just like that."

R. Joseph broke into a big smile and said to Nathalie, "You know, twenty-one years of talking to your brother hasn't been in vain." To R. Haskel, the exchange demonstrated that despite their occasional disagreements, his father recognized that they were on the same page in their approach to Judaism and Jewish communal life. "Which, in fact, we were," he noted. "I believed in the same things that he believed in: a dignified synagogue, with proper decorum that befits a House of God; a modern, centrist approach to Judaism and everything that went with it; tolerance for people with whom we don't agree; and a love for all Jews."

On July 13, two weeks after his stroke, Rabbi Joseph Lookstein died. It was late on a Friday afternoon; R. Haskel, his sister Nathalie, and their mother returned to their parents' apartment to prepare for Shabbat. As his mother set the table, she directed Haskel to R. Joseph's seat. "You sit there – that was dad's seat," she said. "That's where you should sit now." A few minutes later she added, "Well, now you'll finally have a nice office," implying that R. Haskel would move from his much smaller office into R. Joseph's. "In those two comments," R. Haskel observed, "my mother took away a huge burden of guilt which I would have experienced. She matter-of-factly told me what my new role was and that I should assume it without guilt." In the months and years following his father's death, R. Haskel often turned to his mother for advice, whether on personal matters or on the contents of his sermons.

Groomed for more than two decades to inherit from his father the mantle of rabbinic and communal leadership, R. Haskel was professionally and temperamentally well suited for this role. He had, in fact, already been gradually filling his father's shoes as R. Joseph's day-to-day involvement in KJ and Ramaz diminished in his later years. Over the course of his 21 years as assistant rabbi, R. Haskel had assumed increasing responsibility for programming, mastered the techniques of running the KJ prayer service, and perfected the art of the sermon. He had also played a significant role in the many administrative functions that his father had assumed, including financial matters such as budget preparation and fundraising. On his tenth anniversary as assistant rabbi, R. Haskel expressed his gratitude for his "upbringing in a rabbinic household where the entire family lived *rabonus....* To see the example of one who lives his rabbinate day and night, who avoided any outside interest that was not germane, who was absorbed in and totally committed to his singular role of rabbi in Israel – as preacher, as teacher, as 'pastor'...."[1]

One of the important tasks R. Haskel assumed after his father's passing was tending to the needs of individual members. This was the "*Torat chesed*" that his great grandfather had passed on to his father, and that his father had taught him. R. Haskel understood from early on that this was a role the modern rabbi is expected to fulfill. In an essay he wrote in 1960, shortly after becoming assistant rabbi, he compared the job description of the "old-time" rabbi with that of a contemporary rabbi, and he cited "the function of personal contact" as a major new requirement.

"Visits to houses of mourning, participation in family events and '*simchas*,' routine entertaining of members and friends of the congregation, and a day-to-day concern for people and their problems now serve as the real, perhaps the only, way in which the rabbi can 'make Jews' as it were," he wrote.[2]

Most KJ members seemed to agree that R. Haskel excelled in that area in particular. KJ's office files bulge with testimonials from appreciative members recalling Rabbi Lookstein going to great lengths to visit a sick person, console a mourner, or help someone in distress. A congregant who underwent a lengthy hospitalization, which caused him considerable financial strain, discovered that the rabbi had been secretly paying some of his medical bills.[3] A father on his way to his son's bar mitzvah on the Lower East Side was stranded in a hailstorm when his car broke down on the FDR Drive; Rabbi Lookstein, concerned about the man's tardiness, drove uptown to search for him and rescued him in time for the *simcha*.[4] A Ramaz ninth grader who attended a Passover *seder* at the rabbi's home recalled how after she accidentally spilled grape juice on the Looksteins' tablecloth, the rabbi insisted that everybody spill a little wine on the table so she would not be embarrassed.[5] An unnecessary autopsy and delayed burial of a congregant's parent was prevented by Rabbi Lookstein's swift intervention with city officials, on Shabbat.[6] When a baby was born to a congregant at a New York hospital that did not allow circumcisions to be performed by anyone other than its own surgeons, the hospital was compelled to permit the baby to be taken briefly from the hospital for a traditional *brit mila*, as a result of R. Haskel's behind-the-scenes lobbying efforts.[7] Tribute books presented to Rabbi Lookstein on the occasions of his twenty-fifth and fortieth years in the KJ pulpit, and on his seventieth birthday, overflow with letters citing acts of *chesed* large and small, a word of consolation at just the right moment, a thoughtful gesture just when it mattered most, an unexpected visit to the sick, a *simcha* invigorated by his enthusiastic participation.

Chesed was something that Rabbi Lookstein has not only always practiced, but taught as well. In a 1983 Rosh Hashana sermon titled "If You Were God," R. Haskel proposed that the most appropriate way to emulate God is to "imitate His kindness" by engaging in practical deeds of *chesed*. "I don't want money, I want time," he told the congregation. "No checks; instead, an effort." On Yom Kippur every KJ attendee received a card with twelve fold-down tabs, each tab corresponding to a particular area of *chesed*: hosting Shabbat guests, keeping in contact with the homebound elderly, visiting the sick, consoling mourners, arranging *shidduchim*, assisting the *chevra kaddisha* [burial society], and more – including "Adopt a Beginner: Open your home to a newcomer to Judaism." In 1987 the chesed campaign was expanded to include a *Kol Nidre* night food drive, in which all congregants on their way to the Yom Kippur evening service were asked to deposit cans of food for the homeless in barrels in the KJ lobby. At about the same time, the KJ Social Action Committee began organizing a group of volunteers to take part in the Dorot Food Distribution Project to assist impoverished elderly Jews in Manhattan.[8]

As senior rabbi of KJ, R. Haskel also now took on the responsibility for guarding against moral backsliding among his congregants. In his 1980 Rosh Hashana sermon, which generated a particularly enthusiastic response from congregants, Rabbi Lookstein advocated what he called "*Menschliness* Before Godliness." Too many "in our religiously resurgent Jewish world insist on glatt kosher but not necessarily *glatt yosher* – perfectly smooth lungs in an animal but not perfectly straight behavior in people," he declared, arguing that meticulousness in observance of religious rituals needed to be matched by a similar level of concern for ethics. Yeshiva students selling Regents exams, Orthodox businessmen evading taxes, and *shul*-goers indulging in gossip all make the same mistake of forgetting that Judaism's ethical regulations are as sacred as all the other mitzvahs. "One cannot be a *tzaddik* without being a *mensch* first." He later described that sermon as "probably the most impactful address I have ever delivered" and said it was "the stimulus for many policies and activities in KJ and Ramaz" in the years that followed.[9]

Six years later R. Haskel returned to the subject, but this time from the other side: "If *Menschliness* Before Godliness, Then Why Godliness?" was the title of his Rosh Hashana sermon in 1986. If the main goal of Judaism is to be a *mensch* – "good, kind, caring, honest, respectful, and decent" – then "what difference does it make whether I put a metal cover on my stove on Shabbat or not" – that is, why is it necessary to observe the various Jewish rituals? Rabbi Lookstein pinpointed the three key philosophical arguments for pursuit of Godliness: "Without a sense of God and *mitzvot*, we would have no clear criteria for what is ethical and good; without a belief that *menschliness* is Divinely prescribed, most people would soon become lax in the fulfillment of ethical obligations such as giving charity or visiting the sick; and menschliness is the prerequisite to *kedusha* [holiness], which is the real goal of Judaism.[10]

Curbing ostentatious spending also became an important part of R. Haskel's creed. Luxuries and lavish *simchas* send the wrong message about priorities, he argued. The concept of *hatzne'a lechet*, walking humbly before God, means exercising moderation in all areas of life. Materialism run amok contradicts Judaism. He applauded a proclamation by Israeli rabbis declining to preside at *simchas* where the costs exceeded specified limits.[11] The manner in which bar and bat mitzvahs were celebrated became a matter of particular concern in the 1980s, as wealthier members of the American Orthodox community increasingly indulged in extraordinarily expensive events, sometimes including inappropriate entertainment, when their sons and daughters came of age.

A *New York Times* feature story in 1996, "Mitzvah or Mania?" cast an uncomfortable spotlight on events such as "Mollywood," an over-the-top Academy Awards-themed bat mitzvah celebration, complete with palm trees, singing waiters, and Oscar statuettes. Rabbi Lookstein's subsequent sermon on "Mollywood

Madness" pleaded with his followers to recognize that bar and bat mitzvahs were too often characterized by wastefulness, unhealthy competition ("competition is not a bad thing in sports, scholarship, or business – but competition in consumption?"), and a diminution of *kedusha*, the spirit of holiness that should dominate a Jewish religious event.[12] "Bash Mitzvahs!" a 1998 story in *New York Magazine* about six-figure bar mitzvah extravaganzas, likewise discomfited some members of the congregation, but Rabbi Lookstein titled his March 7, 1998, sermon "Thank You, New York Magazine," arguing that while the article was a "caricature," it also contained "an element of truth [and] should give us pause for reflection." As a measuring stick, he suggested asking, "Would the RaMaZ be comfortable in our celebrations?" The grand scale, immodest attire, and undue emphasis on material pleasure at some of the more lavish events undoubtedly would have alarmed their rabbinical namesake, he contended.[13]

On several occasions over the years Rabbi Lookstein felt compelled to appeal to Ramaz parents to "emphasize the 'Mitzvah' part of the celebration rather than the 'Bar' aspect."[14] "Some celebrations that are being held may be acceptable for adults, depending upon one's preferences, but they are not appropriate for Middle School age children," he wrote. "Children do not need a dinner-dance for their bar and bat mitzvah. Children do not need a quasi wedding to celebrate their coming of age religiously...it is inappropriate to invite children to celebrate a bar and bat mitzvah at an adult dinner party that features disco dancing and social dancing."[15]

Another major area of new responsibility for R. Haskel as senior rabbi was fundraising. Most synagogues have either a paid director of development or at least volunteer fundraisers from among the congregation. At KJ, by contrast, responsibility for fundraising has always been invested solely in the rabbi. At the time that Rabbi Lookstein took over from his father, the annual synagogue appeal raised approximately $100,000, which constituted about 20 percent of the synagogue's yearly budget. It is testimony to Rabbi Lookstein's success that by 2008 the appeal raised more than $1.5 milllion annually, representing about 40 percent of the budget. Major construction projects requiring astronomical sums have been made his responsibility: R. Haskel raised most of the $10.5 million needed to build the new upper school during 1977–1980, and all of the $35 million for the new middle school during 1998–2000. A contemplated major expansion of the lower school and synagogue in will necessitate raising tens of millions.[16]

The rabbi explained his strategy for "Running a Successful Annual Synagogue Appeal" in the pages of the Rabbinical Council of America's newsletter *Resource*, in which veteran pulpit rabbis share with their younger colleagues the benefit of their experiences. "I hate fundraising," he began. "I am uncomfortable asking others to give to my shul. I get terribly anxious as the time launching the Annual Synagogue Appeal approaches." But he proceeds nonetheless, because doing so is "critical to the life of the congregation"; there is nobody more effective at the task than the rabbi, since he is (or is supposed to be) the most revered and trusted member of the community; and because if a rabbi is immersed in fundraising, lay leaders will be comfortable inviting him to play more of a role in budget and policy matters.

The secret to KJ's success, he wrote, was first that it did away with the traditional practice of holding the annual appeal at the time of the *Kol Nidre* service on Yom Kippur eve. "We used to do this at KJ also until the late 1940s. Then my father changed it. In the first year he doubled the results" and subsequently the returns continued to increase until by the mid-1990s they had reached close to 40 percent of KJ's budget. R. Haskel urged his colleagues to "recognize that *Kol Nidre* night should be devoted to prayer and repentance. Charity should not come from a mass appeal, but from a personal approach.... Spend five minutes on a silent appeal and get on with *kedushat hayom* [the sanctity of the day]."

The annual appeal process begins with the rabbi's review, each spring, of the KJ membership list, to select those who are able to give most generously. A letter is mailed to each one. It includes an invitation to a meeting in the rabbi's home and a pledge card. Some donors immediately return the card with a check; others opt to attend the meeting, which can have as many as 60 to 70 people in attendance. The majority of those who attend the first meeting make their contributions on the spot. The day after the meeting, letters go out to the pledgers, thanking them for their generosity. This same process is repeated for a second meeting. Seventy-five percent of the final total comes from the two meetings. The remainder is contributed as a result of letters and calls from the rabbi just before Rosh Hashana and Yom Kippur and then again toward the end of the calendar year.

"Jews are taught by our religion to be generous," he wrote, concluding his recommendations on an optimistic note. "Most will respond to a sincere, hardworking rabbi who has the congregation's needs at heart. A successful annual synagogue appeal will not happen overnight. It needs consistent, systematic, and energetic hard work year after year. With such an effort the results will grow, the congregation will thrive, and the rabbi will feel his commitment of time and personal energy has been most worthwhile."[17]

✠ NOTES

1. RHL, "A Milestone and the Reflections It Inspires" (sermon delivered by Rabbi Haskel Lookstein on his 10th anniversary in the rabbinate of Kehilath Jeshurun, June 15, 1968), File: Sermons, KJ. Ferziger, in "Lookstein Legacy," argued that the phenomenon of Joseph Lookstein succeeding his grandfather-in-law and then in turn being succeeded by his own son demonstrated that a "Lookstein dynasty" had taken shape. The subsequent decision of R. Haskel's son Joshua to choose a different career path demonstrated otherwise.

2. RHL, "The Rabbi: Then and Now – A Comparison," 16 April 1960, File: Rabbi Haskel Lookstein, KJ, p. 4.

3. Mayer Moskowitz Testimonial, 25th Anniversary Tribute Book, KJ.

4. Ira M. Miller, "Rabbi Haskel Lookstein: A Personal Tribute," 25th Anniversary Tribute Book, KJ.

5. Testimonial by Alexandra Pike, in "A Tribute to Rabbi Haskel Lookstein in Honor of His 70th Birthday" (New York: Kehilath Jeshurun, 2002).

6. Testimonial by Martin Sanders, in "A Tribute to Rabbi Haskel Lookstein," op. cit.

7. Testimonial by Bonnie and Isaac Pollak, in ibid.

8. "Chesed Means Caring," Chavrusa (Yeshiva University Rabbinic Alumni newsletter) XVIII:2, February 1984, pp. 1–2; RHL, "'If You Were God...' (A Rosh Hashana Sermon)," KJB LI:2 [3 October 1983], p. 5; "Chesed Campaign Adds New Dimension to Synagogue Life," KJB LI:2

(3 October 1983), p. 4; "Massive Food rive Set for Kol Nidre Night," KJB LVII:1 (15 September 1989), p. 2.

9. Rabbi Haskel Lookstein, "If *Menschliness* Before Godliness Then Why Godliness? (Rosh Hashana 1986), KJB LIV:4 (19 December 1986), p. 3.

10. Ibid.

11. Walter Ruby, "The Material Evidence Against Materialism," *Jewish World* 14–20 May 1999.

12. Lang Phipps, "Mitzvah or Mania?" *New York Times*, 21 April 1996; Rabbi Haskel Lookstein, "Mollywood Madness – Implications for Us All" (sermon), 29 April 1996, File: Sermons, KJ.

13. Ralph Gardner, Jr., "Bash Mitzvahs!" *New York Magazine*, 9 March 1998; Rabbi Haskel Lookstein, "Thank You, *New York Magazine*" (sermon), 7 March 1998, File: Sermons, KJ.

14. Rabbi Haskel Lookstein to Ramaz parents, December 1982, File: Ramaz, KJ.

15. Principal's Letter, 27 October 2004, File: Ramaz, KJ.

16. RHL Interview, 12 February 2008.

17. Rabbi Haskel Lookstein, "Running a Successful Annual Synagogue Appeal," *Resource* [RCA Newsletter, undated], KJ.

✂ VI. THE ACTIVIST

Political or social activism was hardly the hallmark of American Orthodox rabbis in the 1960s. While a number of Conservative and Reform rabbis participated in the civil rights movement or protested U.S. involvement in the Vietnam War, their Orthodox counterparts typically regarded such causes as too far removed from Jewish concerns to justify their involvement. Haskel Lookstein, while not personally active in those battles, early on recognized a connection between traditional Jewish concepts and modern social struggles. In a May 1966 sermon, which was the subject of a sizable article in the *New York Times*, he argued that the Talmud advocated principles similar to that of the civil rights movement. "It is the Talmud that says that no man is free if he must live in a segregated community, whether that segregation is the creation of law or the result of informal social consensus," he declared. "It is the Talmud that states that no man is free unless he has economic opportunity, a chance for employment, the social possibility to work in any geographical and economic area in accordance with his God-given and acquired talents."[1] In 1971 he was one of the few Orthodox rabbis to publicly endorse Cesar Chavez's battles for the rights of farm workers, and he urged his KJ members to boycott nonunion lettuce. Technically, all lettuce was kosher, he acknowledged, but lettuce produced "under exploitative conditions" should be regarded as nonkosher. Years later, during his tenure as president of the New York Board of Rabbis, R. Haskel engineered the adoption of a resolution urging "all Rabbis and their congregants" to boycott nonunion grapes, declaring such produce to be in violation of "ethical kashrut."[2]

Although some of Rabbi Lookstein's statements or writings during that period echoed the social justice pronouncements of his non-Orthodox colleagues, he was not prepared to take an active role in the causes that interested them. In retrospect, he attributed his reluctance to both the burden of his recently assumed new responsibilities at KJ and Ramaz, and the general attitude in the Orthodox community – which he shared to some extent – that they were not "Jewish issues." As will be seen below, when an indisputably Jewish issue later emerged, Rabbi Lookstein rose to the challenge.

In the aftermath of the Communist revolution of 1917 in Russia, Jewish religious and communal life there was decimated. Most Jewish schools and synagogues were shut down, the Hebrew language and Zionist activity were banned, many prominent Jews were subjected to show trials and executed, and emigration was prohibited. Russia's Jews could neither live as Jews nor leave. Until the 1960s, the American Jewish community exhibited relatively limited interest in the treatment of Soviet Jews. This indifference was the result of a lack of information about the condition of Soviet Jewry, sympathy for the USSR because of its alliance with the United States against the Nazis, and a general reluctance to raise Jewish issues in the public arena. But a wave of show trials and Soviet government-sponsored antisemitism in 1963 stirred concern in the U.S. Jewish community and led to the creation of two grassroots activist groups, the Student Struggle for Soviet Jewry [sssj] and the Cleveland Council on Soviet Antisemitism. In subsequent years additional councils along the Cleveland model were established in other cities, and they came to form the Union of Councils for Soviet Jews [ucsj]. The *Jews of Silence*, a book by Elie Wiesel about the plight of Soviet Jewry, published in 1966, also helped arouse public interest.

This protest movement gained momentum after the 1967 Six Day War, when a growing number of Soviet Jews, emboldened and inspired by Israel's victory, sought permission to emigrate to the Jewish state. In 1969 a militant approach to the issue was adopted by another grassroots U.S. protest movement, the Jewish Defense League, which advocated violence against Soviet diplomatic targets in the United States. The activities of sssj, ucsj, and JDL elicited sympathy from a significant segment of American Jewry, although these groups exercised little power in the organized Jewish community. During the 1960s major Jewish organizations exhibited only limited interest in the Soviet Jewry issue, and the American Conference on Soviet Jewry, the established groups' official mouthpiece on the issue, was provided with little in the way of resources or staff. But the activists' protests, combined with growing interest in the issue among the Jewish public, the media, and the U.S. Congress, compelled major Jewish organizations to become more involved in Soviet Jewry activity starting in the early 1970s. The American Conference on Soviet Jewry, reconstituted as the National Conference on Soviet Jewry, finally was given appropriate funding. A second organization, the Greater New York Conference on Soviet Jewry, was created by the major Jewish groups at about the same time and became the focal point for Soviet Jewry activity in the New York area, the movement's most important base of operations. The National Conference and Greater New York Conference favored a more cautious approach than the activists, often preferring quiet diplomatic contacts to public rallies.

American Orthodox Jews tended to be disproportionately involved in Soviet Jewry activism. The sssj's founders and leaders included R. Haskel's friends, Rabbis Shlomo Riskin, Yitz Greenberg, and Avi Weiss, and a majority of sssj activists in the New York City area – the group's largest branch – were students from Yeshiva University or modern Orthodox day schools such as the Manhattan Talmudic Academy (Y.U.'s high school), the Yeshiva of Flatbush, and later Ramaz.[3] Students from separatist yeshivas, however, were not a common sight at Soviet Jewry rallies; their rabbis tended to regard demonstrations as an unjustified diversion from Torah studies.[4] In addition, a minority of well-known Orthodox rabbis, such as Pinchas Teitz of New Jersey, David Hollander of Brooklyn, and Arthur Schneier of Manhattan, claimed that public protests could result in a backlash against Soviet Jews by the Kremlin. They emphasized the value of quiet diplomacy and visits by American rabbis to Jewish communities in the USSR.

Rabbi Lookstein and kj took an active interest in the subject early on. After the aforementioned 1964 Men's Club meeting featuring a film about Soviet Jewry, kj's Shachar teen group held its own showing of the film and then drafted a petition of protest to the Soviet government. The following year the Men's Club hosted a presentation by Rabbinical Council of America president Rabbi Israel Miller about his recent visit to the USSR. Shortly before Pesach in 1966 the KJ newsletter featured a full-page appeal to congregants to add to their *seder* table "a matzah of oppression – an additional matzah which will not be eaten and which will symbolize the plight of our brethren in the Soviet Union." KJ was one of the first synagogues to adopt this practice and it helped legitimize such activities in the American Jewish community. In the fall of 1966 R. Haskel's sermon on the weekly portion of Noah compared that biblical figure's reputation for selfishness to the selfishness of "people who refrain from joining protests in behalf of three million Russian Jews for fear of aggravating relations between the United States and the Soviet Union." During the intermediate days of Passover in 1967 Ramaz set up a Soviet Jewry protest tent in front of the United Nations headquarters and held a 24-hour vigil. The following year the KJ newsletter included a clip-out petition to the U.N. Secretary General about the persecution of Soviet Jews; more than 1,000 people signed it.[5]

KJ took part in protests against the mistreatment of Jews in other countries as well. When the Iraqi government executed a group of Jews on trumped-up espionage charges in January 1969, Rabbi Lookstein responded by spearheading a large protest rally. Only a small portion of the estimated 20,000 demonstrators could fit inside Kehilath Jeshurun; the bulk of the crowd spilled into the street outside. After listening to speeches by an array of public figures ("the interfaith character [of the event] was particularly heartwarming in a city beset by tensions between various racial and economic groups," Rabbi Lookstein wrote afterwards), the protesters marched to the Iraqi Mission to the United Nations to express their outrage over the persecution of Iraqi Jewry.[6]

In view of Rabbi Lookstein's later clashes with the *New York Times* over its coverage of Israel, it is interesting to note that it was the 1969 rally for Iraqi Jews that triggered his first dispute with the

Times. In a blistering letter to the editor (which was not published), Rabbi Lookstein took the *Times* to task for its "grossly misplaced emphasis" on a few minor skirmishes between the police and the demonstrators. In a line that foreshadowed his own skirmishes with the *Times* years later, Rabbi Lookstein wrote to the editors: "Does coverage of the news require that the reporter consistently accentuate the negative and deemphasize the positive?" The curt reply from the *Times* foreshadowed the editors' responses to the later Lookstein protests: "We are sorry to learn that you were displeased" with the *Times*' coverage of the event, "but are glad you wrote to give us your views."[7]

Rabbi Lookstein's involvement in the Soviet Jewry movement intensified in late 1970 and early 1971, after he was visited in his synagogue office by Malcolm Hoenlein, director of the nascent Greater New York Conference on Soviet Jewry. Hoenlein was recruiting young rabbis to the cause, and Rabbi Lookstein agreed to serve on the group's executive committee. During the next year a newly organized committee, Kehilath Jeshurun for Soviet Jewry, sponsored a series of activities that reflected the congregation's growing commitment to Russia's Jews. On Purim, special prayers for Soviet Jewry were added to the service. On Passover, families again added the "matzah of oppression" to their *seders*. In September KJ hosted a community-wide memorial service for the victims of Babi Yar, site of a Nazi massacre of Soviet Jews in 1941, featuring the leading congressional champion of Soviet Jewry, U.S. Senator Henry Jackson. R. Haskel and KJ actively promoted the Jackson-Vanik Amendment, a congressional initiative linking U.S. trade with the USSR to Jewish emigration, which helped pressure the Soviets to permit more Jews to leave during the early 1970s. On Yom Kippur of 1971, KJ members held a prayer service for Soviet Jewry near the United Nations. Shortly before Hanukka that year, R. Haskel urged congregants to forgo giving their children typical gifts and instead present them with tickets to the upcoming "Freedom Lights for Soviet Jewry" event at Madison Square Garden; some 500 tickets were sold through KJ and Ramaz.[8]

For Rabbi Lookstein, the turning point in his activism for Soviet Jewry came in the spring of 1972, when his friend Rabbi Louis Bernstein, president of the Rabbinical Council of America, proposed that R. Haskel travel to the Soviet Union. Bernstein himself had been to the USSR, as had R. Haskel's friend and colleague, Ramaz administrator Noam Shudofsky (together with his wife, Nechi). They believed Rabbi Lookstein, with his outgoing personality and devotion to *chesed*, would be well suited to bring encouragement and spiritual succor to Russia's Jews. Rabbi Bernstein also wanted Audrey to participate, knowing from experience that a couple would be more effective than a lone rabbi. The Looksteins agreed. "I learned from my in-laws that whenever possible, the rabbi and his wife should go together to public events," Audrey noted. "From both the personal and professional point of view, it was a formula that was successful for them, and I tried to follow that example – although I couldn't have anticipated that it would mean going to the Soviet Union." With assistance from the RCA and Yehoshua Pratt, an Israeli Consular official and Ramaz parent, Rabbi and Mrs. Lookstein mapped out an itinerary that would ensure maximum interaction with refuseniks in Moscow, Leningrad, and Kiev.

They arrived in Leningrad on September 20, bringing books and religious articles (including four sets of *lulavim* and *etrogim*) to give to local Jews. They also brought a large supply of canned tuna fish and soup cubes, which would be their main source of kosher food throughout their thirteen days behind the Iron Curtain. They each lost more than fifteen pounds over the next two weeks.

Two days later, on Sukkot, the Looksteins attended services at the Leningrad Synagogue. Word of their arrival had spread quickly in the local Jewish community and more than 1,000 people attended services, no doubt some of them motivated to come because of the rare visit by a young American rabbi. Requesting the honor of reading the *haftorah*, R. Haskel proceeded to put emphasis on each word "as if I were *davening ne'ila*," he said. Officially he could not deliver a sermon in the synagogue, since he was in the Soviet Union as a tourist, not a visiting rabbi. Nonetheless, he gave what he later called "a political address via the *Tanach*." He chose as his subject Ezekiel's vision of the valley of the dry bones, which is normally read and discussed on Shabbat *hol ha-moed* rather than on Sukkot, but it struck R. Haskel as unusually relevant, given the circumstances. Speaking in Yiddish – which he had studied that summer in preparation for the trip, and to which he had also grown accustomed in Rav Soloveitchik's classes – "I said to them, Like those bones, you thought you were dried up, finished, but God says, 'I will bring you out of your graves and plant you on your land, I promise and I will do it.'"

He and Audrey ate with members of the congregation in the synagogue's *sukka*, "which looked like it would hold about 75 people, but by the second day somehow there were 300 jammed into it." He made *kiddush* and *hamotzi* for the congregation, and during the meals taught the words and tunes to various "*zmirot* of redemption," that is, Shabbat table songs with verses pertaining to the ingathering of the exiles and similar themes.

At one point Rabbi Lookstein was approached by a 96-year-old man who, upon hearing the rabbi's last name, suspected they might be related. It took only a few moments of matching relatives' names to discover that the man, Mikhail Abramovich Lokshin, was the brother of the rabbi's grandfather, Yaakov Shachna Lokshin, from the town of Simyatitch. They both had tears in their eyes as they embraced and marveled at the phenomenon of kin reuniting after so long.[9] "It was an incredibly emotional experience for everyone in that jam-packed *sukka*," the rabbi noted.

In the streets outside the Leningrad synagogue the rabbi and Audrey met with several refuseniks, conversing as they strolled so as not to attract attention. (A lovers' lane near the St. Isaac's Cathedral proved useful, as the couples were "too busy with their own affairs" to pay them any mind.) While in Leningrad, they also delivered a *lulav* and *etrog* to a Lubavitcher Hassid who was too ill to come to the synagogue.

From Leningrad they traveled briefly to Kiev, "a very hostile and tightly controlled city" where, for the first time, Rabbi Lookstein realized they were being followed by a KGB agent. Meeting *aliya* activists in Kiev proved complicated because the activists were denied access to the Kiev synagogue, but the rabbi was able to share with them a copy of a letter to KJ members Rosalie and Harry Kleinhaus, which refuseniks had dictated to them by telephone two weeks earlier and which had appeared in the *New York Times* the day the Looksteins left the United States. While in Kiev, the Looksteins visited the Babi Yar massacre site. The Soviets' refusal to acknowledge the Jewish identity of the victims or permit the erection of monuments on the site fueled international controversy in the late 1960s. "Babi Yar was of course a terrible disappointment," Rabbi Lookstein wrote afterwards. "There is nothing to see, which I guess is something too."[10]

The Looksteins then proceeded to Moscow for the last days of the Sukkot holiday. On *hol ha-moed* and Hoshana Rabba, the rabbi *davened* and gave classes in both of the city's synagogues. But the main event was Simchat Torah. Taking over the evening service, Rabbi Lookstein exhorted the crowd of 1,500 – twice the number that normally filled the synagogue – to sing and dance. A *Washington Post* correspondent who was on hand reported:

> Inside the temple, the singing and dancing was encouraged by an American rabbi, Rev. Haskel Lookstein of New York City. He repeatedly tried to arouse the congregation to sing more loudly, remarking that Jews in New York were trying to sing loud enough to be heard in Russia and asking the Moscow Jews to reciprocate in kind.[11]

The crowd responded with enthusiasm. "They were waiting for an experience, and the synagogue establishment was simply not capable of giving it to them," he wrote. "I therefore tried my best, with some pretty good results."[12] Those results were repeated the next morning, when a comparably huge crowd, some of them undoubtedly attracted by word of the previous night's celebration, erupted in prolonged singing and dancing. Yearning to reconnect to their Jewish roots and inspired by an American rabbi who had come thousands of miles to be part of their lives, the Jews of Moscow turned that Simchat Torah into an event of a lifetime – for themselves and for Rabbi Lookstein. "In going around the synagogue, I was able to shake hands with hundreds of Jews who whispered their words of encouragement, hope, warning, prayer, etc., to me," he recounted. "Of course, I tried to respond to each in an individual way."[13]

The Looksteins' final days in Moscow, after Yom Tov, were spent meeting with Jewish activists, in particular the family of Roman Rutman, for whom, remarkably, the rabbi conducted both a conversion and a wedding. Rabbi Lookstein brought Rutman a *siddur, tallis, tefillin*, and Jewish books that he smuggled into the USSR, and he spent hours teaching him how to pray, recite grace after meals, observe Shabbat, and keep kosher. Rutman's wife, Lena, considered herself a Jew but had a non-Jewish mother, so Rabbi Lookstein organized a conversion ceremony at the *mikva* of the Moscow synagogue and then, immediately afterwards, conducted a Jewish wedding for them in their home. Numerous prominent activists and refuseniks filled the tiny apartment although, in a reminder of grim reality, one of their closest friends, Vladimir Slepak, could not attend because he was in prison for seeking to emigrate. Rabbi Lookstein left the Rutmans with a tape recording of the Shabbat prayer services and assorted *zmirot*. In his subsequent report to the Rabbinical Council of America on his trip, R. Haskel noted that in addition to their well-publicized desire to emigrate, "their willingness as students points up a very serious interest on the part of many of these activists in growing Jewishly and expanding their Jewish education and experience."[14] The Looksteins left Moscow "under very close surveillance," and some of their rolls of film were confiscated by a customs officer who, oddly enough, spoke fluent Hebrew as well as English.[15]

In choosing Rabbi Lookstein for the mission, the RCA

leadership secured for itself a meticulous reporter with a keen eye for detail. This characteristic was important, because the Soviet regime's tight controls made it impossible for the outside Jewish world to receive anything but the sketchiest of information about Soviet Jewish life in general, or about the needs of the activists and refuseniks in particular. Upon his return from the USSR, the rabbi composed a highly detailed, fourteen-page, single-spaced memorandum not only chronicling his experiences but providing specific, practical advice on how future *shlichim* should conduct themselves.

He offered crucial guidance for making one's way through the labyrinth of synagogue officials in each city, who ranged from sincerely pious to paid agents of the KGB. Visitors would need to know, for example, that at the main Moscow synagogue, Motel the Shochet was "quite trustworthy," but Shmuel the Shochet, he cautioned, was "less trustworthy." Reb Sholem is "a brilliant *lamdan*" [learner] who once tutored Rabbi Joseph Soloveitchik; but Ephraim Kaplun, who runs the synagogue, "is a big *am ha-aretz* [ignoramus]," and if he were given religious articles for distribution to the needy, he would sell them on the black market for wildly inflated prices.[16]

Rabbi Lookstein's report also included precise directions for finding the synagogues in each city; detailed advice on how to relate to the synagogue officials ("Try to make friends immediately with the heads of the synagogue; indicate that you have heard a great deal about their work and you value it greatly"); a list of what type and quantity of religious articles to bring, how to distribute them ("nothing whatsoever should be given to any official in any synagogue – it is absolutely like throwing it in the trash basket, or worse"), and how to pack them so as not to attract attention from customs officials (in the middle of the suitcase, equidistant from all sides); a list of kosher nonperishable foods to bring along "in order that one should not starve in the Soviet Union"; how to smuggle messages out of the USSR, and tips on reducing the likelihood that customs officials will scrutinize one's luggage on the way out, such as "stalling with exchanging currency back into dollars, so that there is very little time left for the examination of baggage"; and suggestions on how to persuade nervous synagogue officials to permit conversion ceremonies at the *mikva* ("a few rubles will go a long way toward getting their silence") and how to perform weddings under unusual circumstances (for example, "memorize the *ketuba* [religious marriage contract] before you go to the Soviet Union"). He also included advice on how a visiting couple might maximize the fact that there are two of them, such as walking separately to and from the synagogue in order to speak with twice as many people, and standing on separate lines at customs in order to determine which officials were less scrupulous.[17]

Finally, Rabbi Lookstein's report stressed a significant point that departed somewhat from the public emphasis on the issue of emigration: while the main goal of Russian Jews was to leave the USSR, "they do not know when their ultimate goal of *aliya* will be reached." Thus "it is necessary for them to live a little bit for the present as well. They want to deepen their Jewish experience beyond the purely national and social…. They hunger for God and religion; we must help to satisfy that hunger." The struggle for Soviet Jewry, he argued, needed to take place on two levels simultaneously: an international political battle for the right to emigrate, and a more personal campaign, within the Soviet Union, to bring Jewish knowledge and practice to individuals while they wait – often for years – for exit permits. The visiting rabbi and *rebbitzen* must be prepared to "go to the homes of activists and spend long periods of time with a family or a small group," teaching them basic Judaism. "Much can be accomplished even in a matter of days, and future visitors can follow up on the initial education which is given."[18]

Rabbi and Mrs. Lookstein themselves accomplished much in their sixteen days behind the Iron Curtain. Their willingness to undertake such an arduous journey boosted the morale of a downtrodden community that had been virtually cut off from the outside world for more than half a century. Rabbi Lookstein's take-charge personality energized and inspired the Simchat To-rah crowds. In their private meetings with Soviet Jews and in the classes that the rabbi gave in the synagogues, the Looksteins shared Jewish knowledge with eager audiences. They also col-lected valuable information about the plight of individual *aliya* activists for use in the American Jewish community's battle for the right to emigrate. And they provided their sponsor, the Rab-binical Council of America, with an invaluable eyewitness account to help guide future emissaries.

As much as the trip accomplished for Soviet Jews, Rabbi Lookstein looked back upon it as an experience that affected him just as deeply:

> The visit was a turning point in my life. Before we left the U.S., my uncle, Bernard Fishman, said to me, "Hack, make the most of this trip because it will change your life. You will never be the same after it. What you experience will have a profound impact on you for the rest of your rabbinic career and your personal life." He couldn't have been more accurate. I truly began to feel that it was my responsibility to help Jews wherever they might be.[19]

The journey to the USSR in 1972 transformed R. Haskel into a deeply committed activist for Soviet Jewry. While he had felt concern for Russia's Jews prior to the journey, now their situation seemed much more real, and urgent. He saw, up close, the all-en-veloping atmosphere of intimidation in which Jews lived. He was followed by the KGB. He was strip-searched at the airport. His film had been confiscated for no reason. After this brief, bitter taste of life for Jews in Russia, he was no longer content to adopt the stance of the typical American rabbi, sympathetic but too busy with other responsibilities to become more than tangentially involved in an ongoing protest movement. Rabbi Lookstein now felt connected to Soviet Jewry in a profoundly personal way. Every time he read in the newspapers about the plight of a refusenik or a harsh new

Soviet decree, he connected it to his own powerful memories of people and places that he had seen firsthand.

The congregants at KJ and the students and faculty at Ramaz soon learned that the Soviet Jewry struggle was not some flash-in-the-pan cause for their rabbi but rather reflected a profound commitment that he had undertaken, and which he fervently hoped they would share. In a letter to KJ members shortly after his return, Rabbi Lookstein reported that "it would be an understatement to say that these were the most important, inspiring, and productive days in our entire lives.... Our experience has drastically changed our lives. Perhaps it can have an effect on yours as well." He and Audrey subsequently provided a full report on their trip to a standing-room-only audience in the KJ auditorium.[20]

In the weeks and months that followed, Rabbi Lookstein and Noam Shudofsky initiated a series of projects that moved the Soviet Jewry issue to the top of the agenda of both the synagogue and the school, while simultaneously bringing it to wider public attention as well. KJ's "Kehilath Jeshurun for Soviet Jewry" committee was now rejuvenated and helped implement the new projects. The first was a rally by yeshiva students near the United Nations, to coincide with International Human Rights Day. Although conceived and to a large extent organized by Rabbi Lookstein, he realized that the students' protest would be far more effective if it took place under the auspices of mainstream Jewish organizations. He also understood that partnering with the established Jewish leadership, which was sometimes reluctant to engage in street rallies, could help redefine the communal consensus as to what kind of protest tactics were acceptable. At his request, the Greater New York Conference on Soviet Jewry agreed to serve as the main sponsor of the students' rally.[21] This episode illustrates the unique role that R. Haskel was beginning to assume in the Soviet Jewry movement. He was a Jewish leader who embraced activist tactics yet operated from within the established Jewish leadership. By doing so, he helped make activism a legitimate part of the Jewish agenda by bringing to it the imprimatur of the Jewish establishment while at the same time leading large numbers of KJ members and Ramaz students to become activists.

At the synagogue, Rabbi Lookstein sought to ensure, first and foremost, that Soviet Jewry was always on the minds of his congregants. It soon became difficult to walk into the Kehilath Jeshurun building without being reminded of their plight, thanks to the uniquely redesigned bulletin board on the front of the building. Routine information about upcoming events was moved down, and the top half of the marquee was devoted to a message pertaining to Russia's Jews. "It's human nature to forget last month's news," the rabbi explained. "My goal was to keep the issue in front of the people all the time."[22] The messages on the board, which would change periodically, highlighted a particular Soviet Jew by name and announced the number of months since he or she was first denied the right to emigrate, or a similar statistic. When Natan Sharansky was sentenced to thirteen years in prison in 1977, the bulletin board began to note the number of Sabbaths in which he had been imprisoned and how many more he had to go. That message remained, with the number updated weekly, until Sharansky was released eight and a half years later. "It was not very hard to have such a bulletin board, and it helped keep the tragedy in the forefront of the minds of the Jewish community," according to Rabbi Lookstein. "It was exactly the kind of thing I wrote about in my book – the sort of thing that American synagogues should have done during the Holocaust, but didn't." Soon after becoming president of the New York Board of Rabbis in 1979, Rabbi Lookstein sent an appeal from the Board to rabbis throughout the city, complete with a photograph of the KJ marquee, urging them to do something similar at their synagogues.[23]

During the services themselves, references to the plight of Soviet Jewry became commonplace. An extra psalm was added at the end of every *shaharit* service as an expression of solidarity with Russia's Jews, and after becoming president of the RIETS Alumni Association in 1982, R. Haskel urged attendees at the group's annual convention to do likewise in their own synagogues.

The Chicago Rabbinical Council quickly adopted the proposal, as did other agencies and synagogues.[24] Rabbi Lookstein, together with Rabbi Joshua Bakst, dean of the Ramaz Upper School, composed a "Prayer for Soviet Jews," in Hebrew and English, which was added to KJ's *Yizkor* service booklet. The prayer asked God to rescue "the remnant of Thy people who are victims of repression and persecution in the Soviet Union." Significantly, nearly half of the seventeen-line prayer focused not on Soviet Jewry but on the need for activism by Jews abroad and the positive impact such activism had on American Jews. "Strengthen our resolve to stand in solidarity with them, to strive for their deliverance, and to struggle for their freedom," the prayer pleaded. "Help us to understand that as we dedicate our efforts for their redemption we simultaneously redeem ourselves. The battle for their survival... raises our sense of purpose, uplifts our lives, and gives noble meaning to our existence."[25]

The idea that Soviet Jewry protests helped not only the refuseniks but the protesters themselves was both an unexpected benefit of the movement and an indication of how central a role the Soviet Jewry cause had come to play in the lives of many KJ members. Rabbi Lookstein perceived the Soviet Jewry struggle not merely as an occasional activity alongside numerous other activities in his congregants' daily routines, but rather as a core part of their lives as Jews. Moreover, Soviet Jewry activism also infused younger Jews with a sense of confidence that they might otherwise lack. "I remember taking part in a march down Fifth Avenue around 1973," R. Haskel said. "At about 55th Street, as the marchers passed a church, I heard two of my daughters, who were in sixth or seventh grade and were marching in the front, chanting, 'We are Jews, we couldn't be prouder, and if you can't hear us, we'll yell a little louder!' I thought to myself, 'What a difference between now and when I grew up.' In the 1930s and 1940s, when we carried our Hebrew books to school, we would hold them with the covers facing inward so nobody would see were Jews." At Ramaz in those days, R. Joseph insisted that a yarmulke be regarded as an "indoor garment," to the point that students reportedly were told to remove their yarmulkes before exiting the building during fire drills, reflecting an attitude that was not uncommon among American Orthodox Jews.[26]

"My father used to say, 'In the 1940s we walked around like question marks, bent over' – but in the 1970s, we were starting to walk around like exclamation points," R. Haskel noted. "The Soviet Jewry movement played a major part in bringing about that change, along with other factors such as the Six Day War and the ethnic pride movements among blacks and other minorities. They said 'Black is beautiful!' We were starting to think, 'Jewish is beautiful too!'"[27]

Many former refuseniks who visited the United States spoke from the KJ pulpit. Eliahu Essas, Roman Rutman, Vladimir Slepak and Alexander Luntz were among the synagogue's guest speakers on Shabbat or Yom Tov. On the High Holidays a large poster of a refusenik would be placed on a chair next to the ark. "I would speak about the person on the poster and express my hope and faith that one day he or she would be there to join us," Rabbi Lookstein said. "We had a poster of Sharansky there a number of times and spoke about him. I was convinced that one day the poster would be gone and Sharansky himself would be sitting there."

Rabbi Lookstein first met Sharansky when he and Audrey returned to the USSR for Sukkot in September 1975, again under the auspices of the Rabbinical Council of America. They were accompanied by Mario Merola, district attorney of the Bronx. Jewish organizations often sought to include U.S. political figures on such trips, both to sensitize officeholders to the plight of Soviet Jewry and to put additional pressure on the Soviets.

It turned out to be "an extraordinary trip," in fact "much more productive even than our first one, which we thought it would be impossible to equal." The second time around, "you not only know what to do but you are also received with greater enthusiasm by the Jews."[28] The most remarkable difference between the first trip and the second, the rabbi and Audrey immediately discovered, was the increased pride and boldness of the refuseniks. Whereas in 1972 the atmosphere was almost completely one of fear, now they found that while the fear was not gone, there was also "confidence…the conviction of these people that they were doing the right thing and that in the not too distant future they would be reunited with their people in the land of Israel." He described the refuseniks they met in 1975 as "the only free people in the Soviet Union." They were, he wrote,

> the only ones who are not intimidated by the "System." They have contempt for the KGB and its mission. They walk freely in the streets speaking Hebrew and English. They speak without hesitation in their apartments except when they are saying something which is politically very sensitive or strategically significant. I had the feeling as I walked with them through the Soviet Union that the blessing of *zokef kfufim* ["He who helps the bent stand straight"] had already been realized for these heroic individuals. They are no longer bowed. They stand upright for Israel, for Judaism, and for the Jewish People.[29]

As they did previously, the Looksteins began their mission in Leningrad, where they were still widely remembered. At the Leningrad synagogue, and outside it, they were frequently greeted, in Yiddish, Hebrew, or English, with comments such as "You didn't forget us," "Thank you for coming back," "Come again next year," and "Let's come together again next year and be together – but not here!" Rabbi Haskel's great-uncle, Mikhail Abramovich Lokshin, whom he had met in the Leningrad synagogue in 1972, was there, too – "now three months away from his 100th birthday." Once again the rabbi read the *haftorah* on Yom Tov, putting special emphasis on all references to Jerusalem. His uncle, with tears streaming down his cheeks, stood next to him at the *bima* throughout the reading. More than 1,500 people attended, some 300 of whom crowded around the *bima* to be closer to Rabbi Lookstein and be part of the experience of hearing this American Jewish leader bring them words of hope for redemption.[30] R. Haskel made *kid-dush* and *ha-motzi* in the overcrowded *sukka*, and during the meal led the hundreds of congregants in singing *zmirot*. As he did in 1972, he offered comments on Ezekiel's dry bones vision, but this time speaking more explicitly about Soviet Jews being set free and reaching Israel. At one point Audrey spotted six men who appeared to be KGB agents entering the courtyard, with two of them staying to listen to his talk in Yiddish. She quickly signaled the rabbi to cut his remarks short. "Fortunately, my Yiddish is so inadequate that in retrospect I don't believe they understood my speech," he said later. "Nevertheless, it was a frightening experience."[31] They had another apparent encounter with the KGB later on in the trip, in Riga. Believing they had been followed while walking back to their hotel one afternoon, and suspicious that the KGB might be eavesdropping, they began writing notes to each other in the room instead of speaking. After a while, there was a knock at the door, and a man claiming he had to repair something, removed and inspected a part on the window sill. The Looksteins suspected that the KGB, knowing they were in the room but not hearing any voices, thought that the listening device they planted in the room was not working.[32]

After meeting with his Soviet counterparts to press them on the plight of Soviet Jewry, District Attorney Merola joined the Looksteins for a meeting with refuseniks in a Leningrad apartment. Merola "listened intently" as they described their experiences, R. Haskel recalled. "It is one thing for them to tell it to an American rabbi and quite another for them to tell it to an Italian Catholic district attorney who they feel carries some weight in American governmental circles. This may very well have been the most significant role that Mr. Merola filled during his visit to the Soviet Union."

The discussion introduced the Looksteins to an important new problem facing Soviet Jewry: the growing number of Jewish émigrés choosing to go to the United States instead of Israel.

About 40 percent of all Soviet Jews were "dropping out," and the rates had reached 70 percent among Jews from Leningrad and Moscow. These activists feared that the Soviet authorities were intentionally giving visas only to Jews whom they believed would go to America. Their doing so would enable the Kremlin to completely shut off Jewish emigration, with international acquiescence, by claiming that the high rate of emigration to the United States proved it was "not a humanitarian matter but rather an emigration of a bunch of selfish Jews who do not like Communism and who would rather live in the rich lands of the West." This unexpected problem would vex Soviet Jewry activists in the United States in the years to follow.[33]

Several nights later the Looksteins enjoyed Shemini Atzeret dinner in the Moscow home of refusenik Vladimir Slepak, with a number of fellow activists on hand, among them Natan Sharansky. Years later Sharansky recalled how, at that first meeting, R. Haskel taught him how to do the ritual washing of the hands before a meal (*netilat yadayim*) and say the appropriate blessing. "What was so unusual was not the *brakha* itself, but rather his way of teaching it to me – as though he were a young, innocent child, excited by a newly acquired knowledge and eager to share this knowledge with another person."[34] Sharansky had another vivid memory of his first meeting with Rabbi Lookstein: a lecture in which R. Haskel spoke about Jewish heroes in ancient times. "He explained that Jewish heroes, as opposed to Greek heroes, were portrayed at times as physically weak, people full of doubts and uncertainties, but that they always prevailed because of their will, determination, and soul. This message, presented during an underground meeting of Jewish refuseniks, definitely struck home."[35] For his part, Rabbi Lookstein was impressed by Sharansky's ability to follow the lecture, which was lengthy, dealt with complex ideas, and was delivered in advanced Hebrew. "Yet it was clear from the many questions Sharansky asked me afterwards that he understood the lecture precisely," he said. Sharansky's wife, Avital, had been forced to leave the USSR the day after their wedding in

1974 and in Israel was beginning to embrace religious observance. "He told me that he had been receiving letters from Avital that contained references to the philosophy of Rav Kook, and he did not understand what she was saying," R. Haskel recalled. "I told him not to worry about learning Rav Kook's philosophy, he had more basic aspects of Judaism to learn, and he could always deal with Rav Kook at some later point."

Over the course of the next few days R. Haskel and Sharansky began what would become a close and long-lasting friendship. They spent four to five hours together each day for three days in a row, at one point walking for about three miles together, from one side of Moscow to the other, as they conversed.[36]

It was standard practice for emissaries to the USSR, on the last day of their trip, to leave their personal *tallit* and *tefillin* behind for a Soviet Jew to use. Rabbi Lookstein gave his to Sharansky. Since Sharansky had not embraced religious observance, he replied frankly that he could not promise he would put them on. R. Haskel was not fazed. "I said to him, 'Maybe you'll want to put them on tomorrow, or maybe next week, or in a year, or when you get to Israel. But whatever the case, I would be honored if you would take them. He gave in." Rabbi Lookstein also gave him a copy of *The Jewish Catalog* (a 1970s how-to book about basic Jewish practice and culture), which included a diagram of how to don *tefillin*, but thought it would be helpful if he also showed him directly how to do it. "When he had them on, he looked positively angelic, I just had to take a photo of him," he recalled. "Later I showed it to Zeesy Schnur, director of the Greater New York Conference on Soviet Jewry. I had no idea she was going to blow it up and make it into a poster for the next Solidarity Sunday rally."[37]

In his later description of that evening at the Slepaks' apartment, R. Haskel wrote, "I allowed myself to eat the bread so that I could teach them how to wash, make *ha-motzi* and *bensch*." Before the Looksteins' earlier trip, RCA officials had explained that they were guided by a *halakhic* ruling according to which in the entire period of such a mission to the USSR the rabbi should consider himself to be in a situation of *pikuach nefesh* (i.e., lives are in danger, so he can transgress certain commandments in order to help them) or at least *pidyon shvuyim* (redemption of captives, which similarly justifies briefly transgressing halakhic obligations).

In this instance, R. Haskel opted to partake of bread that was not certifiably kosher, for the sake of the higher immediate objective of teaching the refuseniks mitzvahs that they would observe for years to come. Rabbi Lookstein could have declined to eat the bread, but doing that would have both undermined his ability to teach them about the relevant laws and also caused his hosts and their friends considerable embarrassment by in effect declaring that their food was not kosher. In another instance affected by this principle, the Looksteins both carried their passports with them on Shabbat, even though there was no *eruv*, because they were in a dangerous situation in which an American passport could prove critical to their safety.[38]

In the meantime, the Looksteins experienced another unforgettable Simchat Torah in the USSR. The scene at the Moscow synagogue was remarkable:

> Outside of the synagogue we saw 10,000 young people dancing in the streets. They started at 6:00 P.M. and did not finish until midnight. The sight had to be seen to be believed. Every place we looked they were singing and dancing and talking and simply identifying with Judaism. Needless to say, we lost our voices within 20 minutes trying to teach melodies and sing together with them outside.

Aliya activist Alexander Luntz later recalled how Rabbi Lookstein "stood in front of the Moscow synagogue and spoke loudly on behalf of the State of Israel – something that most of those who visited us from the Free World (and, unfortunately, many Soviet Jews those days) were afraid to do. Moral support, in our struggle with the KGB, that's what we needed most, and Haskel was very good at that."[39]

After Yom Tov, the Looksteins "took a cab to God knows where and ended up at the apartment of Ina and Yuli Kosharovsky," who, like most Soviet Jews, had been married in a civil ceremony. Now they wanted to be married under a *huppa*, with R. Haskel officiating and 75 refuseniks participating in a Jewish wedding for the first time in their lives. "Imagine my chagrin – and terror – when I discovered that both the bride and groom had been previously married. There was no possibility of obtaining a religious divorce in Moscow. A Jewish wedding was virtually out of the question, but how was I going to explain this to a group of activists who could not possibly understand my 'technical' considerations?" After further questioning, however, Rabbi Lookstein discovered, "to my absolute delight," that Ina's first husband had died and Yuli's first wife was not Jewish, thus making a Jewish divorce unnecessary. He wrote a *ketuba* from memory and proceeded to conduct the wedding with a bottle of Carmel wine that the rabbi had brought with him to Russia "just in case." "We sang and we danced for about a half hour…. [T]here wasn't a dry eye in that room."

At a *shiur* the following night, refusenik Mark Asbel introduced Rabbi Lookstein by referring to the Kosharovsky wedding. "I am 43 years old," he said, "and last night was the greatest experience in my entire life – to witness a *huppa* ceremony, to be with a rabbi who would sing with us, dance with us, and feel with us, was an unforgettable experience." Asbel presented the Looksteins with a simple Russian art object, on the back of which all of the refuseniks who were at the wedding had signed their names, and he invited the additional refuseniks who were in the seminar on Monday night to do likewise. "That art object," R. Haskel noted, "is the most precious possession we have in our home."[40] Another young activist who attended the wedding was Eliahu Essas, who at the time was nonobservant. Speaking at KJ many years later, Essas said that as he left the wedding together with several friends, "We were so moved by the experience that we said to each other, 'There must be something very powerful in this religion, something that is worth learning more about.'" Essas would go on to become not only a *ba'al teshuva*, but also the leader of a large and influential *ba'al teshuva* movement inside the Soviet Union.[41]

The Looksteins arrived at the airport for their flight home together with District Attorney Merola, whose presence, they assumed, would afford them a certain amount of protection against aggressive searches by the Soviet customs officials. What happened, however, is that Merola, as a government official, was quickly waved through customs without inspection. He proceeded to board the plane, not realizing that the Looksteins were receiving very different treatment. "The customs people were waiting for us," the rabbi recalled. "They took apart every piece of material in our suitcases, looking for God knows what. Of course they found nothing, but they did succeed in making us miss our plane." The wait for the next flight was four and a half hours. As the frustrated couple could do nothing but "sit around feeling sorry for ourselves," R. Haskel recalled, "I suddenly began to cry. Audrey asked me why. I told her, 'Here we are crying because we have a four hour wait to get out. Just seven hours ago we left people who have been waiting five and a half years to get out.'"[42]

Under Rabbi Lookstein's leadership, the Kehilath Jeshurun for Soviet Jewry committee undertook a wide range of activities, some public and others behind the scenes. Committee members made regular telephone calls to individual Jews in the USSR, to boost their morale and find out the latest information about visa denials, imprisonments, and supplies that were needed. Op-ed pieces and letters to the editor were submitted to the press. Members of Congress and professional associations were lobbied. Packages of clothing, reading materials, and other permitted items were mailed to refuseniks, while articles that could not be sent through the postal system were given to tourists to smuggle into the USSR. A telegram bank barraged Soviet officials with protest messages. Funds were raised for a variety of purposes, from over $30,000 to send Alan Dershowitz and Nuremberg prosecutor Telford Taylor to the Soviet Union to aid prisoners of conscience, to a sum of several thousand dollars that was used to ransom a Russian Jew. Cultural activities were also undertaken, such as sponsoring performances of Elie Wiesel's play *Zalmen*, about Soviet Jews, and supporting a ballet recital by two former refuseniks.[43]

The committee was also in charge of mobilizing the KJ-Ramaz community to take part in the Greater New York Conference's annual "Solidarity Sunday with Soviet Jewry" march through midtown Manhattan. In a typical year 500 or more people assembled in front of KJ and then walked to Fifth Avenue to join the tens of thousands of protesters in the main march.

In the summer of 1979 the Greater New York Conference asked Rabbi Lookstein to chair the following year's event. As associate chairman of the Greater New York Conference, R. Haskel had played an important role in previous Solidarity Sundays, particularly in the area of mobilizing day school principals to send their students to the march. His Conference colleagues also remembered, with appreciation, how he persuaded prominent Manhattan rabbis to withdraw their synagogues' advertisements from the *New York Times* for one month to protest the *Times*' decision to relegate its coverage of the 1976 Solidarity Sunday rally to page 61.[44]

Accepting the Conference's invitation to chair the 1980 march, Rabbi Lookstein, with his characteristic attention to detail, oversaw the long series of meetings, strategy sessions, kickoffs, publicity events, and other preparatory work that preceded each year's march. The 1980 effort "did not begin so auspiciously," he later noted. "Apathy was high in almost every community and organization" because of the absence of any specific new crisis to which Solidarity Sunday could be a response. Indeed, as work began in the autumn of 1979 for the next year's rally, the number of Jews permitted to leave the USSR reached an all-time high, in response to the unrelenting pressure of the American protesters and the Kremlin's desire to improve its public image in advance of the 1980 Olympic games in Moscow. The relaxation of emigration restrictions proved to be temporary, however, and Solidarity Sunday's sponsors made headway with an intensive publicity campaign that included radio spots by Barbra Streisand and Judd Hirsch, solidarity resolutions in the U.S. Congress and New York State legislature, speaking tours by former refuseniks, and an all-night teach-in by spirited teens from Young Judea. Overcoming both a two-week transit strike and inclement weather on the day of the march, these efforts generated a crowd of 75,000 to 100,000, crowning a year of high-level Soviet Jewry awareness and protest activity in the run-up to the rally.[45]

Not surprisingly, the Greater New York Conference prevailed upon Rabbi Lookstein to chair the 1981 march as well, and it proved even more successful than the previous year's event, in part because R. Haskel maintained a detailed accounting of the strengths and weaknesses of the previous year's effort. His notes from 1980, and the way in which he utilized them the following year, mimic almost precisely his style of management at Kehilath Jeshurun, where the pros and cons of a particular adult education course or an Israel Independence Day program are carefully recorded in memos from the rabbi to himself and then trotted out the next time around to ensure that mistakes are not repeated. "Youth comprise a large percentage of the audience each year," one of his memos pointed out. "How can we make the program more attractive to them?" The suggestions that followed clearly reflected R. Haskel's success at infusing the Ramaz School with Soviet Jewry content. The list included placing an empty chair for a Prisoner of Zion at every school assembly; posting Soviet Jewry-related announcements on all school bulletin boards; organizing a Soviet Jewry poster contest; and inviting former refuseniks to speak to the students.[46]

Ramaz high school students embraced Soviet Jewry activism early and vigorously. Possessed of the natural idealism of youth, inclined toward activism because of their principal's ethos of *chesed* and social concerns, and fortuitously situated just eleven blocks from the main Soviet diplomatic office in New York, the Soviet Mission to the United Nations, Ramaz high schoolers

quickly became the vanguard of student activism for the Jews of
the USSR.

To facilitate his students' participation in Soviet Jewry activities, Rabbi Lookstein implemented a policy that was most unusual
in the day school world: he canceled classes whenever there was
a major rally. "The educational value of this active performance
by the children will transcend in importance anything that they
can possibly learn that day," he once explained. "If there is any
meaning to the word[s] *lo ha-midrash ikar ele ha-ma'aseh* [the real
point of learning is to act], it surely would refer to an act of this
kind."[47] As Natan Sharansky later put it, "Demonstrations and rallies were part of the Ramaz curriculum."[48] "Other schools would
send home permission slips for the parents to let their kids go to
the zoo," Dean of Admissions Daniélle Gorlin Lassner recalled.
"We would send home permission slips to go to demonstrations."
Solidarity Sunday "was practically a required school day," one
student remembered.[49]

R. Haskel made no bones about his conviction that his students' participation in a Soviet Jewry demonstration was more
important than the Torah learning they would have been doing
during that time. In one 1972 letter to day school principals urging them to bring their students to a Soviet Jewry demonstration,
Rabbi Lookstein did not argue that the rally was a one-time diversion from regular studies justified only by a particular emergency; rather, he asserted that the demonstration would make a
"maximal contribution" not only to the cause of Soviet Jewry but
also "to the image of Yeshiva education."[50] In the rabbi's view, the
prevalent image of day schools as insular and uninterested in the
world around them was unfortunate. Participation in the rally
would demonstrate a social conscience and a level of concern
about other Jews that R. Haskel feared was often lacking in the
Orthodox community. From his perspective, activism in support
of Soviet Jewry was itself a positive Jewish value and therefore
precisely what day school educators should encourage, even at
the occasional expense of other schoolwork or classes.[51]

When the Greater New York Conference staged a "Shofars for Freedom" ceremony near the United Nations, Ramaz students did much of the shofar-blowing. When the mayor of Moscow visited New York, Ramaz students wearing prison uniforms set up tables near the United Nations and ate a meal of hard bread and water, to demonstrate the diet Soviet Jewish prisoners endured. When a Soviet art exhibit came to the Metropolitan Museum of Art, 700 Ramaz students from grades one through twelve rallied outside. When the Moscow Circus performed at the Felt Forum, Ramaz students dressed as clowns, acrobats, and Soviet Jewish prisoners in cages staged a mock circus in front of the building.[52]

Daily life in Ramaz was permeated by the Soviet Jewry struggle. Students recall an atmosphere of "eating, sleeping, and breathing Soviet Jewry all year round." The hallways were plastered with posters of refuseniks. Former Prisoners of Zion spoke at the school. A special plea for Soviet Jews was added to the *birkat ha-mazon* [Grace After Meals]. Referring to the latter, R. Haskel once wrote, "It is all part of consciousness raising. This is the very thing that Jews did not do during the Holocaust."[53]

"I was 14 years old [and a student at Ramaz] when [Rabbi Lookstein] came back from the Soviet Union and told us about a brave man named Anatoly Sharansky," alumnus Rivka Rosenwein later wrote in the *Wall Street Journal*. "My first consciously political act was to attend a rally on behalf of him and other 'refuseniks.'"

> My friends and I learned grass-roots politics through annual lobbying trips to Washington and letter-writing campaigns to congressmen, ambassadors and three presidents.... My high school graduating class voted unanimously to dedicate its yearbook to Anatoly Sharansky.[54]

"Sharansky Day" at Ramaz in March 1978 provided a snapshot of the role that the Soviet Jewry cause had come to play in Ramaz. To mark the one-year anniversary of Sharansky's imprisonment, all classes and activities highlighted Sharansky's plight. The 400 students in the high school fasted for the entire day, and even the elementary schoolers undertook a partial fast. In French class, students learned the French words for "granting a pardon" and studied the original French version of a statement by Elie Wiesel about the persecution of Soviet Jewry. In English class, the students read poems about imprisonment in various countries. In their Judaic Studies classes, the Ramaz students focused on such subjects as communal fasts in response to crises, Psalms that relate to human suffering, the *halakhot* of redeeming captives, and the obligation of a Jew to help fellow Jews. Social Studies classes compared the persecution of Jews in the USSR to the treatment of other religious minorities there, the diet given to Soviet prisoners, and due process in the Soviet legal system. Many students spent part of the day – and two additional days – on nearby street corners, gathering signatures on petitions in support of Sharansky. In an address to a student assembly, Rabbi Lookstein pointed out that during the Holocaust many American Jews had carried on "business as usual" despite the plight of European Jewry; he praised the Ramaz students for their very different response. The school day concluded with an address by Avital Sharansky.[55]

The most extraordinary chapter in the history of Ramaz and the Soviet Jewry struggle unfolded in the autumn of 1982. Frustrated that Sharansky "was dying in prison without even a voice being raised in his behalf," Rabbi Lookstein conceived a new plan for attracting attention to Sharansky's plight. He explained to a series of school assemblies that each day, one class in the high school would fast during the day and spend their lunch hour davening in front of the Soviet Mission. The money saved by the school on the food would pay for small weekly advertisements in the *New York Times* about Sharansky's plight. "While Jews suffer, our lives cannot simply go on as usual," he implored them. After one of the assemblies, juniors Leonard Silverman and Andrew Lassner approached the rabbi with an idea of their own: in addition to the afternoon service, they wanted to have a *minyan* at the Soviet

Mission every morning at 7:30. "The idea sounded interesting," Rabbi Lookstein recalled, "but I didn't know whether I could impose this additional burden on the students." Privately the rabbi was somewhat skeptical, noting such inconveniences as having to bring a Torah scroll and table every Monday and Thursday. He and other faculty and administration members could take turns joining them so there would always be an adult in charge, but if Leonard and Andrew wanted to pursue it, they would have to recruit the students. They did. When the first *minyan* was held the next day, 21 students took part. The following day there were 33, and by the third time there were 50. Day after day, rain or shine, students walked from Ramaz to the Soviet Mission for the *shaharit* service.

On the twenty-fourth day, Avital Sharansky, who was visiting New York City briefly for meetings and protests, joined the students. Until that point the police guarding the Mission had chosen not to interfere with the *daveners*, even though a city ordinance prohibited demonstrations on that block earlier than 9:00 A.M. For whatever reason, on the twenty-fourth day the police decided to enforce the law. Right in the middle of the *Shemoneh Esrei* prayer, when Jewish law prohibits any movement of one's feet, the police captain announced that all the participants were under arrest. Rabbi Lookstein employed his best stalling tactics in order to give the students time to finish the *Shemoneh Esrei* and in anticipation of the arrival of a camera crew from the local ABC-TV affiliate, which had indicated it would cover that day's prayers since Avital Sharansky was on hand. They did arrive just in time, and with cameras rolling, the Ramaz students finished their service by reciting two special Psalms for Sharansky. Still wearing their *taleisim* and *tefillin*, Rabbi Lookstein, Ramaz teacher David Bernstein, and 65 students, all under arrest, were marched down the block to a nearby police station.

R. Haskel himself had been arrested on one prior occasion: in 1976 he, together with SSSJ leader Rabbi Avi Weiss and 28 other rabbis, chained themselves to the gates of the United Nations as

part of a Soviet Jewry protest. The wife of one of his fellow protesters wrote to Rabbi Lookstein afterwards:

> Some wives are thrilled when their husbands give them a fur
> coat, a diamond bracelet, or a gold pin. Yesterday Sol gave
> me his Summons of Arrest and no gift in the world could
> have given me more pleasure. I'm very proud of Sol's par-
> ticipation in your demonstration, but you – you have given
> me a more precious gift. You've given me back my hope, my
> optimism for the future....[56]

The Ramaz students, who ranged in age from seventh graders
(including Joshua Lookstein) to seniors, were apprehensive yet
remained "serious and sober," as Rabbi Lookstein put it. "They
refrained from improper behavior in front of the cameras. They
were really outstanding." All 67 detainees were released after a
short time without any charges being pressed. The television crew
was waiting for them outside the station house and interviewed
several of the students; Amanda Newman and Josh Rochlin
"spoke movingly about why they felt it was important to participate in this protest."[57] R. Haskel recalled:

> The entire experience could only be described as a *Kiddush
> Ha-Shem*. Boys and girls of junior and senior high school age
> *davened*, chanted, and pleaded with God and with man for
> the safety and well-being of a heroic Jew 6,000 miles away.
> The entire demonstration was carried out with dignity and
> propriety. The students spoke intelligently and compassion-
> ately about their cause.... It was good publicity for Sharansky;
> it was also an unforgettable experience of solidarity with a
> suffering Jew on the part of sixty-five young men and women
> who will never forget what they did and why they did it.

For Rabbi Lookstein too it was unforgettable, and in a more personal way. "I devoted four years of my life to writing a doctoral

dissertation on the subject: 'What Were American Jews Doing While Six Million Died?'" he noted. "The answer to that question is 'not much'.... [B]usiness went on pretty much as usual.... There were no daily services outside on the street conducted by students or by adults.... Maybe Ramaz students have learned the lesson. Maybe they are even teaching us a lesson."

Rabbi Lookstein himself provided the students with the ideal role model for learning those lessons. The research for his dissertation had both sensitized him to American Jewry's disappointing record and energized him to ensure that past mistakes would not be repeated. One episode in particular epitomized the extent to which he had internalized the importance of that history. One autumn shortly before Yom Kippur he received a phone call from Zeesy Schnur at the Greater New York Conference on Soviet Jewry, asking him to attend a Jewish leadership summit for Soviet Jewry that would take place in Washington three days before the Day of Atonement. R. Haskel explained that his numerous High Holiday duties made his attendance impossible. "But as soon as I hung up the phone, I remembered how in 1943, three days before Yom Kippur, 400 rabbis left their pulpits and communities and came to Washington to plead for the rescue of Europe's Jews," he said. "It was no doubt a huge inconvenience for them, but they did it anyway. I had written about that episode in my book, and about how tragic it was that it was the only rally in Washington during the Holocaust. How could I do any less?" The rabbi immediately called Schnur back and said he would attend. But as fate would have it, just hours before the summit the Looksteins' daughter Mindy gave birth to their first grandchild, Michael Joseph. R. Haskel planned to cancel his trip to be with Mindy, but she insisted he go. Reluctantly he did so, on condition that when the boy was old enough, she would explain to him that the reason his grandfather could not be with them on the day he was born was that he had to go to Washington to help Soviet Jewry.[58]

R. Haskel had no regrets about the high level of involvement by his students in protest activities, even at the expense of school time. "I always say, 'You should never allow school to interfere with your education.' Some people may think that's downgrading education, but I feel that it's actually upgrading education. Students can get more in an hour at an important demonstration than they can in three hours in class. The fact that our students wanted to do it was, in my mind, a tremendous triumph, because in the end that's what the shul and the school are all about – raising a generation that really cares." He never received any complaints from parents about their children missing classes, or even about the arrests, although after his own first arrest for Soviet Jewry his father expressed dismay that R. Haskel would have a police record. "He warned me that I would be barred for life from ever becoming president of the United States because of my record of arrests. It was a deprivation to which I submitted with great fortitude."[59]

In the wake of the mass arrest, the police agreed to permit the students to hold their morning *minyan* further down the block. So they continued to come day after day, prompting the Soviet Mission to formally complain to the United Nations that "Zionist hooligans are assembling daily in the vicinity of the Mission." Autumn turned to winter and temperatures plummeted, yet 40 to 60 students still came every frigid morning. Finally, on December 13, nearly two months after they began, with the temperature at just 18 degrees and the wind chill factor below zero, the students reluctantly heeded their rabbi's plea to end the vigil. There was, however, an important postscript to the vigil of 1982: in 2006, Ramaz students began *davening* in front of the Iranian Mission to the United Nations every Wednesday morning to protest Iran's Holocaust denial and its support for terrorist groups. Rabbi Lookstein's grandson David was one of the organizers and is a regular participant. The practice has continued through today.

After so many years of prayers and protests, hunger strikes and sit-downs, bulletin board reminders and marches down Fifth Avenue, one day in February 1986 it happened: Natan Sharansky was released from prison and flown out of the Soviet Union. Frustrated by the constant clamor of Soviet Jewry protesters in the

United States and their ability to push the Sharansky issue onto the agenda of Soviet-American relations, the Kremlin finally decided that keeping Sharansky was more of a headache than letting him go. Rabbi Lookstein and the KJ-Ramaz community could justly feel proud of the important role they played in keeping Sharansky in the spotlight and galvanizing the American Jewish community to greater activism. The day before Sharansky's release, R. Haskel heard a brief, vague rumor about the possibility that something might happen, but when the news came over the radio it hit him "like a thunderclap." The Looksteins immediately booked a flight to Israel, even though they were scheduled to go again in just three weeks on a UJA Rabbinic Cabinet mission. "We had always promised ourselves that when he got out, we would drop everything to go see him. And we did."[60]

"The feeling of meeting him, in Jerusalem, after all those years of struggle, was indescribable," R. Haskel said. "It was nothing short of a miracle." After a long embrace, they sat down and Rabbi Lookstein presented Sharansky with a copy of *Were We Our Brothers' Keepers?* The dedication page read: "To Anatoly Scharansky, a dear friend and a heroic Jew. You taught us the meaning of the Biblical command: 'Do not stand idly by while your brother's blood is spilled.' (Leviticus 19:16) One day soon we will present to you in Jerusalem a copy of this book, which you inspired." That day had finally arrived. "It stunned me to realize that only eight months after I wrote those words, it actually came to pass. I had never believed it would happen so quickly," he said. "What was also amazing is that when I handed him the book, Natan said, 'Oh, this was going to be your dissertation.' Even though I am sure I had only mentioned my dissertation topic in passing, he still remembered it, more than eleven years later, and despite everything he had endured during that time."[61]

Two months later Sharansky came to New York City to take part in Solidarity Sunday. Naturally his stop included a visit to Kehilath Jeshurun. The entire student body of Ramaz, nearly 1,000 children, packed the shul. Sharansky sat alongside the ark, in the chair that had held his poster every Rosh Hashana and Yom Kippur. (Photographs of Israeli MIAs now occupy that seat.) R. Haskel invited every student whose parents had gone as emissaries to the USSR to sit directly in front of Sharansky, on the steps leading up to the ark, as a gesture of thanks for their parents' involvement. More than 70 children came forward, vivid testimony to the high level of involvement by Ramaz parents in the Soviet Jewry movement. In his remarks, Sharansky expressed his appreciation to Rabbi Lookstein, Noam Shudofsky, the students of Ramaz, and the KJ membership for all their efforts over the years. He said he was particularly moved to learn of such gestures as the bulletin board in front of the synagogue, the students' daily *minyan* outside the Soviet Mission, and "Sharansky Day" at Ramaz.[62]

When Rabbi Lookstein gave Sharansky his *tallis* and *tefillin* in 1975, he wondered if the young refusenik would ever make use of them or come closer to Judaism in any way. Nearly three decades later at the Kotel, he would by accident discover the answer to that question. KJ's Thanksgiving Week mission to Israel in 2002 coincided with Shabbat Hanukka, and the group *davened* on Friday night at the Wall. Someone in the KJ group informed Rabbi Lookstein that Sharansky was there too. "I looked around and, although it was very crowded and neither of us is very tall, sure enough I spotted his telltale army fatigue hat," R. Haskel said. "He was *davening* with students from Yeshivat HaKotel. The two of us embraced. I could not get over the fact that this man, who when I first met him did not know a *siddur* from a Herman Wouk novel, was now davening fluently, saying *kaddish* – his mother had passed away earlier that year – and everything else. I thought to myself, this is the fulfillment of the extra prayer that we were saying on Hanukka – 'for the miracles and the wonders that You did for our forefathers, in those days, at this time' – only, I thought 'in those days *and* in this time,' because it really was a wondrous sight."[63]

During the final years of the Soviet Jewry struggle, Rabbi Lookstein occasionally found himself at odds with individuals from the Orthodox community who favored a softer approach toward the Soviets. For example, a letter from New York City Councilman Noach Dear to the *New York Times*, minimizing the extent of antisemitism in the USSR, compelled R. Haskel to respond with both a letter to the *Times* and a more strongly worded private letter. "I was appalled by your readiness to judge the extent of antisemitism in the Soviet Union from the relative safety of an office or home here in New York," he wrote to Dear. "Is it fair to sit in New York and decide whether Soviet Jews are right or wrong about the threats being real or not? We had no right to do that fifty years ago, and we have no right to do it today."[64]

On another occasion Adolph Shayevitz, chief rabbi of Moscow, a strong critic of Zionism and the Soviet Jewry protest movement, was brought to the United States by Rabbis Arthur and Marc Schneier for a series of talks in which he essentially defended the Soviet regime. Rabbi Lookstein and his colleagues at the New York Board of Rabbis agreed to meet him so long as it would be strictly in private, "so that there should be no publicity whatsoever about the meeting which might hurt the cause of our brothers and sisters in the Soviet Union." R. Haskel and other officers of the Board of Rabbis presented Rabbi Shayevitz with an array of skeptical questions. Rabbi Lookstein, hoping the meeting could produce something positive rather than be a confrontation, expressed sympathy for "how hard it is for a rabbi with any congregation (and) how much harder it must be when the congregation includes the government officials of the Soviet Union." He then gave Rabbi Shayevitz a small pocket Tanach and asked him to deliver it to the imprisoned Natan Sharansky.[65]

The Looksteins' third visit to the USSR took place in May 1987, when they were sent by the Rabbinical Council of America (RCA) as part of a delegation. This was a period of growing turmoil within the Soviet Union. In response both to its own domestic problems and to the international economic and political pressure over human rights issues – of which the Soviet Jewry campaign was an important component – Soviet Premier Mikhail

Gorbachev had begun instituting a series of reforms known as *perestroika* and *glasnost*, which involved loosening restrictions on freedom of speech, releasing political prisoners, and other significant changes. In response to these reforms, a delegation from the World Jewish Congress undertook what turned out to be a highly controversial visit to the USSR in early 1987, just prior to the RCA mission. To the chagrin of Soviet Jewish refuseniks, the WJC delegation offered to push for a waiver of the Jackson-Vanik Amendment's restrictions on trade with the USSR in exchange for alleged promises by Soviet officials to improve conditions for Russian Jews. After their visit, the WJC representatives suggested that the emigration issue should take a back seat to other concerns such as improving Jewish cultural life in the USSR.[66]

R. Haskel and the RCA delegation became engulfed in related turmoil when one member, Rabbi David Hollander, who preferred quiet diplomacy to public demonstrations, excluded Rabbi Lookstein from meetings with Soviet officials. Rabbi Hollander claimed to have secured Soviet assurances on such issues as opening a kosher restaurant in Moscow and permitting American rabbinical students to study in the USSR and Russian Jewish students to study at an American yeshiva. Rabbi Hollander and his organization, the Union of Orthodox Rabbis (Iggud Harabonim), subsequently urged a boycott of that year's mass rally for Soviet Jewry in Washington and met with Soviet diplomats in the United States to continue discussing issues unrelated to emigration.[67]

In private correspondence, Rabbi Lookstein characterized Rabbi Hollander's actions as "acts of travesty and stupidity" that would "lull people into an absolutely groundless sense of security." Sending "a few hand-picked lackeys" to study in the United States should not be presented as evidence of *glasnost*, he wrote. "That is wonderful for Gorbachev. He couldn't ask for better propaganda. But such statements could be a crushing blow to Soviet Jewish refuseniks" by undermining the chances of them receiving exit visas.[68] His public response to the Hollander group came in the form of an op-ed article entitled "Soviet Jewish Refusneniks Want

Exit Visas Even More Than They Want Rabbis." The possibility of opening a kosher restaurant or sending rabbinical students to the Soviet Union "are interesting prospects but they should not distract us from the main goal of the refuseniks," he wrote. "That goal is emigration. It is their first, second, and third priorities.... Jewish cultural and religious life in Russia is desirable – but emigration is critical."[69]

In a second op-ed piece later that year, urging Jews to attend the rally in Washington, Rabbi Lookstein said that a kosher restaurant in Moscow would "do a lot for Gorbachev and 'Rabbi' Shayevitz but very little for Soviet Jews. What is needed is one thing: free emigration."[70] Returning to a theme that appeared often in his writings and speeches about Soviet Jewry over the years, R. Haskel argued in the op-ed article that an important reason for attending the December 1987 demonstration was the memory of American Jewry's "indifference to Jewish suffering during World War II." The response of American Jews to news of the Holocaust "was pitifully weak. There were no rallies in Washington in December of 1942," despite the confirmation of the Nazi genocide that month. In a letter to the Jewish Week in response to a rabbi's denunciation of the rally, Rabbi Lookstein argued that advocates of that position "sound like the scared Jews of the 1930s and 1940s who said that we should not make loud noises for fear of endangering German Jewry and Polish Jewry.... History has shown us that this view was wrong 45 and 50 years ago (and) it is still wrong today," as proven by the fact that the Soviets had permitted nearly 300,000 Jews to leave in the past fifteen years in response to world pressure. American Jews answered the call in 1987: in the largest rally in U.S. Jewish history, an estimated 250,000 protesters gathered in Washington, D.C., that December.[71]

While Rabbi Hollander urged an emphasis on religious and cultural assistance instead of emigration, Rabbi Lookstein advocated action on both fronts. In addition to his public activism for emigration, R. Haskel urged fellow rabbis to visit the USSR to provide Soviet Jews with religious aid. One of his earliest acts after becoming president of the New York Board of Rabbis in 1977 was to send a letter to all of its members, urging them to visit the Jews in the Soviet Union. Likewise after becoming chairman of the Yeshiva University Rabbinic Alumni Association in 1978, he used his position to press his fellow rabbis to go to Russia, even announcing that he would personally assist Y.U. graduates who were willing to go.[72] After becoming chairman of the RCA's Soviet Jewry Committee, he strongly encouraged RCA member-rabbis to visit the USSR, he raised funds to purchase *tefillin* and other religious articles to be smuggled into the Soviet Union, and he pressed rabbis to urge bar and bat mitzvah children to contribute part of their gift money to sponsor publication of small boxed sets of Russian-language Chumashim to be smuggled into the USSR.[73] The issue was a question of priorities. Between those who, at one extreme, were interested only in emigration, and those at the other extreme, such as Hollander, who wanted to focus solely on cultural matters, Rabbi Lookstein sought a golden mean: continuing demonstrations and other efforts to pressure the Soviets on emigration while simultaneously providing religious and educational assistance to Soviet Jews.

His 1987 visit behind the Iron Curtain reconfirmed for Rabbi Lookstein the wisdom of his dual approach. From the moment he and Audrey arrived and saw the customs officials barely check any of their luggage, they realized that, as he put it, "Yes, there is *glasnost* today in Russia and you can feel it." On their previous trips, "We felt as if we were in a prison. This time we did not have that feeling. We knew we were in a prison but it didn't feel like it."[74] One glance at downtown Moscow in 1987 told Audrey that things were changing. "On our previous visits, everything seemed gray and brown and depressed," she recalled. "But the first thing we noticed this time was how people were wearing brighter clothing, display windows in stores were colorful; it gave us the feeling that Russian society was starting to come alive again."[75]

Among the refuseniks, they found a strong conviction that

with the advent of *perestroika*, a crucial window of opportunity
had opened, and swift pressure on the Kremlin was needed by
American Jewry and the U.S. government to ensure that Prisoners
of Zion were released and exit visas increased significantly. "Unlike during the Holocaust," Rabbi Lookstein wrote in his report
to the RCA,

> we cannot use what Hayim Greenberg called "an ox-cart
> express" while our foes keep the machinery of oppression
> humming. We have to work quickly and not waste a minute.
> I kept thinking of the Talmudic principle that a "mitzvah
> which comes to your hands should not be allowed to go sour."
> It must be done on the moment.[76]

Rabbi Lookstein urged his RCA colleagues to "listen to the refuseniks" in determining how to respond to *glasnost*. "They are there.
They have the facts on the ground.... It's their life, not ours." The
refuseniks feel that "culture and religion ought to be priorities, but
not at the top of the list. The first, second, third, fourth, and fifth
priorities are: emigration, emigration, and particularly emigration
for long-term refuseniks.... A kosher restaurant in Moscow is not
going to solve any problems.... We cannot transform Russia, they
say, but Russia can manipulate us into pushing for something else
other than emigration."[77]

One of the items in the rabbi's hand luggage that the customs
officials never spotted was a videotape of a Solidarity Sunday rally,
something that refuseniks in the Soviet Union had never seen.
"Both of us were scared stiff, knowing that this was sitting in my
carry-on bag," Rabbi Lookstein wrote to a colleague. "For the life
of us, we couldn't figure out what we would say if the customs officials took it out and began to look at it." But they did not, and
the next day the rabbi and Audrey sat with a group of refuseniks
as they watched it. "To see them riveted on that tape for two hours,
watching every nuance, taking in every word, was an incredible

experience for us," R. Haskel recalled. "To see the excitement in Masha [Slepak] when she saw her children and grandchildren [who took part in the rally] was extremely moving."[78]

The meetings the Looksteins held during their week in Russia in 1987 illustrated how much the atmosphere had changed since their last visit twelve years earlier. One group of refuseniks, for example, described plans to begin publishing their previously banned magazine, *Jews in the USSR*, in view of the Kremlin's abolition of censorship. The Looksteins heard complaints about visiting rabbis – not that there were so few, as in 1975, but that while there were many who were visiting Jewish communities in large cities, they were needed in smaller cities as well. Conversations about kosher chickens, Passover matzahs, and Jewish books that were needed focused on the number needed for particular locales rather than the idea of any being available anywhere. Most remarkable was the fact that there was now a sufficient number of religiously observant refuseniks that there were three factions, each with its own particular approach to political, religious, and emigration issues. At a gathering in celebration of Yudi Edelstein's release from prison, the Looksteins marveled at the fact that Yuli, Eliyahu Essas, and a group of about twenty ba'alei teshuva washed with *mayim acharonim*, sang *Shir HaMaalot* to the tune of *Hatikva*, and then "bensched in a most fervent and pious manner. It was something which we never anticipated seeing in the Soviet Union after our visits in '72 and '75."[79]

One morning near the end of their stay in the USSR, while davening at the Moscow synagogue, Rabbi Lookstein was asked to serve as the Torah reader. "I agreed to despite the fact that I wasn't sure I knew the particular *parsha* well enough. Somebody upstairs – the same One who always guides us around when we are in the Soviet Union – improved my memory and I managed to do very well." R. Haskel then made a *misheberach* for a new baby girl, born to the wife of Alexander Kholmiansky, "and we followed the *misheberakh* by singing together with everybody *Siman Tov U'Mazel Tov*. It was just as if we were in KJ here in New York."[80]

On their last day, after a meal with a group of refuseniks, Rabbi Lookstein led the grace after meals. As he did so and glanced around the table, he realized that everyone there had been waiting more than fifteen years to leave the USSR. "As I came to the end of the bensching I began to sing *HaShem Oz L'Amo Yitein*, may God give his people strength and may God bless his people with peace, and without realizing it, both Audrey and I suddenly became choked up," he recalled. "Later on we both realized that we were thinking of the same thing. God has given our people in the Soviet Union an incredible amount of strength. But it is high time that He gave them some peace as well." With continued activism, he was convinced, "Peace will come to all of our friends at this critical hour, a moment in history which none of us dare waste."[81]

The RCA leadership endorsed Rabbi Lookstein's perspective. In effect rebuffing Rabbi Hollander's efforts, the RCA distributed a letter to its constituents urging them to attend the Washington rally, warning that despite *glasnost*, "the overall picture for Soviet Jews remains extremely bleak," and urging the American Jewish community to "continue to apply pressure and express our indignation and protest until there is a true liberalization of emigration policy and the opportunity for a fuller Jewish life inside the Soviet Union." In a letter to Rabbi Lookstein, RCA president Rabbi Milton Polin described as a "canard" Rabbi Hollander's claim that the leading Torah authorities opposed demonstrations (on the grounds that rallies might provoke a backlash by the Kremlin against Soviet Jewry).[82] The RCA also resolved to continue urging its members to take part in missions to the Soviet Union, as Rabbi Lookstein recommended.

Rabbis were not the only ones whom R. Haskel urged to visit the USSR. After returning from his mission in 1972, he initiated a program, administered by Noam Shudofsky, to send KJ members to the Soviet Union. Over the course of fifteen years, more than 50 KJ or Ramaz alumni couples went. Ramaz students went too, on a series of separate missions. Although accompanied by faculty members, the missions still meant sending young teenagers into a distant and hostile country, although by the time of the visits, in 1986 and 1988, conditions in the USSR had eased sufficiently to put most parents' fears to rest.

In early 1989 Rabbi Lookstein was named chairman of the Coalition to Free Soviet Jews (formerly the Greater New York Conference on Soviet Jewry). With *perestroika* and *glasnost* in full swing, Prisoners of Zion were being set free and the rate of Soviet Jewish emigration skyrocketed. By the end of 1989 it would reach an all-time annual high of 70,000. With many refuseniks still denied exit visas and the overall situation so uncertain, the Coalition at first continued many of its previous activities, although Solidarity Sunday was canceled and it seemed inevitable that the organization would shift from demanding emigration to coping with the huge flow of emigrants.

When the Looksteins traveled to the USSR in December of that year, for their fourth and final mission, they saw firsthand the drastic changes that had taken place. Meetings with Jewish activists in Moscow focused on the need to send more emissaries "to bring these people closer to Judaism" in the last months before their seemingly imminent emigration. In Leningrad there were "probably more young people than old people" in the synagogue, a reversal of what the Looksteins experienced in their 1970s visits. More than 700 local Jews were studying Hebrew, and "700 more want to learn but cannot because there are not enough teachers." Preparations were underway to establish a day school. The Looksteins spent a number of days in a smaller city, Kharkov, which had been neglected by most emissaries to the USSR. At a Friday night gathering in the home of a local Hebrew teacher, the Looksteins spent five hours praying, teaching, singing, and guiding the participants through the first Shabbat observance that many of them had ever experienced. (The ritual handwashing and recitation of the appropriate blessings alone took thirty minutes, because none of them had ever done it before.)[83]

Despite the relatively small size of the Kharkov Jewish

community, there were 500 Jews studying Hebrew, and another 300 on a waiting list. The Looksteins met with local activists, assessed their specific needs, and even filed a complaint with the local authorities about careless damage done to the synagogue's water pipes, prompting assurances that the Jewish community would receive better protection. ("What a difference a couple of years can make!" R. Haskel wrote in his report.) As on their previous trips, Rabbi Lookstein spent considerable time showing local activists the basics of Jewish practice: *kiddush, ha-motzi,* Shabbat songs, prayers, *birkat ha-mazon,* and the like. He even managed to perform a wedding before the trip ended.[84]

In a post-trip report co-authored with traveling companions Zeesy Schnur and Ezra Levin of the Coalition to Free Soviet Jews, Rabbi Lookstein grappled with the question of whether the Coalition should continue to exist. Their conclusion was that it was too soon to go out of business. Although there had been many months of large-scale immigration, they could not yet be certain the trend would continue, and it would be too difficult later to rebuild a disbanded organization. Moreover, even if emigration continued at a high rate, the Coalition was still needed to organize American rabbis and other emissaries to go to the USSR to assist in the "Judaization" of a community that had been forcibly assimilated for 70 years. "Jewishness and Judaism are exploding inside the Soviet Union," Rabbi Lookstein told a UJA-Federation meeting called to discuss whether to continue funding the Coalition. "Jews who would never have thought of emigrating to Israel are now doing so. A totally secular Soviet Jew sitting next to a cab driver on our drive in Kharkov told us that he has friends in Haifa and Tel Aviv and therefore he is going to Israel. This young man had as much a connection with Jewishness as I have with being an astronaut.... You and I have a job to do – we have to fuel that resurgence of Judaism that is taking place and make sure that when Soviet Jews arrive in Israel they do not come raw but rather as well prepared as they possibly can be."[85]

Toward that end, the Coalition undertook a number of programs, including a live telephone hookup between Jews in six
Soviet cities and a Ramaz Hanukka assembly ("You have no idea
how beautiful it was for us in Tashkent to hear Jewish children
singing *Hatikva*," a Soviet Jewish woman in that Central Asian region told the interpreter), Torah lessons given by telephone to the
USSR by Ramaz faculty and other rabbis, monthly missions to the
USSR by Hebrew and Judaic Studies teachers, and expansion of bar
mitzvah twinning projects and the sending of books and tapes.[86]
With the final collapse of the Soviet Union in 1991 and the drastic
expansion of services provided by other American Jewish organizations and the Israeli government, the Coalition for Soviet Jews
found its activities supplanted by other agencies that were better
equipped for such efforts. In 1993 the Coalition ceased its regular
operations and became a commission of the Jewish Community
Relations Council. Rabbi Lookstein's two decades of Soviet Jewry
activism had reached their gratifying conclusion.

✢ NOTES

1. "Talmud Is Called Civil Rights Guide," *New York Times*, 15 May 1966; RHL, "'And Proclaim
   Liberty Throughout the Land': A Biblical Prescription for 'The American Dilemma'"
   (sermon), undated (1966), File: Sermons, KJ.
2. Haskel Lookstein, "A Word About 'Kosher' Lettuce," KJB XXXIX:11 (5 February 1971), p. 2; "Are
   California Table Grapes Kosher?" KJB LIV:4 (19 December 1986), p. 6.
3. Glenn Richter interview with Rafael Medoff, 7 March 2008.
4. The term 'separatist' is used here to refer to yeshivas whose philosophy is to keep as separate as
   possible from secular society, in contrast to Centrist, or Modern, Orthodoxy, which advocates
   participation in secular society while maintaining Orthodox religious observance. The term
   haredi is usually used in Israel to designate those adhering to a separatist philosophy, although
   that term has not yet become commonplace in the United States.
5. "Another Capacity Audience Attends Men's Club Meeting," KJB XXXIII:11 (21 November 1964),
   p. 1; "Teenagers Discuss Russian Jewry," KJB XXXIII:16 (1 January 1965), p. 2; "Capacity Audience
   Hears Moving Report on Soviet Jewry by Rabbi Israel Miller," KJB XXXIV:8 (5 November 1965),
   p. 3; "That the Jews of the Soviet Union May Know That They Have Not Been Forgotten...,"
   KJB XXXIV:27 (1 April 1966), p. 3; "Haskel Lookstein, "Noah and Selfishness," KJB XXXV:4
   (14 October 1966), p. 2; "Special Service for Students as Part of Soviet Jewry Vigil Sunday,
   Chol ha-Moed, at U.N.," KJB XXXV:28 (21 April 1967), p. 5; "Our Youth Vigil for Soviet Jewry,"
   KJB XXXV:29 (12 May 1967), p. 4; "Petition on Behalf of Silent Soviet Jewry," KJB XXXVII:11 (6
   December 1968), p. 5; "One Thousand Signatures Sent to United Nations in Behalf of Russian
   Jewry," KJB XXXVII:13 (27 December 1968), p. 1.
6. Haskel Lookstein to the Editor of the *New York Times*, 4 February 1969, File: *New York Times*,
   KJ; "Kehilath Jeshurun Host to 20,000 at Mass Prayer and Protest Meeting for Iraqi Jewry,"
   KJB XXXVII:18 (7 February 1969), p. 1.

7. George Palmer, Assistant to the Managing Editor, to Haskel Lookstein, 19 February 1969, File: New York Times, KJ.

8. "Purim Notes for Parents and Children," KJB XXXIX:13 (5 March 1971), p. 1; "Over 1,000 Attend Babi Yar Memorial at K.J.," KJB XL:3 (8 October 1971), p. 3; "KJSJ Daveners at the Isaiah Wall with Dr. Mikhail Zand," KJB XL:4 (22 October 1971), p. 5; Haskel Lookstein, "A Suggestion for Chanukah," KJB XL:5 (5 November 1971), p. 2; "Freedom Lights for Soviet Jewry," KJB XL:8 (17 December 1971), p. 1.

9. To Rabbi Lookstein's apology for "speaking such a broken Yiddish," the man replied, "No, you speak beautiful Yiddish," prompting Rabbi Joseph Lookstein to later joke, "If you had been speaking Yiddish, he would have said it was beautiful." RHL interview, 16 August 2007.

10. "Report on Visit of Rabbi and Mrs. Haskel Lookstein to the Soviet Union, September 19–October 2 (1972)," p. 2, File: Soviet Jewry, KJ.

11. Robert G. Kaiser, "Soviets Restrict Jewish Celebration," *Washington Post*, 2 October 1972.

12. "Report on Visit of Rabbi and Mrs. Haskel Lookstein to the Soviet Union, September 19–October 2 (1972)," p. 3, File: Soviet Jewry, KJ.

13. Alexander Luntz memoir in *Teacher, Preacher*, p. 72.

14. "Report on Visit of Rabbi and Mrs. Haskel Lookstein to the Soviet Union, September 19–October 2 (1972)," pp. 3–4, File: Soviet Jewry, KJ.

15. Ibid., p. 4.

16. Ibid., pp. 5–6.

17. Ibid., pp. 8–12.

18. Ibid., p. 14.

19. RHL Interview, 16 August 2007.

20. RHL to Members and Friends, 10 October 1972, File: Soviet Jewry, KJ.

21. RHL to Stanley Lowell, 11 July 1972, File: Soviet Jewry, KJ.

22. RHL interview, 25 July 2007.

23. RHL Interview, 18 September 2007; Rabbi Baruch Silverstein and Rabbi Haskel Lookstein to Colleagues, 6 March 1979, File: Soviet Jewry, KJ.

24. Rabbi Joseph Deitcher to Colleagues, 2 November 1982, File: Soviet Jewry, KJ.

25. *Yizkor – Remember: A Service of Prayer*, Congregation Kehilath Jeshurun, pp. 14–15.

26. RHL Interview, 18 September 2007; Jenna Weissman Joselit, *New York's Jewish Jews: The Orthodox Community in the Interwar Years* (Bloomington and Indianapolis, 1990), pp. 21, 160 n.111.

27. RHL interview, 18 September 2007.

28. Rabbi Haskel Lookstein to Joshua Justman, 17 November 1975, File: Soviet Jewry, KJ.

29. Rabbi Haskel Lookstein to various recipients, 8 March 1976, File: Soviet Jewry, KJ.

30. Rabbi Haskel Lookstein, "Report on Visit of Rabbi and Mrs. Haskel Lookstein to the Soviet Union, September 16–October 2, 1975," File: Soviet Jewry, KJ, pp. 1–2.

31. Ibid., p. 2.

32. Audrey Lookstein interview.

33. Rabbi Haskel Lookstein, "Report on Visit of Rabbi and Mrs. Haskel Lookstein to the Soviet Union, September 16–October 2, 1975," File: Soviet Jewry, KJ, pp. 2–3.

34. Natan Sharansky memoir in *Teacher, Preacher*, p. 76.

35. Ibid.

36. RHL interview, 10 January 2008.

37. Ibid.

38. Ibid.

39. Ibid.

40. Rabbi Haskel Lookstein, "Report on Visit of Rabbi and Mrs. Haskel Lookstein to the Soviet Union, September 16–October 2, 1975," File: Soviet Jewry, KJ, p. 8; Rabbi Haskel Lookstein to Joshua Justman, 17 November 1975, File: Soviet Jewry, KJ., p. 2.

41. RHL Interview, 8 January 2008.

42. Rabbi Haskel Lookstein, "Report on Visit of Rabbi and Mrs. Haskel Lookstein to the Soviet

Union,September 16–October 2, 1975," File: Soviet Jewry, KJ, p. 8; RHL interview, 10 January 2008.

43. "A K.J.S.J. Report to Its Members and Friends," KJB, 19 January 1973, p.1; Noam Shudofsky to Fred Grubel, 12 May 1975, File: Soviet Jewry, KJ; Memo, "Telford Taylor Project," 4 March 1975, File: Soviet Jewry, KJ; Raphael Recananti to Rabbi Haskel Lookstein, 2 April 1976, File: Soviet Jewry, KJ; Robbie Bensley to Board Members of Kehilath Jeshurun for Soviet Jewry, 12 December 1975, File: Soviet Jewry, KJ; Mrs. Samuel Eisenstat and Harry Kleinhaus to Members of Kehilath Jeshurun for Soviet Jewry, 18 November 1974, File: Soviet Jewry, KJ; Harry Green and Gilbert Kahn, "Memorandum to the Community," 6 February 1973, File: Soviet Jewry, KJ.

44. Rabbi Haskel Lookstein to Rabbis Judah Cahn, Louis Gerstein, Gunter Hirschberg, Edward Klein, and Ronald Sobel, 5 May 1976, File: Soviet Jewry, KJ.

45. Rabbi Haskel Lookstein, "Solidarity Day 1980 Evaluation: Basis for Discussion" (undated), File: Soviet Jewry, KJ.

46. Rabbi Haskel Lookstein memo to Solidarity Day '81 Committee, 23 September 1980, File: Soviet Jewry, KJ; "September 30, 1980 Solidarity Day '81 Committee Meeting – Summary of Discussion," File: Soviet Jewry, KJ.

47. Rabbi Haskel Lookstein, Draft of Greater New York Conference letter to rabbis (undated), File: Soviet Jewry, KJ.

48. Natan Sharansky memoir in *Teacher, Preacher*, p. 76.

49. Danielle Lassner interview with Rafael Medoff, 27 November 2007; Mindy Cinnamon interview, op.cit.

50. RHL to yeshiva day school principals, 14 November 1972, File: Soviet Jewry, KJ.

51. RHL to yeshiva day school principals, 30 November 1972, File: Soviet Jewry, KJ.

52. "They Speak for Jews of Russia," *New York Daily News*, 4 February 1973, p. 47; Arlene Agus to Rabbi Haskel Lookstein, 28 January 1976, File: Soviet Jewry, KJ; Ramaz News Release, 8 June 1977, File: Soviet Jewry, KJ; Margy Ruth-Davis to Rabbi Haskel Lookstein, 15 October 1976, File: Soviet Jewry, KJ.

53. Shira Baruch interview; RHL to Rabbi Noah Golinkin, 4 June 1986, File: Book, KJ.

54. Rivka Rosenwein, "An Ex-Martyr on Parade," *Wall Street Journal*, 14 May 1986.

55. Elenore Lester, "School Stages All-Day Fast-Protest to Tell Sharansky He's Not Alone," *Jewish Week-American Examiner*, 26 March 1978; "Natalia Scharansky, Wife of Imprisoned Soviet Refusnik, Addresses Ramaz School Student Body in Hunger Strike" (news release), 15 March 1978, File: Soviet Jewry, KJ.

56. RHL, "Thoughts at a Chain-In," KJB XLIV:4 (12 November 1976), p. 3; Bertha Shoulson to RHL, 8 June 1977, File: Soviet Jewry, KJ.

57. RHL interview, 18 September 2007; Rabbi Haskel Lookstein, "The Anatomy of a Protest" (New York: Ramaz School, 1983).

58. RHL Interview, 18 September 2007; "Why We Are Here – Closing Statement of Rabbi Haskel Lookstein at the National Leadership Mission for Soviet Jewry in Washington at the Capitol Building, Wednesday, October 8, 1986," File: Soviet Jewry, KJ.

59. RHL, 18 September 2007; Rabbi Haskel Lookstein, "Acceptance Address Upon Election as Chairman of Coalition to Free Soviet Jews, Monday, January 23, 1989," File: Soviet Jewry, KJ, p. 4.

60. Rabbi Haskel Lookstein, "We Remember Shcharansky," undated (May 1986), File: Soviet Jewry, KJ.

61. RHL interview, 10 January 2008.

62. A note from Elie Wiesel to Sharansky congratulating him on his freedom, urging him to accept Rabbi Lookstein's invitation to speak at Kehilath Jeshurun, noting, "No one has done more for you or for Soviet Jews. Ask Avital, she will confirm this." (Elie Wiesel to Anatoly Sharansky, 9 February 1986, File: Soviet Jewry, KJ.)

63. RHL interview, 8 January 2008.

64. Rabbi Haskel Lookstein to Hon. Noach Dear, 26 March 1990, File: Soviet Jewry, KJ.

65. Rabbi Haskel Lookstein, "A Private Encounter with the Rabbi of Moscow," 14 May 1984, File: Soviet Jewry, KJ.
66. Audrey and Haskel Lookstein, "Moscow's Refuseniks Grapple with Glasnost: A Report on the Views of Soviet Jews, May 5–12, 1987," File: Soviet Jewry, KJ, pp. 3–4.; Henry L. Feingold, "Silent No More": Saving the Jews of Russia, The American Jewish Effort, 1967-1989 (Syracuse, N.Y.: Syracuse University Press, 2007), pp. 269–270.
67. Rabbi Haskel Lookstein to Rabbi Binyamin Walfish and Rabbi Milton Polin, 10 June 1987, File: Soviet Jewry, KJ; Rabbi Milton Polin to Rabbi Haskel Lookstein, 16 June 1987, File: Soviet Jewry, KJ; Rabbi Binyamin Walfish to Rabbi Haskel Lookstein, 6 July 1987, File: Soviet Jewry, KJ; Rabbi Haskel Lookstein to Rabbi BInyamin Walfish, 15 July 1987, File: Soviet Jewry, KJ; Rabbi Haskel Lookstein to Dr. Oscar Z. Fasman, Rabbi Dr. Baruch A. Poupko, and Rabbi Solomon Roodman, 23 July 1987, File: Soviet Jewry, KJ; Rabbi Haskel Lookstein to Rabbi Baruch A. Poupko, 12 October 1987, File: Soviet Jewry, KJ; Rabbi Haskel Lookstein to Rabbi David Hollander, 12 October 1987, File: Soviet Jewry, KJ; Rabbi David Hollander to Rabbi Haskel Lookstein, 22 October 1987, File: Soviet Jewry, KJ.
68. Rabbi Haskel Lookstein to Rabbi Judea B. Miller, 11 June 1987, File: Soviet Jewry, KJ; Rabbi Haskel Lookstein to Rabbi Binyamin Walfish and Rabbi Milton Polin, 10 June 1987, File: Soviet Jewry, KJ.
69. Rabbi Haskel Lookstein, "Soviet Jewish Refuseniks Want Exit Visas Even More Than They Want Rabbis," undated (June 1987), KJ.
70. Several months later, when no such restaurant had yet been opened, Rabbi Lookstein was unsettled by a reference to it in a letter from students' Soviet Jewry group. "No kosher restaurant has been opened," he wrote to the students. "It is the figment of the imagination and public relations of the Soviet Union and one particular American rabbi who feeds off that kind of misleading information." (Rabbi Haskel Lookstein to Student Coalition for Soviet Jewry, 29 February 1988, File: Soviet Jewry, KJ.)
71. Rabbi Haskel Lookstein, "Why I Must Attend Soviet Jewry Rally," New York Jewish Week, 4 December 1987; Unpublished letter to the New York Jewish Week, 22 December 1987, File: Soviet Jewry, KJ.
72. Rabbi Haskel Lookstein to Members of the New York Board of Rabbis, 10 March 1977, File: Soviet Jewry, KJ; Minutes of Executive Committee, Yeshiva University Rabbinic Alumni, 13 December 1978, File: Soviet Jewry, KJ.
73. Rabbi Haskel Lookstein letter to RCA colleagues, August 1988, File: Soviet Jewry, KJ; Rabbi Haskel Lookstein letter to RCA colleagues, 6 October 1986, File: Soviet Jewry, KJ.
74. Audrey and Haskel Lookstein, "Moscow's Refuseniks Grapple," p. 1.
75. Audrey Lookstein interview.
76. Audrey and Haskel Lookstein, "Moscow's Refuseniks Grapple." Greenberg, editor of the U.S. Labor Zionist journal Jewish Frontier, wrote in a 1943 critique of American Jewry's response to the slaughter of European Jewry: "(A)t a time when the Angel of Death uses airplanes, the A(merican) J(ewish)Congress employs an oxcart-express." (The text of Greenberg's article was reprinted in Shlomo Katz, "6,000,000 and 5,000,000 (Notes in Midstream)," Midstream x:1 (March 1964), pp. 3–14.
77. Ibid., p. 4.
78. Rabbi Haskel Lookstein to Zeesy Schnur, 13 May 1987, File: Soviet Jewry, KJ.
79. Audrey and Haskel Lookstein, "Moscow's Refuseniks Grapple," p. 9.
80. Ibid., p. 12.
81. Ibid., p. 13.
82. Rabbi Milton Polin to Rabbi Haskel Lookstein, 14 January 1988, File: Soviet Jewry, KJ. Rabbi Polin included clippings from the Hebrew and Yiddish press citing prominent rabbinical authorities who endorsed demonstrations. The clippings had been sent to him by Rabbi Aaron Shurin, who, interestingly enough, was one of the 500 rabbis who took part in the only rally in Washington during the Holocaust, a rally cited by Rabbi Lookstein in his book, and in many speeches, as a source of personal inspiration to him.

83. Haskel Lookstein, "The Jewish Heart Beats in the Soviet Union," *New York Jewish Week*, 23 February 1990.

84. Rabbi Haskel Lookstein, "Mission to the Soviet Union: December 2, 1989–January 3, 1990," File: Soviet Jewry, KJ.

85. Rabbi Haskel Lookstein, Ezra Levin, and Zeesy Schnur, "Why the Coalition for Soviet Jews in New York Must Continue Its Work," 15 January 1990, File: Soviet Jewry, KJ; "Rabbi Haskell (sic) Lookstein Remarks, Combined Meeting, January 22, 1990," File: Soviet Jewry, KJ.

86. D.J. Saunders, "Shalom to Soviet Jews," *New York Daily News*, 20 October 1989; Haskel Lookstein, "New Realities Demand New Reactions," undated, File: Soviet Jewry, KJ; RHL, "Principal's Letter," 13 December 1989, File: Ramaz, KJ, p .4.

VII. WOMEN'S ISSUES

The original by-laws of Kehilath Jeshurun, which were typical of American Orthodox synagogues established in the nineteenth century or the first half of the twentieth, did not consider women to be individual members of the synagogue and did not grant them the right to vote at the annual meeting. A married couple was considered one member, and a single woman was merely an associate member. In practice, KJ's annual vote was conducted by a show of hands, and no vote was ever seriously contested, so when women, erroneously assuming they had the right to vote, raised their hands along with everyone else, nobody objected. But the principle of inequality remained in place, as did the reality that if they were not members, they could not serve as trustees or officers either. Thus they were legally unable to assume any leadership position in the synagogue. This imbalance would not sit well with Rabbi Lookstein indefinitely.

As a product of the Ramaz system, with its co-educational classes in all subjects from elementary through high school, R. Haskel entered the rabbinate with a sympathy for women's concerns that was atypical of American Orthodox rabbis. His inclination was tempered, however, by the public atmosphere of the late 1950s and early 1960s, in which women were consigned to a subordinate role at home, in the workplace, and in their houses of worship. Among American Orthodox women, such as those who belonged to KJ, there was relatively little sentiment for significant religious or social change. But amidst the rise of feminism and the women's liberation movement in the 1960s and early 1970s, an increasing number of Orthodox women began raising questions about their status in communal and religious life.

In early 1971 R. Haskel declared, in a sermon, that the time had come for Orthodox synagogues, including KJ, to permit women not only to be full individual members but also to serve on their boards. At the next meeting of the KJ board, Max Etra, who had recently retired after nearly three decades as president, upbraided the rabbi for his statements. "Mr. Etra felt that this was a form of propaganda and that it did not belong in the pulpit," the minutes reported. The criticism indicated the persistence among a segment of the KJ community and leadership of old-world attitudes about women's roles.[1]

The gradually simmering debate at KJ over women's concerns emerged full blown in June 1974, when women formally asked the Special Projects Committee for a change in the conduct of the Simchat Torah celebrations. Until then, women had been sitting in the balcony, essentially as spectators, while the men danced with the Torah scrolls below. Jean Blumenthal informed the committee that "all women to whom she had spoken want to be downstairs," in an area separated by a *mehitza*. The minutes recorded: "The time had come, said Jean, when the wishes of the women could no longer be ignored." Several men objected that having the women downstairs would unfairly reduce the area in which men and children could dance. Despite their objections, a resolution allowing women downstairs, with "overflow men" directed to the balconies, was approved by a vote of 12 to 2.[2] In addition, a Simchat Torah Committee was appointed to consider the matter. It subsequently reported to Rabbi Lookstein its view that despite the danger of overcrowding, it was "crucial that female congregants play a much more active role during the services and not be relegated to an observer status upstairs."[3]

But the issue was not yet concluded. At the next meeting of the Special Projects Committee, it was reported that all but one of the officers opposed having women sit downstairs. They claimed that "only a limited number of women" actually wanted to sit there, that the use of the *mehitza* would "severely hamper" the dancing, and that older members would object to having to sit in the balcony. After a vigorous debate, a motion was made to proceed with having an area for women downstairs. It passed, albeit narrowly: six in favor, five against, and one abstention.[4]

The following year Rabbi Lookstein proposed that the Yeshiva University rabbinic alumni devote their entire annual conference to issues such as women's prayer services, women serving as trustees or officers of their synagogues, and the problem of *agunas*, women whose ex-husbands would not grant them a religious divorce [a *"get"*]. The time had come, he urged his colleagues, for a full discussion of "Orthodoxy's response to a basic change in society's attitude toward women and in women's attitude toward themselves." Looking for practical solutions rather than just theoretical discussions, Rabbi Lookstein urged that the conference emphasize "making concrete *halakhic* and programmatic proposals to deal with these issues. We could then take these proposals to the highest rabbinic authorities and try to get specific approval or action upon them." The conference, however, did not materialize.[5]

In 1976 R. Haskel decided the time had come to confront the issue of women serving as members or officers of his synagogue. He asked Rabbi Soloveitchik for a specific ruling on the subject and was told that women could be members. In addition, the Rav ruled that women could also serve as trustees, since trustees deal with corporate issues and women have the same responsibilities as men in those areas. Rabbi Soloveitchik was undecided, however, on the question of women serving as officers, such as president or vice president. Those positions were related to the *halakhic* issue of a king's authority, and in Jewish tradition there is no concept of being ruled by a queen, only a king. As a result, the amended by-laws drafted in 1976 by R. Haskel, together with KJ members Irwin Robbins and Martin Markson, enabled women to serve as both members and trustees but also included this proviso: "By virtue of a *halakhic* opinion of Rabbi Joseph B. Soloveitchik, women shall not be eligible to be officers of the congregation."[6]

A handful of older members at KJ felt uncomfortable about women becoming members or trustees, regarding such changes as an expression of feminism that was too radical for traditional Jewish life. But Rabbi Lookstein's presentation of the Rav's psak [religious ruling] to the board of trustees put the issue to rest and the new by-laws were adopted without incident on May 6, 1976. Ami Texon, a daughter of Rabbi Henry Raphael Gold and president of the KJ sisterhood, was immediately made the first woman trustee.[7]

In the months that followed, there was ample evidence of the changing attitudes within the congregation. The KJ newsletter began publishing bat mitzvah notices, complete with photos of the bat mitzvah girls, just as it had always done for bar mitzvah boys. The first *simhat bat* ceremony for a new baby girl was held at KJ that fall. At the next year's Simchat Torah festivities, "The *Hakafot* [dancing with the Torah scrolls] were never like this before," the newsletter reported. "Round and round the shul we danced – and the women too, for the first time; and they outlasted the men in both song and dance." By 1979 the appeal for attendance at the Father and Son Minyan was titled "Calling Fathers [and Mothers] and Sons [and Daughters]." At about the same time, KJ became the first American Orthodox synagogue to have a female executive director, when Marcia Barany filled the position, albeit on a volunteer basis, for several years.[8]

R. Haskel's efforts regarding women members reflected several important aspects of his personal outlook and agenda. First, that wherever possible, without transgressing *halakha*, Orthodox practice should be brought into line with modern sensibilities. Second, that every effort should made to make Orthodoxy as attractive as possible both to its adherents and to the non-Orthodox. Third, that Orthodoxy should be as tolerant and inclusive as possible.

A dispute in Israel in 1986 brought these issues to the fore. Mrs. Leah Shakdiel, an Orthodox woman, was appointed by the municipality of her small home town, Yeroham, to serve on the local religious council, a government-funded body that administers synagogues and *mikvas*. Until Shakdiel's selection, the religious councils had been the exclusive province of men. The Religious Affairs Ministry and the chief rabbinate sought to block Mrs. Shakdiel's appointment. Rabbi Lookstein regarded the position of the Israeli rabbinical establishment as a minefield. "The establishment has backed itself into a corner" by taking the position that

women cannot serve on such councils "and is engaged in a struggle which cannot be won without very serious losses," he wrote.
One of those losses would be the damage to the public image of
Orthodox Judaism, which would be seen as anti-woman. In addition, keeping Mrs. Shakdiel off the council might have the effect
of alienating young Orthodox women from traditional Judaism.
In the hope of contributing to a resolution of the conflict, Rabbi
Lookstein decided to violate his own self-imposed policy of not
publicly commenting on Israeli internal affairs. "I happen to be
among those who believe that American Jews should not meddle
in the internal affairs of Israel," he explained to a newspaper editor. "If you really want to affect Israeli policy, you have to make
the leap of *aliya* and do it from Israel." In this case, however, he
believed that a public statement by himself and other American
rabbis might help "create an atmosphere in which the religious
establishment could retreat from a position which is so detrimen-
tal to religious life in Israel."[9]

"Without wishing to interfere in the matter," he wrote in a
letter to a number of his rabbinical colleagues, it was necessary
to show Israel's religious establishment "that we have fought this
battle in America and resolved the problem without any losses
whatsoever. Perhaps the example of how the problem has been
resolved here will be of some help in resolving it in Israel." He
asked them to co-sign a statement of protest, and nineteen of the
rabbis he contacted agreed to do so.[10]

The statement they issued argued that while in ritual matters
there were *halakhic* strictures governing women's roles, "in corporate matters [in a synagogue or a religious council], there is a
great deal that can be done and has been done to assure that all
members of the community – men and women – have the same
voice in the corporate affairs of the community.... In America,
most Orthodox congregations recognize the equal responsibility
of men and women in the administrative functions of the synagogue."

Rabbi Lookstein and his colleagues also pointed out that

"almost all Orthodox congregations have equal status for men and women as members; many have women on their board of trustees; and a number have women as officers."[11] KJ, however, was not yet one of the latter. That situation would change in 1999, six years after the Rav's passing, when Rabbi Lookstein decided to revisit the issue after reviewing a *shiur* by Rav Hershel Schachter explaining that Rav Soloveitchik's concerns about women serving as officers did not apply to the actual duties of an officer at KJ.[12] On that basis, KJ's by-laws were changed to permit women to serve as officers. The first woman president of a major Orthodox synagogue was appointed in 1997 (in Englewood, N.J.), and although the phenomenon of women presidents at Orthodox synagogues remains uncommon, there is little doubt that a woman could serve as president of KJ without opposition.

The issue of women's *tefilla* groups arose relatively late at KJ. What was apparently the first women's *tefilla* group in the U.S. Orthodox community was organized at Lincoln Square Synagogue on Manhattan's Upper West Side in 1972. Similar groups were created at other Orthodox synagogues throughout the 1970s and 1980s. Interest in forming such a group at KJ emerged only in the late 1980s. It came from women who had been active in areas of synagogue life in which women typically played a prominent role, such as the *hevra kaddisha*, *bikur holim* [visiting the sick], and adult education. Now they sought to have more personal involvement in such ritual aspects of synagogue life as prayer and Torah reading. In accordance with his general approach of tolerance and inclusiveness, Rabbi Lookstein regarded such groups sympathetically. In his view, "Women should be given every opportunity to express their religious commitment and to be as involved as possible in ritual, as long as it is done within an absolute *halakhic* framework. Whatever *halakha* will allow for women, should be done."[13]

There were murmurings of opposition within KJ from those who feared that a separate women's *tefilla* group, and particularly the prospect of women reading from the Torah at such groups, represented too much of a break from customary practices. R. Haskel checked with a colleague who had once discussed with Rabbi Soloveitchik the permissibility of a women's *tefilla* group at Brandeis University. He told Rabbi Lookstein that "the Rav did not say he was in favor of such a group, but instead said, 'If they're going to do it, here's the way they should do it,'" which included leaving out of their *tefilla* all parts of the regular service that require a *minyan*, and reading from the Torah without the usual blessings.

On that basis, R. Haskel devoted his *Shabbat HaGadol* sermon in 1988 to the question of such *tefilla* groups. The women who participated in the groups were not "a bunch of fanatic feminists looking for their place in the religious sun," he told his congregants. Nor were they "looking for kicks or fights – just for a personal experience in prayer which they cannot find in the balcony…. There are new needs which Jewish women have today to participate personally in *tefilla* as they do in life." Actually, those needs were not entirely new – as he noted in a later sermon, Miriam and the other Jewish women who sang at the Red Sea constituted "the first women's *tefilla* group."[14]

Some limitations were necessary, he ruled: the group's *tefillot* needed to be limited to those sections of the liturgy that did not require a *minyan*; there could be no separate women's reading of Megillat Esther on Purim, an event R. Haskel believed should be experienced by the congregation as a single unit; and the participants in the group must "not make a big public noise about it," so as not to offend prominent rabbinic authorities who strongly opposed women's *tefilla* groups. But with those caveats, he declared that "the time has come to encourage the creation of such a group in our shul."[15]

Not long afterwards, the request for permission to have a women's *tefilla* group was formally presented to the KJ board and approved. In its early days the group attracted 40 to 50 participants, who met once each month on Shabbat morning and proceeded with those parts of the *shaharit* and *musaf* services allowed by the Rav's guidelines. In more recent years, as interest somewhat diminished, the group convened less frequently, usually on the occasion of a bat mitzvah and on Simchat Torah. Students at Ramaz asked for and received permission from Rabbi Lookstein to establish their own women's *tefilla* group. Despite the objections of some faculty members, R. Haskel ruled that the group, which met on Tuesdays, could read from the Torah, without the usual blessings, on any Tuesday when a Torah reading is mandated, such as Rosh Chodesh, Hanukka, or a fast day.[16]

In a major address to a 1993 AMIT Women's conference on gender issues, Rabbi Lookstein spelled out in greater detail the kinds of steps he felt the Orthodox community should take in order to head off "the danger of losing the best women" and "respond to [religious] striving by women in *halakhically* acceptable ways." Girls and boys should not only both learn Talmud, but should learn it together. "Unless they learn it together, the better teachers will go to the boys and the weaker teachers will go to the girls. That's the way it inevitably works out. There is no such thing as separate but equal in education of the races or of the sexes." Women should daven three times daily, whether in the regular *minyan* or a women's *tefilla* group. They should also strive to be part of a *m'zumenet*, a group of three or more women who dine together and can say an introduction to *birkat ha-mazon* afterwards. While not recommending that women wear a *tallis* or *tefillin*, he said the Jewish community "should be understanding about it," noting that two Ramaz girls who wanted to don *talleisim* and tefillin were permitted to do so in the KJ morning minyan. "There is no consensus" at Ramaz in favor of letting a girl wear *tallis* or *tefillin* at the main *minyan*, and therefore he would not grant that permission, but he added, "I wish all of us *davened* with the concentration and seriousness that these young women have."[17]

In several other sermons, and in remarks delivered to a Conference on Orthodoxy and Feminism in 1998, Rabbi Lookstein outlined additional areas where he felt it was possible to be more sensitive to women's needs while not straying beyond *halakhic* boundaries. For example, the blessing thanking God "for not making me a woman," recited by men each morning, could be said silently so as not to offend any women at the *minyan*. At KJ the practice of reciting it silently was introduced but then stopped because it created the impression the blessing was simply skipped. Instead, the problem of sensitivity to women's feelings was solved by beginning the service with the section that starts, "*Rabi Ishmael omeir*," after the *birkhot ha-shahar* (morning blessings, which contain the reference to women) are all said quietly. A mother's name could be included in various situations where it is commonly not mentioned, whether at a baby naming ceremony, on a *ketuba*, or on a tombstone. Women too could say the *birkat ha-gomel*, the blessing recited after a potentially dangerous journey or experience.[18]

In another area of particular concern to women, Rabbi Lookstein was an outspoken advocate of efforts to address the problem of agunas "Rarely does a year pass for me," he wrote in 1983, "without my confronting the tragedy of a woman who is civilly divorced but whose husband, for reasons of spite, hate, avarice, or simply viciousness, refuses to free her to marry a Jew by means of granting a *get*. Similarly, with alarming frequency I share the struggle of a civilly divorced husband to encourage his former wife, sometimes estranged for a decade or more, to accept a *get* and she refuses because of the same kind of negative feelings.... In more than one case tens of thousands of dollars have been demanded by the noncompliant partner."

R. Haskel sought to confront the problem by developing a prenuptial agreement requiring the man to give a *get*, and the woman to accept it, in the event they divorce. In consultation with attorneys, he prepared a draft, which Rav Soloveitchik approved. The project received an important boost from a New York Court of Appeals ruling in February 1983.[19] Rabbi Lookstein decided to use the occasion of his election to a second one-year term as president of the New York Board of Rabbis, in 1987, to launch a major initiative on the *aguna* problem. In his address, he urged his fellow rabbis of all denominations to adopt two procedures: first, to require engaged couples to sign the prenuptial agreement; second, to impose sanctions on recalcitrant spouses, including denial of honors, synagogue membership privileges, and the right to burial in a Jewish cemetery.[20]

Rabbi Lookstein was widely applauded for his thoughtfulness and creativity, but his proposal also ran into a number of obstacles. While Conservative rabbis were generally in accord with their Orthodox colleagues on the need for a *get*, most Reform rabbis regarded the *get* as insufficiently egalitarian, since only the husband can give it. Since they disliked it in principle, they were reluctant to require it as a condition of performing a marriage ceremony. As a corollary, Reform rabbis seemed unlikely to impose sanctions on someone for failing to give a document that they did not require. Several New York area rabbis, including R. Haskel's predecessor as president of the New York Board of Rabbis, were quoted in the press as saying it was "distasteful" to discuss a prenuptial agreement about divorce conditions with a couple just before their wedding.[21]

In a series of speeches and op-ed articles in the months to follow, Rabbi Lookstein appealed to the Reform movement to compromise, explaining that the *halakha* simply could not be altered, and the plight of *agunas* should in this case outweigh the principle of egalitarianism. As for rabbis who hesitated to raise a touchy subject on the eve of a wedding, he pointed out that "most rabbis face far more touchy situations and have to deal with them." The bottom line, he emphasized, was that there were already "between 5,000 and 15,000" Jews, mostly women, being held prisoner by vindictive former spouses. "It is irresponsible of rabbis to act as bystanders in the face of suffering.... Do not be afraid to raise this issue with intelligent couples who are about to marry," he pleaded. "Rather be afraid of the awesome responsibility which all of us assume when we simply do nothing in the face of a growing communal problem."[22]

In response to R. Haskel's proposal, the Board of Rabbis established a committee of two Reform rabbis, two Conservative, and two Orthodox (Rabbi Lookstein and Marc Angel) to examine the issue. After many weeks of debate, the Reform members agreed to a significant compromise, accepting the principle "that as important as egalitarianism may be as a religious principle for some of us, the ability of all our children to marry freely among each other was of greater import to all of us." The committee's recommendation, adopted by the Board of Rabbis in May 1987, called on all rabbis to urge their congregants to provide a get in addition to civil divorce proceedings, called on synagogues to impose sanctions on recalcitrant spouses, and urged rabbis to encourage engaged couples to sign prenuptial get agreements – a complete victory for Rabbi Lookstein's initiative.[23] The Board's executive vice president, Rabbi Gilbert Rosenthal, characterized as "amazing" R. Haskel's success in convincing his non-Orthodox colleagues to accept his position. "It may be that only a man of Rabbi Haskel Lookstein's stature could have achieved what he did. He is truly esteemed by colleagues of all groups."[24]

Seven months later, R. Haskel received, to his surprise, a letter from the executive director of the Reconstructionist Rabbinical Association. It informed him that while the RRA could not, as a matter of principle, pledge to adhere to Orthodox strictures regarding the issue of a get, it was prepared to provide all of its member-rabbis with a list of Orthodox rabbis in major cities "who would be prepared to supervise divorce proceedings for our congregants." He predicted that "many of our members would probably refer couples to the Orthodox rabbinate if a list of competent and sensitive rabbis were made available to them." Rabbi Lookstein described the letter as "one of the most gratifying things I have ever experienced in my life."[25]

✣ NOTES

1. Minutes of Meting of the Board of Trustees, March 25, 1971, p. 8.
2. "Special Projects Committee, Minutes of Third Meeting, Held June 26, 1974," File: Special Projects, KJ, pp. 1–2.

3. Arthur Silverman, Samuel Eisenstat, and Steven Gross to Rabbi Haskel Lookstein, 14 August 1974, File: Special Projects, KJ.
4. "Special Projects Committee, Minutes of Fourth Meeting, Held September 19, 1974," File: Special Projects, KJ.
5. Rabbi Haskel Lookstein to Rabbi William Herskowitz, 24 March 1975, File: Women's Issues, KJ.
6. Amendment to Certificate of Incorporation, for the May 6, 1976, Annual Meeting, File: Incorporation Papers, KJ.
7. RHL Interview, 12 December 2007; "Congregation Votes in Favor of Women Trustees," KJB XLIII:14 14 May 1976, 1; "What Is a Simchat Bat?" KJB XLIV:5 (3 December 1976), p. 4; "It Was a Great Simchat Torah!" KJB XLV:3 (14 October 1977), p. 1; "Calling Fathers (and Mothers) and Sons (and Daughters)," KJB XLVI:6 (5 January 1979), p. 2.
8. The first was "B'not Mitzvah," KJB XLIV:3 (22 October 1976), p. 2; Rafael Medoff interview with Marcia Barany Chonchol, 12 December 2008; Medoff interview with Craig Barany, 11 December 2008.
9. Rabbi Haskel Lookstein to Ari Rath, 24 December 1986, File: Women's Issues, KJ.
10. Rabbi Haskel Lookstein to unnamed colleagues, 25 November 1986, File: Women's Issues, KJ.
11. Rabbi Haskel Lookstein and 19 colleagues to the *Jerusalem Post*, 15 December 1986, File: Women's Issues, KJ.
12. The key point was that a woman could not serve as president only if "the president is authorized to spend significant sums for the congregation without clearance from an executive committee, or a board, or any other authority." (Rabbi Haskel Lookstein, Memorandum to File re: Women Being Officers in a Congregation, 28 April 1999, File: Women's Issues, KJ.)
13. RHL Interview, 12 December 2007.
14. RHL, "And Miriam Sang…Would She Do It Today in Queens?" (sermon), 25 January 1997, File: Sermons, KJ.
15. RHL, "Women's Tefila Groups: Halakhic Issues and Communal Policy" (sermon), 26 March 1988, File: Sermons, KJ.
16. Rabbi Haskel Lookstein to Participants in 11/30 Women's Tefilla Group Meeting, 2 December 1994, File: Sermons, KJ.
17. Gitelle Rapoport, "Appeal for Understanding," *New York Jewish Week*, 14–20 January 1994; Rabbi Haskel Lookstein, "Male and Female He Created Them: A Torah Perspective on Gender Differences – Presented to AMIT Women Seminar, January 9, 1993," File: Women's Issues, KJ.
18. Rabbi Haskel Lookstein, "Words That Hurt or Ignore Women – Panel on Liturgy," Conference on Orthodoxy and Feminism, 15 February 1998, File: Women's Issues, KJ; Rabbi Haskel Lookstein, "Dealing with Women's Issues in Ritual Matters Today – Seuda Sh'lishit – 24 May 2003," File: Women's Issues, KJ.
19. Haskel Lookstein, "The Courts Aid the *Aguna*," Sh'ma, 1983; Rabbi Haskel Lookstein to Alvin K. Hellerstein et al, 26 March 1982, File: *Agunas*, KJ.
20. William Saphire, "Rabbis Urged to Undertake 'A Major Initiative' to Solve the Problem of Religious Divorce," *Jewish Telegraphic Agency Daily News Bulletin*, 26 January 1987.
21. Stewart Ain, "Pre-marital Agreements: Clouds or Umbrellas," Jewish World, 19 June 1987.
22. Haskel Lookstein, "Get Smart: Are Jews Divorced from Reality," Jewish World, June 12, 1987.
23. "A Resolution of the Board of Governors of the New York Board of Rabbis for Presentation to the Membership on May 13, 1987," File: *Agunas*, KJ; Haskel Lookstein, "Good News for Women Seeking Religious Divorce," *New York Jewish Week*, 20 November 1987.
24. Rabbi Gilbert Rosenthal memoir in *Teacher, Preacher*, p. 63.
25. Rabbi David Klatzker to Rabbi Haskel Lookstein, 19 January 1988, File: *Agunas*, KJ; Rabbi Haskel Lookstein to Rabbi David Klatzker, 31 August 1988, File: *Agunas*, KJ.

⅋ VIII. THE ZIONIST

Israel and Zionism always played a major role in the life and thought of Rabbi Lookstein and the institutions he led. He grew up in a strongly Zionist home. Rabbi Joseph Lookstein was a long-time leader of the Mizrachi Religious Zionists of America and shaped the Ramaz School accordingly, with heavy emphasis on Zionist themes in the curriculum and instruction of modern Hebrew. "My father consciously selected teachers who were personally committed to the idea that Hebrew was the national tongue of the Jewish people and a central part of the Jewish national renaissance," according to R. Haskel. "That's why the teachers were so passionate about it, and their passion affected the kids." Beginning with the first bar mitzvah of a Ramaz student, in 1943, R. Joseph delivered his *d'var Torah* first in Hebrew and then in English. R. Haskel continued this tradition, not only at bar and bat mitzvahs but also at weddings of Ramaz alumni.

R. Joseph was also active, during the 1940s, in the pro-Zionist American Jewish Conference and was part of the delegation of Zionist leaders who lobbied at the 1945 founding meetings of the United Nations in San Francisco. In later years R. Joseph was active in an array of Israeli institutions, in particular Bar Ilan University, of which he was a founder and for which he served as president from 1957 to 1967 and as chancellor until 1977.

As the Zionist struggle to create a Jewish state escalated in the aftermath of the Holocaust, it became a frequent topic of discussion and concern in the Lookstein household. Haskel's summers at the strongly Zionist camp Massad were infused with activities relating to Eretz Yisrael, where Hebrew was a major part of conversation and instruction. "I lived Zionism for two months every year from 1945 through 1956," as he put it. One particular episode in the summer of 1945 deeply influenced him:

> I was 13 and a first-time camper at Massad. On Tisha B'Av night the entire camp sat on the floor in Bialik Hall, following the reading of Lamentations by candlelight. At one point

Shlomo Shulsinger, director and founder of Massad, who seemed to me to be a very old man but who was probably no more than 35, began reading *aggadot* from the Talmud about the destruction of the Temple. He wept as he read the Aramaic words which I did not understand. But I will never forget the feeling of this "old" man shedding tears over an event that occurred 2,000 years earlier and speaking about what it meant to lose a Jewish state and how important it was that the Jewish people return to Palestine. If I had to pinpoint when Zionism became an integral part of my identity, it would be that summer night.[1]

A second transformative experience took place two decades later. Shortly after the 1967 war, Audrey proposed that they visit Israel. "I don't think you should step into the pulpit on Rosh Hashana without having seen, firsthand, what happened as a result of the war," she said. R. Haskel was concerned about the expense of the trip and agreed only reluctantly. Visiting reunited Jerusalem and newly accessible holy sites such as Rachel's Tomb, near Bethlehem, and the Cave of the Patriarchs in Hebron was, R. Haskel said later, "a profound experience, even life-altering." Seeing "the amazing transformation of Israel" was "an extremely important moment both in my professional life and in our life as a couple. Audrey was absolutely right."[2]

In an essay commemorating the centennial of the First Zionist Conference, R. Haskel made it clear that his vision of Zionism is based on the idea of "a Jewish State, not just a place where Jews might live." The difference between the two, he wrote, "is not unlike the difference between Jerusalem and Miami Beach." Israel must "clearly maintain its Jewish character." The goal of Zionism from its inception was to have a state "in which Jewish culture would thrive, the Hebrew language would be revived, and Jewish thought, religion, and traditions would predominate."[3]

Along with the mainstream of religious Zionism, Rabbi Lookstein regarded the establishment of the State of Israel as the beginning of the process leading to the messianic era, a conviction he maintained despite the turmoil of later Israeli political developments and the fragmenting of the religious Zionist community over Israeli government policies. "To be sure, the process is slow, there will be fits and starts, and one has to be patient and have faith," he wrote in 1996. "Redemption is like a little child who has to be given time grow." He noted that when Israel was founded, just 6 percent of world Jewry lived in Israel, but by 1996 that figure had grown to 33 percent. "How can this phenomenon not be considered the dawn of our redemption? But it is only the dawn, and one should not expect the sun to be shining as someday it will at high noon. That will take time, perhaps a long time, and patience is necessary."

In the wake of the 1967 Six Day War, with Israel escaping the threat of annihilation and liberating Jerusalem and other significant portions of the biblical Land of Israel, KJ adopted the Israeli chief rabbinate's decision that the *Hallel* prayer, with a full blessing, should be recited on Israel Independence Day. "Surely, there is a need to translate those miraculous deliverances into religious terminology and ritual," R. Haskel wrote in the KJ newsletter. While acknowledging that some segments of Orthodox Jewry rejected the practice as "an unnecessary pronouncement of God's name," nevertheless, "for us at Kehilath Jeshurun, the Chief Rabbi of Israel is good enough. We will take the chance based on his religious decision that praising God for the events of last year will not be viewed by God himself as taking His name in vain."[4]

Rabbi Lookstein saw in the 1990s emigration of Soviet and other Jews further evidence of the redemption process. Just ten years earlier Natan Sharansky and Yuli Edelstein were in prison; now they were members of the Israeli cabinet. Ten years earlier 5,000 Jews were suffering in Syria, 75,000 were "living in peril in Iran," and 25,000 Ethiopian Jews were "living in serfdom and bondage." By 1996 nearly all of them, along with 800,000 Soviet Jews, were living freely in Israel. "These are the living examples… of the dawn of redemption," he wrote.[5]

To this day the Ramaz curriculum and calendar reflect the Looksteins' deep feelings about Hebrew, Zionism, and the State of Israel. The *Ivrit b'Ivrit* Hebrew language instruction opens up traditional Jewish source literature "while at the same time building a way to identify with *Eretz Yisrael*, *Medinat Yisrael*, and *Am Yisrael*," according to R. Haskel. Jewish history classes fortify the students' connection to the biblical Land of Israel, ancient and modern. Israel Independence Day is marked with extensive celebratory activities, including the recitation of the *Hallel* thanksgiving prayer, said with all appropriate blessings, as is customary among religious Zionists. Participation in each year's Salute to Israel parade is mandatory.

As much as Ramaz's leaders were eager to have their graduates attend Ivy League universities, in the late 1970s they increasingly encouraged their students to spend a year between high school and college at a yeshiva in Israel. Indicative of the growing emphasis on spending a year in Israel is the fact that beginning in the spring of 1979 the annual front-page story in the KJ newsletter proudly listing colleges that Ramaz seniors would attend in the fall, for the first time began also announcing the names of seminaries in Israel that some of them would attend in the coming year. This new practice demonstrated both the school's pride in those students' decision and the fact that the number of students doing so had finally reached a level sufficient to merit public acknowledgment. That year 10 of the 59 graduates opted for a year in Israel.[6]

Three years later, in an overview of the school on its forty-fifth anniversary, R. Haskel noted with pride that nearly one-fourth of the senior class [up from 17 percent in 1979] "postponed college for a year to study in the finest Torah institutions in Israel. From there they will go to Princeton, Columbia, Yeshiva, Brandeis, and a host of other fine schools. But first they are deepening their Jewish commitment and learning to love Israel – the Land and the People – in a way for which they have been well prepared at Ramaz but on a level which can only be attained by living in a

Torah environment in *Eretz Yisrael*." By 2006 nearly two-thirds of the senior class opted for a post-Ramaz year in Israel.[7]

A 1987 survey of Ramaz graduates found that 10 percent had immigrated to Israel, and 60 percent of them said their education at Ramaz had influenced their decision to make *aliya*.[8] Another estimate, in 1986, calculated that 20 percent of Ramaz alumni had moved to Israel. The percentage appears to be higher among post-1967 graduates, whose exposure to Israel and Zionism was more intense than those who attended Ramaz in the 1950s and early 1960s, when interest in Israel – both at Ramaz and throughout the American Jewish community – was somewhat more subdued. Over the years R. Haskel himself did not specifically urge students to make *aliya*. "I don't believe in preaching something unless I do it myself," he noted. "Israeli Army officers say, '*Acharai*,' 'After me!' – not '*L'Finai*,' 'You go first!' If I don't do it, I won't ask others to do it."[9]

Rabbi Lookstein's annual appeals for contributions to Israel Bonds and the United Jewish Appeal-Federation likewise have always followed the "*Acharai*" method: it begins with his announcement of his and Audrey's own contribution. Their annual gift to UJA had been $1,800 for some years, but it rose to $6,000 in 1985. The year, the UJA's campaign focused on the airlifts of Ethiopian Jews, caclculating $6,000 as the cost of rescuing one Jew. "I said to myself, how could I not contribute at least that much?" R. Haskel explained. After becoming chairman of the UJA's National Rabbinic Cabinet, he and Audrey increased their annual donation to $10,000. "I consider it my `Jewish tax'-it's my first responsibility, as a Jew in New York, to support what the UJA does at home and abroad." In his UJA position, Rabbi Lookstein led missions to Israel, Europe, Morocco and elsewhere to view first-hand the work of the UJA-funded American Jewish Joint Distribution Committee and inspire his fellow-rabbis to support those efforts. R. Haskel's longtime leadership role in both UJA-Federation and Israel Bonds has typified his deep commitment to Jewish philanthropy at home and abroad.[10]

Given Rabbi Lookstein's proclivity for public political action, it is not surprising that KJ responded to Israel's crises, such as the Six Day War and the 1973 Yom Kippur War, with rallies and vigorous fundraising campaigns, sometimes using tactics already honed in the ongoing Soviet Jewry struggle. During the 1973 war, for example, R. Haskel urged KJ members to celebrate a "present-less Hanukka," by "taking the money that you would normally have spent on gifts and sending it as an additional contribution to the UJA Israel Emergency Fund."[11]

Other Israel-related issues in recent years that prompted KJ rallies included the extended imprisonment of Jonathan Pollard, the plight of Israeli POWs, Iranian support for terrorism, and, most notably, media bias against Israel. The *New York Times* in particular was repeatedly challenged by Rabbi Lookstein for its Mideast coverage. In the summer of 2001, in response to an article in which a *Times* reporter equated Arab terrorists and Israeli victims, Rabbis Haskel and Joshua Lookstein issued a public appeal to Jewish readers of the *Times* to suspend their subscriptions for ten days, from Rosh Hashana to Yom Kippur. "We are fed up with the bias and the distortion and are ready to do something about it," they wrote. Evidently many people agreed; R. Haskel received calls from more than 1,000 readers who said they would join the ten-day boycott. Senior editors of the *Times* quickly invited Rabbi Lookstein to a meeting, at which they admitted the newspaper had made some "mistakes." R. Haskel was not persuaded to drop his protest, but he was pleased that "someone is listening." "In the modern world with its mass societies, mass media, and mass culture, it is natural to draw the conclusion that the voice of the individual doesn't count," R. Haskel wrote later. "We feel that whatever we have to say will not be heard. Frustrated, disappointed, and resigned to our own insignificance we therefore remain silent. Recently, I learned – dramatically – that 'it ain't necessarily so.'" The *Times*' evident concern about the boycott demonstrated that protests can have an impact.[12]

In a follow-up op-ed piece in the *Jerusalem Post*, Rabbi

Lookstein explained to his Israeli reading audience that the boycott of the *Times* should be regarded not only as a protest against media bias, but also as an expression of solidarity with Israel at a time when the rate of American Jewish tourism to Israel had been plummeting because of terrorism fears. "We are with you in this struggle," he wrote. "We will use our voices as effectively as we can. We will travel to Israel as often as we can. We are your family, and we recognize that when things get tough the family must respond." It was a political protest, but it was also an act of chesed. "We know that each of us has a voice. We just have to use it. Many of us are determined to do just that."[13]

Rabbi Lookstein crossed swords with the *Times* again in the spring of 2002, over the newspaper's coverage of the Passover *seder* massacre in Netanya and Israel's anti-terror operations in response. The *Times* further stoked the controversy when its coverage of the Salute to Israel parade featured a front-page photo of a small Arab counterdemonstration. "Is it okay to keep writing things on suffering Palestinians, who are suffering because of the terrorism of their colleagues, and not to give sufficient attention to the victims of terror?" Rabbi Lookstein asked. He urged the Jewish community to boycott the *Times* for an entire month and called upon congregations and Jewish organizations to stop placing paid death notices in the newspaper. Once again, there was an overwhelming response.[14]

The final straw came in the autumn of 2006. In a column in the *New York Jewish Week* Rabbi Lookstein announced that he had permanently canceled his subscription to the *Times*, and he explained why. Earlier that year the Times revealed confidential details of an ongoing U.S. government investigation into how terrorist groups receive funding through European banks. "This seemed to me, at a time when we are at war against terror, as an act bordering on sedition," he wrote. "It was quite literally an assault on the ability of the government to protect us." But it was the *Times'* reporting on the July 2006 Lebanon War that sealed R. Haskel's decision. "Throughout the war and for weeks afterwards, through pictures, headlines, and stories, the *Times* made the Lebanese and Hezbollah the victims and depicted Israelis as disproportionate responders and murderers of civilians." At the same time, a *Times* article about rocket attacks on the Israeli town of Sderot claimed "no serious damage" was done. Rabbi Lookstein knew firsthand that the report was false; he himself had been in Sderot that week. "I saw the damage and the trauma" that the rockets had caused. "Our family has had enough," he concluded. "We will miss a lot of the wonderful features in the *Times*, but we have come to feel, regrettably, that all of its news is not necessarily fit to print – or to read."[15]

R. Haskel and the KJ-Ramaz community also spoke with their feet. In his inaugural address upon his election as president of the New York Board of Rabbis in February 1986, Rabbi Lookstein urged rabbis to lead groups from their congregations on missions to Israel as a way of showing solidarity with the Jewish state and helping its economy. The first KJ-Ramaz mission, led by Rabbi and Mrs. Lookstein, spent ten days in Israel that summer.

Four years later American Jewish tourism plummeted to a new low in the months prior to the first Gulf War. Past KJ president Sandy Eisenstadt, returning from Sukkot in Israel, reported that there were just nine guests in the King David, "a hotel," R. Haskel later noted, "where, in the past, one practically needed to know a government minister in order to get a room during the festival seasons of the year." To counter the impression among Israelis "that they are being abandoned by American Jews," Eisenstadt and Rabbi Lookstein organized a week-long mission to Israel, timed for Thanksgiving weekend so potential participants would not have to commit to missing a significant number of work days. Eighty people took part in "Operation *L'Hitraot* – To See and Be Seen."[16] They received an effusive welcome. A former Ramaz colleague taking the bus to work in Jerusalem heard the news of their arrival on the radio "and began to cry tears of joy." A man approached them in the hotel lobby to say, "You don't know me, but we all know you. It's great that you came. If only every rabbi would come with his congregation." The desk in Rabbi Lookstein's room was piled high with a stack of letters and messages from total strangers praising them for coming. "We saw in that enthusiastic reception the depth of pain and disappointment of our brothers and sisters in Israel.... Every American Jew must plan to visit Israel, must talk with our feet.... Fifty years ago American Jews stood still. We cannot afford to stand still again."[17]

Ten years later, after the eruption of a second major wave of "Intifada" terrorism, Sandy Eisenstadt again returned from Sukkot in Israel to report nearly empty hotels and shuttered restaurants. Preparations for "Operation *L'Hitraot* II" began immediately. To those who stayed away from Israel because of perceived dangers, he responded that the real danger was not going to Israel. "If you or I were in trouble and our family avoided us, how would we feel?" he asked. "That's a real danger."[18] Sixty-seven KJ members joined that mission. In the years to follow, KJ sponsored "Operation *L'Hitraot*" every Thanksgiving and Pesach, often with more than 100 participants.

Another unique *chesed* project, undertaken in the spring of 2002, provided aid to merchants from Jerusalem's Ben Yehuda Street whose businesses had suffered as a result of the tourism drought following that year's wave of suicide bombings. On the bus ride home from a pro-Israel rally in Washington (to which KJ and Ramaz sent 1,500 people) two KJ women leaders, Riva Alper and Stacey Scheinberg, conceived of the "KJ *Midrachov* (the name of the pedestrians–only shopping area in downtown Jerusalem)." With Rabbi Lookstein's strong support, KJ flew seven of the Jerusalem vendors, with their stocks of merchandise, to New York City for a day of business in the 85th Street building. "Despite the rainy weather," one newspaper reported, "the first and second floors of the synagogue were wall to wall with customers all day, from 9 A.M. to 5 P.M., with 115 volunteers – men, women, and children – helping the merchants." In all, some 10,000 people came through the synagogue building that Sunday in May.

"I couldn't have imagined this in my dreams," said Jewels of

Jerusalem proprietor Yuval Boteach. "For months I have not been able to pay my rent at my store, but from today alone I can pay and survive, thanks to these angels." "What this community did is unbelievable," said Uri Shkalim, owner of a women's clothing store. "Even if I had not sold one item, it would have been worth it to be here and see the outpouring of caring." All seven merchants completely sold out their wares and departed with lists of additional orders to ship. Moreover, numerous other Jewish communities in the United States and Canada, hearing of KJ's initiative, made plans to organize similar projects.[19]

Rabbi Lookstein usually steered clear of the divisive Israeli policy issues that attracted American Jewish partisans during the 1980s and 1990s. He always felt strongly that those who do not live in Israel should refrain from meddling in Israeli affairs. For that reason, he responded sharply when a prominent Reform leader, Albert Vorspan, authored an essay in the *New York Times Sunday Magazine* harshly criticizing Israeli policies. R. Haskel chose to reply in the *New York Jewish Week*, since responding in the *Times* itself (even if it would allot him the space) "would be to further confuse American public opinion" by highlighting Jewish divisions. "Vorspan's job, like my job, is to support [the Israeli] government," he argued. "It is the government they chose.... It is their government and, with so much at stake, only they should be criticizing it." Vorspan's "Israel-bashing" might, "God forbid, result one day in a congressional vote" against U.S. aid to Israel, yet Vorspan, safe in his "plush Manhattan offices," would not suffer the consequences of his actions.[20]

In a similar vein, Rabbi Lookstein responded to a public attack on Israel by *Tikkun* editor Michael Lerner in 1989 with a private letter challenging Lerner's statements as "*chutzpah*, and dangerous." "You don't live in Israel," he wrote Lerner. "You don't take the risks that the Israelis take.... If Senators and Congressmen choose to believe you, Michael, Israel will lose financial support and military support.... [I]f something happens to the State of Israel, you...will lose faith, pride, and all the things which we feel about Israel. But the people in Israel will lose their sons, their husbands, and perhaps many thousands of civilians."[21]

Rabbi Lookstein defended the Likud government under Yitzhak Shamir against U.S. pressure for concessions in 1988, not on the basis of whether or not the requested concessions were wise but because "Whether all of us agree with its policies, there is an elected government in Israel [and] that government has the right to make decisions about what is best for the people of Israel." He went so far as to compare American Jewish disputes over the issue to the intra-Jewish quarrels that wracked the community during the Holocaust and undermined government support for Jewish concerns. "If there is one lesson that Jewish history has taught us, it is that Jews have to stand together when confronting danger," he argued. When we did not follow this lesson 45 years ago, we paid a terrible price. Must we pay a similar price today?"[22]

R. Haskel's search for the golden mean in Israel's political scene led him briefly to Meimad, a breakaway faction from the National Religious Party, which took positions close to his own: "centrist religious Zionism," "mutual respect and tolerance" between secular and religious Israelis, and a moderate public face for Orthodox Judaism. The fact that Meimad was founded by his personal friend Rabbi Yehuda Amital and was supported by another friend (and son-in-law of Rav Soloveitchik), Rabbi Aharon Lichtenstein, made the new party even more appealing to Rabbi Lookstein. "Never in my life have I been involved in American or Israeli politics, and I never again expect to be involved," he wrote in a private letter in 1998 supporting the new party.[23]

R. Haskel was cautiously supportive of the 1993 Oslo accords and joined *Shvil Hazahav* [The Golden Mean], a small group of American Orthodox Jewish intellectuals who endorsed the Israeli government's negotiating stance. This action put him at odds with much of the U.S. Orthodox rabbinate, where sentiment toward the Oslo accords generally ranged from skepticism to fervent opposition. In the wake of continued Arab terrorism, however, Rabbi Lookstein in May 1995 urged Israel to suspend its negotiations with the Palestinian Authority, arguing that the Jewish State would become a "prisoner of the peace process" if it made additional concessions despite the PA's failure to act against terror groups. By 1997 he had concluded that "the Arabs do not want peace," although by that time a Likud government was in power, so his position was once again supportive of the Israeli government.[24] On the other hand, reports that the Labor government would in 2001 divide Jerusalem prompted Rabbi Lookstein to host a public rally at KJ, at which he spoke against giving over any parts of the city to Arab rule.[25]

Somewhat paradoxically, the rabbinical sage whom R. Haskel has since the 1990s cited as his most important intellectual mentor after his father and Rav Solovetichik, is an Israeli rabbi who holds views on political and territorial issues far more nationalistic than his own: Rabbi Shlomo Aviner, head of the Ateret Yerushalayim (formerly known as Ateret Cohanim) yeshiva in Jerusalem's Old City. For R. Haskel, Rabbi Aviner's opposition to any Israeli surrender of territory is secondary in importance to his profound commitment to the principles of *derekh eretz* [good manners] and *ahavat Yisrael* [love of fellow-Jews], which R. Haskel regarded as nearly identical to the philosophy of "*menschliness* before Godliness" that he himself always espoused.[26]

❧ NOTES

1. *Hadassah Magazine*, December 1997.
2. RHL interview, 13 February 2008.
3. Haskel Lookstein, "Israel: A Jewish State," *The Reporter* (Women's American ORT), May 1997, p. 42.
4. Haskel Lookstein, "A Religion Which Addresses Our Needs," KJB XXXVI:33 (24 May 1968) p. 2.
5. Rabbi Haskel Lookstein, "I Say the Prayer for the State of Israel," undated (1996), File: Religious Zionism, KJ. The sermon was based on a poem by Rabbi Shlomo Aviner.
6. Compare "Ramaz Seniors Establish Outstanding Record as School Completes 41st Year," KJB XLV:12, 2 June 1978, p. 1 – the last such article to refrain from mentioning students going to Israel – to "Ramaz to Graduate 59 Seniors on June 13; Ten Complete Their Studies in Israel," KJB XLVI:11 (31 May 1979), p. 1, inaugurating the inclusion of Israeli yeshivot, a practice that continues to this day.
7. Rabbi Haskel Lookstein, "Looking Back and Ahead: A View of Ramaz at Age 45" (New York: Ramaz, 1982).
8. Nathalie Friedman, "The Graduates of Ramaz: Fifty Years of Jewish Day School Education,"

in Jeffrey S. Gurock, ed., *Ramaz: School, Community, Scholarship and Orthodoxy* (Hoboken, N.J.: Ktav, 1989), pp. 83–123.

9. Greer Fay Cashman, "Manhattan's Ramaz Orthodox School Celebrates Its Fiftieth Anniversary," *Jerusalem Post*, 29 August 1986.

10. RHL interview, 12 December 2007.

11. "More Than Half a Million Raised for Israel by Kehilath Jeshurun Members," KJB XXXV:32 (9 June 1967), p. 1; Haskel Lookstein, "A 'Presentless Chanukah' This Year?" KJB XLI:7 (7 December 1973), p, 1.

12. RHL, 12 December 2007; Haskel Lookstein and Joshua Lookstein, "Sending a Message to the N.Y. Times," *New York Jewish Week*, 15 June 2001; "The Rabbi Meets the Editor," *New York Jewish Week*, 13 July 2001; Haskel Lookstein, "Your Voice Does Count," unpublished op-ed, July 2001, File: Zionism, KJ.

13. Haskel Lookstein, "The Worst of 'Times," and How to Fight It," *Jerusalem Post*, 5 August 2001.

14. Felicity Barringer, "Some U.S. Backers of Israel Boycott Dailies Over Mideast Coverage that They Deplore," *New York Times*, 23 May 2002.

15. Rabbi Haskel Lookstein, "No More Time for 'The Times,'" *New York Jewish Week*, 15 September 2006.

16. Haskel Lookstein, "Why You and I Must Go to Jerusalem Now" (op-ed), 23 November 1990.

17. Haskel Lookstein, "Talking with Their Feet," *Jerusalem Post*, 4 December 1990.

18. Haskel Lookstein, "The Danger In Not Going to Israel," *New York Jewish Week*, 15 December 2000.

19. Gary Rosenblatt, "Buying Israeli, First Hand," *New York Jewish Week*, 17 May 2002.

20. Haskel Lookstein, "Public Policy Debate Rests with Israelis," *New York Jewish Week*, 27 May 1988.

21. Haskel Lookstein to Michael Lerner, 8 March 1989, File: Israel, KJ; Lerner to Lookstein, 25 April 1989, File: Israel, KJ; Lookstein to Lerner, 8 May 1989, File: Israel, KJ. Lerner responded by accusing Rabbi Lookstein of not having "the slightest understanding of Torah or the Prophets."

22. Rabbi Haskel Lookstein, "Doomed to Watch History Repeat Itself," *New York Jewish Week*, 8 April 1988, p. 22; also see Rabbi Haskel Lookstein, "A Time to Be Silent and a Time to Speak Out," *New York Jewish Week*, 28 October 1988, p. 26.

23. Rabbi Haskel Lookstein to "Dear Friends," 11 October 1988, KJ; Rabbi Haskel Lookstein to Members of Kehilath Jeshurun, 15 November 1988, File: Meimad, KJ.

24. RHL interview, 12 December 2007; Richard Bernstein, "For Jews in America, a Time for New Hope and New Fear," *New York Times*, 3 September 1993; Haskel Lookstein, "Prisoners of Peace, No!" *Jewish World*, 12–18 May 1995; Rabbi Haskel Lookstein, "Ghosts of Destruction," *New York Jewish Week*, 8 August 1997.

25. Hundreds Gather in NY for Pro-Jerusalem Rally," *Jerusalem Post*, 9 January 2001.

26. RHL interview, 12 February 2008. A second Israeli scholar whom R. Haskel regards as a major intellectual influence on him was Nechama Liebowitz, whose *shiurim* he attended in Jerusalem on many occasions, and whose methods for studying Chumash he closely follows.

✢ IX. CENTRIST ORTHODOXY

During the 1970s and 1980s there were increasing indications that a segment of the American Orthodox community was becoming stricter in its religious observance and less tolerant of those who were not as strict. This trend was evidently due to factors such as ba'alei *teshuva* undertaking particularly rigorous observance, modern Orthodox adolescents "rebelling" by becoming more punctilious than their parents, and a growing resentment in the Orthodox community toward the permissiveness of American culture. The shift toward more rigorous observance and separatist attitudes became apparent in areas such as modes of attire, standards of *kashrut*, choice of schools, and attitudes toward non-Orthodox Jews and non-Jews. R. Haskel, by contrast, advocated Centrist Orthodoxy, that is, an Orthodoxy anchored in openness to American culture and a desire to cooperate with other wings of Judaism and members of other faiths. Moreover, he argued that centrism was not merely a default position of quietly refraining from extremism, but rather a principle that needed to be advocated with vigor. "We must be passionate about our centrism," he asserted in one 1987 appeal. Referring to recent clashes between Orthodox and secular militants in Israel, he wrote: "Today, while the extremists are passionate, the centrists are passive. No more! We must be insistent about *ahavat chinam* [unconditional love] in the face of *sinat chinam* [unwarranted hatred] which threatens to destroy us."[1]

For many years the Synagogue Council of America served as a battleground in the struggle between Orthodox separatists and Orthodox advocates of cooperation. As early as 1983, separatist elements within the generally centrist Union of Orthodox Jewish Congregations of America [OU] pressed, behind the scenes, for withdrawal of the OU from the Synagogue Council. They contended that the OU's participation in the Synagogue Council constituted de facto Orthodox recognition of the religious legitimacy of the non-Orthodox groups in the council. Rabbi Lookstein strongly supported Orthodox participation in the council, as did his father, who served a term as its president. "The Synagogue Council of America serves both symbolically and functionally to emphasize the unity that transcends our divisions and the solidarity of the Jewish people that takes precedence over any disagreements," R. Haskel wrote in one of many letters to the OU leadership, urging them to reject the mindset of those Orthodox Jews "who have turned inward to such an extent that the concerns of *Klal Yisrael* [the Jewish People] are not theirs any more. They only find time to criticize, not to support, to disparage other Jews and not to join with other Jews in helping to save Jewish lives." To reinforce Rabbi Lookstein's position, the 1985 annual meeting of Kehilath Jeshurun adopted a resolution that expressed strong support for the OU's continuing to be part of the Synagogue Council. The persistence of rumors of a possible OU withdrawal from the council eventually compelled R. Haskel to warn its leaders bluntly that if they took such a step he would "vote with my pocketbook and with my congregation's pocketbook as well," by withdrawing Kehilath Jeshurun from the OU and working to establish "a new Synagogue Council affiliated with Yeshiva University.[2]

Signs of Orthodox intolerance seemed to be multiplying. On the eve of the High Holidays in 1984, the Agudas Harabonim, a small association of separatist Orthodox rabbis, placed an advertisement in several New York Jewish newspapers, declaring it better to refrain from attending synagogue altogether on Rosh Hashana or Yom Kippur than to go to a non-Orthodox synagogue. Rabbi Lookstein denounced the ad as a "slap [in] the faces of Reform and Conservative Jews" and an attempt to cause them "pain and embarrassment." If the ad's sponsors thought their pronouncement would prevent Jews from committing a sin, they were utterly mistaken, he wrote. "Nobody responds to such teaching. No one responded to it when it was the fashion in Eastern Europe fifty years ago."[3] Moreover, he explained in a later op-ed article in *Jewish Week*, it was wrong to "attack the validity of non-Orthodox movements" when those movements in fact play a positive role in Jewish life. A Reform Jew "attending a temple service on the

Sabbath, even if that service does not conform to *halakhic* standards" was clearly better than that Jew "spending that morning on the golf course or at the beach." An egalitarian religious service "is in my view counter to *halakha*," but "if the Jewish identity of a Conservative Jew is strengthened" by taking part in such a service, surely that is "positive for that particular Jew" and better than having him or her "assimilate and not step inside any synagogue." While "of course we would hope that people would embrace the entirety of Shabbat, without a question half a *challah* is better than none. Such an approach does not repel Jews but rather attracts them. In the long run, there will be more Jews, a heightened Jewish identity, and a greater sense of belonging to a people by virtue of [this approach] than through the demanding proclamations of the Agudas Harabonim."[4]

Additional signs of intolerance abounded. In one instance a prominent Orthodox rabbi who was invited to be honored along with the community's other rabbis at a UJA fundraising dinner said he would attend only if he were listed separately from the non-Orthodox rabbis in the program and seated on a dais that was physically separate from that of the other rabbis.[5] Meanwhile, shortly before Rabbi Alexander Shapiro, president of the [Conservative] Rabbinical Assembly addressed the [Orthodox] Rabbinical Council of America in the spring of 1985, some wives of RCA rabbis received a letter from Orthodox critics urging them to influence their husbands to boycott the event. The letter asserted that the participation of a Conservative rabbi qualified as a desecration of God's name. Rabbi Lookstein, by contrast, not only rejected such views but himself spoke at the Rabbinical Assembly's annual convention in 1995, and even addressed the attendees as "my dear fellow and sister rabbis."[6]

The rotation agreement by which rabbis of different denominations take turns as president of the New York Board of Rabbis by chance resulted in Rabbi Lookstein's elevation to the presidency precisely in the midst of these controversies. He decided to use his inaugural address, in December 1985, to focus attention on the issue of Jewish unity and to propose a possible solution. "[T]he growing polarization that exists in the religious community both here and in Israel" poses "a serious and frightening threat" to the Jewish people, he said. "So many of us are unable to speak to each other civilly. Religious rightists and leftists throw epithets at each other. The extremism that manifests itself on both sides threatens to isolate Jew from Jew and to rend the fabric of Jewish peoplehood so that we will no longer be one people."

Noting the relatively small number of Orthodox rabbis involved in the Board of Rabbis, Rabbi Lookstein bemoaned the fact that "so many of my Orthodox colleagues...want no part of dialogue" with the non-Orthodox. But, he emphasized, there had been statements and actions by the left – by Reform leaders – that were just as unreasonable as those from the right. The 1982 Reform decision to accept as Jewish anyone who has one Jewish parent, whether it is the mother or father, "threatens to tear us apart as a people, because we will no longer have a common ground for agreement on who is Jewish and who is not."

R. Haskel's solution was multifold. To improve the general atmosphere in the Jewish community, he called on both sides to undertake a general "lowering of the strident tones of our rhetoric." He asked Orthodox rabbis "to extend a hand of friendship and love to Conservative and Reform rabbis and not to be afraid to sit down with them" to discuss issues of contention. He asked his Conservative and Reform colleagues to take three specific steps to promote Jewish unity: reconsideration of the decision on one-parent Jewish identity (patrilineal descent); cooperation in finding a method of converting non-Jews to Judaism that would be acceptable to all denominations, including the Orthodox; and acceptance of the principle that every Jewish divorce should be done in a way "that will be acceptable to the Jewish people as a whole," that is, through a get. If it seemed that his prescription for unity was somewhat unbalanced, asking the Conservative and Reform rabbis to take specific steps while asking the Orthodox for something that was "rather unspecific," that would be a mistaken impression, Rabbi Lookstein wrote. In fact, "such a change in attitude on the part of the Orthodox establishment" – a willingness to engage in dialogue with the non-Orthodox on religious issues – "would constitute a very significant shift in outlook." The publication of most of R. Haskel's address in the pages of *Moment* magazine shortly afterwards helped bring his proposals to even wider public attention.[7]

As noted earlier, Rabbi Lookstein subsequently used his address upon reelection as head of the Board of Rabbis in early 1987 to focus even more energetically on the get issue in particular. That stance resulted in the decision of an intradenominational committee in favor of accepting the principle of insisting on a get and sanctioning recalcitrant spouses. But when he announced this victory at the May 1987 RCA convention, R. Haskel received what he considered "a very lukewarm reception." From his perspective, he was "bringing to them a tremendous accomplishment…that indicated the willingness of Reform and Conservative rabbis to meet us on our own terms" on the get issue. "I have persuaded an organization, composed of at least two-thirds non-Orthodox rabbis, to approve and endorse the obtaining of a get by everybody who gets a civil divorce," he pointed out. "Surely this has to be considered a positive result of intergroup cooperation." Evidently not, he discovered. "Unfortunately, the accomplishment was not deemed terribly worthy by my colleagues. It was a depressing experience. But it was probably a necessary awakening for me" in that it illustrated for him how far separatist attitudes were penetrating modern Orthodoxy.[8]

Much to Rabbi Lookstein's chagrin, the issue of relations between Orthodox and non-Orthodox Jews suddenly assumed international dimensions after the Israeli parliamentary election of November 1988. The victorious Likud's ability to form a governing coalition depended on four Orthodox parties, which conditioned their participation on amending the Law of Return to recognize a convert to Judaism only if the conversion were performed according to *halakha*. Although in practical terms the legislation would have affected only the small number of non-Orthodox converts who sought to immigrate to Israel, it would have enshrined in Israeli law the principle that the State of Israel did not recognize non-Orthodox conversions as legitimate. American Reform and Conservative leaders flew to Israel to lobby Prime Minister Yitzhak Shamir and his colleagues against the amendment. Rabbi Lookstein joined them. R. Haskel has always believed "that Americans should not be making decisions for Israelis," but "this time Israelis were making decisions for Americans." As a result, "we had every right – indeed, obligation – to take a very strong position" against the amendment.[9] For him the issue was not the *halakhic* validity of non-Orthodox conversions, which he too could not accept. Rather, what troubled Rabbi Lookstein was the pain that the amendment would cause to large numbers of non-Orthodox Jews, the strains that it would create in the relations between Orthodox and non-Orthodox Jews, and the image of intolerance that would be attached to Orthodox Judaism.

Expecting Israeli officials to be less sensitive to those concerns than to the danger of an anti-Israel backlash, the delegation stressed that "if the State of Israel rejects a large body of people who consider themselves as Jews, those people may very well reject the State of Israel and repudiate our national homeland.... The results in terms of financial support of Israel and, more importantly, political support, could very well be disastrous for our people and for the State of Israel.... No Israeli leader should expose Israel to such a possible loss of support and to the alienation of hundreds of thousands who, being rejected, will react in the manner in which any rejected person would react."[10]

As for the question of how the Israeli government should relate to non-Orthodox converts seeking to be recognized as Jews, "there is no need for a secular government in Israel to deal with these *Halakhic* issues." They should be "left to the chief rabbinate, which has experience in resolving those problems which may arise from time to time," such as when a non-Orthodox convert in Israel seeks permission to marry a Jew. Indeed, if he himself were asked to perform a marriage involving such a person, "I would have to face the *Halakhic* questions regarding their Jewishness" just as the chief rabbinate does, but that could be handled quietly on an individual basis, presumably involving some sort of conversion process acceptable to Orthodoxy.

Drawing on his research about American Jewish responses to the Holocaust, Rabbi Lookstein noted that negotiations between American Zionist and non-Zionist leaders to establish a joint fundraising apparatus foundered in October 1938 when the non-Zionists broke off the talks. A few weeks later the Kristallnacht pogrom devastated German Jewry, and the shaken non-Zionists quickly concluded an agreement for establishment of the United Palestine Appeal (later called the United Jewish Appeal). "What a tragic irony," R. Haskel commented, if "just weeks after the fiftieth anniversary of the terrible pogrom of Kristallnacht the unity of the Jewish people which Kristallnacht created would be dissipated and our people would be torn apart by anger and resentment."[11]

In this controversy too Rabbi Lookstein sought the golden mean, opposing the amendment but also repudiating the "exaggerations and Orthodox-bashing" by some anti-Orthodox elements.[12] He was particularly troubled by a sermon in which Stanley Davids, a Reform rabbi who was part of the delegation to Israel, attacked "the narrow-minded bigotry of 770 Eastern Parkway," headquarters of the Lubavitch movement, which favored amending the Law of Return. The Lubavitcher Rebbe "is a warm, loving Jew…a saintly, deeply religious man, not a narrow-minded bigot," Rabbi Lookstein responded. "It is this kind of Orthodox-bashing which is angering many modern Orthodox rabbis and making the effort to bring us together much more difficult."[13]

R. Haskel also took the opportunity of his exchange with Rabbi Davids to reiterate the importance of leaders from each denomination challenging their own congregants rather than focusing criticism on other groups, a point he had made on numerous occasions. "When I speak in my shul, I blast my own group," he wrote to Rabbi Davids. "I do not talk about what Reform Judaism has done to deeply divide the American Jewish community. I do not blast [Reform leader] Alex Schindler. Rather, I criticize my own colleagues for not being ready to sit down with Alex Schindler and work out a solution to our problems." He urged Davids to likewise spend his time "educating your congregation about the flaws in your own camp rather than inflaming them about the rather obvious and troubling problems in the camps of others." Doing so might result in criticism from some of his congregants, R. Haskel acknowledged, but then, he added, quoting Rabbi Israel Salanter, the famed nineteth-century founder of the Mussar movement, "A rabbi whom everybody likes is not a rabbi."[14]

Rabbi Lookstein made the same point some time later when Rabbi Ismar Schorsch, then chancellor of the Jewish Theological Seminary, publicly alleged that modern Orthodoxy was being overtaken by "the escalating power of ultra-Orthodox values" such as stricter criteria for conversions and taller mechitzas to separate men and women during prayer services. "I wonder why it is necessary for the head of the Conservative movement to pound away at the far right in Orthodoxy," R. Haskel wrote him. "I don't pound away at the far left in Conservative Judaism, and there certainly is a far left. That is a Conservative problem; the far right here in America is largely an Orthodox problem.... This is our struggle, not yours."[15]

Despite their occasional disagreements, Rabbi Lookstein found over the years that there was "a tremendous advantage" to associating with rabbis of other movements. For him, pluralism – which he mockingly called "the P word," to indicate the disdain in which it is held in some Orthodox circles – was not a concession but a valuable experience. "I learned a lot from their perspective, and they from mine," he said. "It was mutually edifying. You naturally develop more respect for people with whom you disagree when you meet face to face." R. Haskel recalled his experiences as a leader of the New York Board of Rabbis and the UJA's Rabbinic Cabinet as "exciting, informative, and in certain ways even formative – for my understanding of the ways other Jews see things."[16]

With his deeply held philosophy of intra-Jewish tolerance and his appreciation for the benefits of interaction with all Jewish denominations, Rabbi Lookstein was well suited for the presidency of the Synagogue Council of America, just as his father had been fifteen years earlier. However, by the time the system of presidential rotation gave R. Haskel the opportunity to serve, the council was beset with institutional troubles. Although it was established (in 1926) for the purpose of fostering unity among American Jewry's religious denominations, its member-organizations came to realize that their theological differences made it too difficult to find substantive common ground. As a result, the council's main function for many years had been to represent U.S. Jewry in dealing with the representative bodies of other religions. That would have constituted a useful occupation except that other, better-funded Jewish organizations such as the Anti-Defamation League and the American Jewish Committee established their own relationships with an array of religious agencies and leaders. In his September 1993 installation address, Rabbi Lookstein acknowledged that the work of the council had come to focus on "the outside world," but he pledged to strive also for higher purpose: to demonstrate how harmoniously we can work together, blending our voices in a symphony of tolerance and understanding rather than creating a cacophony of dissonance by mutual disrespect and mistrust."[17]

Few of R. Haskel's colleagues at the Synagogue Council shared his enthusiasm. Even his mild suggestion for a pre-Rosh Hashana campaign urging every Jew to join a synagogue failed to win approval. The Orthodox groups rejected it on the grounds that the plan was religious in nature, and as a matter of principle they rejected the council's right to play a role in Jewish religious affairs. The Reform and Conservative movements, for their part, insisted that such a campaign was the responsibility of their own congregational associations, not the SCA as a whole.[18] R. Haskel's vision of tolerance and cooperation was colliding with the reality of the member-groups' rapidly dwindling interest in the work of the council and the financial debt the council had accumulated in recent years, which was approaching $200,000. Unable to meet its basic expenses, the council closed down in November 1994.[19]

The struggle over relations between the Orthodox and non-Orthodox soon erupted anew on, of all places, New York City's basketball courts. In 1996 a Solomon Schechter (Conservative) day school applied to join an all-Orthodox basketball league, the Metropolitan Jewish High School League. Administered by a council of principals of the participating day schools, under the auspices of the Greater New York Board of Jewish Education, the league was the framework for basketball competition among Jewish schools in the New York City area. In the discussions within the Principals' Council about the application, opposition to admitting Schechter coalesced around two concerns: that granting it admission would be tantamount to recognizing the legitimacy of Conservative Judaism, and that interaction with boys or girls who were less observant could have a negative influence on the yeshiva students.

R. Haskel, as the Ramaz representative on the Principals' Council, made the case in support of admitting Schechter. Instead of offering a tactical argument, that playing sports with a Conservative school did not constitute recognition of Conservative Judaism, or that opportunities for social interaction at the games were minimal, Rabbi Lookstein decided to take a stand on the principle of cooperation. He argued that the primary concern of day school principals should be to ensure that all Jewish children receive a Jewish education, and while an Orthodox education was desirable, Schechter and other non-Orthodox schools constituted "a very good alternative" for those families that would otherwise opt to send their children to secular schools. His argument was not well received. Moreover, the discussion grew heated, with both sides making remarks that R. Haskel later characterized as "angry, vituperative, and frankly disrespectful." Tempers calmed down only after Rabbi William Altshul, then principal of the Yeshiva of Flatbush, rose and declared, "I don't think this is the kind of meeting at which the Chofetz Chaim would have felt comfortable, and if this doesn't stop, I'm walking out." Tempers cooled, but when the application was put to a vote, the separatists carried the day: the overwhelming majority of the approximately two dozen council members rejected Schechter's application, with only Rabbi Lookstein and a few other principals dissenting. For R. Haskel it was further evidence that the separatist mood was spreading within American Orthodoxy.

Rabbi Lookstein was not, however, prepared to let the matter lie. His persistence may or may not have been influenced in part by his own well-known affection for sports. Rabbi Lookstein's passion for tennis is often remarked upon among KJ members; his fondness for New York's baseball, basketball, football, and hockey teams is so fervent that he sometimes videotapes their games when they conflict with his schedule, in order to watch them late at night while exercising on his treadmill; and even in his 70s he can still sink his patented two-handed set shot in the annual Ramaz faculty-student basketball game. R. Haskel's enthusiasm for Ramaz's sports teams is such that he has often attended their matches wearing a team jersey. Add to all that his strong views on the issue of cooperation between Orthodox and non-Orthodox Jews and it was perhaps inevitable that he would not easily concede defeat in the Metropolitan Jewish High School League affair.

Convinced that the Jewish community had "enough things that divide us ideologically without being divided athletically," Rabbi Lookstein and like-minded colleagues from two other Orthodox day schools announced that they would establish an alternative league together with three area Schechter schools. Theirs would be a league that would uphold the value of Jewish unity. Moreover, by demonstratively spurning the exclusionist trend within Orthodoxy, the new league would project a kinder, gentler image of Orthodoxy to the non-Orthodox world, a long-time Lookstein goal. Despite its noble intentions, the alternative league lasted just one season, because the three dissident Ortho-dox schools simultaneously remained part of the MJHSL, and it proved too stressful for the students to play a full schedule of games in two leagues at once. The controversy, however, was far from over.

The following year the Schechter schools' petition was again turned down by the league, but this time Schechter supporters decided to take their case to the United Jewish Appeal-Federation of Greater New York, the financial sponsor of the Board of Jewish Education. After four years of lobbying, UJA officials eventually agreed, in 2001, to threaten to withhold funding from the board unless the basketball policy was changed. The Principals' Council responded by voting to break the league away from the Board of Jewish Education. Rabbi Lookstein and his allies, for their part, announced that they would try again to create their own league unless the policy of exclusion was canceled. Another round of behind-the-scenes negotiations ensued, and in May 2001 a com-promise was announced. The non-Orthodox schools would be permitted to play in the league on condition that their home games would not be played in their schools, and that Orthodox rabbis would rule on any "matters of *halakha*" that might arise in connection with the games. Ironically, however, after struggling for so many years to gain admission to the league, only one of the Schechter schools actually joined the league. The others refused on the grounds that they did not accept the right of Orthodox rabbis to have the last word in matters of dispute.[20]

One of the next great battlegrounds in the struggle between the factions within Orthodoxy will likely be the issue of conver-sions, another area in which Rabbi Lookstein took a substantial interest in recent years. R. Haskel's approach to the issue of con-verting non-Jews to Judaism was shaped both by his own vision of Orthodoxy as open and welcoming, and by a specific reply that Rav Soloveitchik gave him to the question of how demanding a rabbi should be in deciding whether to convert an applicant. "The Rav's answer was that one should never ask a convert to promise to do a specific mitzvah, because if the answer is no, you cannot go any further in the conversion process," he recalled. "The convert's acceptance of the 613 mitzvas is a general commitment, not a specific reference to any one particular commandment." The rule of thumb, Rav Soloveitchik explained, was that "the rabbi has to be reasonably convinced that the would-be convert is going to lead an observant Jewish life." In recent years, however, a growing number of younger rabbis have adopted a different position, insisting that the potential convert commit in advance, quite specifically, to a fully observant lifestyle. Rabbi Lookstein, by contrast, follows his father's approach. "He would ask a prospective convert, 'Have you come here to embrace Judaism or to embrace a Jew?' If, out of a desire to embrace a Jew – that is, their future spouse – the person is ready to embrace Judaism, then you have to give him or her every opportunity to proceed."

The Lookstein position appears to be in the minority in the Orthodox world. In 2005 the Office of the Sephardic Chief Rabbi of Israel for the first time raised questions about the validity of Orthodox conversions performed in the United States. "There were a handful of instances in which Orthodox rabbis may have proceeded too hastily in converting someone," according to R. Haskel. "But it was a small problem which could have been resolved quietly, on an individual basis." Instead the chief rabbinate called for creation of a single, centralized system of conversions according to strict criteria, to be administered by the Rabbinical Council of America. R. Haskel was a member of the commission appointed by the RCA to examine the chief rabbinate's request. He argued that if Orthodox rabbis adopted unnecessarily strict standards, prospective converts will go to Reform or Conservative rabbis for their conversions and then affiliate with those movements. In the end, however, his was a lone voice of dissent; even the few other commission members who privately agreed with R. Haskel refrained from voicing their views. The commission endorsed the rabbinate's stance, and in late 2007 the RCA agreed to require its members to abide by the more rigorous criteria for conversions.

A similar problem will soon arise with regard to the conversion of the adopted children of nonobservant couples, according to Rabbi Lookstein. "If we tell the parents that their home must be kosher and *Shomer Shabbos* and they must live within walking distance of an Orthodox synagogue, they will not have their child undergo an Orthodox conversion." The result is that the child will receive a Conservative or Reform conversion, and his Jewishness will be recognized by everyone in the Jewish community except the Orthodox. "It's embarrassing to Orthodoxy, and unfair to the couple," in R. Haskel's view. "They have just gone through the agony of infertility and the adoption process, and we are closing the door in their face. We have to remember that 'love thy neighbor as thyself' includes loving nonobservant Jews who have suffered with infertility." Here too the Rav's advice to him was particularly helpful: try to get the parents to be as observant as possible, but the main requirement is that they commit to give the child a Jewish education (i.e., day school). If they make that commitment, the child can be converted.[21]

⌘ NOTES

1. RHL, "It's Time to Turn Things Around," KJB LV:1 (18 September 1987), p. 1.
2. Haskel Lookstein to Julius Berman, 7 December 1983, File: Synagogue Council of America, KJ; Haskel Lookstein to Sidney Kwestel, 1 April 1985, File: Synagogue Council of America, KJ; Haskel Lookstein to Sidney Kwestel, 6 May 1985, File: Synagogue Council of America, KJ; "Resolution on the Involvement of the Union of Orthodox Jewish Congregations of America in the Synagogue Council of America," 1 May 1985, File: Synagogue Council of America, KJ; Haskel Lookstein to Sidney Kwestel, 11 March 1987, File: Synagogue Council of America, KJ; Haskel Lookstein to Sidney Kwestel, 28 May 1987, File: Synagogue Council of America, KJ.
3. Haskel Lookstein, "An Orthodox Response to an Unorthodox Ad," *New York Jewish Week*, 19 October 1994.
4. Haskel Lookstein, "An Orthodox Response to an UnOrthodox Charge," *New York Jewish Week*, 4 April 1997.
5. Rabbi Haskel Lookstein to Rabbi Marc Angel, 7 May 1985, KJ; Haskel Lookstein, "Mending the Rift: A Proposal," *Moment*, March 1986, p. 59.
6. Rabbi Haskel Lookstein and Rabbi Alan Silverstein, "Denominational Jews: Do Our Titles Really Define Us?" Proceedings of the 1995 Convention of The Rabbinical Assembly, p. 5.
7. "Remarks Prepared for Delivery by Rabbi Haskel Lookstein at Annual Meeting of the New York Board of Rabbis, Wednesday, December 18, 1985, 11:00 A.M.," File: Pluralism, KJ; "Mending the Rift," op. cit.
8. Rabbi Haskel Lookstein to Rabbi Binyamin Walfish, 20 May 1987, File: Law of Return, KJ; Rabbi Haskel Lookstein to Sidney Kwestel, 28 May 1987, File: Law of Return, KJ.

9. Rabbi Haskel Lookstein to Dr. Michael Wyschogrod, 28 February 1989, File: Law of Return, KJ.

10. Haskel Lookstein, "We Are One and We Will Remain One: An Orthodox Response to a Political Crisis," undated [November 1987], KJ.

11. Ibid.

12. Rabbi Haskel Lookstein to Dr. and Mrs. Elmer Offenbacher, 15 December 1988, File: Pluralism, KJ.

13. Rabbi Haskel Lookstein to Rabbi Stanley M. Davids, 5 January 1989, File: Pluralism, KJ.

14. Ibid.

15. E.J. Kessler, "Schorsch Touches Nerve with Broadside," *Forward*, 24 July 1998, p. 3.

16. RHL, "Religious Pluralism – An Unorthodox Orthodox View – Adapted from a Presentation to the American Jewish Committee, Tuesday, December 10, 1996," File: Pluralism, KJ.

17. "Installation Address, Synagogue Council of America, September 20, 1993, by Haskel Lookstein," File: Synagogue Council of America, KJ, p. 2.

18. RHL interview, 19 November 2007.

19. Steve Lipman, "Seeking Common Ground," New York Jewish Week, 24–30 September 1993; Debra Nussbaum Cohen, 'Synagogue Council Succumbs to Financial Ills," Jewish World, 2–8 December 1994; Rabbi Haskel Lookstein to The Agency Executives of the Member Organizations of the Synagogue Council of America, 10 October 1994, File: Synagogue Council of America, KJ.

20. Jeffrey S. Gurock, *Judaism's Encounter with American Sports* [Bloomington, 2005], pp. 177–180; RHL interview, 21 January 2008.

21. RHL interview, 23 January 2008.

✣ X. THE TEACHER

Rabbi Joseph Lookstein privately suspected that his son's real reason for becoming assistant rabbi at KJ was to afford him the opportunity "to express his primary love, which was Jewish education."[1] There certainly appears to be at least a grain of truth in that suspicion. As soon as R. Haskel began at KJ in 1959, he began teaching Tanach and Talmud at Ramaz. Within two years he was named Coordinator of Judaic Studies for the high school and was teaching Talmud, Chumash, Prophets, and American Jewish history. "He proved to be a gifted teacher who not only loved to teach but also loved the children whom he taught," R. Joseph noted in 1978. "Even now, when he is preoccupied with so many duties, I can still 'catch' him in the room adjoining his office surreptitiously teaching several boys how to chant the service as officiating cantors. As I look in on him, there is a sly smile on his face which seems to say, 'I know I'm cheating, but I love to do this.'"[2]

The Talmud course that he taught to sophomores in his first year was especially memorable. "I gave them the full gamut of my experience in learning Tractate *Beitza* with the Rav," he noted. "It was a fabulous class, lively and interesting for both them and me." It also provided an early experience in nascent Orthodox feminism. At the time, girls would learn Talmud only through tenth grade and then take typing and home economics in their final two years. "There was a certain 1950s logic behind this structure," he concedes. "How could a girl get a job in those days if she couldn't type? And how could she run a household if she couldn't cook?" But toward the end of the year two girls from R. Haskel's class, Vivian Eisenberg and Shira Neiman, asked the upper school headmaster for permission to continue studying Talmud in the year ahead. "The glass ceiling was broken," R. Haskel recalled. "I was proud that their experience learning Talmud with me contributed to their desire to continue." Their initiative changed the rules; girls were henceforth given the option to study Talmud in eleventh and twelfth grades. Today it is no longer an option; girls are expected to achieve the same prowess in Talmud as the boys. R.

Haskel points with pride to the fact that Vivian and Shira proved to be exceptionally successful in the professional world as well. Vivian earned a PhD in art history and today holds the Feld Chair in Judaica at The Jewish Museum; Shira, an attorney, became the first woman in the criminal division of the U.S. Attorney's Office.[3] They exemplify the type of student that R. Joseph, and his son after him, wanted Ramaz to produce: one who is comfortable and accomplished in both Orthodoxy and the broader community.

Another important manifestation of the Looksteins' progressive views on education has been the Ramaz policy, since the school's inception, of permitting female students to sing publicly throughout their high school years. Most day schools prohibit girls' participation in activities that involve public singing, such as the school chorus or dramatic performances, after they reach the age of bat mitzvah (sixth grade). The *halakhic* basis for the restriction is *kol isha*, the concept that a woman's singing voice is enticing to men. Although most rabbinic authorities hold to that view, there are some *poskim* [*halakhic* decisors] who argue that behavior which is part of everyday public experiences should not be considered enticing. "Since we all hear women's singing voices in various routine settings, we have never considered *kol isha* to be a problem," according to R. Haskel. "At Ramaz, we have always regarded the peforming arts as an important of education and a source of Jewish inspiration for the students. For Ramaz girls to sing is an important part of their Jewishness and religious growth, and to silence their voices would be wrong." The performance of the Upper School Chorus is the centerpiece of each year's Ramaz dinner, "and many former chorus members have gone on to join Jewish a cappella singing groups in college," Rabbi Lookstein noted with pride.[4]

In 1967 R. Haskel was named assistant principal of Ramaz, and two years later, when his father needed to step back, R. Haskel was moved up to acting principal. He began his tenure at the helm of Ramaz with a bedrock commitment to sustain his father's long-standing themes and traditions. Ramaz would continue to stand out as an open institution that warmly welcomed students from a variety of backgrounds and levels of religious observance. In the school's early years this philosophy reflected not only a matter of principle but also a recognition of the reality that few Orthodox Jews lived in the immediate vicinity of the school. In later years, as the Orthodox community of the Upper East Side grew, the percentage of students from Orthodox households increased.

R. Haskel also took care to maintain his father's emphasis on giving girls and boys the same opportunities, teaching *ivrit b'ivrit* (Hebrew language, taught in Hebrew), stressing the importance of Israel, and adhering to a consciously centrist version of Orthodoxy. At the same time, R. Haskel initiated a number of changes designed to bring Ramaz up to date with the latest educational methods. By the time he became principal, in 1971, he could announce that the school had made a successful transition "from a didactic approach to a participatory one." The teachers at Ramaz "have become listeners rather than lecturers," he wrote in a report to the parents. "Students are encouraged to be enthusiastic and active producers of education rather than mere passive products of a 'joyless classroom situation,' to quote Charles Silberman's newly coined phrase. More and more, our school is becoming student dominated and yes, even student run."

For the younger children this philosophy meant stressing "the students' needs rather than the school's curriculum" and "encouraging each child to learn at his own pace…. The teachers serve as guides and counselors." In the Upper School, juniors and seniors in a special program "study Bible and Prophets virtually on their own, with but limited guidance from teachers…. They take far fewer tests, but we are convinced that they are learning much more." In the area of secular studies too the high school underwent notable changes. "[W]e have revamped our English courses so that the students read about problems in life, in society, and in their own personal development," he reported. "The books which revolve around those problems [have thus] become much more relevant to them."

Since "it is well known that students learn more from informal educational opportunities than they do in a classroom," as R. Haskel put it, a major effort was undertaken in the spring of 1970 to increase student interest and participation in non-classroom areas as well – and "the results have been electrifying." An intensified effort to attract high school students to the voluntary morning *minyan* brought participation up to "about twenty five per cent of the male population of our high school" despite the fact that the *minyan* "begins at 7:30 in the morning – quite an 'ungodly' hour for divine worship." Attendance continued to rise during the autumn of 1970, and by the time the *minyan's* faculty advisor, Rabbi Mayer Moskowitz, returned several months later from an illness, "fully one-half of the student body of the high school – one hundred and fifteen boys and girls – attended the morning service. It was one of the most glorious days in the history of Ramaz, and it was organized by students alone."

Another facet of Rabbi Lookstein's "Education for Life" effort was the Senior Project, in which twelfth graders worked for two months "in some kind of educationally productive capacity" in a local hospital, public school, or other institution. A small number of seniors did take advantage of the situation in order to enjoy "a sort of senior 'cop out,'" Rabbi Lookstein conceded, but "the vast majority of the students benefited greatly from the work and brought back testimonials from the various institutions which made them and the school justifiably proud."

R. Haskel made clear in his report that political activism was an integral part of the learning process. When students want to demonstrate for Soviet Jewry or Israel, "far from trying to stifle that demand in the interests of classroom education, our policy has been that under the right auspices, students can learn more about what education really means while walking in a protest march for an hour than they can in a week of study in class." During the turmoil of the spring 1970 Kent State shootings and the escalation of fighting in Southeast Asia, Ramaz students held teach-ins and then went into the streets of the neighborhood, "trying to convince passersby of the justice of their viewpoints." "During the two weeks when these matters were at a boiling point in the country, we saw certain Ramaz students mature almost overnight," Rabbi Lookstein reported. "They became alert to the political currents of the day, sensitive to the issues, and realistic about the options open to the country and to themselves."

While Rabbi Lookstein emphasized the positive aspects of student interest in public policy issues, segments of the KJ-Ramaz community were less than enthusiastic about the positions some of their young people were taking on the controversies of the day, such as the Vietnam War. In 1970, college student Gilbert Kahn, whose father was a KJ trustee, let it be known that he planned to propose a resolution urging U.S. withdrawal from Vietnam at the upcoming KJ annual meeting. President Harry Baumgarten tried unsuccessfully to dissuade him, and Rabbi Joseph Lookstein initially resisted including Kahn's proposal on the agenda. R. Haskel brokered a compromise whereby two resolutions would be considered, one suporting U.S. weapons for Israel and the other calling for an end to American involvement in the Vietnam. Kahn was given several minutes to explain his position. The official minutes of the meeting note that the elder Rabbi Lookstein felt compelled to appeal for "patience and calmness." He reminded the attendees "that people of all ages have opinions to express and that these opinions should be listened to with tolerance, even if we do not share such opinions." After a "heated discussion," as the minutes described it, the board accepted the Israel resolution and shelved Kahn's.[5]

It is not surprising that R. Joseph initially felt uneasy about his son's strong embrace of political activism as an educational tool. In the world to which he was accustomed, not many Orthodox Jews took part in street protests. Moreover, the antiwar movement and college campus rebellions reflected a concerted rejection of authority and tradition, and the embrace of radical social views that were alien to Orthodox Judaism. Yet he gradually came to recognize that the Jewish version of 1970s protests differed in positive ways. "My son holds that when young students march in protest, in defense of the 'prisoners of Zion' or in behalf of Anatoly Sharansky, they are actually studying Bible and performing a mitzvah greater even than the mitzvah of study," R. Joseph remarked in 1978. "He contends that marching enthusiastically and proudly in an Israel Independence Day Parade is a lesson in history, in freedom, in justice, and in Jewish solidarity. Who can differ with that? All credit to him for this practical philosophy of education."[6] In more recent years R. Haskel's philosophy has been reflected in student activities ranging from prayer services outside the Iranian Mission to the United Nations to volunteer work in New Orleans following Hurricane Katrina.

Helping students develop an acute moral sense was always considered a crucial part of a Ramaz education. "We are anxious to inculcate in our students a sense of menschlechkeit [decency], a quality that is often most noticeable in the younger generation by its absence," R. Haskel wrote in 1974.[7] Thus while his father's slogan, from *Pirkei Avot*, had been *Yaffeh Talmud Torah im derech eretz* [The study of Torah is beautiful when combined with *menschlichkeit*], R. Haskel's own preferred guiding slogan for the school was the midrashic statement, *Derech eretz kadma l'Torah*, which he translated as "*Menshlichkeit* precedes Torah" or, as he explained it, "Before you can be a *tzaddik*, you have to be a *mensch*."

Nothing gave the principal more satisfaction than instances of Ramaz students exhibiting morally upstanding behavior. In a 1979 "Principal's Letter" to the parents, R. Haskel proudly reported two instances in which students found large sums of money – $500 in bills in one case, a wallet with $135 in another – and returned them to their owners while refusing to accept a reward. He took equal pleasure in a letter from a parent in 1983 recounting how when his daughter was struck by a car on the way to the school bus, another student left the bus, hailed a taxi, accompanied her to the hospital emergency room, and waited there until the child's family arrived. The parent added that it was not the first time he had heard of Ramaz students acquitting themselves so admirably, noting that recently he had heard of several students who "stopped to help an old woman who was injured or in pain on the street." The parent thanked Rabbi Lookstein for insisting that Ramaz emphasize "ethics and human responsibility."[8]

Ramaz represented only one part of R. Haskel's teaching load. From the early 1960s until 1977 he taught periodically at the Yeshiva University-affiliated Teachers Institute for Women. Beginning in the early 1970s, he occasionally substituted for his father in teaching homiletics to sophomore rabbinical students at Y.U. After his father's passing in 1979 R. Haskel taught homiletics regularly, donating his salary to the university in honor of his father's memory. Several years later, he was named Joseph H. Lookstein Professor of Homiletics. The course covered the full range of a congregational rabbi's speaking duties, such as Sabbath sermons, eulogies, wedding talks, bar and bat mitzvah remarks, and invocations. On many occasions over the years he experienced the gratification of watching a former student deliver a talk according to Looksteinian formulae, including writing out the entire speech and structuring it around three specific points of commentary.

Part of the task R. Haskel set for himself in teaching homiletics was to demonstrate to his students that the Sabbath sermon is a way of teaching the congregation, especially given the likelihood that many in the audience will not learn Torah anywhere else in the week to come. This perspective assumed added importance as the percentage of Orthodox congregants keenly interested in hearing the weekly sermon diminished steadily over the years. One of the first questions Rabbi Lookstein asked his students at the start of each semester was how many of them enjoy listening to sermons. Today only about one-fourth answer in the affirmative, a substantial decline from the 1960s and 1970s. "In those days people came to shul for the sermon and the davening, in that order," according to R. Haskel. "Today the sermon is peripheral." In his view, this trend represents not an ideological shift but a lifestyle change: the triumph of impatience. Just as doubleheader baseball games and double movie features are largely a thing of the past, it does not surprise him that *hashkama minyanim* – speedily recited early morning prayer services with no sermon – have become popular in many Orthodox synagogues over the years.

In addition to its educational value, the sermon serves two other important purposes, according to the Lookstein worldview. One is intellectual: it keeps the rabbi on his toes by challenging him to think deeply about a concept or issue each week. The second is practical: delivering the sermon engenders public respect for the rabbi. It validates him as an informed, thoughtful figure to whom congregants can turn during the week when issues arise or counsel is needed.

Both in his classes at Ramaz and in his sermons at KJ, Rabbi Lookstein felt no compunction about confronting hot-button issues. In 1985, for example, he began teaching a class at Ramaz in sexual ethics, precisely because it was "a subject nobody talks about." Sooner or later, he explained, Jewish teens are going to be exposed to sexual issues through the mass media or other sources, and "they have to know what is the standard of sexual behavior in American society along with the moral and *halakhic* issues, as well as the dangers and risks that attend that standard." The Ramaz course, jokingly referred to by the students as "Sex with the Rabbi," covered such subjects as *nidda* and *mikva*, birth control, premarital sex, homosexuality, abortion, and AIDS. While expressing heartfelt compassion for AIDS victims, R. Haskel remained firm in rejecting the kinds of behavior that can lead to the disease. In one 1991 sermon, for example, he urged congregants to pray for the well-being of the AIDS-afflicted basketball star Magic Johnson. Yet in the same breath, the rabbi praised sports columnist Dave Anderson for being one of the few voices in the athletic world to say openly that Johnson's promiscuity "was, quite simply, immoral." R. Haskel denounced the popular perspective that all consensual sexual relations between adults are morally acceptable. "We do not subscribe to morality by majority," he said. "If the majority cheats a little on income taxes, that doesn't lessen the immorality – only the stigma." If the majority of people engage in, or approve of, promiscuity, that does not lessen its immorality. "Thank God for Dave Anderson," he concluded.[9]

Issues pertaining to gays proved to be particularly complex. R. Haskel never wavered from the Orthodox principle of rejecting homosexual practices. He publicly denounced a lesbian wedding ceremony performed by a leading Reform rabbi in 1995 as "an assault on Jewish marriage and family."[10] In a private letter to the officiating rabbi, R. Haskel made it clear he was not denouncing the women for their private behavior, but rather urging the rabbi to refrain from "celebrating something which if it were done by everybody would mark the end not alone of the Jewish people but of the human race." It was one thing to be tolerant, Rabbi Lookstein wrote, but "quite another to celebrate the lifestyle."[11] Similarly in a 1997 sermon he specifically rejected the possibility that someone could be "fully Jewish and fully gay," that one could "adopt a lifestyle that runs totally counter to Torah and insist that it be called 'fully Jewish.'"[12]

Yet in the years that followed, as he grappled with the phenomenon of gays in the Orthodox community, R. Haskel found himself looking for a more compassionate approach to the issue. He was particularly moved by the 2001 documentary Trembling Before God, about Orthodox gays, calling it "a magnificent film which should touch every Jew in many ways." While rejecting the film's suggestion that biblical verses prohibiting homosexuality should be reinterpreted, Rabbi Lookstein urged his congregants to "understand the pain" of Orthodox gays, "empathize" with the inner conflicts that torment them, and "love all Jews and welcome them into as full a Jewish life as they – and we – can achieve." What this meant in practical terms was that while homosexual behavior could never be acceptable, the principle of chesed requires treating a gay Jew the same as any other Jew.[13]

As the issue of gay marriage became an increasingly prominent topic of public debate, Rabbi Lookstein revisited the topic in a 2004 sermon. On the one hand, he reaffirmed his belief that gay marriage was prohibited by Judaism and harmful to society in general, and he argued that the government should not sanction such unions. At the same time, searching as always for a compassionate approach, he suggested that state and local governments could "give all kinds of people who live together in caring relationships certain privileges that would encourage those kinds of relationships...incentives which might have a beneficial effect upon society." It was a quintessentially Looksteinian solution, one that stayed within the bounds of Jewish law while making every effort to address the real human needs at stake.[14]

❧ NOTES

1. Rabbi Joseph H. Lookstein, "Rabbi Haskel Lookstein – An Evaluation and a Tribute," undated [1978], File: Rabbi Joseph Lookstein, p. 3.
2. Rabbi Joseph H. Lookstein, "Rabbi Haskel Lookstein," op.cit., pp. 3–4.
3. Nieman's father was the aforementioned Hebrew teacher with the good aim who taught R. Haskel in the eighth grade (see p. 377).
4. RHL interview, 14 December 2008.
5. Minutes of Ninety-Eighth Annual Membership Meeting, Congregation Kehilath Jeshurun, Tuesday, May 12, 1970," pp. 7–8 ; Rafael Medoff interview with Gilbert Kahn, 17 November 2008. Rabbi Joseph Lookstein, "Rabbi Haskel Lookstein," op. cit., pp. 6–7.
6. Rabbi Haskel Lookstein, "Where We Are Now and Where We Are Headed: A Look at Ramaz at Age Thirty-Four," undated (1971), File: Ramaz, KJ.
7. RHL, "Principal's Letter," 7 September 1979, File: Ramaz, KJ, p. 4; Rabbi Irving Greenberg to Rabbi Haskel Lookstein, 14 January 1983, File: Ramaz, KJ.
8. Rabbi Haskel Lookstein, "AIDS Education Clarification" (letter), Jewish Floridian, 29 January 1988; "Ramaz Students Learn About Sex, Orthodox-Style," Forward, 3 April 1998; Rabbi Haskel Lookstein, "Thank God for Dave Anderson" (sermon), 16 November 1991, File: Sermons, KJ.
9. Rabbi Haskel Lookstein, "Lesbian Marriage in Great Neck and Concubines in Brooklyn – Has the Jewish Community Gone Mad?" (sermon), 9 September 1995, File: Sermons, KJ.
10. Rabbi Haskel Lookstein to Rabbi Jerome K. Davidson, 1 August 1995, File: Pluralism, KJ
11. Quoted in Rabbi Haskel Lookstein, "'Trembling Before God': The Struggle to Be Gay and Orthodox" (sermon), 10 November 2001, File: Sermons, KJ.
12. Ibid.
13. Rabbi Haskel Lookstein, "What Should Our Attitude Be Toward Same-Sex Marriage?" [sermon], 1 May 2004, File: Sermons, KJ.

✌8 CONCLUSION

Making sense of senseless tragedies is one of the most difficult tasks any rabbi faces. In such situations, a congregation naturally turns to its spiritual leader for answers, but as every clergyman knows, some questions ultimately have no answers and some occurrences cannot be explained. For Rabbi Lookstein each such crisis presented anew the unique challenge of finding meaningful and effective ways to help the Ramaz-KJ family cope with the crisis. Such uniquely trying situations brought into sharp relief the qualities that characterized his career as a rabbinical and communal leader, in particular his emphasis on practical deeds of *chesed* to heal his community's wounds.

On the local level, the single most jarring moment occurred in 1988 when 21-year-old KJ member Alan Brown was severely injured in a swimming accident and became a paraplegic. The tragedy was compounded by the fact that Alan had just finished raising $75,000 for paralysis research in response to an auto accident that had left his best friend paralyzed. Why do such things occur? "There are no answers," R. Haskel said, "certainly not in an individual case, and one who offers them is foolish, blasphemous, and perhaps cruel." Yet, "while there are no answers, there must be a response." That response must begin with prayer, precisely at the moment when it is most difficult to pray. Second, empathy for the victim and his family, "no intrusions or pressure or overdoing it," but finding out their actual needs and meeting them. "We do not wallow in questions that have no answers. We respond with prayer, with help, and with confidence that somehow, in some way, God will help."[1]

When tragedy struck in a different community, R. Haskel's response was not very different. He and Audrey cut short their summer vacation in Florida in 2005 after a tropical storm left the region without electricity for two days. Escaping the discomforts of the blackout and settling back into their cozy Manhattan apartment and familiar daily routine, Rabbi Lookstein found himself pondering the human tendency to take life for granted and not really appreciate what one has until it is taken away. Within days that tropical storm had grown into Hurricane Katrina and destroyed much of New Orleans. "The small lessons we took from our own discomfort and dislocation were still valid," he told the congregation. "But now something much more powerful overwhelmed us." There was no way to explain why it happened, and it was certainly inappropriate for political opponents of the Bush administration to be "playing the blame game, with almost sadistic joy." The answer to the crisis was, simply, to help. "We cannot enjoy life here in New York without sharing our possessions with Jews and non-Jews who need help so desperately.... The first question I must ask is not 'What is Bush doing?' or 'What are the state and city officials doing,' but rather: What am I doing?" To that end, he announced that he and Audrey were personally contributing $1,000 to the United Jewish Communities' Katrina relief fund, and cards for pledges to the fund were distributed throughout the synagogue. "Afterwards we will pray to God for redemption and consolation," he said. "But first, we must give."[2]

A tragedy that was both national and local required a response that was national and local as well. The September 11, 2001, terrorist attacks constituted both a catastrophe on a massive scale and one that took place not in faraway Louisiana but just a few miles down the road from KJ. On the national level, Rabbi Lookstein urged his congregants to fully support the U.S. war on terrorism and recognize it as a fight against Amalek, an implacable foe that can only be destroyed, not merely weakened or imprisoned. Cumbersome airport security checks and other inconveniences would have to be endured without complaint, since America was engaged in a war comparable to the war Israel has been forced to endure for the past six decades. A spirit of patriotism and self-sacrifice was now obligatory. On the local level, the response that he recommended had to be practical. Ramaz students under the leadership of DeeDee Benel, educational director of the student activities, made 1,000 sandwiches and sent them to the rescue teams at the World Trade Center site. The congregation also raised over $75,000 for the families of nine firefighters from the fire station down the block from KJ who lost their lives in the rescue operation. The station commander and his associate were greeted at Shabbat services on Saturday morning, September 15. It was one of the most emotional moments in the history of the congregation.

There was room, too, for another kind of response to 9/11. The attacks were, as R. Haskel put it, "a monstrous assault on *bein adam l'chevro*," the laws governing human interaction. "It is hard to imagine a more heinous violation of elementary principles of behavior toward one's fellow man." The response, therefore, should be "to repair in some significant way our behavior" toward others, such as repairing a broken friendship, providing financial assistance to a person in need, paying bills on time, visiting the sick, and in general "just trying to be nice to everyone."[3]

If there is a single common thread in the multitude of activities and achievements that have defined Haskel Lookstein's personal life and professional career across more than seven decades, perhaps it is embodied by the response he crafted to 9/11: the application of the principle of *chesed*, from the arena of small interpersonal gestures to the grand stage of national and international events.

✯ NOTES

1. Rabbi Haskel Lookstein, "What Shall We Do and What Shall We Say?" (sermon), 9 January 1988, File: Sermons, KJ.
2. Rabbi Haskel Lookstein, "Thoughts After a Catastrophe (After Hurricane Katrina)" (sermon), 3 September 2005, File: Sermons, KJ.
3. Rabbi Haskel Lookstein, "Our World Has Changed: Sermon the Shabbat following 'The Attack on America' 9/11/01," 15 September 2001, File: Sermons, KJ; Rabbi Haskel Lookstein, "Our World Has Changed: Remembering 9/11" (sermon), 11 September 2004, File: Sermons, KJ. The idea was communicated to the rabbi by Daniel Edelstein, a Ramaz alumnus.

Contributors

Hayyim Angel is the Rabbi of the historic Congregation Shearith Israel of New York (the Spanish & Portuguese Synagogue, founded in 1654). He also teaches advanced undergraduate Bible courses at Yeshiva University. He has published more than 40 scholarly articles, primarily in Bible. Twenty of those essays are collected in his book, *Through an Opaque Lens* (2006), and is currently at work on a new book of another twenty essays. He graduated from the Ramaz High School in 1987.

Rabbi Shlomo Aviner is the *Rosh Yeshiva* of Ateret Yerushalayim, in Jerusalem's Old City. A qualified electrical engineer with a Master's degree in mathematics, he was raised in France, where he served as national director of the Bnei Akiva Youth movement. After emigrating to Israel in 1966, he studied under Rabbi Zvi Yehuda Kook at the Mercaz HaRav yeshiva in Jerusalem, where he received his rabbinical ordination. He subsequently served as the rabbi of Kibbutz Lavi, Moshav Keshet and Beit El. He is also a reserve lieutenant in the Israel Defence Forces. Rabbi Aviner is the author of numerous books, including commentaries on Ruth and Ecclesiastes, a Pesach *haggada*, the philosophy of Rabbi Avraham

Yitzhak Kook and Rav Zvi Yehuda Kook, and issues of morality and modesty in Jewish thought.

Rabbi Jack Bieler is Founding Rabbi of the Kemp Mill Synagogue in Silver Spring, Maryland. He has been an administrator and faculty member in Jewish day schools for more than 30 years and has published extensively on the philosophy of Modern Orthodox Jewish education. Currently he is a mentor for the Principals Seminar of the Joseph Lookstein Center of Bar-Ilan University. Between 1974 and 1988, Rabbi Bieler was a faculty member, college guidance counselor, and chairman of the Talmud Department of Ramaz, and served during this period for eleven years as Permanent Scholar-in-Residence for Congregation Kehilath Jeshurun.

Michael J. Broyde is a law professor at Emory University, Chaver (and former director) of the Beth Din of America, and the Founding Rabbi of the Young Israel in Atlanta. He is also the Dean of the Atlanta Torah Mitzion Kollel. Rabbi Broyde has written more than 75 articles, as well as five books, on matters of Jewish law in such publications as *Tradition*, the *Journal of Halacha & Contemporary Society*, *Techumin*, and *Ohr Hamizrach*, and has published op-eds in such newspapers as diverse as the *New York Times*, *International Herald Tribune*, the *New York Jewish Week* and the *Jewish Press*.

Rabbi Mark Dratch is Founder and CEO of JSafe: The Jewish Institute Supporting an Abuse Free Environment, and Instructor of Jewish Studies and Philosophy at the Isaac Breuer College of Yeshiva University. He has authored numerous articles on the interface between Jewish law and contemporary society, focusing especially on issues of domestic violence, child abuse and clergy abuse in the Jewish community. Rabbi Dratch served as a pulpit rabbi for 22 years and was the Associate Rabbi of Kehilath Jeshurun and a teacher at Ramaz Upper School from 1990–1992.

Rabbi Dr. Adam S. Ferziger (Ramaz Upper School '82), is

Gwendolyn and Joseph Straus Fellow and vice chairman of the Graduate Program in Contemporary Jewry at Bar-Ilan University. His publications include *Exclusion and Hierarchy: Orthodoxy, Nonobservance and the Emergence of Modern Jewish Identity* (2005); *Orthodox Judaism: New Perspectives* (2006) [Hebrew], co-edited with Aviezer Ravitsky and Yoseph Salmon; and "The Lookstein Legacy: An American Orthodox Rabbinical Dynasty?" *Jewish History* 13:1 (Spring 1999), 127–149. Prior to embarking on a full-time academic career, he served as founding director of Bar-Ilan's Mechina for New Immigrants and rabbi of the Beit Binyamin Synagogue. He and his wife, Naomi (nee Weiss) live with their six children in Kfar Sava, Israel.

Sylvia Barack Fishman is Professor of Contemporary Jewish Life in the Near Eastern and Judaic Studies Department at Brandeis University, as well as co-director of the Hadassah-Brandeis Institute, and is a Faculty Affiliate of the Cohen Center for Modern Jewish Studies. Her eight books include *Matrilineal Ascent/Patrilineal Descent: The Growing Gender Imbalance in American Jewish Life; The Way Into the Varieties of Jewishness; Double Or Nothing? Jewish Families and Mixed Marriage*; and *Jewish Life and American Culture*. Prof. Fishman's work analyzes the interplay of American and Jewish values, transformations in the Jewish family, the impact of Jewish education, and contemporary Jewish literature and film. Prof. Fishman has enjoyed speaking for and consulting with Rabbi Haskel Lookstein on many occasions.

Rabbi David C. Flatto is an assistant professor of Jewish studies and constitutional law at Penn State University. Rabbi Flatto received a BA and rabbinical ordination from Yeshiva University, a JD from Columbia Law School, and is completing a PhD in the Department of Near Eastern Languages and Civilizations at Harvard University. He has also been an adjunct professor at Yeshiva University, and a visiting researcher at Yale Law School and New York University School of Law. Rabbi Flatto served as Rabbinic

Scholar at Kehilath Jeshurun and Senior Beit Midrash instructor at the Ramaz Upper School from 2000 to 2008. His writings have appeared in the *Yale Law Journal Pocket Part, Yale Journal of Law and Humanities, NYU Law Global Hauser Series, Hebraic Political Studies, Commentary, Tradition* and the *Jerusalem Post.*

Zvi Gitelman, a graduate of the Ramaz elementary school, received his AB summa cum laude from Columbia University, where he also earned his Masters and Doctoral degrees. He is Professor of Political Science and Preston Tisch Professor of Judaic Studies at the University of Michigan. Gitelman is the author, editor or co-editor of 14 books, including, most recently, *Religion or Ethnicity? The Evolution of Jewish Identities* (Rutgers University Press, 2009). His current research is on Jewish identities in Russia and Ukraine and on the USSR in World War Two.

Rabbi Jay Goldmintz is Headmaster of the Ramaz Upper School, where he first began teaching 27 years ago. He has been the recipient of the Board of Jewish Education Creative Teachers Award and the Gruss Excellent Teachers Award and has been a Jerusalem Fellow and contributing editor to the educational journal *Ten Da'at.* He is a member of the advisory board of the Wexner Kollel Elyon and is a Doctoral Fellow at the Azrieli Graduate School of Education. In addition to writing curriculum materials, he has also authored several articles related to Jewish education and religious development which have appeared in *Tradition, Jewish Educational Leadership, Ten Da'at, HaYidion, Jewish Action,* and *Atid.*

Rabbi Dr. Lawrence Grossman is editor of the *American Jewish Year Book* and associate director of research for the American Jewish Committee. He is the author of more than 100 publications on American Jewish history, Jewish religious trends, and issues in contemporary Jewish life, including an essay in the *Rabbi Joseph H. Lookstein Memorial Volume* (1980); the annual article on

"Jewish Communal Affairs" that has appeared in the *American Jewish Year Book* since 1988; and, most recently, "Decline and Fall: Thoughts on Religious Zionism in America" in the Orthodox Forum volume, *Religious Zionism Post Disengagement*. A graduate of Ramaz, he was in the second high-school class taught by Rabbi Lookstein.

Jeffrey S. Gurock, Ramaz '67, is Libby M. Klaperman Professor of Jewish History at Yeshiva University. His most recent book is *Orthodox Jews in America* (2009).

Rabbi Nathaniel Helfgot is Chair of the Departments of Bible and Jewish Thought, *maggid shiur* in Talmud and *Halakha*, and Director of Community Education for Yeshivat Chovevei Torah Rabbinical School in New York City. He is the author of numerous essays in English and Hebrew, as well as the editor of *Community, Covenant and Commitment: Selected Letters and Communications of Rabbi Joseph B. Soloveitchik* (2005) and *The YCT Rabbinical School Companion to the Book of Samuel* (2006). Rabbi Helfgot is the associate editor of *The Meorot Journal* and a contributing editor to *Ten Da'at*, and lectures frequently on Jewish themes in communities throughout North America.

Dr. Arthur Hyman, who holds the PhD. degree from Harvard University, is a Historian of Philosophy who has specialized in Medieval Jewish Philosophy. He is the Distinguished Service Professor of Philosophy at Yeshiva University. He has served as visiting professor at Columbia University, the Hebrew University of Jerusalem, and Yale University. A member of several learned societies he has been the president of the American Academy for Jewish Research and the president of the Society for Medieval and Renaissance Philosophy. He is the recipient of the award for textual studies of the American Academy for Jewish Culture. His numerous publications include *Eschatological Theories in Medieval*

Jewish Philosophy, Philosophy in the Middle Ages: The Islamic, Jewish, and Christian Traditions (co-editor) and he serves as editor of *Maimonidean Studies*.

Richard M. Joel was inaugurated as Yeshiva University's fourth president in 2003. Prior to his appointment, he served as the president and international director of Hillel: The Foundation for Jewish Campus Life for fifteen years. Joel received his BA and JD from New York University, where he was a Root-Tilden law scholar, and has received honorary doctorates from Boston Hebrew College and Gratz College. He was an assistant district attorney in New York, and Deputy Chief of Appeals in Bronx, N.Y. His career continued as associate dean and professor of law at Y.U.'s Benjamin N. Cardozo School of Law. A recipient of the Julius Bisno Award for Excellence Professional B'nai B'rith in 1992 and was the Millender Fellow at Brandeis University's Hornstein Program in 1996. He also served as chair for the campus task force of Birthright Israel.

Dr. Gilbert N. Kahn is a professor of political science at Kean University. While his major area of interest concerns group influence on U.S. foreign policy decision-making, he recently has focused as well on the question of how antisemitism and the Holocaust influence U.S. foreign policy, and decision-makers. He has been a member of Kehilath Jeshurun since his birth. Together with his wife Bernice, they are the parents of two Ramaz graduates, Abigail and Theodore.

Rabbi Jeffrey B. Kobrin is currently the Headmaster of the Ramaz Middle School. A 1987 graduate of Ramaz and longtime friend of the Lookstein family, Rabbi Kobrin has a BA and MA from Columbia University and rabbinical ordination from the Rabbi Isaac Elchanan Theological Seminary and Rabbi Zalman Nechemia Goldberg. Rabbi Kobrin has published in *Ten Da'at*, the *Torah*

U'Madda Journal, and the *Atid*. He lives in Riverdale, New York with his wife and four daughters.

Rebecca Kobrin, Assistant Professor, Department of History, Columbia University works in the field of American Jewish History and modern Jewish migration. She received her BA from Yale University, her M. Phil and PhD from the University of Pennsylvania. Before coming to Columbia, she served as the Blaustein Post-Doctoral Fellow at Yale University (2002–2004). Her forthcoming book *Between Exile and Empire: Jewish Eastern Europe and Its Diaspora* was awarded the Center for Jewish History's Sandra and Fred Rose Young Historian's Award. She is presently a fellow at the Center for Advanced Judaic Studies, exploring the role Jewish immigrant bank failures played in reshaping American finance before the First World War. Her publications on Jewish philanthropy include "Contested Contributions: American Jewish Money and Polish-Jewish Relations in Inter-War Poland, 1919–1929," *Gal-Ed: A Journal of Polish Jewish History* (Fall 2005), 49–62.

Dr. Jonathan Krasner is Assistant Professor of the American Jewish Experience at Hebrew Union College-Jewish Institute of Religion in New York. His articles have appeared in the *American Jewish Archives Journal, Jewish Social Studies, Journal of Jewish Education*, and *American Jewish History*. He is the recipient of a Koret Jewish Studies Publications Program Award for his upcoming book, tentatively titled *The Benderly Boys and the Making of American Jewish Education*, which will be published by Brandeis University Press.

Norman Lamm served as President of Yeshiva University for 27 years until 2003, when he became Chancellor. He continues to serve as the *Rosh HaYeshiva* of its affiliated Rabbi Isaac Elchanan Theological Seminary. He is the author of 11 books, including *Faith and Doubt, Torah Lishmah, Torah Umadda, The Shema, The*

Religious Thought of Hasidism, Seventy Faces and other works, some in Hebrew. He founded the Orthodox Forum – a think tank of and for Modern Orthodoxy with which he is associated – and the journals *Tradition* and the *Torah Umadda Journal*. He formerly served as Rabbi of The Jewish Center in Manhattan, and his first pulpit was as Assistant to Rabbi Joseph Lookstein at Kehilath Jeshurun.

Dr. Bryna Jocheved Levy, who was born in the United States and moved to Israel 28 years ago, is one of the most esteemed Bible teachers in Israel today. A pioneer in the movement for women's Torah study, she was the first woman to earn a doctorate in Bible from Yeshiva University. She is presently a senior lecturer in Bible at Matan: The Sadie Rennert Women's Institute for Torah Studies in Jerusalem, and is founder and director of the Joan and Shael Bellows graduate program in Bible and Biblical Interpretation at Matan, a joint program with Hebrew University. Levy's most recent creative endeavors include her new book *Waiting for Rain: Reflections at the Turning of the Year* (JPS, 2008) and a number of websites commissioned by George Blumenthal and the Center for On Line Jewish Studies, which may be found at *www.cojs.org*

Rav Aharon Lichtenstein grew up in the United States, earning his rabbinical ordination at Yeshiva University, and a PhD in English Literature at Harvard. He is committed to intensive and original Torah study, and articulates a bold Jewish worldview that embraces modernity, reflecting the tradition of his teacher and father-in-law, Rabbi Joseph B. Soloveitchik. In 1971, Rav Lichtenstein answered Rav Yehuda Amital's request to join him at the helm of Yeshivat Har Etzion in Alon Shevut, Israel. He is a source of inspiration for a wide circle of Jewry, for both his educational attainments and his intellectual leadership.

Deborah Lipstadt is Dorot Professor of Modern Jewish and Holocaust Studies at Emory University, Atlanta. Her book, *History on Trial: My Day in Court with A Holocaust Denier* concerns her London libel trial against David Irving who sued her for calling him a Holocaust denier. Her *Denying the Holocaust: The Growing Assault on Truth and Memory* examines the history of Holocaust denial. As an historical consultant to the United States Holocaust Memorial Museum, she helped design the section dedicated to America's response to the Holocaust. Dr. Lipstadt has also written *Beyond Belief: The American Press and the Coming of the Holocaust*, which examines the American press response to the news of the persecution of European Jewry. She is currently writing a book on the Eichmann trial.

Joshua Lookstein is the Director of Foundation Relations at UJA-Federation of New York. He recently concluded five years as the Executive Director of the S. Daniel Abraham Foundation. Prior to joining the Foundation, he served as Assistant Rabbi at Congregation Kehilath Jeshurun, as well as on the Judaic Studies faculty of the Ramaz School. He received his rabbinic ordination from the Rabbi Isaac Elchanan Theological Seminary, and a Masters in Jewish History from the Bernard Revel Graduate School. He is a Board Member of the Jewish Funders Network, Yeshivat Chovevei Torah, and Areyvut, and serves on the Advisory Council of the Taglit-birthright israel Foundation. He is a member of the New York Board of Rabbis, the Rabbinical Council of America, and the International Rabbinic Fellowship. He is the favorite son of Rabbi Haskel and Audrey Lookstein.

Vivian B. Mann is Director of the Masters Program in Jewish Art at the Graduate School of the Jewish Theological Seminary, and Curator Emerita at the Jewish Museum, New York. She is the author of numerous articles on medieval art and Jewish art. Her latest book, *Art and Ceremony in Jewish Life: Essays in Jewish Art History* was published in 2005. She has been the recipient of a Woodrow Wilson National Fellowship, a National Endowment for the Arts Fellowship for Museum Professionals, and two

Fellowships from the National Endowment for the Humanities, among other awards. In 1996, Dr. Mann was a Fellow at The Institute for Advanced Studies of The Hebrew University, and in 1999, she received the Jewish Cultural Achievement Award in Jewish Thought from the National Foundation for Jewish Culture. She graduated from Ramaz High School in 1961, where she studied Talmud with Rabbi Lookstein.

Dr. Rafael Medoff is founding director of The David S. Wyman Institute for Holocaust Studies, which focuses on America's response to the Holocaust. He is the author of ten books on American Jewish history, Zionism, and the Holocaust, and has contributed to numerous scholarly journals, encyclopedias, and other reference volumes. His most recent book is *Blowing the Whistle on Genocide: Josiah E. DuBois, Jr. and the Struggle for a U.S. Response to the Holocaust* (2008).

Peter N. Miller (Ramaz High School '82) is Dean of the Bard Graduate Center in New York City. His main field of research is the history of historical research with a focus on the Provençal antiquary Peiresc (1580–1637) and the later history of the relationship between antiquarianism and the modern cultural sciences. He is also the author of books on opera and intellectual life in seventeenth-century Venice, and political thought in eighteenth-century England.

Rabbi Adam Mintz is an adjunct professor in Jewish History at Queens College and the immediate past president of the New York Board of Rabbis. He lectures widely on a variety of topics in Jewish History and his weekly streaming video, "This Week in Jewish History," is featured on the internet at *www.rayimahuvim. org*. Rabbi Mintz served in the pulpit rabbinate for over twenty years, including serving as Associate Rabbi at Congregation Kehilath Jeshurun from 1992–1996, and is one of the founders of Kehilath Rayim Ahuvim in New York City. He is the editor of *Jewish Spirituality and Divine Law* (2005).

Michael B. Oren is a Senior Fellow at the Shalem Center in Jerusalem and a professor in the Program of Jewish Civilization at the Georgetown University Foreign Service School. He writes frequently on Middle East issues for publications such as the *Wall Street Journal*, the *New York Times*, and *The New Republic*, of which he is a contributing editor. Dr. Oren is the author of *Six Days of War: June 1967 and the Making of the Modern Middle East*, and *Power, Faith, and Fantasy: America in the Middle East, 1776 to the Present*, which were both *New York Times* bestsellers. He has lived in Israel for thirty years, has served as a government advisor and as an officer in the Israeli army.

Prof. Jonathan J. Price is professor of Classics and Ancient History at Tel Aviv University. He is the author of two books and numerous articles and reviews on Greek, Roman and Jewish history, historiography, and epigraphy, with a special emphasis on the writings of Flavius Josephus. He lives in Jerusalem with his wife, Naomi Schacter (a niece of Haskel Lookstein), and their five children.

Sandra E. Rapoport is coauthor, with Shera A. Tuchman, of *The Passions of the Matriarchs* (2004) and *Moses' Women* (2008). Through a weaving of biblical text and midrashic intertext, her books bring to life the untold stories of the women in the books of Genesis and Exodus. Ms. Rapoport was a litigating attorney and management consultant before turning full-time to her passions for writing and Bible study. Her articles have appeared in law reviews and in several periodicals including *Commentary*, and she also lectures on biblical subjects. She and her husband, Sam, have been members of Congregation Kehilath Jeshurun for the past eighteen years, where Sandra has been a student in Rabbi Lookstein's Wednesday morning Torah *shiur*. She is currently working on her third book.

Rabbi Moshe Rosenberg, a product of Kehilath Jeshurun and Ramaz Elementary School, is the son of Rabbi Israel D. Rosenberg, who served as Ritual Director of Kehilath Jeshurun from 1954 to 1990. Rav Moshe is Rav of Congregation Etz Chaim of Kew Gardens Hills, and a member of the Judaic Studies faculty at the SAR Academy. His forthcoming book, *Morality for Muggles*, examines eternal themes through the prism of Torah, literature, and, particularly, the Harry Potter novels.

Jonathan D. Sarna is the Joseph H. & Belle R. Braun Professor of American Jewish History at Brandeis University and director of its Hornstein Jewish Professional Leadership Program. He also chairs the Academic Advisory and Editorial Board of the Jacob Rader Marcus Center of the American Jewish Archives in Cincinnati, and is chief historian of the National Museum of American Jewish History in Philadelphia. Author or editor of more than twenty books on American Jewish history and life, his most recent book is entitled *A Time to Every Purpose: Letters to a Young Jew*. His *American Judaism: A History* won the 2004 Everett Family "Jewish Book of the Year Award" from the Jewish Book Council. From 1960 until his parents moved to Boston in 1965, Jonathan Sarna was a pupil at Ramaz.

Rabbi Hershel Schachter is the Nathan and Vivian Fink Distinguished Professional Chair in Talmud at Yeshiva University, where he concurrently serves as the Rosh Yeshiva of the Rabbi Isaac Elchanan Theological Seminary and the Rosh Kollel of the Marcos and Adina Katz Kollel. He is the author of numerous articles, three books of Talmudic and *Halakhic* essays (*Eretz HaTzvi*, *B'Ikvei HaTzon*, and *Ginas Egoz*), two books on the life, thought, and views of Rabbi Joseph B. Soloveitchik (*Nefesh HaRav* and

MiP'ninei HaRav) and has edited several volumes of the shiurim of the Rav.

Rabbi Dr. Jacob J. Schacter is University Professor of Jewish History and Jewish Thought and Senior Scholar, Center for the Jewish Future, Yeshiva University. A PhD recipient from Harvard University and rabbinical ordination from Mesivta Torah Vodaath, he served as a pulpit rabbi for nearly thirty years in pulpits in the Boston area and in New York City and was the founding editor of the *Torah Umadda Journal*. In addition, he has authored and edited seven books and has published over sixty articles and reviews. His new Hebrew edition of the autobiography of Rabbi Jacob Emden will be completed in 2009.

Natan Sharansky is an internationally renowned human rights activist, political leader, and author. Imprisoned in the Soviet Union in 1977 for his activity as a dissident and spokesman for the Soviet Jewry movement, he was released as part of an East-West prisoner exchange and permitted to emigrate to Israel in 1986. Sharansky is the author of three critically-acclaimed best-sellers, *Fear No Evil* (1988), *The Case for Democracy: The Power of Freedom to Overcome Tyranny and Terror* (2004), and *Defending Identity: Its Indispensable Role in Protecting Democracy* (2008). From 1996 to 2005, Sharansky was a Member of Knesset, and served, successively, Minister of Industry and Trade, Minister of the Interior, Minister of Housing and Construction, and Minister for Jerusalem and for Diaspora Affairs. He presently chairs the Adelson Institute for Strategic Studies, a division of the Jerusalem-based Shalem Center.

Rabbi Meir Y. Soloveichik is Associate Rabbi at KJ. He is a graduate of Yeshiva College *summa cum laude* and received his ordination from the Rabbi Isaac Elchanan Theological Seminary at Yeshiva University, where he was also a member of the Kollel

Elyon. Rabbi Soloveichik studied philosophy of religion at Yale University's Divinity School and is currently a doctoral candidate in philosophy of religion at Princeton University.

Rabbi Joseph Telushkin is the author of *Jewish Literacy: The Most Important Things to Know About the Jewish Religion, Its People and Its History*. The most widely selling book on Judaism of the past two decades, *Jewish Literacy* has been hailed by leading figures in all the major movements of Judaism, and was brought out in a new edition in 2008. Telushkin is currently working on a project he regards as his life work, a three-volume comprehensive study of Jewish Ethics and their applicability to daily life. The first volume (published in 2006), *A Code of Jewish Ethics: You Shall be Holy*, won the Everett National Jewish Book Award for book of the year. Volume 2, *Love Your Neighbor as Yourself* (from which his essay in this volume is drawn), is due out in 2009.

Shera Aranoff Tuchman has been teaching weekly classes in biblical commentary at Kehilath Jeshurun for fifteen years. These lectures culminated in the publication of two books, *Passions of the Matriarchs*, and *Moses' Women* (2004, 2008), co-authored with Sandra Rapoport. Dr. Aranoff Tuchman was recently interviewed on the CUNY television series "Jewish Women in America." Besides studying and teaching Bible, which is her passion, she is a dermatologist in private practice in Manhattan and at Lenox Hill Hospital. Shera and her husband, Alan Tuchman, have been members of Kehilath Jeshurun over twenty-five years. Their children Ari, Micole and Andy, all graduated from Ramaz High School.

Dr. Harlan J. Wechsler is founding Rabbi of Congregation Or Zarua in New York City. He was a member of the philosophy department of the Jewish Theological Seminary for over thirty-five years and has published widely in the field of Jewish ethics and the history of Jewish philosophy. Rabbi Wechsler is past Chairman of the Board of the HealthCare Chaplaincy, and was instrumental in the development of chaplaincy as a career option for rabbis. Author of *What's So Bad About Guilt* (Simon & Schuster) and *Old Is Good*, a study of old age in Rabbinic literature, Rabbi Wechsler's most recent paper was "So That The Centre Will Hold: Shmuel David Luzzatto's Commentary to the Torah" delivered at the International Meeting of the Society of Biblical Literature in 2008. Rabbi Wechsler and his wife, Naomi Friedland-Wechsler, are parents of two Ramaz graduates.

Rabbi Avi Weiss is Founder and President of Yeshivat Chovevei Torah, the Modern and Open Orthodox Rabbinical School, and Senior Rabbi of the Hebrew Institute of Riverdale, a congregation of 850 families. He is also National President of AMCHA – the Coalition for Jewish Concerns, a grassroots organization that speaks out for Jewish causes. Rabbi Weiss was recently named by *Newsweek* magazine as one of the fifty most influential rabbis in America. Rabbi Weiss is author of *Women at Prayer*, a *halakhic* analysis of women's prayer groups; *Spiritual Activism: A Jewish Guide to Leadership*; and *Repairing the World* (2008) as well as *The Haggadah for the Yom HaShoah Seder*. He has also authored numerous papers, articles and editorials in journals and newspapers around the world.

Elie Wiesel was fifteen years old when he and his family were deported to Auschwitz. He described that experience in his best-selling book *Night*, first published in 1956 and subsequently translated into more than thirty languages. He has authored more than fifty other books, and has received numerous literary awards. A leading international spokesman for human rights, Mr. Wiesel has worked on behalf of Soviet Jews and Israel, helped the relatives of "the Disappeared" in Argentina, spoken out for the Cambodian Boat People and victims in Rwanda, Ethiopia, Kosovo, and Central America, and fought against apartheid in South Africa. His efforts have earned him the United States Congressional Gold Medal (1985); the Presidential Medal of Freedom (1992); the rank of Grand-Croix in the French Legion of Honor (2001); an honorary Knighthood of the British Empire awarded by Her Majesty, the Queen (2006); and, in 1986, the Nobel Peace Prize. Mr. Wiesel has been the Andrew W. Mellon Professor in the Humanities at Boston University since 1976.

Dr. Avivah Gottlieb Zornberg has recently published *The Murmuring Deep: Reflections on the Biblical Unconscious* (Schocken, 2009) which includes her essay appearing in this volume. She is the author of two previous books on Bible and Midrash: *The Beginning of Desire: Reflections on Genesis* (which won the National Jewish Book Award in 1995) and *The Particulars Rapture: Reflections on Exodus.* She lives in Jerusalem, where she teaches in several institutes of Jewish Studies. She also lectures widely in the United States and Great Britain.

Jubilee Volume Patrons

The publication of this historic work was made possible through the generous support of the following;

Anita & Jordan Abowitz
Diane & Robert Abrams
Ellen & Mitchell Agoos
Nicole & Raanan Agus
Lenore & Eugene Alpert
Lillian & Alan Applebaum
Barbara & Harvey Arfa
Jonathan Art
Karine & Eric Attias
Louise & Sidney Banon
Gladys Baruch
Shira & Larry Baruch and Family
Ellen Baumgarten
The Baumgarten Family
Ilana & Daniel Benson
Deborah & Barry Berg
Sara & David Berman

Brenda & Albert Bernstein
Renee & Michael Bernstein
Barry Best
Marisa & Michael Bevilacqua
Barbara & Jonathan Blinken
Deborah & Richard Born
Elana & Aryeh Bourkoff
The Braiterman & Mandelker Families
Mark Brecker
Devora Brickman
Marie & Robert Briefel
Ruth Brod
Fran & Benjamin Brown
Doina & Lawrence Bryskin
Elias Buchwald
Tova & Norman Bulow
Roberta Caplan

Mindy & Jay Cinnamon and
 Family
Sherry & Neil Cohen
Carole & Seymour Cohen
Hollace & Steven Cohen
Rachel & Barry Cooper
Michelle & Eric Creizman
Vivian & Larry Creizman
Sharon Dane
Ann Davenport and Family
Rochelle & Mayer Davis
Rita & Fred Distenfeld
Elisabeth & Alan Doft
Arlene & Avrom Doft
Abigail & David Doft
Suzanne & Jacob Doft
Shlomit & Chaim Edelstein
Suzanne & Samuel Eisenstat
Randi & Howard Eisenstein
 and Family
Lillian & Elliot Eisman
Pamela & Adam Emmerich
Barbara & Abe Esses
Rebecca & Evan Farber
Estanne & Martin Fawer
Marilyn & Leonard Feingold
Miriam & Eric Feldstein
Florence & Philip Felig
Maria Finkle
Lynne & Joshua Fishman
Martine & Leo Fox
Sheila Freilich & Alan
 Manevitz
Anne & Natalio Fridman
Marylene & Alan Friedman

Arthur Friedman
Helen & Sidney Friedman
Ronalee & Russell Galbut
Lauren & Martin Geller
Ira Gober
Jane & Ishaia Gol
Dale & Saul Goldberg
Sarah & Martin Goldman
Tamar & Eric Goldstein
Yonina & Eric Gomberg
Ruth & David Gottesman
Trudy & Robert Gottesman
Rebecca & Laurence Grafstein
Wendy & Sholem Greenbaum
Jeanette & Mikhail Grinberg
Georgette & Steven Gross
Nicole & David Gruenstein
Rae & Stanley Gurewitsch
Jill & James Haber
Pearl & Zev Hack
Lori & Alan Harris
Hashkama Minyan of Cong.
 Kehilath Jeshurun
Fanya Gottesfeld Heller
Hedwig & Joseph Heller
Michele & Ari Hering
Kathy & Jonathan Herman
Ronnie & Samuel Heyman
Rochelle & David Hirsch
Elie Hirschfeld
Alexandra & Moshe
 Hocherman
Ann & Jerome Hornblass
Mildred Hostyk
Dina & Marshall Huebner

Wendy & Sidney Ingber
Terry & Michael Jaspan
Suzanne & Norman Javitt
Barbara & Manfred Joseph
Deborah & David Kahn
Judith & Hirshel Kahn
Ilana & Mitchell Kahn
Ellen & Rob Kapito
Jessica & Adam Kaplan
Jennifer & Michael Kaplan
Karin & Joel Katz
Keren Keshet
Barbara Braffman & Benjamin
   Klapper
Rosalie & Harry Kleinhaus
Ruth & Lawrence Kobrin and
   Family
Gloria & Richard Kobrin
Yvonne Koppel
Bertha & Henry Kressel
Randy & Mitchell Krevat
Melanie & Andrew Kule
Wilma & Stephen Kule
Seryl & Charles Kushner
Vivianne & Robert Kurzweil
Amy & Darren Landy
Naomi Lazarus
Jane & Don Lebell
Madeleine & Mark Lebwohl
Elena, Jay, Talia, Danielle &
   Jacob Lefkowitz
Sheila & Wallace Lehman
Jane & Reuben Leibowitz
Jody & Elie Levine
Sheila & Jeffrey Levine

Sharon & Asher Levitsky
Jane & Michael Lewittes
Jean & Armand Lindenbaum
Belda & Marcel Lindenbaum
Leora & Richard Linhart
Janice & Saul Linzer
Deborah & Robert Lipner
Judy & David Lobel
Audrey Lookstein
Joshua Lookstein
Susanna & Steven Lorch
Hannah & Edward Low
Ruth & Edward Lukashok
Jay K.R. Lunzer
Rochelle & Eugene Major
Vivian & David Mark and Ian
Caroline & Morris Massel
Monica & Aaron Meislin and
   Family
Paula and David Menche
Perla & Julio Messer
Mindy & Fred Miller
Naomi Miller & Bathia
   Churgin
Judith & Ben Milstein
Joyce & Edward Misrahi
Janet & Mark Mittler
Wendy & Adam Modlin
Frank Morgenstern
Marilyn Meltzer & Sheldon
   Muhlbauer
Ruth & David Musher
Jessica & Jason Muss
Helen Nash
Sara & Joseph Nathanson

Carol & Mel Newman
Rebecca & Noah Nunberg
Lisa & Edward Ostad
Judith & Daniel Ottensoser
Anita & Robert Payne and
    Family
Carol & Ralph Perlberger
Janelle & Sheldon Pike
Barbara & Terry Plasse
Bonnie & Isaac Pollak
Helen & Daniel Potaznik
Suzy & Larry Present
Lauren & Mitchell Presser
Dina & Douglas Propp
The Propp Family
Gabrielle Propp
Sandra & Samuel Rapoport
Monique & Andrew
    Rechtschaffen
Hilda Riback
Diana & Ira Riklis
Sue & Win Robins
Pamela & George Rohr
Laurel & Lawrence
    Rosenbluth
Marian & William Rosner
Jennifer, Jeffry & Sam Roth
Florence & Robert Rothman
Amy & Howard Rubenstein
Naomi Ickovitz & Steven
    Rudolph
Victoria & Daryosh Sakhai
Susan & Martin Sanders
Evelyn & Salomon Sassoon
Sheira & Steven Schacter

Barbara & Bernard Scharfstein
Stacy & Ronald Scheinberg
Sidney Scheinberg
Miquette & Morton Schrader
Paul Schulder
Hillary & Jeremy Schwalbe
Janie & Robert Schwalbe
Leana & Bernard Schwartz
Erica & Robert Schwartz
Debbie & Shelly Senders and
    Family
Rina & Amnon Shalhov
Ruth & Irwin Shapiro
Susan & Scott Shay
Sara & Simon Shemia
Judith & Isaac Sherman
Deena & Adam Shiff
The Shudofsky Family
Alejandra & Ariel Sigal
Donna & Arthur Silverman
    and Family
Adina & Michael Singer
Alice Smokler
Eva & Jason Sokol
Phyllis & Mark Speiser
Meg Rosenblatt & David Stein
Melvin Stein
Robyn & David Stonehill
Surie & Robert Sugarman
Randi & David Sultan
Dorothy, Andrew, Zoe, JoBeth
    & Tanner Tananbaum
Laurie Tansman
Judith Tanz
Carla & Steven Tanz

Nadia & Yuli Tartakovsky
Susan & Robert Taub
Adele & Ronald Tauber
Elizabeth & Joshua Trump
Phyllis & Jonathan Wagner
Deborah & Raymond Ward
Ellen & Sanford Ward
Diane Wassner
Grace & David Weil
Lynn Weinstein

Kim Gantz Wexler & Sanford
    Wexler
Judy & Philip Wilner
Rita & David Woldenberg
Barbara Zimet
Gail Suchman & Jerald
    Zimmerman
Cathy Zises
Seymour Zises & Andrea
    Tessler